Social Development

To my grandchildren
Heather, Becky, Kirsty, Emily

Social
Development

H. RUDOLPH SCHAFFER

University of Strathclyde

Blackwell
Publishing

350 Main Street, Malden, MA 02148-5018, USA
108 Cowley Road, Oxford OX4 1JF, UK
550 Swanston Street, Carlton South, Melbourne, Victoria 3053, Australia
Kurfürstendamm 57, 10707 Berlin, Germany

First published 1996 by Blackwell Publishing Ltd
Reprinted 1997, 1998 (twice), 1999, 2000 (twice), 2001, 2002 (twice), 2003

Library of Congress Cataloging-in-Publication Data

Schaffer, H. Rudolph
   Social development / H. Rudolph Schaffer
       p.   cm.
   Includes bibliographical references and index.
   ISBN 0–631–18573–9 (hardback) — ISBN 0–631–18574–7 (paperback)
   1. Socialization. 2. Child development. I. Title.
   HQ783.S27   1996   96–3614
   305.23'1—dc20   CIP

A catalogue record for this title is available from the British Library.

Set in 10.5 on 12.5 pt Ehrhardt
by Best-set Typesetter Ltd, Hong Kong
Printed and bound in the United Kingdom
by T. J. International Ltd, Padstow, Cornwall

For further information on
Blackwell Publishing, visit our website:
http://www.blackwellpublishing.com

Contents

Figures

Tables

Preface

The task of a textbook is to present a state-of-the-art account of its chosen field. What do we know now, what insights have we achieved, where are we going? To answer such questions one cannot merely present a litany of facts; it is also necessary to say something about the general aims, intentions, and theoretical concerns that underpin the studies carried out, as well as to indicate the kinds of methods used to obtain the findings presented. To do all this for the field of social development, and do it in a reasonably concise and readable manner, is my objective in this book.

Any body of knowledge with which students are expected to become familiar needs, of course, to be continuously updated. As far as social development is concerned that need is a particularly pressing one just now, for the field has changed dramatically in the recent past. Who could, for example, have predicted just a short period ago that our conception of the socialization process – a central theme in any account of children's development – would need such drastic reformulation? At one time it all seemed so straightforward: children (so it was asserted) are shaped by their parents' rearing practices; they assume whatever characteristics are assigned to them by means of adult rewards and punishment; and to account for any individual child's development one need look, therefore, no further than the parents and their particular socializing actions. But consider where we stand now: increasingly we have come to realize that children are capable of exerting a marked influence over their own development; it has become clear that, far from being at the mercy of whatever external forces they happen to encounter, children actively select and shape their own environment; and as we come more and more to appreciate the child's own striving nature so we also have had to question whether parents are in fact as all-powerful as we thought at one time and whether their role in the developmental process ought not therefore to be reconsidered. There are several reasons for this change in orientation: first, negatively, the finding that the relationship between parental rearing practices and children's psychological attributes is at best a tenuous one and that the former cannot therefore predict the development of the latter with any degree of certainty; second, the growing influence of behavior genetics, with its demonstration of the marked effects that inherited aspects can under certain conditions exert on children; and finally, the realization that even very young children are already actively construing and interpreting their experiences and that these facets of their inner life can play a powerful role in guiding their behavior. All in all, a major rethink has been necessary.

There have been other recent changes with profound effects on the way in which we now study and think about children's social development. Take the relationship between theory and practice – two aspects that at one time were thought of as quite separate enterprises. Academics were expected to confine their studies to "pure" research; they could then hand the knowledge thus acquired down to practitioners working on applied problems; and it was left to the latter to adapt these findings as best they could to the messy life outside the laboratory. That distinction has largely disappeared: for example, as has repeatedly been shown, research in real life settings such as day care centers or neighborhood gangs can come up with findings that address not only immediate practical problems but also may contribute to our knowledge of wider concerns involving the role of substitute attachments or the nature of peer relationships. A continuous to-and-fro between theoretical and practical issues is thus set up, producing one integrated body of knowledge. Or take the increasing tendency in developmental research to pay attention not just to products but also to processes – to ask questions, that is, not only about *what* the end results of development are but also *how* they are brought about. To know, for example, that certain kinds of families are likely to produce aggressive, undersocialized children is useful; it is only a first step, however, and especially if we intend to helpfully intervene in such families a knowledge of what actually goes on there is essential. Social interaction analyses are thus becoming an increasingly accepted part of social development research.

There is one general trend that is particularly noteworthy, and that is the increasing tendency to link up and integrate topics that had previously been considered in isolation, and so do justice to the interconnectedness that characterizes social life and social behavior. The following are some examples:

- Until recently children's relationships to such significant others as mother, father, and siblings were examined one at a time, as though each exists in isolation and their total impact on the child can be expressed by the sum of their separate effects. We now appreciate that we must also take into account the relationship between these relationships: what goes on between mother and child is affected by what goes on between father and child; for that matter it is also affected by what goes on between mother and father – as shown vividly by research on the way marital conflict spills over onto the parents' treatment of their children.
- A similar consideration applies to the various life settings – home, school, peer group, etc. – in which children spend their time. These too were previously examined quite separately, but children do not lead their lives in separate boxes: what happens in one may have considerable implications for what happens in another, as seen most clearly in the mutual effects that children's scholastic and family experiences have on each other. The nature of the links between these

diverse settings and their conjoint effect on the child's development must therefore be traced.

- A further example refers to the various levels at which social development can be examined. At one time this was investigated almost exclusively at the level of the individual (when do infants begin to smile? are boys more aggressive than girls? are preschoolers capable of altruism?). But questions about social processes may be asked at various other levels too, such as those of interpersonal interactions, of relationships, of groups and of society in general, and recent years have seen a great burst of research dealing with these matters too. The various levels, however, are all interrelated: thus, in order to fully understand the behavior of individual children one must take into account the fact that each child is embedded in certain kinds of interpersonal relationships, is part of a particular family and belongs to a given culture. The importance of such contextual factors has now been duly recognized; increasingly attempts are being made to trace the influence of one level upon another; and the use of multilevel explanations is gradually becoming more common.

I have tried to do justice in my narrative to these complexities and to present the child as an inhabitant of a heterogeneous social world – a world where, for instance, it is no longer sufficient (as was thought at one time) merely to describe the relationship with the mother as though that could account for all there is in the child's developing personality. Children have fathers too, as well as siblings; they spend much of their time with peers and at school; impersonal agencies like TV and other media impinge on them as well; and all these external influences act jointly with those stemming from each child's individuality. No wonder that our research designs are becoming more and more complex and our conclusions increasingly hedged in by qualifications! What is perhaps particularly significant in this respect is the realization that so many of our findings are culture-specific, that is, that a great deal of what goes on between child and caretakers as described for samples in the West is based on values and practices that turn out to be very different in other societies. Cross-cultural data, being more difficult to get access to, are slower in forthcoming and less widely known than Western-only findings; they are essential, however, in helping us to preserve a proper appreciation of the relative nature of much of our research material, and have therefore been introduced in diverse relevant places in this book as reminders of that relativity.

The book is addressed to students of psychology and other social sciences with no or only limited knowledge of child development. It covers the age range up to and including adolescence, with a somewhat greater emphasis on the earlier years – for the simple reason that rather more goes on during that period than subsequently in other comparable time spans. The content is organized according to themes, but these themes follow a rough developmental progression. At first, however, we shall pay attention to the manner whereby research findings are obtained, for findings are a function of the methods used to procure them, and to attend only to the former without some acquaintance with the latter can easily lead to misunderstanding. Throughout the book I have set aside "cases," i.e. illustrations of specific points that need to be dealt with in greater detail and thus require a change in pace. At the end of each chapter a fairly full summary will be found which can be used for rehearsal and revision purposes.

I am deeply grateful to the many colleagues with whom I have been associated over the years in both teaching and research, who have discussed and argued and instructed and occasionally also agreed with me. I am also most grateful to Angela Kerigan, my secretary throughout this enterprise, who helped me in so many ways and who despite the invention of the word processor still had the unenviable task of having to decipher a good many handwritten notes. And I am especially grateful to my students, who over the years were the victims of my various teaching experiments in Social Development courses. Thankfully, they were far from passive victims and this book has benefited enormously from their comments, complaints, and suggestions.

Rudolph Schaffer

Acknowledgments

The author and publishers gratefully acknowledge the following for permission to reproduce copyright material:

The British Psychological Society, for figure 30, which originally appeared in E. J. S. Sonuga-Barke et al. (1993), "Inter-ethnic bias in teachers' ratings of childhood hyperactivity," *British Journal of Developmental Psychology*, *11*, 187–200;

Elsevier Science Ltd, for figures 33 and 34, which originally appeared in M. Rutter (1989), "Pathways from childhood to adult life," *Journal of Child Psychology and Psychiatry*, *30*, 23–51;

Erlbaum (UK), Taylor & Francis (UK), for figure 2, which originally appeared in R. A. Hinde (1992), "Human social development: an ethological\relationship perspective," in H. McGurk (Ed.), *Childhood social development: Contemporary perspectives*;

Harvard University Press, for figure 1, which originally appeared in J. Kagan (1978), *Infancy*; copyright © 1978, 1980 by the President and Fellows of Harvard College;

Lawrence Erlbaum Associates, Inc., for figure 3, which originally appeared in L. W. Sander et al. (1979), "Change in infant and caregiver variables over the first two months of life," in E. B. Thomas (Ed.), *Origins of the infant's social responsiveness*;

Charles and Daphne Maurer, for revised figure from D. Maurer and C. Maurer, *The World of the Newborn*, 1988.

Plenum Publishing Corp., for figure 10, which originally appeared in M. Lewis and J. Brooks-Gunn (1979), *Social cognition and the acquisition of self*;

the Society for the Psychological Study of Social Issues, for figure 28, which originally appeared in G. H. Elder and A. Caspi (1988), "Economic stress in lives: Developmental perspectives," *Journal of Social Issues*, *44*, 25–45;

the Society of Research in Child Development, for figure 25, which originally appeared in J. B. Kupersmidt and J. D. Coie (1990), "Preadolescent peer status, aggression and school adjustment as predictors of externalizing problems in adolescence," *Child development*, *61*, 1350–1362.

The publishers apologize for any errors or omissions in the above list and would be grateful to be notified of any corrections that should be incorporated in the next edition or reprint of this book.

Chapter 1

The Study of Social Development

The Questions Posed

"How kids get on with other people" is perhaps not a bad definition for the study of social development; the trouble is that instructors like their students to use long words and complex sentences and, more to the point, to be as precise and informative as possible in conveying meanings. Let us therefore suggest instead that social development refers to the behavior patterns, feelings, attitudes, and concepts children manifest in relation to other people and to the way that these various aspects change over age.

Traditionally, psychological functions have been classified under three headings: cognitive, affective, and social. In some respects the distinction, especially that between cognitive and social, still serves a purpose – otherwise I would hardly have written a textbook with the present title. What has become increasingly clear is that the distinction is nothing like as absolute as was thought at one time. Take the above definition of social development. Children have *feelings* about other people – an obvious statement, especially so when we consider the extremely intense emotions children in their early years express in their relationships with people, but one which reminds us that social behavior is rarely a cold-blooded affair and is frequently charged with great love or hate, affection or hostility, fear or anger. All behavior has an emotional tone to it, whether it is expressed by an adult or a child and whether it is directed to the social or the physical world. Whether children are more emotional than adults is debatable, though there can be no doubt that they tend to have less control over emotional displays and their feelings are therefore more readily expressed and observed. What also cannot be doubted is that the most intense emotions are to be found in the context of interpersonal relationships rather than in interactions with things: the joys and tensions of family life are ample testimony to that. A strict dividing line between social and emotional functions thus has little meaning.

In many respects the same applies to social and cognitive functions. When psychologists investigate the latter in their own right they generally study them vis-à-vis physical stimuli; however, in so far as cognition is concerned with the way in which individuals think about the world it is obvious that other people must be included in that world. Thus our definition of social development includes the notion of children's *concepts* about others, so that justice is done to the notion that children perceive, remember, think about, interpret, and construe the behavior of other people (and of themselves). They use, that is, cognitive functions in order to guide their behavior in the social world. No wonder the topic of *social cognition* has become an important area for investigation, for any social action must as inevitably entail cognitive processes as it must inevitably be emotionally toned. Thus, while the investigation of social development is focused on interpersonal aspects of children's behavior, both cognitive and affective aspects are included in the study of such aspects.

Studying Children and Studying Development

Why are people interested in children's development?

Roughly speaking, there are two main reasons. The first is an interest in children per se. One wants to find out what children are like at particular ages: how competent they are in managing interpersonal relationships with other people, how they can best be influenced to conform to the demands of society, what variation one can expect from one age to another in their behavior in social situations, and what accounts for the great differences one sees in all such respects among children. The motivation to ask such questions may be theoretical or practical – to extend our knowledge of children or to be of help to them. On the one hand, a psychologist may, for example, wish to determine the extent to which a newborn baby is already differentially tuned in to the human voice, paying more attention to that than to any other sound of similar intensity, in order to establish whether we arrive in the world with certain preadapted mechanisms for social intercourse. Knowledge such as this serves to throw light on the means that first enable children to enter society; it constitutes one building block in a theory of human development that psychologists are attempting to construct. On the other hand, questions may also be asked for purely practical reasons. Do 1-year-old children require the constant availability of the mother, thus making it ill-advised for women with children of this age to go out to work? Are 5-year-olds capable of functioning in groups as large as 20 or more children, or ought classes in kindergarten and primary school to be broken down into smaller units? At what age should one begin to provide sex education, including information about topics such as AIDS? These are "real world" questions and the answers to them should lead to some form of action designed to improve the lot of children. Not that the distinction between theory- and practice-driven inquiries is necessarily an absolute one: knowledge about the differential sensitivity of babies to the human voice may be useful in designing devices for soothing fretful babies; equally, observing the effects of day care on 1-year-old children while the mother goes out to work contributes not only to action but also to our knowledge of the nature of sociability at that age. In any case, whatever the motive, the interest lies in children *as* children and they are thus investigated for their own sake.

The other reason for studying children's development relates to *development* rather than to *children*. The object is to learn about the nature and end product of the developmental process; indeed one's interest may have nothing to do with children but lie instead in adults. There is a strong belief, often regarded as "commonsensical," that the child is father to the man, that is, that the circumstances of childhood shape the course of personality development and that our experiences in early life determine the type of individual we become. Childhood is thus studied to throw light on adulthood; the final product is to be understood by investigating the conditions which gave rise to it. Freud, more than any other writer, was responsible for propagating this view; it was his conviction that adult psychopathology has its roots in early experience and, in the context of a complex theoretical framework, he outlined the way in which such experience continues to reverberate within the individual and may account for the nuances of normal as well as abnormal psychological growth. Freud's developmental theories have not fared well in the light of subsequent scrutiny; the particular infantile experiences he considered as crucial have not turned out to be so, and the whole issue of early experience has (as we shall see later) turned out to be far more complex than originally thought. Nevertheless, it is impossible to believe that, to some extent at least, we are not creatures of our past and that, for example, the kinds of relationships established with parents during the formative years do not have some sort of influence on the kinds of relationships we establish in maturity. Thus childhood is scrutinized on the assumption that it will provide the key to questions about adults' individuality.

It could be argued that, in so far as we are dealing with social *development*, it is change over age that is our primary concern. Such change is, of course, what makes children so fascinating – the fact that they gradually become less dependent on parents, that other-control in due course gives way to self-control, that they develop the capacity for friendship, that understanding the rules of social living increasingly comes to regulate their behavior, and so forth. Children change in just about every sphere of activity, and to document and explain these changes is the overarching aim of developmental psychology. It may therefore seem somewhat ironic that a great many studies by developmental psychologists are in fact not developmental at all; they examine some specific age group in its own right without apparent consideration of what comes before or after, and thus without explicitly adopting a developmental perspective. Such work is, however, valuable not only for the light it sheds on children's behavior at particular ages; it is also essential to any effort to arrive at a developmental formulation, for if we are to make statements about change we need to know just what it is that changes. Intimate knowledge of specific age groups provides a series of cross-sections; developmental theories weave together these cross-sections and cannot therefore be formulated without knowledge of *what* changes into *what*.

Description and Explanation

Any attempt to understand human behavior must concern itself with both "what" questions and "why" questions. The "what" type involve description: What do the phenomena one is interested in look like? Under what circumstances do they manifest themselves? In what way do they vary according to age, sex, or culture? "Why" questions, on the other hand, are concerned with explanation; they seek to elucidate why people behave as they do and thus refer to the underlying processes and causes of behavior.

Psychologists have been much criticized in the past for failing to become properly acquainted with the phenomena they were investigating, because in their anxiety to do "respectable" laboratory work they missed out on the descriptive stage and so tried to explain aspects of behavior that they had not yet investigated in their real-life settings. What applies to psychology in general applies to the study of social development too: under the overwhelming influence first of behaviorism and then of social learning theory, attention throughout the 1950s to the 1970s was focused almost wholly on the *mechanisms* whereby developmental change is brought about – mechanisms such as drive reduction, reinforcement, and observational learning, which were applied to children's behavior and the actions of their caretakers as explanatory principles and analyzed under laboratory conditions. Thus experiments were conducted which demonstrated that the rate of smiling in infants can be increased by following each smile with some social action by the experimenter – a pat, a smile, or a few words, which were then regarded as a "reward" and considered to model the way in which parents shape the course of their child's development (Brackbill, 1958). Or take the huge number of experiments inspired by Bandura and Walters (1963) on the role of imitation: children would, for example, observe an experimenter perform some stipulated aggressive action in a laboratory; if the child then imitated that act the finding was regarded as demonstrating that observational learning can bring about developmental change and as pointing to the mechanism whereby parents influence their children. Thus the argument began with some theoretical expectation; this was then put to experimental test in a laboratory, and the conclusions drawn there were finally applied to the real-life situation in which parents reared their children. Even then, however, there was no attempt to observe parents and children in order at least to confirm the laboratory observations. Empirical data were thus confined to what experiments yielded; the constraints imposed by studying "children in strange situations with strange adults for the briefest possible periods of time" (as Bronfenbrenner, 1977, once characterized the prevailing methodology) were not considered. The notion that one should *start* with the real-life situation in order to become intimately acquainted with the phenomena of interest was not taken into account during this period.

Yet things have changed, and probably more quickly in developmental psychology than in any other branch of psychology. The reason lies partly in many people's urgent need for descriptive information about age changes. Parents, teachers, and others responsible for children's upbringing require to know *what* children can do at *what* ages under *what* circumstances, and though that need has always been there they are now increasingly aware that psychologists are the people who ought to deliver these goods. Psychologists in turn have found that there is a ready market for this type of information; the public has little interest in whether infants can be conditioned or whether 5-year-olds can imitate a strange adult in a university labora-tory, but people do want to know when they can expect their babies to start recogniz-ing their mothers, in what way they can best influence their children to conform to parental demands, and how children perform under different classroom regimes. It is all very well to demonstrate that certain phenomena like operant conditioning *can* occur, but the pressure on psychologists is to provide answers to problems concerned with phenomena that *do* occur.

The other main reason for a change to a more descriptive orientation is the influence of ethology – that branch of biology concerned with the description, classification, and analysis of animal behavior (see Hinde, 1982, for a detailed ac-count). In the ethological tradition description comes before explanation: it is re-garded as essential that the scientist spend a period in the field in order to provide a detailed descriptive picture of the animal's behavior under natural conditions before aspects of that behavior are then analyzed under laboratory conditions. Thus the imprinting phenomenon, the process whereby the young of certain species come to form close attachment bonds with the first moving object encountered after coming into the world, was initially described in great detail by Lorenz (1935) as it occurred in the animals' natural settings; only subsequently was a more analytic approach taken when investigators asked questions about the precise stimuli evoking the imprinting response, the period during which the bond could be formed, its reversibility, and so forth. As studies of human ethology have shown (e.g. Blurton Jones, 1972), it is in the field of children's social development that the ethological approach has exerted its greatest influence – partly because of its historical link with an evolutionary orientation (see Bowlby's, 1969, account of attachment theory) but mainly because its insistence on a sound descriptive basis came to the notice of developmental psychologists just as the disillusionment with a primarily experimen-tal approach began to set in.

One further reason for the change is to be found in technological innovation. Natural behavior, and especially interpersonal behavior where one may need to keep an eye on several individuals simultaneously, is highly complex and varied. The traditional operant conditioning experiment focuses on only one specific response, be it a pigeon's pecking or a baby's smile; to record the incidence of such responses requires little ingenuity. However, to describe how a 4-year-old child joins a group of other 4-year-olds – the precise strategy adopted, the sequence of responses, the behavior of the other children in welcoming or rejecting or ignoring the newcomer – all that requires highly sophisticated observational techniques, and especially so because some of the phenomena one is attempting to capture may be subtle and fleeting. Fortunately the advent of film and video technology has greatly eased the task of describing such behavior; not only can a much fuller record be obtained at the time but by means of repeated and, if necessary, slow motion replay justice can be done to even the most intricate and transient behavior patterns. Add to that the advent of computer analysis and hence the possibility of handling large amounts of data referring to a wide range of simultaneously recorded responses and one can appreciate that the technical limitations which not so very long ago made many kinds of descriptive investigations virtually impossible are no longer an insuperable obstacle.

The ability to obtain highly detailed descriptive accounts becomes particularly important in the study of social interaction. Any phenomenon can, of course, be investigated at many different levels of detail, from the molar to the molecular, from merely noting that it has occurred to describing the most minute specifics. In social interactions, however, a great deal of the exchange between participants occurs at split-second speeds: the signals they provide each other and the manner in which they interweave their responses often only become clear when special techniques such as frame-by-frame analysis or slow motion replay of filmed material are used – even though, as participants ourselves in everyday situations, we are obviously aware of this split-second world. What applies to adults applies to children too: even babies are already involved in exchanges with parents that may be based on minute actions occurring at extraordinarily rapid tempos (see Schaffer, 1977, for examples). To have the means of gaining access to such information can be extremely illuminating in understanding the nature of social interaction.

One point needs stressing: an emphasis on description should not be taken to imply a blind data-gathering exercise; just because one is attempting to become acquainted with people's natural behavior under natural conditions does not neces- sarily mean that one is launched on some aimless trawling for facts. Descriptive research, if it is to be of any use, must be guided research, where the investigator has particular questions in mind to which answers are sought. The questions may be formulated more loosely than the hypotheses that guide experimental research; they are essential nevertheless if the investigator is to avoid being swamped by information. Thus the questions serve to narrow the descriptive focus; in turn, however, their presence means that certain assumptions will have been made as to what is worth observing. The notion of an "open mind" may seem admirable in principle; in practice there is no such thing and in research, while the investigator ought always to be alert to the unexpected, it is a virtual impossibility.

Descriptive data can serve various purposes, but two in particular stand out. In the first place, such information may be required for its own sake – to "get the feel" of a particular set of phenomena, to establish norms and so learn what is typical at various ages, to analyze a global category such as "play" or "aggression" and thus find out its actual behavioral manifestations or, on the contrary, start off with the constitu- ents and, by seeing "what goes with what," set up a classification system. The second main purpose is to generate hypotheses which may then be put to the test under experimèntal conditions. A hypothesis is sometimes nothing more than a grand name for a hunch; even then, however, it should be stated as precisely as possible if one is to verify it. The dividing line between descriptive and experimental phases of research is, in fact, not as distinct as may appear at first sight. For one thing, in the course of experiments opportunities may arise for gathering descriptive data, and though the generalizability of the data beyond the laboratory situation will need to be ascertained any information additional to the specific experimental measures may well be pertinent in throwing light on what is being investigated. And for another, during field observations hypotheses can sometimes be tested, e.g. that one particular phenomenon (such as a raised level of aggression) always follows another (such as viewing violence on television), or that a particular behavior pattern is more likely to occur under one set of environmental conditions than under some other condition (such as immature play behavior in overcrowded environments). Nevertheless, the basic point is that the two kinds of research serve different functions: one to answer "what" questions and the other "why" questions.

The "why" types of question are addressed to various issues. In child psychology one of the main points of interest naturally concerns the reasons for developmental change. Descriptive research can tell us that there are age differences and provide details regarding the nature of these differences. But how does it come about that children first start showing signs of self-awareness some time in the course of the second year of life? Or that role taking skills develop sharply at the end of the preschool period? Or that at entry to adolescence there is a marked increase in the intimacy that characterizes friendships? What processes are responsible for producing these changes? Such questions about the mechanisms behind psychological growth are at the very heart of developmental psychology; it is therefore hard to acknowledge that we still know relatively little that will help to answer them – children get more competent with age, but why?

Other "why" questions concern the reasons for individual differences between children. Why, for example, is one child more sociable than another? Nature? Nurture? Some sort of combination of the two? Why do some children develop deviant conditions such as delinquency or autism? And even with regard to something as basic as the nature and limits of parental influence on the course of children's personality development – here too there is still much controversy and a great deal to be learned. Indeed any attempt to answer questions concerning causation, however important and fascinating these problems may be, has so far met with only limited success. But perhaps this is not really surprising, for to a large extent it is a reflection of the sheer complexity of the phenomena we are trying to understand and the many influences that jointly play a part in accounting for any particular outcome. All aspects of psychological development are multi-determined; disentangling the many factors involved is a considerable task, and it is therefore hardly surprising that as yet our knowledge about the nature of children's behavior far outstrips our knowledge about the causes of that behavior. The case concerning the effects of mothers' employment on children provides an example of the complexity that characterizes so many real-life situations.

The case of maternal employment

Over the last few decades there has been a very large increase in the number of mothers who are employed outside the home, the increase being greatest among those with preschool children. There are many who deplore this trend, believing that it is tantamount to deprivation of maternal care at a time when children need their mothers' attention most, that it drastically weakens the bond with the mother and that it may be the cause of many of the ills of society. Research was therefore undertaken, with the initial expectation that it would yield straightforward answers in terms of "good" or "bad" and so provide clear-cut guidelines to those needing to make decisions on this issue.

In fact, the history of work in this area has been one of locating a seemingly ever-increasing number of variables that exercise some sort of moderating effect on the outcome. The following are among the main ones (see Gottfried & Gottfried, 1988; L. W. Hoffman, 1989):

1 *The child's age.* There are suggestions (though disputed) that maternal employment during the child's first year may have more deleterious effects on the growing relationship with the mother than can be found at other ages.

2 *The child's sex.* According to some studies the consequences of having an employed mother differ for boys and for girls, with the former more likely to show adverse effects.

3 *The child's temperament.* As with any kind of experience, the impact is not uniform across all children but is mediated by various aspects of the child's personality.

4 *The mother's motivation,* i.e. whether the mother actually wants to go out to work or is forced to do so by financial necessity, has

been found to affect the child, presumably through the kind of mood produced in her by these circumstances.

5 *The effect on the mother's self-image,* i.e. whether her morale is boosted by having an intellectually and socially satisfying job, may in turn have implications for the relationship with the child.

6 *The mother's ability to cope with role strain.* The possibility of overload as a result of multiple responsibilities is one of the more common problems that employed mothers must face; how successful they are in coping with it affects the child.

7 *Support from father.* This refers not only to practical help with child care and housework but also to agreement with the mother's original decision to work outside the home, and thus determines the family atmosphere in which the child is reared.

8 *Number of hours worked.* While the relationship between the length of the mother's daily absence from home and the effects on the child is not a linear one, various negative effects have been found when the number of hours exceeds full time.

9 *The quality and consistency of the child's substitute care,* both of which have turned out to be among the most important considerations in evaluating the effects of maternal employment.

10 *The outcome measures employed to assess the effects on the child.* Literally dozens of such measures, reflecting all sorts of aspects of intellectual and social development, have been investigated. What applies to one aspect need not apply to another, as the experience may produce different effects on different functions.

There is evidence that each one of the above variables plays some part in shaping the outcome. As a result, sweeping generalizations as to whether maternal employment is good or bad for young children cannot be made. Admittedly, there is now general agreement that such an experience need not produce the ill effects feared by some; indeed, some studies have even found children of employed mothers to have certain advantages over those of nonemployed mothers. What can be concluded is that a simple cause-and-effect model, where maternal employment is the cause and the nature of children's development the effect, is too simplistic. The mother's employment is embedded in a context of a great many other family variables, each one of which needs to be taken into account. It produces its effects not directly but through an altered pattern of relationships, and to understand how particular consequences are produced a family perspective must therefore be adopted – one that is considerably more complex than the linear cause–effect model previously regarded as adequate.

Topics Investigated

Among the huge number of questions that one can raise about social development only a certain number are selected for attention by research workers and their clients at any one time. Periodically these change: new topics come to the fore and form rallying points for scientific excitement as old ones are discarded like last year's out-of-fashion clothes. What determines the choice of topics?

There are a number of factors, but among these one of the more important is the influence of the major theoretical frameworks predominant at the time. One of the functions of a theory is to throw up new questions that need to be answered by appropriate empirical data: psychoanalytic theory, for example, drew our attention to the possibly crucial role of infant rearing practices and thus gave rise to a great deal of research on the relationship between parental care patterns and children's personality development; Piagetian theory gave prominence to the alleged egocentrism of young children and brought into being a wave of work on the ability of children to accommodate their behavior to the requirements and characteristics of others; and ethology threw a completely new light on the formation of attachments, stimulating much research into an old problem but from a very different perspective. In each case new questions are formulated, the attention of the research community is accordingly redirected and it becomes positively fashionable to work in an area that is generating so much intellectual excitement.

Another factor that determines the direction of research refers to the availability of methods and techniques to undertake investigation into certain problems. Consider the whole area of psychological functions in infancy – for long a closed book as far as empirical research was concerned because the customary methods of obtaining data about human beings (interviews, questionnaires, tests, etc.) were obviously inappropriate and there was thus no apparent "way in" as far as such very young children were concerned. No wonder the state of the infant's mind was subject to wild and contradictory speculation! It was not till Fantz (1961), Lipsitt (1963), Papousek (1961), and others decided to use whatever minimal response capacities infants do have – selective looking, sucking, head turning, and various physiological indices of arousal – that it became possible to begin proper empirical research on topics that had remained dormant until then. Thus the visual preference technique, as perfected by Fantz, enabled work to be carried out on infants' face perception and to answer such questions as the extent to which newborns are already selectively attuned to human stimuli, the particular aspects of the face to which they are responsive at various ages, and the ability to discriminate familiar and novel social stimuli and its development over the course of infancy (Fantz & Nevis, 1967). Similarly the development of a means for assessing various qualitative aspects of attachment behavior through Ainsworth's construction of the Strange Situation technique (Ainsworth, Blehar, Waters, & Wahl, 1978) enabled a whole range of questions concerning individual differences in infants' attachment formation to be examined.

The choice of topics is, however, not merely determined by what is happening within the ivory tower of academic research. Increasingly pressures from society are playing a part in that choice, and especially so at a time of rapid social and technological change. The examples of divorce, day care, homosexuality, drug abuse, and TV violence are but some of those that spring to mind. All these raise questions of a practical nature, though in tackling them the psychologist may well use the findings obtained also to extend knowledge of theoretical issues. The to-and-fro between theory and application is much to be welcomed by both parties involved – by practitioners because they can base their decisions about individuals on guidelines provided by objective research rather than on assumption and guesswork, and by academic research workers because the problems they are requested to investigate are "real" ones. In any case pressures from society can exert a powerful influence on the direction of work, often leading to results that are theoretically meaningful and practically useful at the same time.

Theories change, for having outlived their usefulness they are replaced by new ones. Methods change, in that increasingly sophisticated techniques become available for use in research. And the problems that society throws up also change: maternal employment was not an issue that caused much concern 50 years ago; drug abuse by teenagers is a relatively new phenomenon; and child abuse by family members, though probably as old as the family itself, has only relatively recently reached the public conscience. As a result of all these changes the questions which demand an answer from research also change from time to time, and especially so because of another force at work, namely the inexorable advance of knowledge itself. As old problems are dealt with new ones appear, often in the very process of attempting to solve the previous ones. Infants are found to be perceptually competent to a degree not previously attributed to them: so what is that competence used for in learning to form relationships with others? Preschool children are found to be nowhere near as egocentric as Piaget had suggested, but what are the limits of the prosocial behavior of which they are capable and what are its origins and determinants? Measures of temperament have been perfected which can now be applied to even very young children and seem to indicate various inborn tendencies that are fairly stable over time; we can now go on to ask about the way such tendencies affect the parents and their treatment of the child. That hackneyed phrase "pushing out the frontiers of knowledge" is in fact a highly appropriate one which emphasizes what is after all one of the most important aspects of any scientific endeavor, namely that it never stands still.

There are, it is true, some topics that have been on the agenda for a long time, for their complexity is such that there are no easy answers. The most obvious example is the nature–nurture controversy – the extent to which behavior is shaped by forces inherent in the child from birth as opposed to forces emanating from outside the child and referring to the particular experiences that child is exposed to. Yet here too, despite the complexity of the question, progress has been made: to appreciate this one only needs to consider the extreme statements on behalf of *either* nature *or* nurture made by such protagonists as Gesell (1933) and Watson (1925) and compare them with the position currently adopted by behavior geneticists (e.g. Plomin, 1990; Scarr, 1992). As we shall see later, nature and nurture are no longer seen as separate, opposing forces; they interact in a variety of highly intricate ways which demonstrate that the either-or position makes no sense when discussing psychological functions.

One general trend in the study of social development which deserves special mention refers to the way in which the focus of interest has increasingly widened as our knowledge has grown. Early studies of children's social behavior were essentially concerned with the children as *individuals*: they treated social behavior as a property of the child and the questions they set out to answer dealt accordingly with such issues of individuality as the age when children first reach particular milestones (the first smile, the onset of fear of strangers, the beginnings of cooperative behavior, and so on), the differences between groups of children (are boys more aggressive than girls? are only children less sociable than children with siblings?), and the nature of individual differences (whether the rate of social development parallels that of intellectual development, whether aggression is a unitary trait, and so forth). Such questions may be perfectly proper and worth while; however, by themselves they are not sufficient because they miss out what most people regard as the essence of social behavior, that is, the *to-and-fro between individuals*. It is only comparatively recently that this to-and-fro has become a topic of interest in its own right; the focus, that is, has widened beyond events *within* individuals to the study of the interactions and relationships *between* individuals. Thus the dyad (e.g. of mother and child) became the basic unit of interest rather than the individual; subsequently the focus widened still further to larger, polyadic groups such as the family or the peer group, on the assumption that what goes on between any two individuals is also a function of other, concurrent interactions and relationships in which each participant is involved and that systems as a whole (such as families and peer groups) must therefore be the unit of study. However, even at that point one cannot draw hard and fast lines of demarcation: families in turn are part of wider social structures such as the neighborhood or the cultural group to which they belong, and what goes on between family members is very much a function also of characteristics of these wider systems. The story of the study of social development in recent years is thus very much a matter of increasing awareness of the importance of *context*, that is, the realization that the behavior of individual children is given meaning by the relationships in which the child is embedded, that these relationships in turn are embedded in systems such as families, and that these too can only be fully understood within the context of the society of which they form a part. Admittedly in practice one cannot study everything and one has to draw the line somewhere. To answer a question such as about the age when infants first begin to smile discriminately at familiar people it may be adequate to take only the individual child as the unit of study; and yet, even here, one must consider the possibility that the behavior of their caretakers may influence that age, and also the fact that the nature of caretakers' behavior as well as the number and identity of these caretakers is determined by the society of which they are a part. If one is fully to understand the onset of infants' discriminate smiling and also be able to generalize beyond the particular cultural group observed it does become necessary to take into account the wider context in which individual behavior takes place.

Conceptions and Preconceptions

The search for insight into the nature of social development is not merely a search for a lot of facts about children's behavior with other people, haphazardly collected and haphazardly put together. Like any scientific enterprise it needs to be selective in the direction it takes, and for that purpose it requires guidance. A theoretical framework can provide such guidance: theories such as psychoanalysis or social learning theory have exercised enormous influence on the kinds of topics that have been selected for study and the kinds of interpretations that have been put on the findings. Establishing such theories, deriving hypotheses from them, putting these hypotheses to the test and modifying the theory according to the results obtained – all this seems like a highly rational, intellectual exercise and no doubt corresponds to the stereotype of how a scientist goes about the business of science: detached, objective, and cold-blooded.

Reality is rather different, and to understand what has been learned about social development so far we need to consider *how* we have learned it. We need, that is, to take into account the various influences over and above the push of theory that propel the scientific enterprise. Above all, we need to be aware of the value judgments, assumptions, and preconceptions that may play a vital part even in selecting the kind of theory considered to be congenial and worth backing. This applies to all science but especially so to the social sciences in general and psychology in particular. The preconceptions may stem in part from the personal history and experience of the individual scientist, but they also reflect the values that are prevalent at that particular time and in that particular place.

Changing Images of Childhood

What is a child? There is no absolute answer to this question; it is relative to the socioeconomic conditions of each society, to the current state of medical and scientific knowledge and to the religious and philosophical dogmas to which most people subscribe at that time. Each society, that is, constructs its own image of childhood, and the needs and abilities ascribed to children, the forces that account for developmental change and hence also the role caretakers are supposed to fulfill – all these are to a large extent a function of that image.

The point is made by the historical accounts of childhood that writers such as Aries (1973) and de Mause (1974) have published. Consider the advice on child rearing by Susanna Wesley, the mother of the British evangelist John Wesley, writing in the 18th century:

> I insist upon conquering the wills of children betimes; because this is the only foundation for a religious education . . . Heaven or Hell depends on this alone. So that the parent who studies to subdue [self-will] in his children, works together with God in the saving of a soul: the parent who indulges it does the devil's work. This, therefore, I cannot but earnestly repeat, – Break their wills betimes; begin this great work before they can run alone, before they can speak plain, or perhaps speak at all. Whatever pain it costs, conquer their stubbornness; break their will, if you would not damn the child . . . Therefore (1) Let a child, from a year old, be taught to fear the rod and to cry softly. In order to do this, (2) Let him have nothing he cries for; absolutely nothing, great or small; else you undo your own work. (3) At all events, from that age, make him do as he is bid, if you whip him ten times running to effect it. (from Newson & Newson, 1974)

To us this seems like undue harshness, even outright cruelty; such treatment, however, was part and parcel of the Puritan ethos that pervaded every aspect of the society in which Mrs Wesley lived – an ethos that was preoccupied with sin and that compelled parents to stamp out sin in their children by punitive and authoritarian measures in order to save them from eternal damnation. Looking back, it is easy to condemn; nowadays, however, we are living in a different social climate where life is less harsh and where a more relaxed, positive view of childhood can be taken. Contrast the views of two 20th-century child-rearing experts with those of Mrs Wesley:

> Children do not need teaching as much as they need love and understanding. They need approval and freedom to be naturally good. (Neill, 1962)

> Your baby is born to be a reasonable, friendly human being. (Spock, 1948)

All these views express *philosophies* of child rearing; they are not the hard-and-fast conclusions derived from some objective research inquiry and are thus based more on some general feeling about childhood and its purpose, indeed about human nature generally, than on any empirical knowledge. Such philosophies can change drastically as society changes. During the Industrial Revolution at the beginning of the 19th century children from the poorer classes in England were sent from as young an age as 5 to work in factories and down mines, spending 12 or even 16 hours a day under conditions that to us seem quite appalling (Kessen, 1965) but that at the time gave little concern to employers, the general public, or even the children's parents. Society needed all the workers it could get; families depended on the earnings of all their members, even the youngest; and the notion that children have educational needs that ought to be given priority was not yet widely accepted. Given the economic conditions at that time, the image of the child as a *worker* prevailed above all else. Whether the subsequent change in that image was due to the advent of a more enlightened view of childhood, or whether it was because the economically oppressive conditions of that period changed for the better is open to debate. In any case, within the space of a few decades, and despite assertions such as that by one mine owner, that "for miners' children a practical education in the collieries is superior to a reading education" (Kessen, 1965), school replaced the workplace as the "natural" setting for young children and education was seen as a child's "right."

Even today, despite the spread across the world of Western norms of behavior, the diversity of child rearing practices among different cultures is still instructive. In each case children are brought up to fit in with some image of the ideal member of that society: needs and abilities are read into the child accordingly and the role of the caretaker is then interpreted in the light of these alleged needs. Take a society like that of the Kaluli, a tribe living in a remote and isolated part of Papua New Guinea, where communal living is the norm, where families spend the major part of their daily lives together with the rest of their tribe rather than in the privacy of their own home, and where child care is shared out among different adults to a far greater extent than is customary in the West. As described by Schieffelin and Ochs (1983), Kaluli mothers rarely engage in dyadic forms of interaction with their infants. Episodes of mutual gazing do not occur; instead of facing their babies and talking to them directly the mothers orient the infant outwards so that it can be seen by and see others that are part of the social group. Where the social group rather than the mother–infant dyad is the basic unit in society such treatment makes sense, however aberrant it may seem to us at first sight. Fostering emotional dependence on *one* individual is considered as inappropriate in that community; the more a mother can help her child to become oriented to the group as a whole the more she can prepare it for the kind of life it will lead there. The mother treats the infant as though she sees it as belonging as much to the social group as to herself.

A comparison of children's treatment by preschool staff in three different cultures, China, Japan, and the United States, makes the same point (Tobin, Wu, & Davidson, 1989): each society constructs its own ideas as to what childhood is about and in what direction children should be steered, and then brings up its children accordingly. Take the practices observed in Chinese preschool centers. In all respects children there are required to conform to the common purpose and to value the group above the individual. From the earliest years on they are taught to play cooperatively with others and not to fight for individual possession of toys. To Western eyes an excessive amount of regimentation takes place, to the extent that children are all directed to go to the bathroom at the same time. Contrast that with preschool practices in America or Europe, where the stress is very much on individualism and where there is an underlying assumption that children are basically *unalike* and need to be treated accordingly.

Scientific endeavors to understand children's development are not immune from such assumptions. The psychologist is, after all, part of a particular culture, brought up to cherish certain values and to hold to certain belief systems, which will influence professional every bit as much as private activity. This is perhaps inevitable; it may even be regarded as desirable in that communication of psychological knowledge to the rest of society would be so much more difficult if one did not operate within a common framework of values. But at the very least we need to be aware of this influence – on the topics that are selected for study, on the theories put forward to make sense of findings, even on the kind of measures used to express particular concepts. How we conceptualize and assess children's social competence provides one example.

The case of social competence

In recent years the notion of social competence has become a frequently used concept to express a desirable end result of child development. As such it certainly has intuitive appeal; however, it is also so global an idea that it is no wonder that different writers have put forward different definitions for this concept (see Schneider, 1993, for a review). Various aspects of children's social behavior have been suggested as representing the essence of competence, some more vague than others – the capacity to interact effectively with the environment; the attainment of relevant social goals; the ability to engage effectively in complex interpersonal interaction; specific skills such as friendship formation and being able to join in with others; and certain outcomes such as popularity and peer acceptance. As Dodge put it in 1985, the number of definitions of social competence seems to approach the number of investigators in the field – a situation that has changed little today.

Divergencies in definition lead to divergent ways of measuring, and the choice often seems to depend on value judgments that remain unexpressed and implicit. Take what was one of the first and most influential attempts to provide a means of assessment, namely a scale proposed by Harter (1982) for children of elementary school age and forming part of a more general competence scale (the other parts refer to cognitive competence and physical competence). The social competence scale comprises the following items (each of which children are asked to check for themselves):

- have lot of friends
- popular with kids
- easy to like
- do things with kids
- easy to make friends
- important to classmates
- most kids like me

As an index of what a socially competent child should be the items clearly refer to a particular ideal, that is, an extroverted, active, popular, and happy-go-lucky child (it is also relevant that the social competence scale turned out to be highly correlated with the physical competence one, which referred primarily to being good at sports – i.e. prowess at athletics is part of the picture). It follows that the child of a naturally more introverted disposition is penalized as relatively incompetent, though whether a large number of friends is "better" than having just a few friends, especially when no account is taken of the depth of the relationships, is surely debatable.

The role of value judgments as to what should be included in such a scale is obvious, and especially when one considers what else could be

included. As Harter acknowledges, the emphasis is on popularity rather than on social skills; children's behavior in large groups is given priority over their intimate one-to-one contacts. The child, moreover, is seen as a behaving rather than as a thinking being: excluded from consideration are such qualities as maturity of decision making in social situations, accuracy of judgments about other people, and understanding of and empathy with others' motives; also excluded are prosocial aspects such as helping, sharing, tolerance, and willingness to cooperate.

Many other measures of social competence have since been proposed, some based on conceptual schemes that emphasize quite different aspects of competence (e.g. Dodge, Pettit, McClaskey, & Brown, 1986; Waters & Sroufe, 1983), though social popularity remains one of the more common (Hubbard & Coie, 1994). In each case, however, certain assumptions are made about the nature of childhood and about the kind of personal qualities that ought to be fostered, with cultural bias prominent among these assumptions. Disagreement among research workers about findings may then turn out to reflect value judgments rather than differences concerning theoretical or purely technical matters.

Major Theoretical Frameworks

There are, of course, more formal guides in the search for knowledge about children's development than value judgments and preconceptions, and scientific theories in particular serve this purpose. Theories are sets of propositions that make sense of isolated facts by relating them to more general principles; they order whatever information has already been obtained and guide the search for further information. Thus a theory is essentially a tool to enable one to think about a body of facts; the tool is discarded when it is no longer found useful, that is, when it ceases to make sense of new information or when hypotheses derived from the theory are not borne out on testing.

In the field of child psychology theories vary greatly in scale – from megatheories that cover great ranges of developmental phenomena and were adhered to with almost religious fervor by their followers to far more modest propositions with the aim of doing justice to just a highly limited set of observations. The former, of course, are better known; they are of interest not only for the specific constructs they offer but also for the particular view of childhood each represents. Let us briefly look at the more influential ones; detailed accounts can be found elsewhere (e.g. A. L. Baldwin, 1980; Crain, 1992); here we will only give the highlights of each and particularly consider its bearing on the study of social development.

(1) *Psychoanalytic theory* Of all psychological theories that put forward by Freud is popularly the best known. This is hardly surprising: it touches on virtually every aspect of behavior and society; its tone and content, with its emphasis on the irrational and emotional and particularly the sexual side of human nature, made it quite sensational at the time of its appearance; and it was linked to a therapeutic method that promised to alleviate many disorders for which there was then no other cure.

Freud was no student of child behavior; his concern was with adult patients whose neurotic conditions he attempted to understand and resolve. However, he came to the conclusion that the roots of such disorders – indeed of all behavior in maturity – are to be found in events occurring in early childhood and that his task as a therapist was therefore to retrace the course of development and to confront his patients with those events. The view of the young child which Freud thus came to form on the basis of the retrospective information offered by his patients was of a basically self-seeking creature – one driven by primitive impulses that the child initially sought to gratify at all cost. However, society cannot function if its members live according to such a pleasure principle, and it is therefore the task of parents to help the child develop appreciation of outer reality and to learn means of delaying and inhibiting impulse gratification. How this is accomplished forms the principal part of Freud's developmental theory.

Freud liked to think in terms of mental entities, that is, components of the mind that represent particular sets of functions. Accordingly he proposed that the child starts life with an *id*, which is the source of all selfish impulses requiring immediate gratification and which is thus governed by the pleasure principle. In due course, however, two other entities emerge: the *ego*, which is turned toward the outer world, functions according to the reality principle and is thus able to exercise restraint over the child's primitive impulses in the light of realistic information, and the *superego*, which is made up from parental prohibitions and other exhortations that become internalized and so enable the individual to exercise self-regulation by means such as feelings of guilt. Much of childhood is a painful struggle between these three structures – in fact conflict is an all-pervasive theme that the deeply pessimistic Freud ascribed to all aspects of development: conflict between the pleasure principle and the reality principle, conflict between the individual and society and conflict between id, ego, and superego. The early years, according to this view, are thus a far cry from that happy, carefree period of innocence that so many others have depicted for childhood. No wonder that (at least according to Freud) so much can go wrong during those years and account for so much pathology later on!

The conflicts that children experience between their strong inner needs on the one hand and the demands of parents and society on the other hand occur according to a definite timetable of bodily growth, as given by the succession of oral, anal, phallic, latency, and genital stages. In each the child's interests are dominated by particular physical functions, and in each the child requires the "right" sort of experiences if it is to pass through that phase successfully. For example, during the oral stage, when activities such as sucking, mouthing, and biting predominate, it is especially the way in which parents deal with the feeding situation that will determine the psycho-logical outcome for the child. Too much or too little gratification, punishment for thumb sucking, too early or too sudden weaning – these are the sort of parental rearing practices that may make it impossible for the child to cope properly with the developmental demands of that period, leaving the individual fixated at that point and resulting in symptoms such as compulsive eating or addictive smoking which indicate that even during adulthood that person is still coping with an infantile conflict.

Appropriate parental treatment is thus one prerequisite for coping with tension and violent emotion. Another lies in the development of *defense mechanisms*, that is, psychological means which children employ in order to avoid such difficulties. *Repression* is probably the most important of these mechanisms; it is the means whereby unbearable memories are driven into the unconscious and need thus no longer be confronted. Another common defense mechanism is *regression*, as seen when in the face of a stressful event such as a sibling's birth a child retreats to the comforts of babyhood. And a third is *identification*: confronted by parental disap-proval of impulse gratification the child, rather than incur punishment and lose the parents' love, incorporates their standards and, as it were, becomes the parent. Defense mechanisms clearly serve a vital function: they prevent excessive anxiety arising from the various conflicts to which the child is exposed and make the task of adjustment to environmental demands easier. Yet there may also be a price to pay: a repressed memory, for example, will remain active and manifest itself indirectly through symptoms, and these in turn may produce difficulties and problems of adjustment. Whether such memories can emerge in later years, either spontaneously or by the use of particular techniques during therapy, and how reliable such memo-ries are, is an issue of great importance, especially to the alleged perpetrators and victims of sexual abuse. There is no doubt that sexual abuse of children is tragically common; it has to be concluded, however, that so far there is no scientific evidence to demonstrate the authenticity of repressed memories that are subsequently recov-ered (Brewin, Andrews, & Gotlieb, 1993; Loftus, 1993).

Freud's theory no longer arouses the intense reaction (devotion *or* hostility) that it did at one time. In a sense that is a measure of its success: it has been assimilated into thinking about human nature and concepts such as unconscious motivation and infantile sexuality (broadly interpreted as sensuality) are widely accepted. Not that all of Freud's formulations have been accepted – far from it, and from our point of view it is perhaps particularly significant that it is his developmental notions that have fared worse when subjected to more orthodox empirical tests than those applied by Freud himself. In particular, the idea that certain experiences represent infantile traumata that will be associated with specific personality characteristics and problems later on in life has received no confirmation (Orlansky, 1949; Caldwell, 1964): particular infant-care practices do not have an unvarying psychological effect that manifests itself in later life. Also Freud's belief that initially the infant is characterized only by various biological needs (for food, warmth, and pain reduction) and becomes interested in other people merely because they are experienced as sources of gratification for these needs remains unsubstantiated: on the contrary, there is every indication that from the beginning children are attuned to their social world and preadapted to pay special attention to and interact with other people (Schaffer, 1984). And finally, however useful Freud's emphasis on the first few years of life may have been, the notion that early experience is irreversible and that we remain victims of our past is no longer credible (A. M. Clarke & Clarke, 1976); as we shall see later on, Freud greatly overestimated the power of the past and saw personality development as much too rigidly predetermined.

What Freud did achieve was to provide a counterweight to the behavioristic ideas about child development that were emerging at about the same time. As the section on behaviorism below will show, the behaviorists' view of the child was a very different one: cold-blooded, based on learning principles, missing out on all the agony and tension of growing up. Freud, coming to child development via his neurotic patients with their intense fears and anxieties and anger, had other ideas: to him it was the emotional aspects of children's minds that were of prime importance. Much of value followed from that: the emphasis on children's sensuality, the need to consider the part played by unconscious forces, the search for the mind's defenses and the importance attached to the quality of early parent–child interaction. Whether and in what way that quality affects the kinds of relationships established later on in life remains controversial and is a topic still under investigation. What Freud certainly inspired was the great interest shown by subsequent workers (and the general public) in the developmental origins of all sorts of psychological functions: the operation of conscience; the formation of attachments; the appearance of sex role behavior; the channeling of the child's aggressive drives; the construction of a self-image; the motivation underlying altruistic behavior, and so forth. And in addition, such general themes as the stage-like nature of development, issues of continuity and discontinuity and the relative role of biological and experiential factors in development also owe to Freud the impetus which his speculations provided to other thinkers.

(2) *Behaviorism*　At about the same time that Freud put forward his views, that is, around the beginning of the 20th century, a very different conception of human nature and its development emerged in America, due primarily to the influential

writings of John B. Watson (1913; 1928). In some respects the parentage of behaviorism goes back to John Locke (1693), who wrote one of the earliest advice-to-parents books because, as he put it, "I myself have been consulted of late by so many who profess themselves at a loss of how to breed their children . . ." and also because "the early corruption of Youth is now become so general a complaint" (17th-century echoes of only too familiar modern day complaints!). In that book Locke suggested that the child's mind is initially like a blank slate, a *tabula rasa*, which could only be inscribed by experience, and it was up to parents to provide that experience in the form of learned associations and habits. The developed personality, that is, is a function of what has come to the child from outside and is composed primarily of the many tiny building blocks representing individual learned experiences.

Locke was a philosopher, with no empirical basis to his proposals other than a few ad hoc observations. Watson, on the other hand, lived at a time when psychology was just emerging as a scientific discipline, and he came to the study of children via experimental investigations of rats with the strong conviction that the psychology of human beings, every bit as much as that of animals, should be based on overt, observable behavior and not on mysterious inner, mental events. Much of psychological writing at the time relied on introspection for its raw data; without denying the reality of mental events Watson considered them to be outside the realm of scientific study and fit only for unchecked speculation. Thus while Freud considered the "real" child to be represented by its inner life Watson attempted to redirect attention to what was external and open to examination by any observer.

The notion that only overt behavior can be the province of the psychologist was one of Watson's messages. The other was the same as Locke's: the environment determines behavior; the building blocks of human development are learned associations (between stimuli and responses, according to Watson); and a child at birth can therefore be regarded as infinitely modifiable. As Watson (1925) put it in a much quoted passage:

> Give me a dozen healthy infants, well-formed and my own special world to bring them up in and I'll guarantee to take any one at random and train him to become any type of specialist I might select – doctor, lawyer, artist, merchant-chief and, yes, even beggar-man and thief – regardless of his talents, penchants, tendencies, abilities and vocation and race of his ancestors.

It is thus the task of parents to ensure that children are provided with the right learning experiences – indeed their responsibility according to the Watsonian view is an awesome one, and Watson had no hesitation in laying down how this should be discharged, i.e. by avoiding hugging, kissing, and other forms of overt affection (condemned by him as "mawkish and sentimental") and replacing them by matter-of-fact, unemotional ways. Such advice probably tells one more about Watson's personality and upbringing than about psychology; the emphasis on modification through experience, on the other hand, was taken up avidly by the learning theorists, led by Clark L. Hull and B. F. Skinner, who wanted to transform psychology into a science as hardnosed and respectable as physics and who found Watson's principle of human beings' infinite modifiability through experience to provide a most congenial framework within which to operate.

Some of Watson's early efforts were devoted to demonstrating that experience, through a process of association, can indeed modify behavior. The best known example is provided by Little Albert, a 9-month-old infant who was shown a rabbit on several occasions at the same time as being subjected to a very loud noise. His fear of the latter quickly generalized to the former, so that he cried even when the rabbit appeared without the accompanying noise. This was considered a paradigm not only for the acquisition of fears but for the growth of behavior generally, and again shows Watson's conviction that parents can make of their children what they will (as well as demonstrating that ethical considerations were not allowed to interfere with the conduct of his experiments on even very young children!).

Watson went further, however, in that he also attempted to locate the mechanism whereby the child's learning and development are made possible. He found the solution, he thought, in Pavlov's work on the conditioned reflex – a notion that was subsequently developed to form the foundation for the considerable edifice of American learning theory, with its twin devices of classical and operant conditioning. Classical conditioning involved the pairing of stimuli, as in Little Albert's case, and was directly derived from Pavlov's experiments on dogs who learned to salivate at the sound of a bell that had been repeatedly paired with food. Operant conditioning came to be linked to Skinner's work (1953) and the demonstration that behavior can be controlled by its consequences: children, that is, expand their behavioral repertoire because they learn that certain responses are followed by reward; other responses are eliminated because they are followed by punishment. Thus Skinner, like Watson, saw the true causes of children's development to lie in the external environment and moreover considered the relationship between the individual's behavior and its reinforcement to be the primary mechanism for developmental progress; to change a child's behavior one must change the reinforcement, and parental rearing practices must therefore be interpreted in this light.

Behaviorism was enormously influential for a large part of the 20th century, yet its legacy has proved to be more methodological than substantive. Skinner in particular insisted on the need for tightly controlled experimental techniques, whether the subject is a pigeon in the renowned Skinner box or a child in a laboratory setting, and his writings gave rise to a whole industry of research on topics such as social reinforcement, devoted to plotting the way in which adult approval or disapproval shapes various facets of child behavior (see Stevenson, 1965, for examples). Methodologically such work was in many respects highly sophisticated; its analytic approach also had the advantage of stimulating interest in the observation of the more fine-grained aspects of children's behavior and its environmental concomitants. And yet one must also conclude that it was features of the learning theorists' methodology that constituted one major reason for the eventual downfall of their view, for the insistence on control resulted in the neglect of real-life settings in favor of laboratory studies, where children carried out meaningless tasks like dropping marbles into boxes, accompanied by the carefully predetermined noises of approval or disapproval from strange adults serving as experimenters. Ecological validity was sacrificed to experimental rigor; increasingly doubts were raised as to the meaningfulness of findings obtained in such a manner.

The other main reason for dissatisfaction with behaviorism lay in its "empty child" philosophy. Watson's boast that he could make any child into whatever he chose it to be – doctor or lawyer, beggarman or thief – was, fortunately for him, never put to the test; had it been he would quickly have come up against the individuality which resides in even the youngest infant. The unidirectional view of socialization, where parents mold their children into any shape they like, has had to be abandoned in the face of growing evidence of *child effects*, that is, the influences that children from birth on exert over parents by virtue of their own temperamental and other individual characteristics (R. Q. Bell, 1968). The concept of the child as a passive recipient of other people's stimulation could therefore no longer be upheld; parent– child interaction, as we shall see, has turned out to be a much more intricate process than Watson and Skinner depicted it to be. And one further cause for dissatisfaction with behaviorism concerns what is, after all, its primary assertion, i.e. that the student of development must remain outside the child and refuse to acknowledge the opera- tion of inner mental processes. With the advent of cognitively oriented theories such as that of Piaget it became increasingly difficult to maintain that the child was not actively selecting, interpreting, and processing stimulation; the empty-child notion therefore grossly misrepresented reality. Thus behaviorism was eventually aban- doned as providing too mechanical an account; it put all its eggs into the reinforce- ment basket as the means whereby development proceeds; and it saw the transaction between child and caretaker as a wholly one-sided affair and so failed to do justice to the role of children as active agents in their own upbringing.

(3)   *Social learning theory*   Dissatisfaction with behaviorism took various forms, and initially was seen in the efforts by a group of individuals brought up in the learning theory tradition (Neal Miller, John Dollard, Robert and Pauline Sears and their associates) to marry their concepts with ideas derived from psychoanalysis. These two theories are, of course, very different in many ways; however, it was hoped that the shortcomings of each would be compensated for by the advantages of the other – in particular, that by translating psychoanalytic ideas into learning theory terms one would be able to put the former to empirical test and at the same time preserve the dynamic character of Freudian ideas so sadly lacking from behaviorist concepts.

The best known example of such efforts is the study reported by Sears, Maccoby, and Levin (1957), which set out to determine the kinds of relationships that exist between parental rearing practices and children's personality characteristics. The particular relationships investigated were hypothesized largely on the basis of psy- choanalytic propositions but explained by invoking mechanisms derived from learning theory. For instance, individual differences in children's aggressiveness were thought to relate to the extent of parental restrictiveness, the effect brought about – as Freud had suggested – by the frustration engendered in the child by parents' punitive demands. Similarly, variations in children's dependency behavior were said to derive directly from the warmth and nurturance with which their parents treated them, particularly in infancy, reinforcing the child's efforts to obtain attention and gratification from the parent. In order to investigate hypothesized links such as these Sears and colleagues interviewed nearly 400 mothers about their rearing methods, as well as about the child's behavior, and examined the pattern of correlations thus obtained. The results yielded a lot of useful data about the mothers' rearing methods; however, their contribution to the understanding of children's personality development was disappointingly limited. As shown by the small size of the correlations between parental measures and child measures, explaining personality development on this basis turned out to be an unpromising approach.

There are a number of probable reasons for this failure: the concentration on the mother as the sole source of experience; the reliance on interviews as the only method for obtaining information; a conception of characteristics such as dependence and aggressiveness as unitary entities; and above all the assumption that parental rearing (as an input variable) is wholly responsible for the nature of children's psychological development. As we shall see later, the socialization process is vastly more complex: it is multi-determined, with children's own characteristics being one of the major influences to be taken into account. Sears and colleagues, in keeping with learning theory tradition, concentrated on external experience as shaping children, assuming, for instance, that it is feasible to establish direct causal links between mothers' child rearing practices and the children's behavior. In short, the study reflected the general consensus at that time that child development is largely to be explained by whatever it is that mothers do to children – a unilateral view of the relationship which, in retrospect, was probably the most important reason for the failure to obtain a convincing pattern of correlations.

Dissatisfaction with traditional learning theory as an account of psychological development also took other forms. Most noteworthy was the social learning theory created by Bandura (1977; Bandura & Walters, 1963), which was an attempt to preserve all the conceptual and methodological rigors of the earlier approach and continue its emphasis on learning processes, but at the same time to do justice to the fact that we can learn from other people by merely observing and imitating them. Observational learning was thus promoted to the role of prime mechanism whereby children acquire a behavioral repertoire that equips them for social living: a great deal of psychological development can be explained, Bandura believed, by the simple act of watching suitable models and subsequently reproducing their behavior. Freud too had stressed the role which identification with others plays in children's development, and he too had singled out the motive to be like the parent as a significant force in their growth. Bandura, however, in keeping with the behaviorist tradition, considered the psychoanalytic account too loaded with mysterious and unobservable processes – hence his attempt to set up the concept of imitation as a more narrowly defined but observable type of learning. This also had the advantage, as compared with the bit-by-bit procedures of trial-and-error learning accounts, that the acquisition of whole sequences of behavior could be explained; it had the further advantage over psychoanalytic accounts that the phenomenon could be brought under experimental control and thus investigated under laboratory conditions.

Bandura's theory resulted in a great deal of empirical effort to closely examine the nature of observational learning and the conditions under which imitation occurs. In a typical study (see Bandura, Ross, and Ross, 1961) children would watch an adult play with a large, plastic clown (a "Bobo doll"), treating it (for no obvious reason) in an aggressive manner and displaying various quite specific hostile actions towards it. When the children were subsequently given a chance to play with the Bobo doll their behavior was found to be far more aggressive than that of children who had not observed the adult; moreover, they displayed similar specific actions to those observed in the model. Similar results were obtained when children watched filmed rather than live sessions, even when the actors were cartoon characters rather than human beings. Nevertheless, certain characteristics in the model, such as perceived power or affection, were found more likely to elicit imitation; also the consequences of the observed actions, that is, whether they were rewarded or punished, affected the likelihood of imitation. The phenomenon, moreover, was not confined to aggression but was also demonstrated to occur with such other behavior patterns as altruism and gender-appropriate activity.

These experiments were believed to represent what happens in real life. Children are, of course, continuously exposed to models and have plenty of opportunity to acquire particular action patterns through imitation. In this process reinforcement can hardly play the mechanical role proposed by traditional learning theory, and though Bandura originally attempted to persevere with the notion of reinforcement somehow stamping in observed acts it is one of the features of his theory that in time it became less and less behavioristic and more and more able to accommodate internal, especially cognitive, processes. Thus Bandura agreed that self-reinforcement by the child might be just as important as external reinforcement: the child, that is, does not passively get pushed around by environmental rewards and punishment but actively evaluates the observed actions and their possible consequences. Social learning theory thus came to pay increasing attention to the mental events that mediate between observation and reproduction of an act; after all, the fact that children select what to imitate and that imitation may not occur for quite some time after observation indicates such processes as attention, retention, and motivation to be at work, and their operation should not be neglected. Increasingly also Bandura came to believe that much of the child's efforts could be seen as aimed at increasing the feeling of self-efficacy – a feeling that is both the result and the organizer of the individual's actions (Bandura, 1982, 1986) and that again draws attention to the child as actively participating in its own development.

It is very much to Bandura's credit that he thus freed himself from the constraints of behaviorism and came to adopt a much less mechanistic view of the nature of psychological development. The amount of work stimulated by his social learning theory is impressive, as is its methodological rigor. Yet it is also the case that that same rigor was responsible for the increasing doubt that crept in regarding the validity and meaning of the empirical data obtained. The laboratory settings chosen for the studies, and the procedures adopted for the experiments, are so far from real life that one must question whether the findings are representative of real behavior. Imitation obviously occurs and is surely an important means whereby children learn; whether that learning takes place in the way suggested by these studies remains uncertain because one cannot automatically generalize from the laboratory to the outside world. A further problem with the theory is that it is essentially *a-developmental*: the hypothesized processes underlying observational learning are identical whatever the child's age. One must contrast this account with Piagetian theory which puts the child's cognitive transformations in the course of development at the very core of any attempt to understand that development: in the face of similar experiences children of different ages interpret and react to what is happening to them in radically different ways. The lack of a developmental framework means that all age groups are treated as equivalent by Bandura and robs his theory of the impact that both Freud and Piaget have had.

(4) *Piagetian theory*   It may seem strange to include in a discussion of social development a theory wholly concerned with cognitive functions. Piaget certainly paid almost no attention to social factors; his child lived in a world virtually devoid of people where development progressed on the basis of transactions with inanimate objects. The fact that these objects were often arranged and manipulated by other people, and the fact that of all features in the environment it is those people that are of most fascination to the child, received no mention. There are some rare exceptions, such as Piaget's assertion that it is through interaction with peers that the child eventually grows out of egocentrism, yet the very fact that egocentrism played such a prominent part in the theory meant that a picture emerged of a solitary being cocooned in its own business and isolated from all other beings.

And yet Piagetian theory has had a profound influence on our understanding of social development, if only indirectly. Let us consider some of the reasons:

(a)   Piaget radically transformed our thinking about the nature of development, above all by showing that a child is not just a miniature adult – psychologically the same but endowed with rather less knowledge, who is then supposed to acquire that knowledge bit by bit, like the accretion of inches that account for physical growth. According to Piaget children are not so much quantitatively as qualitatively different from adults, and change takes place in a predictable sequence of stage progressions. It is true that the latter assertion has probably encountered more criticism than any other part of Piagetian theory (e.g. from Donaldson, 1978): cognitive development does not appear to take place in the great steps that Piaget's writing would lead one to expect. Nevertheless, there are ample demonstrations that at different ages children do think about the world in qualitatively different ways; thus the manner in which they organize information shows predictable changes during the course of development, in particular in the way in which the child can increasingly cope with abstractions. This, of course, has implications for the understanding of children's concepts of people which are unlikely to differ radically from their concepts of objects; the field of social cognition (a sort of halfway house between the cognitive and the social areas) has consequently greatly benefited from Piagetian ideas.

(b)   Piaget more than any other theorist countered the behaviorist view of the passive child, molded by whatever experience it encounters. On the contrary, the Piagetian child is from the very beginning an active agent in its own development, seeking and selecting appropriate stimulation and thereby helping to create its own environment. This, as we shall see, is vital to the understanding of socialization processes: bringing up a child is not a matter of molding an inert blob of clay but more like a negotiation process with a partner who has ideas of his or her own. Thus on the one hand development, according to Piaget, depends on an innate timetable that periodically makes new forms of adaptation possible; on the other hand, for these to come about the child must encounter the "right" kinds of experiences, i.e. forms of stimulation that are meaningful in terms of the present stage of understanding reached by the child. It is here that one should introduce the role of sensitive adults, willing to ensure that children do have appropriate experiences and that they can progress to the next stage – a role that Piaget himself neglected, preferring to put the onus on the child's own efforts to seek relevant experiences, but which nevertheless fits well into his general formulation. It is thus not surprising that Piagetian ideas have had a considerable influence on educational theory; the interplay of maturational readiness and challenging experience forms an interactional model that characterizes the teaching–learning process most appropriately.

(c)   Social and cognitive functions are not, as we have emphasized, two utterly distinct sets of processes but are reciprocally dependent. The most common assumption about their relationship is that cognitive development is in some way more basic, and that certain social functions cannot make an appearance until their cognitive underpinnings are in place. However this may be, one reason for the interest in Piagetian ideas lies in the possibility of "explaining" various developments in the social sphere by the preceding emergence of corresponding cognitive achievements. Take, for example, the fact that somewhere around the third quarter of the first year of life infants first show signs of separation upset (Schaffer, 1958). The baby, that is, no longer behaves to the mother as though "out of sight is out of mind" but shows active efforts to retrieve her and in other ways remains oriented to her even though she is no longer perceptually present. It is significant that around this same age Piaget has found infants first to become capable of searching for a missing object; whereas previously a cover dropped over a desirable toy would immediately result in infants giving up all signs of orientation to that toy, now they will lift the cover and retrieve it. The infant, that is, has acquired the *object concept* (as Piaget, 1952, called it), i.e. the notion that things have a permanent existence in time and space independent of the child's own perceptual awareness of them. This is regarded as a general mental development and among its repercussions is the onset of separation upset, i.e. the ability to miss the absent mother. Cognitive advance thus facilitates social advance. There are other such general developments with social implications, for example the onset of *decentration* towards the end of the preschool period (Piaget, 1929). Up till then children have difficulty in focusing on more than one aspect at a time: their attention is "centered" on whatever is the most prominent feature in their awareness and cannot be deployed flexibly. One result is egocentrism; children are over-whelmed by their own perspective and cannot at the same time take into account other people's perspectives. Not until the cognitive capacity for decentration devel-ops can children free themselves of their own, dominant point of view and under-stand the feelings and roles of others. This particular Piagetian proposal has met with much criticism, at least with respect to its timing; it does, however, show again why those interested in social development have examined Piaget's theory in their search for explanatory concepts. Whether the primacy of cognition over social development is in fact correct remains an open issue: it is at least conceivable that social experience facilitates such cognitive developments as the emergence of the object concept (Schaffer, 1987) rather than the other way round.

(5) *Ethology*   It is probably more accurate to designate ethology as a general ori-entation to the study of behavior than a definite theory about behavior and its development. Yet its influence has been great, and especially so with respect to certain aspects of social development such as attachment formation and peer rela-tions. Methodologically too it has been highly influential, in that the swing away from controlled experimentation to observation under natural conditions has been due to no small extent to the example set by ethologists.

Ethology began as a subdiscipline of biology, concerned primarily with the evolu-tion and function of behavior in animals (Hinde, 1982; Archer, 1992). Its founding fathers are Lorenz (1935) and Tinbergen (1951), who argued that the behavior of different species could best be understood in terms of the nature of their adaptation to the natural environment in the course of evolution, that each species was thus distinguished by its own behavioral patterns just as it was distinguished by sets of physical characteristics, and that a primary task of the biologist was to study these behavior patterns as they could be observed in the natural habitat. In the course of undertaking this task ethologists have provided not only a great deal of fascinating descriptive material about the behavior of animals but also a number of stimulating theoretical insights and highly serviceable constructs. Nevertheless, it would be misleading to suggest that there exists a unitary ethological theory; rather, there are a number of orienting attitudes which, according to Hinde (1987), include an empha-sis on the need for description at different levels of behavioral complexity and on the importance of asking questions about function and evolution as well as about devel-opment and causation (and interestingly, Hinde also adds to the list of attitudes a sense of humility which should be engendered by the diversity of nature).

In their analysis of behavior ethologists placed special emphasis on the concept of *fixed action patterns* – the sets of behavioral responses with which any given species is endowed to help it adapt to its given environment. The best known example relates to the *imprinting* phenomenon: the tendency of certain species of birds such as chicks and ducklings to follow the first moving object encountered after hatching. The following response is an unlearned behavior pattern which normally ensures that the young animal will become attached to (imprinted on) the parent bird and, by remaining in its proximity, ensure protection and survival. In fact the crucial element of the stimulus eliciting the fixed action pattern (referred to as the *sign stimulus*) consists of some primitive cues that, in the case of imprinting, are part of the parent's appearance but may be found in a much wider range of environmental objects – hence the experimental demonstration by ethologists that imprinting can be elicited in chicks by such diverse things as moving boxes, footballs, and human beings (Sluckin, 1972).

These observations are important for a number of reasons. First, they do away with the common but artificial distinction between instinctive and learned behavior: a fixed action pattern may be instinctive but its functioning still depends on the individual learning the characteristics of the object with which it is to be associated. Thus species appear to have *innate* predispositions to *learn* – i.e. they are endowed with built-in biases which make the animal more likely to acquire certain associations that have served an adaptive purpose in the evolution of that species. In the second place, ethologists placed much emphasis on the timing of learning: the concept of *critical periods* was advanced because of the conviction of the earlier workers that learning such as following a particular stimulus object could only take place in sharply delimited developmental periods. Later work demonstrated that the critical nature of these periods had been overstated and that they were more suitably called *sensitive periods*; nevertheless, the timing of learning in relation to the developmental course of the individual received some useful emphasis. Third, the work on lower species inspired a great deal of valuable research on human children, designed to search there too for sets of fixed action patterns and their eliciting sign stimuli. Work on infants' sucking and smiling responses turned out to be particularly successful in this respect. And finally, ethological work served to draw attention to the role of the *context* in which individuals are observed, and in particular to the importance of starting from a base of "natural" behavior, i.e. that occurring in the individual's normal environment rather than in artificial settings such as laboratories. Not that ethologists eschewed laboratory analysis; on the contrary, they demonstrated the value of a continuous to-and-fro between natural description and experimental analysis. Observation in a natural context, however, had to come first, as otherwise the richness of that context would be missed and wholly artificial phenomena might be singled out for study.

The application of ethological principles to the study of human social behavior has sometimes resulted in rather crude and overdrawn analogies from one species to another. Human behavior cannot be explained merely on "naked ape" lines, nor can the complexities of the developing personality be solely accounted for by specific experiences in critical periods. But the so-called human ethologists (e.g. Blurton Jones, 1972) have not only used their orientation to produce much new and interesting material but have also widened our conceptual horizons by taking into consideration the biological basis of all human behavior. The infant does not arrive in the world as an "empty" organism; it brings with it, first, its own individuality but in addition it comes equipped with the vast heritage of its forebears which is reflected every bit as much in its behavioral repertoire as in its physical appearance.

Theory Today

The student confronted by a plethora of theories may understandably get impatient with what at first sight appears to be contradiction and confusion, and may well wish that the psychologists would put their house in order and come up with one generally agreed theoretical framework to explain social development. But we have our excuses! Developmental psychology is, comparatively speaking, still a very new scientific endeavor, and with knowledge only just beginning to accumulate it is to be expected that different ways of conceptualizing that knowledge will be tried out. Theories are, after all, only tools, to be used to further our understanding and to be discarded if they turn out not to serve that purpose. Thus behaviorism, at least in its extreme form, has been found wanting; above all it does not do justice to the active, striving nature of the child and to the mental structures which are to be found in even the youngest infant. Similarly, certain parts of psychoanalytic theory are no longer regarded as useful, either because they rely on concepts that are too vague and untestable (such as libido or death wish) or because they have been put to empirical test but not been confirmed (such as the theory of infantile trauma as a cause of later psychological disturbance).

In any case, the various theories we have listed are not always as contradictory as they may seem, for they take as their starting point different aspects of psychological development and thus address themselves to different phenomena: psychoanalysis to the emotional life of young children, behaviorism to learning through association, social learning theory to imitation, Piagetian theory to thinking and ethology to instinctive behavior. It is true that the proponents of a particular theory may then overextend it and apply it to other psychological phenomena, as seen in the efforts of behaviorists to reduce the whole of mental life to the formation of associations. But however dogmatic their assertions may sound, the various theoretical formulations are really only hypotheses which in due course will be examined and, if not confirmed, discarded.

We can also not escape the fact that theory building, like all other aspects of the scientific endeavor, is by no means a coldly logical affair but one intimately imbued with personal considerations. What if Freud had been a jolly, cheerful, contented man instead of someone suffering all his life from periodic anxiety and bouts of depression, as a result of which he was driven to preoccupation with the inner life and to attempts at self-analysis (Jones, 1953–7)? What if J. B. Watson had had a happy childhood instead of being deserted by his father and brought up by a strict, narrowly religious mother who showed little overt affection to her son (D. Cohen, 1979)? Would he still have preferred to work with rats rather than with human beings and to investigate outer behavior rather than inner thought and feeling? Would he still have disregarded individuality and the role of mother love? In addition one must take into account the particular sociohistorical factors which affect each writer: the Victorian mores, for example, which held sway in Freud's youth and which surely played a part in accounting for his preoccupation with morality and guilt, plus the prevailing anti-Semitism which made him less inclined to toe the line and more prepared to question commonly held beliefs; or the emphasis in America, the home of learning theory, on the idea that "all citizens are created equal," leading to a ready acceptance of a developmental theory based on similar achievement opportunities for everyone. However, the zeitgeist changes and with it the kinds of theories that creative individuals propose and which the scientific community and society generally find acceptable. The progress of knowledge per se is, of course, largely responsible for theoretical change; however, that progress takes place in a personal and social context that also plays a powerful part in the nature of theory construction.

There is at present some skepticism as to the usefulness of the sort of meta-theories that we have examined above, and currently most explanatory efforts take a far less ambitious form. They deal with more limited topic areas, such as the development of attachments or the formation of peer groups, and no longer set out to encompass such great ranges of psychological functions as was previously the case. The meta-theories are, of course, of more than just historical interest: they have guided our attention to all sorts of phenomena (the role of early experience, the existence of sensitive periods, the importance of imitation, and so forth) which are of interest in their own right and can fruitfully be investigated without necessarily fitting them into one or other major theoretical framework. And in addition the theories have also given impetus to the perfecting of various methodological tools required to investigate developmental processes, such as longitudinal methods (owing much to the emphasis of psychoanalysis on the effects of infantile experience on later behavior), controlled laboratory experiments (closely associated with behaviorism and learning theory), interview techniques (used – controversially – by Piaget), and a range of sophisticated observational methods devised in the first place by ethological workers.

Methodological Considerations

Findings produced by research are not merely a function of what is "out there," i.e. the topic investigated, but also of the particular methods employed to obtain these findings. Different methods do not necessarily produce identical results, even though they may be dealing with the same topic. If, say, we want to investigate the nature and extent of bullying among school children, we have a choice among a considerable variety of techniques for obtaining the required information. We can observe children directly, say, in playgrounds; or we can hold interviews and ask them about incidents of bullying; or we can distribute questionnaires designed to obtain the necessary data. If we opt for observation, the question arises which of various available techniques (e.g. time sampling or event sampling) is to be used, in what setting, at what time, and how long for. If interviews or questionnaires are chosen, who is to be targeted – teachers, parents, or the children themselves? And which of various types of interviews or questionnaires is appropriate, given the kind of information wanted? Add to that the need to decide on a particular group of subjects (in terms of age, sex, ethnicity, and so forth), as well as the need subsequently to select among various possible ways of data reduction and statistical treatment – and it becomes abundantly clear that there are indeed a great many ways of investigating the "same" problem, and that differences in conclusions reached about bullying by different investigators may well be a function of the methods chosen. Results cannot be divorced from the techniques used to obtain them; each technique adds its own distinctive flavor to the conclusions reached; and some insight into the *process* of research is therefore necessary in order to understand its *products*. Before we look at what has been found out about social development let us therefore briefly examine the nature of the research enterprise generally and consider how it has been applied to the study of social development in particular.

The Nature of Research

All scientific research, in whatever field, is characterized by a number of features which together distinguish it from less objective ways of arriving at conclusions. Thus research may be described as empirical, systematic, controlled, quantitative, and public.

    1. *Empirical*   Conclusions are based on information obtained directly through experience; this is available to all and is therefore verifiable. One can contrast this with hunches, guesswork, and armchair theorizing; such procedures may have a part to play at some points of the research process but they are strictly subject to checking by empirical means.

    2. *Systematic*   The research process is carried out according to an explicit plan (the research design). This specifies all phases and aspects of the study and is adhered to throughout, so that methods of investigation do not merely depend on private whim and inclination.

3.   *Controlled*   If the aim is to arrive at explanation of the phenomena being investigated, alternative explanations must be ruled out. It may therefore be necessary to adopt such devices as the inclusion of control groups which are not exposed to a particular condition but are similar in all other respects, or make use of double-blind procedures in order to guard against the influence of prior expectation.

4.   *Quantitative*   While there is a very definite place for descriptive research yielding purely qualitative data, quantification is essential for any purpose involving comparison of groups or conditions or treatments. It has the advantage of accuracy and enables one to establish with confidence that there is, for example, a difference between groups or that one treatment is more effective than another.

5.   *Public*   All aspects of an investigation, its methods as well as its findings, must be available to scrutiny, so that it can be replicated by others. If there is a failure to obtain the same results it should then be possible to locate the reasons for the divergence.

There are many avenues to knowledge, including those of the poet and the mystic. But when one wants to investigate the consequences for young children of parental divorce or compare the effectiveness of two ways of presenting instructional material or ascertain the conditions under which antisocial behavior develops one is not likely to turn to poet or mystic. Social action needs to be based on social science research; the checks inherent in objective inquiry are an essential safeguard without which conclusions remain in the realm of the imaginary.

Yet research does have its limitations. Let us consider some of these as they apply to the study of children's development:

(1)   *Methodological constraints*   The first concerns the point we have just emphasized, namely that findings are always a function of methods. Apparently contradictory conclusions are therefore reached by different research workers. One of the best known examples is to be found in the controversy regarding egocentrism in young children: Piaget's belief that egocentrism holds sway right up to the end of the pre-operational period (i.e. age 7 or so) was largely based on one particular test – the three-mountain model that children had to imagine being viewed by other people from different angles (Piaget & Inhelder, 1956). But as Donaldson (1978) has argued convincingly, for preschool children such a task is meaningless and therefore much too difficult; given another but meaningful task which also measures the ability to take another person's point of view children of a much younger age can be found to produce non-egocentric answers. In addition there are questions as to whether egocentrism is one unitary entity that can be assessed with one measure or whether it is an umbrella term for several different and not necessarily related characteristics, each of which needs to be assessed in its own right (Cox, 1986). Thus again we find that research findings are specific to the methods employed and that conclusions derived from any one study are accordingly constrained. One way round this problem is to adopt a multimethod approach: if the same conclusion is reached via several different

techniques one can have greater faith in it than would be justified when operating from a more narrow basis.

(2) *Sample constraints*   Research results are also limited by the particular sample that is chosen for investigation. Ideally the sample should be "representative" – a term often employed to designate the notion that one should be able to generalize the results of the study to *all* children. Taken literally as designating children in all parts of the world, such a notion is virtually nonsensical: what applies to one culture may not apply to others and accordingly needs to be checked repeatedly. Even at a less ambitious level a sample that is representative of some specific group (all middle class families in the United States with an employed mother, or all 10-year-old British children) still requires such great resources that few can afford to mount such an investigation. Progress in knowledge therefore rarely depends on the execution of one definitive study based on one all-embracing sample; what is much more likely to happen is that an investigator will choose a sample that happens to be convenient (located in the nearest nursery school, or an obliging youth club, or even one's own family) without any pretense of general representativeness. It is then up to others to replicate the findings on other samples, even though each of these may be just as unrepresentative; however, the very fact that identical conclusions are reached from the study of a diversity of groups, despite the singularity of each, gives one confidence in the generality of these conclusions. Thus the notion of object permanence was first put forward by Piaget on the basis of results obtained from his own children – an N of 3, living in a Swiss middle class family! The findings have subsequently been replicated many times with other specific groups of children from different social classes and ethnic groupings in various parts of the world; they are now accepted as describing a feature of development that one can safely assume to be universal. Nevertheless, until such replication has taken place one cannot assert that findings are applicable beyond the specific group studied.

(3) *Time constraints*   One can also not assume that findings obtained at one particular period of time can be generalized to other periods. This applies particularly to any function closely influenced by the social setting in which the child is reared: customs change and what applies to one generation may not apply to the next. Each set of findings should therefore be evaluated in the context of the time period in which they were obtained. There is thus a need for periodic updating of research findings, at least of those that are likely to be affected by changes in social climate. This makes progress of knowledge an arduous business; in this respect too caution is clearly called for in claiming results to be "representative."

(4) *Ethical considerations*   There are all sorts of interesting questions one can pose about human development, yet with quite a few of these the only immediate way of obtaining an answer is to subject children to procedures that are generally regarded as ethically unacceptable. The case of the hired twins is an example.

The case of the hired twins

In the 1930s and 1940s much effort was devoted to attempts to determine whether children's early development was primarily due to maturation or to experience. This is a "big" question to answer empirically, but one way to tackle it – so it was thought – is to ask what would happen if children are deprived of all their usual experiences and brought up under conditions of minimal stimulation. Would they still reach the usual milestones of development at the normal times? Would the first smile still appear around 6 weeks, would they still begin to grasp objects around 4 months, would they start to vocalize, sit up, stand, and walk at the usual ages?

Wayne Dennis and his wife Marsena (1941) put this to the test by hiring a pair of twins born to a mother who was unable to provide for them. They came to the Dennises when they were 36 days old and stayed with them throughout the first year, when they were returned to their mother. During this time they were kept in a room in the Dennis home under carefully controlled conditions of minimal stimulation. The room contained little furniture; a screen was placed between the infants' cribs so that they could not see each other; and through the window they were able to look at only sky and tree-tops. They were kept there at all times except for feeding and bathing and for some purposes of assessment. No toys were provided until the infants were almost a year old. They rarely saw anyone other than Dennis and his wife, who had the sole care of the twins.

The regime to which they were subjected involved keeping all social stimulation down to a bare minimum. If either infant cried the cause was investigated; if it was a cry for attention it was not answered. All adult acts that could conceivably be imitated – smiling, vocalizing, clapping hands, etc. – were rigidly avoided. The children were not spoken to at all for the first six months; they were not petted or cuddled; they were not put into sitting or standing postures, nor were they given any practice in reaching for an object. No action of theirs was ever encouraged or discouraged, rewarded or punished. In this way it was hoped to establish whether behavioral development would occur normally despite the infants' care being reduced to the minimum which would ensure their comfort and physical well-being.

Probably the most stimulation the twins got was through the assessments of their development which Dennis periodically applied. These appeared to show that throughout the first year the children's development followed the usual course, and that the milestones were reached within the expected age range. They were retarded with respect to a few responses that required practice, such as reaching for an object, sitting without support and supporting the weight of the body upon the feet. Even these readily appeared once opportunities for practice were afforded. In short, the "experiment" came down on the side of maturation as the main force behind early development.

It is inconceivable that such a procedure could take place now. A very different ethical climate prevails these days, which would ensure that no deliberate interference involving the taking away of opportunities and stimulation could occur. In fact there are other ways of looking at the same problem, particularly by making use of "experiments of nature," and indeed Dennis himself made use of some of these such as examining infants in highly depriving orphanages or infants in other cultures subjected to such practices as being bound to cradle boards. Ironically, these gave answers rather different from those obtained from his study of the twins he had hired: they indicated that stimulation is essential for normal development and that severe retardation occurs when it is reduced to a minimum. Whatever the reason for the normal development of the twins, the exercise had in fact been a waste of time, producing results not confirmed by subsequent work. Yet even if it has produced some important insights, there is no doubt that nowadays we would not believe that the end justifies the means.

Professional organizations for psychologists, such as the American Psychological Association and the British Psychological Society, these days have strict codes of conduct which their members are expected to follow when carrying out research, and studies involving children in particular are expected to be conducted with due respect for the well-being of subjects. Where one draws the line between the acceptable and the unacceptable is, of course, often difficult to establish and may change from time to time. For example, in the 1960s and 1970s there was much interest in the experimental analysis of punishment and its effects on children (Walters & Grusec, 1977). Many of the relevant studies used the so-called resistance-to-temptation paradigm, in which children were left alone in a laboratory with a desirable but forbidden toy and then punished by a hidden observer each time they touched the toy, usually by means of a sudden loud noise or a blast of air or some other aversive stimulus (even mild electric shocks have been employed). Whatever the benefits of these experiments in terms of knowledge gained, they raise grave issues concerning, first, the deliberate use of punishment (however mild), and second, the deception of children by putting them in temptation situations and spying on them. Such studies are no longer carried out; while there is no harm in the experimental analysis of behavior as such (however awesome a phrase that may be), this can usually be done in ways not detrimental to the participants. Yet ethical issues do arise even in observational studies. If, say, one wants to investigate the nature of parenting, should one inform the parents beforehand of one's intention to observe them, thereby risking the distortion of their natural behavior, or is it acceptable to conceal the truth for the sake of obtaining a realistic picture but being open to the charge of deception? Here too there have been changes: an investigator in the 1960s, for instance, would probably have had few qualms about inviting mothers and children to a laboratory, leaving them in a waiting room under the pretense of not being ready and then observing them through a one-way mirror. Does the end justify the means? Nowadays a firm "no" is the answer; investigators are more likely to search for other ways of putting the mother at ease while respecting her right to privacy. Deception is actively discouraged, even at the price of making research sometimes more complex and longer drawn-out.

(5) *Investigator effects* Research is always a personal enterprise, that on human beings especially so. It is carried out by individuals closely identified with their work who have hopes, expectations, and ambitions that may well color what they do and what they find. Established research procedures are supposed to eliminate such subjective influences; this, however, is easier said than done. There are accepted safeguards: control groups, random allocation, double-blind procedures and so forth, yet even with these in place the need for vigilance against often quite unconscious bias remains. In psychology, where measures tend to be very much "softer" than in the physical sciences, it is somewhat easier for subjective expectation to affect results – an influence all the more pernicious because it is mostly quite unconscious. The same applies to the influence of value judgments. Take research on the effects on

children of parental divorce. The early work on this topic was done at a time when there was still a definite social stigma attached to divorce and when there was little doubt in anyone's mind that the consequences for children were bound to be wholly and severely negative. As a result investigators looked only for such negative effects; their inventories were accordingly loaded with questions about fears and aggression and school failure; the possibility that the escape from a conflict-ridden family atmosphere could also bring about positive effects was not considered. Only later, in a different social climate and with different social values, were research instruments designed without that particular bias.

Given these various constraints on research it is apparent that independent replication of findings is essential. There have been some spectacular failures to replicate work that at first sight seemed highly competent in execution and most promising in the insights it provided but which in retrospect, after other studies had obtained different results, turned out to be blemished in some of the ways described above. Replication is not a popular undertaking because any researcher worth his or her salt prefers to embark on something original rather than repeat what others have done. Nevertheless, advances in knowledge and any social action that may result therefrom require a more solid basis than single, unconfirmed studies.

Research Design

The kind of findings one obtains from a study depends to a considerable extent on the form of that study, i.e. on the research design employed to answer the question posed. Some understanding of the main kinds of design found in developmental research is therefore useful to anyone wanting to learn about the conclusions reached by that research.

The two most common questions asked in developmental psychology are:

1   How does behavior change over age?
2   What are the determinants of behavior and its development?

Different strategies tend to be chosen to provide answers to these questions.

Charting behavioral change can be thought of in terms of plotting growth curves. Just as one may plot such curves for children's height or weight, so any psychological function (digit span, vocabulary comprehension, impulsiveness, and so forth) can be measured and traced over age. Admittedly, measuring aspects of behavior is usually more complex than measuring height or weight, for the agreed scales and the equivalent units which can be used to assess a child's physical development do not exist for most psychological functions. The problem of finding comparable measuring tools for different ages is certainly far greater in any attempt to assess behavioral change: scales yielding results in inches or kilograms can be applied equally to a 2-year-old and a 20-year-old, but if one wants to trace the development of, say, intelligence or aggression or sociability the type of measuring tool appropriate to one age group may be quite inappropriate at another age. This makes it difficult to express psychological change in quantitative terms and accounts for the preponderance as yet of qualitative descriptions of the different age groups. Nevertheless, plotting change over age is an aim of much developmental work, which can yield data about such aspects as the norms of development, the age when particular functions first emerge or level off or even deteriorate (as in old age), the regularity or irregularity of growth, and the way in which different functions compare in their developmental course (e.g. short-term as opposed to long-term memory among the aged). In all such studies age as such is, of course, not an explanation of change: children do not, for example, become more independent *because* they are older; age is only an "indicator variable," that is, it highlights the fact that change is occurring at certain periods and in a particular manner, and it therefore remains incumbent on the investigator to search for the processes that are actually responsible for the changes observed.

The two main research strategies employed to answer questions about the nature of behavioral change are the *cross-sectional* design and the *longitudinal* design. In the former, different groups of children are seen at different ages; in the latter the same group is followed up and seen at different ages. There is no question that longitudinal studies are preferable if one wants reliable information about change, for in making age comparisons one can be certain that the only thing that has changed is age and that this is therefore the operative factor to take into account when attempting to explain any differences found. In a cross-sectional design the investigator may try very hard to make the different age groups as comparable as possible, yet once all the more obvious variables have been controlled for (sex, social class, ethnicity, and anything that previous research or common sense suggests as related to the outcome) there may still be a great deal of variance between the groups that is not accounted for.

However, the longitudinal method does have its drawbacks too. For one thing, there is the danger of sample loss: the longer the follow-up period the greater is the danger that children move away or do not wish to cooperate any more or become unavailable for some other reason. The remaining sample may then be no longer representative of the original group. For another, the nature of the tests used for assessment purposes may change in the course of the follow-up period: new and more efficient methods may come on the market, presenting the investigator with the dilemma of continuing with outmoded tests or changing over to a method not strictly comparable to that used hitherto. But the greatest drawback of the longitudinal design is a purely practical one: it takes a long time and thus requires expensive resources to mount such an investigation. Not that all follow-up periods extend over the whole of childhood or even over several years: a longitudinal study could take place over a quite brief period, enabling the investigator to trace some quite specific change known to occur at a particular point of development. For example, wariness of unfamiliar people and objects is known to set in around the age of 8 or 9 months; a longitudinal study designed to shed light on the manner of this development can usefully be carried out by investigating infants at monthly intervals between 6 and 12 months (Schaffer, Greenwood, & Parry, 1972). Or take the changes in psychological well-being that have been found to occur in many children around the ages of 11 and 12, when they must cope not only with puberty but also with the stresses of changing from one type of school system to another. As Hirsch and Rapkin (1987) showed, a longitudinal study following up children over the transition from elementary to junior high school and involving just a one-year period can produce some illuminating insights into the way in which self-esteem is affected by such a sudden life-change. In general, however, given the expense and time commitments involved in most longitudinal studies, it is perhaps not surprising that cross-sectional studies are more common and that much of our information derives from this type of research.

Investigating the determinants of behavior and its development is the other main problem facing child psychologists. Here we get into the realm of explanation, where questions are asked about the effects of x on y. Some of the most interesting questions refer to those where x relates to some event or condition early in life and y to the outcome in terms of adult personality – interesting, but unfortunately particularly difficult methodologically. Ideally, a longitudinal research design is required to answer such questions, but again the practical difficulties of time and expense make this kind of study a relatively rare occurrence in the literature. A short cut is to obtain information about the early event retrospectively, that is, to see the subjects at only one point of time and gather data about both the alleged cause and the effect simultaneously. But however tempting this short cut may be, the fallibility of human memory is such that relying on it for anything but the crudest data about the early events may well produce misleading information – and even at a crude level the memory of mothers, for instance, about their children's past has been shown to be often quite inaccurate (Wenar & Coulter, 1962).

A further difficulty about making statements regarding the effects of early experience on later personality functioning is that the early event can rarely be considered in isolation: its effects will be attenuated, amplified or modified in some other way by later events (Rutter & Robins, 1990). We shall discuss this topic in detail in chapter 8; here let us just note the methodological implications. Studying an individual at some point in infancy, say, and then only once again 20 years later is clearly not going to be sufficient to throw light on the final outcome. Given the multiple influences on that outcome, if one wants to make cause-and-effect statements the child needs to be followed up and investigated during the intervening period as well so that information can be obtained about the way in which later experiences come to entwine themselves with the earlier one and jointly produce some particular kind of psychological end result.

Considering the methodological complications of long-term research, it is not surprising that far more work has been done on the immediate determinants of behavior. Are father-custody boys better adjusted than mother-custody boys? Can preschool children empathize more easily with positive than with negative

emotional expressions in other people? Is reasoning more effective than power assertion in getting children to comply with parental requests? Are children more likely
to solve problems when working jointly with a peer or when alone? Whether an
answer is sought by means of laboratory experiments or field studies, the approach in
each case is an a-temporal one, in that the determinants of behavior are sought in the
here-and-now and the complications associated with the passage of time are thus
avoided.

Yet there are other complications that cannot be avoided. One of the most common questions in child psychology concerns the effects on children of parental
behavior – the style of discipline adopted by the parents, their warmth and sensitivity, their work pattern, their agreement with respect to child rearing, and so
forth. The literature is replete with studies reporting associations of one kind or
another of parental measures with child measures, yet association is all that they
indicate. The correlations reported do not permit one to make causal statements: for
instance, the fact that parental reasoning is associated with child compliance does not
necessarily reflect the greater effectiveness of this technique over any other but may
be due to children who are naturally compliant eliciting this kind of behavior from
parents rather than some more forceful behavior. The cause-and-effect sequence
is thus from child to parent rather than vice versa; the correlations do not permit
one to choose between the two alternatives. This is a problem of interpretation
that pervades all research carried out by means of field studies: for instance, the
association between amount of violence viewed on television and child aggression
may not stem from the effect of the former on the latter but from the disposition of
aggressive children to select more violent programs in their television viewing;
similarly an association between parents' harsh punitive treatment and children's
antisocial behavior may be interpreted in either direction of the cause-and-effect
sequence.

The use of laboratory experiments does permit one to tease out causes and effects.
By controlling and systematically varying the assumed causal factors it becomes
possible to reach unambiguous conclusions about etiology in a way that field studies
do not allow, and for certain purposes this is a great advantage. Yet the experimental
approach also has its problems, in particular the fact that the conclusions are specific
to the laboratory setting and that one cannot automatically assume they can be
generalized to real-life settings. The lack of "ecological validity" of the laboratory has
rightly received critical attention (e.g. by Bronfenbrenner, 1977); on the other hand
the artificiality of the setting, the stimuli presented and the procedure adopted can be
minimized by imaginative treatment and a proper appreciation of the requirements
and habits of one's subjects. And, perhaps even more to the point, the purpose of
certain kinds of experiment may have nothing to do with any immediate resemblance
to real life: their aim may be to ascertain the relationship between sets of variables in
order to derive general principles which are only then applied to naturally occurring
events – in the same sense that a physicist obtains results under "pure" conditions in
a laboratory, and these enable him then to explain real life situations taking place in

rather "messier" conditions. Under such circumstances the so-called artificiality of the laboratory is neither here nor there.

Both the field approach and the laboratory approach have advantages and disadvantages; which of the two was used for any particular purpose must be taken into consideration when evaluating the conclusions of any given study. They represent the principal methods for investigating the determinants of development; however, there are others such as, in particular, so-called "quasi-experiments" which partake of the characteristics of both field and laboratory studies. These are based on some naturally occurring variation, that is, one which takes place in real life and over which the investigator thus has no experimental control but which can nevertheless be taken advantage of for research purposes. For example, variations in quality of care offered to young children occur among day care centers; this situation can be used in order to ascertain the effects of such variation on children's development and, by carefully describing the way in which centers differ, even to isolate the specific parameters of care responsible for the effects observed (e.g. Fox & Fein, 1990). Or one may examine the effects on children of natural disasters such as earthquakes or bush fires (e.g. Burke et al., 1982; McFarlane, Poliansky, & Irwin, 1987), in order to investigate the effects of a stress much too horrendous ever to reproduce in a laboratory. For that matter the naturally occurring variation among cultures can also form a rich source of information; as cross-cultural psychologists have shown (e.g. LeVine et al., 1994; Whiting & Edwards, 1988), the divergent child rearing practices of different societies can be examined in order to ascertain the extent to which developmental patterns do take a universal form despite this diversity, as well as whether particular culture-specific rearing patterns produce particular psychological outcomes.

There are other approaches which further add to the research worker's armory – for example field experiments, where a controlled study is performed but in a natural field setting, thus retaining the twin advantages of control and ecological validity though often at the cost of some reduction in both these aspects. But whatever the approach, the main point remains: findings are always a function of methods; conclusions from a given study are therefore constrained by the research design employed, and answers (for example to questions about causation) cannot be obtained from research not set up to provide them.

Obtaining and Analyzing Findings

At all stages of carrying out a piece of research investigators have to make choices – such as the scale of the topic to be investigated, the research design to employ for the study, the number and kind of subjects to include and the setting in which to see them, and the particular techniques most appropriate for obtaining the required data. Each choice will influence the end result; each therefore needs careful consideration.

This certainly applies to the techniques selected to obtain the data. In the study of social development, and especially so with respect to socialization processes, there has been much debate about the relative merits of interviews and questionnaires on the one hand and direct observation on the other. The former were the principal tools up to the 1960s; their advantages are that information can be obtained speedily and hence from a large number of subjects; they can cover considerable ranges of time and investigate situations that might be inaccessible to outside observation; and they can explore feelings and subjective perceptions as well as overt behavior. For a time interviews and questionnaires were almost the sole means of finding out what transpires between parents and children; the complex and once highly influential models of the child rearing process proposed by writers such as Becker (1964) and Schaefer (1959) were based almost wholly on what parents said they did rather than on what they were observed to do.

Increasingly, however, it became apparent that there are also disadvantages to obtaining information through such a parental filter. Any form of self-report can be subject to a *social desirability set*, i.e. the tendency to present oneself in a favorable light. Thus, consciously or not, a mother answering questions on topics such as punishment may be swayed by prevailing social norms and by what she believes the interviewer to regard as acceptable behavior; her information will accordingly be distorted. In any case her emotional involvement with the child may well prevent her giving a purely objective account: the very intimacy that provides her with the best opportunities for describing the relationship also makes her a suspect reporter. To cope with these problems interviewing techniques have been developed whereby such distortions can be minimized, even though they may not be completely eliminated. And similarly, attempts have been made to deal with another problem characterizing much of the earlier use of interviews, namely the tendency to ask only about modal behavior (i.e. what the mother *usually* does), thereby missing the many nuances that give behavior its reality and eliciting instead global, summarizing answers. By asking, for instance, about events in the last 24 hours, or requiring parents to give very detailed information regarding the child's behavior in some specified situation, an attempt can be made to get away from vague description and nearer to the details of real life, even though one still needs to rely on the accuracy and veracity of the informant.

The advantages and disadvantages of observational methods are in many respects the obverse of those found in the interview and questionnaire approach. Observational methods can yield objective, quantitative data; they are geared to specific time-and-place situations; they can cover behavior in great detail (particularly if recorded on film or video); but by the same token they cover only limited samples of behavior and therefore involve a great deal of effort if wider coverage is required. In addition the influence of observer effect must be taken into account: when people know they are being observed they may not behave in a typical manner, and the social desirability set may thus occur here too. By and large, therefore, observation yields greater accuracy and objectivity but at the cost of economy of effort.

It is apparent that there is no such thing as a perfect method: each has certain characteristics that color the kind of conclusions which emerge from a given study. This becomes even clearer when one looks at the different types of observational or of interview/questionnaire methods. Observation, for instance, can be carried out by event sampling or time sampling; time sampling can take various forms such as one-zero, point or interval sampling; and the results obtained from different methods applied to the same sample of behavior are by no means necessarily identical (Altmann, 1974; Bakeman & Gottman, 1987). Choice of method depends, of course, on the question to which an answer is being sought: information about children's night waking, for example, will almost certainly have to be derived from parental reports; the nuances of a mother's communicative behavior and its integration with the child's ongoing activity, on the other hand, will require the fine-grained detail that only observational data can provide. But there are other topics where a real choice of methods is feasible, and then the relative advantages and disadvantages of each need to be weighed up by the research worker but must also be taken into account by anyone wanting to understand the conclusions of the study.

Once the data have been collected there are further choices to be made as to how to collate, summarize, and present the findings. Take a set of observations on the way in which mothers teach their children some particular task. One way of reducing the body of data and making sense of it is by means of ratings: judges, that is, assign each mother to a particular point along a continuum, the continuum representing some dimension considered crucial to the teaching process (directiveness, interference, amount of modeling, sensitivity, etc.). The number and identity of dimensions may be decided on an a priori basis, or they may arise from inspection of the data. The ratings are thus global statements about the mothers' behavior; in so far as they depend on subjective judgments a check on interrater reliability is essential. Such global statements have the advantage of economically summarizing a lot of information; at the same time, however, they are a big step removed from behavioral reality in that they contain a large element of interpretation, as found in the choice of dimensions, in the definitions attached to them and in the assignment of individual mothers to particular ratings.

The same body of findings can also be dealt with by sticking to the behavioral data obtained from the mothers and treating them in terms of the frequencies (or, for certain purposes, durations) of the particular categories of behavior recorded. Again, of course, choices will have had to be made as to the identity of those categories and their relative breadth: for example, a category labeled "restrictiveness" may be established by grouping together all instances of a mother's discouragement, verbal and physical interference, and directiveness; alternately verbal and physical instances may be kept separate and two types of restrictiveness thus distinguished; or behavioral counts may be kept at a much more microscopic level by sticking to categories such as mothers' use of the word "no," their physical manipulation of the child's hands during the task or their resort to slapping. The creation of meaningful observational categories to express the behavior of individuals has received much attention (Bakeman & Gottman, 1987); there has also been considerable discussion as to ways of combining individual measures to form dyadic measures such as synchrony or reciprocity (e.g. Hinde & Herrmann, 1977).

It is clear that each aspect of methodology adds its own distinctive contribution to the results obtained, and the use of multimethod approaches is recognition of this fact. Rather than argue, for example, whether observation or interview is the best technique, one can profit from the particular advantages of each and combine them. Observation may well be the most appropriate means for plotting an individual's behavior in a given situation; interviews, on the other hand, will serve to explore that person's perception of that same situation and so provide additional insights. Put the two techniques together, consider the way in which they converge, and one may have a much richer interpretation of the events recorded.

Summary

- The study of social development is concerned with the behavior patterns, feelings, attitudes, and concepts that children manifest in relation to other people, and with the way all these aspects change with age.

The Questions Posed

- There are two main reasons why we want to learn about development: first, because we want to find out about children *as* children and investigate their characteristics at particular ages; second, because we are interested in the nature and end products of development and want to learn how childhood experience contributes to adult personality.
- Developmental studies involve both "what" questions and "why" questions. The former aim to provide descriptive information, i.e. *what* children can do at *what* ages under *what* circumstances. The latter are concerned with the reasons for developmental change and for the existence of individual differences between children.
- Among the very large number of questions one can raise about social development only certain ones are selected for attention at any one time. Their choice depends in part on the influence of currently prevalent theories, in part on the availability of methodologies, and in part also on the needs of society to find solutions to the practical problems of modern-day childhood.

Conceptions and Preconceptions

- Scientific attempts to understand children's development are by no means immune from value judgments and assumptions, often unconscious in nature, about the make-up of children. These vary according to both time period and culture, and can exercise considerable influence on the character of psychological research, including its techniques and procedures.

- Theoretical frameworks serve as formal guides in the search for knowledge about children's development. The major ones that have guided child psychology in the past are psychoanalysis, behaviorism, social learning theory, Piagetian theory, and ethology. Currently, however, such meta-theories are less influential than explanatory efforts dealing with more limited topic areas.

Methodological Considerations

- Findings produced by research depend in part on the methods used to obtain the findings. To understand the products of research on social development it is therefore necessary to gain some insight into the process of research: its nature, its uses, and its limitations and constraints. Thus the distinction between cross-sectional and longitudinal methods to chart the course of behavioral development needs to be appreciated, as must the respective advantages and disadvantages of laboratory and field approaches and of observational and interview techniques. Each type of methodology adds its own distinctive flavor to the conclusions reached and should therefore be taken into account when evaluating findings.

Chapter 2

Biological Foundations

If we want to explain why children develop as they do we find that two broad categories of influences are generally evoked: those stemming from the child's bio-logical endowment and those referring to environmental effects. To say both play a part is easy; to spell out their respective contributions and describe how these interact is as yet by no means easy. Great progress is now being made as a result of the efforts of behavior geneticists, yet the nature–nurture issue remains an intensely controver-sial one.

Why it should arouse such passion, why so many writers have found it necessary to take sides and why in the course of the history of science there have been such swings of emphasis is puzzling. After all parents, who are perhaps the most interested parties in such a discussion, supply both aspects: nature through the genes they pass on to the child and nurture through their rearing practices. Either way they know they are deeply implicated in the child's development. Perhaps now, as knowledge accumulates, the debate will become less passionate, and especially so as it is becom-ing increasingly apparent that the either–or basis to past discussions is in many respects quite misleading. Take the belief that everything inborn is immutable while all acquired characteristics are modifiable – a dichotomy that is demonstrably false. For example, a genetically determined condition such as PKU (phenylketonuria), which would normally give rise to a severe form of mental handicap, can be elimi-nated by suitable action at the right time; on the other hand phobias, acquired during an individual's lifetime, are sometimes extraordinarily difficult to eradicate. More generally, it is also now impossible to maintain that the issue is one of nature *or* nurture. As far as psychological characteristics are concerned, there is no instance of nature being the sole determinant: any aspect of behavior (other than such primitive reflexes as the knee jerk) requires an environment in which to develop and to function. And equally any form of learning inevitably takes place in the context of an individual's inborn endowment that will help to determine how, when, and what is acquired. All development is thus a matter of nature *and* nurture.

Most of this discussion has taken place with respect to the development of intel-lectual aspects of behavior. The origins of social aspects, however, are just as much in need of analysis (Plomin, 1994a). The question whether the human child is *born* social or *made* social preoccupied many writers until quite recently; we are now moving beyond such meaningless discussion, having realized that every individual arrives in the world already *preadapted* for social life in the same sense that babies are preadapted to breathe and to take in food, but that subsequent experience in the particular culture to which the baby belongs will build on that foundation and vastly extend the child's repertoire. Feeding patterns and breathing have evolved in our species because we need them for survival; behavior that brings the infant into contact with its caretakers is just as essential and has thus also evolved as adaptive. The nature of social preadaptation as found in humans generally is thus one issue for study; the nature of individual differences is another. Newborns are not all identical; the facts of individuality are obvious from the beginning and affect how the child is treated by others. It is here in particular that the techniques of behavior genetics are of use in throwing light on the nature of that individuality and on its interweaving with environmental influences.

Evolutionary Perspective

How can we explain the course of human development? One way is to phrase the answer in terms of *proximate* (or immediate) causes, the other is to resort to *ultimate* (or remote) causes. The former predominate in psychological inquiry, where the question "why" about the developmental course is usually answered by examining influences that are currently affecting the individual or, at most, have played a part in that person's earlier history. Contrast that with the longer-term perspective, adopted more commonly by biologists, which provokes questions about the evolution of behavior and so examines the way in which particular response patterns have come into being in the course of the millions of years that constitute the history of the species. In this book we shall be mainly concerned with problems of proximate causation; proper understanding of developmental processes, however, requires also an awareness of the longer-term perspective and we shall therefore first turn to that.

Adaptation, Selection, and Survival

Evolutionary theory, as originally put forward by Charles Darwin (1859), was a massive attempt to explain how the form and function of all characteristics of every species have come into being. The basic principle proposed by Darwin to account for this process was that of *natural selection*, that is, the notion that members of a species differ from one another in their genetic endowments and that those variants which equip an organism particularly well to cope with the exigencies of the environment will be the most likely to be preserved in the struggle for existence and so become the prevailing type. Evolution by natural selection may thus be represented as the survival of the fittest, though this is not the popular notion of "nature, red in tooth and claw" where the struggle for existence leads to deadly combat. Such combat usually occurs between members of *different* species, whereas Darwin was concerned with the slow and gradual process whereby members of the *same* species show different rates of survival and reproductive capacity. Genetic variability within each species makes it possible for characteristics advantageous for survival to be perpetuated, in that individuals possessing them are most likely to succeed in reaching maturity and reproducing themselves. In so far as such characteristics are inherited they can be passed on to offspring who in turn will have a competitive advantage; over generations, therefore, species will gradually become better adapted to the environment in which they live.

Darwin's account of evolutionary mechanisms has not remained unchallenged; in particular there has been much discussion as to whether certain characteristics are selected because they are adaptive for individuals (as Darwin believed) or for the species as a whole. The idea that whole *groups or populations* compete and replace one another through evolutionary time (Wynne-Edwards, 1962) has not been upheld; in so far as the genes selected for are passed on from parent to offspring, an explanation in terms of selection acting primarily on *individuals* appears more plausible. Yet there are some facts that do not fit this account, in particular acts of cooperation or of altruism such as parents willing to sacrifice themselves for the good of their offspring. Some characteristics (and parental behavior is especially noteworthy in this respect) evolve despite the fact that they are costly to the individual in terms of survival and are of benefit to others. Evolutionary theory has therefore been extended by the principle of *kin selection* (Hamilton, 1964), which proposes that natural selection works not only through the advantages conferred on individuals but also through those conferred on other genetically similar individuals. A characteristic that is disadvantageous to individuals might thus be selected nevertheless if enough kin, particularly closely related kin, will benefit. Selection can, under certain circumstances, favor those actions that increase the survival of closely related persons even at a cost to the individual; what matters is that *genes* can thereby be preserved by being passed on to the next generation.

Such ideas have been incorporated into the theories put forward by sociobiologists such as E. O. Wilson (1975) and Dawkins (1976). Sociobiology represents an attempt to organize the facts about the adaptive significance of social behavior in animals and, by extension, in human beings; as Wilson put it, it is "the systematic study of the biological basis of all forms of social behaviour, including sexual and parental behaviour, in all kinds of organisms, including humans." Its starting point is the belief that behavior is dominated by a genetically based urge to produce the maximum number of successful offspring, either directly or by favoring one's next of kin. Parental love, for instance, is adaptive because it ensures that parents will invest in the child in a manner that maximizes the parent's "fitness," involving the extent to which genes succeed in projecting copies of themselves into future generations. In just the same way the child loves its parents because such an attachment enhances its own chances of ultimate evolutionary success: the infant's proximity-seeking and affectionate behavior will mobilize parental protection and thereby ensure its survival and ultimate ability to produce its own offspring. Individuals who function better socially may be better perpetuators of their genes and are more favored by natural selection than those who are less successful. What matters above all, however, is the maximizing of *inclusive fitness*, i.e. the total of individuals' reproductive success through their offspring *plus* that of their relatives.

Sociobiology has aroused much controversy, some of it politically motivated because of the belief (a mistaken one, according to sociobiologists) that it is determinist in character and thus denies human flexibility and the possibility of equal opportunities. However this may be, from a scientific point of view it represents an attempt to understand how and why social behavior has evolved in all its forms, including cooperation, conflict, mating, and parental behavior. By drawing on evolutionary theory, population ecology, and ethology it seeks to extend Darwinian ideas and to accommodate facts left unexplained by Darwin (as seen, for example, in the concept of "reciprocal altruism," which maintains that individuals will help others, even at some cost to themselves, if they can expect similar help in return). According to Wilson, quite specific predictions can be set up on the basis of sociobiological principles which can then be put to the test, in the human as well as in other species. However, the extent to which these principles can do justice to human flexibility and cultural variation is still a matter of much controversy.

From our point of view three aspects of evolutionary theory are worth emphasizing:

1   evolutionary theory applies as much to behavioral as to structural characteristics;
2   the adaptation of a species is always to a particular kind of environment;
3   the old innate-versus-acquired distinction has no place in this account.

As to the first point, it is true that structural characteristics initially received most attention (the neck of the giraffe is a much-quoted example of the adaptive value of a characteristic that enabled those with the longest necks to have access to the most leaves in trees and thus to have the best chance of survival). Yet, as Darwin himself pointed out, all aspects of organisms are subject to the same selective processes, functional as well as structural, including such psychological characteristics of the human species as feeling, thought, and language. Thus behavior patterns can be analyzed in the same way as anatomical structures and physiological reactions; they are subject to the same principles of evolutionary pressure, and in particular those present in the very earliest stages of life lend themselves to the kind of study that can profit from knowledge of biological concepts and cross-species comparison. Certainly the question as to the nature and functioning of species-specific patterns which play a part in the development of human social behavior has evoked much discussion and research, and we shall give some examples below when we turn to work on such social signaling systems as smiling and crying and on emotional expressions.

The second point draws attention to the fact that each species is adapted to a quite specific environment – its *ecological niche*, so that it can survive by means of its structural and functional characteristics in that environment. Individuals need to be studied in the context of their natural habitat if one is to understand the evolutionary value of particular characteristics. It was this consideration which impelled Darwin to devote several years of his voyage on the *Beagle* to work in remote parts of the earth in order to collect details not only about many kinds of plants and animals but also about the habitats in which these organisms were to be found. Evolutionary change is, after all, not brought about by some internal force located solely within organisms; it proceeds through the interaction of organisms and their ecosystems. Understanding the former means dovetailing them with the latter. This is particularly important because the habitat is not necessarily static: environmental conditions may change, sometimes relatively suddenly (e.g. because of human interference with ecological and climatic conditions) and favor new sets of species characteristics. Modifiability in relation to altering circumstances is thus at a premium in evolution; the "fit" of the physical and behavioral characteristics of a species is a dynamically changing concept in that all sorts of environmental conditions (unavailability of certain kinds of food, drought, a rise or fall in temperature, etc.) can make previous forms of adaptation no longer appropriate and, under extreme circumstances, even lead to the extinction of a species. Psychologists at one time tended to preoccupy themselves with individuals in isolation; one of the advantages of cross-fertilization with biological thinking has been to draw attention to the importance of *context* in the development of any organism, including that of the human child. For most species the natural environment varies slowly and changes little; not so for human beings where the ever-increasing rate of technological advance means that the relationship between individual and environment is increasingly unstable, and where it is therefore all the more important not to study individuals in isolation but to take into account the setting in which development occurs.

The third point refers to the degree of modifiability of species-specific behavior patterns as a result of individual experience. The fact that a particular behavior pattern is part of the individual's genetic endowment does not mean that it remains fixed for ever more in its original form. Apart from such primitive reflexes as the knee jerk and the eye blink all human behavior is modifiable; the extent of possible change, however, varies. Hinde (1983) has made the useful distinction between *environmentally stable* and *environmentally labile* characteristics, the former referring to those behavior patterns that are relatively little influenced by variations in the environment and the latter to patterns much influenced by such variations. This is, of course, not a dichotomy but a continuum, and any particular behavior pattern may move up or down this continuum according to the individual's developmental stage: at some points of the life cycle, that is, the behavior pattern may be more open to environmental influences than at others – a good illustration, let us note, of the uselessness of a rigid innate–acquired dichotomy. Some biological constraints always exist, the only question being their extent and timing.

Cross-species Comparison

It is a basic tenet of evolutionary theory that there are continuities between animals and human beings. Human characteristics, Darwin maintained, are derived from animal sources by the force of natural selection; there is no qualitative discontinuity between the human and other species, and impetus was thus given to the idea that one can learn about children's development by studying that of animals.

There is no doubt that such a comparative approach has its uses – for one thing because humans *resemble* animals and for another because they *differ* from them. The resemblance was spelled out by Darwin (much to the consternation of his fellow-Victorians); the infant's cry for food, for example, he considered to be analogous to the cry for food of the nestling-bird, because of similarities both in the function of this behavior pattern and in its instinctive nature. The point of the analogy, it should be noted, was not to make superficial comparisons at a purely phenotypical level; it was rather to derive general principles of behavioral functioning and origin. The comparative method is thus useful for evaluating the generality of a hypothesis across the different species, and it was this which impelled Darwin, in the course of his own work, to collect information from a very wide range of organisms, from plants to human beings.

According to Hinde (1974), the advantages of the comparative method are threefold:

1   animals are useful for developing methods of study that can then be adapted for the study of human beings;
2   particular problems can be investigated in animals where ethical considerations prevent human work;
3   research on other species can give rise to principles the relevance of which to human beings can then be assessed.

The first two points refer to matters of convenience; the third is the essential one which provides the basic motivation for the use of comparative methodology. The gap between humans and animals is, of course, great; nevertheless, studies of other species may yield valuable hypotheses that can then be tested out on human beings. But whatever the advantages of a comparative approach there are also dangers, in particular the tendencies to *anthropomorphism* (ascribing human-like qualities to animals) and *zoomorphism* (ascribing animal-like qualities to humans) – in brief, the mindless generalization of findings from one species to another. Accounts of children's social development have been particularly prone to this, as seen in the case below.

The case of physical contact

There is a longstanding belief that physical contact between mother and child plays an important part in early human development, and that to be fondled, held, stroked, and cuddled are essential ingredients in the formation of infant attachments. Ribble (1944), for example, suggested that the baby's tactile need is similar to hunger for food and has to be gratified through personal stimulation involving touching and skin-to-skin contact. Such contact, she maintained, is an essential precondition to psychological and physical growth in the early months of life; failure to achieve it is a form of deprivation with possibly serious consequences.

It is not easy to obtain empirical backing for such a claim, and results from animal studies were therefore eagerly fastened on by child care experts, in particular work by Harlow and his associates on rhesus monkeys (e.g. Harlow, 1958; Harlow & Zimmermann, 1959). Infants of this species are equipped with a powerful clinging response, which is used from immediately after birth to make contact with the mother who, in turn, provides a fur that can easily be clung to. In a series of experiments Harlow showed that *contact comfort* is a much more powerful motive for bringing about the infant's attachment to the mother than provision of food: animals given the choice between a wire model of a mother and a cloth model spent nearly all their time on the latter, despite the fact that they obtained food from the former. When frightened by something strange the infants rushed to the cloth model and clung to that; when separated from the cloth model, but not the wire model, they showed considerable disturbance. As Harlow concluded, contact comfort appears to be a variable of critical importance in the development of affectional responsiveness to the mother.

These results were generalized to human infants, for example by Casler (1961) who maintained that tactile stimulation is the most essential ingredient of mothering; physical contact, that is, was seen by many as the primary mechanism whereby the attachment to the mother is brought about. Such a claim, however, neglects the totally different structure and functioning of the two species. Whereas infant monkeys are provided with a powerful clinging response that enables them to take an active part in making contact with the mother, the grasping reflex of the human infant is of little use for that purpose. Human babies are equipped with different means of bringing about the mother's proximity, e.g. crying; in addition, as a series of experiments by Korner showed (Korner & Grobstein, 1966; Korner & Thoman, 1970), they are much more likely to be comforted by kinesthetic than by tactile stimulation. Picking up a crying baby, as is well known, is a soothing experience; by experimentally teasing apart the various stimulus components of picking up Korner demonstrated that it is the moving about of the child which produces the effect rather than the tactile stimulation provided. And one further consideration is that by no means all infants like physical contact: some actively resist all forms of cuddling and yet form perfectly satisfactory attachments to their mothers, who manage to find other but quite acceptable ways of relating to the child (Schaffer & Emerson, 1964b).

It is apparent that physical contact does not play the same role in human development as it does in that of the rhesus monkey (and most other primates) and that automatic extrapolation from one species to another is not justified. In monkeys clinging is used to achieve a particular end, i.e. to remain in proximity to the mother. In humans other means are used; the end is the same and it is that which has generality, but in order to achieve it each species has available its own mechanisms, these having evolved to fit in with the general characteristics of that species. This is not to deny that tactile contact cannot play an important part in human parent–child interaction; on the contrary, as Stack and LePage (1996) have shown, infants are sensitive to even quite subtle changes in mothers' touching during normal face-to-face interaction, this being a highly effective means of bringing about attentiveness, reducing negative affect and maintaining positive affect. However, the precise part such contact plays in humans is distinctive to the needs and characteristics of our own species and not those of any other.

The same terms – aggression, attachment, parental care, etc. – are customarily used by us to describe the social behavior of both animals and human beings. The reason we do so is that they serve the same function, not that they necessarily take the identical form. We cannot therefore simply transfer knowledge of their phenotypic expression or of the stimulus conditions that elicit, maintain, and terminate the respective behavior patterns from one species to another. These patterns need to be investigated in their own right for each species; what we have learned from animals may therefore be useful for hypothesis formation in the study of human development, but automatic generalization is not justified.

Social Signaling Devices

The term *fixed action pattern* has been used by ethologists to denote relatively simple and stereotyped actions that are activated by certain quite specific stimuli. They are "prewired," that is, they form part of the individual's genetic endowment and are usually, but by no means necessarily, functional early on in life. Prewired does not, however, mean the pattern is immutable (indeed some prefer the term *modal action pattern* for this reason); it may be modified and extended as a result of environmental interaction and thus differs from reflexes which cannot be so changed. Rather, prewired means that the behavior is evolutionarily based and is preadapted to serve a particular function essential for survival.

Each species, including the human, has its own repertoire of fixed action patterns. Take the baby's *rooting response* (Prechtl, 1958), which refers to the single directed turning movement towards the source of stimulation (usually the mother's breast) that is elicited whenever a limited area around the baby's mouth is touched. Occasionally the response takes the form of rapid side-to-side movements; in either case the purpose is to come into contact with the nipple and enable the infant to commence feeding. Rooting is present from birth (i.e. it is prewired); in due course, however, it becomes less mechanical in that the infant is capable of employing it in a more flexible and purposive manner as part of the whole sequence of feeding behavior, including such other innately organized activities as sucking and swallowing.

Obtaining food is, of course, essential for the infant's survival, but so is obtaining the caretaker's attention and ensuring her proximity. It is therefore not surprising to find that the human infant comes into the world with a number of devices the function of which is to display certain differentiated signals that typically elicit particular kinds of response from caretakers. The two most obvious are smiling and crying.

(1)   *Smiling*   The smile is a peculiarly *social* response. It enhances the attractiveness of the infant and ensures further attention on the part of the parent, thus leading to a whole chain of interactions. Although present from birth it is initially vague in form and occurs as much when the infant is alone as when with another person; only from the second month on is the smile usually elicited in interpersonal contexts, commonly by the sight of another person's face. In fact, as a series of investigations (Ahrens, 1954; Kaila, 1932; Spitz & Wolf, 1946) have made abundantly clear, the stimulus sufficient to evoke the smile is at first something of a much more primitive nature than the face, i.e. merely a pair of eyelike dots. A mask containing nothing but such dots will result in the infant smiling just as surely as the sight of the mother's face. In this way one can show that the other person's mouth or facial expression play no part in eliciting the smile from infants in their second and third months; at that time infants still have such limited capacity to process information from the environment that they are unable to attend to the face as a whole and instead abstract from it the very simple configuration of the two eyes. These constitute a *key stimulus* that is innately linked to the fixed action pattern of the smile, in the same way that, for example, the pecking response of the young herring gull is released by nothing more complicated than the red dot which is found on the beak of the parent. In both cases biologically important stimulus–response sequences are part of the innate endowment of the species, serving functions that ensure the offspring's survival. Thus the smile increases the infant's attractiveness and so its chances of care and protection. It is significant, however, that the smile is not wholly tied to a visual key stimulus, for smiling can also be seen in blind babies (Freedman, 1974), where it is évoked by a gentle touch or a soft sound. Some degree of flexibility appears to be built into the human system.

(2)   *Crying*   The baby's cry is another built-in social signaling device of obvious communicative usefulness. Detailed analysis (e.g. by Wolff, 1966) has shown crying to be a highly organized and complex response, where each cry is made up of four phases (expiratory, rest, inspiratory, rest), the relative timing of which may vary and so give rise to several quite distinct types of cry (see table 1). Different information is thus carried by these patterns and mothers quickly come to distinguish them and to react accordingly (though other adults, men as much as women, have been found to be just as adept and responsive; Frodi, Lamb, Leavite, & Donovan, 1978). As with smiling, the eliciting conditions in the early weeks of life are primitive: pain, hunger, movement restriction, discomfort, and so forth, and only with increasing age will the range of stimulus conditions giving rise to crying also increase. Terminating conditions too are initially simple, e.g. rocking and other forms of kinesthetic stimulation,

swaddling, feeding, and so on. In the young infant crying is a purely reactive pattern; it is only towards the end of the first year that infants come to appreciate the communicative value of their behavior and begin to use it purposely.

Signaling devices such as smiling and crying are examples of the *social preadaptation* found in human infants. They are innate communicative behavior patterns that serve to bind the child at the beginning of life to its caretakers. These in turn must, of course, show reciprocal responsiveness for the bond to develop; it is significant, however, that mutual adaptation is brought about in the first place by nature. Smiling in the early weeks is automatically triggered by the sight of the parent's eyes; because parents love to see their babies smiling they are more likely then to pay them continued attention. Crying arouses the parent (the pain cry in particular); as a result parents are provoked to act in some appropriate manner. In that sense the human child is adapted for social life from birth on, even though the baby itself has no conscious appreciation as yet of its actions and their consequences. In due course, largely as a result of cognitive maturation and socializing influences, devices such as smiling and crying will become more complex and sophisticated communicative patterns. We shall take up their developmental course later on; here we wish to make the point that already at the start of life the child is provided with means, determined by its genetic endowment, whereby participation in social interactions is possible.

Biological Basis of Emotional Development

In any form of social interaction the communication of the participants' emotional state plays a central role, and especially so at the earliest, nonverbal stages when it may be the only way for parents to "read" their children and correctly interpret their needs. There are obvious advantages therefore for a child to arrive in the world already equipped to provide a range of emotional signals to guide caretakers' behavior.

Table 1   Characteristics of three cry patterns

	Time (in seconds)		
Cry phase	Hunger cry	Anger cry	Pain cry
Expiratory	0.62	0.69	3.83
Rest	0.08	0.20	3.99
Inspiratory	0.04	0.05	0.18
Rest	0.20	0.11	0.16

Source: Adapted from Wolff (1966)

It is perhaps ironic that a feature of human behavior as intimately familiar as emotion should have given rise to so much scientific uncertainty. There are disputes about the number of discrete emotions that can be identified, about their developmental timetable, about the manner of their modification through experience, about their relationship to cognitive processes, about their physiological substrata and even about their definition. What no one denies is the central role emotions play in the regulation of both individual and interpersonal behavior. At an individual level, feeling state is the paramount component of which we are aware and which tells us something about our own psychophysiological reaction to life events. At an interpersonal level we rely on the overt signs that accompany another person's emotional states, and though both gestural and voice cues can be used for this purpose it is facial expression that usually provides the most reliable information.

Emotional facial expressions can be viewed as fixed action patterns that have been selected in the course of evolution as useful signaling behaviors (Malatesta, Culver, Tesman, & Shepard, 1989). There are several assumptions here: first, that the basic emotional expressions are universal, second that they are innate, and third that even in infancy emotional expressions correspond to those in adults and that adults can therefore accurately read the child's state. Though there are some residual doubts about each of these statements it seems highly probable that all are accurate.

The universal nature of facial expressions was of great interest to Darwin (1872). From early on in his career Darwin believed that such expressions could well be part of human beings' inherited behavioral repertoire, having evolved from response patterns useful in the struggle for survival: anger, for example, is characterized by the lowering of eyebrows (useful for enhancing visual acuity by shielding the eyes from direct sunlight), the flaring of nostrils (facilitating rapid intake of oxygen), and an open mouth display that may have originally functioned to bare teeth ready for biting (Campos, Barrett, Lamb, Goldsmith, & Stenberg, 1983). He therefore collected data from other cultures in order to establish the universality of emotional expressions; he also obtained information about the reactions of mental patients to emotional events; and in addition he observed his own children during their infancy in order to establish whether their emotional expressions were homologous to those of adults. Such information convinced him that there is indeed continuity across both ages and cultures in the way that emotions are expressed and, moreover, that there is also some degree of continuity across different primate species. Emotional expression, Darwin concluded, is almost certainly a product of evolution, having become part of our inheritance because of its central role in social interaction.

In more recent years rather more sophisticated methods than those used by Darwin have borne out these conclusions. Cross-cultural evidence has shown that the emotions expressed by people in diverse societies, including some with minimal outside contact, are highly similar to those expressed by people living in the West (Izard, 1977; Izard & Malatesta, 1987). Thus Ekman and his colleagues have found members of many different societies, both literate and preliterate, to show the same facial expressions under similar incentive conditions, e.g. when asked to pose the expression appropriate to receiving news of someone's death. Similarly, Western observers have no difficulty in accurately interpreting the expressions of members of preliterate societies (Ekman, 1972; Ekman & Oster, 1979). Considerable agreement thus emerged with respect to such emotions as happiness, sadness, surprise, fear, anger, and disgust. This is despite the socialization pressures which each society brings to bear on the way in which emotions are displayed: as Ekman (1972) found, Americans and Japanese in public often follow very different social rules in their emotional reactions to the same stimulus situation; while alone, however, their facial expressions when experiencing fear, disgust, and distress are the same. Universality, it is true, does not automatically indicate an innate origin; as Ekman and Oster (1979) have pointed out, the reason for common patterns could be common species-typical learning experiences. However, in the absence of evidence for such learning experiences explanations in terms of genetic origin are more convincing.

Whether infant emotional expressions correspond to those of adults depends in the first place on the possibility of being able to identify discrete facial expressions in the early weeks of life – a controversial matter, in that it raises the whole issue of the nature of emotional development and its timetable. Bridges (1932), in some of the earliest work on this subject, concluded that initially emotions are nothing but undifferentiated excitement and that only later on will the infant become capable of expressing discrete emotions: distress at 3 weeks, delight at 3 months, anger at 4 months, disgust at 5 months, and fear at 7 months. Here she differed from a still earlier writer, J. B. Watson (1919), who declared that infants are endowed with three primary emotions – rage, fear, and love – and that all other emotional responses develop on the basis of the individual's conditioning history. The argument about early differentiation is still in progress; however, while former theories relied on impressionistic observations that allowed plenty of room for subjective interpretation, more recent work has profited from the development of objective and reliable assessment schemes which score emotional expression from the details of facial movement. The two most widely used schemes are Ekman and Friesen's (1978) Facial Action Coding System (FACS) and Izard's (1979) Maximally Discriminative Facial Movements Code (MAX) – both very detailed analytic techniques which attend to the precise appearance and movement of distinct muscle configurations in different regions of the face and which then identify the corresponding emotion on the basis of the sum or pattern of the individual scores. Simplified versions of these schemes are now available, as are adaptations for use specifically with infants. Despite some reservations about the neglect of nonstandard facial movements by these scoring methods (Fogel et al., 1992) their application does make it far more likely that a number of distinct emotional expressions can be discerned from the beginning and that others appear in the course of infancy according to some genetically determined timetable. Much of the relevant information comes from studies that have placed infants in situations designed to arouse particular emotions: the administration of some bitter tasting substance, the removal of a biscuit, the unexpected disappearance of a toy, or the stress of being inoculated. By recording the infants' reactions and subsequently having them scored by observers ignorant of the eliciting conditions it becomes possible to demonstrate, first, that certain specific emotions are found even in newborn babies and, second, that these correspond to what adults would regard as responses appropriate to the situation. It seems highly likely, therefore, that there are quite specific links between particular emotional feelings and particular facial expressions, and that these links are of innate origin. Darwin's proposal, that emotional expressions are part of our common inheritance and that a variety of distinct emotions are to be found from early on, is thus given credence by modern research techniques.

One of the most detailed treatments of emotional development has been provided by Izard (1971, 1977; Izard & Malatesta, 1987). According to his Differential Emotions Theory every individual is equipped with nine basic emotions, i.e. interest, joy, sadness, surprise, anger, disgust, contempt, fear, and shame, each of which is linked to a particular neural substratum, is overtly expressed in a distinct manner, and is associated with a specific feeling tone. The three components (neural, motor-expressive, and mental) are innately linked; they provide each emotion with its distinctive overt and subjective form and, initially at least, the three are organized in a rigid and stereotyped manner. Basic emotions all have unique adaptive value; each has, on the one hand, certain biological functions of a regulatory nature and, on the other hand, social functions of a communicative nature. They emerge at the time of the life cycle when they first become adaptive to the individual; thus some are present from birth: the behavior associated with disgust, for example, is already adaptive in early infancy in the expulsion of distasteful substances. Emotions, however, are not totally separate from other aspects of behavior: their developmental course takes place in synchrony with perceptual, motoric, and cognitive development, and though they constitute the primary motivational system for human behavior, the complexity and flexibility of emotions is in turn greatly enhanced by developments in the individual's cognitive and language systems. Though modifiable by subsequent experience, in particular through the socialization practices of caretakers, the essentially distinctive nature of the various emotions means that in early development they figure prominently in the child's ability to communicate needs and establish affective bonds with others.

We shall turn to the socialization of emotions at a later point. Here the emphasis is on the manner in which emotions and their expressions are innately organized and from early on provide a bridge between the child and its caretakers. Not everyone agrees with the details of Izard's Differential Emotions Theory: Campos and his colleagues (Campos et al., 1983; Barrett & Campos, 1987), for instance, criticize Izard for confusing emotional *expression* with emotional *experience* and suggest that all basic emotions are present from birth rather than emerging at specific points of development. Emotions, they stress, are not reified wholes that appear only when some criterion (such as a specific cognitive achievement) is met; rather, each emotion should be seen as a *family* of features, none of which is a *necessary* index that provides sufficient information for us to infer emotionality. Thus the features (including particular facial movements, actions, physiological patterns, and adaptive functions) may be intrinsic but they are not invariant; their association is not as rigid as may appear from Izard's theory but will vary according to the particular circumstances of each encounter by the individual with the environment.

At this relatively early stage of research into emotional development it is not surprising to find differences in opinion and emphasis. What is certain is that emotional displays are among the first means whereby child and caretaker communicate with each other, thanks to the presence of various specific inborn means of expressing different emotional feelings. The powerful role which this form of communication plays becomes particularly evident in cases of pathology when, for one reason or another, emotional signals fail. This is illustrated in the case below.

The case of emotional expressions in some atypical children

For proper communication between parent and child it is necessary that the child be capable of providing clear signals, so that the parent can recognize them easily and respond to them appropriately. Unfortunately this is not always possible.

Take blindness. Fraiberg (1977) has provided some vivid descriptive data to show how blind babies appear to give misleading cues to their caretakers because of the "blank" look that they habitually wear. The extremes of emotions, such as great happiness or unhappiness, can easily be discerned in their faces, but as far as more subtle emotions are concerned they have an impoverished repertoire of facial signs, as a result of which they may give the impression of a lack of interest or feeling, primarily because the eyes fail to provide the usual cues. However, Fraiberg goes on to show that this is in fact a misleading impression: emotional cues are often discerned more reliably by watching the blind child's hands. When the mother gives the child a new toy the face may register lack of interest; if she switches her attention to the child's hands, however, a different message is conveyed, for these may be very busy indeed exploring and becoming acquainted with the toy. Similarly when a toy drops on the floor: the child may look bored and the mother may therefore take no action; the hands, however, tell a different story for they are searching and feeling everywhere. Not all emotions can be easily communicated through this alternate channel; in any case, parents with blind babies have the task of reorienting themselves and learning to pick up emotional signals by different means.

In Down's syndrome children too, such reorientation is necessary. The emotional expressions of such children have been described as "dampened" (Cicchetti & Sroufe, 1976): they tend to remain unresponsive where other children smile and to smile where others laugh; laughter is only elicited by the most vigorous forms of stimulation such as bouncing on the knee. Reactivity to stressful situations, such as being left alone by the mother, is also diminished. This places an extra burden on parents, yet one which most are able to compensate for spontaneously. Thus Sorce and Emde (1982) found that mothers of Down's syndrome children are much more likely to respond even to low-intensity emotional signals than mothers generally do – as though they had recalibrated their responsiveness threshold to ensure that the child was not deprived of interactional experience as a result of an inherently depressed level of emotional signaling. Other mothers confronted by the same Down's syndrome children did not respond so readily, suggesting that the recalibration was a matter of experience and also showing that such children will continue to encounter difficulties in communicating with other people.

That adults are sensitive to the emotional cues which infants show in their facial expressions cannot be doubted. Communication, however, ought to be a reciprocal process in social interaction, and so the question arises as to how soon infants show sensitivity to others' expressions. Darwin believed that such sensitivity is also an inborn tendency; however, infants in the early weeks of life lack the visual ability to make the fine discriminations which are necessary for the recognition of specific facial expressions (C. A. Nelson, 1987). It is not till the age of 2 or 3 months that infants begin to scan both the internal and the external features of another person's face; before then attention tends to be confined to gross characteristics such as eyes and hairline and all faces are thus treated alike. Once infants have the requisite visual skills, however, it becomes evident that others' expressions can have a marked effect on them. Confronted by mothers who, for experimental purposes, have been asked to remain quiet and unresponsive for a period, infants from 3 months on look puzzled and show signs of unhappiness (Trevarthen, 1977; Tronick, 1989). Simulated depression on the part of the mother also produces gaze avoidance and crying (Cohn & Tronick, 1983). As, furthermore, it has been demonstrated that by at least 5 months of age infants have become capable of reliably differentiating such emotions as anger, fear, and sadness (G. M. Schwartz, Izard, & Ansal, 1985), we can conclude that sensitivity to the emotional states of others appears early, is linked to the development of visual skills and plays an important part in regulating the behavior of infants and their communication with adults.

Cultural Evolution

The process of biological evolution is based on changes in genes and is thus extremely slow. A much faster process is that of cultural evolution, which is based on the transfer of knowledge from one individual to another and in particular from one generation to another. The one has given us particular kinds of bodily and mental capacities; the other determines how we use those inherited capacities.

Biological and cultural evolution go hand in hand. To quote Konrad Lorenz (1966):

Man's whole system of innate activities and reactions is phylogenetically so constructed, so "calculated" by evolution, as to *need* to be complemented by cultural tradition. For instance, all the tremendous neuro-sensory apparatus of human speech is phylogenetically evolved, but so constructed that its function presupposes the existence of a culturally developed language which the infant has to learn. The greater part of all phylogenetically evolved patterns of human social behaviour is inter-related with cultural tradition in an analogous way.

Thus culture is not in any way opposed to evolution nor does it attempt to undo its work. Quite on the contrary, social change occurs within the biological framework characterizing the human species, and the mechanisms of change, though based on different processes, are similar. As Stebbing (1982) puts it, those societies which have used their inherited capacities more efficiently have been able to acquire more food and to defend themselves better, thus improving their chances of survival and reproduction and crowding out less efficient societies. Their greater efficiency was perpetuated by cultural transmission: the processes of socialization, teaching, and learning became vital to progress and came to be recognized as important areas in their own right. And just as inherited properties evolved through biological processes and came to differentiate various species, so culturally developed social norms have come to characterize particular groups of human beings and differentiate them from one another.

The concept of *culture* refers to those aspects of life that are specific to particular societies and that are transmitted from one generation to another. Societies pride themselves on their traditions and there is thus considerable pressure on individuals to conform, much of it mediated by the particular child rearing practices adopted by the society. The culture thus provides a context for development, setting the goals to be achieved and the tasks to be performed by its individual members. The topic of socialization will form a major theme in this book; here let us note that the recent emphasis on cultural determinants of development has at the very least ensured that psychological growth is no longer studied in isolation but as dependent on the social setting in which the child is reared. This has indeed been one major use of cross-cultural research: instead of glibly assuming that whatever is found by investigators working in Western societies has universal applicability, cross-cultural studies can provide information both about similarities and about differences according to cultural mores, and thus yield insights into the role of experience in development. The sequencing and timing of cognitive achievements as postulated by Piaget has been a particularly popular topic from this point of view (Dasen & Heron, 1981); in the study of social development, too, findings concerning similarities as well as differences can be illuminating. Take separation protest, known to occur first around the age of 7 to 8 months in Western infants (Schaffer, 1984): as Konner (1982) has pointed out, the onset of this developmental phenomenon occurs at virtually identical ages, whether the sample is drawn from the Kung San of Botswana (who have 24-hour mother–infant physical contact in a dense social context), Indians living in a remote Guatemalan village (where there is high mother–infant contact in relative isolation), a large Guatemalan town (less mother–infant contact with more social stimulation), an Israeli kibbutz (mother–infant contact on afternoons and weekends), or various subcultures of the United States (see figure 1). Given the regularity

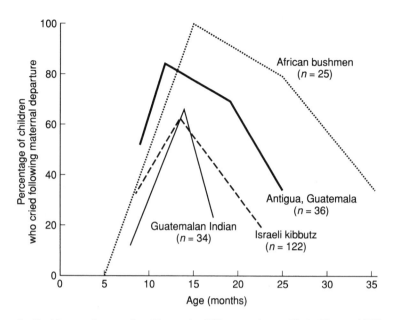

Figure 1   Incidence of separation distress in different cultures (from Kagan, 1978)

of timing despite variation in environmental input it is tempting to conclude that the appearance of this milestone is dependent on a biologically determined timetable.

It is, however, the *differences* among societies that have received most attention, for they show how culture can steer the course of development into channels defined as appropriate by the society concerned. For instance, where peer interaction is valued and infants are accordingly given far more contact with age mates than is customary in the West, children show levels of social interaction the complexity of which has been considered quite beyond the maturational stage of such young children on the basis of Western studies (Zaslow & Rogoff, 1981). Or again, cultural differences in family roles enable one to examine the influence which fathers (in comparison with mothers) play: Morelli and Tronick (1992), for instance, have shown that among the Efe (pygmy) people of Central Africa fathers' involvement with their young children differs in both form and extent from what has been described for the typical Western family, suggesting that the father–child relationship is primarily a cultural construction shaped by the requirements of each society. And to take one more example, the development of sex role behavior has also been profitably examined from a cross-cultural perspective. For instance, it has been found that not only in Western but in many other societies girls are generally more nurturant than boys in their relationships with younger children (Edwards & Whiting, 1977), giving rise to the speculation that this is a biologically determined characteristic inevitably linked to gender. Among the Luo community in Kenya, however, where the care of infants is assigned to boys, no sex difference is found: girls are no more nurturant than boys, suggesting instead that this is a characteristic associated with a certain kind of upbringing (Ember, 1973). Cultural variations thus provide the opportunity to examine the sources which influence particular developmental outcomes.

Human beings are continuing to change, but that change is the result of cultural rather than biological evolution. The rate of change, moreover, appears to be accelerating, due above all to the influence of technology on our lives. Take family life and the role of the sexes. At one time biological factors ensured that there was strict segregation in the parts which men and women played: men, due to their greater physical strength, hunted, toiled in the field, and conducted war; women, by virtue of childbearing and breastfeeding, were tied to the home and responsible for child rearing and household tasks. Technology has changed all that. Food production has increasingly become a mechanized process and is less dependent on sheer physical strength; in similar vein the conduct of war increasingly involves pressing buttons rather than person-to-person combat, and so also calls for different skills from those which our ancestors required. As to child care, consider something as simple as the feeding bottle: its invention meant that the mother was no longer the only person fit to look after babies; fathers could do so just as well. Add to that the development of labor saving household devices: central heating, washing machines, microwaves, precooked foods, and so on; consider the consequent great reduction in the time required for household chores, and it is no wonder that in the last few decades women have increasingly sought employment and fulfillment outside the home and are competing with men for jobs previously regarded as a male monopoly. Even childbirth is being transformed as a result of technological advances: for one thing, the advent of safe forms of contraception means choice in the timing and spacing of children and indeed in whether to have children at all; for another, advances in reproductive technology mean that children can be brought into the world by surrogate mothers and, no doubt in the not too distant future, spend their prenatal life in artificial wombs. As a result, within the space of a very brief period of time profound changes have taken place in our ideas about the functions which men and women can perform in family and society and also in our concept of parenthood. Because of such advances as artificial insemination by donor and the implantation of fertilized ova in another womb it is possible for the genetic mother, the woman who bears the child, and the psychological mother to be three different people. Add to that the fact that the child's genetic father may be a different person from the psychological father, and it becomes clear that there are many possible combinations of individuals who are relevant to the child's conception, birth, and upbringing, and that consequently the notion of parenthood becomes vastly more complex and fragmented. Cultural changes may thus appear to override biological endowment; however, let us bear in mind that it is also part of our biological inheritance to have a considerable degree of flexibility built into our nature, and that it is this which enables us to benefit from technological advances and make choices such as whether to have children and how to rear them. Or to put it another way: human genotypes are characterized above all by great phenotypic flexibility and can therefore easily be modified by whatever experiences individuals encounter or create for themselves.

The Genetics of Behavior

Our heredity provides us with two kinds of characteristics: those common to all human beings and those that distinguish us as individuals. These can refer to the same structures: for example, our genetic endowment provides each one of us with a brain which, among other things, enables us to solve problems and acquire language; however, that endowment is also responsible for producing considerable differences from one person to another in the speed of problem solving and language acquisition. The science of genetics, which goes back at least to the 19th century, is concerned with both; the discipline of behavioral genetics, which is of very recent origin, addresses itself exclusively to the latter.

There are many misconceptions about the implications of genetics for knowledge about human development. Rutter (1992) lists a number of these, among which the following are particularly relevant here:

1. *"Strong genetic effects mean that environmental influences are not important"* This is not so, primarily because the environment may bring about considerable changes in the mean level of a characteristic while genetic effects continue to account for individual variability. Thus children from disadvantaged families will show a rise in IQ level when adopted into more advantaged families, demonstrating the general effects of a stimulating environment; the range of individual differences in IQ of these children, however, is very much more closely related to the range found among their biological parents than that of their adoptive parents, indicating the continuing role of genetic factors.

2. *"Genes provide a limit to potential"* This is true to only some extent, for the statement neglects the role of the environment. As the example of adopted children's IQ shows, genetic factors do affect potential but only in any given environment. Change the environment and the potential is changed too.

3. *"Genetic research is only about hereditary influences and has nothing to say about environmental influences"* As we shall see in greater detail below, this statement is also not true. Behavioral genetics has as much to say about environmental as about genetic effects; given the right research strategies it is possible not only to show the intimate interaction of the two kinds of influence but also to distinguish them and estimate the extent of their relative contribution.

4. *"Nature and nurture are separate"* This is perhaps the most common misconception, i.e. the belief that nature and nurture operate quite separately. In the psychological field in particular this does not occur: both genes and an environment are necessary for an individual to develop. As Scarr and Weinberg (1980) put it,

"everyone must have both a viable gene complement and an environment in which the genes can be expressed over development. No genes, no organism; no environment, no organism." Thus individuals' genetic endowment may predispose them to be susceptible to particular kinds of environmental influences; equally, it may lead them to select and construct certain kinds of environment compatible with their endowment.

5. *"Genetic influences diminish with age"*   It has become apparent that the relationship of genes to age is a much more complex one; the belief that hereditary factors are most evident in the early stages of development and that environmental influences become progressively more important as the individual grows older cannot be supported. For certain characteristics this may be so; for others not, if only because the characteristics may take time to manifest themselves. Age at puberty, which is the obvious example, is largely under genetic control; equally there are indications that differences in intelligence are *more* explicable by genetic factors in older than in younger children.

One further point needs to be made (and the example of age at puberty illustrates it). Genes are not just concerned with static characteristics but also with developmental change. The physical and psychological timetable that we observe in the course of children's development is primarily set by the individual's innate nature. Extreme deviations in the normally expected environment may upset that timetable and produce gross delay, but the emergence of particular characteristics and the sequence in which they appear are primarily a function of the genetic blueprint with which the child arrives in the world. Thus genes are implicated as much in change as in continuity of development.

Mechanisms of Genetic Transmission

Knowledge about the nature and operation of genes has been accumulating rapidly in recent years. Quite apart from the theoretical implications which this knowledge has for understanding human development, there is also growing appreciation of its practical value. *Prenatal screening*, aimed at the detection of hereditary conditions in utero, and *gene therapy*, making possible the replacement of defective genes, are but two of the measures which can now be taken and which bring nearer the day when many inherited diseases, including various forms of mental handicap, can be eliminated. Genetic engineering brings with it a great many ethical hazards but also much potential benefit.

Genes, the basic units of hereditary transmission, are segments of *chromosomes*, rod-shaped structures along which the genes are arranged like beads on a necklace (see table 2 on p. 67 for a summary of key terms used in genetics). Every cell in the human body, with the important exception of the germ cells (i.e. male sperms and female ova, known collectively as *gametes*) contains identical sets of 46 chromosomes, and as each chromosome includes about 20,000 genes there are nearly 1 million genes in each one of these cells. The genes are composed of DNA (deoxyribonucleic acid), a threadlike molecule shaped like a long double spiral staircase (a double helix) which has the ability to copy itself. This takes place whenever a new body cell is required for growth or tissue replacement: in a process known as *mitosis* an existing cell divides, whereupon the chromosomes are duplicated and each half of the dividing cell receives one of the duplicates. New cells, as well as old ones, thus have the full complement of 46 chromosomes.

Gametes, however, contain only 23 chromosomes each, with no pairs. When such a cell divides a process referred to as *meiosis* occurs, which ensures that these chromosomes do *not* double. On conception, when a male sperm penetrates the wall of an ovum and thus fertilizes it, forming a single cell, the 23 chromosomes in the sperm and the 23 in the ovum combine and form the beginnings of a new organism with the full complement of 46 chromosomes. Thereafter the fertilized cell divides in half repeatedly, duplicating each chromosome and then distributing one of the duplicates to each half of the dividing cell. In this way it is ensured that every cell in the growing body of the fetus contains an identical set of chromosomes, half descended from the mother and half from the father. Mitosis continues throughout fetal life, producing thousands of cells in the embryo. In time these cells begin to form themselves into groups, each characterized by a particular chemical process and each assuming a special function: some as part of the nervous system, others as part of the musculature, still others to form bones, and so on, until a complete organism is eventually produced.

The formation of these specialized cells is controlled by the genes. By means of the chemical messages contained in the DNA they ensure the production of specific proteins within each cell. Each gene is responsible for the production of one particular chemical substance, controlling the timing of its release as well as its nature and so directing the course of the organism's growth. The *genotype*, i.e. the total collection of an individual's genes, may be regarded as the blueprint for the assembly and regulation of the proteins which are the building blocks of our bodies; the end result is the *phenotype*, i.e. the observable characteristics, physical or psychological, displayed by the individual. The distinction is an important one, for the same genotype may give rise to different phenotypes depending on environmental influences: height, for example, is a genetically determined characteristic that nevertheless is intimately dependent on the nutrition an individual receives during the period of growth. The phenotype is therefore the characteristic which results from the interaction of an individual's genetic constitution with the environment.

Under some circumstances individual genes may act alone to produce a phenotype; in others they act jointly with other genes. The latter, known as *polygenetic inheritance*, applies to virtually all psychological characteristics; thus the development of intelligence, for instance, has been estimated to depend on at least 150 genes. However, behavioral characteristics as such are only indirectly regulated by genes; what is inherited is a susceptibility by virtue of particular bodily structures. Thus a person may inherit a volatile autonomic nervous system and as a result be more liable to develop a neurotic personality; the latter as such, however, is not inherited but will emerge given particular kinds of environmental experiences that act in conjunction with the genetic susceptibility. In so far as psychological traits are largely a function of physical characteristics genes only *indirectly* affect behavior.

Some of the messages conveyed by the genes refer to common human attributes; they ensure that each of us is provided with the kind of nervous system, physical appearance, and so forth that define our species-specific characteristics and distinguish us from other species. Other messages refer to aspects of individuality, that is, those that distinguish each of us from other human beings and ensure that every human being is genetically unique and unlike any other person on earth. This uniqueness is brought about by the incredibly large number of different ways whereby the 23 chromosomes from the father and the 23 from the mother can combine, resulting in an enormous range of different configurations of characteristics. During meiosis, when a pair of chromosomes segregates, it is a matter purely of chance which of the two chromosomes will end up in a particular gamete. Moreover, as each pair of chromosomes segregates independently of all the other pairs there are very many different combinations that could result from the meiosis of a single germ cell. It has been calculated that an individual parent could produce more than 8 million different gametes of which no two will be genetically alike. Taking into account the other parent's 8 million, the child which the couple produces will be one of 64 trillion possible combinations! Even this is not the end of the story, due to a process known as *crossing over* which occurs during meiosis and which describes the exchange of *some* portion of the genetic material between pairs of chromosomes, as a result of which the number of possible combinations of genes in each set of 23 chromosomes is increased even further and the number of different gametes produced by an individual extended well beyond the 8 million mark.

Genetic variability is essential to evolution. It also provides us with an account of the mechanisms whereby physical and psychological uniqueness is brought about (for further details from a psychological point of view see Plomin, Corley, DeFries, & Fulker, 1990). Such uniqueness characterizes even siblings, for every child inherits only half of each parent's genes. The exception is *monozygotic* (or identical) twins, for each such pair develops from a single fertilized egg which splits into two, both having identical genotypes. *Dizygotic* (nonidentical) twins result from two eggs fertilized at the same time by different sperms and therefore resemble one another no more than other siblings.

Methods of Behavioral Genetics

It is essential to bear in mind that behavioral genetics does not set out to determine how much of a characteristic is due to genetic factors and how much to the environment; instead it aims to assess the relative contribution of heredity and environment

Table 2 Summary of key terms used in genetics

Term	*Definition*
Canalization	The extent to which genetic endowment limits developmental outcome to just a few possibilities
Chromosomes	Threadlike structures in the body's cells made up of genes
Crossing over	The exchange of genetic material between pairs of chromosomes
DNA	Deoxyribonucleic acid – a long threadlike molecule shaped like a double helix that runs along the length of each chromosome
Dizygotic twins	Nonidentical twins, who develop from separate ova
Gametes	Sperm and ova
Genes	Segments of DNA in chromosomes that are the hereditary blueprints for development
Genotype	An individual's genetic endowment
Heritability	The amount of variability in a trait that is due to genetic differences among individuals
Meiosis	The process of cell division that produces gametes
Mitosis	The process of cell division taking place in all cells other than gametes
Monozygotic twins	Identical twins, who develop from a single ovum
Phenotype	The overt result of the operation of genetic influences, functioning in a given environment
Polygenetic inheritance	The joint operation of several genes in producing a particular phenotype

to the *differences among individuals*. Thus the focus is on what accounts for variability among people with respect to a given characteristic, and not on the causes of a particular mean value for that characteristic in a population. For example, it has been found that vocabulary is one of the most highly heritable aspects of cognitive ability (Plomin, DeFries, & McClearn, 1990). This does not, however, enable one to say that the commonly found superiority in vocabulary among females over males is of genetic origin. Such a difference could well be due to socialization factors; the methods of behavioral genetics do not address the issue of the relative contribution of the two sets of influences to group differences. For that matter they do not deal with the question of the causes of behavior in any particular individual, i.e. whether one specific person's ability is due largely to heredity or to environment. Instead, the *heritability* of vocabulary refers to the fact that individuals in a given population differ on scores on vocabulary tests and that these differences are influenced by genetic differences. One of the fundamental aims of behavioral genetics is to assess the extent of that influence relative to that of environmental factors.

To do so, three basic methods have been used: family studies, twin studies, and adoption studies (see Plomin, 1990, and Plomin & McClearn, 1993).

(1) *Family studies*   Genetically related individuals should be similar phenotypically to the extent that genes influence particular behavior patterns. Different types of family relationships should therefore yield different estimates of heritability: children should resemble their mothers and fathers more than their aunts and uncles; full siblings should be more alike than half-siblings and cousins, and so forth.

One example of such an approach can be found in the study of schizophrenia. In an overview of over 40 different studies, Gottesman (1993) calculated the risk of developing this mental disorder for various categories of relatives (table 3). The risk for the children of schizophrenics is relatively high, being nearly 13 times that for the general population. For siblings it is about 9 times as high, whereas for relatives further removed it is considerably lower. It is highest by far, however, for monozygotic twins: should one twin develop the disorder the risk rate for the other twin is 48 percent. On the face of it there is a definite tendency for schizophrenia to run in families, leading to the assumption that the condition is hereditary.

However, on the basis of these data alone that assumption is not justified. The problem with family studies lies in their inability to sort out genetic from environmental influences. Families live together and share experience; the closer the relatives

Table 3   Risk estimates of schizophrenia for relatives of schizophrenics

Relationship	Risk (%)
General population	1
First-degree relatives:	
Parents	6
Siblings	9
Children	13
Second-degree relatives:	
Uncles/aunts	2
Grandchildren	5
Third-degree relatives:	
First cousins	2
Monozygotic twins	48

Source: Adapted from Gottesman (1993)

are the more likely it is that they live in the same environment. By itself such an approach cannot therefore lead to definite conclusions, though it is useful in giving rise to suggestive evidence.

(2) *Twin studies* In order to avoid the confounding of genetic and environmental effects comparisons of monozygotic (MZ) and dizygotic (DZ) twins have been re- sorted to. MZ twins are genetically identical; DZ twins are no more alike genetically than ordinary siblings, i.e. they share on average 50 percent of their genes. On the assumption (not wholly justified) that both sets of twins share environmental influ- ences to the same degree any difference between the sets should reflect the operation of a genetic component. That is, phenotypic difference between MZ twins must be due to environmental factors alone, whereas in DZ twins it reflects the combined effects of hereditary and environmental factors. As seen in table 4, the resemblance of MZ twins is in fact very much greater with respect to virtually all psychological characteristics that have been examined than that found for DZ twins, suggesting the presence of genetic influences on these characteristics.

The bulk of the work involving MZ–DZ comparisons has concerned the effects of heredity on intelligence. The evidence for such effects is strong: in a review of 30 studies which had examined intelligence scores Bouchard and McGue (1981) found average correlations of 0.85 for MZ and 0.58 for DZ twins; the latter figure is similar to that for ordinary siblings. What is interesting is that it is not only the absolute *level* of intelligence (usually measured by IQ) but also the *pattern* of intellectual growth that shows this picture. In the Louisville twin study (R. S. Wilson, 1983), which followed up nearly 500 pairs of twins and their siblings from infancy to adolescence, it was found that the profiles of developmental spurts and lags over time showed considerably greater resemblance in MZ pairs than in DZ pairs. This was particularly marked in early childhood, when the rate of gains is sharpest and the spurts and lags most pronounced; even in adolescence, however, the sequence still appeared to be subject to maturational processes that are gene-controlled. According to Wilson, "the message from these results seems clear: there is a strong developmental thrust in the growth of intelligence that continues through adolescence and is guided by an

Table 4 Correlation coefficients for monozygotic (MZ) and dizygotic (DZ) twins for various psychological characteristics

	MZ	*DZ*
IQ	0.85	0.60
Personality	0.50	0.20
Childhood behavior problems	0.80	0.60
Vocational interests	0.50	0.25
Social attitudes	0.65	0.50

Source: Adapted from Plomin (1994b)

intrinsic template or ground plan. The template is rooted in genetic processes that act throughout childhood and adolescence."

However, the assumption that DZ pairs share experiences to the same degree as MZ pairs and that therefore the only difference between the two kinds of twins is in their genetic make-up must be questioned. Evidence from observational studies (e.g. Lytton, 1980) has shown that identical twins are more likely to be treated identically by parents and peers than nonidentical twins, especially when the latter are different sex pairs. MZ twins are also more likely to imitate one another. As a result heritability estimates will become inflated. An extension of the twin design provides one way of dealing with this problem. This involves studying not only groups of MZ and DZ twins reared together but also twins reared apart: if MZ twins resemble one another to a greater extent than DZ twins even when brought up in a different environment then one is on much safer ground in arriving at conclusions about the operation of genetic factors. The drawback is, of course, that there are so very few instances of twins reared apart, and even then their environment may not differ greatly. A study by Tellegen and colleagues (1988) is therefore particularly valuable, in that it is based on a relatively large sample of four groups of twins, that is, MZ twins reared together, DZ twins reared together, MZ twins reared apart, and DZ twins reared apart. As adults all were given a standardized personality questionnaire yielding a number of scores on specific scales which in turn could be combined into three higher order factors, i.e. positive emotionality, negative emotionality, and constraint (roughly corresponding to what others have termed extraversion–introversion, neuroticism, and psychoticism). Table 5 shows the mean correlations for the twin pairs on these three personality characteristics. It is clear that MZ twins resemble one another even when reared apart from early childhood on, and that this resemblance is greater than that found among DZ twins, even when these have been reared together in the same family. Personality differences, it appears from these results, are due more to genetic than to environmental factors. Other twin studies point in the same direction: Rushton, Fulker, Neale, Nias, and Eysenck (1986), for instance, obtained measures for altruism and aggression on five scales administered to a large group of adult MZ and DZ twins, and found the MZ twins to be far more closely related than the DZ

Table 5   Personality characteristics of monozygotic (MZ) and dizygotic (DZ) twins reared apart (A) and reared together (T)

	Mean correlations of scores by twin pairs			
	MZ-A	*DZ-A*	*MZ-T*	*DZ-T*
Positive emotionality	0.34	−0.07	0.63	0.18
Negative emotionality	0.61	0.29	0.54	0.41
Constraint	0.57	0.04	0.58	0.25

Source: Adapted from Tellegen et al. (1988)

twins (correlations in the range of 0.40 to 0.54 and 0.04 to 0.25 respectively). Strong genetic effects are thereby indicated, despite the general belief that these two traits are mostly shaped by socialization experiences.

(3) *Adoption studies*   Another way to investigate genetic effects on individual differences and sort them out from environmental influences is to study children brought up from an early age by parents other than those who conceived them, and to compare their psychological characteristics with those of both their biological and their adoptive parents. Similarity to the former is assumed to indicate genetic influences; similarity to the latter indicates environmental influences. Not that this research strategy is altogether problem-free: for one thing, biological parents cannot always be traced or may not wish to be tested; for another, selective placement often occurs whereby children are assigned to adoptive parents who resemble the biological parents. However, most experiments of nature bring with them certain difficulties and limitations, and it is then up to the scientist to identify these and constrain generalizations accordingly.

Again most attention has been given to the effect on intelligence. A finding common to virtually all studies is that the correlation of adopted children's IQ with the IQ of their biological parents is significantly greater than that with the IQ of the adoptive parents. Take the Texas adoption project (Horn, 1983), based on 300 families, some with several adopted children (see table 6): the intelligence scores of these children correlated more strongly with those of their biological mothers, even though they had never lived with these women, than with their adoptive parents who had raised them. Individual differences in intelligence are thus largely controlled by hereditary factors; on the other hand findings from the same study showed that the *average* IQ of the children was more similar to that of the adoptive parents, and that this applied especially when the biological mothers were of low IQ. Moving a child from a disadvantaged home to a more privileged and stimulating home may raise IQ by as much as 15 or 20 points, demonstrating the importance of environmental effects; the fact that *individual variability* remains more closely related to the biological mothers' scores underlines the continuing role of genetic factors. Add to that the fact that the mental development of unrelated children adopted into the same family

Table 6   IQ correlations of adopted children with their adoptive and biological parents

	Correlation with adopted children's IQ
Adoptive mother's IQ	0.17
Adoptive father's IQ	0.14
Biological mother's IQ	0.31

Source: Based on Horn et al. (1979)

in infancy will show zero correlation in adolescence (Scarr & Weinberg, 1983), and there is clear indication that intelligence moves to an end point that is powerfully affected by developmental genetic processes.

As far as personality measures are concerned, the evidence from adoption studies is less clear than that from twin studies. Findings from the Texas adoption project (Loehlin, Horn, & Willerman, 1981, 1989) showed a striking lack of resemblance for people living together, regardless of genetic relationship, suggesting that neither heredity nor environment was influential in shaping personality traits. Other studies have found somewhat more evidence for genetic influences. Henderson (1982), for instance, by combining the results of three adoption studies, showed that the average correlation for extraversion and for neuroticism scores was 0.15 for biologically related individuals but near zero for adoptive family members – a modest but significant indication of hereditary factors at work. Rather more definite indications come from findings which show that genetic factors may play a part in the development of criminality (Mednick, Moffitt, & Stack, 1987): adopted sons whose biological fathers are convicted criminals have been found to be more likely to become criminals themselves than other adopted sons, irrespective of whether the adoptive fathers engage in such activity. However, this does not apply to less severe delinquency, which is often merely a transient phenomenon among juveniles. Surprisingly, there is also a suggestion that such a highly specific behavior pattern as amount of television viewing in young children can be genetically influenced (Plomin, Corley, DeFries, & Fulker, 1990): the viewing times of 3- to 5-year-old adoptive children, when compared with those of their biological parents on the one hand and those of their adoptive parents on the other, indicate a significant resemblance with the biological parents' times despite the fact that there had been no contact with them since early infancy. Again a psychological characteristic usually ascribed wholly to socialization influences appears to be significantly affected by hereditary factors.

Nature–Nurture Interface

The study of human behavior genetics is still at a very early stage. Nevertheless, a number of conclusions have arisen from its findings, though some are rather more tentative and controversial than others.

(1)   *Virtually all psychological traits show some evidence of genetic influence*   That even attitudes such as authoritarianism or conservatism, or interest such as reflected in television viewing time, are in part genetically transmitted goes against the common belief that experience, in the form of parental rearing practices in particular, is wholly responsible for shaping such characteristics. This belief, however, is based on assumption rather than evidence; recent findings show that individual variability in virtually all behavioral aspects examined is *to some extent* under genetic influence.

It is, however, also becoming apparent that the extent of this influence varies both according to age and to trait. As far as age is concerned, the widespread assumption that genes exert their strongest influence at the beginning of life and that after infancy environmental factors become progressively more important has not been borne out. On the contrary, in the case of intellectual development follow-up data obtained by both twin and adoption studies show that genetic influence *increases* with age (Loehlin, Horn, & Willerman, 1989; Plomin & DeFries, 1985): in infancy about 15 percent of the variance in scores on developmental tests is due to genetic differences; later in childhood estimates of genetic influence on IQ scores are closer to 50 percent. As Plomin (1987) concludes from a review of relevant studies, "whenever the relative magnitude of genetic variance changes during development, its impact increases rather than decreases." While not enough information is available to include characteristics other than intelligence in this generalization it is evident that genes are not necessarily operating at full throttle immediately after birth, to be slowed down subsequently by the impact of the environment. Such a notion is much too simplistic; it neglects, for example, the fact that some genetically determined functions (e.g. sexual behavior and certain cognitive abilities) do not emerge until later stages of childhood. The interplay of genetic and experiential forces over the course of development assumes a much more complex form than that.

The complexity is increased further by differences among traits in their susceptibility to genetic influence. Physical and intellectual characteristics on the whole show such influence to a more marked degree than social and personality characteristics, though the greater reliability of measures available for the former two may at least in part account for this difference. Nevertheless, there is impressive evidence, ranging from studies of temperament in infants to investigations of personality dimensions in adults, that characteristics associated with introversion–extraversion on the one hand and neuroticism on the other are strongly affected by heredity at all ages (Eaves, Eysenck, & Martin, 1989). Individual differences in sociability and shyness, for instance, representing a basic component of introversion–extraversion, are already evident in infancy and show marked genetic influence; similarly individual differences amongst infants in emotionality, a central aspect of neuroticism, have been demonstrated to be strongly affected by genetic factors. Aspects of personality not directly related to these two pervasive dimensions appear to be rather less under genetic control: masculinity–femininity and tolerance of ambiguity, for example, were found to show relatively little hereditary influence in a study of adolescents (Loehlin, 1982). Nevertheless, the investigation of twins in particular, including those reared separately, has made it impossible to escape the conclusion that genetic endowment plays a considerable part in accounting for the nature of personality differences.

(2) *Nonshared environmental influences are of greater importance than shared environmental influences* No example exists of any psychological characteristic that varies entirely as a result of genetic differences; 40 to 50 percent of variability is the

maximum that can be accounted for in this way. But as we have already stressed, behavioral genetics is not merely concerned with hereditary factors; ironically its contribution to the understanding of environmental influences is at least as great. The same body of literature that deals with hereditary influences can also highlight the role of environmental variation and, as an additional bonus, has been able to analyze it into its component parts.

A finding with far-reaching implications is that two such components need to be distinguished, i.e. shared and nonshared environmental influences, and that it is the latter rather than the former which requires our attention in any attempt to understand the course of personality development. *Shared* influences are those common to all children growing up in the same family; they describe that family in terms of such characteristics as social class, educational level, number of books in the home, and child rearing philosophy, all of which act to make members of the family similar to each other. *Nonshared* influences, on the other hand, are those that are not common to all family members, acting instead to make them different from one another. They represent those experiences that are unique to each sibling: the parents' preference for one child over another; their differential treatment of each child because of the child's own inherent characteristics; the position each child occupies within the sibling constellation; the child's exposure to particular extrafamilial influences such as certain peer groups or teachers; and idiosyncratic experiences like accidents or illnesses (Dunn & Plomin, 1990). What is suggested, on the basis of various studies by behavior geneticists (reviewed by Plomin & Daniels, 1987), is that most of the environmental influences critical to psychological development are of the nonshared kind and are not the shared influences which have hitherto received most attention from psychologists. Consider, for example, adopted children who are reared in the same family but originate from different sets of parents and are thus biologically unrelated to each other. Despite the fact that these children are brought up in the same environment (by the same adoptive parents, in the same home atmosphere, in the identical neighborhood, and so on) their mutual resemblance is around zero. The experiences that they have in common do not make them alike. Family influences matter, of course, but the most important forces shaping individual development are those that are specific to each child rather than general to an entire family.

There are several implications to this proposal, the most important being that research on the developmental antecedents of personality development should shift its focus from the study of between-family variables to the study of within-family variables. The former have in fact yielded few significant relationships with aspects of children's development (Maccoby & Martin, 1983); it is now becoming apparent that this failure may well be the result of searching in the wrong direction and that the unit of environmental transmission is not so much the family as such but rather the various microenvironments within families. Thus, instead of making one global assessment per family of, say, its social status or of the typical child rearing techniques adopted by the parents and relating these measures equally to all siblings in a comparison across different families, behavioral geneticists propose that more than one child per family should be studied in order to pinpoint the environmental sources of differences between children in the same family. Traditional variables such as parental warmth or control, which have yielded few insights into child development in the context of across-family designs, can thus be employed in order to search for *differential* parental behavior to siblings within the same family. Variation of parental behavior from one sibling to another rather than some measure of absolute level characterizing that parent would thus be expected to have major impact on children's development (Plomin, 1994b).

The amount of research supporting such a shift in focus is so far fairly limited. What cannot be denied is the fact that common family influences have on the whole failed to predict child outcomes (Scarr, 1992). As we have seen, unrelated children adopted into the same family do not resemble each other in any aspect of psychological development despite growing up in the same home. Even biologically related siblings (other than MZ twins) show limited resemblance, suggesting that the *common* experiences to which they have been exposed from infancy on are of much less power than had previously been assumed. This negative argument does not detract from the importance of its conclusions; the potential of the new line of inquiry proposed is considerable. It draws attention in particular to the need to investigate the *differential* experiences children have within the *same* family setting. The findings obtained so far suggest that siblings can indeed encounter considerably different environments in terms of their treatment by parents, as well as their interaction with each other and with others outside the family, and that the nature of their differential treatment may be closely related to the psychological adjustment of each sibling (e.g. Daniels, Dunn, Furstenberg, & Plomin, 1985). As Dunn and Plomin (1990) conclude from their summary of the relevant research, it appears to be not so much the *absolute* but rather the *relative* amounts of children's experiences that affect developmental outcome – relative, that is, to what each individual child perceives itself to be experiencing in comparison with others, especially with siblings. Behavioral geneticists concede that shared environmental influences do account for some psychological differences between individuals, but believe that it is high time that nonshared influences were given their due recognition.

(3) *Within the range of "good-enough parenting" children's development depends primarily on heredity* This proposition, put forward by Scarr (1992), is probably the most controversial of all those advanced by behavioral geneticists. Children of course require supportive and affectionate parenting; in the absence of opportunities to use their inherent capacities development cannot occur. Scarr maintains, however, that as long as this is provided development depends primarily on inherited characteristics. Only families that fall outside the range of what has been referred to as the *average expectable environment*, i.e. that which is normal for the species, are unlikely to promote proper psychological growth – something to be seen, for example, in those that subject their children to extreme deprivation or abuse. Thus low-quality environments affect development, but environments in the adequate to superior

range have few differential effects and instead function primarily as support for the individual child's inherited capacity. It is therefore at the negative extreme that environments are at their most powerful.

The notion that ordinary differences between families have few effects on children's development as long as they receive good-enough parenting is an unpalatable argument for many and has aroused some fierce opposition (e.g. Baumrind, 1993; Wachs, 1993). It should be borne in mind, however, that it is *differential effects* that are at issue; parents are far from being reduced to nonentities and only their impact on the child's *individuality* is thereby challenged. According to Scarr, given that most children in Western societies are provided with plenty of opportunities it stands to reason (supported by research evidence) that individual differences in psychological development depend more on the person's inherent characteristics than on environmental pressures and opportunity. There is certainly little evidence that family environments, except the worst, have significant effects on the development of psychopathy or any form of common behavioral disorder (Plomin & Daniels, 1987). In the average expectable environment the experience of varied stimulation can promote normal human development; all such experiences present functionally equivalent opportunities. Environments are essential for development to occur but they need not cause variations among individuals. As Scarr and McCartney (1983) argue, nature has not left essential development at the mercy of experiences that an individual may or may not encounter; the only necessary experiences are those that are widely available to the species and that the vast majority of children can expect to come upon. It is only under extreme conditions, such as gross deprivation, that experience will diminish the role of genotypes.

(4)   *Children's genetic make-up directly affects their rearing environment*   Scarr (1992; see also Scarr & McCartney, 1983) has taken her argument further still by proposing that the basic component of the relationship between child and family should be construed in terms of genotype→environment, that is, that people, by virtue of their genetic make-up, construct their own environments.

Again traditional psychological theory is challenged thereby, for during childhood in particular the environment (as represented by parental socializing techniques) used to be seen as "causing" the nature of individual development. However, the cause–effect sequence may run in the opposite direction: according to Scarr's proposal each child constructs a reality from the opportunities afforded by caretakers in keeping with its own talents and predilections; it is the latter that determine the nature of the environment to which the child in turn responds. In this sense genes drive experience; environments are a product of the person.

There are three kinds of genotype→environment effects which Scarr distinguishes:

a   A *passive* kind, which refers to the fact that parents provide both heredity and experience for their biological offspring, as a result of which genes and environments are inevitably correlated (e.g. number of books in the home and amount of reading engaged in by parents will be positively correlated with children's progresss in literacy-related activities). Children's experiences are therefore constructed from opportunities that are correlated with their personal characteristics.

b   An *evocative* kind, whereby a child elicits responses from others according to its genotype. These responses then further reinforce the child's genetically based behavior, thus shaping development in ways that correlate with the genotype. Smiley, active babies, for instance, tend to receive more attention from others than passive babies; as a result the original tendency will be strengthened in that infants are encouraged actively to seek out and participate in further social interaction.

c   An *active* kind, where each individual chooses what environments to attend to, seek out and even create. Such *niche-picking* is highly selective and is undertaken in order to function in settings that are compatible with the motivational, personality, and intellectual aspects of the individual's genotype. The more environmental opportunities there are the more likely it is that such activity will be undertaken; it is also more likely to be evident at later stages of childhood when adolescents move out from the family and increasingly make their own choices.

(5)   *Genetic factors influence environmental measures*   One of the most common approaches to understanding the nature of psychological development is to measure some aspect of children's environment and then relate it to some aspect of child behavior. Thus parental sensitivity is related to the security of children's attachment; number of books in the home is related to children's reading ability; the parents' disciplinary practice is related to the children's moral behavior. In each case the environmental measure (usually some aspect of the home or of the parents' child rearing practices) is regarded as "out there," that is, it is assumed to be an external force which is imposed on the individual.

This assumption too has been challenged by behavior geneticists (Plomin, 1995; Plomin & Bergeman, 1991). Aspects of the environment, they point out, may not be "pure" but contaminated by genetic influence, and especially so because the most important environmental aspects refer to people related to the child. Such people share genes as well as environment with the child; to assume that home–child correlations are wholly due to the latter type of influence is not justified. Thus parental sensitivity is a trait that is affected, to some extent at least, by the parent's genetic make-up; this in turn is shared with the child. It cannot therefore be automatically regarded as an index of the environment. Number of books in the home may reflect the parents' intelligence; this too is shared with the child. Disciplinary technique is also a function of parental personality and is therefore similarly linked to the child's behavior via genetic factors. In short, genes can passively create correlations between measures of the family environment and measures of child behavior, in contrast to interpretations of active shaping of children's development by parental practices. The latter view may be valid; the former must also be considered.

Thus the process of transmission from parent to child can take two forms: a *direct* one through the environment or an *indirect* one through correlation with parental genotypes. Children may be shy because they have shy parents; this can be brought about, on the one hand, by parents shielding their child from contact with others and also by the example they set through their own behavior, or on the other hand by means of passing on to the child their genes. Thus ostensible measures of the environment may be affected by genetic influences; child rearing practices, family life, and home conditions may all be a function of parental genotype and linked to child characteristics through genetic mediation rather than through direct environmental impact (or, of course, through both). Using the methods of behavioral genetics it is possible to determine the size of these effects, in particular by comparing adoptive with nonadoptive families. If genes play a part in the association between so-called environmental measures and measures of children's development then such associations should be significantly greater in nonadoptive (biologically related) families. Take a study by Coon, Fulker, DeFries, and Plomin (1990): in a sample of children from the Colorado adoption study, including both adoptive and nonadoptive families, measures of IQ at age 7 were correlated with an assessment of the home environment as given by two standardized scales, each of which provided a series of measures of various specific aspects of the home environment. Comparing the correlations between these environmental measures and the children's IQs as found in adoptive and nonadoptive families, it emerged that those in the latter group were for the most part significantly higher. To illustrate, the total score for one of the scales correlated 0.31 with IQ in the nonadoptive families; in the adoptive families the correlation was only 0.08 – a significant difference, indicating that genetic effects were primarily responsible for bringing about the association. In general, it has been estimated that about half of environment–development relationships in biological families are in fact mediated genetically (Plomin, Loehlin, & DeFries, 1985); the usual assumption that parental behavior affects children's development solely through experience cannot therefore be sustained.

The various conclusions we have listed represent some of the principal insights gained from the recent wave of research on human behavioral genetics. Some should perhaps be regarded more as hypotheses than as firmly established findings; all, however, point to new directions that research and theory ought to take when attempting to understand the role of families in children's development. As a result it is now necessary (to pick out some of the main points) to reconsider the relationship between individual and environment during development; to rethink the nature of the environmental forces that exert a formative influence on children; and to reformulate the processes whereby heredity and experience jointly lead the person to maturity. In particular, it is necessary to reconsider both the nature and the extent of parents' influence on children's development, for there are strong indications that these influences, in the form of training and example, are considerably less powerful than was formerly believed by psychologists and is still believed in popular circles.

Bases of Individuality

Psychological differences are already apparent in newborn babies. Pre- and perinatal events may in part be responsible, but except in cases of major pathology their influence is a temporary one, confined to the early weeks or months of life. Genetic factors, on the other hand, play a continuing role in the shaping of individuality; to a considerable extent they account for the inherent characteristics which make people distinctive from the beginning of life on; they thus provide the "biological givens" which children bring into the world with them and which have an important effect on how other people respond to them. Clearly such biological givens need to be identified and investigated.

We shall examine here what has been learned about two aspects, namely temperament and sex. The former refers to a diverse set of dimensions of constitutional origin along which people can be ranged, representing an attempt to do justice to the earliest constituents of personality. The latter is usually treated as a dichotomy (though with questionable justification), but it too is a basic aspect of individuality – consider that the first thing a parent wants to establish after birth is the child's sex! Both temperamental characteristics and sex provide children with the beginnings of an identity in the eyes of others; however, their genetic basis should not be taken to mean that their behavioral expressions are of an immutable nature: on the contrary, the contribution of experience and the manner in which the social environment interacts with the biologically determined characteristics is now widely acknowledged and represents a major area of research.

Temperament

According to two of the best known contributors in this area, "temperament may best be viewed as a general term referring to the *how* of behavior. It differs from ability, which is concerned with the *what* and *how well* of behaving, and from motivation, which accounts for *why* a person does what he is doing. Temperament, by contrast, concerns the *way* in which an individual behaves" (Thomas & Chess, 1977). It can thus be equated to the term *behavioral style*. While not everyone can agree that the how and the what can so easily be kept apart, the definition does serve to draw attention to those stylistic aspects of behavior that have some consistency over different situations and that refer to the emotional vigor, tempo, and regularity of an individual's customary activities. Several general characteristics distinguish temperament:

1 it refers to a set of individual differences which emerge early in life;
2 it shows some stability over time;
3 it is pervasive across a wide range of situations; and
4 it shows some evidence of heritability.

In addition, it must be emphasized that temperament is about general dispositions and not about discrete behaviors.

The study of temperament has focused on a number of issues.

(1)   *Constituents*   There has been much discussion about the number of dimensions which make up the concept of temperament, as well as the identity of these constituents. There is reasonable agreement concerning broader components, but the more specific elements remain subject to lively debate.

We shall single out two of the most influential schemes. The first is that which arose from the New York longitudinal study, carried out by Thomas & Chess (1977). This is based on a group of 138 individuals who were followed up from birth into adulthood, with a massive amount of data gathered periodically by a variety of means from parents, teachers, and the children themselves. Thomas and Chess became convinced that whatever developmental changes in behavior they observed over this period occurred against a background of continuity, and that this could best be expressed in terms of a number of temperamental dimensions which they identified partly by inductive content analysis of parental reports and partly by quantitative

Table 7   Categories of temperament proposed by Thomas and Chess

Category	Definition
Activity level	Extent of mobility in everyday situations, and the diurnal proportion of active and inactive periods
Regularity	The predictability of any function, such as feeding patterns and sleep–wake cycles
Approach–Withdrawal	The nature of the infant's initial response to a new stimulus, whether displayed by mood or motor activity
Adaptability	The ease with which infants' behavior can be modified in a desired direction
Threshold of responsiveness	Intensity level of stimulation required to evoke a discernible response
Intensity of reaction	The energy level of responses, irrespective of quality or direction
Quality of mood	Amount of pleasant, joyful, and friendly behavior, as contrasted with unpleasant, crying, and unfriendly behavior
Distractibility	The effectiveness of extraneous stimuli in interfering with ongoing behavior
Attention span	Length of time a particular activity is pursued

Source: Based on Thomas & Chess (1977)

techniques such as factor analysis. The nine dimensional categories are listed and described in table 7.

From these dimensions Thomas and Chess derived a further three-way typology, considered to be of particular relevance to children's interactions with the social environment:

a *Easy* children are characterized by regularity of behavior, positive approach responses to new stimuli, high adaptability to change, and mildly or moderately intense mood that is preponderantly positive. Such children quickly develop regular sleep and feeding schedules, easily adapt to such new experiences as starting school, are positive to strangers, and generally accept frustration with little fuss. About 40 percent of the Thomas and Chess sample fell into this category.
b *Difficult* children are those at the opposite end of the spectrum; they are those with irregularity of biological functions, negative behavior to new experiences, difficulties in adapting to any change, and intense and often negative mood expressions. Problems about feeding and sleeping are thus more common, as are difficulties in adjusting to new routines, people, or situations. About 10 percent were found to belong to this group.
c The third category is made up of *slow-to-warm-up* children, who are characterized by a combination of negative responses of mild intensity to new stimuli and slow adaptability after repeated contact. Thus on first exposure to something strange they may show the characteristics of a difficult child; unlike the latter, however, they gradually come to show quiet and positive interest like an easy child. Approximately 15 percent of Thomas and Chess's sample were so labeled.

Not all children fit into these three categories, for some show a combination of traits that makes them difficult to classify. What is more, the three constellations represent *predominant* rather than invariable reactions; some situational variability is allowed for. According to Thomas and Chess, however, they are "real" entities, detectable from the beginning before parental action could have created them, even though subsequent interaction with the social environment may modify their behavioral expression. To a limited extent therefore temperament is socially constructed; on the other hand, Thomas and Chess became convinced that a genetic component underlies the variations of behavior observed by them and that an objective biological foundation thus constitutes the foundation of children's distinct dispositions.

Subsequent work by others has confirmed some aspects of the Thomas and Chess scheme but not others. The concept of "difficultness" has attracted most support; on the other hand there is doubt whether the nine temperamental scales can realistically be seen as psychometrically meaningful, separate dimensions. Buss and Plomin (1984) are amongst the skeptics and have put forward an alternate scheme which has also attracted considerable attention and empirical support. According to their proposal only three dimensions can be reliably identified, namely emotionality, activity, and sociability (hence the acronym for their scheme of EAS):

a   *Emotionality* refers to strong arousal in response to stimulation, as expressed in both behavior and psychophysiological affect. Young infants, it has been demonstrated, can be reliably arranged along this dimension, whether one considers their expressions of distress, fear, or anger. It seems likely that in later development emotionality will come to form the core of one of the two most consistently identified dimensions of personality, i.e. neuroticism.
b   *Activity* relates to motor tempo and vigor. This is one of the most firmly established constituents of temperamental variability – a clear indication of behavioral style, evident early on and showing at least some stability over age. The active child seems to provide its own source of energy and may thus be easier in some respects for parents to care for than the inactive child who is largely dependent on others to provide the initiative. In either case the child's constitutional disposition can have definite social consequences.
c   *Sociability* describes the extent to which the individual prefers the company of others as opposed to being alone. The child high on sociability can be expected to seek attention from and the company of other people, to initiate contact with others for its own sake and to be forthcoming even with strangers. The child low on this dimension, on the other hand, is shy and solitary: other people are avoided, especially if they are unfamiliar, and the child makes few attempts to seek out the company of others. The second major dimension identified for personality structure in older individuals, i.e. extraversion–introversion, is thought to be a consequence of variations in early sociability.

Other temperament schemes have also been put forward, based on other conceptual approaches and identifying other dimensions. These divergencies are due partly to different theoretical assumptions and partly to different methodologies – a situation typical of an area of research in the early stages of development. In due course there will be agreement to adopt whatever scheme turns out to be most *useful* – useful, that is, in terms of predicting behavior and in terms of providing insight into the psychological processes that account for individual differences.

(2)   *Measurement*   How to assess temperament, particularly in very young children, has turned out to be a matter of considerable difficulty. The three main methods used are parental reports, home observation, and laboratory assessment.

Parental reports, obtained either through interview or (more often) by means of structured questionnaires, have been the most common way of obtaining information. This method has many advantages: parents have the most intimate knowledge of their children and can provide summaries over a lengthy period of time; parents also have the opportunity to observe their children in a wide range of natural settings and can thus report on what is typical; and by the use of questionnaires the relevant data can be obtained quickly and in a standardized manner. The question is, however, whether parental reports are sufficiently objective and free of bias or whether they reflect the characteristics of the parent to an undue degree. This debate has centered in particular on the concept of difficult temperament, where J. E. Bates (1980) has argued that such a concept needs to be recast as a social perception rather than as a within-the-individual characteristic – an argument bolstered by the often quite modest agreement between mothers and fathers and (even more so) between parents and observers, but one vigorously resisted by Thomas, Chess, and Korn (1982) who believe there is sufficient evidence to suggest that there is a definite reality to the concept. Certainly questionnaires are generally constructed in such a manner as to ask for reports of specific everyday behaviors rather than of global temperamental qualities; this is likely to reduce bias though it may not eliminate it. Thus the most reasonable conclusion is that both subjective and objective factors enter into parental reports, and while it is tempting to deplore the presence of subjective bias it is also worth bearing in mind that for certain purposes parental perception is more useful and predictive than objective assessment of child temperament (J. E. Bates, 1983).

Direct observation of children has advantages and disadvantages that are the obverse of those of parental reports. On the one hand it is less subject to bias; on the other it is time-consuming and covers only a limited span of the child's natural behavior. This applies even more so to the third method, *laboratory assessment*, which involves presenting the child with some specific stimuli under controlled (and therefore artificial) conditions. Such a technique may be useful when focusing on some quite specific and well defined temperamental quality; the tendency to inhibition, for instance, has been usefully investigated in this way (Kagan, Reznick, & Snidman, 1986). For purposes of wider ranging assessment such an approach has little to recommend it. Much depends therefore on the purpose to which the measurement of temperament is to be put. If the focus is on personality assessment, say in a clinical context, parental report is almost inevitably the only method that is practicable. For in-depth research, on the other hand, the other two methods may be more feasible.

(3) *Heritability* Temperament, according to most conceptions, has an inherited component. This does not mean, of course, that it is immutable; it indicates that there is a genetic basis which may then be modified and transformed by life experience.

The evidence for such a genetic basis is, however, still patchy. It is strongest for the three components of the EAS approach (Buss & Plomin, 1984): both twin and adoption studies give credence to the notion that emotionality, activity, and sociability are strongly influenced by individuals' genotypes. As seen in table 8, MZ twins show greater resemblance in these characteristics than DZ twins; similarly such more specific behaviors related to temperament as fear, smiling, crying, attention demands, and temper displays have been found to show MZ/DZ differences (Goldsmith & Campos, 1982; Plomin, 1986). Admittedly, parental reports may be influenced by the

Table 8 Correlation coefficients obtained by monozygotic (MZ) and dizygotic (DZ) twins on the three components of the EAS temperament scale

	MZ	*DZ*
Emotionality	0.63	0.12
Activity	0.62	−0.13
Sociability	0.53	−0.03

Source: Adapted from Buss & Plomin (1984)

parents' knowledge of the twins' identity or nonidentity; it is therefore worth noting that both home observations (Plomin & Rowe, 1979) and laboratory studies (Goldsmith & Campos, 1986) have confirmed such differential resemblance. The fact that MZ/DZ differences may vary according to age does not vitiate the heritability argument; as we have already seen, genetic factors are more influential at some ages than at others and are by no means constant in their operation. At the beginning of life in particular genetic influences on temperament are difficult to spot: in a study of neonates, for example, Riese (1990) found no clear evidence for their operation and concluded that such environmental influences as intrauterine and perinatal factors were of greater importance at that time. Moreover, according to R. S. Wilson and Matheney (1986) little evidence of heritability emerged from laboratory assessments of twins' temperamental qualities right through the first year: only during the second year did higher MZ than DZ correlations begin to appear, as did more consistent age-to-age changes.

(4) *Stability* While a genetic basis does not preclude change, some consistency over age is to be expected. Conceptions of temperament generally imply such consistency; a trait that shows drastic changes in the course of development is likely to be excluded from the temperament domain.

On the whole the evidence supports the existence of some rather limited degree of stability (McDevitt, 1986), though the variation in findings from one study to another makes generalization hazardous. More global aspects of temperament tend to show greater stability than more narrowly defined ones: Pedlow, Sanson, Prior, and Oberklaid (1993), for instance, found substantial continuity from infancy to 8 years in a number of widely defined temperament factors such as inflexibility, approach, and rhythmicity; on the other hand Kerr, Lambert, Stattin, and Klackenberg-Larsson (1994), investigating the more narrowly conceived trait of inhibition, found stability to be confined mainly to those of their subjects lying at the two extremes of this continuum. By and large, the less specific, situational, or contextual the level of analysis is the easier it is to demonstrate continuity. As with all personality characteristics, the ability to predict from one age to another depends also on the age from which prediction is made and on the length of the interval from one age to the next.

Table 9   Interyear correlations for easy–difficult temperament scores

Years		Years		Years		Years	
1–2:	0.42*	1–3:	0.26*	1–4:	0.07	1–5:	0.05
2–3:	0.37*	2–4:	0.24*	2–5:	0.20*		
3–4:	0.29*	3–5:	0.14				
4–5:	0.44*						

*Statistically significant beyond 0.05.
Source: From Thomas & Chess (1986)

Take findings by Thomas and Chess (1986) for their nine categories: in the first five years of life six of these showed significant (though mostly low) correlations from one year to the next; for the 1-to-5-year period only three were significant; and for the period from 1 year to adulthood just one category reached significance. Prediction improved somewhat when an overall easy–difficult temperament score was constructed by taking the means of the scores of the five categories making up this constellation: the correlation between age 4 and adulthood, for example, reached 0.37. Within the preschool period, as we can see from table 9, stability coefficients vary according to time interval: where this is only 1 or 2 years correlations are significant; beyond that the size of the coefficients declines. However, easy–difficult is a catch-all concept that tells one little about the specific manifestations of temperament at different ages and their susceptibility to environmental influences; thus a considerable realignment may occur in temperamental qualities with age and yet not be reflected in a global easy–difficult measure which could remain stable.

In general, the issue of stability is a highly complex one where a lot of work still needs to be done to unravel the different influences at work. As Prior (1992) has put it, enormous variability in estimates can be found in the literature; these depend on a large number of factors including age and sex of the child, the identity of the traits assessed for stability, time between assessments, the type of assessment method used, and the relative level of homogeneity of the sample investigated. In addition the stability of the social environment must be taken into account: where that remains constant stability of individual traits is clearly more likely.

(5)   *Prediction of behavioral adjustment*   One of the reasons for interest in the early manifestations of temperament is the belief that these differences have clinical implications with respect to later development. If, to some extent at least, temperamental qualities endure they may provide clues to subsequent psychological functioning and be of use in predicting pathology. Early detection could thus lead to timely remedial action.

A large number of studies have examined possible relationships between early temperament and later behavioral adjustment. From her review of such studies Prior

(1992) concluded that the relationships found have generally been no more than moderate in strength. To some extent they depend on age at initial assessment: prediction from infancy is hazardous but becomes more effective as the child grows older. Thus Thomas and Chess (1982) found that temperament scores from age 3 on were significantly correlated with the presence or absence of a psychiatric diagnosis in early adulthood; before that age no such relationship was evident. To some extent findings also depend on the aspects of temperament used for prediction purposes, for not all are equally useful in this respect. Most attention has centered on the syndrome of difficult temperament as a high risk factor, and there are various indications that this is indeed related to later incidence of behavior disorder (Thomas, Chess, & Korn, 1982). In general, it appears that it is easier to make predictions about children at the extremes of the temperament range; for the majority in the middle the relationship is not so clear.

In any case, the pathway from early temperamental manifestations to later behavioral adjustment is by no means a direct one. As Thomas, Chess, and Birch (1968), in an overview of their longitudinal study, concluded:

> A given pattern of temperament did not, as such, result in a behavioral disturbance. Deviant, as well as normal development, was the result of the interaction between the child with given characteristics of temperament and significant features of his intrafamilial and extrafamilial environment. Temperament, representing one aspect of a child's individuality, also interacted with abilities and motives, the other two facets, as well as the environment, in determining the specific behavior patterns that evolved in the course of development.

Prediction, that is, cannot merely be based on temperament considered in isolation; certain temperamental qualities may act as predisposing influences, but it is only in combination with other factors, particularly those in the child's social environment, that the individual's constitutional make-up can have a significant impact on developmental outcome.

(6) *Social implications*   The real significance of temperament lies in the effects it produces on other people. Different temperaments produce different reactions: an irritable, fretful infant will provoke a caretaking pattern that differs radically from that elicited by a calm, easy infant; a highly reactive child will require different parental treatment compared to that given to an unresponsive one. Temperamental characteristics thus fall under the heading of *child effects* – those aspects of children's individuality which directly influence the way others respond to them; these responses in turn may modify the child's behavior, and a bidirectional set of influences is thus set in train that not only determines the nature of the immediate social interaction but also produces cumulative effects on the course of development.

However, the meaning which a given temperamental characteristic has for other people can vary considerably from one person to another. A highly active infant may resist the mother's cuddling – not because it rejects the contact per se but because of a dislike of movement restriction (Schaffer & Emerson, 1964b). Most mothers readily appreciate that the child's behavior merely reflects a particular temperamental characteristic and will quickly adjust their behavior accordingly by offering different kinds of contact. A few mothers, however, will attach a different meaning to the infant's resistance: they will interpret it as a form of rejection and so continue their attempts to cuddle the infant despite the latter's obvious dislike and distress. Whatever the reasons for such insensitivity may be, a situation is set up where the child's inherent characteristics are not matched by what the mother has to offer and where "goodness of fit" is thus lacking.

Goodness of fit is the concept put forward by Thomas and Chess (1977) to describe the circumstances where the properties of the environment (with particular reference to the demands, expectations and attitudes of caretakers) match the child's temperamental and other characteristics. When such a match between individual and environment occurs, optimal development is possible. Conversely, poorness of fit is found when the characteristics of individual and environment do not match; distorted development and maladaptive functioning may then occur. Thus in the "right" rearing environment the temperament of even a difficult child need not result in behavior problems; equally, an easy temperament is no guarantee of a problem-free childhood if parents persist in making unrealistic demands. Not that goodness of fit (according to Thomas and Chess) necessarily implies an absence of stress and conflict: these are inevitable concomitants of the developmental process. However, when they are consonant with the child's capacities the consequences are constructive; when they are dissonant in relation to that particular child unfavorable developmental consequences may occur.

The goodness of fit concept has been criticized for being vague and offering few guidelines for further research (Campos et al., 1983). It does have intuitive appeal, however, and serves to emphasize the fact that temperament is not meaningful without reference to the social context. Temperament may have a within-the-individual basis; nevertheless, it cannot be considered independent of the particular interactions with others in which it manifests itself. This is well illustrated in a study by Dunn and Kendrick (1982a, 1982b) of children observed both before and after the birth of a sibling. There was clear evidence that throughout the mothers behaved differently with children of different temperament. For instance, in families where children were described as "unmalleable" or "negative in mood" children received less attention from the mothers: thus mother and child spent less time jointly attending to the same focus of interest, and the mothers helped and showed things to their children less frequently. Temperamental differences were also associated with differences in the children's reaction to the mother's interaction with the baby: unmalleable and emotionally intense children were more likely to protest and less likely to ignore this interaction than other children. In marked contrast, however, temperamental differences did not account for the wide differences in the quality of interaction between the siblings; other aspects such as the nature of the child's relationship with the mother and the way in which the mother had explained the baby to the child were of greater importance. Thus temperamental differences mattered in the relationship with the mother; they were of little account in the relationship with the sibling. Temperament, it appears, is not a characteristic independent of the relationship in which it is observed; the social context in which it is manifested must also be taken into account.

This applies not only to the interpersonal but also to the cultural context. According to some reports it is possible to detect ethnic differences in temperamental characteristics of newborn babies: Freedman (1974), for instance, found that American babies from Chinese and Japanese families were less perturbable, better able to soothe themselves and less emotionally labile than American babies of European stock. Given such early appearance it seems probable that these differences are genetically determined. More to the point, however, is the observation that any given temperamental quality can assume different meanings in different cultures. Take a study by deVries (1984) of Masai babies in southern Kenya, whose temperamental characteristics had been assessed early on. When severe famine conditions struck that community it was found that the babies most likely to survive were those whose temperament had been considered "difficult," i.e. fussy, unadaptable, and intense; quiet and undemanding babies, on the other hand, were at much greater risk – presumably because it is the fussy infants who are most likely to receive attention and be fed. In the West a difficult temperament is generally regarded as maladaptive and therefore undesirable; under other cultural circumstances, however, it can assume a different functional value and may not be regarded as stressful by parents. Or take some results from the Thomas and Chess study comparing native-born middle class children in New York with a Puerto Rican working class sample also living in New York (Thomas et al., 1982). In the former group behavioral maladjustment at age 5 was found to be associated with a difficult temperament rating; no such association existed in the latter group. The most likely explanation may lie in the differences in maternal child care attitudes and practices prevalent in the two samples: the middle class mothers tended to be more demanding with respect to feeding, sleeping, and adaptation to new situations and people – demands which are especially stressful for "difficult" children; in the Puerto Rican sample, on the other hand, these children were not subjected to such pressures and were thus no more likely to develop behavior problems than other children. High activity, however, was a significant indicator in the Puerto Rican group, for living in overcrowded conditions such behavior was much more likely to be considered as intolerable and therefore subject to parental demands for change.

The implications of temperamental differences for social development cannot be doubted; the manner whereby they operate, however, is complex. The effects of such differences on parents varies according to the individual parent's interpretation of the child's behavior; that interpretation in turn is determined by the parent's own personality, values, and preferences, and these tend to be a function of the particular culture to which the individual belongs. But the link between temperament and developmental outcome draws in other influences: temperament does not function on its own but in conjunction with other, mediating variables. This is illustrated by a study of the relationship between children's temperament and the type of attachment developed to the mother (Crockenberg, 1981): irritability in infancy was found to be highly predictive of insecure attachments, but only in combination with two other factors, namely maternal insensitivity and low social support for the family. Presumably an irritable infant is less rewarding to rear, but especially so for mothers who have difficulty in coping anyway – partly because of their own psychological make-up which predisposes them to insensitivity and partly also because they are socially isolated and therefore under greater stress. Under these circumstances the relationship is more at risk, whereas this need not apply to an easier child even when cared for by an insensitive mother and in an unsupportive environment. Again we see that multiple indices are necessary if one is to predict developmental outcome with any degree of confidence.

Given the interweaving of temperamental with social interactive forces it is not surprising that early temperament assessments do not show total stability throughout development or that they do not unfailingly predict later behavioral adjustment. On their own they can hardly be expected to provide infallible pointers to the future; it is only when taken in conjunction with other, experiential factors that temperamental characteristics can be seen to influence the developmental course. This applies in particular to the middle of the temperamental range; however, even in children at the extremes (e.g. very difficult or very easy) the nature of life experience must be taken into account in any attempt at explaining the end result.

The case of the "difficult" child

For obvious practical reasons most attention has been given to the category of difficult temperament. It is here that some of the fiercest arguments have taken place with respect to definition, measurement, stability, and prediction; here too, however, the need to take into account the social context is evident.

A study that illustrates well the intricate interweaving of temperamental with environmental factors is that by Wolkind and de Salis (1982), which set out to predict the types of children most likely to develop behavior problems. Temperament scores, along an easy–difficult range, were obtained when the children were 4 months old and related to the extent of behavior problems at $3\frac{1}{2}$ years. A significant relationship was found, i.e. preschool children with many behavior problems had also generally been assessed as "difficult" in infancy, mainly because of their excessive crying and resistance to the mother's efforts to establish regular feeding and sleeping routines. The most severely affected preschoolers, however, were those who not only had a difficult temperament but also had a mother with psychiatric symptoms (mostly depression). It seems that the *combination* of the two factors, that is, a vulnerable disposition and an environmental stress in the form of a sick parent, is most likely to give rise to behavior problems – a point supported by the fact that children of an easy temperamental disposition were strikingly unaffected by their mothers' depression. Yet once again we find that the cause-and-effect sequence turns out on further examination to be even more complex, for there were indications that the mothers' depression was, at least to some extent, affected by the child's disposition: those women who had difficult infants often complained, when the children were 14 months old, that they were physically extremely tired and worn out, and it was these women who subsequently were most likely to develop psychiatric symptoms. Wolkind and de Salis accordingly speculate that difficult children may make their own contribution to the environmental stress that will in turn affect them later – possibly because their mothers are more exhausted and possibly also through a loss of the mother's self-esteem caused by looking after a difficult baby. This may then contribute to the development of the mother's psychiatric condition, which then adversely affects the child.

Temperamentally difficult children are thus more vulnerable to the development of behavior problems – but it is only in conjunction with particular environmental circumstances that such a disposition actually gives rise to problems. Wolkind and de Salis make an analogy with the conditions that produce earthquakes: it takes both a fault line in the earth and an external strain to produce tremors. Similarly a mother's psychiatric disturbance (the external strain) may lead to behavior difficulties in the child, but only

if that child is of a particular temperament (the fault line). A difficult child need not, of course, have difficult family relationships: thus Thomas and Chess (1977) describe a boy who was one of the most extreme cases of difficult temperament in their sample but whose father took a delight in his son's "lusty" characteristics and who helped his rather more anxious wife to treat the boy with patience and tolerance. As a result of optimal handling by the parents as well as a stable environment the boy avoided behavioral difficulties; what is more, later assessments showed him to have moved from the difficult end of the temperamental scale towards the easy end. In this case, therefore, goodness of fit resulted in some degree of discontinuity; in other cases, as Thomas and Chess (1986) point out, the specific dynamics of the person–environment interaction may produce quite different patterns of stability or instability. Add to that the fact that there are age changes in what parents define as "difficult" behavior: as Carey (1986) found, a trait such as distractibility may be seen as an advantage in handling an infant but as a disadvantage when dealing with a schoolchild. Given such circumstances, it is no wonder that predictiveness of a difficult temperament early on is not strong enough to justify preventive screening (J. E. Bates, 1986): there are just too many unpredictable experiential events lying ahead of each individual!

Sex Differences

An individual's sex, together with age and ethnicity, is one of the main ways whereby we categorize the people we meet. Like temperament, it is a basic aspect of individuality, with profound social consequences. From birth on people respond differently, in certain respects at least, to males and females, these differences depending on the way each culture defines the role played by the sexes in society. The physical development of males and females begins to take distinctive pathways soon after conception; once the child is born that distinctiveness may act as a cue to others and determine the socialization practices they adopt. Biology and culture thus interact in defining how an individual eventually becomes a man or a woman.

Sexual dimorphism is the term used to refer to bodily differences between males and females. It is applied in particular to anatomical structures concerned with reproduction but also to some of the secondary sexual characteristics such as beards and breasts. Sexual dimorphism is based on chromosomal differences between men and women. As we saw earlier, chromosomes in body cells are in pairs, where the members of each pair are similar in size and in the genes they contain. Among the 23 pairs of chromosomes, however, there is one exception, namely the two sex chromosomes. These differ in males and females: in males one of the pair is a large chromosome, designated X, and the other one a much smaller one, designated Y; in females, on the other hand, both members of the pair are X chromosomes.

At conception a female egg unites with a male sperm to form a single cell with 23 pairs of chromosomes. One of these, the sex chromosome pair, determines the child's sex. The sex chromosome provided by the woman is always an X, whereas the man's sperm cells may have either an X or a Y. The pairing of an X-carrying sperm with an egg will result in a girl; the pairing of a Y-carrying sperm with an egg, on the other hand, will produce a boy. The father's sperm therefore determines the child's sex. Initially the gonads, or sex glands, of embryos are all the same; from the seventh week, however, they begin to differentiate and sexual dimorphism first appears. In the presence of the Y chromosome testes develop which start secreting a hormone (testosterone) that triggers the formation of male genitals. Where such a hormone is not present female genitals develop. Intriguingly, there are suggestions that prenatal hormones also differentially affect some aspects of brain development in males and females and that later psychological differences between the sexes could therefore have their origins in this very early form of sexual dimorphism. For that matter, there have also been attempts to explain the later development of heterosexual, bisexual, or homosexual orientations in terms of particular patterns of prenatal hormones (Money, 1987). All such explanations, however, remain controversial.

A considerable number of physical differences between the sexes appear after the seventh prenatal week and gradually become fully apparent in the course of childhood. Some of these concern the appearance of the two sexes: thus males are taller than females, have broader chests and develop facial hair; women, on the other hand, are wider in the pelvis and have a higher ratio of fat to muscle. These differences act as cues in everyday life and enable us to identify a person as male or female – a categorization which may then lead to differential behavior towards that person according to culturally specified norms. Or take another type of interweaving of biological with environmental forces: men are endowed with greater muscular strength; society therefore expects them to undertake heavier work; this will further accentuate the physical difference; that difference will also lead men to certain occupations and lifestyles not usually adopted by women. The two sets of influences, biological and cultural, thus combine in producing distinctive sex roles.

Are there behavioral differences between the sexes that are directly linked to genetic factors? The question of men's and women's psychological make-up has been the subject of speculation throughout the ages and has attracted sweeping generalizations galore. It has also, however, attracted considerable research. In their 1974 book

Maccoby and Jacklin examined over 2,000 studies, most published in the preceding ten years, which had looked at sex differences in behavior, and concluded that among the many psychological functions investigated only four were supported by reliable evidence, one from the personality-social domain, the others of a cognitive nature:

(1) *Aggression*   At all ages and across cultures physical aggression tends to be greater in males than in females. The difference is not large but has frequently been reported (Eagly, 1987; Hyde, 1984). In some studies no sex differences have been found, but reports of greater female aggression are extremely rare. Research on animals has also shown the male to be the more aggressive in many species. Hormonal influences, with particular reference to the male hormone testosterone, have been implicated in this difference but the evidence is far from conclusive (Huston, 1983).

(2) *Verbal ability*   Girls tend to perform better than boys on tasks involving verbal skills. This becomes especially evident from about the age of 11; even early on, however, it is apparent that girls begin to speak and learn to read earlier. Explanations have mostly centered on the part played by brain lateralization: it is generally considered that in the course of development the two hemispheres of the brain become progressively specialized, with the left processing mainly verbal and the right spatial information. However, it has not been satisfactorily established that left hemispheric growth is faster and more advanced in females than in males (Kinsbourne & Hiscock, 1983).

(3) *Spatial skills*   Males tend to perform better on tasks involving visuospatial abilities, though there is some doubt whether this difference appears before adolescence. Again hemispheric lateralization has been implicated; more frequently, however, a direct genetic cause has been evoked as explanation by associating spatial ability with a recessive gene on the X chromosome. Such a gene is sex-linked: if the gene occurs in a male it will always be expressed because it is paired with a Y chromosome which cannot overrule it, whereas in a female it will only be expressed if the same recessive gene also occurs on the other X chromosome. Both hemophilia and color blindness, conditions occurring primarily in males, have been explained in this way; as far as spatial ability is concerned, however, no definite proof is yet available (Boles, 1980).

(4) *Mathematical ability*   Males tend to be superior in solving mathematical problems. This difference does not appear till later on in childhood; it is in any case the least firmly established among the four in being less general and not as great. An overlap with spatial skills may help to account for the difference; however, an even more plausible explanation is that social expectations and educational practices are responsible, in that girls (for reasons nobody has satisfactorily explained) are generally considered by society to lack mathematical aptitude.

Not everyone accepts Maccoby and Jacklin's conclusions, some denying the existence of acceptable evidence for sex differences in any aspect of behavior while others wish to add to the list of four functions put forward by these authors. There are, for example, some indications that males are characterized by a greater activity level than females, but this is by no means a universal finding (Eaton & Enns, 1986). On the whole the material published since Maccoby and Jacklin's 1974 review detracts from rather than supports the reality of the four sex differences singled out by them. However, there is one further difference which has become apparent as a result of more recent research which should be considered because of its important psychological implications:

(5) *Physical and psychological vulnerability* Males are more vulnerable than females. This applies primarily to the early stages of development; it is most notable with respect to physical aspects but has its counterpart in mental development too. Thus more male fetuses are spontaneously aborted during pregnancy than female: according to some estimates about 140 males are conceived for every 100 females but only 106 boys are born for every 100 girls. Males continue to be at greater risk for a variety of disorders: they are more susceptible to prenatal and perinatal complications; more boys than girls die in infancy; and throughout life men remain more at risk for many diseases and accidents. Such differential vulnerability has its counterpart in psychological development: thus in determining what kinds of children are most susceptible to stress sex has quite consistently emerged as a predictor (Schaffer, 1990). For example, in a study by E. E. Werner and Smith (1982) conducted on the island of Kauai, Hawaii, of almost 700 children who were followed up from birth to early adulthood boys were found to be less resilient in the face of a wide variety of stresses, psychological as well as physical. More boys than girls experienced perinatal complications; a greater proportion of boys died in infancy; and subsequently more boys than girls suffered serious physical defects or illness requiring medical care. In addition throughout the first decade of life boys were found to react more adversely to the effects of poverty, family instability, and lack of educational stimulation in the home. Females overall appeared to cope rather more successfully with a wide variety of stresses than males. This pattern is typical of many other reports: family discord, divorce, parental mental illness, maternal employment and father absence have all been found to produce a greater incidence of adverse reaction in boys than in girls (Zaslow & Hayes, 1986). Over a large part of childhood the incidence of behavior problems, emotional maladjustment, learning difficulties, antisocial behavior, and neurotic and psychotic disorders is therefore greater among males. No satisfactory explanation exists for such differential vulnerability (Archer & Lloyd, 1985), nor for the fact that at puberty a reversal occurs, in that females from then on show greater vulnerability.

What has become clear is that any generalization about masculinity and femininity is bound to be hazardous. For one thing, these concepts are not unidimensional; they are made up of a great many components which do not necessarily vary together from one individual to another. For another, they are not necessarily polar opposites; more recent discussions of the concept of *androgyny* have drawn attention to the fact that both males and females possess a mixture of so-called masculine and so-called feminine psychological characteristics and that the distribution of these is far from bipolar. And finally, whatever part genetic determinants play it is clear that there is considerable malleability in psychological sex characteristics: what is regarded as desirable for each sex varies among cultures and over time. Each society defines sex roles in its own way and socializes children accordingly. As Margaret Mead (1935) showed, departures from Western norms can be great indeed. Among the Tchambuli, a tribe in New Guinea, sex roles are reversed in comparison with our stereotypes: women assume responsibility for fishing, trading, and other work which generates income, and are generally the dominant partners, whereas men spend their time on artistic activities and on adorning themselves. Among the Arapesh, another new Guinea tribe, both sexes behaved in a "feminine" way, rejecting all aggressive behavior in favor of a more gentle lifestyle; among the Mundugumor, on the other hand, just the opposite trend prevailed, in that both sexes favored highly aggressive behavior and brought up their children accordingly.

That there are socialization pressures to conform to cultural norms as to what is appropriate behavior for each sex cannot be doubted. We shall describe these practices later on in this book; here the question arises as to how these social influences interact with biological influences and what the relative contribution of each is. Providing an answer is no easy undertaking, though one possible way of determining the factors necessary for normal psychological sex development is to examine what happens when the course of physical development is in some way deviant, as illustrated below.

The case of atypical sex differentiation

The vast majority of children are born as boys or as girls, and are assigned to their sex on the basis of their genitalia. In a few cases such differentiation is not so clear cut. Such cases sometimes give rise to considerable human suffering both in the individuals involved and in their families; they can, however, help to throw light on the factors that control sexual development.

Some of these abnormalities and their psychological implications have been described in detail by Money and Ehrhardt (1972). Perhaps the most striking concerns a pair of identical male twins, one of whom at the age of 7 months lost his penis as a result of surgical mishap during circumcision performed by means of electrocautery. Reassignment as a girl was recommended to the parents, and after considerable agonizing they followed the advice and changed name, clothing, and hairstyle when the child was 17 months old. This was followed in due course by surgical changes designed to convert the boy into a girl, with hormone treatment following at puberty in order to bring about the development of feminine sexual characteristics.

Of particular interest is the fact that, psychologically, the child soon developed distinctly feminine attributes and in this respect became very different from her twin brother. According to Money and Ehrhardt this was largely due to her treatment by the parents, who made a point of emphasizing her femininity by dressing her in frilly frocks, providing her with bracelets and hair ribbons and encouraging her to help with the housework. As a result the girl (unlike her brother) became neat and tidy, interested in clothes, proud of her long hair, and dainty in her appearance, and while her brother wanted toy cars for presents she preferred dolls and other such "feminine" toys and activities. On the other hand she was described as tomboyish, in that she had abundant physical energy and tended to be dominant with other children.

Money and Ehrhardt describe other such cases where sexual identity is ascribed arbitrarily or counter to the child's genetic sex. One such concerns a baby born with ambiguous genitalia who was genetically a male but assigned female sexual identity by the parents in the second year. Again feminine traits and interests emerged; the early indications at any rate suggested that biological sex was overridden by the way in which the parents treated the child. In an attempt to investigate the respective roles of nature and nurture more systematically Money and Ehrhardt examined pairs of hermaphrodites (individuals born with ambiguity of reproductive structures), each pair matched to be identical chromosomally and gonadally but differing in their sexual assignment, in that one member of each pair was brought up as a male and the other as a female. According to the authors, examination of the psychological outcome of these pairs showed that "the contrast between two such young adult individuals in gender role and gender identity is so complete that the ordinary person meeting them socially or vocationally has no clues as to the remarkable contents of their medical history." Social assignment, they conclude, is the primary determinant of sexual identity and sex-appropriate behavior, though they add the rider that this needs to take place within the first three or four years. After such a "critical period" change-over becomes very much more difficult.

Not everyone agrees with these conclusions. For example, Imperato-McGinley, Guerro, Gautier, and Peterson (1974), and Imperato-McGinley (1979) argue, first, that hormones exert a more powerful influence on sexual identity than upbringing and, second, that reassignment can be accomplished later on in the course of development. They cite a group of children found in the Dominican Republic who were born with an enzyme deficiency resulting in a feminization of their genitals. As a result they were brought up as girls; however, when these children reached puberty they developed both primary and secondary male sexual characteristics (penises, facial hair, deep voices, and so on), whereupon they were reassigned and treated as male from then on. According to Imperato-McGinley and his colleagues this transition was made successfully and a new identity as males was assumed by all these young people – an achievement attributed to the influence of prenatal and pubertal testosterone. Nature, according to these authors, was able to assert itself despite the influence of early upbringing.

Any conclusion about the respective roles of biological and environmental influences on the formation of sexual identity is bound to be hazardous at the present state of knowledge. Extreme statements, such as "biology is destiny," can be ruled out; any model of psychosexual development must allow for the interplay of biology and environment. There are, for example, suggestions that visuospatial ability (where males tend to excel) may be biologically controlled through brain lateralization processes (N. S. Newcombe & Baenninger, 1989) and so give boys a head start. For one thing, however, when parents and teachers find a particular child to show proficiency in some area they are likely to provide encouragement and opportunities so that the child can develop further in this respect, and for another the child for his or her part will develop a sense of competence and pride in the relevant achievements which in turn will lead to further achievements. The end result is thus multidetermined, though a kickstart is provided by biological elements. This is likely to apply to other behavioral sex differences too. Take the greater aggressiveness of males. This too is likely to have a biological basis, though the evidence is admittedly indirect. Thus experimental administration of male hormones to animals is known to raise the level of aggression; more aggressive males tend to have higher levels of androgens than less aggressive males; and girls who receive excess male hormones prenatally tend to indulge in the kind of rough-and-tumble play that is more characteristic of boys (Ehrhardt & Baker, 1974). Again, however, any conclusion about hormones "causing" male aggressiveness is likely to be simplistic. As Maccoby and Jacklin (1974) argue, prenatal hormone levels may simply predispose boys to learn certain kinds of behavior more readily; opportunities for rough-and-tumble play, for instance, would therefore be seized upon with greater enthusiasm. This in turn creates social stereotypes about the two sexes, so that boys will be confronted by expectations that they will then want to live up to. It is, of course, conceivable that the way in which biological and social forces intertwine differs from one psychological function to another, but some form of intertwining is almost bound to be the rule.

Summary

Evolutionary Perspectives

- Psychological explanations of human development are usually phrased in terms of proximate (or immediate) causes. However, explanations in terms of ultimate (or remote) causes must also be recognized, including those that played a part in the evolution of human behavioral development.
- Three aspects of evolutionary theory need to be emphasized: first, that evolution concepts apply as much to behavior as to structure; second, that an individual's functions must always be related to the context (the "ecological niche") to which the species is adapted; and third, that a rigid distinction between what is innate and what is acquired is meaningless in this account. Evolutionary theory has also given impetus to the use of cross-species comparisons in developmental study, but while there are considerable advantages to such an approach the danger of unjustified generalizations across species must also be recognised.
- Different species are equipped with different sets of fixed action patterns as part

of their behavioral heritage. In human beings social signaling devices, such as crying and smiling, are examples of these patterns; they ensure that the infant is preadapted to obtain attention from caregivers and so fulfill an essential survival function.

- The ability to communicate emotional state is another biological device serving to bind child to caregiver from birth on. Facial expressions corresponding to different emotions appear to be innate, universal, and of the same form in infants as in adults. Not all emotions are present from the beginning; they emerge at the time of the life cycle when they begin to serve useful regulatory and communicative functions. Infants from an early age on are also sensitive to other people's emotional displays.

- Biological evolution is supplemented by cultural evolution – a process very much speedier, based on transfer of knowledge from one individual to another and from one generation to another. Just as the former produces different species through genetic change so the latter gives rise to different cultures through socialization practices. As cross-cultural research has shown, psychological development is profoundly affected in certain ways by the social setting in which a child is reared; it cannot therefore be studied in isolation or on the assumption that whatever is found in Western society has universal applicability and is innate.

The Genetics of Behavior

- The basic units of hereditary transmission are the genes. These are segments of chromosomes, represented in every cell of the body. The genotype is the sum total of an individual's genes and describes the overall pattern of inherited characteristics. However, the function of genes depends on their interaction with the environment, the end result being the phenotype, i.e. the observable characteristics of an individual.

- Behavioral characteristics are only indirectly regulated by genes, as these act solely on physical structures. The latter provide a genetically based susceptibility that will emerge given particular kinds of environmental experience.

- The science of behavioral genetics is concerned with the investigation of those characteristics that distinguish us as individuals. It assesses the relative contribution of heredity and environment to the creation of such individual differences, and for this purpose uses three main methods: family studies, twin studies, and adoption studies.

- Findings by behavioral geneticists show that virtually all psychological characteristics are genetically influenced, though the extent of that influence varies from one trait to another. In no case, however, does it account for more than about half the variability among individuals, the remainder being due to environmental influences. Among the latter, those of a nonshared kind, i.e. the experiences that are unique to individual family members, by and large exert a greater influence on

psychological development than shared experiences, i.e. those common to all members of a family.
- Just how much influence parents exert over their children's development has been called into question by some of the behavioral genetic research, with the proposition that within the range of "good-enough parenting" development depends primarily on heredity. Less controversial is another proposition, namely that by virtue of their genetic make-up children affect how their caregivers treat them and thus help to construct their own environment.

Bases of Individuality

- The inherent characteristics which account for our individuality include temperament – a term used to refer to an individual's behavioral style. Among the various schemes put forward for classifying temperamental qualities, that by Thomas and Chess has received most attention. As illustrated in particular by their category of "difficult" temperament, these qualities have social implications, in that they affect the way other people respond to the child. To produce optimal development, therefore, a "goodness of fit" is required between the child's inherent characteristics and the caregiver's treatment.
- A person's sex is also a basic aspect of individuality that has profound social implications. Sexual dimorphism starts at conception; it is based on chromosomal differences between males and females and directly accounts for the physical characteristics of the two sexes. The existence of sex-linked psychological differences remains controversial; the most likely candidates are aggression, verbal ability, spatial skills, mathematical ability, and physical and psychological vulnerability.

Chapter 3

Constructing the First Relationships

The establishment and progression of interpersonal relationships is a basic theme in social development. Children form many kinds of relationships to many kinds of partners: mothers, fathers, grandparents, siblings, peers, teachers, and so forth. It is, however, the very first relationship, usually to the mother, that has attracted most attention. This is in part because it is so intriguing to find out how a child at the very beginning of life can master such a highly complex task as the establishment of a relationship to another person; it is also because of the longstanding belief that the first relationship acts as a prototype for emotional relationships in later life. While the evidence for the latter assertion is as yet limited, wanting to understand the emergence of the first relationship in its own right is reason enough to devote time and effort to its investigation.

We all know about relationships from personal experience, yet defining and objectively investigating them is no easy task. This is because we do not directly observe a relationship – we infer it. What we observe are *interactions*, i.e. the behavior of individuals participating in some joint activity. Relationships are built up from interactions; however, this does not mean that relationships are simply the sum of lots of specific interactions (Hinde, 1979): a relationship has characteristics of its own, such as faithfulness or involvement or devotion, none of which can be applied to any one specific instance of interaction. For that matter interactions have properties which do not apply to individuals: synchrony, for example, describes what goes on *between* individuals and cannot be inferred from the behavior of the two participants studied in isolation.

It is therefore useful, as Hinde (1992) has argued, to distinguish between various levels of social complexity, ranging from the whole of society at one end to physiological processes at the other (see figure 2). Each level has certain characteristics which are not relevant at any other level; hence trying to understand relationships by applying propositions derived from the study of individuals (as social psychologists attempted to do at one time) is a profitless undertaking. And equally, we need to make a sharp distinction between the study of interactions and the study of relationships: the former are a here-and-now phenomenon, the latter imply continuity over time and are more than the sum of a series of interactions. At the same time, however, the

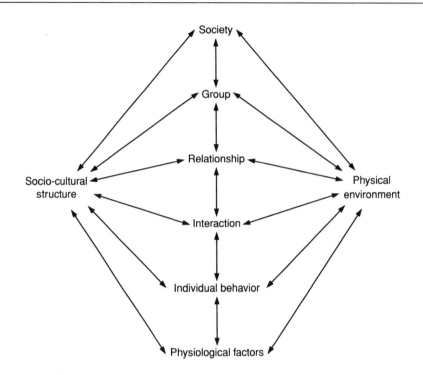

Figure 2   Relations between successive levels of social complexity (from Hinde, 1992)

levels are all reciprocally connected; to fully understand the quality of relationships, for example, one must take into account both the group or family in which that relationship is embedded and the individuality of each of the participants, as well as the influence of the sociocultural milieu and of the physical environment.

Early Interactions

In any interpersonal interaction the separate activities of the participants are coordinated in such a way that one can refer to them as a single, unitary entity: a conversation, a game, a fight or any other joint activity that is equally dependent on the behavior of both participants. Among adults such coordination occurs easily and smoothly; at the beginning of life, on the other hand, the ability to fit one's behavior to that of another person is still very limited and whatever coordination occurs must therefore initially depend on the adult partner.

Stages in Interactional Development

How coordination is accomplished and the developmental changes that occur in this respect in early life can best be considered within the framework outlined in table 10.

Table 10 Stages in parent–infant interaction

Stage	Starting age (months)	Developmental task
1 Biological regulation	0	To regularize the infant's basic biological processes such as feeding and waking–sleeping states and harmonize them with parental requirements
2 Face-to-face exchanges	2	To regulate mutual attention and responsiveness in face-to-face situations
3 Topic sharing	5	To incorporate objects into social interactions and ensure joint attention and action to them
4 Reciprocity	8	To initiate intentional actions directed at others and develop more flexible and symmetrical relationships
5 Symbolic representation	18	To develop verbal and other symbolic means of relating to others and reflect upon social exchanges

The scheme is based on the sequential reorganizations that periodically occur in the child's mental life during the first two years. Psychological development, as has become increasingly apparent, is not a matter of slow and gradual quantitative expansion; instead, the child's behavior will from time to time, quite spontaneously and relatively suddenly, show transitions to new levels of functioning that are, in certain respects at least, *qualitatively* different from preceding levels. This is most evident in infancy, where development is marked by the relatively frequent emergence of new abilities each of which brings about new modes of adaptation on the part of the child. Such changes have implications not only for the child but also for the parents and the role that they play: jointly they have to address whatever developmental task the advent of each stage produces. We shall spell this out in greater detail below, using the sequence outlined in table 10 as guideposts for discussion. Here let us just note a more general point, namely that the type of interaction characteristic of each stage is primarily determined by the child's developmental agenda and that whatever requirements parents may have need to be introduced in the context of that agenda.

Biological Regulation

The most urgent requirement during the first weeks is to regulate the infant's basic biological processes such as feeding and sleeping, and it is around these functions that many of the first social encounters take place. To stabilize these and to establish a mutually convenient timetable is the initial developmental task for both parent and child.

Such adaptation can take place surprisingly quickly. Take feeding, where the schedule adopted depends, on the one hand, on certain internal periodicities that determine the infant's hunger and, on the other hand, on the preferred timetable of the parents (which includes, amongst other things, eight hours uninterrupted sleep). In a classical study by Marquis (1941) the hourly changes in activity of two groups of infants was investigated during the first 10 days of life. One group was fed according to a regular three-hour, the other according to a regular four-hour schedule. After just a few days each group had already developed a peak of restlessness just before its respective feeding time – a finding which became particularly obvious when the three-hour group was subsequently shifted to a four-hour schedule and so had to wait the extra hour for the feed. The infants' hunger rhythms, it seems, had become regulated by the particular experience of each group.

Or take infants' sleeping patterns. In the first weeks sleep tends to occur in many short periods, distributed throughout the day and interspersed by periods of wakefulness that are even shorter (Parmalee, Wenner, & Schulz, 1964). Very soon, however, both sleep and waking begin to assume a different pattern: individual periods become longer, they are less randomly distributed within each 24-hour interval, and in due course they become organized in a diurnal pattern. Detailed round-the-clock recordings by Sander and colleagues (1979) illustrate this shift: by the end of the first postnatal week more than half of the longest sleep periods now occur during the night while motility and crying peaks have shifted to daytime. By the end of the first month of life this pattern has become definitely established (figure 3).

Such changes occur as the result of parental actions designed to shape the infant's inborn periodicities – actions such as waking the infant up early from an afternoon nap or keeping it awake longer in the evening, so ensuring more sleep during the night hours. How this is done depends on each set of parents and child; as Sander found, the mutual adaptation which took place was highly specific to each parent–child pair. He demonstrated this in a "cross-fostering" experiment, when infants awaiting adoption were looked after by one nurse for the first 10 days and then changed over to the care of another nurse (Sander, Stechler, Burns, & Julia, 1970). It was apparent that a definite rhythm had already been established after 10 days between each infant and the first caretaker, which then became disrupted, resulting in large increases in crying and feeding difficulties before another set of adaptations became established with the second caretaker.

Face-to-face Interactions

Around 2 months of age infants reach a transition point in their development, heralded by a sharp increase in visual efficiency (Aslin, 1987). As a result they become much more aware of their external environment, and in particular of other people. Direct eye contact with the partner can now be made, periods of rather more prolonged gaze ensue and the first social smiles can be elicited. For the next few

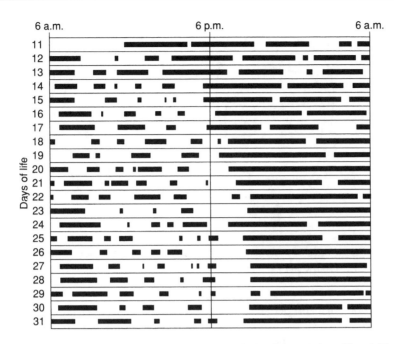

Figure 3 One baby's sleep and awake periods, for each day between days 11 and 31: solid lines represent sleep (from Sander et al., 1979)

months social interaction occurs primarily in the context of face-to-face encounters, and it is there that the infant begins to learn the rules which govern such interactions. The main developmental theme at that time is the regulation of mutual attention and responsiveness.

Before 2 months of age infants are only minimally aware of faces. This is largely because of the so-called *externality effect* – the tendency of infants to attend to the boundaries of stimuli and neglect the interior (Aslin, 1987). Gross features such as the hairline and the region around the eyes are looked at, i.e. whatever is perceptually most salient captures the young infant's interest and holds it to the exclusion of all else. Examining the face as a whole by scanning all the various internal contours is a later and more gradual development (figure 4). It is as though the infant's capacity to take in information is at first severely limited and the ability to attend to an increasing number of facial features only becomes possible with maturation and experience.

This means that initially an infant will not be aware of those features that distinguish one person from another; visually at least, people are all alike to infants in the first few weeks. There are indeed suggestions that at first infants have no appreciation of faces *as* faces. By using the *visual preference technique* (Fantz, 1961), that is, by simultaneously confronting an infant with two stimuli and measuring the amount of attention paid to each, it has been shown that not till 2 or 3 months of age can the

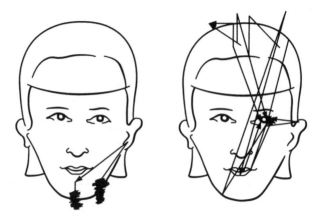

Figure 4 Scan lines of a human face by 1- and 2-month-old infants (from Fogel, A., & Melson, G. F., 1988, *Child Development*. St Paul, MN: West Publishing)

representation of a "proper" face be discriminated from one of a face with its features scrambled (figure 5). Before that infants find both stimuli equally interesting; only thereafter is the proper face preferred (Maurer, 1985). Presumably it takes several weeks of exposure to people plus the necessary maturation of the visual system for recognition of faces to become possible.

The same trend is evident in the development of the smiling response. As we have already seen, smiles are at first triggered by nothing but another person's eyes: all other features of the face are irrelevant. With increasing age, however, infants come to require more and more of the face before a smile will appear (see figure 6): by blocking off parts of the face, or by using models or drawings, it can be shown that from 3 months on they also attend to the facial outline; at 4 months all internal

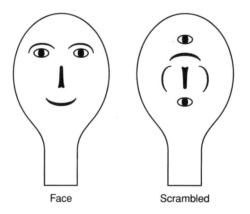

Face   Scrambled

Figure 5 Stimuli used in face recognition experiments (from Johnson & Morton, 1991)

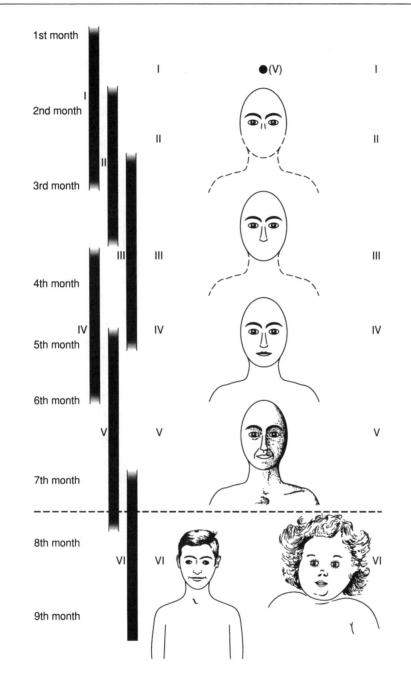

Figure 6   Conditions for evoking smiling in infants up to the ninth month (from Ahrens, 1954)

features are apprehended; after 5 months they respond also to the particular emotional expression of the other person; and from approximately 7 months the most important change of all takes place, as from then on smiling is no longer indiscriminately elicited by all faces but only by certain familiar ones.

In real interactions, however, the other person's face is not an immobile stimulus but one that almost constantly moves, signals, and communicates, and moreover does so in conjunction with the infant's actions. Thus the typical mother–infant interaction illustrates a synchrony of the two partners' behavioral rhythms, even though the contribution of each is of a distinctive nature (Schaffer, 1984).

(1)   *Infants*   bring to the interaction certain biologically based cycles of attention–nonattention (Lester, Hoffman, & Brazelton, 1985) that serve to make the infant more predictable to the adult. One can observe this in the child's looking patterns during face-to-face interaction: for a few seconds the infant will look at the adult, then turn away, then look back, and so forth in a continuing cycle. The length of each looking-at or looking-away period may vary somewhat, and though the rate of fluctuation shows certain regularities their sequence is indicative of the infant's efforts to regulate arousal level (Stern, 1985). Attending to another person is an arousing experience; the young infant cannot sustain such excitement for long, thanks to the on–off nature of looking; however, excitement can be controlled by the use of time-out periods.

(2)   *Mothers*   (and most other adults) are intuitively aware of the need to help the infant modulate the level of arousal and will accordingly synchronize their stimulation with the child's on–off periods. In a face-to-face situation the mother generally looks at the child almost continuously, thus providing a "frame" (as Fogel, 1977, has described it) within which the infant's gazing may cycle to and fro. This enables the mother constantly to adjust the timing, nature, and intensity of her stimulation in the light of the infant's condition. During looking-at periods, for instance, the mother will do her best to keep the infant interested with exaggerated facial displays or rhythmic and repetitive vocalizations; during looking-away periods, on the other hand, she will respect the child's need for time-out by ceasing her stimulation but remaining watchful in order to help the infant to resume the next cycle of activity.

Unlike the interactions of adults, there is thus at first an asymmetry in adult–infant exchanges. The mother is almost constantly ready for interaction; it is left to the infant to determine whether interaction in fact takes place. Yet even within the first few months developments take place which bring greater symmetry to infants' social encounters. These are largely the result of maturational changes in the neurophysiological organization of infants' visual control, which permit infants to shift their attention voluntarily in contrast to the "obligatory" attention observed previously (Rothbart, Ziaie, & O'Boyle, 1992). As Kaye and Fogel (1980) found when studying a group of infants at various points in the first six months, such control can be observed in the infants' greater ability to sustain attention and to switch readily from one focus to another on their own initiative rather than being dependent on and merely reactive to the mother's actions. Thus, by virtue of this greater spontaneity, they will in due course become more of an equal social partner.

The case of "still-face"

The intricate to-and-fro of mother and infant in face-to-face encounters has been likened to a waltz, in that the partners are able to move in close synchrony on the basis of a shared program and in prompt response to each other's steps. But what if one of the partners does not accept the invitation to the waltz? What does the infant do when the mother does not behave in the customary way?

A number of investigators have asked mothers deliberately to distort their usual behavior by adopting a "still-face," that is, by remaining silent and expressionless while seated opposite the infant (e.g. Cohn & Tronick, 1983; Tronick, 1989). Descriptive accounts show very clearly that infants as young as 2 or 3 months are disturbed and upset by such behavior. When the mother fails to greet them in the usual way they sober and look warily at her, giving a brief smile and, when that is not reciprocated, they look away from her. They then alternate brief glances at her with glances away, occasionally smiling but in an increasingly wary manner. The glances away become longer and longer, until the infant eventually withdraws altogether by orienting face and body to the side and staying turned away from the mother. Some infants become overtly distressed under such conditions, and both distress and wariness may continue for a while when the mother is asked to resume her usual responsive behavior.

The significance of these observations lies in their implications for understanding the effects of maternal depression on infants. The mother's unresponsiveness is then "for real" and, being continuous, can be expected to have greater consequences for the child. Depressed mothers have difficulty tuning in to the infant's behavior, picking up cues and responding appropriately. They thus no longer provide the contingent responsiveness which infants require in order to learn about the to-and-fro of social interaction, and it is therefore not surprising to find that such infants develop various behavioral disturbances: they are more likely to cry, be withdrawn and show a general lack of energy, even with people other than the mother. The emotions they customarily display tend to be negative ones such as sadness or anger rather than positive ones like joy and interest (Pickens & Field, 1993). Thus their behavior mirrors that of the depressed mother and suggests that they are in danger of developing an overall distorted style of social interaction if interventive action is not taken (Field, 1987). Interestingly, there are indications that mothers suffering from depression but with employment outside the home are much more positive in relating to their infants and behave towards them more like nondepressed mothers than is the case with mothers without outside occupation (Cohn, Campbell, Matias, & Hopkins, 1990).

The respective roles of mother and infant in these early face-to-face interactions is illustrated by another feature, namely *turn-taking*. This is seen most clearly in vocal exchanges. Among adults turn-taking is, of course, an essential characteristic of a conversation: if both partners were to talk simultaneously any communication would be virtually impossible. Adults, however, are highly skilled at sequentially integrating their individual contributions and know the rules whereby speaker and listener periodically exchange roles. Such knowledge can hardly be attributed to young infants, yet recordings of their vocal exchanges with mothers show clearly that a turn-taking pattern is already present in the early months (Schaffer, 1984). Infant and adult, that is, alternate their contributions, rarely vocalizing simultaneously and managing their exchanges of speaker–listener roles with great precision. What is also apparent, however, is that this is brought about primarily by the mother's action in skillfully inserting her contributions in the pauses between the bursts of vocalizations produced by the infant. As we have seen, mothers are highly attentive to their infants in face-to-face encounters and can therefore time their vocal interventions in such a way as not to interrupt the baby. The mother, that is, allows herself to be paced by the infant and thereby takes responsibility for converting the encounter into something that sounds almost like a conversation. It is she therefore on whom the onus falls for sustaining the interaction.

Turn-taking characterizes other forms of early interaction too, and one of these becomes apparent when one observes mothers and babies during feeding. The infant's sucking response has been shown (e.g. by Wolff, 1966) to be a highly intricate activity organized as a burst–pause pattern – i.e. the infant sucks in bursts, pauses for a while and then resumes sucking with another burst. As Kaye (1977) has shown, this temporal patterning is highly suited for incorporating feeding into a more general social interaction sequence, for mothers tend to interact with their infants in precise synchrony with the burst–pause pattern. During bursts they are generally quiet and inactive; during pauses, on the other hand, they jiggle, stroke, and talk to the infant (figure 7). Thus the mother fits in with the baby's natural sucking rhythm, accepts the opportunities to intervene offered by pauses, and in this way sets up a turn-taking pattern in exactly the same way as seen in vocal interchange.

We can draw two conclusions from these observations. In the first place the temporal, on–off organization of infants' behavior lends itself well to social interaction because of the opportunities it offers for the adult's intervention. Such response organization is an aspect of the infant's preadaptedness for social life: it provides the possibility of to-and-fro interchange. And in the second place the observations draw attention to the importance of adults' willingness to make use of these opportunities by playing a complementary role to the infant, fitting in with its behavioral organization and treating the child's behavior as if it were already intentionally communicative. Given such willingness, infants from a very early age are provided with the chance of learning about the nature of mature social interaction formats by being directly involved in them and so acquiring in due course the skills necessary to act as a full partner.

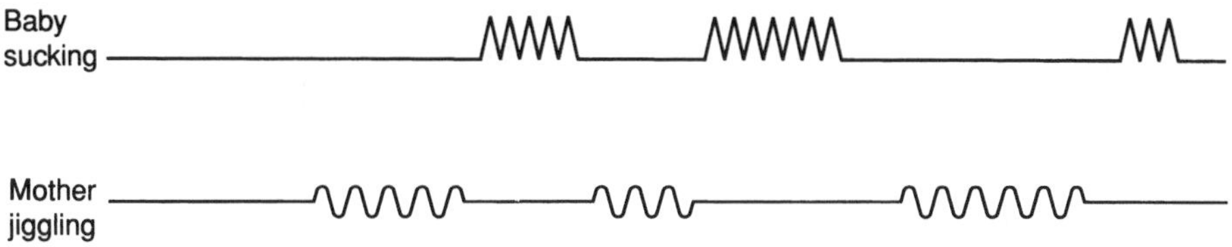

Baby
sucking ⎯⎯⎯⎯⎯⎯⎯⎯⎯⎯⎯⎯⎯MWM⎯⎯⎯⎯MWWM⎯⎯⎯⎯⎯⎯⎯⎯M⎯

Mother ⎯⎯⎯⎯⎯⎯⎯⎯⎯wνν⎯⎯⎯⎯νν⎯⎯⎯⎯⎯νννν⎯⎯⎯⎯⎯
jiggling

Figure 7 Baby's sucking bursts interspersed by mother's activity

Interactive Style

Each adult–child pair tends to develop its own distinctive manner of interaction. When trying to understand such distinctiveness it is useful to distinguish three kinds of influence, namely those stemming respectively from the cultural context in which the child is brought up, from the personality of the adult, and from the characteristics of the child.

(1) *Cultural influences*   Until quite recently the literature on adult–infant interaction was almost wholly derived from investigations of North American and European samples. What was found was considered to be applicable to all normal parent–infant pairs, to the extent that findings common to such studies were often attributed to biological origins. Recent anthropological reports suggest the need for a more cautious approach and point to the importance of taking into account the cultural context in which relationships develop.

Take the Gusii people of Kenya, whom LeVine and his colleagues (1994) studied and directly compared with a group of American mothers living in Boston. The relationship between the African mothers and their infants was marked by the comparatively little face-to-face interaction that could be observed; what there was tended to be slow, unchanging, and devoid of affect. Bouts of play and talk were extremely brief; a mother's most common response to her baby's gaze or vocalizing was to look away. The reason for a mother adopting such behavior was thereby to avoid or dampen down any excitement in the infant; instead of deliberately seeking the peaks of arousal that her Western counterpart builds up in face-to-face interactions the Gusii mother aims to keep her infant calm at all times and prevent it getting involved in exciting social interactions. Emphasis is instead on holding and physical contact, even during sleep – forms of interaction that soothe rather than arouse. The mother thereby follows a cultural agenda: the objective behind such an interactive style stems from her need to return to working in the fields at an early stage of the child's life, for then the infant will be handed over to the care of older children and must therefore be sufficiently calm and manageable for them to be able to cope. A close attachment with the mother is also avoided because babies are born at very close intervals; again, having a manageable child makes it easier for the mother to attend to the new baby.

What happens between mother and infant is thus by no means rigidly laid down by biological requirements; characteristics that at first appear to be universal turn out to be culture-specific. Even in the early months infants are already being prepared for the requirements of social life that prevail in the particular society into which they were born; the interactions to which they are introduced and from which they learn the norms of behavior serve to integrate them into their cultural group and its specific customs.

(2) *Adult personality* Infants as young as 4 weeks already behave differently with their mother, their father, and a stranger (Yogman et al., 1976). To some extent this can be explained by the adult's confidence in handling the baby; to a large extent it reflects various individual characteristics of each person. Emotional expressiveness, speed of movement, responsiveness, tenseness, playfulness – these and many other personality attributes differentiate people and help to produce distinctive interactive styles.

Most attention has been given to the differences between mothers and fathers in the way in which they relate to young children. In many families the parents perform different tasks: caretaking is mostly assigned to the mother while the father concentrates primarily on play. Yet it is not only a matter of *what* the parents do but also *how* they do it. As has been repeatedly shown (e.g. Clarke-Stewart, 1978; Lamb, 1977; Power & Parke, 1982), fathers' play tends to be much more physically stimulating, vigorous, and abrupt, whereas mothers provide more verbal stimulation, more object play, and in general a more gentle and predictable kind of input. With respect to affection and contingent responsiveness, on the other hand, mothers and fathers tend to be alike.

Exposure to different individuals, each with his or her own distinctive manner of relating to the child, is beneficial in helping children to develop a varied repertoire of interactive skills and learning with whom and under what circumstances each set of skills is appropriate. This is one advantage of having two parents: though they may agree on the basic principles of child rearing, mother and father are inevitably different personalities and therefore provide different experiences to their children. From the beginning the infant's social world is thus characterized by interpersonal diversity and thereby offers suitable preparation for coping with the multiple relationships that the child will establish in due course.

(3) *Child characteristics* The nature of interactive episodes depends on what *both* participants bring to the encounter, whatever their age. Thus the inborn temperamental characteristics of even the youngest infant will help to shape the course of the interaction and influence the behavior of the other person. Take activity level, one of the basic dimensions of temperament. The highly active infant – almost continuously on the go, squirming in the parent's lap, wanting change and stimulation – elicits a very different type of behavior from the adult compared with an inactive infant, content to lie quietly and signaling only rarely for attention. Given a

sensitive parent who will adjust her actions to those of her child's the course of the interaction will run smoothly; however, when the child's characteristics are such that adjustment is a difficult task the relationship becomes a much more awkward one to establish.

This is seen most clearly when the characteristics which the infant brings into the world take a markedly deviant form (Field, 1987). Congenital abnormalities such as the various forms of mental handicap, pre- or perinatal complications resulting in brain injury, and sensory disorders often represent a formidable challenge to the parent in the attempt merely to conduct ordinary social interactions with the infant. When the infant's behavior is so disorganized as to be unpredictable and to lack clear communicative messages to which the parent can respond, or when the infant is emotionally either unresponsive or, on the contrary, hyperresponsive, it can be extraordinarily difficult for the adult to judge the amount, form, and timing of appropriate stimulation. For instance, the behavioral periodicities of attention–nonattention normally observed in face-to-face interaction may be disrupted, and under such circumstances the task of coordination of adult and child cycles will then be a much more arduous one which will make far greater demands on the parent's sensitivity and patience. Depending on the nature and severity of the child's condition proper interpersonal exchanges may eventually develop; in the early stages, however, interactions could well leave both partners confused and dissatisfied.

The case of premature babies as social partners

Prematurely born babies, being of low birth weight, are an at-risk group whose survival and physical health are the first consideration. Over and above that, however, there are psychological problems associated with both cognitive and social functioning which may well right themselves in due course but which in early infancy add to the burden of care. Premature newborns have been described as behaviorally disorganized, less predictable, less adaptable, overreactive to some forms of stimulation and underreactive to other forms, and in addition less attractive in appearance – all characteristics that have profound implications for their early social development.

Eckerman and Oehler (1992) list four ways in which the circumstances of the beginnings of social development differ for such infants:

1   Social interactions begin at a much earlier point in development. The infant may consequently not be ready as yet to process the sights and sounds provided by parents.

2   Prematures, especially those of very low birth weight, may not only be immature but also sick. In particular, they may be at risk for the development of neurological disorders which will cause further irregularities in their behavior.

3   The period following birth may be one of great stress for the parents; their behavior too will thus be altered.

4   Social interactions begin under quite different physical constraints, imposed by the intensive care nursery in which such infants are initially reared. Parents have only limited contact with the infant; they are often intimidated by the equipment that forms a

necessary part of such an environment; and they may also feel that their role is only a minor one, being of less significance than that of nurses and doctors.

It is thus not surprising that early parent–infant interactions, as observed for instance in face-to-face situations, take a different form compared with those involving full-term infants (Eckerman, Oehler, Medvin, & Hannan, 1994; Minde, Perrotta, & Marton, 1985). Synchrony is more difficult to establish because of abnormally high or low thresholds to stimulation; the infant's attention is more difficult to elicit and maintain; and the mother's attempts to provide the infant with extra stimulation through talking and touching may result merely in greater irritability. Under such conditions some mothers may feel rejected and withdraw; special efforts to coach them will then be required (Field, 1987).

Yet prematures, even in the early weeks of their lives, are already responsive to some forms of social stimulation: speech, for example, can maintain them in the awake and visually attentive state that is presumed conducive to social interaction (Eckerman & Oehler, 1992). Thus, whatever initial difficulties there may be, such infants do have the potential to be rewarding social partners, and indeed the great majority catch up within the first three to six months of postnatal life.

From Nonverbal to Verbal Communication

From the very beginning infant and parent mutually influence each other. On the one hand infants provide cues to their caretakers which convey messages about their state and requirements; it is essential to their welfare that these are then correctly picked up by the adult and appropriately responded to. And on the other hand how adults behave may exert an influence on infants from an early age, even when that takes a very primitive form such as that described by Sullivan (1947) as *contagion* – a means whereby a mother's tension can be picked up and responded to by her baby, primarily through bodily cues when held, which can then have marked effects on the nature of their interaction.

Whether it is appropriate to refer to these early exchanges as "communication" is a matter of definition. If communication involves an *intention* on the part of the participants to influence each other then clearly such exchanges do not qualify. It is only gradually that young children learn about the message value of their behavior, i.e. that their actions have predictable effects on others and result in shared meanings, and it is thus only in the later stages of infancy that they come to use these actions in a planned and deliberate manner. Earlier exchanges, where adult and infant engage in nonverbal dialog, have therefore sometimes been referred to as *protocommunications*, in the belief that they share some features of later communication and may even be a necessary precursor but do not yet qualify to rank with the real thing.

The growth of intentionality is one trend which transforms early interactions and which makes for greater symmetry in the roles played by adult and child. Another is the greater flexibility of the child's attentional capacity, as a result of which social exchanges are not merely confined to face-to-face situations but can incorporate objects (third parties, as it were) as well. And finally there is the transition from nonverbal to primarily verbal means of communication as the child becomes increasingly capable of symbolic representation. We shall trace these trends in the following discussion.

Topic Sharing

Every social interaction has a topic to which the participants address themselves, and for communication to take place there must be mutual agreement as to the nature of that topic. During the first few months, when face-to-face interactions prevail, adult and infant are primarily concerned with events arising within the dyad itself: attention, that is, focuses on such things as the facial expressions or the sounds or movements of the partners, providing the infant with opportunity to learn about other people and the mechanisms of directly interacting with them.

At around 5 months of age a marked and relatively sudden change occurs. The emergence of manipulative abilities means that infants now turn increasingly to the world of things – objects that they can grasp, handle, and act upon and with which they can stimulate and amuse themselves. Kaye and Fogel (1980), following up a group of infants over the first half-year, found a drop in visual attention to the mother from 70 percent of session time at 6 weeks to 33 percent at 26 weeks: as the mothers reported, direct face-to-face interaction was no longer as appropriate at the older age as previously, and instead their task was now to share with the child events external to the dyad such as toys and objects and whatever else fascinated the infant as a result of its mental horizon expanding. How to structure the interaction around such external topics is the main issue to which adult and infant must now address themselves.

As far as infants are concerned, attentional capacity at this age is still very limited, with the result that they can attend *either* to an object *or* to a person but not to both. Watch a play session with a 6-month-old infant: the child is totally absorbed in whatever toy it is handling at the time, apparently oblivious of the mother until she makes a move to attract attention to herself, whereupon the infant briefly switches from toy to mother before returning to the toy once more. Attention, that is, tends to be deployed *successively* to object and person; games such as give-and-take which rely on *simultaneous* attention to both are still beyond the child's capacity. If there is to be topic sharing it is therefore up to the adult to take the initiative and convert an *infant–object* situation into an *infant–object–adult* situation.

Mothers use a variety of procedures for this purpose. Take the phenomenon of *visual coorientation* – a term used to indicate the joint attention of two or more people to some common focus. In a study by Collis and Schaffer (1975) mothers and infants were confronted by a display of toys in a laboratory observation room and their behavior videorecorded from behind a one-way window. Analysis of the recordings showed, in the first place, that mother and infant were more often than not attending to the same toy at the same time – the phenomenon of visual coorientation. Second, it was found that almost invariably this was brought about by the mother closely monitoring the infant's gaze direction and then, almost automatically, following the gaze to look at the same toy. The infant, that is, took the lead by spontaneously looking from one toy to another and so determining the choice of topic; the mother thereupon ensured that the topic became a *shared* one. The infants themselves, up to the age of 10 months, rarely followed the mother's gaze; it is not till the end of the first year that another person's gaze direction becomes a meaningful signal to the infant. And in the third place, such topic sharing frequently led to further interaction: the mother, for instance, would not only look at the toy but also point to it, name it, and comment upon it, and in this way elaborate upon the object of mutual interest and incorporate it in a more complex exchange with the infant.

The last point is a particularly important one, for it draws attention to the usefulness of introducing new material to children in the context of their own selected focus of interest. We shall have more to say about this when we discuss below the role of *joint involvement episodes* – certain kinds of social interaction which begin with establishing a common attentional focus and which the adult then uses to extend the child's behavioral repertoire and so help to reach higher levels of competence. However, the role which such episodes play in children's cognitive socialization can already be seen in infancy. Take language acquisition, with particular reference to the learning of object names. As Collis (1977) has shown, a great deal of verbal labeling of objects goes on during visual coorientation: the mother, that is, uses the infant's spontaneous interest in a particular toy as the context for naming that toy and, by carefully timing her production of the name to coincide with the child's appropriate attention, she ensures that the child has every opportunity of learning the correct association between object and verbal label. The importance for semantic development of having verbal and visual input synchronized is self-evident.

Reciprocity and Intentionality

Some of the most profound changes to be found in children's development occur at around 8 or 9 months. A "blossoming" of abilities (as Bretherton, McNew, & Beeghly-Smith, 1981, have referred to it) takes place then, in that a considerable range of new capacities emerges at this age, transforming the child's behavior and making it vastly more flexible, more coordinated, and more purposive than in previous months (for examples see table 11). In particular, the child now becomes capable of coordinating several activities that formerly could only be performed separately: person-directed acts, for example, can be inserted into play with objects, so that the infant is no longer confined to attending to mother *or* toy but can combine diverse events into one coordinated sequence. Taken in conjunction with such Piagetian developments as the beginnings of object permanence and the ability to

Table 11   Examples of new capacities emerging around 8 months of age

Invokes adult help in performing a task with an object
Obeys simple requests
Imitates demonstrated actions on objects
Points to objects and follows the pointing gesture of an adult
Plays peek-a-boo, hiding own face for another to watch
Holds cup to doll's mouth
Opens and closes book, looking at mother after each move
Follows adult's visual gaze
Shakes head or says "no" in refusal
Begins to use conventional labels for objects. Names persons and pets
Demonstrates affection by hugging and kissing
Plays at carrying out adult activities (mopping floor, driving car, etc.)
Shows toes when these are named by mother
Plays "appropriately" with cup, spoon, and saucer

Source: Adapted from: Trevarthen & Hubley (1978), Bretherton et al. (1981)

differentiate means from ends, the cognitive changes taking place in the third quarter of the first year have profound implications for social behavior, making the child into a more equal partner increasingly able to act reciprocally and intentionally in social encounters.

One of the best contexts for tracing these changes are adult–infant *games*. The great majority of parents play games such as patacake, peekaboo, give-and-take, and horsie (Gustafson, Green, & West, 1979) for the sake of the enormous pleasure children obviously get from them. However, games are also useful because they provide a setting in which infants can acquire social skills, for they are conventional, oft-repeated routines requiring the mutual involvement of the two participants and are based on clear rules, of which turn-taking and repetition of rounds are the most common. Thus they provide infants with the opportunity to learn to anticipate the next move, to integrate their behavior with that of the other person, and periodically to exchange roles – all aspects common to every form of social interaction. Indeed writers such as Bruner (1983) have proposed that games have an essential role in facilitating language acquisition, for they share some of the same characteristics as are found in conversations (e.g. turn-taking) and, like language, are made up of constituent parts in a particular order that can be varied to some extent without breaking the basic rule on which they are based. Experience of playing games, according to this argument, makes it therefore easier to understand the requirements of linguistically based conversation.

As infants get older the role which they play in games changes and becomes more active and more sophisticated. Take Bruner's (1977) description of the development of give-and-take games. Up to 8 months or so the infant's participation is limited to "take": the mother offers the toy, the infant takes it and the sequence ends with the child dropping the toy. After that age the game ceases to be so one-sided: now the infant may begin the sequence by showing or offering the toy to the mother, or may hand it to her at her request. The exchange is still hesitant, with the infant constantly checking between object and mother as though not sure of the right procedure. By the end of the first year, however, the game has definitely become established as a set of routines, the infant having learned the basic rule that the roles of giver and taker are reciprocal and also exchangeable. Still later the infant increasingly dares to depart from the basic routine and to introduce all sorts of variations without, however, breaking the essential rules on which the game is based.

Games thus serve as an index of the developmental changes that occur in infants' cognitive and social abilities. One way of testing these abilities is to interrupt the alternating sequence by the adult's failure to take a turn and then examine the child's response to such rule breaking. Ross and Lollis (1987) recorded the behavior of infants during interruption periods at various ages between 9 and 18 months and found that even the 9-month-old infants already understood some elements of the structure of games: they appeared puzzled, turned from object to adult, and in various ways attempted to get the partner to continue participation. With age such behavior became more marked: for example, the frequency of infants taking the adults' turn on their behalf increased four-fold over the nine months of the study. The children's understanding of the overall structure of the game thus became more and more evident, as did their ability actively to preserve that structure.

These observations highlight two features which are essential characteristics of mature social interchange: reciprocity and intentionality.

(1)   *Reciprocity* refers to the knowledge that an interaction needs to be sustained by the action of *both* partners and that, moreover, their roles need to be coordinated and can be interchanged. The 6-month-old infant may enjoy a game with an adult but only in a purely passive capacity as spectator; the 12-month-old infant, on the other hand, is able actively to participate in the game and ensure that it is no longer a one-sided performance.

(2)   *Intentionality* also appears towards the end of the first year. The ability to plan one's behavior and anticipate its consequences is a highly sophisticated accomplishment; it is also a necessary one for full participation in social interaction. Communicative acts may be evident from birth on: the young baby can convey its state and requirements by means such as crying; however, it is not till 8 or 9 months that such acts come to be employed in a planned and deliberate manner. Intentionality is admittedly a nebulous concept that is difficult to operationalize. E. Bates, O'Connell, & Shore (1987) used three criteria to examine communicative behavior in episodes where a child is attempting to obtain an object:

a   *Gaze alternation*: the child looks back and forth from object to adult – as though expecting the adult to help out in some way.

b   *Repair of failed message*: if an initial gesture or vocal signal fails to move the adult into action the child will repeat, augment, or substitute signals until the goal is obtained.

c   *Ritualization of gestures*: an action such as reaching which was previously used as a genuine attempt to obtain the object becomes transformed into a ritualized movement (e.g. an abbreviated grasping motion or an open-and-shut gesture with the hand) directed at the adult, with no function except as a signal.

Behavior patterns such as these indicate that communicative behavior is used in an intentional manner and that the child has become capable of understanding how signals can be used with the express purpose of influencing another person.

Using Gestures

Towards the end of the first year a considerable expansion takes place in the range of devices available to the infant for communicating with others. In particular, even before words appear, children begin to use gestures, that is, nonverbal means of conveying messages that are conventional in form and are universally recognized.

One of the earliest examples is pointing. According to Fogel and Hannan (1985) pointing-like gestures can already be seen in 3- to 5-month-old infants, but at that age it is merely a spontaneous display of interest or attention. Up to about 9 months of age there is no indication that infants understand the meaning of the gesture: when another person points they are unable to follow the direction of the pointing finger and instead look at the finger itself (C. M. Murphy & Messer, 1977). Thereafter they begin to follow correctly, but only under "easy" conditions, i.e. when finger and target are near to each other in the same part of the visual field. Infants' own use of pointing as a means of indicating something of interest also emerges around this time; it is noteworthy that it appears in the same form in all cultures, i.e. with arm and index finger extended, with no suggestion that it is in any way learned or imitated. Initially, however, the gesture takes the form of "pointing-for-self," i.e. the infant points to the target but without checking whether the other person is following the gesture. "Pointing-for-others," as a communicative phenomenon indicative of the child's desire to share the object with another person, emerges later (H. Werner & Kaplan, 1963). By looking from object to person and back again infants show that they can now integrate the two foci of interest into the same activity, thus providing yet another demonstration of the important role which the development of this ability plays in social interchange.

The same phenomenon can also be seen in the development of other gestures such as showing or offering objects to another person (Fogel, 1991). Before 10 months infants may hand a toy to the mother in the course of play, but do so without taking their eyes off the toy. Subsequently they not only offer the toy but, by looking to and fro between object and mother, clearly signal that the toy is *for* the mother. Give-and-take games can then also develop: the toy is incorporated into a social interaction sequence in which the child shows a clear understanding that holding out an object to another person is part of a reciprocal chain in which taking is the counter-part to offering. The gesture is thus intentionally employed as a communicative device.

In the second year of life gestural behavior undergoes a further development, namely the use of nonverbal gestures to *symbolically* represent objects and events, with the aim of communicating these to other people. A flower, for instance, may be represented by sniffing; an aeroplane by holding out the arms sideways; a dog by panting; food by smacking lips, and so forth. In a study of 11-month-old infants, followed up regularly for a nine-month period, Acredolo and Goodwyn (1988) found an impressive degree of symbolic gesturing to develop during this time. Altogether they located 81 different gestures, of which those in table 12 are some examples. Some had been purposefully taught by adults but others had been spontaneously developed by the child, usually in the course of social interaction. Most of the gestures depicted the function rather than the form of the object to which they referred. Not surprisingly, however, their use decreased as language acquisition proceeded and the children became capable of replacing the gesture by a verbaliza-tion. Thus the two systems, gesturing and language, have a common communicative function; indeed both arise at about the same time and in similar contexts, and children advanced in the use of one also tend to be advanced in the other.

The case of deaf children's sign language

Just how powerful the push to communicate is can be seen by examining children in whom the verbal channel is blocked on account of deafness. Such children do not develop the usual linguis-tic means of communicating; they may be taught a conventional system of gestural signing such as ASL (American Sign Language) or BSL (British Sign Language), but as a number of studies (e.g. Goldin-Meadow & Morford, 1985) have shown, even in the absence of any teaching or any models to imitate most of these children will quite spontaneously construct their own gestural system.

For instance, Goldin-Meadow and Morford investigated a group of deaf children unable to acquire language and not exposed to any con-ventional manual sign language, and compared their communicative skills with a number of hearing children. They found that each of the deaf children generated a gesture system that was comparable both in content and in form to the early spoken system developed by the hear-ing children. For example, the deaf children first developed single gestures to denote specific ob-jects or actions – just as the hearing children used single words as their first step in language acquisition. The deaf children then proceeded to link together gestures into "sentences" in just the same way as hearing children string words together, and in time these gestures increased both in number and complexity. All this without tuition or example! The hearing children, of course, also developed gestures but these were not as complex as those of the deaf children and gradually decreased as language took over as the main communicative means. When children do have a model to imitate the learning of gestures proceeds very rapidly. Bonvillian, Orlansky, and Novack (1983), in an investigation of the hearing children of deaf parents who used sign language for communication, found that the children's first recognizable sign was produced at 8.5 months, the tenth sign at 13.2 months and the first sign combination at 17.0 months. In contrast, children learning to speak normally do not attain the equivalent milestones for spoken language until two or three months later.

Verbalization has many advantages over any manual system and it is not surprising that it normally replaces gesturing. However, in children incapable of language it does provide a means of communication that is remarkably sophisticated for something that may be developed quite spontaneously.

Social Referencing

A young infant confronted by a strange object or person will stare fixedly for a brief while and will then take some form of action – approach under some circumstances, withdrawal under others. In either case the action is determined by whatever transpires between child and stimulus in those first few seconds.

In children after the age of 9 or 10 months a new pattern is observed. The child will not merely look at the object but also at the mother or whatever other familiar person is present before taking action. The purpose of such looking is to seek cues from the other person's expression or behavior that will guide the child's appraisal of the situation. Thus the nature of the eventual response is determined not only by the child's perception but also by the reaction of others; that information comes to be integrated into the child's understanding of the event.

This phenomenon is referred to as *social referencing*. As a typical study we can take that by Klinnert (1984), who examined the reactions of 12- and 18-month-old

Table 12 Examples of gestures observed in 1- to 2-year-old children, categorized according to function

Object signs	Sniffing gesture for "flower"; panting for "dog"; arms stretched out for "aeroplane"
Requests	Smacks lips, to show wants food; knob turning gesture, to show wants out through door; up–down movement of hands, to show wants play piano
Attributes	Blows, to indicate "hot"; raises arms, to indicate "big"; waves hands back and forth, to indicate "many"
Reply	Opens palms, meaning "I don't know," or also shrug of shoulders
Events	Waving one hand (=bye-bye) when someone leaves; clapping to stand for baseball games

Source: Adapted from Acredolo & Goodwyn (1988)

children when confronted by three novel toys. Novelty means uncertainty, and not surprisingly most children looked at the mother after each of the toys was first produced. The mothers, having been carefully instructed beforehand, then posed either a smiling or a fearful or a neutral expression, the experimenter's interest being in the extent to which the child's subsequent behavior appeared to be influenced by the mother's emotional reaction. The results indicate that such influence was indeed at work, becoming more marked over the three trials: when the mother's face showed joy the children moved away from her and closer to the toy; when she showed fear they withdrew from the toy towards the mother; and when her expression was neutral they assumed an intermediate position.

It is clear from studies such as this that social referencing provides an important avenue for the communication of feeling, and that it becomes particularly useful in situations of uncertainty. As Feinman (1982) has stressed, it is not a form of imitation: the child looks to the adult for cues as to how to interpret the situation, but these cues are integrated into the child's own understanding of the event and so do not necessarily involve identical reaction. Social referencing is, moreover, selective: though mothers and fathers may be equally used for this purpose (Hirshberg & Svejda, 1990), a person who is not a customary source of security is unlikely to exert such influence. It is thus an active mental process whereby the child attempts to make sense of the world and uses trusted adults for this purpose. According to Bretherton (1984) social referencing involves a form of mental sharing and indicates that young children are able to see other human beings as having a psychological as well as a physical presence; it is one of the earliest signs that children impute mental states to others and are thus developing a "theory of mind," However that may be, what is apparent is that once again the ability to combine object and person and the information emanating from each separate source into one integrated course of action underlies this development, making possible a much more deliberate and complex response compared with that of the younger infant who reacts only to the person *or* the object.

The Emergence of Language

Sometime around the middle of the second year another profoundly important milestone is reached when children first become capable of symbolic representation. As Piaget (1950) has so carefully documented, from then on children no longer function entirely at the level of overt actions performed on concrete objects; instead these actions and objects can be represented internally in symbolic form. Of the various manifestations of this new capacity the use of language as a set of shared symbols is the most prominent, and henceforth social exchanges increasingly assume the form of conversations. Not that children are incapable of verbalizations before then; however, the isolated words that appear in most children at the end of the first year are not used as yet as *representations* of the objects to which they refer: when children see the object they produce the name in an associative manner but cannot generate it in the absence of the object. Verbal labels, according to Piaget (1951), are merely "semi-signs" at that time; only from the middle of the second year on will children discover that the label can be differentiated from its referent, act as its substitute, and be used for communicative purposes. The sudden spurt in vocabulary growth which takes place at that time (Goldfield & Reznick, 1990) may well be connected with that discovery.

The ease and speed with which children acquire language from the second year on is most impressive. What remains uncertain is how they do so; in particular, the extent to which the development of language is dependent on other people's actions is a matter of much debate (Kuczaj, 1986). That other people do play some part is obvious: after all, children brought up by English-speaking parents learn to speak English while those brought up by Chinese-speaking parents learn Chinese. Imitation thus clearly plays some part. However, more controversially it has also been proposed that the most significant and, initially at least, the sole settings in which the child is exposed to language are the dyadic get-togethers of the child with a sensitive adult who is prepared to take a number of actions regarded as crucial to language acquisition, and that language development is therefore crucially dependent on certain kinds of social input.

We can refer to these dyadic sessions as *joint involvement episodes* (or JIEs for short), and consider them as the principal context for socialization in the early years (Schaffer, 1989, 1992). In JIEs the two participants, adult and child, pay joint attention to, and jointly act upon, some specific topic. The topic may be an object, a toy, or another environmental feature, though as children grow older topics are increasingly likely to assume a symbolic, mainly verbal form and the JIE then becomes a conversation. The assumption is that when a child has plentiful opportunity to experience such intimate one-to-one involvements with an adult, and when that adult is prepared to be sensitive to the child's needs, requirements, and abilities, it becomes possible for the child to try out the first attempts at communication and obtain the necessary support and feedback for further progress.

There are a number of studies which indicate that the amount of children's involvement in JIEs is correlated with various indices of their language growth. For instance, Tomasello and Todd (1983) videotaped mother–child dyads periodically at home in a play situation, beginning at the child's first birthday and continuing for six months, and found that the amount of time spent by the dyads in JIEs over this period was an excellent predictor of children's vocabulary growth. Children, that is, who spent more time in joint interaction with their mothers developed larger vocabularies, and while cause-and-effect statements cannot easily be derived from correlations a number of lines of evidence produced by the authors support the argument that these episodes did have a facilitative effect on the child's early language development. A similar finding comes from a study by Wells (1985; Ellis & Wells, 1980), based on a large number of preschool children from whom speech samples were periodically obtained at home by means of radio microphones and related to the particular settings in which they occurred. A significant relationship was found between the rate of language development at $2\frac{1}{2}$ years and the proportion of speech addressed by the mother to the child in such contexts of shared activity as joint book-reading, talking, play, or doing housework together. These and other studies support the hypothesis that the amount children become involved in joint interactions with the parent has a direct bearing on the development of their language competence – a relationship receiving further support from studies of twins who must share the mother's attention and who, in the initial stages at any rate, tend to lag behind in language acquisition.

The case of language development in twins

Studies of twins have pointed to two conclusions: first, that the language development of such children is well behind that of singletons, and second that twins have fewer opportunities for verbal exchanges with their parents (e.g. Lytton, Conway, & Sauve, 1977; Bornstein & Ruddy, 1984). The latter has been regarded as responsible for the former. This is illustrated in a study by Tomasello, Manule, & Kruger (1986) in which 6 pairs of twins and 12 singletons, all in their second year, were observed at home with their mothers. Language tests showed that the twins scored lower on all measures. What was also found, as shown in table 13, was that the language learning environment was very different for twins. When one compares the first two columns of the table it is apparent, first, that the total amount of speech addressed by mothers to individual twins in one-to-one situations was far less than that addressed by mothers to singleton children, second that episodes of joint attention (JIEs) took up but a fraction of the time for individual twins compared with singletons, and third that the talk to twins was considerably more directive in nature. In short, the conditions to acquire language were much less favorable for the twins – a situation little

changed when one also takes into account the mothers' speech addressed to both twins simultaneously.

These results, according to Tomasello et al., are not due to any special characteristics of the mothers or the children but reflect rather "the nature of the twin situation and the special demands placed on the mother in such triadic interactions, where she has to allocate finite resources and divide them between two children." It has often been found that first born children develop language skills at a faster rate than later born children – presumably because the mother can devote herself entirely to one child. Yet even in a family containing several siblings it is easier for the mother to allocate attention when each child is at a different developmental level and thus has different needs and requirements. When two (or more!) children are at the same level they are likely to be treated as a unit and thus experience fewer one-to-one interactions. What is more, given the additional stress on the mother of caring for twins it is perhaps not surprising that her speech becomes controlling rather than eliciting in nature, and is thus characterized by a style that has been found less conducive to language learning.

Table 13 Speech addressed to singletons and to twins

	To singleton	To individual twin	To individual twin plus to both
No. of maternal utterances	198.5	94.9	141.0
Maternal directives (%)	33.0	62.0	69.0
Time spent in joint attention (seconds)	594.0	57.0	208.0

Source: Adapted from Tomasello et al. (1986)

If one-to-one interactive situations do play a vital role in the child's acquisition of language, it becomes necessary to specify more closely the precise processes within such situations that are responsible. Adults may play a supportive role, but just how do they do so? Various suggestions have been advanced, of which the following are the most noteworthy:

(1) *Adopting "helpful" speech styles* As already mentioned, the general style of child-directed speech which individual adults adopt appears to be related to children's linguistic progress. A highly directive style, particularly one where the adult deliberately sets out to "teach" the child to speak, actually interferes with language development (K. Nelson, 1973; Olsen-Fulero, 1982). A mother, on the other hand, who is willing to listen, watch, and interpret the child's behavior, who follows rather than leads and who (paradoxically) is tolerant of her child's "wrong" words is thereby likely to facilitate vocabulary growth – presumably because the child is thereby *motivated* to participate in verbal exchanges and not discouraged by continuous attempts at correction (C. Howe, 1981).

(2) *Use of attention eliciting techniques* Among efforts to specify more precisely the nature of the parent's input that facilitates children's language growth, a series of studies by Bornstein (1985; Tamis-LeMonda & Bornstein, 1989; Vibbert & Bornstein, 1989) are noteworthy. The particular aspect of behavior singled out in these studies was the mothers' encouragement of their children's attention to objects and events in the environment by, for instance, pointing, naming an object, or demonstrating how something works. Individual differences among mothers in the frequency with which they engage in such activities were found to be closely related to various measures of children's language comprehension and production in the second year – a relationship not dependent on the overall frequency of social exchange between mother and child or on the amount of mothers' talk in general. It seems that the efforts of the mothers to elicit their children's attention have a specific use in making the representational nature of language more salient to the child. By incorporating the words in shared activities the child learns that the words stand for things and, more specifically, which words stand for which things.

(3) *Timing of verbal input*   There is a general tendency for the mothers of language learning children to carefully time their talk about objects to coincide with the child's interest in the object (Collis, 1977; Messer, 1978). Such close synchronization of verbal input (in particular supplying the name of the object) with the child's focus of attention gives the child the best opportunity to extract from the situation information about the relationship between word and referent; it can therefore be expected to facilitate vocabulary growth. There are several indications that this is so. For example, M. Harris, Jones, Brooks, and Grant (1986) compared maternal speech to two groups of 2-year-old children, one showing a normal and the other a slow rate of language development. Particularly notable among the differences found was the fact that mothers of slow children made fewer references to objects which were currently attended to by the child, as well as more references to objects not being attended to. Similarly Tomasello and Farrar (1986), when examining the speech of mothers to children aged 15 to 21 months in the context of joint attention, found that individual differences in the mothers' timing of references to objects currently being attended to by the child were positively correlated with the size of the child's vocabulary at 21 months. It seems likely that these differences reflect variations among mothers in sensitivity and that they account for the variation in children's language development. Such a causal link cannot, of course, be definitely proven by studies such as these. However, it is made more likely by findings from a study by Dunham, Dunham, & Curwin (1993) in which an experimenter taught 18-month-old children novel words either when the child's attention was already spontaneously on the relevant object or when it was elsewhere and therefore had first to be switched to the object. By such experimental manipulation it was possible to show that the former strategy was more successful than the latter. Starting where the child is, and providing verbal input carefully timed to coincide with the child's interest, appears therefore to be an important ingredient to early language acquisition.

(4) *Involvement in formats*   According to Bruner (1983) continuity between preverbal and verbal communication is based on the child's participation in "formats." These are the standardized, oft-repeated routines of which the infant–adult games that we have already discussed are the best example. Such preverbal formats contain a number of design features which they share with language, and it is Bruner's belief that frequent involvement in them in infancy gives the child the opportunity to learn these features early on and thus enter the world of language with ease. For example, formats such as games are composed of a set of constituent acts which occur in definite sequences but can be varied within limits – a characteristic shared with the grammatical ordering of sentences. Formats are systematically arranged according to such rules as turn-taking – a further feature which the child can transfer to participation in verbal exchanges. And game formats also provide children with the opportunity of learning to attend to whole sequences of acts all of which refer to the same topic – again a skill required in conversations. Thus the common features of preverbal and verbal communication, as supported by routinized and

familiar settings, are said to provide the child with a great deal of language-relevant knowledge long before speech becomes a possibility. By providing formats such as games parents can show children that certain kinds of order exist in these early interchanges; with the appearance of language the child is primed to find order in verbal communication too. Bruner's argument is an interesting one; let us note, however, that it is based entirely on analogy: whether participation in early preverbal formats is a *necessary* condition for language acquisition, as Bruner suggests, is not established.

(5) *Speaking motherese*   In talking to young children adults quite automatically adjust the manner of their speech to the child's ability to comprehend. The style of such adult-to-child speech has been referred to as "motherese" – misleadingly so, as it is not only mothers but virtually anyone who will adopt it when confronted by a young child. Motherese has many features, referring to syntactic, semantic, pragmatic, and phonological aspects, some of which are listed in table 14. In sum, they make speech to children simpler, briefer, more repetitive, and more attention-worthy than speech to adults, and the extent of such fine-tuning varies according to the child's age (or more precisely, linguistic stage): parents, that is, speak at the level their children can comprehend and with remarkable sensitivity adjust their speech according to the child's progress (Sokolov, 1993). Whether they thereby actually *teach*

Table 14   Some features of "motherese"

Phonological characteristics
   Clear enunciation
   Higher pitch
   Exaggerated intonation
   Slower speech
   Longer pauses

Syntactic characteristics
   Shorter utterance length
   Sentences well formed
   Fewer subordinate clauses

Semantic characteristics
   Limited range of vocabulary
   "Baby talk" words
   Reference mainly to here-and-now

Pragmatic characteristics
   More directives
   More questions
   More attention devices
   Repetition of child's utterances

children to speak is more problematic. Although motherese is found in most cultures it is not universal: it is, for example, not used by parents in one particular Mayan society and yet children there acquire language normally (Pye, 1986). For that matter, the speech of depressed mothers to children lacks some of the features of motherese; these children too do not appear to be handicapped thereby (Bettes, 1988). On the other hand it is noteworthy that features of motherese such as simplifying, exaggeration, and slowing can be found even in mothers' signing to deaf children – again, presumably, in order to make easier the communicative task of such children (Masataka, 1993). It may be that motherese facilitates language learning but is not necessary for it. Probably its most important characteristic is that it is attention-worthy – a conclusion substantiated by the finding that even 2-day-old infants already prefer to listen to it as opposed to adult-directed speech (Cooper & Aslin, 1990).

That parents can make language meaningful and its acquisition pleasurable cannot be doubted. What is much less certain is whether involvement in social interactions of a particular kind (e.g. Bruner's formats) are a *necessary* condition to language acquisition. Again cross-cultural findings are useful here. The Kaluli of Papua New Guinea rarely engage their infants in dyadic communicative interchanges: their mothers treat them as "having no understanding" and thus tend not to address them verbally. Even later on, when mothers do begin to talk to their children, they do not use motherese but rather a highly directive style consisting mainly of "one-liners" that do not call for any verbal response. Yet despite the lack of one-to-one verbal experience and of adult sensitivity in adapting verbal input to the child Kaluli children become speakers of their language within the normal range of development (Schieffelin & Ochs, 1983).

The push to communicate with others is intense: where there is a handicap, such as deafness, children will overcome it by finding means other than verbal ones; where cultural concepts of infants preclude giving much verbal experience language development still takes place. Above all children want to relate to others; language is one means of doing so, and children therefore work hard at making sense of others' verbal messages and at learning to convey their own. There are ways of socially facilitating such development; however, it is also increasingly likely that there are diverse pathways into the linguistic community and that one must be wary of considering any one as the "right" one.

Attachment: Nature and Development

Defining and Characterizing Attachment

The ability to form relationships has been a major focus of study in developmental psychology; work on the child's first relationship in particular has become an important growth area in recent years. That relationship is generally referred to as an *attachment*, which we can formally define as a *long-enduring, emotionally meaningful tie to a particular individual*. The object of the attachment is generally someone (most often a parent) who returns the child's feelings, creating a tie that can be extremely powerful and emotionally laden in both directions.

Let us also note at the outset that a distinction is generally made between *attachment*, the behavioral system within the individual which organizes the child's feelings towards the other person, and *attachment behavior*, the overt means of expressing those feelings. The former can, of course, only be deduced from the latter. In addition, a distinction has also sometimes been made between attachment as a system existing *within* individuals and attachment relationships which exist dyadically *between* individuals.

Attachments in young children are characterized by the following features:

1 They are *selective*, i.e. they are focused on specific individuals who elicit attachment behavior in a manner and to an extent which is not found in interactions with other people.
2 They involve *physical proximity seeking*, i.e. an effort is made to maintain closeness to the object of attachment.
3 They provide *comfort and security*, these being the result of achieving proximity to the attachment object.
4 They produce *separation distress* when the tie is severed and proximity cannot be obtained.

Proximity seeking is at the heart of attachment. It is the most obvious overt manifestation in young children, and though subsequently the attachment system becomes a vastly more complex network of sentiments, feelings, attitudes, and beliefs its evolutionary and developmental basis is, quite simply, the need to be near the parent. The biological significance of such a motive in helpless and immature individuals is clear: care, protection, and security are guaranteed thereby, at least if the parent reciprocates the child's feelings. The attachment object thus functions as a safe haven from which the child may venture forth to explore the environment and to which it can return in the face of uncertainty and danger. Emotional bonds between infant and parent, based on proximity seeking, are to be found in all higher animal species whose young are initially in a relatively helpless state and thus in need of care and protection. This is most vividly seen in the phenomenon of *imprinting*, the process of attachment formation found in certain species of birds which we described in chapter 1.

Bowlby's Theory

The most comprehensive and influential account of attachment formation is that given by John Bowlby (1969, 1973, 1980). It is based on concepts derived from a number of sources such as psychoanalysis, information theory, and control theory, but above all it is influenced by ethology, with its emphasis on the evolutionary origins and biological purposes of behavior. However, while most ethological work had previously concerned itself with relatively simple behavior patterns in animals, Bowlby extended it to encompass far more complex functions involving the development of social relationships in humans.

The young child, according to Bowlby, is "biologically biased" to develop attachments to its caretakers by virtue of its genetic endowment. A close bond with the caretaker, particularly in the distant past of the history of humanity when predators spelled real danger, ensures survival; its importance to the species is thus every bit as great as that of such other inborn behavior systems as feeding and mating. For the sake of survival the infant must therefore be equipped with the means of bringing about and maintaining the parent's proximity, these taking the form of attachment responses such as crying, clinging, and following. These will, of course, only be effective if the parent reciprocates the child's behavior, hence the development of a parental attachment system that emerged in complementary fashion in the course of evolution. Nowadays we may no longer be plagued by predators, but attachment behavior continues to be activated by perceived danger, just as it is terminated by perceived safety. The *biological* function of attachment is thus the protection of the young; the *psychological* function is to provide security. Accordingly infants are genetically "wired" to maintain proximity to the mother and to signal to her for attention and help at times of distress, and mothers for their part are programmed to respond to such signals.

In the course of the first two years in particular attachments go through some marked developmental changes. Bowlby has proposed a four-stage framework for viewing these changes, outlined in table 15, which shows how the character of attachments develops as behavior becomes increasingly organized, flexible and intentional. Initially infants display a range of diverse responses, which Bowlby grouped under two headings:

1   *signaling behavior*, i.e. crying, smiling, and babbling;
2   *approach behavior*, i.e. clinging, following, and reaching.

Such behavior is at first purely indiscriminate: for instance, the smiling response, as we previously saw, is elicited by *any* human being in the early weeks. What unites the responses is their biological function: from the beginning all serve to promote proximity to the parent. By bringing the infant close to a protective caretaker they make the provision of comfort and security more likely.

In due course infants come to distinguish their regular caretakers from other people, and as a result familiar people will elicit attachment responses more readily and more intensely than strangers. Yet the change is not a profound one: it is based on perceptual recognition alone and infants remain indiscriminate in accepting care and attention from anyone. It is not till the third quarter of the first year that

Table 15 Phases of the development of attachment

Name	Age range (months)	Principal features
1 Pre-attachment	0–2	Indiscriminate social responsiveness
2 Attachment-in-the-making	2–7	Recognition of familiar people
3 Clear-cut attachment	7–24	Separation protest; wariness of strangers; intentional communication
4 Goal-corrected partnership	24 on	Relationships more two-sided: children understand parents' needs

unequivocal indications of full-blown attachments appear: for one thing, the diverse attachment responses now become focused on certain specific individuals only; for another, unfamiliar people are likely to be greeted with wariness or even fear. Separation upset appears at this age, i.e. the infant protests at the absence of attachment figures and so shows that an *enduring* bond has come into existence. From this point on caretakers are no longer interchangeable; the child is now capable of forming interpersonal relationships, and attachment responses are henceforth organized into coherent attachment systems focused on particular individuals.

Once attachment relationships have emerged they undergo further change which takes place largely in tandem with cognitive developments. Children become increasingly sophisticated in their ability to behave intentionally, plan their actions in the light of goals and take into account the feelings and goals of the other person. They now form what Bowlby referred to as *goal-corrected partnerships*: crying, for example, is no longer a purely automatic reaction to some internal state; instead it can be used deliberately with the specific aim of summoning the mother, and can be expressed flexibly in that the child adjusts its intensity according to the mother's nearness and reaction. If one kind of attachment response does not succeed then the child can substitute another: calling, crying, following are all interchangeable means to be employed for the sake of the same goal. The child, Bowlby suggests, functions like a *control system*, that is, an apparatus that serves to bring about some end wired into the machine, tests out whether that end has been achieved or not, and on the basis of feedback information then makes a new attempt should this be necessary. A thermostat, set to bring about and maintain a particular temperature, is a very simple type of control system; the child is a vastly more complex example in that it can use many different types of attempts to bring about the goal and, moreover, can reflect upon them and consciously change them. In either case, however, the system takes account, first, of the wired-in goal (a certain temperature in one case; the mother's proximity in the other), second, of whatever feedback information is available about the external state of events (the actual temperature; the mother's whereabouts), and third, of the discrepancy between goal and reality, and then takes action accordingly in order to reduce the discrepancy. Thus attachment shifts from a reliance on very simple, automatically activated reactions to any adult to an increasingly complex, goal-corrected system aimed at specific, differentiated individuals.

One further development, which has received increasing attention from research workers in recent years and to which we shall refer in more detail below, concerns what Bowlby referred to as *internal working models*. As children become capable, from about the second year on, of representing the world to themselves in symbolic form, they form models of themselves, of significant others and of the relationships they have with these others. Such models are increasingly used to guide the child's actions; they enable it to anticipate the other person's behavior and plan an appropriate line of response. Internal working models are built up on the basis of experience vis-à-vis particular attachment figures and reflect the quality of the relationship with that figure. A warm, accepting mother will give rise to an internal working model in the child which depicts the mother as a source of security and support; as a result the child will expect the mother to be predictably available as a haven of safety and develop positive emotions towards her. Such expectations are then likely to be transferred to other people. Once formed, therefore, the model is imposed like a template on to new interactions; if, however, experience repeatedly disconfirms the child's expectations (because, say, the quality of the mother's relationship changes for the worse) the model will need to be adapted and reformed.

Internal working models, according to Bowlby, are constructed of all important aspects of the world. None, however, are as important as those involving the child's interpersonal relationships. This is especially so because the child's model of the self is built up through such relationships. A punitive, rejecting mother will leave the child with a sense of failure and lack of worth: if the self is not acceptable in the eyes of the attachment figure the experience will have negative impact on the way in which the child construes its own image. Thus the working models of self and attachment figures develop in complementary fashion, and the attachment relationship consequently has psychological implications well beyond the relationship itself.

Onset of the First Attachment Relationships

Empirical investigations, mostly under the influence of Bowlby's theory, have paid particular attention to the first emergence of the attachment relationship. There is general agreement as to when this occurs and much has also been learned about the way in which the relationship manifests itself during its earliest stages.

The most clear-cut criterion for determining that a young child has formed an attachment to a particular person is to see what happens when the child is separated from that individual and put in the care of others. In the early stages of attachment formation the child has little capacity as yet for tolerating separation; frequent confirmation of the mother's whereabouts is required and prevention from attaining the mother's proximity, particularly in unfamiliar situations, is therefore a stressful experience giving rise to distress and efforts to regain the mother by crying and searching. At the same time other people's attention is refused: the child shows that people in general are not interchangeable and that attachment behavior has come to be focused on certain individuals only.

Using the criterion of *separation distress*, there are indications that children first become capable of missing the absent person at around 7 or 8 months. Observations of children admitted to hospital (Schaffer, 1958), left in everyday separation situations such as with an unfamiliar babysitter (Schaffer & Emerson, 1964a) or separated from the mother in a laboratory setting (Kotelchuk, Zelazo, Kagan, & Spelke, 1975) all agree that up to that age infants show no orientation to the missing mother and are content with the care of even unfamiliar people. From the third quarter of the first year on, however, separation distress is evident; the infant no longer merely responds to the mother when she is physically present but actively seeks her when she is not. At about the same time fear of strangers first emerges: unknown individuals are no longer greeted indiscriminately but treated warily or even actively avoided (figure 8).

An important milestone of social development is thus to be found in the third quarter of the first year. Up to that point infants are by and large indiscriminate;

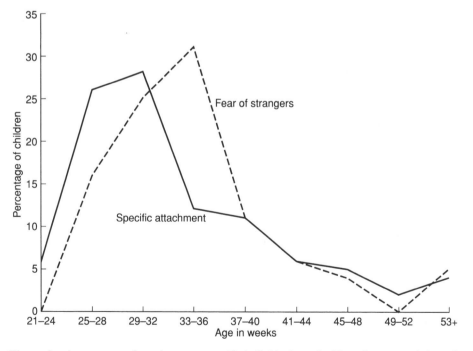

Figure 8   Age at onset of attachment to specific individuals, and of fear of strangers (adapted from Schaffer & Emerson, 1964a)

caretakers are not missed when absent. It is only from about 7 or 8 months that infants seek the proximity of just certain individuals and show wariness and proximity avoidance of others. Attaining this milestone appears to be relatively independent of experience, for there is remarkable similarity across a wide range of cultures and child rearing practices in the age when separation distress first appears (Konner, 1982). Children blind from birth, as well as those reared in day nurseries during infancy and so having relatively limited contact with the mother, also reach this milestone at comparable ages. The subsequent course and behavioral manifestations of these functions may differ according to the finer details of child rearing, but not their age at onset, which appears to be maturationally determined.

We know little about what goes on in the central nervous system that can account for children suddenly becoming capable of forming focused relationships to others. We do know, however, that such a capacity requires certain cognitive prerequisites: in particular children must have developed, first of all, a *recognition memory*, enabling them perceptually to differentiate the attachment figure from other people, and second, the notion of *object permanence*, which makes it possible for the child to form relationships that endure over time.

Recognition memory develops very early on, though just how early depends largely on the sensory modality of the infant which one examines for signs of recognition – vision, smell, or hearing. The literature on *visual* recognition is far from unanimous as to the age when infants first show signs of differentiating the mother from a stranger (C. A. Nelson & Ludemann, 1989), due largely to differences in the procedures and stimulus conditions employed by the various investigators. It does seem, however, that reliable visual discrimination, based on the whole face, is not possible before about 3 months. On the other hand, recognition based on *smell* is evident much earlier on. By holding a pad on each side of an infant's face, one pad containing breast milk from the mother and the other breast milk from another woman, Macfarlane (1975) was able to show that by the age of 6 days most infants were able to discriminate one from the other. They did so by turning towards the mother's pad; in so far as young infants prefer the familiar to the unfamiliar they showed thereby that they recognized the mother's odor and turned towards it. Two-day-old infants, on the other hand, showed no such discrimination; evidence of learning had not yet appeared. As far as *hearing* is concerned, such evidence is, astonishingly, to be found at even earlier ages, i.e. as soon as one can test for it in newborn babies. In a series of studies by DeCasper and his colleagues (e.g. DeCasper & Fifer, 1980; DeCasper & Spence, 1986; DeCasper et al., 1994) it emerged that newborn babies were able to discriminate the mother's voice from that of another female. As the infants had had only a few hours of contact with the mother their learning must either have taken place very rapidly immediately after birth or occurred in the womb. In so far as the auditory apparatus of the fetus is already functioning in the last weeks of pregnancy the possibility of prenatal learning must be taken seriously – a view that is reinforced by DeCasper's further finding that fetuses who had heard the mother repeatedly recite a particular nursery rhyme over a four-week period were able to discriminate that rhyme from another, unfamiliar one when audiotapes of both were played through the mother's abdomen. Learning while still in the womb, one must conclude, appears to be a definite possibility.

Recognition memory involves the ability to compare perceptual input with a stored representation and is therefore a fairly sophisticated cognitive skill, yet one that can appear very early in life. Just how early seems to depend on the sensory modality involved; in any case it is evident long before the onset of focused attachments. Merely being able to recognize the mother does not mean a "real" relationship has been formed to her yet; for that other prerequisites are required.

Object permanence is one such prerequisite. This is the ability to remain aware of an object even in its absence. As Piaget (1954) showed, initially infants behave on the basis of "out of sight, out of mind": in an object hiding test they will show no orientation to the object the moment it is no longer perceptually present (see figure 9). It is not till they reach Piaget's sensorimotor stage IV, usually at around 8 months, that they become capable of searching for the missing object, thereby demonstrating that they remain oriented to it despite its absence. *Person permanence* involves the same ability but as shown towards another human being; it too may be assessed by means of hiding tests. There is some disagreement as to whether or not person permanence precedes the appearance of object permanence (S. M. Bell, 1970; Jackson, Campos, & Fischer, 1978); in any case, the third quarter of the first year is indicated as the crucial period for its emergence and it is also then, as we have seen, that separation distress first becomes evident – a behavior which also indicates the child's ability to miss the absent person.

Knowledge that people continue to exist when they are out of sight is clearly critical to the establishment of enduring relationships with them. The child must be able to count on the other person to be continuously available and not to suddenly disappear entirely from its life. Recognizing an individual is not enough; this refers merely to the ability to differentiate familiar from unfamiliar persons while they are present. Person permanence, on the other hand, is based on a rather more sophisti-

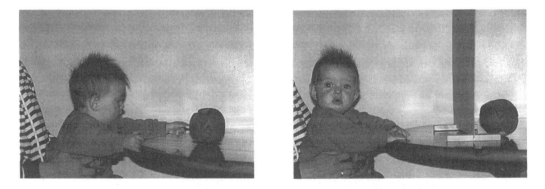

Figure 9 "Out of sight, out of mind": 6–month–old child in object hiding test

cated cognitive ability, namely *recall memory*, i.e. the ability to spontaneously retrieve a central representation of an absent person or object. Recognition develops before recall; the spontaneous access to the memory store implied by the latter process does not appear until several months after the former. Both are prerequisites to the formation of focused attachments; no wonder that these are not in evidence until both cognitive processes are in place.

Fear of strangers too depends on cognitive developments (Schaffer, 1966, 1974). There is some dispute as to how common such a reaction is in infants (Rheingold & Eckerman, 1973), but this reflects the considerable variability in the manifestation of the response. In part this depends on how the other person behaves: the more the stranger encroaches on the infant and the more speedily this is done the more likely it is that fear will be evoked (Morgan & Ricciuti, 1969). In part it depends also on the looks of the stranger: by comparing infants' reactions to unfamiliar adults, midgets, and children Brooks and Lewis (1976) were able to demonstrate that it is facial appearance more than height that causes wariness, for the infants showed as much negative affect to the midgets as to the adults yet behaved positively to other children. And finally it also depends to a considerable extent on the child's temperamental characteristics: a genetically influenced trait, variously labeled "shyness" or "inhibition," accounts for much of the variability among young children in their response to strangers (Kagan, Reznick, & Snidman, 1987). In general, however, there is a tendency from about 7 or 8 months for infants to no longer respond positively to all strangers. The initial reaction to the sight of an unfamiliar person is one of wariness rather than fear, i.e. the infant ceases all activity while closely watching the other person (Schaffer, 1974). Presumably a process of cognitive appraisal goes on during this interval, depending on which the infant may then either relax and even approach the stranger or, on the contrary, show fear and withdraw. The ability *not* immediately to approach unfamiliar people is thus another achievement characterizing children's early social development.

The case of infantile autism

Some children, it appears, are constitutionally incapable of forming an attachment at all. They suffer from the syndrome of infantile autism, a condition characterized above all by a severe impairment in the ability to form social relationships.

Autism was first described by Kanner (1943), who was especially struck by the tendency of affected children to avoid all eye contact with other people. In addition autistic children do not cuddle or respond to affection and have prob-lems in communicating with others. In some there is a complete failure to develop language; in others speech may be delayed or never progress beyond two- or three-word sentences; while in still others various linguistic abnormalities occur such as a confusion between "you" and "I" or echolalia (the exact repetition of others' speech). There may also be such other symptoms as repetitive movements, a resistance to change, and an obsessive insistence on sameness (Howlin & Yule, 1990).

Kanner regarded autistic children as having an "innate inability to form the usual, biologically provided affective contact with people." He thus drew attention to an inborn predisposition to form social relationships which is missing in these children. The unfortunate suggestion, advanced at one time, that the condition is due to parental lack of affection has turned out to be quite without foundation: there is no evidence that parents are in any way responsible. The precise cause has yet to be located; there is, however, general agreement now that autism has an organic, possibly genetic, base and that children are *born* unable to form normal social attachments (Bishop, 1993).

Object Choice

To whom do infants become attached? According to Bowlby (1969) there is an inbuilt bias – *monotropism*, as he referred to it – initially to form an attachment to just a single person, normally the mother. All other attachments appear only subsequently and will be of minor significance compared with the basic one. Thus by nature infants are said to be incapable of forming more than one emotionally meaningful relationship at first, and any child care arrangement that involves more than one principal caregiver is likely to be harmful. The uniqueness of the mother–child unit is thus given prominence by this argument.

There is in fact no empirical support for the concept of monotropism. As soon as infants become capable of forming focused attachments they can direct them to several individuals. Of 60 infants studied throughout the first 18 months by Schaffer and Emerson (1964a) almost one-third directed their initial attachments to more than one person, some even selecting as many as five. By 18 months the majority were attached to several individuals. While the mother was by far the most frequently so selected, the importance which others came to assume in these infants' lives, with particular reference to fathers, was also very evident (see table 16). Although the most intense attachment was generally formed to the mother, this was by no means inevitable: fathers especially were also found to be the child's principal attachment figure, even when they were available for only a limited part of the day.

Others (e.g. L. J. Cohen & Campos, 1974; Lamb, 1977) have confirmed that as soon as infants become socially discriminative they establish attachments with several individuals simultaneously. As the anthropologist Margaret Mead (1962) once pointed out, this is all to the good: it means that in those societies where life is precarious the child is "insured" for possible loss of the mother, for there will be greater continuity of care arrangements and less likelihood of trauma when other familiar caretakers are immediately available. There is certainly no biological necessity for parenting to be confined to one person; the strict division of labor, whereby child care was wholly assigned to women, no longer prevails as it did at one time; fathers especially are far more involved in the rearing of their children and, largely due to the great increase of mothers going out to work, shared child care arrange-

Table 16   Percentage of infants forming attachments to particular individuals

Individual	At onset of attachment	At age 18 months
Mother	95	81
Father	30	75
Grandparent	11	45
Other relative	8	44
Sibling	2	24
Other child	3	14

Source: Adapted from Schaffer & Emerson (1964a)

ments have become common. What is more, cross-cultural data also help to put the issue in perspective: as Weisner and Gallimore (1977) point out, amongst all human societies on whom we have relevant data mothers function as exclusive caretakers of their children in only 3 percent and as predominant caretakers in only 60 percent of societies. There is no indication from investigations conducted in these societies (such as that illustrated in the case of the Efe pygmies) that shared care is diluted care, that it will lead to a weakening of the tie with the mother and that it must therefore be regarded as psychologically damaging.

The case of the Efe pygmies

In a series of reports Tronick and Morelli (e.g. Tronick, Morelli, & Winn, 1987; Morelli & Tronick, 1992) have provided some vivid descriptive data about the child care arrangements found in a society very different from the Western norm. The Efe pygmies are a seminomadic people living in the forests of Zaire in central Africa, where they form bands of 6 to 50 members that are the primary community into which a child is born. During the first year or so infants experience multiple caretaking: for instance, while the mother is working other women will pick up a crying baby and comfort it by putting it to the breast, whether they are lactating or not. Only if this is not successful will the mother be fetched. Access to a breast is almost constant and on demand, and the infant is thus nearly con-

tinuously held in close bodily contact by any one of a number of women. Even when the mother is present she is not the sole caregiver: for example, the observers noted that in a one-hour session a 4-month-old was transferred nine times among six different people. The average number of caretakers for the group of infants as a whole was 14.2, with a range from 5 to 24. From the second year on the infant has a more focalized relationship with the mother, but it remains in the context of relationships with other familiar and willingly available individuals.

Given the life of the Efe there are many advantages to such a child care pattern. Amongst these Tronick and his colleagues list the increased likelihood of adoption should the mother die (and mortality rate there is high), the increased overall quality of care received, the relief of a busy mother from some caretaking chores, the greater sense of security of the infant and the wider and more varied social exposure which infants experience. There are few if any psychological costs: infants form multiple attachments and so acquire various sources of security; this helps in forming strong group identification which, in that environment, is highly adaptive.

Such comparative material illustrates well that a great range of child care practices are possible within the limits set by our biological make-up. The primary relationship need not be an exclusive one; the form it takes is fashioned by what is appropriate in each society, and the child's attachment development in turn will be shaped accordingly, again as suits that particular society.

Irrespective of how many attachment objects are chosen by a young child, what determines the choice of any one? On the whole it is easier to list factors that do *not* play any part than pinpoint those that do. For example:

1   Individuals other than the child's biological parents may be selected, e.g. adoptive parents (B. Tizard, 1977), day care staff (Goossens & van IJzendoorn, 1990), or the metapelet, i.e. the professional caretaker employed in an Israeli kibbutz to rear children (Sagi et al., 1985).

2   The main attachment figure need not be a female. Male (fathers in particular) can elicit strong attachments (L. J. Cohen & Campos, 1974) and may be just as competent at parenting as females (Schaffer, 1990). The individual's sex is thus irrelevant.

3   Satisfaction of the child's physical needs by, for example, the provision of food also plays no part in attachment choice. Individuals who have never participated in physical care routines may nevertheless elicit strong attachments (Schaffer & Emerson, 1964a).

4   Continuous daily care is yet another factor that one can exclude. Some minimum quantity of interaction is obviously required, but as studies of employed women have shown (e.g. Gottfried & Gottfried, 1988) a mother may be apart from her child for several hours each day and yet remain a source of security and comfort.

What does appear to matter in object choice is the *quality* of the interaction. The provision of fun and playful stimulation is one such qualitative aspect: individuals associated with this kind of interaction are sought after and missed when absent – hence the popularity of fathers. And another aspect is the sensitive responsiveness of the adult in relating to the child – a possibly important quality in determining the nature of attachments to which we shall return below.

Later Developments

In the post-infancy period a gradual decline occurs in the child's need for the proximity of attachment figures. Children can move further away in order to play and explore, remain out of eyesight for increasingly longer periods and show greater tolerance of separation. Rheingold and Eckerman (1970) demonstrated this trend over age when they recorded the distance children were prepared to move from the mother while playing out of doors: at one year the average distance observed was 6.9 meters, at 2 years 15.1 meters, at 3 years 17.3 meters and at 4 years 30.6 meters. The mother may remain a haven of safety, but it is not one in which the older child has to spend a major portion of its time. Curiosity about the outside world becomes an increasingly powerful motive; only when something frightening appears will the child retreat back to the mother and seek the reassurance of her presence.

The interplay of several behavioral systems is thereby illustrated. Increasingly the child's activities in social situations can be understood in terms of the way in which systems such as attachment, exploration, and wariness interact. The distinction between such systems, according to Bowlby (1969), rests less on their overt manifestations, for the same act may be employed in the service of any one of them, and much more so on the purpose, biological and individual, for which they are employed: proximity seeking, curiosity, and proximity avoidance respectively. Each system has its own genetically determined characteristics, but in the course of development children become capable of using each in increasingly flexible fashion and of coordinating them all into flexible overall plans.

The major reason why children are able to distance themselves more and more from the mother (or other attachment figure) is that cognitively they become sufficiently advanced to form mental representations of the mother which, so to speak, they carry with them and to which they can relate in her absence. Consider a 10-year-old's response to separation (in hospital, say, or in summer camp): such a child has no difficulty in visualizing the mother in the customary setting of home, can appreciate the temporary nature of the separation and is able to anticipate the eventual reunion. The 2-year-old, on the other hand, needs constant confirmation of the mother's whereabouts: such a child can tolerate brief separations (at least under benign circumstances) but the mental representation of the mother is not firm enough to withstand longer absences and requires frequent updating. Proximity seeking of the real mother remains an overriding goal; her symbolic representation has as yet limited use.

The development of attachments in the post-infancy period is thus closely linked to the formation of *internal working models*. As we saw above in the account of Bowlby's theory, these are gradually built up from the child's specific experiences with attachment figures; they come to represent the pertinent attributes of each and the kind of relationship that has developed with that individual. The following are their most salient characteristics (Main, Kaplan, & Cassidy, 1985):

1   Internal working models are mental representations that include emotional as well as cognitive components.
2   Once formed, they exist outside consciousness.

3   Their development is shaped by the outcomes of the infant's proximity seeking experiences.
4   Basic differences in the nature of working models exist between individuals whose proximity seeking attempts in infancy were consistently accepted and those whose proximity seeking was blocked or inconsistently accepted.
5   Internal working models after the first year tend to be stable but are by no means impervious to the influence of further relationship experiences.
6   The function of internal working models is to provide rules for the individual to guide both behavior and feeling in relation to significant others. They make it possible to forecast and interpret the other person's behavior and so plan one's own behavior in response.

We can conclude that the later course of attachments is shaped by three kinds of developments. In the first place, the attachment system comes increasingly to interact with other behavioral systems; instead of each functioning in isolation they will form organized wholes. For example, an infant when frightened will retreat; at a somewhat older age the child will retreat *to the mother* – proximity avoidance and proximity seeking become coordinated. In the second place, social activity is no longer played out on a wholly overt level in here-and-now situations; with the development of representational capacity children can regulate their actions according to both past experience of previous encounters and anticipation of future actions, as contained in their internal working models. And in the third place, children gradually become capable of taking account not only of their own aims and intentions but also of those of the other person; they can now appreciate that they share a relationship with that individual and thus form what Bowlby called a *goal-corrected partnership*.

Attachment: Individual Differences

The bulk of empirical research on attachments has been devoted to the investigation of qualitative aspects, with particular reference to the differences among young children in the *security* of their initial attachment relationship. Much of this work is due to Mary Ainsworth and her colleagues (1978) and their provision of a procedure, the "Strange Situation," whereby attachment security can be assessed.

Security–Insecurity

Ainsworth devised the Strange Situation as an experimental procedure which, by subjecting children to a series of relatively mild stresses, highlights their use of and feeling about the attachment object. The procedure consists of seven episodes (outlined in table 17) which take place in an unfamiliar room and which give observers the

Table 17   The Strange Situation

Episode	Persons present	Events
1	Mother, infant	Infant explores; mother watches
2	Mother, infant, stranger	Stranger enters; is first silent, then talks to mother, then plays with infant
3	Infant, stranger	Mother leaves. Stranger interacts with infant
4	Mother, infant	Mother returns and settles infant; stranger departs
5	Infant	Mother leaves. Infant alone
6	Infant, stranger	Stranger enters, interacts with infant
7	Mother, infant	Mother returns and settles infant; stranger departs

opportunity to describe the child's behavior alone with the mother (or other attachment figure), being confronted by a strange adult, being left with the stranger by the mother, being left entirely alone and being reunited with the mother. Each episode lasts about three minutes, though it can be curtailed if the child becomes too distressed. The focus is primarily on how the child deals with the cumulative stress and the use that is made of the mother in her presence and especially on reunion after one of the separation episodes.

According to Ainsworth, children's reactions to this situation can be classified into three basic attachment types: *secure* (type B), *insecure/avoidant* (type A) and *insecure/resistant* (type C). Table 18 gives further details. Thus the *securely attached* child plays happily while near the mother, does not have to check on her presence all the time, can use her as a safe base from which to explore, and will show positive interest in strangers. The *insecure/avoidant* child is relatively unaffected by the mother's whereabouts and ignores her when reunited after a separation, actively resisting attempts to be comforted and accepting attention as readily from the stranger as from the mother. The *insecure/resistant* child has much more difficulty in an unfamiliar situation, clinging to the mother and not exploring freely. Separation produces a lot more upset, and on reunion a mixture of contact seeking and contact resisting occurs in response to the mother.

These three types are considered to represent fundamental differences in the way in which social relationships are first established; in particular, the degree of security in the first attachment relationship is thought to be the most influential ingredient in the creation of children's internal working models of relationships generally and will thus help to shape all intimate interpersonal bonds formed by the individual in future years. The original threefold typology has been amended somewhat, first by introducing subdivisions into the existing categories and then by adding a fourth, completely new category referring to *insecure/disorganized* (type D) infants (Main &

Solomon, 1985). Most studies, however, are primarily concerned with the difference between secure and insecure children.

Type B (secure) children have generally been found to be the most common (about 65 percent in the majority of studies conducted in the United States). Perhaps this is as well, for they are said to represent the optimum in terms of mental health and developmental success. However, there are *cross-cultural variations* (van IJzendoorn & Kroonenberg, 1988), which have led some writers to question the meaning of the Strange Situation in societies other than the North American one and the values that we attach to the different categories. As seen in table 19, the most marked variations are to be found in the percentages classified into either of the two main insecurity categories. For example, Japanese children rarely fall into the avoidant category but are relatively frequently assessed as resistant. This could be because infants in Japan are almost continuously in contact with their mothers; the separations imposed on them in the Strange Situation would therefore be experienced as far more stressful and likely to result in the intense and inconsolable crying which is part of the specification of the avoidant category. One must therefore wonder whether Strange Situation findings tell us anything about the fundamental nature of Japanese children's attachments or whether they merely reflect the unusual demands of the particular setting in which they are assessed.

Table 18 Types of attachment security

Type	Behavior in Strange Situation
Securely attached	Child shows moderate level of proximity seeking to mother. Upset by her departure, greets her positively on reunion
Insecurely attached: avoidant	Child avoids contact with mother, especially at reunion after separation. Not greatly upset when left with stranger
Insecurely attached: resistant	Child greatly upset by separation from mother. On her return difficult to console; both seeks comfort and resists it

Table 19 Cross-cultural variation in distribution of attachment types

	Percentage of attachment type		
Country	Secure	Avoidant	Resistant
Great Britain	75	22	3
Japan	68	5	27
Germany	57	35	8
United States	65	21	14

The case of day care children's attachment

Controversy regarding the nature of Strange Situation behavior and the meaning one should attach to it has been particularly fierce with respect to children in day care. Much research has now been devoted to studying such children in order to ascertain whether daily separation from the mother is harmful and especially whether it weakens the bond with the mother. By and large the results have shown up no ill effects: provided certain conditions are met, with special reference to the stability and quality of the care received, children are not harmed by daily separations from the mother and may well benefit from them in certain respects (Schaffer, 1990).

There is, however, one exception, arising from work carried out by Belsky and Rovine (1988). These investigators concluded that there is a heightened risk of infants developing insecure attachments to the mother if the child has been in day care for at least four months beginning before the first birthday and for more than 20 hours per week. Under such conditions a child is more likely to show indications of emotional maladjustment as reflected in the relationship with the mother, and though a large number of the children at risk develop secure attachments those who do not do so represent a larger proportion of children than is found among children remaining at home.

If this is indeed the case there are consider-able implications for child care practice and policy. The problem is that the findings were exclusively obtained from one assessment technique, i.e. the Strange Situation, and there are those (e.g. Clarke-Stewart, 1989) who do not believe that this is an appropriate technique for children in day care. The Strange Situation is based on the assumption that repeated separation from the mother puts children under stress and thus highlights their security seeking attempts. Day care children, however, are used to such separations; they may therefore not experience stress, and when they respond to the mother's return in the Strange Situation with indifference they may be demonstrating independence and self-reliance, and not the "avoidance" and "resistance" that are responsible for getting them classified as insecurely attached.

We are thus confronted not with a difference in findings but with a difference in interpretation of findings. Is the day care infant's behavior in a reunion situation a sign of developmental precocity or of emotional disturbance? It is possible that the Strange Situation procedure is not psychologically equivalent for children of working and of nonworking mothers. If that is so it becomes even more important to ensure that any conclusions are based on a variety of assessment techniques and do not depend on just one that may involve the making of value judgments.

A further reservation concerns the possible role of the child's *temperament* on attachment classification: as Kagan (1982) has suggested, vulnerability to stress generally might account for observed differences in the Strange Situation rather than qualitative variations in attachment security. This question has been much debated (e.g. Lamb, Thompson, Gardner, & Charnov, 1985; Belsky & Rovine, 1987; B. E. Vaughn, Lefever, Seifer, & Barglow, 1989) but remains unsettled. It is unthinkable that an individual attribute as general as temperament would not affect behavior in any situation; on the other hand it may be no more than one influence among several. In this respect the finding that attachment classification may vary according to the adult with whom the child is observed is especially noteworthy, indicating that temperament cannot be a sole cause: relationship influences must also be taken into account.

The *stability* of attachment classification, both over time but with the same person and with different individuals but at the same time period, has received much attention. When a child lives in a stable, relatively stress-free family situation there is considerable stability in attachment classification, at least in the short term. Waters (1978) assessed children's behavior in the Strange Situation both at 12 months and at 18 months, and found that only 2 children out of 50 changed their security category. One of the drawbacks of the Strange Situation is that it is applicable only within a narrow age range, i.e. around the first half of the second year, and long-term stability is thus more difficult to assess. However, Main and Cassidy (1988), with the help of a variety of age-appropriate measures, rated children's attachment security at age 6 and found significant correlations with Strange Situation assessments previously obtained in the children's second year for the child–mother relationship; correlations for the child–father relationship were rather less impressive. On the other hand, B. Vaughn, Egeland, and colleagues (1979) found changes over time to be much more common in a sample of economically disadvantaged families, even though the period covered was only of six months duration. As a result of social stresses experienced by the families during this time (illness, unemployment, etc.) children were likely to change from the security category to one of the insecurity categories; absence of stress, however, did not necessarily result in a change in the reverse direction. A similar pattern of instability was uncovered by Thompson, Lamb, & Estes (1982) in a middle class group of families: in response to major changes in social circumstances, such as the mother taking on employment, children were likely to change their Strange Situation classification, the change taking place in either direction, i.e. from security to insecurity or vice versa. Only 53 percent of the children obtained the same attachment classification at 19 months as they had obtained at 12 months. Qualitative aspects of children's attachments are thus far from immune from outside events, at least in the early years; presumably parents are psychologically affected by these events and, if these take an undesirable form, become less responsive and sensitive to their children. The altered nature of the parent's interactions with the child may cause the latter to feel differently about the parent, which in turn will be reflected in the kind of Strange Situation behavior that leads to particular security classifications. It is not till after the preschool period, when internal working models become more firmly established and resistant to change, that stability becomes more marked.

On theoretical grounds stability of attachment classification *across persons* need not be expected, in so far as Ainsworth considered the classifications to reflect something about *relationships* and not about children. There is certainly no guarantee that a given child's attachments are all of the same quality: Israeli kibbutz children, reared primarily by a professional caretaker (metapelet), develop an attachment type to the metapelet that may bear little similarity to that shown to either the mother or the father; for that matter, the attachment type shown by different children to the same metapelet has been found to vary from one child to another (Sagi et al., 1985). Studies which have compared children's attachments to mother and father have come up with somewhat differing results. However, Fox, Kimmerly, and Schafer (1991), putting together all the data from 11 such reports, arrived at three conclusions:

- Infants classified as secure to one parent are unlikely to be classified as insecure to the other parent.
- The specific type of insecurity tends to be similar from one attachment object to another: an infant categorized as either resistant or avoidant with one parent is likely to receive a similar categorization with the other parent.
- Despite these statistically significant trends there is nevertheless a minority of instances where discordance is shown, either in the security-or-insecurity classification or in the resistant-or-avoidant classification.

It appears therefore that in a majority of cases one can expect children to have similar kinds of attachments to both parents – possibly because of similarity among the parents in their styles of interaction with the child, possibly also because of influences from the child (such as stable qualities of temperament) which consistently emerge in all social interactions. Nevertheless, concordance of attachment type across different relationships is not a *necessary* condition: whatever is measured in the Strange Situation is specific to particular relationships and reflects the nature and history of that relationship.

Antecedents: The Sensitivity Hypothesis

According to Ainsworth, the main reason for qualitative differences in children's attachments lies in the nature of their interactive experiences with the mother. In particular, she hypothesized that the extent to which attachments are characterized by security or insecurity is determined by the extent of the mother's sensitive responsiveness in handling the infant during the early months. Based on a longitudinal study of infants throughout the first year Ainsworth, Blehar, Waters, and Wahl (1978) showed that mothers who responded in a sensitive manner to their infants' signals in situations such as feeding, face-to-face play, physical contact, and distress episodes will have securely attached children; failure to provide such responsive handling will result in one of the two types of insecurity. Each attachment type is thus said to be associated with a particular kind of mothering:

- *Type B (secure)*   the mothers of these infants are easily able to pick up the child's signals and communications and respond to them promptly and appropriately. They are readily accessible to the child and are warm, cooperative, and accepting in all exchanges.

- *Type A (insecure/avoidant)*   these mothers tend to be psychologically unavailable, in that they are not tuned in to the child's signals and are withdrawn and neglectful. Their general style of interaction is marked by insensitivity and rejection.
- *Type C (insecure/resistant)*   the mothers of these infants tend also to be insensitive but in an inconsistent fashion, sometimes responding positively and at other times rejecting the child's bids for attention.

The proposed link between early maternal behavior and subsequent child attachment security (the "sensitivity hypothesis") has received some but by no means unanimous support from other studies. Lamb and colleagues (1985), after reviewing various studies that have examined the hypothesis, concluded that there was general support for the link between sensitive parenting and the development of type B attachments, at least when studies were conducted in the United States. The evidence for particular kinds of parenting associated respectively with types A and C, on the other hand, was found to be much more variable and less convincing. Grossmann, Grossmann, Spangler, and Unzner (1985), in a study of families in North Germany, found Strange Situation categories to be predicted by assessments of maternal sensitivity carried out when the infants were aged 2 and 6 months but not, inexplicably, by assessments when they were aged 10 months. These investigators also found a much greater incidence of type A (insecure/avoidant) children in their sample than usually reported for American samples (49 instead of 21 percent); they also did not find the mothers of this group of children to be any less sensitive than those of type B (secure) children. Cultural factors are thought to account for these differences in findings: the German families investigated by Grossmann et al. tended to emphasize early self-reliance in their child rearing practices and as a result showed a less responsive pattern of mothering. For the same reason the children were more likely to behave in an independent fashion in the Strange Situation and thus, when assessed on scales based on different cultural values, be labeled as insecure/avoidant.

One problem with many of the earlier studies is their reliance on subjective ratings for the measurement of maternal sensitivity. More recent studies have attempted to operationalize this concept in terms of specific, observable interactions – but again with mixed success (Belsky & Isabella, 1988). To take a typical example, Isabella, Belsky, & von Eye (1989) examined whether early mother–infant encounters are marked by *interactional synchrony*, i.e. the extent to which they are reciprocal and mutually rewarding. All instances of co-occurrence of infant and maternal behaviors, as recorded during home observation sessions, were scored as either synchronous, neutral, or asynchronous: thus a mother promptly responding to her infant's cry would be considered an example of synchrony and reflect the mother's sensitivity to her child's needs. When synchrony scores were related to children's attachment classifications at 1 year it was found that securely attached dyads had shown a considerably greater incidence of synchronous interactions than insecurely attached dyads – but only at two of the three observation points, i.e. at 1 and 3 months and not at 9 months. As in the Grossmann study, a puzzling degree of inconsistency throws doubt over the hypothesized sensitivity–security link. Maybe, as Isabella (1993) has suggested, the trouble is that maternal sensitivity is not a stable trait, and if that changes from one age to another it is hardly likely to provide a satisfactory explanation for infants' attachment security.

It is highly likely, of course, that attachment security is not just determined by parental behavior but that other factors also play a part. One possibility concerns *child effects*, i.e. the influence which the child's individuality exerts on the mother's behavior from birth and which will thus in due course affect the quality of attachments. High-risk infants, namely those who are born prematurely and of low birthweight, are of particular interest, for their behavior is at first more disorganized and less predictable and will thus place a much greater burden on a mother's capacity for sensitivity. Yet follow-up studies of such children have shown no indication that they are also at risk for attachment insecurity (Easterbrooks, 1989; Frodi & Thompson, 1985): their distribution over the various Strange Situation categories is similar to that of fullterm infants. Taken in conjunction with the previously mentioned findings about temperament, which has also not yet shown any clear-cut association with attachments, one must conclude that the question of antecedents of attachment quality cannot be answered by looking at child effects alone, any more than by looking at maternal caregiving alone (Schneider-Rosen & Rothbaum, 1993).

What is much more likely is that a number of factors need to be considered in conjunction, and that their *joint* effect predicts the formation of attachments rather than the effect of each on its own. This is well illustrated by Crockenberg (1981), who found that infants' irritability (a quality assessed in the newborn period which might well have considerable influence on mothers' handling of the child) did not by itself show any association with particular attachment classifications. However, when combined with the extent to which mothers received social support from relatives and others an association did emerge: mothers with highly irritable infants who also received little social support were most likely to have infants who developed insecure attachments; mothers with good support from kin, on the other hand, were able to cope with their difficult infants who then developed secure attachments. Presumably the combination of stress occasioned by the child's condition and the mother's isolation resulted in her becoming unresponsive and this in turn brought about the child's insecurity. Assessment of maternal responsiveness to distress at 3 months showed a relationship to attachment security at 12 months, but the effects were evident only when social support was low. Thus the consequences of such behavior on the part of the mothers could only be understood in the context of other important variables. Once again the link between early parental behavior and the development of secure attachments is shown to be rather less firm than was thought at one time. As van IJzendoorn, Juffer, & Duyvesteyn (1995) have put it: "The empirical impact of sensitivity on attachment appears to be only modest and not in accordance with its central position in attachment theory."

Consequents: The Competence Hypothesis

A further claim made on behalf of individual differences in attachment quality, as assessed by the Strange Situation, is that they predict behavior differences in other contexts and at later periods. Thus children classified as secure at age 1 are said to be more competent and mature in a great range of social and cognitive functions in subsequent years when compared with children assigned to any of the insecure groups (the "competence hypothesis"). The security typology has been said to predict a remarkably wide range of psychological functions, including:

- *personality characteristics*, e.g. self-esteem, self-knowledge, enthusiasm, resilience;
- *peer relationships*, e.g. sociability, friendliness, cooperativeness, empathy, popularity;
- *relationships with adults*, e.g. independence, confidence with strangers, compliance;
- *emotional aspects*, e.g. positive affect, negative affect, frustration tolerance, impulse control;
- *cognitive aspects*, e.g. maturity of play, persistence in problem solving, curiosity, attention span;
- *adjustment*, e.g. antisocial behavior, psychopathy.

In every instance the hypothesis investigated by the large number of studies that have examined this problem was that securely attached children are "superior" in comparison with insecure children, and in many instances this expectation was borne out.

However, as with the antecedents of security so with the consequents: the link is far from firmly established (Lamb et al., 1985). There are just too many exceptions to the positive findings that did emerge, such as unpredicted sex differences or age differences that do not make theoretical sense. In addition we have failure to replicate particular patterns of results across different studies; positive findings for some measures yet negative ones for others in the context of the same investigation; and reports of differences between the secure group and one but not the other insecure groups. Take a study by M. Lewis, Feiring, et al. (1984), which set out to predict psychopathology at age 6 from Strange Situation classifications at age 1. For boys such a relationship was found, in that a greater incidence of behavior problems was reported among those classified as insecure. However, this relationship did not occur in girls; moreover, even in boys prediction from early attachment status met with only limited (though statistically significant) success. As Lewis and colleagues point out, early attachment security does not guarantee later invulnerability, nor does an insecure attachment mean the child is doomed.

Prediction over a period of several years is always hazardous, and especially so because of the uncontrolled influence of intervening events. As Lamb and colleagues (1985) point out, the strongest evidence for the predictive validity of the Strange

Situation comes from studies of children brought up under conditions of family and child care stability. Under such circumstances the kind of parenting they receive in later years is likely to be of the same quality as that experienced in infancy, and a more economical explanation would then be that it is *current* rather than early patterns of child–parent interaction that account for the child's personality development. For example, in a study by Jacobsen, Edelstein, & Hofman (1994) it was found that securely attached children had better cognitive performance right through into adolescence than insecurely attached children. However, there is no reason to believe that the family situation of these children was any different in adolescence than in early childhood; the relationship of later cognitive functioning to early attachment assessment may thus merely exist because of the influence of a continuing pattern of certain kinds of family relationships.

But prediction also depends on how sound the measure is from which one is attempting to predict. This raises the question of the *validity* of the Strange Situation. The procedure as a whole lasts 21 minutes, but assignment to a particular security category depends almost wholly on the two reunion episodes, i.e. on two extremely brief samples of behaviour. That the Strange Situation has been so successful in forward prediction is astonishing, given that personality assessment in general usually requires an extended and representative sample of behaviour. Certainly any diagnostic attempt aimed at individual children should be based on multiple assessment: the Strange Situation alone cannot be regarded as a sufficiently sound basis for such a purpose. Also assessment of particular groups, such as children reared in atypical families or attending day care, ought to include a variety of techniques and not (as has so frequently been the case) put all eggs into the Strange Situation basket. Indeed for some groups, such as Down's syndrome children (B. E. Vaughn, Goldberg, et al., 1994) there are doubts whether this procedure is applicable at all. As a research tool the Strange Situation has certainly generated a lot of interesting work; here too, however, it has its limitations. In particular, some of the claims that have been made with respect to both the responsiveness and the competence hypotheses have turned out to be much too grandiose and are not firmly supported by the available evidence. Children no doubt differ in the quality of the attachment relationships they form; however, the issue of the antecedents of such differences and their consequences is nowhere near as straightforward as has been suggested by many attachment enthusiasts.

Intergenerational Continuity?

Under the influence of the Strange Situation paradigm research on attachments was initially almost wholly confined to the first two years. It was part of Bowlby's theory, however, that the formation and management of attachment relationships is not just a developmental task for infancy but that it is a lifelong issue: attachments continue into adulthood even though the circumstances that elicit attachment behaviour change. The ways in which attachments are expressed also change; nevertheless, Bowlby proposed that there is a coherence in the attachment organization which is largely determined by early experience and preserved over time.

More recent work has followed up these ideas, though in order to move beyond the age period where the Strange Situation is regarded as appropriate new measures of attachment had to be devised. A number of these are now available, both for older children and for adults, including separation situations specifically devised for preschool children, series of drawings depicting separation experiences, attachment story completion tasks, and Q-sort techniques (Greenberg, Cicchetti, & Cummings, 1990). By means of such tools one can examine the question of stability of attachments over a wide age span and also consider a number of conceptual issues inherent in Bowlby's theory.

One such issue refers to the possibility of intergenerational continuity in parenting experiences. As we saw, early attachments result in the formation of internal working models which, according to Bowlby, incorporate the child's view of those relationships and which increasingly come to determine the nature of other social bonds formed in subsequent years. Though such models may be affected by later events Bowlby considered that under normal circumstances they remain stable and indeed become resistant to change. If that is so, there must be a strong possibility that the care received by a mother from her own mother, and the type of attachment formed by her in early childhood, will in turn influence the formation of attachments by her child. As Bowlby (1973) put it (perhaps somewhat dogmatically, considering the lack of empirical data at the time he was writing):

> Because . . . children tend unwittingly to identify with parents and therefore to adopt, when they become parents, the same patterns of behaviour towards children that they themselves have experienced during their own childhood, patterns of interaction are transmitted, more or less faithfully, from one generation to another.

Do people parent their children as they were parented? The problem of intergenerational continuity is an intriguing one but also methodologically a most difficult one to investigate – not least because one may need to wait 30 years or so for observational results to come in (Ricks, 1985). However, one might argue that it is not so much the objective facts of being parented but rather the way in which the individual construes these facts, i.e. the nature of the internal working model that is formed, which will determine that person's behavior as a parent. Accordingly Mary Main and her colleagues (Main, Kaplan, & Cassidy, 1985) have developed a technique for assessing such models in adults, enabling them to investigate their nature in parents and relate them to children's attachment formation. The *adult attachment interview* consists of a series of questions designed to elicit the individual's experiences of attachment relationships in childhood and the way in which that person considers these experiences as an influence on later development and on present functioning. In fact it is not so much the content of these recollections as the way in which they are conveyed that Main regards as significant, with particular reference to their emotional openness and coherence. Classifying each interview as a whole, Main proposed the following categorization of parents' current status with respect to attachment:

- *Autonomous*: individuals so classified discuss their childhood experiences frankly and coherently, acknowledging both positive and negative events and emotions.
- *Dismissing*: such individuals seem cut off from the emotional nature of their childhood, denying especially their negative experiences or dismissing their significance.
- *Preoccupied*: these individuals are overinvolved with what they recollect, appearing so overwhelmed that they become incoherent and confused in the interview.

The first group has also been labeled as secure, while the other two have been classified as insecure (for a fuller review of this and other instruments designed to assess attachment in adults, see Crowell & Treboux, 1995).

There have been a number of attempts to link up these categories of mothers' attachment status with the groupings produced for their children in the Strange Situation. According to Main and colleagues (1985), autonomous mothers tend to have secure children, dismissing mothers have avoidant children and preoccupied mothers have resistant children. Table 20 gives further details. Comparing the children's attachment types, as given by the Strange Situation at age 1, with the mothers' categories obtained five years later from administering adult attachment interviews, Main was able to confirm such a cross-classification. The concordance rate of 0.61 found by her is by no means a perfect match: other influences are also clearly at work; it is nevertheless high enough to suggest that some sort of link does exist.

Table 20   Cross-classification of mothers' and children's attachment status

Classifications		
Mother	*Child*	*Nature of mother–child relationship*
Autonomous	Secure	Mother's mind not taken up with unresolved concerns about own experience, therefore free to be sensitive to child's communications
Dismissing	Avoidant	Mother reluctant to acknowledge own attachment needs and therefore insensitive and unresponsive to child's needs
Preoccupied	Resistant	Mother confused about her attachment history and thus inconsistent in her treatment of the child

Source: Based on Main et al. (1985)

It is, of course, possible that such results are affected by selective recall on the part of the mothers, i.e. that the recollections of their childhood are influenced by their current experiences with their own child. A study by Fonagy, Steele, and Steele (1991) is therefore of particular interest, for these investigators administered the adult attachment interview before the birth of the child. Ninety-six pregnant women were thus classified; at age 1 their children were categorized on the basis of their Strange Situation behavior; and the two groupings so obtained were compared. Table 21 summarizes the results. A three-way match of 66 percent was found; the concordance was particularly impressive for the autonomous mother–secure child pairing. Only the preoccupied category failed to predict the child's attachment status.

Table 21 Mothers' prenatal adult attachment interview classification and children's Strange Situation classification

Children's classifications	Mothers' classifications		
	Dismissing	*Autonomous*	*Preoccupied*
Avoidant	15	8	7
Secure	5	45	5
Resistant	2	6	3

Source: Adapted from Fonagy et al. (1991)

It seems therefore possible that the way in which a mother construes her own relationship history is an important influence on the kind of relationship that the child establishes with her. Let us stress that it is not the *actual* experiences of the mother in early life that are said to be responsible – given the retrospective nature of the research such an assertion cannot be made. It is rather how the mother, as an adult, *views* those early experiences. Thus the proposal is that a mother's internal working model, built up during her childhood and tapped in adulthood, will affect the way in which she interacts with her child, as a result of which the child will then form a particular kind of attachment with her. Again we must stress that other influences will also be at work, interacting with those of the mother's model in complex ways. Some degree of intergenerational continuity, together with the processes whereby it is produced, is nevertheless at least hinted at by the currently available research.

Summary

Early Interactions

- The earliest social interactions revolve around the infant's need for biological regulation of basic processes such as feeding and sleeping. Mutual adaptation of infant and caretaker begins at birth and occurs with surprising speed during the early weeks of life.

- The main developmental theme during the next phase is the regulation of mutual attention and responsiveness, as found primarily in the context of face-to-face interactions. Infants bring to these interactions certain biologically based cycles of attention; parents adapt their behavior to these, thereby ensuring a synchronization of the two sets of actions as seen, for instance, in early turn-taking behavior.
- Each adult–child pair develops its own distinctive interactive style. This is shaped by three sets of factors, i.e. cultural influences, the adult's personality, and child characteristics.

From Nonverbal to Verbal Communication

- With progressive expansion in attentional capacity infants become increasingly able also to incorporate objects in their social interactions. How to bring about topic sharing then becomes a major theme for adult and child.
- Towards the end of the first year a blossoming of abilities occurs, with behavior becoming more purposive, flexible, and coordinated. These developments can be traced in the way adult–infant games change with age, in particular in the way they become more reciprocal and intentional.
- Increasing coordination is also responsible for developments in communicative skills at that time. This is seen in the beginning of gesturing and in the social reference phenomenon, both of which involve coordinating attention to the partner with attention to an external event.
- With the onset of symbolic representation social interactions become increasingly verbal in nature. Language abilities develop primarily in one-to-one encounters (joint involvement episodes), in which adults can sensitively adapt their input to the child's capacities.

Attachment: Nature and Development

- Attachments, as formed in infancy, are long-enduring, emotionally meaningful ties to particular individuals. They involve seeking the physical proximity of the parent and thus obtaining care and protection while still in a helpless state.
- John Bowlby's attachment theory is based on the biological significance of the child's emotional ties. Children are said to be genetically biased to develop attachments to their caretakers, and accordingly are equipped with such responses as crying, clinging, and following. Initially these are employed indiscriminately; in due course they become focused on specific individuals and organized into coherent attachment systems. With the development of intentionality and planning

ability, goal-corrected partnerships appear; the child, moreover, becomes capable of forming internal working models which enable the attachment relationship to be mentally represented.

- Focused attachments first become apparent around the age of 7 or 8 months. The ability to recognize familiar individuals appears much earlier; however, it is not till the second half-year that infants become capable of person permanence, i.e. the ability to remain oriented to individuals even in their absence. This is a necessary prerequisite of attachment formation.
- Even in infancy attachments can be formed to several individuals. Their choice depends on the quality of the interaction with them rather than on such factors as the sex of the person or the total amount of time spent together.
- With the development of internal working models children become capable of tolerating gradually lengthening periods of separation; they can also increasingly take into account other people's intentions and thus form more balanced and flexible relationships.

Attachment: Individual Differences

- Ainsworth's "Strange Situation" is a technique used to highlight individual differences in the quality of infants' attachments. Three basic attachment types are generally used to classify these differences: secure, insecure/avoidant, and insecure/resistant. According to Ainsworth the differences are related to the degree of the mother's sensitivity during interactions in early infancy; it is likely, however, that other factors such as temperament also play a part. It has furthermore been suggested that the three attachment types predict a wide range of psychological competencies in later childhood, generally in favor of securely attached children; again, however, the link is not firmly established.
- Attachments remain a lifelong issue, but for age periods beyond infancy assessment techniques other than the Strange Situation have had to be developed, including the adult attachment interview. By this means it has been possible to show that some degree of intergenerational continuity occurs, in that a mother's internal working model of her early attachment experiences tends to influence the way she interacts with her children and therefore the type of attachment they in turn will form to her.

Chapter 4

Sense of Self:
Sense of Other

Children are active processors of the experiences they encounter. Their own behavior is far from being an automatic reaction to environmental stimulation; it is the result of vigorous attempts to make sense of what is happening to them. Thus in any social situation children will monitor, reflect upon, and evaluate the information presented to them; and how they then respond is closely dependent on such evaluation.

In understanding their experiences in interpersonal situations children are helped by forming *social concepts*. These are tools which enable them to make sense of their experiences in encounters with other people, and for this purpose they must above all form concepts of themselves, of the people with whom they interact, and of the interpersonal relationships which emerge. We have already referred to this process in discussing Bowlby's internal working models which the child forms of itself and of significant others – models which are the result of the child's attachment experiences and which increasingly come to regulate interpersonal behavior. The formation of such mental representations begins early on, in that they are evident at least from the beginning of the second year. But the formation of the self and of concepts of other people is a long-drawn-out developmental process that continues through much of childhood; at any one point it is dependent both on the individual's cognitive level and on past social experience, and as the child gets older it reaches increasingly complex levels in an orderly progression. Much has been learned in recent years about the nature of that progression, with particular reference to the formation of self-concepts, and to these we turn first before considering children's concepts of other people.

The Self

Of all social concepts that of the self is the most basic. It enables the individual to adopt a particular stance from which to view the world – a source of reference which mediates social experience and which organizes behavior towards others. It has a key role because it determines how each of us construes reality and what experiences we seek out in order to fit in with the self image. Thus to understand the nature of child development in general and of any given individual in particular the self must be taken into account.

It is true, of course, that the self is essentially a private affair – indeed *the* most private of all aspects of personality. Yet as a result of much research it has become increasingly possible to externalize and measure many of its features and thereby demonstrate the role they play in individuals' lives. Thus the self is no longer just the subject of philosophical speculation but a topic for empirical investigation, as a result of which an outline of how it emerges and grows during childhood can now be provided. However, what has also become apparent is that the self is by no means a simple, unitary concept but rather a complex system of different constructs, each of which needs investigating in its own right. The principal constituents of the self-system will be mentioned below; however, there is one basic distinction which was introduced over 100 years ago and which has guided thinking ever since, namely that made by William James (1892) between the "I" and the "me." The "I" is the *self-as-knower*, that which organizes and interprets experience in a purely subjective manner. It is something which we regard as continuous over time and distinctive in comparison with others, and which thus provides us with a particular self-identity. The "me," on the other hand, is the *self-as-known*, i.e. the object of our perception when we contemplate ourselves. It is whatever results from our efforts at self-awareness, including all those categories we use in order to define ourselves – age, gender, race, psychological characteristics, possessions, etc. James predicted that the "I" would remain elusive to empirical investigation and would continue subject to philosophical treatment alone. He has not been completely borne out in this respect; on the other hand there is no doubt that much more research has examined the "me" than the "I" and that our knowledge of developmental aspects in particular is most advanced with respect to the cognitive basis of children's self-concepts, i.e. self-understanding.

Self-awareness: The Emergence of Self

Infants are generally assumed to possess no sense of self in the early months of life; such a sense can only be constructed through experience, particularly through experience with other people. As George Herbert Mead (1934) put it:

> The self has a character which is different from that of the physiological organism proper. The self is something which has a development; it is not initially there, at birth, but arises in the process of social experience and activity, that is, develops in a given individual as a result of his relations to that process as a whole and to other individuals within that process. . . . The self, as that which can be an object to itself, is essentially a social structure, and it arises in social experience.

Whether interacting with others is indeed the crucial factor that creates the self remains an unproven, though plausible, assumption. Mead's other assertion, that children start off without a sense of self in the early months of life and develop it gradually, does receive empirical support, above all by the work of Michael Lewis and his colleagues (e.g. Lewis, 1990; Lewis & Brooks-Gunn, 1979).

Building on William James's "I–me" distinction, Lewis differentiated between two aspects of the self: the *existential* and the *categorical* self. The former is the first to appear; it refers to a feeling of being distinct from all else and of possessing continuity over time. A primitive sense of separateness, Lewis argued, is already evident by 3 months; a sense of continuity (or self-permanence) emerges at about 9 months. Self-awareness, as measured by the ability to visually recognize oneself, appears during the second year, and it is only then that the first signs of the categorical self become evident, i.e. the ability of children to define themselves in terms of such categories as age, sex, and size.

By far the most attention has been given to the emergence of the capacity for visual self-recognition. For this purpose a spot of rouge is surreptitiously applied to the child's nose and the child then put in front of a mirror. If children are able to recognize that the mirror image is of themselves they will reach for the spot on their *own* nose, not the nose in the mirror; they can then be regarded as possessing a sense of self-awareness. In studies reported by M. Lewis and Brooks-Gunn (1979), no children under the age of 1 touched their noses; such behavior first appeared at 15 months and was seen in most infants by 21 months. These results are very similar to those obtained in a previous study by Amsterdam (1972), – see figure 10.

How do the infants manage to recognize themselves? There are two kinds of clues they may be using: *contingency clues*, derived from the fact that the mirror image moves precisely in tandem with the child's own movements and is thus contingent upon them, and *feature clues*, i.e. such stable physical features as facial and bodily appearance which the child may have come to associate with itself. It is not possible from mirror studies to tell which kind children are using; however, Lewis and Brooks-Gunn were able to separate out their respective roles in a series of further experiments using other media such as videotapes and photographs of the children. Thus a TV image of the child may either be presented live (and therefore contingently) or taken from a film obtained a week earlier (and thus excluding contingency); in addition the child's response to the TV image of another child may also be investigated. Still photographs too exclude contingency; signs of recognition can therefore only be based on feature clues, though of a static kind. By examining children's responses to these various stimulus conditions Lewis and Brooks-Gunn were able to demonstrate that self-recognition is not a sudden, all-in-one development but that it unfolds gradually in the course of the first two years. Signs of self-recognition became evident from 9 months on: infants, for instance, showed greater interest in their own TV image than in those of others. It was also clear that early recognition was initially based exclusively on contingency, and though responsiveness to such clues was at first tentative it increased steadily in the course of the second year. Responsiveness to feature clues was a later development, emerging at around 15

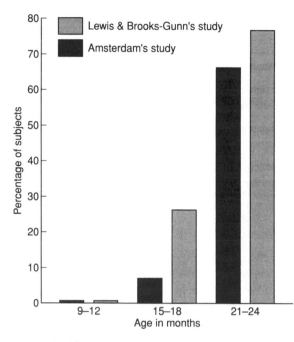

Figure 10   Percentage of subjects (by age) exhibiting mark recognition in two studies (from M. Lewis & Brooks-Gunn, 1979)

months: only from then on were children able to show differential behavior to their own pre-taped TV image compared with that of another child. Table 22 presents an outline of the major advances which these results point to in the emergence of self-awareness in the first two years.

Visual recognition is, of course, not the only indication of self-awareness, though it has the advantage of being applicable from very early on. Another source of evidence comes from children's speech: from the second year on children use self-related terms such as "I" and "me" and are able to understand as well as say their own names. Surprisingly, "I" and "you" are used correctly from the start and not inter-changed despite the inversion required when listening to another person's use of personal pronouns. Children also quickly become able to refer to themselves by their own name and use that interchangeably with "I." It seems that by the time these linguistic developments appear the child has already a fairly well developed sense of self-identity and can therefore immediately employ these verbal devices appropri-ately in the service of the self.

A third source of information concerning these early manifestations of the self is the extent to which children act differently according to whether or not the self is engaged. For example, when a child is praised for success or blamed for failure, can one discern signs of an emotional response such as pride or shame? We shall have

Table 22 Stages in the development of self-awareness in the first two years

Age (months)	Behavioral indications
0–3	Interest in social objects, but no self–other distinction
3–8	First sign of self-recognition, based on contingency clues, but still tentative and unreliable
8–12	Emergence of self-permanence. Recognition of self through contingency. Emergence of feature recognition
12–24	Consolidation of basic self categories (age, gender, etc.). Feature recognition without contingency

Source: Based on table 9.1, p. 227, in M. Lewis & Brooks-Gunn (1979)

more to say about such emotional aspects later; here let us note that these can be used to index the development of children's self-consciousness about their own behavior. The same applies to refusals of help and deliberate non-compliance to an adult's requests, which can be interpreted as signs of self-assertion and are thus again a means of assessing the existence of an active self-system. These various indices all point to the second year as the period of first emergence and subsequent rapid development (Kagan, 1981); this is the crucial period when the self-system is formed and when it starts increasingly to dominate behavior.

However, two provisos are called for. First, even during the second year of life not all behavioral indices develop simultaneously: a systematic progression can be found in the order in which various developments occur. We have already seen that self-recognition based on contingency clues appears before that based on feature clues and that the latter comes to replace the former. Bullock and Lutkenhaus (1990) applied a considerable range of measures of the self-system to children between 1 and 3 years of age, and found a developmental course according to the type of assessment employed. In particular, indices that involve immediate and visible aspects of the self (e.g. physical appearance) make an earlier appearance than nonvisible aspects (e.g. the child's name). This is understandable, for more sophisticated cognitive mechanisms are required to process the latter than the former. The other proviso refers to developments preceding those found in the second year, the role of which should not be overlooked. This point is well made by Case (1991) when he argues that the self *in implicit form* emerges already in the early months, namely from a sense of "agency": the infant, that is, learns that through its own actions it can affect the behavior both of other people and of objects and is thus an agent of change. This realization is a precursor of the "I" self, derived from the child's participation in events with people and objects. Similarly, foundations for the "me" self are laid by the infant's monitoring of its own activities: watching the movements of its own hands, for example, leads in due course to the formation of mental representations of the hands and, combined with the knowledge that the hand is under the infant's own control, will eventually help in establishing the child's body image – a vital constituent of the self-concept.

Thus even the initial emergence of the self-system is a complex process, where different constituents first become evident at different ages and where it would be dangerous to talk in terms of a "no-self" period being followed by a "self" period. To some extent general cognitive developments set the stage, e.g. the ability to go beyond individual experiences and span time and place must have emerged before the notion of self-permanence becomes possible. To some extent also a child's particular social experiences are likely to shape the course of early self development, though how this is brought about and what the link is between particular experiences and individual differences in these first manifestations of the self-system remains uncharted territory.

Self-concept: Children's Views of Themselves

We all have an image of the kind of person we believe we are. To some extent this reflects how others view us – the "looking glass self," as Cooley (1902) referred to it. But largely it is a matter of our own construction, determined by each individual's values and predilections, as a result of which greater emphasis may well be placed on some aspects than on others and which often lead to distortions when compared with others' views of that individual. The product of our constructive efforts is the *self-concept*; this refers to the cognitive aspects of the self-system and expresses the subjective knowledge people have of themselves as psychological and physical beings. It is the answer to the question "Who am I?"

The self-concept is far from static. It changes as a result of the continuous process of self-observation that we all indulge in (the "I" watching the "me"). It is affected by experience, especially of success and failure and the feelings of competence or incompetence derived therefrom. However, most changes occur in the course of childhood, for it is then that the foundations of the concept are laid and it is then that the individual is most vulnerable to other's evaluations. The way in which children conceive the self varies to some extent according to age and depends on the stage of cognitive growth achieved. As a result it is possible to describe the progression of self-concepts during childhood in terms of a number of developmental dimensions, summarized in table 23.

The first two dimensions indicate trends that are readily evident. Young children's concepts are simple affairs; thus they may think of themselves as "good" or as "bad," as "clever" or as "stupid," as "strong" or as "weak," and not make any finer discriminations. Only later on will they realize that there are variations between each pair of such extremes, and it is also only with increasing age that they appreciate the importance of context and extenuating circumstances, so that one can, for instance, be clever at some things and stupid at others. At younger ages children are also much

Table 23   Summary of developmental changes in self-concept

	From	To	Description of change
1	Simple	Differentiated	Younger children form global concepts; older children make finer distinctions and allow for circumstances
2	Inconsistent	Consistent	Younger children are more likely to change their self-evaluation; older children appreciate the stability of the self-concept
3	Concrete	Abstract	Younger children focus on external, visible, physical aspects; older children focus on internal, invisible, psychological aspects
4	Absolute	Comparative	Younger children focus on self without reference to others; older children describe themselves in comparison with others
5	Self-as-public	Self-as-private	Younger children do not distinguish between private feelings and public behavior; older children consider private self as "true self"

more likely to be inconsistent in their views of themselves – largely because they tend to focus on the here-and-now of behavior and do not see either themselves or other people in terms of underlying dispositions responsible for producing consistency over time and place. Failure at some task, for instance, is not regarded as having any implications for subsequent performance and children's ability to predict future behavior is thus poor in the early years (Ruble, 1987).

The *concrete–abstract* dimension has attracted more research than any of the other developmental trends. Earlier studies (e.g. Broughton, 1978; Guardo & Bohan, 1971; Montemayor & Eisen, 1977) seemed to indicate a clear-cut progression in children's self-descriptions from the use of outer, visible characteristics to the use of inner, psychological attributes. Asked to provide answers to the question "Who am I?" younger children respond by describing their physical appearance ("I am fair, have blue eyes, and am a bit skinny"); they might also list their possessions and favorite toys and mention their name and address. Only from the age of 7 or so will children also refer to psychological characteristics such as abilities, beliefs, and dispositions. This trend increases sharply in early adolescence when a much greater preoccupation with the self becomes evident and when inner emotions and social motives are much more salient in self-descriptions ("I am moody and rather lonely but I try to be helpful to others"). Even adolescents may still use concrete terms and cite their name and sex, but whereas younger children may consider their unchanging name as a reason for the constancy of the self older children appreciate names as mere labels and use psychological attributes instead as the main indicators of self-identity.

More recent work, however, has introduced some refinements to the concrete–abstract shift. For one thing, according to Damon and Hart (1988) self-descriptive terms in childhood can more usefully be assigned to a four-fold categorization, i.e. *physical, active, social,* and *psychological* characteristics. Physical and psychological refer respectively to the concrete and abstract terms distinguished in earlier work. However, according to Keller, Ford, and Meacham (1978) in young children's self-descriptions it is *activity* terms that usually predominate ("I like watching TV"; "I help my mum"; "I wash my hair myself"). Over 50 percent of responses by the 3- to 5-year-olds whom Keller and colleagues questioned fell into the activity category – considerably more than those referring to body image. Children at this age, one must conclude, think of themselves more in action than in static terms – a trend still evident in mid-childhood (Damon & Hart, 1982). *Social* self-descriptive terms are those which identify a child in terms of family and peer relationships ("I have a mother who goes out to work"; "I am quite popular with other kids"); these are frequently mentioned qualities in mid-childhood and may be extended to the child's feelings of belongingness to particular groups and organizations such as a school, a gang, or a church (Damon & Hart, 1988).

The relative salience of these four sets of characteristics changes with age. According to D. Hart and colleagues (1993), systematic shifts occur in the centrality to the self which 6- to 16-year-olds attach to each set. As we see in figure 11, physical characteristics rapidly decrease in importance during mid-childhood and matter less to children than those defining activity characteristics. Up to early adolescence the most significance is attributed to social characteristics: interpersonal relationships, that is, are perceived as constituting the core of the self – a finding which helps to explain why young adolescents become so distressed when such relationships are damaged or terminated. However, from mid-adolescence there is increasing concern with psychological characteristics as the individual turns inwards and comes to think of the self primarily in terms of personal traits and dispositions. Thus a move from concrete to abstract conceptions can still be discerned, though it takes a rather more complex form than a shift along a simple continuum.

The other refinement which more recent work has brought to our understanding of developmental shifts is, more fundamentally, to throw doubt on the total absence of young children's ability to use psychological constructs in self-description (P. H. Miller & Aloise, 1989). As Wellman and Gelman (1987) point out, a distinction should be made between two kinds of such constructs: *internal states*, which are temporary and common to all (such as "feeling happy," "wanting a drink," and other similar attributions of emotions and intentions), and *dispositions*, i.e. enduring characteristics like aggressiveness or intelligence whereby individuals can be differentiated. Awareness of the former is already evident by age 3, and it is only awareness of the latter that cannot be found till age 7 (Eder, 1990). We shall return to this issue when discussing children's conceptions of other people, but here let us note that the distinction does not by any means disconfirm the concrete-to-abstract shift: momentary states may be mental entities but are linked to specific instances of external, here-

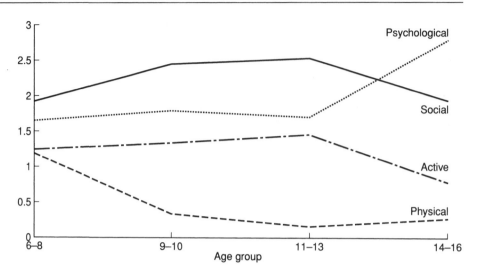

Figure 11   Average salience scores for four sets of self-descriptive characteristics at different ages (from D. Hart et al., 1993)

and-now behavior; dispositions, on the other hand, require a combination of several observations into more global categories and are thus more demanding on the child's cognitive capacity.

The *absolute–comparative* dimension listed in table 23 refers to children's increasing awareness of the role of the social environment in self-formation. Whereas initially children focus entirely on themselves when asked for their characteristics, using absolute terms such as "smart" or "fast," from mid-childhood on there is an increasing tendency to make comparisons with others ("smarter than most other kids in my class"; "faster than Jimmy"). As Ruble (1987) has shown in a series of studies, children are not affected by comparative standards till the surprisingly late age of 7 or 8. Before then they may have some capacity for comparing themselves with others, at least when the differences are highly salient and concrete, but in self-evaluation any form of social comparison does not seem to be natural or of high priority. For example, in a ball-throwing task Ruble gave children feedback on their own performance as well as information about other children's performances. When asked to evaluate their own achievement in the task children under the age of 7 rarely took note of how others had performed; from age 7 on comparative references appeared with increasing frequency. However, not till age 9 was the information provided about other children used consistently and systematically (with remarks such as "I must be pretty good because I beat all the others"). According to Ruble, children under the age of 7 use social comparison information only to judge appearance and action, whereas older children are capable of evaluating competence and ability and will therefore make a point of seeking out any comparative data that throw light on their own status. If this is so, the concrete-to-abstract shift appears also to underlie the emergence of the different kinds of social comparisons, at least in the achievement-related contexts investigated by Ruble. And once a child is able to make such comparisons the opinions of others will play an increasing part in shaping answers to the question "Who am I?"

The final developmental change, that from *self-as-public* to *self-as-private*, can also be regarded as depending on the growing ability to handle abstract, invisible characteristics. Some aspects of the self are considered by children to be private at quite an early age: according to Flavell (quoted by Maccoby, 1980), if someone stares into the eyes of a child and asks "Can I see you thinking in there?" children as young as 3 are already able to say "No" (though their explanations tend to take the form of "Thinking can't be seen because the skin is over it"). However, the idea of a wholly private, separate self is a rather later development. According to Selman (1980) children younger than 6 cannot distinguish between private feelings and public behavior; from about 8 they do make the distinction and, moreover, regard the private self as the "true" self. Further developments continue into adolescence: young adolescents, Selman proposed, are "aware of their own self-awareness" and know that they can consciously monitor their own self-experience – hence the considerable increase in self-consciousness that one so often sees then. At that time adolescents tend to believe that one has control over one's thoughts and feelings and that public behavior ought therefore to be a matter of private volition; only in the later years of adolescence will it become apparent that conscious and unconscious experience need to be differentiated and that there are consequently some limits to the exercise of self-control. The construction of the private self is thus an ongoing process that continues right through adolescence, until the individual finally comes to appreciate the limits of self-awareness and self-control.

The case of puberty and its impact on the self

Given the considerable changes that occur with the onset of puberty, the question "Who am I?" suddenly assumes renewed importance. It so happens that a number of changes coincide at that time: cognitively, the child moves from concrete to formal operational modes of thinking; educationally, a change of school generally occurs around then; and, above all, physically the child's appearance undergoes a number of marked changes. In so far as the latter occur relatively suddenly it is no wonder that children become self-conscious and overly critical at that time about their body image and public impression.

This is especially so because there are considerable variations among children with respect to the timing of these changes. Girls mature sooner than boys: the growth spurt, for instance, occurs about two years earlier in girls. But there are also large individual differences within each sex: menarche, for example, may appear as early as 9 or as late as 16 years of age. To be the first or the last in one's peer group to reach such a milestone can present difficulties, particularly at a time when social comparison is prominent. This applies not only to physical appearance but also to the new sexual functions which now come into being as a result of the hormonal and somatic changes. Sexuality is often experienced as problematic; when it has reached some members of a peer group but not others the problem cannot easily be shared but is more likely to be a source of private concern, thus increasing self-consciousness and the difficulties of readjustment.

The psychological effects of early and late maturation have been documented as part of a longitudinal growth study conducted at the University of California (see J. J. Conger, 1991). For boys the effects tend to be more marked than for girls. Thus boys who mature earlier have a number of advantages over their late-maturing counterparts: they are more likely to be treated as responsible by adults as well as by peers and so more often assume leadership roles; they have greater strength and skill in activities such as sport; they get credit for earlier heterosexual encounters; and as a result they become more self-confident and assured than late-maturing boys, who may well develop feelings of inferiority and wonder when they may ever stop being a mere child. Follow-up studies have indicated that the personality differences between the two groups may persist into adulthood, when early maturers have been found to be more respon-

sible, cooperative, and sociable than the late maturers, though also less insightful, perceptive, and creative (Livson & Peskin, 1980). Among girls, however, differences in age at maturation produce fewer psychological effects. Those who mature early have been found to be more independent and more popular; on the other hand they tend to be more concerned about and less satisfied with their body image and also to have more problems at school than those who mature late. Yet by and large the differences appear to be less extensive and more variable than is the case among boys.

At whatever age maturation takes place, uncertainties about self-identity are common in the transition from childhood to being an adult. It is, however, not only the young person who needs to adapt but also other family members, and how they do so may well have further implications for the development of adolescents' self-identity (Feldman & Brown, 1993). Family relationships tend to change as a consequence of the child's puberty (Paikoff & Brooks-Gunn, 1991), and how parents come to terms with their children's new sexual status will help to determine how the children themselves think about their identity and about their place in society.

Self-esteem: Children's Value of Themselves

Self-esteem refers to an individual's feelings of his or her own worthiness and competence. It is thus the evaluative aspect of the self-system and is related to the image of an ideal self that we all have: where there is little discrepancy between the ideal and the perceived real self the individual will experience high self-esteem; where the discrepancy is great, on the other hand, low self-esteem is the result. Individuals can be ranged along the continuum from high to low; the position for a given person is, however, not necessarily static, for we are constantly monitoring our behavior and assessing the extent to which it falls short of the standards we have set ourselves. Nevertheless, self-esteem is at its most volatile during its initial formation in childhood and remains easily influenced by experience right through adolescence.

Is self-esteem a global entity, summarized by one score, or is it specific to a number of domains of behavior each of which may give rise to a different assessment? A series of studies conducted by Harter (1987) suggests that the issue is not a clear-cut one and that, in a sense, both alternatives are true. Harter distinguished between five domains: scholastic competence, athletic competence, social acceptance, physical appearance, and behavioral conduct. Children were given separate rating scales asking about how *important* it is to do well in each domain in order to feel good about oneself as a person; they were also asked how *competent* they considered themselves in each of the domains. The discrepancy between the scores for perceived competence and the importance attached to that quality was considered as a measure of self-esteem, in that it reflects the extent to which children see themselves as meeting their own standards. In addition Harter also administered a global self-worth scale, asking children how much they liked themselves as people.

The results show that children's self-esteem can vary considerably from one domain to another. Knowing about a child's feelings in one does not necessarily tell one anything about that child's feelings in any of the others. Merely to average them out would thus be misleading. At the same time children do also have a global feeling of self-worth which expresses a general evaluation not tied to any specific area of competence. What is interesting is that this, unlike the domain-specific feelings, does not emerge until the age of 7 or 8: only then can children stand apart from themselves, as it were, and assess themselves independently of performance in particular situations. Once again, it seems, the developing ability to move away from a purely concrete view and adopt more abstract conceptions underlies this change.

One commonly reported developmental change in self-esteem involves the *identity crisis* which, according to Erikson (1963), many young adolescents undergo as they become uncertain about their present and (even more so) their future status and in consequence attempt to reevaluate their personal identity and goals. As we saw above, the physical changes brought about by puberty are accompanied by psychological changes; a sometimes intense period of introspection follows in which the individual attempts to define anew his or her role in life, and the uncertainty experienced at that time is reflected in feelings of unworthiness and self-doubt. Though there is some question whether adolescent identity crisis is as common and as severe as Erikson suggested, the dip in self-esteem during the early stages of adolescence is, in Western culture at least, a commonly described phenomenon (e.g. McCarthy & Hodge, 1982; O'Malley & Bachman, 1983). In part, this is a reaction to a changing body image, and expressions of dissatisfaction with what the young person now possesses are common in early adolescence. In part, it is also the need to think about future choices of occupation and the many uncertainties attached to that; young people know that such choices are imminent and crucial, yet are often fearful of the consequences of whatever course they adopt. As Erikson put it, they are led to conclude that "I ain't what I ought to be, I ain't what I'm gonna be, but I ain't what I was," and as a result of such confusion they come to doubt their self-worth and, for a time at least, become fearful of the future.

The nature of individual differences in self-esteem, and the origins and consequences of such differences, has not surprisingly aroused a lot of research interest. In a classical study Coopersmith (1967) investigated self-esteem in 10- to 11-year-old boys and administered a questionnaire with items such as "I am proud of my school work" and "I find it hard to talk in front of the class." On the basis of their answers to such questions, Coopersmith categorized the boys into those with high and those with low self-esteem. The two groups, he found, could be distinguished by the kinds of relationships they had with their parents. Thus boys with high self-esteem had parents who were extremely accepting of their children, who nevertheless set clearly defined limits of the boy's behavior, and who enforced these limits but within them allowed their children considerable freedom. Coopersmith also found that the parents of boys with high self-esteem themselves tended to have high self-esteem. The boys with low self-esteem, on the other hand, generally had parents who related to them in a rejecting, distant manner and were either autocratic or over-permissive in their treatment of their children. As a result, presumably, the boys felt unappreciated and hence developed a poor opinion of themselves.

Parental behavior is, of course, not the only source of individual differences in self-esteem. As Harter (1987) has shown, the relationship of children's self-esteem with other sources of social support must also be taken into account (table 24). Classmates in particular play an important part in mid-childhood and early adolescence, though it is interesting to note from these findings that the influence of parents is by no means supplanted by that of the peer group as is sometimes maintained. The boosting of confidence, or its deflation, is affected by whoever happens to be significant in a child's life at any given period. Not that self-esteem is wholly accounted for by external influences: what standards are set, how the child feels about meeting them or failing to meet them and the precise implications this has for self-esteem depend to a considerable extent on individual children themselves. For that matter, there are indications from the work of behavior geneticists that the perception of self-worth may be affected by hereditary influences. By examining a large sample of adolescent sibling pairs differing in genetic relatedness, i.e. twins, siblings, and step-siblings, McGuire and colleagues (1994) found, first of all, that family influences of a shared nature (parental education, social class, family size, etc.) accounted for little of the

Table 24   Correlations of self-esteem and four sources of social support

	Age	
Source of support	*8–11*	*11–13*
Parent	0.42	0.45
Classmate	0.46	0.42
Friend	0.38	0.30
Teacher	0.36	0.27

Source: From Harter (1987)

variance in these young people's feelings of self-worth, whereas nonshared environmental influences, i.e. experiences specific to individual children, showed a substantial effect. In addition, however, genetic factors also turned out to play a significant part: it appears therefore that in some way yet to be determined children's inborn nature intertwines with certain kinds of life experiences to produce a particular kind of self-perception. In this respect too the "looking-glass" view of self-development is insufficient to explain all nuances.

As to the kinds of consequences that follow from developing different degrees of self-esteem, Coopersmith's study again provides some useful information. Boys with high self-esteem were by and large less conforming, more creative and academically more achieving than other boys. They have also been described as more assertive and as having a more highly developed sense of self-efficacy (Bandura, 1982). According to Harter (1987), the most important consequence of self-esteem is its influence on the individual's general emotional state, for it is this which in turn affects level of motivation and interest in age-appropriate activities. This is best seen in the oft-demonstrated and close association of low self-esteem with depression – an association that Harter found to be as typical of children as it is among adults.

The case of girls' mathematical ability

Children's self-esteem has many implications, and among these their scholastic progress is prominent. This is well illustrated by discussions about the origins of girls' alleged inferiority in mathematics.

A sex difference in performance on mathematics tests has been consistently reported by a large number of studies (Lips, 1988). The difference is not apparent in the early years of schooling but emerges at the start of adolescence. It is not large except in the upper reaches of the range, where the higher the score the greater is the ratio of males to females (13 to 1 at the top, according to findings by Benbow and Stanley, 1983).

Is the difference due to nature or nurture? The issue is far from settled, but there are some persuasive arguments that experience plays at least some role. Take a study by Entwisle and Baker (1983), who tracked 1,100 children over the first three grades of school, i.e. well before sex differences in mathematics can be expected

to appear. Periodically the children's marks in arithmetic and English were obtained and checked against the previously ascertained expectations by both the children and their mothers. The actual marks showed no sex differences for arithmetic; in reading the girls did rather better than the boys. However, whereas all children were fairly realistic in their expectations as far as reading achievement was concerned, this was not so with respect to arithmetic: boys tended to be overly optimistic; girls overly pessimistic. What is more, at least in middle class families, the mothers' expectations mirrored those of their children: they expected more from boys in arithmetic than from girls, but vice versa in the case of reading. As other research has also shown, parents generally expect higher achievement from sons than from daughters in mathematics; it is likely that this is based on sex role stereotypes as to what is appropriate for males and females and is conveyed to children at home throughout the school years. According to other studies (e.g. Leinhardt, Seewald, & Engel 1979) teachers too convey this message by indicating that they have greater expectations from boys compared with girls in achievement on mathematical tasks.

It is significant that this sex difference is specific to white ethnic groups and could not be found among Hispanic or black children (Schratz, 1978), and that the superiority in mathematical achievement of children in Japan and China over children in the United States by far outweighs any gender gap within these countries (H. W. Stevenson, Lee, & Stigler, 1986). As far as white cultural settings are concerned,

however, we must conclude that girls receive a very definite message telling them that they are inferior in the mathematical field – a message with obvious implications for their self-esteem. As Dweck (1986) has argued, this affects above all girls' interest and motivation; the fact that bright girls in particular more frequently attribute failure in mathematics to their own lack of ability than boys and are more frequently thrown off course by failure, supports the belief that their self-confidence has been undermined and that they have internalized others' messages of their supposed mathematical ineptitude.

The Emotional Self

One significant feature of the self concerns the intense emotions surrounding it. There are few more acute sources of feeling than those experiences and evaluations which in some way reflect upon ourselves, be those feelings positive or negative. Anything to do with one's self-esteem is, of course, inevitably affect-laden; in addition, however, studies of such directly self-referring emotions as shame and pride can help to explain the way in which self-consciousness develops in childhood and the part it plays in regulating behavior.

As M. Lewis (1992) has argued, such emotions occur when the self evaluates the self. Shame results when the self is found wanting with respect to some personal standard or social convention; it can be a painful emotion with sometimes devastating effects. Pride also involves the evaluation of one's performance against some standard, though in this case it signals success in meeting the criterion. Both emotions are more than just temporary states, for they can have lasting consequences for the individual's self-esteem. Studies of their developmental course can thus throw further light on the emergence of the self.

There are, according to Lewis, two cognitive abilities which are prerequisite to the appearance of pride and shame:

1. *The capacity for objective self-awareness*   Some of the primary emotions, such as fear and anger, do not require this and so appear early on in infancy. However, secondary emotions such as pride and shame (as well as guilt and embarrassment) involve self-consciousness and cannot therefore emerge until the individual has formed an objective view of the self. This, as we saw earlier, develops in the second year of life, as indicated by self-referential behavior in the spot-on-the-nose test.

2. *The ability to recognize and maintain standards of conduct* As Kagan (1981) has shown, this too first appears in the second year of life: it is then that words such as "can't," "dirty," or "broken" can be found in children's speech, and it is then that one first finds such behavioral clues as distress when the child cannot imitate a model's action or smiling when it does succeed.

One cannot therefore expect self-referential emotions to appear until the end of the second year when both the above cognitive capacities are in place. Empirical studies bear this out (M. Lewis, Sullivan, et al., 1989; M. Lewis, Alessandri, et al., 1992): when given difficult tasks that they managed to solve children above this age, but not before, showed all the behavior one associates with pride – they raised their eyes, smiled, looked triumphant, and threw up their arms. Failure resulted in signs of shame: eyes were lowered, the body collapsed, and negative comments were made by the children about their performance. Thus children from age 2 or 3 years on are capable of self-evaluation and will react with the appropriate emotion. According to Stipek, Recchia, and McClintic (1992) the developmental course of such self-evaluation can appropriately be thought of in terms of three stages:

1   Given some particular goal (e.g. being able to make a spinning top work or to correctly insert all the shapes into a sorter), children under the age of 2 years obtain pleasure from their achievement but take little notice of any adult reaction to what they have accomplished.
2   After age 2 children increasingly show a need for adult approval: they call the mother's attention to some achievement or look up at her as soon as they have completed a task. Thus they behave as though they desire and are able to anticipate a positive reaction from the adult and depend on her approval.
3   Finally, towards the end of the preschool period, children gradually become more autonomous: their self-evaluation is no longer entirely dependent on an adult's reactions; success and failure are now responded to in terms of the child's own standards and the child need not constantly refer to somebody else for approval.

In conclusion, let us think of the self as a "theory" that each one of us develops during childhood about who we are and how we fit into our society. The functions of the theory are to help us seek out particular experiences that fit in with our self-image, make choices among alternative courses of action, and experience pleasure or displeasure in evaluating the results of such actions. The theory is a complex one; it contains a great many constituents (self-awareness, self-concept, self-esteem, and so forth) all of which need to be knitted together, and it is characterized by both cognitive and emotional features. As we have seen, the theory is built up gradually during childhood, taking different forms at different developmental stages. Initially the content of the self is closely dependent on the way other people react to the child, but with age an increasing trend towards autonomy becomes evident as the individual comes to rely more on his or her own standards. This trend continues throughout childhood; however, the process is by no means a straightforward linear one: in early adolescence, for example, it wanes as young people's reliance on peer group approval again becomes marked. Nor is it a process that is ever complete, for at no time can the self function as a wholly closed system; how others respond to the individual will affect self-evaluation and esteem throughout life. Thus the self begins largely as a socially constructed entity; in due course it attains a certain degree of autonomy; at no point of the life course, however, can the question "Who am I?" be answered without any reference to other people's evaluations.

Knowledge of Others

To function properly in society it is essential that we develop ways of construing the behavior of other people. It is hardly surprising that much of everyday life is taken up with thinking about others: if our own behavior is to have some effect we need to understand the individuals at whom it is directed and be able to anticipate how they may react. In particular, we need to think about *relationships* between people and about the rules that govern these relationships; the social world, after all, presents such a bewildering diversity that some sort of order needs to be imposed on our experience if we are to make sense of it. How this is done is part of the field of *social cognition* – the study of how we perceive, mentally represent, and make inferences about other people.

Investigating how such social skills emerge and develop during childhood has formed a major part of the study of social cognition. A widespread assumption, that general principles of cognition can also be directly applied to thinking about the social world, characterized much of the earlier work on this topic; children's levels of cognitive development, that is, were said to determine their understanding of people according to the same principles that determine their conception of the physical world. Piagetian stages in particular were used to explain children's social behavior, as seen above all in the belief that up to the age of 7 children's interpersonal relationships are characterized by *egocentrism*, that is, the inability to consider any point of view other than one's own. This belief is now largely discredited; as we shall see below, there is a large body of evidence to show that even very young children are capable of a degree of social understanding that any strict application of Piagetian theory could not account for. There is no doubt that levels of cognitive development do influence children's understanding of people, but people differ from physical objects in having intentions and feelings, in being capable of spontaneous behavior and in therefore impinging on the child in ways very different from those of an object. Social cognition thus needs consideration in its own right, even though it may share certain characteristics with nonsocial cognition, and caution is therefore required in generalizing from one sphere to the other.

Self–Other Relationships

Which occurs first, a sense of self or a sense of other? Or do they both emerge simultaneously and develop in parallel? Empirical evidence is scarce, primarily for methodological reasons: self-awareness can be assessed by means such as the spot-on-nose test, but nothing analogous has been developed for assessing the existence of other-concepts. It is true that M. Lewis and Brooks-Gunn (1979) found that children detected the spot on their mothers' noses at an earlier age than on their own noses; nevertheless, these authors maintained that the development of sense of self and sense of other emerge at the same time. In this they followed a well established theoretical tradition: J. M. Baldwin (1987), for instance, argued with great conviction that self- and other-concepts arise simultaneously from social interactions, that both develop in the same fashion and that both share the same features. This is also the view taken by psychoanalytic writers (e.g. Mahler, Pine, & Bergman, 1975): they too maintain that the two concepts, absent in the early stages of infancy, appear subsequently as parallel developments and in isomorphic fashion out of the undifferentiated interaction between mother and child.

The little empirical evidence that does exist suggests that matters may be rather more complicated. We see this in a study by Pipp, Fischer, and Jennings (1987), in which children between 6 months and $3\frac{1}{2}$ years were given a series of tasks to assess both knowledge of self and knowledge of mother. The tasks tapped two different domains: *feature recognition*, i.e. the ability to recognize someone's appearance, and *agency*, namely the understanding that individuals are active, controlling agents in their dealings with the environment. Assessment of the former included questions about perceptual recognition and verbal identification of the self and of the mother, as well as the spot-on-nose test applied to both individuals; testing the latter focused on the child's ability to act on the appropriate individual when asked, for example, to pretend to feed either self or mother. As the results show, the order in which the two concepts of self and other emerge depend on the task: for feature recognition knowledge of mother preceded that of self; for agency, knowledge of self appeared before knowledge of mother. Perhaps this is to be expected: infants see their mothers more than they see themselves and thus have more opportunity to become familiar with the mother's appearance; on the other hand they have far more experience of themselves performing actions and are thus more likely to develop an earlier sense of their own agency than that of another person. It seems there is no simple answer to the question which comes first – it all depends on what aspect of self- and other-concept one is investigating. What is more, cognitive differentiation of self and other may appear relatively early, i.e. by the second year; emotional differentiation, on the other hand, does not take place till several years later. As Harter and Barnes (1981) found, 3- to 4-year-old children automatically attribute the same emotion to their parents that they themselves experience: when they are happy the parent is said to be happy too, when they are sad the parent is also sad. Only older children can appreciate that different people can experience different emotions at the same time.

According to some writers, however, what is primary is neither the self-concept nor the other-concept but a concept of the *relationship* between child and adult. This point has been most clearly developed by attachment theorists such as Bretherton (1985) and Main, Kaplan, and Cassidy (1985). According to their proposal, it is not a matter of first constructing notions of self and of other and only then gradually working out some sort of relationship between the two; rather the process works the other way, in that self and other are experienced in the context of event-based relationships and are constructed out of these dyadic experiences. Children's initial awareness is thus of undifferentiated relationships; it is these that give rise to the first internal working models, and models of self and attachment figure only become constructed as separate entities thereafter. Even then, however, the two cannot be understood without reference to each other, for they represent obverse aspects of the same relationship. The rejected child, for example, will not only develop a working model of the parent as rejecting but also one of him- or herself as unworthy and unlovable; the accepted child, on the other hand, will develop working models of both self and other in correspondingly positive tones.

All this is speculative; however, there is some indirect support to show that the quality of children's first relationships with other people is reflected in the nature and growth of their self-concept. For instance, according to Schneider-Rosen and Cicchetti (1984) securely attached infants tend to develop self-awareness (as assessed by the ubiquitous spot-on-nose test) at a faster rate than insecurely attached infants. Similarly Pipp, Easterbrooks, and Brown (1993) have reported that 20-month-old children who are securely attached have a more highly developed featural knowledge not only of themselves but also of both mother and father than insecurely attached children. Both sense of self and sense of other thus reflect the quality of the relationship between child and adult, and though these findings do not address the issue of primacy of development they do indicate how closely concepts of self, of other, and of self–other relationships are intertwined.

The case of maltreated children's self-development

If there is indeed an association between the quality of children's primary social relationships and the nature of their self-concepts, it should be especially evident where such relationships are markedly deviant. One such example refers to children with a history of maltreatment by their parents.

Maltreated children are known to manifest a wide variety of more or less profound psychological disturbances. Among these is lowered self-esteem. In a study of such children aged 5 to 11 during two weeks spent in day-camps with nonmaltreated children, Kaufman and Cicchetti (1989) found the former to score significantly lower on measures of self-esteem than the latter; they also found them to be more withdrawn and to show other disturbances in peer relationships. It may well be that low self-esteem and disordered relationships with other children influence each other in a mutually self-perpetuating manner: thus children with low self-esteem are more likely to be withdrawn and have difficulties in making successful social contacts, thereby increasing their sense of failure and lack of belief in themselves.

There are other indications that the self-concepts of children maltreated by their parents may develop in deviant ways. Thus such children have been described as displaying feelings more appropriate to younger children (Aber & Cicchetti, 1984), as having negative images of themselves (Kinard, 1980), and as talking less about themselves and their internal feelings (Cicchetti & Beeghly, 1987). However, not all aspects of the self-system are equally affected: the development of visual self-recognition during the second and third years of life was found by Schneider-Rosen and Cicchetti (1991) to develop at the same time as that in other children. This aspect, it seems, is primarily dependent on biological maturation and relatively immune to even such extreme experiences as parental maltreatment. It is significant, however, that in the same study maltreated children, when confronted by their mirror image, showed some intensely negative emotional reactions; even at this young age these children already appeared to be more reluctant to accept themselves in positive and confident terms.

We must conclude that the rejection which is implied in parental treatment is highly likely to give rise to disturbances in self-development. The deviant relationship experienced by the children thus has its counterpart in the way in which these children come to think about themselves.

Differentiation of self from other is a slow and long-drawn-out process that occupies much of childhood. The most detailed account of this progression has been provided by Selman (1980), who put forward a model detailing the way in which children become capable of coordinating their own point of view with those of other people and thus develop appropriate role playing skills. Selman presented children with stories depicting various social and moral dilemmas, and by means of semistructured interviews probed the ways in which children interpret such situations. From the answers so obtained he concluded that children's social understanding evolves through a series of stages, summarized in table 25. This shows that children gradually progress from an egocentric stage, when they are unable to step outside their own skin or even see any need to consider another's perspective, to becoming able at least to appreciate that others do have points of view and that these may be different from their own. Initially such realization is somewhat inflexible: the child can consider various viewpoints sequentially but cannot interrelate them by considering them simultaneously. Eventually people's perspectives can be thought about in an increasingly abstract fashion, in that they no longer need to be tied to specific individuals but are formulated in terms of viewpoints attributed to social groups ("the generalized other"). They are also thought about in an increasingly objective manner, in so far as children can consider others' viewpoints without having to relate them to their own. These stages, according to Selman, form an invariant sequence: children progress through them all in the order stated. Each stage

Table 25 Selman's stages in self–other understanding

Stage	Age (years)	Type of understanding
0	3–6	Egocentric: no awareness that others may interpret the same situation differently
1	5–9	Recognition of different perspectives, but cannot relate perspectives to each other
2	7–12	Can reflect on another person's point of view, but still not consider own and another's perspective at same time
3	10–15	Different perspectives can now be considered simultaneously. Own viewpoint can be reflected upon from that of another person
4	12–adult	Specific points of view can be compared with that prevalent in society generally, i.e. with an abstraction ("the generalized other")

represents a qualitatively distinct way of looking at the social world; at each children are provided with a particular strategy of thinking about themselves in relation to other people.

There are some problems with this account, most of which arise from the fact that it is closely tied to Piagetian stages of cognitive development. Piaget, as we have already mentioned, overestimated young children's egocentrism; to suggest that up to the age of 6 or so children are wholly unable to take another person's perspective into consideration is too sweeping a generalization. In addition Selman tells us nothing about how children progress from one stage to another and in particular what part social experience plays in this development; he only tells us about the structure and does not explain the dynamics. On the other hand the general trends he describes are undoubtedly to be found: children do gradually become able to consider several notions simultaneously; they can increasingly cope with abstractions; and the ability to handle experiences objectively, without constant reference to the self, does increase over age. And finally Selman has shown that self- and other-concepts are so closely intertwined in the early years that it is not till adolescence that the differentiation process can be regarded as complete.

Describing People

When children are asked to provide descriptions of other people – their best friend, say, or a next-door neighbor – two things become clear from their accounts: first, that there are marked developmental changes in the nature of their descriptions and second, that these changes parallel in many respects those we have previously noted for self-description.

Consider the difference between the following two accounts (taken from Livesley & Bromley, 1973) of children's friends:

> (*7-year-old*) "He is very tall. He has dark brown hair, he goes to our school. I don't think he has any brothers or sisters. He is in our class. Today he has a dark orange sweater and gray trousers and brown shoes."

> (*15-year-old*) "Andy is very modest. He is even shyer than I am when near strangers and yet is very talkative with people he knows and likes. He always seems good-tempered and I have never seen him in a bad temper. He tends to degrade other people's achievements, and yet never praises his own. He does not seem to voice his opinions to anyone. He easily gets nervous."

Serveral differences immediately become apparent. For one thing, the younger child's account is briefer and less differentiated. It is also stated in absolute terms, lacking the comparative statements ("even shyer than I am") contained in the second account. The older child is able to make allowance for different circumstances (e.g. shy with strangers but talkative with well-known people); in addition, this boy introduces gradations ("tends to") into his judgments and acknowledges uncertainty ("seems to"). Above all, however, personal qualities are almost wholly absent from the younger child's account: the individual is described in terms of physical appearance and clothes rather than the psychological attributes on which the older boy focuses.

We see here the same developmental trend that we noted in children's self-descriptions, i.e. the trend that proceeds from a primarily concrete to an increasingly abstract descriptive style – though here too more recent research has not found the distinction to be as absolute as earlier work had claimed. Nevertheless, studies of *person perception* (as this topic is often referred to) have shown that the way in which children view others can usefully be thought of as progressing through three developmental stages (for relevant studies see P. H. Miller & Aloise, 1989; Shantz, 1983):

1   Up to the age of 7 or so children describe others in terms of external characteristics – their looks, their actions, their possessions, and where they live. If they do refer to psychological aspects they use global terms such as *nice* or *good*; however, these are employed egocentrically ("nice to me") and refer to here-and-now behavior, with no indication that they may represent lasting dispositions.

2   From 7 or 8 on (at the same age that we noted a shift to occur in the self-system) children show a marked increase in the use of trait terms (shy, anxious, clever, etc.) in their accounts of other people. They continue to describe visible features, but now assume that behind the external facade there are psychological qualities which transcend here-and-now behavior. But the traits are merely listed; they are

not integrated into an overall personality organization, and allowance for different circumstances remains rare.

3   In early adolescence a further step is taken, for now accounts of other people
become much more sophisticated. Qualifying terms, such as "sometimes" or
"quite," appear; judgments are made relative to situation and circumstances; and
there are attempts to resolve contradictions within the context of the individual's
total personality. Increasingly people are also assessed in comparative terms,
whether in relation to other individuals or to some general standard adhered to by
society.

A study by Barenboim (1981) illustrates these changes. Children between 6 and 11
were interviewed and asked to talk about three persons they knew well. Their
descriptive statements were assigned to three categories: *behavioral comparisons* (such
as "Billy runs a lot faster than Jason" or "She draws the best in our whole class");
psychological constructs (e.g. "He's a real stubborn idiot" or "Sarah is so kind"); and
psychological comparisons ("Linda is real sensitive, a lot more than most people").
As figure 12 shows, marked age changes appeared in the extent to which the three
kinds of descriptors were used. Behavioral comparisons, the most frequent category
at age 6, increased in frequency up to age 8 but thereafter declined. Psychological
constructs, initially virtually absent, began to increase markedly from age 7 on,
becoming the most common way of describing others after 9 years. Psychological

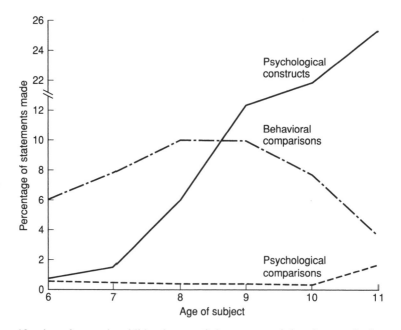

Figure 12   Age changes in children's use of three types of descriptors of other people
(adapted from Barenboim, 1981)

comparisons remained low up to the age of 10 and began to appear more frequently thereafter.

These findings confirm the switch in middle childhood from a reliance on behavioral terms to the increasing use of psychological descriptors. They also point to a developing tendency to make use of comparative judgments: when Barenboim in further work extended his inquiries to the age of 16 he found a sharp increase of statements in the psychological comparison category between 10 and 16. Thus both the ability to switch to a more abstract mode, when the child can view others in terms of their inner attributes, and a growing use of comparative statements are highlighted by these results.

What is responsible for these developmental shifts in other-description? The timing of the two principal changes, around 7 years and in early adolescence, may provide a clue, for it is then that major realignments in cognitive functions have been postulated to occur. At the earlier age children enter the period of concrete operations and become capable of appreciating the invariant nature of objects – as seen, for example, in their ability to conserve such properties as number and mass. Instead of being swayed by whatever concrete perceptual evidence happens to impinge on the child at the moment, children can now integrate diverse bits of information over time and look for consistencies in object properties. In the same way people, we can assume, are no longer seen in terms of separate incidents of behavior; the new ability allows the child to think of others in terms of lasting dispositions that remain relatively stable over time. The ability to appreciate *character constancy* has, according to Rotenberg (1982), two aspects: stability, i.e. the belief that personality remains constant over time, and consistency, the belief that an individual's identity does not change despite changes in overt appearance. In a study of children between 6 and 9 years Rotenberg found both aspects to be acquired at a similar rate over this age range, with stability ahead of consistency. Both were also significantly correlated with scores on tests assessing number and mass conservation, thus providing support for the hypothesis that character constancy is, in part at least, a product of cognitive development, with particular reference to the ability to conceptualize invariant properties.

The second developmental shift in the nature of other-description, that occurring in adolescence, also coincides with a major cognitive change, namely from the period of concrete operations to that of formal operations. At that time children become much more capable of dealing with abstractions and relationships; they no longer have to rely on concrete observations but can think about assumed entities and anticipate future events. Again these developments have their counterpart in social cognitions: adolescents can form hypotheses about people, see them in much more complex terms which acknowledge the interaction of personal disposition and situational factors, introduce qualifications into their assessments according to circumstances, and think about the relationships between people even when these people are unknown to the young person. However, we cannot be certain that cognitive changes are wholly responsible for changes in children's concepts of others; it may be that social experience also plays a part: Higgins and Parsons (1983), for instance, have suggested that shifts in the child's social life such as entry to school or transfer from elementary to secondary education necessitate changes in social cognition which could be reflected in the way other people are thought about.

Attributing Internal States to Others

The ability to appreciate other people's internal feelings and the knowledge that their overt behavior is governed by various inner motives are essential to "reading" others and thus to mature social functioning. If young children were able to attend only to outer characteristics they would not have such skills at all; if they were wholly egocentric they would automatically attribute their own feelings and motives to others. It seems, however, that neither of these propositions is wholly true.

Take the capacity for *empathy*, i.e. the emotional responsiveness which an individual shows to the feelings experienced by another person. The first signs of this appear surprisingly early. Zahn-Waxler and Radke-Yarrow (1982) trained mothers to keep records of what their children did when witnessing naturally occurring expressions of emotion in other people; the children were also observed when an adult feigned mild distress. It was found that even 10-month-old children, the youngest included in the study, showed some reaction by either intently watching the other person or, in about a third of the incidents, showing signs of distress themselves. Over the next year distress signs declined; instead children increasingly attempted actively to intervene by touching or patting the other person. The increase was marked from about 18 months on: children verbally expressed sympathy, offered objects, made suggestions or fetched another person to help. They also increasingly imitated the signs of distress witnessed, as though trying out these emotional expressions in order to comprehend them better.

The capacity for empathy, we can conclude, is present very early on; with increasing age it becomes more complex in its manifestation and more useful in the results it produces. According to M. L. Hoffman (1988) these changes can be summarized in a four-level developmental scheme:

1 *Global empathy* In the first year children may match the emotion they witness, e.g. by crying when another infant is crying, but the emotion is involuntary and undifferentiated.
2 *Egocentric empathy* From the second year on children actively offer help. The kind of help offered is what they themselves would find comforting and is in that sense egocentric; nevertheless, the child at least responds with appropriate empathic efforts.
3 *Empathy for another's feelings* In the third year, with the emergence of role-taking skills, children become aware that other people's feelings can differ from

their own. Their responses to distress may thus become more appropriate to the other person's needs.

4 *Empathy for another's life condition* By late childhood or early adolescence children become aware that others' feelings may not just be due to the immediate situation but stem from their more lasting life situation. Empathy may also be found with respect to entire groups of people (the poor, the oppressed, etc.) and thus transcend immediate experience.

It is hardly surprising that the developmental course of empathy is such a protracted one, for it is a complex concept depending on both cognitive and emotional growth. According to Feshbach (1987), three components make up this construct: (1) the child's ability to experience emotions, (2) the cognitive ability to discriminate emotional cues in others, and (3) the more mature cognitive skills entailed in assuming another person's perspective and role. The capacity for empathy may be there from infancy on, but it requires cognitive developments to transform it into a properly functioning behavior pattern. It might seem highly likely that it is also dependent on the child's socializing experience, but efforts to relate individual differences in children's empathy to such aspects as parental affection, type of disciplinary technique, or the parents' own displays of empathy have met with mixed success. Nevertheless, in a review of such studies Barnett (1987) concluded that when all the evidence is taken together it does seem likely that empathy thrives in an environment that (1) satisfies the child's own emotional needs but discourages excessive self-concern, (2) encourages the child to identify, experience, and express a broad range of emotions, and (3) provides numerous opportunities for the child to observe other people's emotional responsiveness.

The research on empathy suggests that young children are by no means socially inept and that they have greater appreciation of other people as thinking and feeling individuals than was thought at one time. The same conclusion is provided by studies of children's spontaneous talk about other people's internal states (e.g. Bretherton & Beeghly, 1982; J. R. Brown & Dunn, 1991). These show that from about the third year on children have at least some awareness of the desires and emotions both of themselves and of others, that they can comment on motives and infer at least some mental states, and that some time during the preschool period they begin to discuss how their own or another person's state has been caused or may be changed. The following excerpts illustrate these abilities:

- "You sad, Mommy. What Daddy do?"
- "I give hug. Baby be happy."
- "Katie not happy face. Katie sad."
- "Christie fell down. Hurt self."
- "If I cry I'm mad. If you cry I'll be mad."

All these come from transcripts of children not yet 3 years old, and although the child's own internal states are initially more often mentioned than those of other people there are enough of the latter to show that such children cannot simply be labeled as egocentric. On the contrary, they can at times show a remarkable understanding of someone else's psychological condition, even if their ability to act appropriately is limited. Once again we also see the need for caution in applying the notion of a developmental shift from concrete to abstract (or from external to internal, or from physical to psychological) conceptions of people. As P. H. Miller and Aloise (1989) concluded, such a trend surely occurs in some sense at some time in development, but it is not as general and the switch is not as late as previously held. Earlier research tended to underestimate children's abilities because of the reliance on free verbal description (e.g. "Tell me about . . ."); when less demanding methods such as forced-choice questions are used it becomes evident that preschool children do show awareness of mental entities, even though their knowledge is not as accurate or complex as that of older children and tends to be confined to *states* that are operative at the time to the exclusion of stable, permanent *traits*.

The usefulness of the ability to talk about internal states and its implications for children's social interactions are points emphasized in a study by J. R. Brown and Dunn (1991) of a group of children periodically investigated in their homes between 2 and 3 years of age. Their findings show, first of all, that not all internal states are equally easily grasped: desire terms (want, need, etc.) and feeling state terms (sleepy, bored, happy, etc.) are already to be found in the talk of 2-year-olds; mental state terms (know, think, pretend, etc.), on the other hand, do not appear till later and are less frequent (table 26). Throughout the year of the study children referred most often to their own internal states; at age 2 only 4 percent of such references were to other people, but by age 3 this had gone up to 25 percent, indicating a sharp increase of interest in the feelings and desires of others. What is also clear, however, is that the ability to talk about inner states has profound implications for children's social interactions, adding greatly to their effectiveness as teasers, comforters, and deceivers, as well as excusers of their own and other's actions when in trouble. Most of all, as children approach the age of 3, they now have the opportunity to share and negotiate interpretations of events with others and can talk about their respective understanding of the psychological causes of behavior. The scope of social interactions becomes vastly extended thereby.

Table 26   Frequency of references to internal states (for 100 conversational turns)

	Children's age (years)		
	2	*$2\frac{1}{2}$*	*3*
Desire terms	5.4	6.0	9.4
Feeling state terms	3.2	3.7	5.4
Mental state terms	0	0.1	0.7

Source: Adapted from J. R. Brown & Dunn (1991)

It is these social interactions, of course, and especially conversations with parents, that in the first place provide children with the opportunity to learn to talk about inner states. Take this discussion between a mother and her $3\frac{1}{2}$-year-old son:

Child: Why is Billy [*a baby brother*] crying?
Mother: Because he is tired but just can't get to sleep.
Child: Does that hurt?
Mother: Yes, I suppose it does.
Child: But going to sleep doesn't hurt me.
Mother: You cried when you were a baby and were tired.
Child: Does Billy have a pain?
Mother: Well, being tired is I suppose a sort of pain.
Child: There (*patting the baby*), you go to sleep and the pain will stop.

As Dunn, Bretherton, and Munn (1987) found in a study of children 18 to 32 months old, conversations with mothers at home tend to contain a great many references to feeling states such as fatigue, pleasure, pain, and distress – all topics of considerable interest to children and often raised in emotionally highly charged contexts. As the children observed got older both their own use and also the mothers' use of such references increased; what is more, the amount that mothers talked about feelings was significantly related to the amount that their children talked about them. There were also some intriguing hints of sex differences: mothers talked more about feelings to girls, and from 24 months on girls talked more about them than boys. Again the use to which such talk can be put became evident: the children did not merely use feeling terms to comment on inner states but also to explain both their own and other people's behavior and to influence what others were doing. Thus from the age of 2 on children show some understanding of feeling states and can use this understanding in their relationships with family members.

Children's Theory of Mind

The knowledge that others are thinking and feeling beings becomes more sophisticated and coherent with age. For example, at age 4, but not generally before, children begin to understand that the same world can be experienced in different ways by different people and that each person may therefore have a distinctive belief about reality. The ability to infer mental states in others and to see them as the basis for overt action has been regarded as evidence that children have a "theory of mind" (Astington, Harris, & Olson, 1988; Wellman, 1990). Such a theory enables the child to explain observable events (people's actions) by postulating unobservable entities (beliefs, desires, etc.); it is thus a device for understanding social behavior.

There has been some dispute as to the origins of this device, in particular whether a theory of mind is inborn or comes to be constructed in the early years. There is general agreement, however, that it is not till the age of 4 or so that reasonably sophisticated versions of a theory of mind become evident. To demonstrate this the *false belief* paradigm has been used, as illustrated in a landmark study by Wimmer and Perner (1983). Children aged 3 and 4 years were presented with stories, acted out with dolls and toys, in which a character holds a belief that the child knows to be false and thus different from his own. The question is whether the child can correctly

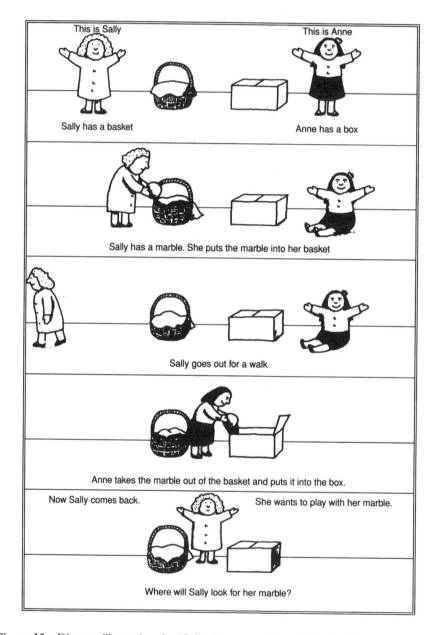

Figure 13   Diagram illustrating the "Sally-Anne" test (from Frith, 1989)

predict the character's action given the false belief. An example is the "Sally-Anne" task, a story about two girls playing together. Sally places a marble in a basket and then leaves the room, whereupon Anne moves the marble to another location. Sally returns and looks for the marble. The child being tested is then asked where Sally will look (see figure 13). Nearly all 3-year-olds will state that she will look in the new location where they themselves know the marble has been put; they cannot, that is, attribute a false belief to Sally and use that to predict her action. From 4 years on, however, children give the correct answer: they can appreciate that others may have beliefs which do not accurately reflect reality and that their behavior will reflect such false beliefs. Such an insight is achieved by all normal children; it seems, however, that certain kinds of social experience can expedite this development. According to Perner, Ruffman, and Leekam (1994) children from large families, with many siblings, become competent in this respect earlier than other children: it seems that the particular experiences involved in sibling interactions are such that they can draw the child's attention to the other's state of mind and so foster the development of insight into others' mental states.

Thus till about 4 years of age children go on the assumption that there is only one world out there, i.e. the one that accords with their own experience, and that other people will therefore act in the way the child would. As the Wimmer and Perner study shows, such children cannot as yet mentally represent to themselves alternative models of a particular event: one their own, the other an incompatible one describing another person's false belief about that event. At around 4, however, a novel cognitive skill emerges in that now children acquire the ability to represent another person's conflicting view; they also become capable of understanding another's absence of knowledge. They have come to realize, that is, that what is in our mind is only a *representation* of reality and therefore not necessarily an accurate image, and that a representation which the child knows to be false may nevertheless and quite justifiably be considered as true by another person.

While most theory-of-mind research has examined belief-dependent *actions* (such as Sally's search for her marble), the same concepts can be applied to the development of children's insight into belief-dependent *emotions* such as surprise. People experience surprise when something occurs that they had not believed would occur; to gain understanding of such an emotional state children must learn that surprise rests on an individual's prior belief. By telling children stories about individuals who had various prior expectations and encountered various outcomes and then asking each child about that individual's reaction, Wellman and Banerjee (1991) found signs of rudimentary understanding already at 3 years; however, they also found that in the following two years considerable improvement took place in that children became increasingly accurate and consistent in their judgments. Discrepancies in the precise age when children become capable of insight into mental states may be due to differences in methodologies; what is clear is that somewhere in the 3- to 5-year range children acquire understanding of how various end results, such as actions and emotions, are produced and that the ability to mentally represent other people's psychological states (i.e. to think about thinking, or "metarepresentation") lies at the heart of this development (Leslie, 1987).

These new abilities do not, of course, just appear out of the blue; they depend on various precursors evident at earlier ages. According to P. L. Harris (1989) the acquisition of a theory of mind requires the following prior developments:

1   *Self-awareness*, with particular reference to the child's own mental states. As we have noted, this is evident at quite an early age and can be seen in children's comments about their feelings and desires. Such an ability represents a basic prerequisite for the understanding of mental operations generally.

2   *The capacity for pretence*. From the second year on children are able to engage in make-believe play, including pretend play with dolls whom the child endows with various mental states. A powerful imagination is thus already at work – again a prerequisite for being able to work out how other people function.

3   *The ability to distinguish reality from pretense*. While pretend play may merely involve children projecting their own feelings on to dolls and other materials, the ability to see that others are not just an extension of the child's desires is a later and more sophisticated development. Only when this appears will children no longer confuse the mental states imputed to other people with their own mental states. There is evidence that this does not become reliably established until the fourth year; it is only then that children can imagine another person's beliefs and feelings even though they are not the child's own.

Theory-of-mind research is important because it draws attention to the fact that quite early on in development children construe not only themselves but also other people as thinking and feeling beings. The "theory" they develop is not a conscious one; it is rather an intuitive grasp about human action – a practical knowledge which develops gradually but has its beginnings in the first few years. According to Wellman (1990) those beginnings are evident from about $2\frac{1}{2}$ to 3 years of age, when children show that they can differentiate reality from mentality and distinguish an object from the thought about the object. They know, for example, that you cannot lick the *image* of an icecream; they also know that that image will not melt, can be made to change color and taste and, unlike the real thing, can be safely parked in one's pocket. Thus from the third year on children are aware of thoughts and wants as a special category; it is not till about 4, however, that they learn how these thoughts are connected with the real world, i.e. how particular experiences give rise to particular images and beliefs and how these internal states in turn give rise to particular actions. It is this development (assessed by false belief tests such as the Sally-Anne story) which is widely regarded as indicating the beginnings of true theory-of-mind skills.

Once a child is capable of representing to itself the mental states of another person social interactions assume a much more sophisticated form. As Perner (1988) has pointed out, the social significance of human interaction generally depends on the mental states of the participants. Thus the observation *George kicks Michael* is on its own of limited meaning; to understand it we need to know George's motive – whether he intended to hurt Michael, or to have fun with him, or to draw his attention to something, or whether the act was an accidental one. Only such further information, which goes beyond the act itself, can give meaning to this encounter, and Michael's response will thus crucially depend on his understanding of George's intention. For this purpose he requires theory-of-mind skills, in that these enable him to go beyond the overt action and make inferences about the other child's mental state which brought it about.

The case of autistic children's theory of mind

One area where theory-of-mind concepts have been usefully employed is the syndrome of autism. This, as we previously noted, involves a severe and apparently inborn impairment in the ability to form proper social relationships and, according to one recent proposal, may be due to a specific cognitive deficit which prevents the development of a theory of mind (Frith, 1989; Happe, 1994).

A study by Baron-Cohen, Leslie, and Frith (1986) illustrates this deficit. Three groups of children – autistic, retarded, and normal – were asked to arrange sets of pictures in their proper sequence so that they would tell a story. Some of the stories dealt with simple mechanical themes, e.g. a man kicking a boulder down a hill which then falls into the water below. Other stories concerned social interactions which did not involve the attribution of mental states, e.g. a child taking an icecream away from another, who then bursts into tears. On both these tasks autistic children performed as well as the other two groups. A third set of stories did require attribution of mental states, e.g. a boy was shown stealing a girl's teddybear while her back was turned, followed by the girl turning round to discover the unexpected loss. On these stories the autistic children did far worse. When the children were subsequently asked to narrate the stories the same pattern was found: on the first two pairs of tasks autistic children described what was happening in the same way as the other children; on the third task their account contained hardly any references to the characters' beliefs, intentions, and feelings which gave the story its true meaning, and instead stuck to the description of their overt behavior.

These results suggest that autistic children have a specific problem with respect to understanding other people's internal states. This is confirmed by their failure on the Sally-Anne test (Baron-Cohen, Leslie, & Frith, 1985), as this too reveals their lack of insight into the way in which others think about the world. Such children are therefore at a grave disadvantage in predicting people's behavior in everyday social life; although they can cope with many simpler aspects of social life (Baron-Cohen, 1991) they are unable to truly understand how others function because of the failure to develop a theory of mind.

Sex Role Development

One of the earliest social categories that children learn to apply both to themselves and to other people is maleness–femaleness. Gender is a fundamental aspect of an individual's self-concept; it is also predominant in any assessment made of another person. It tends to be the first thing that a parent wants to know about a newly born baby; thereafter the child's treatment depends very much on which sex it belongs to. No wonder this category is so influential in children's conceptions of the social world, and no wonder (as summaries of research make clear, e.g. Golombok & Fivush, 1994) it develops very early. Take the following findings:

- In late infancy children can already distinguish faces by gender.
- By 2 years children verbally label themselves and others as male or female.
- Sex-stereotyping in children's choice of toys is found by 2 or 3 years of age.
- From about 3 years children prefer to play with same-sex peers.
- Around 3 or 4 children begin to develop some rigid stereotypes as to what occupations (e.g. doctor or nurse) and what activities (e.g. car repair or cooking) are "right" for males and for females.
- By 5 they associate certain personality traits with males and others with females (e.g. toughness; gentleness).

How children develop such conceptions has been a matter of much debate. Parents, teachers, other children, television – all such socializing influences clearly play a part in making the child aware that sex differences matter and that the child is expected to conform to whatever stereotypes are prevalent at that time and at that place. But, in this respect as in all others, the child is no passive recipient of information: as is now widely recognized, children quite early on begin actively to search for a *rule* about the way that males and females are expected to behave. Whatever information is received will thus be actively interpreted and selectively applied by children to their own and other people's behavior. Rule formation becomes increasingly evident during the preschool period, though it may not be till later that the child can verbally formulate the rule. Initially these rules may be considered as moral absolutes which must be rigidly adhered to; only in later childhood will they be understood as social conventions that can be flexibly applied. All along, however, they act as guidelines which enable the child to fit in with the requirements of society regarding the behavior of males and females.

Before we proceed, a word about terminology. "Sex" and "gender" have been defined in various ways by different authors, the distinction being usually based on biologically versus socially determined aspects. However, the distinction has been applied inconsistently; it is in any case a difficult one to sustain in practice. We shall therefore use the two terms interchangeably. Table 27 lists some other terms commonly used in this area, together with their definitions.

The Nature of Psychological Sex Differences

Research attempting to clarify the development of sex roles has for the most part focused on three areas: preferences for particular toys and play activities, the development of personality characteristics, and the choice of playmates.

Table 27   Some common terms used in the sex role literature

Term	Definition
Androgyny	The psychological merging of masculine and feminine qualities (from the Greek *andro* = male and *gyne* = female)
Gender concepts	The understanding of what males and females are expected to do
Gender constancy	The realization that biological sex is invariant despite superficial changes in appearance
Gender identity	Correct labeling of self and others as male or female
Gender schema	A cognitive structure whereby individuals organize information about gender
Gender stability	Understanding that a person's sex remains constant throughout life
Sex role behavior	The performance of actions that match the social definition of sex role
Sex role concepts	As gender concepts (see above)
Sex role knowledge	Knowing what behavior patterns are regarded as appropriate for males and females
Sex role stereotypes	The over-extension of gender (sex role) concepts
Sex typing	The process whereby sex-appropriate behavior and beliefs about sex roles are acquired

Sex differences in *toy preference* are a well established phenomenon. Boys tend to play with trucks, blocks, and guns; girls with dolls, soft toys, and domestic articles. A study by M. O'Brien and Huston (1985) illustrates this trend. Children aged 1 to 3 were given sets of play materials which (according to adults' ratings) included "male," "female," and "neutral" toys. The results show a clear pattern of sex-typing play. Among the boys even the youngest tended to choose masculine toys and there was little change in this respect after 20 months of age. For girls acquisition of same-sex play pattern was a more gradual process which became increasingly pronounced. In both sexes a distinctive pattern of sex-typed play was evident well before the age of 3. It is, however, not till later that children become consciously aware that some toys are thought of as more appropriate for one sex than the other (Weinraub et al., 1984): behavior thus precedes understanding.

The tendency for girls to lag behind boys in toy preference has been found in other studies too (e.g. Blakemore, La Rue, & Olejnik, 1979). It has also been observed that girls are more likely to play with masculine toys than boys are with feminine toys – again an indication of less pronounced sex typing in girls' early development. Richardson and Simpson (1982) analyzed 855 letters written by children in the 5- to 10-year range to Santa Claus and found that the toys requested showed a clear sex-typing effect. For example, 43.5 percent of the boys but only 8.2 percent of the girls wanted some form of vehicle, whereas 27.4 percent of girls and just 0.6 percent of boys asked for a doll. The letters also showed that a greater number of girls than boys wanted "opposite sex" items. Whether this is due to a "social desirability" factor, as some have speculated, in that male characteristics are more valued and boys are therefore under greater pressure to conform to cultural stereotypes than girls, remains uncertain. As we shall see, the role of adults' expectations and socializing techniques in bringing about sex-appropriate play behavior is still a contentious issue, and another explanation should therefore not be ruled out, namely that inborn personality characteristics of a sex-linked nature may account for differential toy preferences. Boys, that is, tend to be more active and aggressive; girls more passive and nurturant, and both consequently choose those toys that lend themselves best to such behavioral tendencies.

The differentiation of the sexes on the basis of *personality characteristics* has attracted a very considerable body of research. Cultural stereotypes have been subject to much change in recent decades, yet males are still portrayed as active, dominant, aggressive, and confident; women as passive, submissive, fearful, and compliant. However, of all these aspects only *aggression* can be regarded as attracting some research support for such stereotypes (Archer & Lloyd, 1985; Eagly, 1987; Maccoby & Jacklin, 1974, 1980). From about 2 or 3 years on boys have quite consistently been found to exceed girls in aggressive behavior. This may display itself in "play fighting," in rough-and-tumble and (despite some beliefs to the contrary) in verbal as well as in physical aggression. Such a phenomenon has been observed in nearly all other societies and occurs in most (though not all) species. As is the case with all such characteristics, there is a great deal of overlap between the sexes in the distribution of aggressiveness and it therefore requires large samples to bring out the difference (Hyde, 1984). The same applies to another characteristic that some, but by no means all, investigators believe to differentiate the sexes, i.e. *activity level*. In those studies where there is a difference it is almost always boys who are the more active sex (Eaton & Enns, 1986). Given greater male aggressiveness and possibly greater activity level, it is perhaps not surprising that boys and girls choose toys and engage in types of play activity that reflect their respective proclivities (Golombok & Fivush, 1994).

This may apply also to the third area that has yielded sex differences, i.e. *playmate choice*. As has been demonstrated with an impressive degree of consistency, children play primarily in same-sex groups. The following conclusions emerge from the research on this phenomenon (Maccoby & Jacklin, 1987):

- Sex segregation in children's grouping is evident from about 3 years on, emerging (according to some evidence) somewhat earlier among girls than among boys.
- During mid- and late childhood same-sex preference becomes increasingly marked.

- It is a spontaneous phenomenon and one not easily changed by adult pressure.
- Observations on children in other societies show it to be near-universal; it occurs also among at least some subhuman primates.

Figure 14, based on observations obtained by La Freniere, Strayer, and Gaulthier (1984) of preschool children at play, illustrates the developmental trends of sex segregation. A sharp, overall increase was found in this study between ages 1 and 6, though at 28 months boys were still behaving at near-chance level while the girls were already choosing same-sex playmates in nearly 70 percent of cases.

Why do children prefer to play with others of the same sex? We cannot be sure of the answer, and though Maccoby and Jacklin (1987) have advanced various possibilities they conclude that the phenomenon is probably multidetermined. But one factor to consider takes us back to the personality characteristics which tend to differentiate the sexes, i.e. aggressiveness and activity level. Together these two traits may well produce an incompatibility of play styles: boys like rough-and-tumble and attempt to establish dominance relationships; girls prefer a quieter, more equitable manner. Both sexes thus choose companions (as they choose toys) who fit in with these tendencies and with whom they are therefore more comfortable. It is therefore not surprising that all-boy and all-girl groups tend to develop very different styles of interaction. As analyses of verbal exchanges have shown, in male groups a preponderance of commands, threats, boasts, and noncompliance can be found; among girls

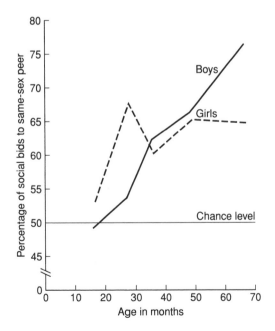

Figure 14 Preferences of boys and girls aged 1 to 6 years for same-sex playmates (based on La Freniere et al., 1984)

agreement, turn-taking, and acknowledgment of others' contributions are frequent. In the one case the emphasis is very much on dominance; in the other it is largely concerned with social binding (Maccoby, 1990). This difference continues into adolescence and beyond.

Any statement about psychological sex differences must be made with care. Gender is without doubt a fundamental social category, yet the overlap between males and females with respect to any behavioral attribute remains noteworthy – *vide* the tomboyish girl and the effeminate boy. However, according to one school of thought, most notably represented by Bem (1974, 1981), the very notion of masculinity and femininity being opposite ends of the same continuum is a mistaken one; instead the two should be regarded as separate dimensions both of which can be found in any one of us. An individual scoring high on one dimension and low on the other is sex-typed; if high on both the person is considered *androgynous* whereas someone low on both is *undifferentiated*. This scheme, and the concept of androgyny in particular, has given rise to much heated debate but also to quite a lot of empirical work. There is little sign of androgyny before the age of 9 or 10; in adolescence, however, when previously rigid ideas about sex roles become more blurred, between a quarter and a third of individuals tested have been classified as androgynous (Hall & Halberstadt, 1980). According to some reports the androgynous person tends to be better adjusted and have higher self-esteem; however, closer examination suggests that it is primarily the masculine component that contributes to this rather than the mixture of masculinity and femininity (Taylor & Hall, 1982). Thus, what is psychologically so desirable is whatever it is that the masculinity items of the sex role inventories measure and not the combination as such of the two kinds of sex-typed items.

Development of Gender Concepts and Sex Role Knowledge

In tracing the development of psychological sex differences we shall examine three topics, i.e. the emergence of gender concepts, the acquisition of sex role knowledge, and the relationship between understanding of sex typing and sex-typed behavior.

Gender concepts, i.e. the realization that people are either male or female, make their first appearance in the second year but do not complete their development for several years thereafter. This is because at least three different aspects are involved, each emerging at a different time (see table 28). As Slabey and Frey (1975) demonstrated, the first to appear is *gender identity*, namely the ability correctly to label self and others as male or female. From 18 months on children already notice some of the characteristics (hair and clothes in particular) which differentiate the sexes; from the age of 2, given a picture of a boy and one of a girl, they can pick out the correct one when asked "Which one is you?"; and soon thereafter they can give the appropriate response when asked "Are you a boy or a girl?"

However, there is more to understanding gender than accurate identification. The second step is *gender stability*, when the child realizes that a person's sex remains

Table 28 Sequential understanding of gender

Step		Age of appearance (years)	Sample questions asked	Characteristics
1	Identity	$1\frac{1}{2}$–2	"Are you a boy or a girl?"	Correctly labels self and others as male or female
2	Stability	3–4	"Will you be a mummy or a daddy when you grow up?"	Understands people retain the same gender throughout life
3	Constancy	6–7	"If a boy puts on a dress, will he be a girl?"	Aware gender not dependent on changes in appearance (e.g. hair, clothes)

Source: Based on Slabey & Frey (1975)

constant throughout life. When Slabey and Frey asked questions such as "When you were a baby, were you a little boy or a little girl?" and "Will you be a mummy or a daddy when you grow up?" children were unable to give correct answers till the fourth year. The third step is taken later still, i.e. not till age 6 or 7. This is *gender consistency*, namely the realization that maleness and femaleness do not change despite modifications in the external cues that normally give rise to identification. A girl, that is, is still a girl even when she cuts her hair short and wears boys' clothes. Thus only when children appreciate that an individual's sex is constant over time *and* that it is constant across situations can one conclude that gender understanding is completed.

The three-step sequence appears to be a universal one, in that it has also been observed in children from a considerable variety of other cultures (Munroe, Shimmin, & Munroe, 1984). It is somewhat more advanced in children's understanding of their own as opposed to other people's gender (Leonard & Archer, 1989), presumably because parents and others draw a child's attention more to its own sex-specific characteristics than to those of others. And there are suggestions that the whole sequence is underpinned by cognitive development: gender constancy, for example, involves the same mental processes as the concept of conservation, in that both require the ability to neglect irrelevant perceptual transformations in arriving at the judgment that the fundamental qualities of people and things remain the same across time and situation. As Marcus and Overton (1978) showed, when children aged 5 to 8 are tested for both gender constancy and conservation of quantity, they tend to succeed on the former only when they can already master the latter.

Sex role knowledge is demonstrated by the development of concepts and stereotypes as to how males and females are supposed to behave and what activities they should undertake. This is assessed by, for example, reading a list of activities (sewing, fighting, cooking, giving kisses, playing with trains, etc.) and asking the child about each whether a boy or a girl would do this. Here too the evidence demonstrates that even quite young children already have definite ideas as to what is appropriate for males and what for females. Take the following assertions by children aged $2\frac{1}{2}$ to $3\frac{1}{2}$ years:

- "Boys hit people."
- "Girls talk a lot."
- "Girls often need help."
- "Boys play with cars."
- "Girls give kisses."

In a study by Kuhn, Nash, and Brucker (1978) children were read statements such as "I am strong" and "When I grow up I'll fly an airplane," and were then asked to select which of two dolls, a male and a female one, had said that. As the results show, even 2-year-olds already had some knowledge of sex role stereotypes, though it also became clear that both sexes tended to believe mostly positive things about themselves but negative things about the opposite sex.

As children get older their knowledge of sex-appropriate characteristics increases. According to Best et al. (1977), who investigated stereotyping among children in the United States, England, and Ireland, such an increase occurs steadily throughout the 5- to 11-year period. At all ages, however, and in all three countries male stereotypes were developing at a faster rate and in more detail than female stereotypes – presumably because of the greater emphasis that our society puts on male conformity to prevailing expectations and the greater freedom allowed to females in defining their role.

Certainly by mid-childhood sex stereotyping is well established, though there is some doubt as to subsequent trends. According to some investigators (e.g. Katz & Ksansuack, 1994) older children become more flexible in their attitudes: whereas the young child considers rules about behavior as absolute requirements and is thus quite intolerant of cross-sex activities, the older child realizes that such rules are only social conventions and therefore adopts more flexible concepts and fewer stereotypes. Yet it has also been suggested that in adolescence, at a time when children develop a new consciousness of all that goes with sex, an intensification occurs of gender-related expectations and that sex role attitudes then revert to their previous rigidity (Galambos, Almeida, & Peterson, 1990). A U-shaped developmental trend would thus be indicated, though whether this is indeed the course that sex stereotyping takes is still far from certain. The problem lies in the fact that no one study has investigated this course over the whole of childhood and adolescence; instead different age groups have been examined in different studies, each using different assessment tools that make generalizations across investigations impossible. And to add yet another complication, sex stereotypes refer to various components, i.e. the toys, possessions, clothes, actions, occupations, and traits considered appropriate for males and females, and the developmental course of all these is not necessarily the same: knowledge of masculine and feminine traits, for example, is not fully matured by age 7 when most of the other components are already well established (Serbin & Sprafkin, 1986).

The relationship between understanding of sex typing and sex-typed behavior is the third area that requires attention. Do children have to possess knowledge of sex typing before they can behave in sex-appropriate ways? Do gender concepts *cause*, or at the very least *influence*, sex-typed preferences? If the formation of gender concepts is a necessary precondition then it should at least precede the development of sex-typed actions, and according to several reviews (e.g. Huston, 1985; C. L. Martin, 1993) this does seem to be the case. For example, Fagot (1985) found that children aged 2 who are able correctly to label the sexes spend 80 percent of their time in same-sex groups, whereas children not yet able to label spend only 50 percent in such groups. Also, according to Fagot and Leinbach (1989), early labelers are subsequently more sex-typed in their toy choices and have greater knowledge of sex stereotypes. It does seem, however, that the level of gender understanding required to influence preferences need be no more than rudimentary. C. L. Martin and Little (1990) administered tests for all three aspects of gender concepts (identity, stability, and consistency) to children aged 3 to 5, as well as tests for clothing and toy stereotypes, toy preferences, and peer preferences, and found that children require only gender *identity* for their preferences and knowledge to be influenced. Merely being able to differentiate and label the sexes may thus make children more aware of the difference and guide their behavior accordingly.

Yet in other respects the link between understanding and behavior is not so clear – on the contrary, from some studies it appears that children can act without knowing. For instance, according to Perry, White, and Perry (1984) children aged 2 to 5, tested both for knowledge of sex role stereotypes and for sex-typed activities, demonstrated the latter well before the former. Boys' knowledge lagged behind their development of preferences by about a year; among girls the trends were more obscure. And N. Eisenberg, Murray, and Hite (1982), who observed 3- to 4-year-old children at play and then questioned them about the reasoning for their selection of particular toys, found few references to sex role stereotypes. Children mostly justified their choices in terms of what the toy could do and how this fitted in with their preferred activities, and not in terms of conscious attempts to act in accordance with learned stereotypes. Thus among preschool children there is no evidence to suggest that gender understanding, at least in any conscious and articulated form, is a necessary precondition to sex-differential behavior – indeed one may wonder whether the influence is not in the opposite direction, i.e. whether children's monitoring of their own and others' behavior might not lead to the development of such cognitive structures as gender concepts and hence to awareness and understanding.

This does not mean that these cognitive structures, once they are formed, do not exert an influence on sex-typed behavior – quite on the contrary, there is every indication that the possession of sex stereotypes may affect an individual's attention to and processing of information relevant to the behavior of the sexes and thereby act as a guide to action. Selective imitation, for example, occurs in children according to sex stereotypes: as Perry and Bussey (1979) demonstrated, 8- and 9-year-olds will choose neutral objects (an apple or a pear, or a pencil or an eraser) selected by adults of the same sex while avoiding those selected by opposite-sex adults. Sex stereotypes may also play a part in academic choices: the notion "maths is not for girls" has no doubt inhibited many a girl from pursuing this subject, affecting her self-perception of competence and preferences. As spelled out by *gender schema theory* (which we shall discuss further below), once children develop schemas, i.e. cognitive representations of the way things are supposed to operate, they will encode and remember information consistent with these mental structures and act accordingly. Sex stereotypes are a form of schema; once in being they will guide action so that a child will behave in conformity with learned standards and with social expectations.

Social Influences on Sex-typed Behavior

As we saw in chapter 2, some psychological sex differences appear to have a biological basis: in these cases genetic and hormonal factors provide the substratum on which behavioral differentiation occurs. But few doubt that a child's experience also plays a crucial part and that parental expectations and rearing practices especially are used for "gender indoctrination," as a result of which children are steered towards the adoption of certain culturally stipulated sex stereotypes. How this occurs has been the subject of much discussion.

From the beginning parents' treatment of a child is influenced by the child's sex. The name given to a baby, the clothes (blue for a boy and pink for a girl), the toys and furnishings – all continually serve as reminders that the child belongs to one category or the other. For example, in a study of middle class infants' bedrooms Rheingold and Cook (1975) showed that the boys' rooms had been filled with toy vehicles, sports equipment, guns, and animals (both toy and live); girls' rooms, on the other hand, were more likely to contain dolls and dollhouses and to be decorated with floral wallpaper and lace. Parents actually perceive boys and girls to be different, even when there is little objective ground for such differences. Thus when J. S. Rubin, Provenzano, and Luria (1974) asked parents to describe their newborn babies they referred to their sons as stronger, bigger, better coordinated, and more alert; daughters were considered to be smaller, softer, more finely featured, and less attentive – and yet, objectively speaking, there was little difference between the boys and girls in terms of their general appearance.

The different expectations that adults bring to their social interactions with boys and girls are most clearly illustrated by studies which manipulate people's beliefs about a child's sex. For example, Condry and Condry (1976) showed a group of adults a videotape of a 9-month-old infant who was either introduced as a boy ("David") or as a girl ("Dana"). The infant was shown responding to various emotion-arousing stimuli such as a jack-in-the-box and a buzzer, and the adults were asked to describe the emotion displayed. The type of description given was clearly influenced by the child's presumed sex. For example, the response to the jack-in-the-box, though neither clearly positive nor clearly negative, was labeled as *anger* by those who believed the infant was a boy but as *fear* by those who thought of it as a girl. Other studies (Frisch, 1977; C. Smith & Lloyd, 1978), using a similar paradigm, have also demonstrated the power of preconception: infants believed to be girls tend to be given dolls and provided with lots of personal stimulation; the same infants passed off as boys are given hammers and guns and played with in a more vigorous style that encourages gross motor activity.

As has frequently been reported, the interaction styles adopted by parents to their sons and daughters respectively differ in a variety of ways. The main differences, together with illustrative studies, are summarized in table 29. The most firmly established finding is that concerning toy choice: boys in particular are discouraged from playing with the "wrong" (i.e. feminine) toys. All other areas mentioned, however, have also been found to attract the efforts of parents to steer their children into sex-appropriate directions. Take the expression of emotion: as analyses of parent–child conversations have shown, adults are much more ready to discuss feelings with girls than with boys (e.g. Kuebli & Fivush, 1992), thereby helping girls more readily to orient to their own and others' emotions and conveying the message that it is quite acceptable for them to do so. Boys tend to receive another message,

Table 29 Socialization areas in which adults adopt different interaction styles to boys and to girls

Socialization area	Findings	Reference
Toy selection	Adults encourage children to choose sex-typed toys	N. Eisenberg et al. (1985) Fagot & Hagan (1991)
Play style	Boys encouraged in and girls discouraged from engaging in vigorous, active play	Fagot (1978) Tauber (1979)
Dependence	Girls' help-seeking responded to more favorably than boys'	Fagot (1978)
Aggression	More attention paid to aggression and assertion by boys than by girls	Fagot & Hagan (1991)
Emotions	Verbal and behavioral expression of emotion tolerated more in girls	Kuebli & Fivush (1992)
Control	More verbal and physical prohibitions shown to boys	Snow et al. (1983)
Task assignment	Boys are given "male," girls "female" household tasks	White & Brinkerhoff (1981)

namely that emotions are not a subject for overt discussion among males and should therefore be pushed into the background. It is therefore clear that from the early years parents are actively involved in their children's sex typing.

Parents are, of course, not the only social agents to influence children's sex typing. Teachers, peers, and the media also exert pressures on boys and girls to conform to particular stereotypes. Peer pressure in particular is significant, for though it may begin early it also continues throughout childhood into adolescence and is sometimes fiercer and more demanding for conformity than adult pressure (Huston, 1983). Even quite young children can be scandalized when a child adopts sex-inappropriate behavior (Langlois & Downs, 1980), and for a boy in particular there is no greater condemnation than to be known as a "sissy." But then boys are under greater pressure anyway, especially from fathers who tend to be much more intolerant of "girlish" behavior in their sons than of "tomboyish" behavior in their daughters (Siegal, 1987).

To what extent and in what way can such social influences account for children's sex typing? According to two theoretical accounts they play the crucial, or as stated by some the sole, determining part:

1 *Learning theory* explains sex typing in terms of reinforcement principles: sex-appropriate behavior is rewarded, sex-inappropriate behavior is punished. The former is accordingly learned and retained while the latter becomes extinguished. Direct tuition is thus the primary mechanism.
2 *Social learning theory* emphasizes imitation as the main mechanism. Children are said to learn about sex roles from observing adult and peer models, and because they are reinforced for paying selective attention to same-sex individuals they are more likely to imitate them and adopt their sex-typed behavior patterns. Here too sex role development is regarded as resulting from the action of the external environment.

It is not difficult to find evidence that appears to support these explanations. Certainly adults selectively use rewards and punishment (usually in the form of approving or disapproving comments) when children choose particular toys or engage in particular sex-linked activities. For example, Langlois and Downs (1980) observed mothers and fathers at play with their preschool children in the presence of both "masculine" and "feminine" toys (respectively soldiers or cars and dollhouses or cooking utensils). Parents generally responded positively to the use of same-sex but negatively to the use of cross-sex toys, thereby presumably perpetuating their children's sex role differentiation. According to Fagot (1985), who observed a playgroup containing 2-year-olds, such sex-differentiated behavior was not found in the teachers in charge of the group; their part, however, was taken by the other children who gave any of their members engaging in sex-appropriate behavior positive feedback of one kind or another but negative feedback for sex-inappropriate behavior. The message from these 2-year-olds was particularly clear in the case of boys, who were thus quickly given the chance of learning "what is not male" and dropping that from their repertoire.

Similarly with imitation, the role of which can be seen by anyone who cares to observe a family at work and at play: boys are encouraged to behave like father, repairing things and engaging in the heavier physical tasks, while girls are more likely to be delegated to the kitchen in order to observe mother's activities there. These activities are then repeated in the games children play. Fatherless families, where boys lack such opportunities for same-sex imitation, would thus be regarded as detrimental to the children's sex role development.

There are, however, problems with explanations that put all their eggs into the social influence basket. Let us list the main ones:

- Any account based on reinforcement encounters the usual problem of such explanations, i.e. that of viewing development in terms of a mechanical stamping in and out, without taking heed of the child's own interpretation.
- Children's development of sex typing occurs early and in a very emphatic way, yet the total amount of reinforcement experience that children encounter is not all that great. Even children treated in a unisex fashion by their families develop such stereotypes.
- There is not a great deal of systematic evidence to suggest that children selectively attend to same-sex models or that they are more likely to imitate them. The role of observational learning is oversimplified, especially as that too misses out the child's interpretation.
- Strong and consistent imitation of same-sex models appears after rather than before the appearance of sex-typed behavior.
- Despite some earlier supportive evidence for a link between fatherless families and boys' atypical sex role development, it is now generally agreed that such a link is not a necessary one.
- Finally, there is the ever present problem of stipulating cause and effect. The fact that adults treat children differentially according to their sex does not mean that any behavioral differences in the children are the effects of such treatment; they may, on the contrary, be its cause.

The last point deserves elaboration. To illustrate it, let us look at some results from a study by Snow, Jacklin, and Maccoby (1983), in which fathers were observed interacting with their 1-year-old sons and daughters in the presence of various disaster-producing objects such as a pitcher full of water and a vase containing flowers. As we see from table 30, fathers of boys were considerably more prohibitive than fathers of girls, the number of prohibitions issued by the former greatly exceeding those of the latter with respect to both physical and verbal interventions. However, when we look at the children's spontaneous attempts to touch the tempting objects we find that boys made significantly more such attempts than girls: by 1 year of age, that is, there were already marked sex differences in behavior, possibly of inherent origin, that could have been the *cause* of the fathers' differential treatment of boys and girls. A similar conclusion emerges when the same father–child pairs were observed in a play situation containing various harmless toys. As table 30

Table 30　Fathers' behavior to boys and girls and the children's spontaneous behavior (mean frequencies)

	Boys	*Girls*
In the presence of tempting object		
Father prohibits	3.91	0.69
Child spontaneously touches	2.13	1.31
In play situation		
Father offers toy	3.50	4.54
Child spontaneously contacts toy	38.93	34.16

Source: Adapted from Snow et al. (1983)

shows, the girls' fathers were found to make rather more attempts to encourage their children to play than the boys' fathers, but as it was also found that the boys were more likely spontaneously to contact the toys than the girls the fathers' behavior may once again be seen as a response to sex-specific characteristics already in the children.

Given the need to take into account the role of inherent characteristics in the child, and given the need to consider the child's own interpretation of its treatment, it is apparent that any explanation of sex typing based on environmental forces cannot survive on its own. Instead, such forces must be considered in conjunction with both biological and cognitive factors.

The case of sex role development in nontraditional families

If processes such as imitation play as big a part in the acquisition of sex roles as social learning explanations propose, children who do not have the necessary role models available would show distorted or, at best, delayed development in this respect.

Examination of various kinds of nontraditional family environments indicates that this is not the case. Take fatherless families, where the absence of an adequate masculine role model ought to have considerable adverse implications for boys' sex role development. Some earlier results seemed to suggest that this is indeed the case, with particular reference to reduced aggressiveness and less stereotyped choice of play objects (Huston, 1983). A more recent review (M. R. Stevenson & Black, 1988), based on a more systematic analysis of all relevant studies, indicates different conclusions. Few, if any, differences between boys reared with or without a father emerged from this overview, and especially so when only the best-designed studies were taken into account. There are some suggestions that boys in father-absent families are less sex-stereotyped in their behavior, but the overall difference tended to be small and of little real import.

Children reared in gay or lesbian households constitute an even stronger test case. Girls or boys, brought up in an environment of two same-sex partners but of the opposite sex to themselves, can be said to be under strong social pressure to develop unconventional sex roles. However, as a review by C. J. Patterson (1992) makes clear, virtually no differences have been found between such children and children of heterosexual parents. As Patterson put it: "The development of gender identity, of gender role behavior, and of sexual preferences among offspring of gay and lesbian parents was found in every study to fall within normal bounds." Take a report by Bailey et al. (1995) on the sexual orientation of the adult sons of gay fathers. More than 90 percent of these sons identified themselves as heterosexual, and as the amount of time the sons had spent living with their fathers bore no relationship to their sexual orientation it seems unlikely that imitation or any other kind of environmental transmission played a part in their sexual development.

A similar conclusion emerges from investigations of children in other nonconventional families, e.g. where husband and wife reverse roles (Radin, 1982) or where parents have avant garde views and strongly promote sexual egalitarianism in their children's upbringing (Weisner & Wilson-Mitchell, 1990). Once again it emerges that such children develop the usual sex identities at the usual times and that variations in family patterns were not related to the children's behavior and preferences. One must conclude that sex role development is a highly robust phenomenon that is not easily thrown off course by atypical social experience.

Children's Gender Construction

While learning theory accounts of sex role development stress experiential factors, other explanations concern themselves primarily with cognitive factors. Such theories are based on the belief that changes in children's cognitive capacities underlie the development of sex-typed behavior.

Cognitive-developmental theory, as formulated by Kohlberg (1966), used Piagetian concepts to understand sex role development. Cognitions about gender, according to Kohlberg, are primary: children cannot be expected to show sex-typed behavior until they have formed the necessary mental structures required to understand gender. The most important aspect of such understanding is the realization that gender is constant; not until children have grasped the notion that they are masculine or feminine for ever will they consistently behave in a sex-typed manner. From then on the gender construct functions as an organizer of behavior; it is the means for ensuring that the child acquires only those response patterns that fit in with this vital aspect of the self-image. Actions are thus selected on the basis of their consistency with gender identity.

In accord with Piagetian ideas, Kohlberg considered that gender constructs do not have to be taught to children but emerge spontaneously. Children, it is generally agreed, are very ready to classify the information they encounter in their environment; the formation of categories helps to handle and make sense of the multiplicity of stimuli which make up their everyday experience, and gender is one of the earliest and most useful social categories formed. Once in existence, such a category is filled with information that is relevant to gender: appearance, clothes, activities, psychological characteristics – all are spontaneously classified according to gender, and specific tuition on the part of adults plays little part in this process. Thus it is only *after* the formation of gender constructs that children come to attend to and imitate same-sex models – a formulation different from social learning accounts which see imitation as primary and required *before* gender categories can be constructed.

The notion that gender concepts need not be taught directly but that children construct them on their own has received much support. However, Kohlberg's theory has one fundamental weakness: the developmental timetable proposed is not borne out by empirical observations. Gender constancy, as we have already seen, does not appear until about 6 years, but long before that children already show clear signs of sex-typed behavior. The proposal that a mature understanding of gender is a necessary precondition for sex typing cannot therefore be upheld, and the relationship between cognitive constructs and behavior needs to be restated.

Gender schema theory has attempted such a restatement, and has also set out to combine the most acceptable features of cognitive-developmental and social learning theories (Bem, 1981; C. L. Martin & Halverson, 1981). There are two principal differences between this account and Kohlberg's: first, the attainment of a mature gender construct is not regarded as a necessary precondition for gender-linked behavior, and second, considerably greater emphasis is given to the information processing functions of gender schemas.

The term *gender schema* is applied to the naive theories people have concerning the characteristics of males and females. Schemas begin to develop early on, i.e. as soon as children realize there is a difference and begin to label themselves accordingly. As schemes become more differentiated so the child's sex-linked behavior and attitudes become increasingly differentiated; however, construct and behavior are thought of as developing in parallel rather than consecutively and gradually rather than in the stepwise fashion envisaged in accounts tied to the emergence of gender constancy at age 6. According to Serbin, Powlishta, and Gueko (1993), even in mid-childhood there is still not a complete coherence between *know* and *act*, possibly because the former, represented by the child's schema about gender, is primarily a function of cognitive maturity whereas the latter, i.e. sex-typed preferences, tends to be influenced by environmental factors. Social factors thus receive due acknowledgment: they play a part in that they influence the activation of gender schemas and provide content for them; differences between children can therefore be attributed to socialization experiences.

However, it is mainly to cognitive aspects that gender schema theorists have turned in their attempts to account for the development and functioning of children's sex-linked behavior and understanding. While complete coherence between *know* and *act* may be a relatively late development, schemas do at least start fairly early on to influence the way in which children attend to, interpret and remember information that is relevant to gender issues. For example, young children will show more interest in novel toys when they are labeled as appropriate for their own sex than when they are labeled as inappropriate (Cobb et al., 1982), indicating that even preschoolers can use knowledge of the sex-appropriateness of objects to guide their choices. School-aged children are able to use knowledge of a person's sex to make inferences about that individual's abilities, preferences, and traits (C. L. Martin, 1989). And once schemas are formed they may affect how gender-related information is subsequently remembered: as C. L. Martin and Halverson (1983) found, children shown pictures of sex-consistent and sex-inconsistent activities (e.g. respectively a boy playing with a train and a girl sawing wood) were better able to remember the sex-consistent pictures, while for sex-inconsistent pictures the information was often distorted by changing the sex of the actor involved. Thus recollections were changed in order to make them consistent with the sex stereotypes which the children had developed. In general, a gender-related memory bias appears to be operative in children: thus pictures and words culturally defined as "feminine" are remembered better by girls than by boys; those culturally defined as "masculine," on the other hand, are remembered better by boys (Liben & Signorella, 1993).

Gender schemas, once fully developed, are highly complex structures which are made up of sets of different components that come to be increasingly coordinated in the course of development (C. L. Martin, Wood, and Little, 1990). Such components include the particular role behaviors, physical characteristics, occupations, and traits which are customarily associated with each gender; thus every component is mentally represented both in a masculine and a feminine version. Fairly early on in development children, knowing whether an individual is male or female, can correctly infer the particular components that belong to that gender; going from label to component is thus a relatively easy task. Inferring one component from another is more difficult, as Martin and colleagues showed for children in the 4- to 10-year range. Told about a person of unspecified gender who manifested some particular sex-linked characteristic (referring to behavior, appearance, job, etc.) and asked to predict other sex-linked characteristics that one can expect to find in such a person, children were found to make only gradual progress in their inferential abilities. Inferences for the opposite sex were found to be particularly difficult. Martin and colleagues therefore suggest that children's gender schemas appear to develop through three stages:

1 In the first stage children learn what kinds of things are associated with each sex. The gender label is thus linked with particular components ("men have short hair," "girls play with dolls," etc.).
2 In the second stage, beginning around 4 to 6 years, associations between components become possible: knowing that a child likes to play with dolls enables inferences to be drawn about appearance and other such characteristics. However, this is as yet limited to children's own gender, i.e. to those with interests like their own.
3 Only in the third stage, from about 8 years on, are children able to show the same ability for the opposite sex, having mastered the gender concepts of both masculinity and femininity and thus having at their disposal the full range of stereotype knowledge.

Summary

- Children form social concepts, especially of themselves and of the people with whom they interact, in order to make sense of their experiences in interpersonal situations.

The Self

- The self acts as a source of reference when interacting with others. It is a complex system of different constructs, as illustrated by William James's distinction between the "I," or the self-as-knower, and the "me," or the self-as-known.
- One aspect of the self is self-awareness. As measured by the ability visually to recognize oneself, this appears in the middle of the second year. It is also then that self-related terms appear in children's speech, as do signs of self-consciousness.
- Another aspect is the self-concept. This is the cognitive feature of the self-system; it is constructed by children as an answer to the question "who am I?" Its nature changes in the course of childhood along a number of developmental dimensions, namely from simple to diffentiated, from inconsistent to consistent, from concrete to abstract, from absolute to comparative, and from self-as-public to self-as-private.
- A third aspect is self-esteem, i.e. the feelings children have about their own worthiness. Self-esteem is much influenced by children's social experiences; it is thus far from static over age and also varies according to function domain. But a "looking-glass" view of self-development, according to which children merely reflect others' opinions, is insufficient: for one thing, children form their own evaluations of their worthiness, and for another self-esteem is also influenced by genetic factors.
- Intense emotions surround the self. This is seen in children's capacity to experience pride and shame – emotions which first appear at the end of the second year when children become capable of self-evaluation.

Knowledge of Others

- The development of children's ability to understand other people shows certain parallels with self-development. Whether one occurs before the other remains uncertain; according to some, what is primary is the *relationships* between self and other. What is certain is that the differentiation of self from other is a long-drawn-out process, described in detail by Selman's stage scheme.
- As studies of children's person perception have shown, the same developmental trends are found in the description of other people as in self-description. This is seen, for instance, in the trend from a primarily concrete to an increasingly abstract descriptive style.

- Quite young children already do have some capacity to understand that other people have internal feelings. Signs of empathy with others' distress, for instance, are evident even in infants, though the developmental course of this capacity occupies most of childhood.
- Children's spontaneous talk about others' internal states also starts at a very early age, i.e. from at least the third year on. Conversations with parents provide a context for discussion about such states and give young children the opportunity to develop insight into the reasons for others' behavior.
- The ability to infer mental states in others and see these as the basis of action is regarded as evidence that children have a "theory of mind." Such a theory becomes increasingly complex over age; as shown by the *false belief* paradigm, a particularly important progression occurs around 4 years when children become able to appreciate that others can have mental representations of a particular event that are different from their own.

Sex Role Development

- Gender is one of the earliest and most fundamental aspects of both self- and other-description, and at quite a young age children begin actively to search for the rules governing the way in which males and females should behave.
- The development of psychological sex differences has mostly been investigated in three areas: toy preferences and play activities, personality characteristics, and choice of playmates. All three show differentiation according to sex from the early preschool period on, though more so in the case of boys than girls.
- Children's concepts of gender involve understanding of the identity, stability, and constancy of a person's sex, the three aspects developing in that order over the first 6 or 7 years.
- Sex role knowledge, i.e. knowing how the sexes are supposed to behave, is evident from about 2 years on. By mid-childhood sex stereotyping is well established, especially for males. Such understanding of sex typing influences children's sex-typed behavior, though the latter can also occur before the former develops.
- From birth on parents treat boys and girls differently. Other social influences, such as peers and the media, also come to play a part. It is unlikely, however, that the development of sex-typed behavior can be wholly explained in environmental terms.
- Changes in children's cognitive capacities have been proposed by two theories as accounting for the development of sex-typed behavior. One is Kohlberg's cognitive-developmental theory, which emphasizes gender constancy as the essential precondition for sex-typed behavior; the other is gender schema theory, which allows for a much looser and more varied connection between *know* and *act*.

Chapter 5

Families, Parents, and Socialization

The three terms in the title of this chapter – family, parents, and socialization – are inextricably intertwined. Socialization is a process that takes place primarily in families, and within the family it is carried out through the agency of parents. The aim of socialization is to fit children into their particular society; accordingly they must acquire the behavior patterns which are acceptable in that society. But society is an abstraction; parents are therefore called upon to act as the agents for the transmission of cultural norms and they do so by first introducing their children to the requirements of family life. Every family has its rules – rules that determine the division of labor among its members, the nature of eating and sleeping arrangements, the way in which individuals address each other, the sharing of resources such as the television set or the most comfortable chair, and so on. The fact that in many respects the family mirrors the society of which it is a part means that these rules can subsequently be carried forward and applied to life in other social groups. However, socialization is not just a coldly intellectual affair of formally learning dos and don'ts; families are also characterized by the considerable emotional intensity with which they conduct much of their business. Coping with love and hate may not be explicitly taught to children; the socialization of emotions is nevertheless one of the most important experiences that family life provides.

Families as Systems

Children's development inevitably takes place in particular contexts, and for the vast majority of children the family is the first and most important context for physical and psychological growth. Families are ideally suited for the bringing up of children: they are small, intimate groups, making it easy for children to acquire consistent rules of behavior; they are linked to various outside settings (other families, work, leisure, and so forth) to which children can gradually be introduced; and they are usually composed of individuals deeply committed to the child whose security and care can therefore be guaranteed. The family is thus the basic unit within which the child is introduced to social living.

Just what a family is has become a lot more difficult to state than was the case just a few decades ago. Traditionally, the family was regarded as a permanent unit containing a married couple and their children, with the father playing the role of breadwinner and the mother that of homemaker and caretaker of children which the couple had jointly brought into the world. This has changed: divorce, single-parent families, cohabitation, employed mothers, role reversal among husband and wife, blended families – these are the signs that many former conventions have now been abandoned, for the family is by no means a static unit for ever set in one particular form. The implications of these changes for children have caused much concern; however, research on nontraditional families has shown that psychologically healthy personalities can develop in the context of a great variety of social groupings and that conformity to one specific norm is by no means essential to children's well-being (Schaffer, 1990). Take a study by Eiduson and colleagues (1982; see also Weisner & Wilson-Mitchell, 1990), in which children from four different social backgrounds were investigated, namely those from single-mother families, from "social contract" (i.e. unmarried) couples, from families living in communes and from traditional two-parent families. A wide variety of social, intellectual, and emotional aspects of behavior was assessed in these children; none, however, yielded any differences between the groups or gave any indication that living in any one type of social setting was more beneficial than in any other. C. J. Patterson's (1992) review of children brought up in gay or lesbian households leads to a similar conclusion, for here too there are no indications that such children are in any way psychologically harmed by being part of such a unit. From a child's point of view it seems that a family can take a great many forms and still function as a secure base for healthy development.

Principles of Systems Theory

A useful way of thinking about the family and the influences it has on its members is by means of *systems theory* (Minuchin, 1988; Sameroff, 1983). The basic principles of this approach, which are applicable to all systems (biological, economic, psychological), stress the following characteristics:

- *Wholeness*   A system is an organized whole that is greater than the sum of its parts. Its properties cannot therefore be understood by merely studying the functioning of individual components; attention must also be given to the totality.
- *Integrity of subsystems*   Complex systems are composed of subsystems that are related to each other. Each such relationship may also be regarded as a subsystem and studied in its own right.
- *Circularity of influence*   Within a system the pattern of influence is circular rather than linear. All components are mutually interdependent; change in one has implications for all others. Statements such as "A causes B" are therefore insufficient because components affect each other in reciprocal fashion.

- *Stability and change*   The systems that are of interest to the psychologist are *open*, i.e. they are affected by all sorts of outside influences. In so far as each system tries to maintain a state of stability, change tends to be resisted; if this proves not possible the system as a whole has to change, even if in the first place the external influence affects only one of the components.

As applied to child development in general, a systems perspective insists that *all* aspects of the child and of the developmental context are equally important and need to be understood in their entirety. This may be more easily said than done; it is, however, in relation to family functioning that systems theory has gained most acceptance.

From a systems perspective a family can be thought of as an integrated whole composed of two kinds of components: the individual members and the relationships between the members (figure 15). The family is more than the sum of these components: it is a dynamic entity in its own right. Knowing everything about the individual members and about their relationships does not reveal anything about the operation of the whole. Different kinds of statements can thus be made at three levels: family, relationships, and individuals. Figure 15 refers to a two-parent family with one child; if another child is added the system becomes considerably more complex, and not just because of the addition of one more member and the consequent extra dyadic relationships but also because of the added possibility of triadic relationships and thus the formation of another layer of subsystems. In so far as such a family contains 4 members, 6 dyads and 4 triads, as well as the family system as a whole, there are 15 units altogether which can be described. Add to that the fact that the family is itself embedded in a wider social system and thus is a unit in interaction with other units in the community, and one can appreciate how complex an undertaking it is to provide a full description of the family as a functioning system.

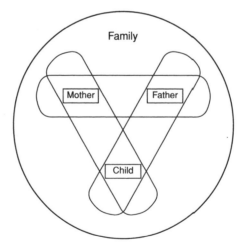

Figure 15   The family and its subsystems

We shall turn to the external relationships of the family later on; for the present our focus is on its internal functioning. As figure 15 makes clear, any one individual belongs not only to the family as a whole but simultaneously participates in several subsystems such as the spousal, the sibling, and the parent–child system. Each of these has distinctive properties; each can be a meaningful unit for inquiry, and each can be affected by happenings in other relationship subsystems.

Mutual Influences within Families

Circularity of influence is one of the basic principles of systems theory listed above. A model that applies this to the family is one proposed by Belsky (1981) and depicted in figure 16. A child's behavior affects and is affected by the parents; it also affects and is affected by the relationship between mother and father, and that in turn affects and is affected by the nature of their parenting activities. Thus each aspect of the system is mutually involved with every other aspect.

Empirical investigations have generally concentrated on just some aspects of this mutual influence process. Most attention has been given to the way in which the quality of the parents' marriage is related to the child's progress, on the assumption that a good marital relationship is likely to be associated with a satisfactory parent–child relationship which in turn is related to optimal development in the child. When, on the other hand, parents do not get on with each other the relationship with the child can also be expected to deteriorate: a parent may be so caught up in the marital conflict that he or she neglects the child or, on the contrary, attempts to compensate for the frustrations of the marriage by overwhelming the child with demands for affection and attention. The evidence bears out these expectations (Easterbrooks & Emde, 1988; N. B. Miller et al., 1993) but also draws attention to the complexity of

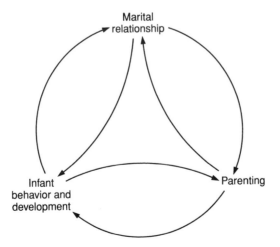

Figure 16   Belsky's model of mutual family influences (from Belsky, 1981)

influence processes. Take a study by Brody, Pillegrini, and Sigel (1986), in which mothers and fathers were observed while interacting with their school-aged children in a dyadic problem solving situation. Parents who reported being contented with their marriage were found to differ in their interactive techniques from discontented parents; however, the effect varied according to parent and type of measure (see table 31). In the contented group mothers and fathers used similar techniques; none of the measures employed showed up any significant differences between parents. In the discontented group, however, fathers were found to be distinct in providing significantly less positive feedback (e.g. praise and approval) and being considerably more intrusive (i.e. interrupting their children's activity and doing things for them rather than allowing them to discover their own solutions). Their wives, on the other hand, not only provided more negative and less positive feedback when compared with contented mothers but also tended to structure the interaction more by frequent questioning and verbal management techniques such as commands and emphatic suggestions. From the child's point of view the discontented parents thus adopted strategies that resulted in a very much less effective learning situation than that created by the contented parents. What transpired in the one relationship had implications for the nature of the other relationship.

An association between marital quality and children's development has frequently been reported. Goldberg and Easterbrooks (1984), for instance, found that parents characterized by low marital adjustment more often had children who had formed insecure attachments to them than was the case with parents reporting high marital adjustment. Presumably a tension-free marriage makes it more likely that the parents relate to their children in a sensitive manner and this in turn might bring about secure attachments. Yet, in keeping with a systems approach, one must also consider the path of influence working in the opposite direction and in a circular manner. Thus the nature of the child may affect the kind of parenting provided and also the quality of the marital relationship – a situation seen most clearly where the child is "difficult" to rear by virtue of being handicapped (e.g. Korn, Chess, & Fernandez, 1978; Floyd & Zmich, 1991). Under such circumstances the strain of parenting such a child can

Table 31 Means of maritally contented and discontented mothers' and fathers' behavior in a problem solving situation

Behavior category	Contented parents		Discontented parents	
	Mothers	Fathers	Mothers	Fathers
Positive feedback	13.60	14.89	12.64	9.99
Negative feedback	2.38	2.28	3.00	3.33
Questions	16.73	18.54	21.19	17.95
Intrusion	3.02	2.46	2.50	4.70
Verbal management	16.68	19.55	21.80	18.72

Source: Adapted from Brody et al. (1986)

have repercussions on the marital relationship which will then deteriorate, producing tensions that in turn create an aversive environment for the child to grow up in and that make the child even more difficult. Simple linear cause-and-effect statements thus do no justice at all to the reality of such family situations.

Let us note one further complexity: the child's relationships with mother and with father are not necessarily affected to the same degree by marital problems. A study by Belsky, Youngblade, Rovine, and Volling (1991) illustrates this. A group of 100 families were followed up from before the pregnancy to the child's third birthday, and information was obtained periodically both about the child's relationship with each parent and about the relationship between the parents. It emerged that marital quality was more closely associated with aspects of fathering than of mothering: where the marriage showed signs of deteriorating the fathers' behavior towards the child became more negative and intrusive while the child grew increasingly disobedient to the father. The mother–child relationship, on the other hand, showed few difficulties; it appeared to be buffered in such a way that marital problems had very much less impact than was the case with the father–child relationship. Perhaps this is because mothers' parental role is much more precisely spelled out by social convention than is the case for fathers, so that the behavior of the former to their children is less easily influenced by events outside the relationship. Alternately, it may be that women are just better at keeping their various relationships in separate compartments than men, who are more inclined to show a general pattern of relating – positive or negative – that is equally applied to spouse and child.

It is, of course, not only the marital and the parent–child relationships that mutually influence each other; the same applies, for example, to the way in which the mother–child relationship affects and is affected by the relationship between siblings. As has been repeatedly demonstrated (e.g. Brody et al., 1986; Hetherington, 1988), families in which parents are harsh, punitive, and erratic in their treatment of children are characterized by high levels of hostile, unaffectionate interactions between siblings. The sibling relationship is also influenced by the marital relationship: where there is a lot of discord and lack of cohesion between parents one generally also finds more conflict between siblings (Brody, Stoneman, McCoy, & Forehand, 1992). The family, we can therefore conclude, is a network of relationships all of which function in an interdependent manner – a conclusion with the important practical implication that therapeutic efforts designed to bring about psychological improvement ought to be directed at the family generally and not at isolated individuals or relationships.

Stability and Change

Families are open systems, affected by outside events. How they organize themselves and how they function are thus determined not only by the members' individual personalities and relationships but also by the impact of happenings in the external world – economic upheavals, political change, technological developments, war and peace, and other such far-ranging events. Seen from a historical perspective (Hareven, 1984) the family is a dynamic entity well capable of adapting to changing circumstances, and in the course of the 20th century in particular the family has undergone drastic transformation. The so-called "traditional" family is no longer regarded as the norm to which everyone must aspire: as a result of extraneous influences such features as the institution of marriage, the procreation and care of children, the role of women within the family, and the way in which couples divide their responsibilities between them have been redefined to a quite drastic degree.

Seen from the perspective of individual families, coping with change enforced by new circumstances is a challenge that must frequently be met. A father becoming unemployed, a mother taking on a job for the first time, a grandparent coming to live with the family, an older child leaving home, a parent or child developing chronic illness – each requires adaptation and reorganization, and even though the event may initially involve only one individual the effects inevitably reverberate throughout the system. This is most obvious with drastic happenings such as death, divorce, remarriage, or a teenage pregnancy; yet the same applies at less drastic levels, for instance when a child reaches some new developmental milestone such as beginning to walk, starting school, or reaching puberty, all of which have some effect on the family as a whole and on all its individual components.

The more drastic events have, not surprisingly, received most attention, for then established patterns may no longer be adaptive and the balance of relationships needs to be renegotiated. A good example is *transition to parenthood* – a period when the arrival of a new family member can markedly alter the behavior of existing members and the nature of their previous relationships. For the parents the effects are most marked in the case of a first baby; subsequent babies have implications for siblings but produce fewer pressures for adaptation in the parents. The adjustments to be made at that time have been categorized as follows (Sollie & Miller, 1980):

1. The *physical demands* on the parents made by a young baby are the most obvious source of stress. Interrupted sleep in particular is a drain, but all aspects of caring for a highly dependent child need to be accommodated within the normal household and other routines that the parents continue to pursue.

2. The *emotional costs* of being responsible for a helpless being are experienced, by some parents at least, as even more draining than physical demands. Joy and satisfaction may be uppermost; nevertheless, the knowledge that the child's life and well-being depend on the parents' appropriate caretaking activities, together with doubts they may have about their own competence, represent a source of strain that often needs considerable efforts of adjustment.

3. *Restrictions of other opportunities*, such as those associated with leisure and work, inevitably follow new parenthood. A different lifestyle must therefore be adopted: a mother may have to give up employment, with financial consequences for the family; both parents are very much less likely to engage in activities outside the

home; and day-to-day life thus involves a different, usually more narrow set of routines to those the parents were used to previously.

4. *Strains in the marital relationship* have frequently been found following birth. Jealousy, disruption in sexual relationships, and the stresses resulting from the three factors mentioned above all play a part in bringing about difficulties in the existing pattern of the husband–wife relationship. Again it is important not to give a misleadingly pessimistic picture: the shared joy in the child can be a powerful binding force too. But the dyad has now become a triad and it follows from all we said about families as systems that the husband–wife relationship will now inevitably change its nature and manifestation.

The capacity of couples to negotiate the transition to parenthood, and in particular their ability to avoid the strains on the marital relationship, can vary greatly (Belsky, 1984). A number of factors have been implicated in such variation, such as the age and maturity of the parents, their relationship with their own parents, the amount of social support available to them, and (most of all) the level of marital satisfaction existing before the baby's arrival. Where that level was low the marriage is unlikely to improve: couples with many conflicts before the birth tend to have many conflicts after it as well, and where there was little sharing of responsibilities in the home beforehand marital satisfaction afterwards is likely to be low and the transition to parenthood accordingly a more difficult undertaking (C. P. Cowan & Cowan, 1992). In addition the nature of the child may influence the course of the parents' adaptation: where a child is "difficult" in temperament or premature or handicapped, the parents will not only experience the transition as more stressful but, in more vulnerable marriages, may drift further apart (Belsky, 1984).

In most families, however, the transition is accomplished well, even though a considerable amount of rearrangement of customary living patterns has to take place. This is seen, for instance, in the sex typing of new parents. According to Feldman and Aschenbrenner (1983) new mothers become *more* and new fathers *less* sex-stereotyped after the child's birth. Mothers, that is, increasingly engage in a greater range of traditionally female activities; the fathers, however, also show a greater involvement in such activities by assuming responsibility for certain child care tasks and helping out with cooking, cleaning, and washing. The sheer pressure of work involved in looking after a baby means that many fathers feel that the traditional division of labor into "masculine" and "feminine" tasks would put too great a burden on their wives and that the transition to parenthood can only be successfully accomplished if such tasks are redistributed. As Levy-Shiff (1994) found when following up couples from pregnancy into the child's first year, some decline in marital satisfaction is common following the birth, especially among women. The extent of the decline, however, depends largely on the father's involvement with the baby, especially in caregiving activities: where there is a high level of involvement the decline is slight or even nonexistent; where it is low and there is no willingness to redefine sex roles the transition to parenthood tends to be more difficult.

In families where there is already a child the arrival of a new baby is likely to disturb the previously established balance in rather different ways. Just how this happens is seen in Dunn and Kendrick's (1982a) study of a group of families who were followed up from the mother's pregnancy until the second child was 14 months old. The baby's birth had a dramatic effect on nearly all of the older children (mostly around 2 to 3 years old at the time): while there was interest in and affection for the baby there was also much disturbance and unhappiness. However, there were also changes in many aspects of the child's relationship with the mother: in particular, the incidence of confrontations increased whereas the time mother and child spent together in joint play markedly decreased. Demands and naughtiness from the older child increased most at times when the mother was caring for the baby; as a result a much greater proportion of the mothers' talk than had been observed before the baby's arrival consisted of prohibitions, thus greatly altering the general tone of the relationship. How the child behaved towards the baby depended largely on the kind of relationship the child had previously had with the parents: a close and intense relationship, especially between mother and daughter, was generally associated with relatively greater hostility to the baby; a more detached relationship, on the other hand, tended to give rise to a higher level of warmth and friendliness to the new arrival.

The problems observed reflect the emotional impact that a sibling's birth has on young children, and though the disturbance becomes less marked with time the initial rearrangement represents a considerable crisis for the majority of children. The baby's arrival is not a matter of just adding another member to the family whereupon life continues pretty much as before. On the contrary, the behavior of each of the individual family members changes, as does the relationship between them. And for that matter a new set of relationships has to be established, namely with the baby – a task especially onerous for the older child. Given the sharply reduced availability of the mother and the almost inevitable jealousy felt when the baby receives the parents' attention, it is perhaps surprising that young children do manage in time to relate to the younger sibling in a largely positive manner and that the family can eventually establish a new balance of relationships.

The case of stepfamilies

One increasingly common example of a drastic reorganization of family life is found when a parent remarries and the children now find themselves as part of a stepfamily. The need to absorb the stepparent in the existing system, to form a new relationship and to rearrange existing ones can sometimes impose considerable strain on children which, in turn, may affect the newly formed marital relationship. What happens at that time, and what help one can provide to make the transition easier, has been subject to much research (see, for instance, Cowan & Hetherington, 1991; Pasley & Ihinger-Tallman, 1984).

Let us take as an example a longitudinal study by Hetherington (1988) of the effects on children of divorce and its aftermath, including remarriage by the custodial parent. For these parents (mostly mothers) remarriage usually brought with it considerable beneficial effects — effects from which not only they profited but also, indirectly, their children. Loneliness, anxiety, economic worries, and household disorganization all diminished and higher ratings of happiness were reported. Much depended, of course, on the kind of relationship established with the new spouse: remarried mothers of sons in particular benefited from a warm, supportive relationship with the stepfather. It was also found, however, that continued involvement by the child with the divorced, noncustodial father, even after six years, led to positive outcomes for the children.

However, the relationship between stepfather and stepchild differed in certain respects from that of biological fathers and children. Many of the stepfathers tended to adopt one of two extremes: either they were highly involved with their stepchildren (though often in a rather restrictive manner) or, more commonly, they tended to be emotionally "disengaged," being somewhat distant and inattentive and giving the mother little support in child rearing. However, this might well have been in response to the child's attitude, for in the early stages of remarriage many children saw the stepfather as an intruder and rival. Girls in particular were often reported as adopting a sulky, hostile manner, rejecting the stepfather no matter how hard he tried.

Over time this situation improved somewhat in the case of boys; some of the young boys especially formed intense attachments and warm, companionate relationships with the stepfather. In cases where remarriage did not occur till the child was 9 or 10 years old, acceptance and a positive relationship were on the whole more difficult to achieve. In the case of girls, however, the relationship often deteriorated: the stepdaughters viewed the stepfather as hostile, punitive, and unreasonable, while the stepfathers became increasingly impatient with the girls' difficult behavior and viewed them increasingly in a negative light.

Reformation of a family clearly brings with it a great many difficulties, and perhaps it is more surprising that so many newly married couples and their children succeed in forming a new unit than that some fail. A great many variables help to determine the eventual outcome and generalizations are therefore difficult. Let us note one common finding, however: the more complex the composition of the new family is the more problems are generally reported. Thus, when the stepfather too brings children from a previous marriage who then need to be incorporated into the household the likelihood of conflict is all the greater. The more new relationships have to be formed the greater is the burden of readjustment; blending together a complex system is clearly a more challenging task than is found in a simpler one.

The Nature of Parenting

It is widely assumed that parenting influences children's development. The nature of that influence has not in fact been easy to demonstrate; earlier input–output models, whereby parents are thought to shape passive children and so be wholly responsible for the outcome, are now known to be simplistic. Whatever effects parents do have are mediated by other aspects, in particular characteristics of the child and those of the social and physical context in which development occurs. Nevertheless, the parental contribution is clearly a crucial one and whatever goals and characteristics parents bring to the interaction with the child need to be described and analyzed.

Let us first turn to the goals of parenting. According to LeVine (1974, 1988) it is useful to distinguish between three basic goals that all families have, implicitly or explicitly, in bringing up their children:

1 *survival* – to ensure that the child remains alive and healthy and lives long enough eventually also to produce children;
2 *economic welfare* – to help the child acquire the skills and knowledge required for economic self-sufficiency as an adult;
3 *self-actualization* – to foster the abilities that are needed to satisfy various cultural values such as those concerned with morality, prestige, and personal fulfillment.

These three goals form a hierarchy: parents can only attend to the latter ones if the former, more basic goals, are first satisfied. Survival is, of course, the most essential of all; in societies where infant mortality is great parents' energies are primarily devoted to keeping their children alive, and there is little time left to teach anything but those skills that are required for finding food, keeping warm, and staying away from predators. When survival can be taken for granted parents' primary task is to foster whatever qualities are needed in their society for economic self-sufficiency, and only when that has been attained can child rearing be principally devoted to those much more sophisticated skills that bring about individual self-fulfillment.

All parents bring to their task certain attributes that, together with the characteristics of the child and the context, determine their child rearing behavior. We can usefully distinguish between:

• *universal attributes*, i.e. those common to all human parents which can be regarded as part of the heritage of our species;
• *culture-specific attributes*, namely those that are specific to particular societies and thus distinguish one grouping of parents from another;
• *individual attributes*, which differentiate one parent from another within cultural groups and can therefore be considered as an expression of the individual's personality.

Most attention has been given to individual attributes, but before discussing these we shall examine what has been learned about the other two kinds.

A Cross-cultural Perspective

A comparison of parental practices in different cultures is often undertaken in the belief that it will help to sort out the universals from the specifics in child rearing behavior (Bornstein, 1991). When a particular parental pattern is found in all social environments, irrespective of variations in customs and beliefs, it is assumed to be genetically determined; when differences are found among cultural groups the influences of learning experiences are said to be at work.

There can be little doubt that parenting does have a genetic basis. Each species is equipped with particular mechanisms whereby parents provide care for their offspring and ensure their survival in a manner that is appropriate to the animals' physical make-up and the habitat they occupy. In lower species this may take a very specific form: among herring gulls, for instance, the parent bird offers food to the young by holding out its beak after alighting on the nest; the young, programmed to peck at the red dot on the beak, will thus obtain whatever morsel the parent has brought. In rats the mother, soon after birth, produces a chemical substance the odor of which is highly attractive to the pups; by means of this innate mechanism the mother can ensure that her young will seek her out and be able to differentiate her from other rats. In human beings too there is a genetically determined bias in parents to maintain proximity and provide care to their offspring, even though it may not take as rigid a form as found in lower species: as ethologically oriented theorists like Bowlby (1969) have argued, human parents, like those of other species, are also set to give care and provide protection for their children by virtue of their innate nature; they too are programmed to respond to the signals which the child sends in particular ways that bring about precise coordination with the child's behavior.

Yet, in comparison with lower species, the human parenting system has built into it a considerable degree of flexibility in the way in which care and protection are expressed, even during the earliest stages of the child's life. Take feeding: there is great variability in the means (breast or bottle) whereby an infant is fed; in the frequency of feeding (whenever the child cries or according to some predetermined schedule); in the identity of the feeder; and in the age at weaning. Cultural comparison is particularly helpful here in highlighting the extent of variability and also in throwing light on the conditions underlying it. The identity of the person responsible for feeding is an example. As we saw in chapter 3, when considering the Case of the Efe Pygmies (p. 136), multiple caretaking arrangements are the norm in some societies. Thus among the Efe a crying baby may be put to the breast by any woman, even a nonlactating one – an arrangement eminently sensible under conditions of communal living where, moreover, a high mortality rate makes it advisable for the child to form attachments to several individuals. Contrast this with Western practice, where living in small, isolated family units cuts down on the number of available caretakers and where there is little need to insure against the potential loss of the mother by forming a large number of attachments. Among humans feeding is thus not an inbuilt prerogative of the child's mother; instead each society works out its own system of care distribution in the light of its particular requirements and values.

Considerable anthropological material is available to illustrate how the diversity of such cultural requirements and values has affected parental behavior. Among the Gusii people in Kenya child rearing practices aim to produce quiet, docile children

– something desired by the mothers so that they can easily hand their babies over to child nurses and get on with their heavy work load. Hence infant care is marked by much soothing and use of measures intended to avoid crying (LeVine et al., 1994). This is a common pattern in agricultural economies where survival is precarious and obedience a much valued trait in adults: in poverty stricken villages in India, for example, where sons are the only source of economic security when the parents are too old to work, much child rearing effort is devoted to instilling in the sons a strong sense of filial obligations and of loyalty to parents – an effort that does not, however, take any coercive form as sons are consistently given preferential treatment over the much less valued daughters (L. W. Hoffman, 1988). Domestic organization, economic need, environmental risk, social beliefs and priorities – these are among some of the forces that account for the differences in parental practices that can be found among cultures.

Such differences are evident even among cultural groups living and working together in the same locality. In a study of mothers' perceptions and beliefs concerning child development Pomerleau, Malcuit, and Sabetier (1991) investigated Haitian and Vietnamese families who had settled in Montreal, together with a group of indigenous Quebec families. Each mother was asked to indicate the age at which she believed that children acquire various abilities (walking, talking, etc.) and the age when mothers ought to initiate certain child rearing activities such as introducing the child to books or getting him/herself to feed independently. Table 32 gives examples of some of the numerous items put to the mothers and shows clearly the marked differences that appeared between the three groups. In particular, Quebec mothers by and large expected children's abilities to emerge considerably earlier than the other two groups of mothers; similarly they also believed that parents should exert

Table 32   Beliefs about child development by mothers from three cultural groups

	Haitian	*Quebec*	*Vietnamese*
A. Mean age (in days) when mothers ought to initiate specific activities			
Talk to child	38.0	4.2	71.6
Show first book	781.6	363.9	476.3
Take bottle unaided	217.2	154.3	217.0
Dress self	1,010.6	776.5	843.5
B. Mean age (in days) when mothers believe children first acquire various abilities			
Hear	27.6	4.9	52.8
See	30.4	18.9	48.2
Recognize mother	62.4	37.6	78.3
Think	405.1	91.8	609.0
Understand words	292.4	215.6	267.3

Source: Adapted from Pomerleau et al. (1991)

child rearing pressures at earlier ages. These answers reflect the dominant belief values held by the three cultural groups about children: thus the Quebec mothers expressed the Western idea that infants are potentially competent beings who need help, however, to enhance the development of already present abilities, whereas the other two groups adopted a rather more "laissez faire" attitude towards the early introduction of stimulation activities by parents.

The case of Japanese mothers' child-directed speech

It has been suggested that one universal attribute of parental behavior is the adoption of a particular speech style when talking to young children. Such a style (sometimes referred to as "motherese"; see chapter 3, p. 125) is designed to make it easier for children to comprehend what is said to them and can be found in a wide range of societies and different language communities (Ferguson, 1978).

In an investigation of Japanese and American mother–child dyads Fernald and Morikawa (1993) paid attention both to the universals and to culturally determined variations in the mothers' speech while playing with their children aged 6, 12, and 19 months at the time. A standard set of toys was supplied for the use of all couples. Analysis of the recordings showed that both sets of mothers simplified their speech in various ways, that both engaged in frequent repetition and that both used vocal attention-attracting devices such as nonsense words. Both groups also adjusted their speech to the child's age by, for example, using less simplified and less repetitive speech with older children.

However, there were also some marked differences and these applied in particular to the extent and manner of object reference. Japanese mothers were less likely to talk about the toys present than the American mothers; when they did talk about them they were less likely to label them; and when they did label them they tended not to use the specific adult form of the word for the object but various of a large number of "baby talk" possibilities, thus making it more difficult

for the child to acquire an object label (indeed at 19 months the Japanese children had a significantly smaller noun vocabulary than the American children). In general, Japanese mothers focused their children's attention less on the toys and emphasized the names of the toys less frequently and less consistently than was seen in the American group.

Two contrasting cultural orientations lie behind these different speech styles. As has frequently been shown (Bornstein, 1989), the Japanese are convinced that children start life as basically independent beings that must be socialized into dependence; their rearing practices are therefore geared to attaching the child firmly to the family and fostering the child's bonds with others. In contrast, American mothers see infants as dependent and interpret their task as helping the child to acquire habits of independence. Thus Japanese mothers emphasize social routines that bond child to mother; American mothers, on the other hand, foster a more impersonal orientation by involving the child in object play. As Fernald and Morikawa show, these cultural differences are reflected not only in the amount of object speech but also in the way in which toys are referred to. An American mother might say: "That's a car. See the car? You like it? It's got nice wheels." The Japanese mother, referring to the same toy, would say: "Here! It's a vroom vroom. I give it to you. Now give it to me. Yes! Thank you." To the Japanese mother the object name is of little importance; what matters to her is to teach the child the cultural norms for polite speech, and the toys are merely a means of involving the child in rituals of social exchange that will bring mother and child more closely together. Child-directed speech thus contains certain universal features that express a general parental sensitivity to the requirements of all language learning children, but it is also a means of transmitting very early on in a child's life values that are specific to particular cultural groups.

Parental Styles

Even within cultural groups there are great differences among parents in their child rearing practices. This is a matter of common observation; how to conceptualize these differences, however, has not proved an easy task. A great many dimensions have been proposed along which parents can be ranged: sensitivity, affection, directiveness, warmth, permissiveness, acceptance, punitiveness, responsiveness, and so forth. A parent's standing along a particular dimension might be measured by means of a standardized questionnaire that would include items such as:

- "The earlier a child is weaned from its emotional ties to its parents the better it will handle its own problems."
- "Children should be encouraged to tell their parents about it whenever they feel family rules are unreasonable."

The parent would then be expected to indicate the strength of his or her agreement or disagreement with the statement, and on the basis of all answers given be assigned an overall score for that dimension. Alternately parenting has been investigated by means of interviews, in which questions would be put such as the following, designed in this case to assess a parent's restrictiveness:

- "Sometimes a child will get angry at his/her parents and hit them and kick them or shout angry things at them. How much of this sort of thing do you think parents ought to allow in a child? How do you handle it when X [the child's name] acts like this?"

The answer to each question would then be rated and here too the aggregated score considered as an indication of the parent's standing along the dimension measured.

There has been much lively discussion about the appropriateness of such techniques for measuring parental attributes, also about the nature of the dimensions assessed and their usefulness in predicting aspects of children's development. Most attention has been given to two major dimensions, for these have emerged consistently from a large number of studies as encompassing a wide range of parental behavior (Maccoby & Martin, 1983). These are:

- *Permissiveness/restrictiveness*, which refers to the amount of freedom that parents give to their children. At one end of the continuum parents tolerate almost everything a child does and have no definite rules that are consistently enforced. At the other end parents impose a great many restrictions on their children and ensure that rules are always obeyed.
- *Warmth/hostility*, which describes the amount of love that parents show to their children. Warm parents freely express their affection, readily show approval and praise, and clearly enjoy their children. Hostile parents are cold, ignoring, and uninterested; they tend to belittle their children and get no pleasure out of their company.

The two dimensions are reasonably independent, so that any number of combinations between them are possible. Indeed it is now widely agreed that parental dimensions have little meaning if treated in isolation but that, if one is concerned with the impact on the child, they must be considered in combination with other dimensions. A highly permissive mother, for example, will affect her child very differently according to whether her permissiveness is expressed in the context of a loving or a hostile relationship. If one combines the two basic dimensions of parenting four patterns emerge (see table 33) which, according to Earl S. Schaefer (1959), can most appropriately be labeled democratic, neglecting, overprotective, and authoritarian, each of which represents a quite distinctive parental style. It is these styles, rather than the isolated dimensions, that are said to show associations with child behavior.

Table 33   Parental styles resulting from combining the dimensions of permissiveness/restrictiveness and warmth/hostility

	Permissiveness	*Restrictiveness*
Warmth	Democratic	Overprotective
Hostility	Neglecting	Authoritarian

The most extensively researched scheme for categorizing parental styles arises from work by Diana Baumrind (1967, 1971, 1973). By means of interviews and observations Baumrind obtained data about the child rearing practices of the mothers and fathers of 134 preschool children, focusing initially on four dimensions of parental behavior: control, nurturance, clarity of communication, and maturity demands. However, she too found that parenting can best be described in terms of *combinations* of dimensions, and she accordingly produced a taxonomy based on the following patterns:

- *Authoritarian parenting*, marked by the assertion of parental power and a rather detached attitude. These parents rarely solicit the child's opinion, rarely praise or show pleasure at the child's achievements, tend to be directive and demanding any may use scare tactics to control the child. They expect their orders to be obeyed without explanation.

- *Permissive parenting*, characterized by love and affection but also by the exercise of only limited control. Such parents demand less achievement from the child, are mostly lax about rules, tend to be somewhat inconsistent about discipline and generally consult the child about decisions and explain the reasons for family rules. On the whole they see themselves as a resource to be used by the child, not as an active agent responsible for altering the child's behavior.
- *Authoritative parenting*, which combines relatively high levels of both warmth and achievement demands. While these parents exercise firm control over their children they do so mostly in a non-punitive manner, encouraging verbal give and take and respecting the child's own wishes. They communicate standards of conduct in a clear manner but do not hem the child in with excessive restrictions, and to achieve their objectives they are just as likely to use reason as power. Affection is expressed more often and in a warmer manner than in the other groups.
- *Rejecting-neglecting parenting*, which is essentially a disengaged style. Such parents are neither responsive to their child nor in any way demanding. They do not monitor the child's activities, are not supportive and tend to provide little structure for understanding the world or the social rules required to live in it. They may either be actively rejecting or else neglect their child rearing responsibilities altogether.

Each parental style is, according to Baumrind's further findings, associated with a particular pattern of child characteristics. Children of authoritative parents have been found to be the most competent: they tend to be more self-reliant, keen to achieve, socially responsible, content, self-controlled, and cooperative with both adults and peers than children from any of the other groups. Children of permissive parents are more likely to be aimless, lacking in self-assertiveness, and generally uninterested in achievement; those of authoritarian parents tend to be surly, defiant, dependent, and socially incompetent (especially in the case of boys), while children from rejecting-neglecting homes tend to be the least mature of all in both cognitive and social spheres. These differences are evident right through childhood: even in adolescence Baumrind (1991) found that those most competent and self-regulated and least likely to have drug problems tend to have authoritative parents. Having such parents seems to be a good thing! Neglectful parenting, on the other hand, must give rise to most concern: as Steinberg and colleagues (1994) found, this parental style has more deleterious consequences for adjustment in adolescence than any other style. However, just how these associations come about remains to be clarified. In her earlier writing Baumrind seems to assume that parental practices are wholly responsible for producing particular child characteristics; subsequently, however, she acknowledged that children's personality and also their sex play a part in affecting the outcome and that a unidirectional view of the parent–child relationship is clearly not adequate.

Certain temperamental characteristics in children may well elicit particular parental styles: parents confronted by a hyperactive child, for instance, could be forced into adopting a highly controlling, authoritarian pattern whatever their inclination may be.

In certain respects, yet not in others, parents show considerable consistency in their behavior in the course of a child's development. A study by McNally, Eisenberg, and Harris (1991) illustrates this well. During a follow-up of children between the ages of 7 and 15 the mothers were asked to fill in a child rearing questionnaire at approximately yearly intervals. Overall a high degree of consistency was found in what the mothers reported: the individual differences between them in the child rearing attitudes they adopted remained quite stable even when comparing the beginning and the end of the eight-year period, presumably because they were based on deep-seated beliefs and goals. However, it was also found that the group as a whole changed in certain respects: for example, in mid-adolescence there was a general increase in maternal control behavior; over the whole age span a decrease occurred in the overt expression of affection, and at the same time there was an increase in emphasis on children's achievement. These changes in the mothers' behavior can be understood as responses to developmental changes taking place in the children: general parenting values remain relatively constant but the specific practices enacted in service of these values do vary because of the changing requirements of the child. This explains why Dunn, Plomin, and Daniels (1986) found considerable consistency in the behavior of mothers with two children when observed with each child at the same age: they were just as affectionate, playful, and responsive with the younger one at age 12 months as they had been with the older one at 12 months. However, when observed with the *same* child at different ages, i.e. at 12 and 24 months, there was little stability in the mothers' behavior. Dependent babies and restless toddlers present different challenges to a mother, and some mothers are more content with one than with the other. Though a parent's overall style may remain constant over time specific response patterns such as responsiveness and playfulness are likely to change in keeping with the child's developmental stage and with the parent's reaction to that stage.

Mothering and Fathering

Up till now we have talked of parenting without distinguishing between mothers and fathers. Yet the way in which males and females carry out their parental task and the roles they play vis-à-vis the child differ in a number of respects.

As a large number of studies have shown (e.g. Lamb, 1981; C. Lewis, 1986; Parke, 1981), fathers adopt a manner of interacting with their young children that is considerably more physical and active than that adopted by mothers. Rough-and-tumble play, bouncing, chasing, tickling, tossing the child in the air – these are some of the favorite tricks in many fathers' repertoires. Mothers, on the other hand, are gentler, less abrupt, tend to make greater use of toys during play, respond more contingently to the child and use verbal rather than physical forms of interaction. Mothers, moreover, assume different responsibilities, for in the great majority of cases they are the principal caregivers – despite the social changes in male and female roles that have taken place in the last few decades. Thus children learn from early on that each parent has a distinctive function: father that of playmate, mother that of provider. No wonder, as C. Lewis (1986) found, that when children want fun they are more likely to turn to father but when they are frightened they will usually turn to mother!

Are such sex differences biologically based? For that matter, are women endowed to be children's "natural" caretakers? Anthropological evidence shows that in the great majority of societies women play the major role in child rearing, yet the fact that in a small but significant minority child care is evenly distributed among mothers and fathers suggests that there is nothing predetermined about maternal and paternal roles (M. M. West & Konner, 1976). Even among animals it is not true that it is inevitably the female who is solely responsible for the rearing of offspring: in several species it is the paternal animal that takes an equal (and in a few cases even a major) part of the responsibility. Also the argument that mothers are "primed" by hormonal changes at birth to engage in caretaking turns out to be unsubstantiated; most of the work on such changes has been done with animals and is of doubtful relevance to human beings.

It seems more likely that social convention accounts for whatever differences are observed among mothers and fathers; when fathers do assume the principal responsibility for their children such differences should therefore disappear. This is borne out by a study by Field (1978) in which fathers who were their baby's primary caretaker were compared both with fathers who were secondary caretakers (the traditional role) and with primary caretaking mothers. When observed in a standardized parent–infant interaction situation the differences found were mainly between the primary caretakers (mother *or* father) on the one hand and the secondary caretakers on the other. Fathers belonging to the former group, that is, adopted a behavioral style with the baby that set them apart from other fathers and instead resembled that usually adopted by females. It seems that it is the differential amount of experience parents have with their child rather than their sex that accounts for whatever differences one normally finds between mothers and fathers.

In any case the notion that fathers are necessarily less competent with and less responsive to their children receives no support from research. In a study described by Parke (1981) fathers, observed while feeding their babies, were found to be just as sensitive as mothers in interpreting and responding to the baby's cues and signals such as spluttering, spitting up, or pausing: they, like mothers, reacted by momentarily stopping the feed, looking closely to check and then taking the appropriate action. Despite the fact that these fathers were less experienced at feeding they behaved as promptly and competently as the mothers and also managed to get just as much milk down the baby. There is also little support for parental sex differences from studies using physiological measures to assess responsiveness to young children: men and women, confronted by a crying or smiling baby, have generally been found to show similar arousal patterns as measured by heart rate, blood pressure, and skin conductance (Berman, 1980). In a study conducted with children Berman and Goodman (1984) found no difference in responsiveness to babies among children aged $2\frac{1}{2}$ to 5 years; from age 6, however, differences did emerge in that girls began to show greater responsiveness – a finding interpreted by the authors as indicating the influence of social learning on the children's developing sex role behavior. There is thus no firm evidence to suggest that females are biologically programmed to respond more readily and to a greater extent than males.

Parental Belief Systems

Bringing up children is not merely a matter of what parents *do*; it is also a matter of what they *think* about their task. At one time the emphasis was all on the doing; as Parke (1978) pointed out, psychologists credited mothers with about as much cognitive complexity as they did babies. Yet parents do have preconceptions and do form theories, implicit or explicit, about the nature of children, about the forces responsible for development and about their own role in this process. To understand parenting it is therefore necessary not merely to observe parents but also to ask how they feel, what they hope for and what they believe about the development of their children.

Parental belief systems are likely to play a major part in determining parental practices, which in turn influence children's behavioral development as well as the belief systems which children themselves come to develop. This is illustrated in figure 17; the sequence of influences is that which has so far guided research on this topic. Yet it is important to emphasize that this may well be an oversimplification: arrows may also go in the opposite direction. Take the relationship between belief and action: as Goodnow and Collins (1990) point out, actions can come about without

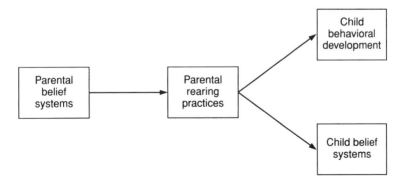

Figure 17 The relationship of parental belief systems to rearing practices and children's development

much grounding in thought, and at least some aspects of child rearing may therefore be cobbled together on an ad hoc basis rather than stemming from any particular cognitive orientation. That comes later; it appears as a rationale and justification for the actions that have already been carried out. The relationship between belief and action is thus a bidirectional one. This applies also to other links in figure 17; in particular it is highly probable that children, and the experience of bringing up a certain kind of child, will affect how parents theorize about the process, and though research has so far only concerned itself with the link from parental beliefs to child development, the possibility of influences in the opposite direction must also be considered.

The research on parental belief systems has been guided by four general questions (S. A. Miller, 1988):

1   What is the nature of parents' beliefs?
2   Where do parents' beliefs come from?
3   How do parents' beliefs affect their behavior towards children?
4   What is the relationship between parents' beliefs and children's development?

The first question, that concerning the *nature* of beliefs, has attracted most attention. Much of it has examined how parents think about the process of development in general. What part does heredity play and what part experience? Are children passive recipients or active constructors? To what extent do parents influence children's development? To obtain answers to such questions various instruments have been developed, usually questionnaires in which a number of developmental achievements are listed which parents are asked to explain. Thus C. A. Martin and Johnson (1992) give details of a 30-item scale in which questions such as the following, together with alternative answers, are posed:

What makes children act independently?

- They reach a stage when they can do things alone.
- Parents praise them for doing things on their own.
- They have a desire to experiment with new ideas and actions.

The response options represent respectively a belief in the importance of maturation, of learning and of the child's own initiative, and the scale as a whole can therefore yield an indication of the parent's predominant belief in one or the other type of developmental determinant.

There are great variations among parents in the kind of "naive psychology" that they employ to understand development, even within the same cultural grouping and indeed even within the same family. Most parents lay rather more stress on environmental than on innate influences, though this may vary according to the child's age and the particular ability under consideration. What is clear is that parents generally do have definite beliefs about development – beliefs which they often regard as definite truths or obvious factual statements about children. What is more, there is usually a marked coherence about their beliefs: the parent who stresses the role of maturation in accounting for some developmental achievement is likely to give the same explanation for other achievements (S. A. Miller, 1988).

The second question about parental beliefs, that concerning their *origins*, has for the most part been examined by attempting to find the factors associated with individual differences in belief systems. Do parents and nonparents hold varying views? Are mothers and fathers distinct, or the young and the old? Basically, all these comparisons involve the role of child rearing experience; however, the expectation that a greater amount of such experience leads to beliefs associated with more accurate knowledge about development or with more sophisticated views has not received unequivocal support (e.g. Holden, 1988; Ninio, 1988). The reason presumably lies in the part that other, more weighty influences play in shaping beliefs.

Two such influences can be singled out. The first refers to the *cultural background* of parents. On the whole the members of any one society tend to have much in common in their ideas about the means and ends of child rearing; members of different societies, however, have different sets of values and will accordingly view children differently. Such a view can be reflected in the language which people use to describe children: when Harkness and Super (1992) compared the words contained in parental talk about children in two cultural settings, i.e. metropolitan America and rural Kenya, they found that the largest group of words in the Americans' descriptions referred to cognitive capacities ("intelligent," "smart," "inquisitive," etc.), whereas among the Kenyan parents primary emphasis was given to concepts dealing with children's obedience and helpfulness (e.g. "respectful," "polite," "good-hearted"). The difference is no doubt related to the sort of demands which each cultural setting makes on its members: getting ahead matters in the competitive West but cooperating with one's group is essential in rural African societies. Such cultural pressures shape parental ideas as to what qualities should be fostered in children; that they succeed in translating ideas into action is illustrated by Harkness and Super's observation that the American children they observed were far more verbally precocious and adept at imaginative play than the Kenyan children; the latter, on the other hand, were able to take sole responsibility for supervising a baby at the age of 5 and could cook dinner for an entire family at the age of 8.

The other influence involves the particular *personality structure* which each parent brings to the task of rearing children. According to Sameroff and Feil (1985) there are systematic differences among parents in the way in which they conceptualize the nature of child development. These differences lie not so much in the content as in the form of parents' explanations, with particular reference to the degree of sophistication with which they explain the nature of development. For instance, presented with a story about a girl, Anne, who is not doing as well in school at math and spelling as her brother Mark did at the same age, people will offer explanations that vary in complexity, from a lack of any causal account, to the use of a single cause, to being

Table 34 Levels of concept development in parental explanations of a child's school failure

Level		Example
1	No explanation	"I don't know, she just is failing"
2	Single cause is presented	"It seems she just daydreams instead of doing her work"
3	Two or more influences mentioned	"She doesn't have ability and so she avoids competing with her brother. Seems like a fear-of-failure situation"
4	A variety of processes are coordinated	"She may not be as interested in math as Mark. She is artistic in temperament. Could be that feeds into sex role stereotypes in how the family responds, which magnify her preferences compared with Mark"

Source: Based on Pratt et al. (1993)

able to view the problem as the outcome of several interacting influences (table 34). Such explanations reflect the cognitive style of the individual; they have been found, for example, to be associated with the way in which people think about social life generally (Pratt et al., 1993) as well as with various other measures of personality functioning (Sameroff & Fiese, 1992). How parents think about child development, it seems, is closely related to the kind of people they are.

The *parental belief–parental behavior link* is the third issue that research has examined. Not that there are many studies that can provide informative findings, though those that can mostly present a positive association. In general, that is, more sophisticated belief systems tend to be related to the kinds of child rearing practices that promote greater competence in children. Yet the relationship is neither a close one nor a consistent one, showing unexpected variations from one setting to another and between mothers on the one hand and fathers on the other (Sigel, 1992). Perhaps this should not surprise us, for how parents act in a particular situation at a particular time depends not only on their general philosophy about child rearing but also on a great many other factors such as the demands of the immediate problem confronting them, the child's behavior, the presence of others, and so forth. Under the circumstances the belief–behavior association can hardly be expected to be one-to-one.

The same consideration applies when we turn to the final question posed, i.e. the *parental belief–child development link*. Again the relatively few studies that have examined the link have found associations in the expected direction. For example, C. A. Martin and Johnson (1992) investigated the relationship between mothers' belief systems and the accuracy of children's self-perceptions, and found that the mothers with the most sophisticated beliefs had children with the most developed sense of self. There are also indications that children's IQs are linked to the nature of their mothers' belief systems (Sameroff et al., 1987) and, for that matter, that parental beliefs in due course come to shape children's own beliefs about the nature of child development (Holden & Zambarano, 1992). But again it would be naive to expect the relationships to be close, if only because parental beliefs exert their influence through parental behavior and that, as we noted, is affected by many additional factors. And yet, as S. A. Miller (1988) points out, the very fact that beliefs express certain overarching orientations may mean that they can be more predictive of children's development than highly specific parental actions: the fact that a parent values, say, curiosity is not something that can be conveyed through single actions but only through a cumulative history of interaction with the child, and it is at this level that parental belief systems exert a guiding influence.

The case of parents' belief clashes

What if a child's two parents do not see eye-to-eye as far as child rearing is concerned? What are the consequences for the family and for the child of disagreements in parental beliefs?

A study by Block, Block, and Morrison (1981) examined this issue. Each parent of a 3-year-old child was asked independently to complete a questionnaire detailing his or her goals and values in bringing up the child. By comparing the responses of mother and father an index of agreement could be worked out which was then related to other aspects of family functioning. Two findings are noteworthy. First, the index predicted the future course of the marriage: the greater the disagreement between the parents the more likely it was that they would divorce in later years. Second, the index related to various aspects of the children's adjustment: in boys in particular more immature social relations, poorer impulse control and less effective ability to cope independently were found to become more likely with increasing disagreement. In a follow-up of these children in adolescence (B. E. Vaughn, Block, & Block, 1988) the association between early parental agreement and child functioning was still evident.

In a family where parents adopt the same orientations towards child rearing they are more likely to provide an environment that is structured and predictable and where children are therefore more secure. Boys in the early years are generally more in need of such an environment than girls; its absence will thus affect them to a greater extent. In addition, however, a clash of parental belief systems may well signal other marital tensions, and it is the absence of general harmony in the home that could therefore be related to the children's lack of adjustment.

Deficits of Parenting

Expressions of public concern about deviant and inadequate parenting are frequently heard. Just how widespread such phenomena are cannot easily be established; what is clear is that there is an urgent need to understand their nature, their causes and their consequences. Child abuse, both in its physical and sexual form, has attracted most publicity, but let us bear in mind that there are many other manifestations of parenting that are also clearly harmful, such as rejection, neglect, ridiculing, denigration, the setting of unrealistic goals, and the use of erratic discipline. We can regard all these as different forms of *psychological abuse*, a syndrome that has attracted much less research than its physical counterpart because of the obvious difficulties of identifying cases. Yet it has been suggested that psychological abuse is not only more prevalent but also more destructive than physical abuse; indeed, in so far as the latter is generally accompanied by psychological manifestations such as rejection or denigration, it is possible that it is these that are primarily responsible for the ill-effects observed in abused children rather than the actual bodily harm produced (S. N. Hart & Brassard, 1987).

Any attempt to understand the causation of pathological parenting can usefully start with the following classification, proposed by Belsky and Vondra (1989), of the influences that shape parental behavior generally:

1   the parents' individual characteristics and resources
2   the child's characteristics
3   the social context of the relationship

Parental characteristics are the contribution which the parents make to the interaction with the child, largely as a result of their own developmental history. There has for long been concern that the inadequately parented child will become the inadequate parent, and that a vicious circle is thus set up that brings about continuity across generations. The evidence provides only partial support for such a contention. Take a study by Dowdney and colleagues (1985) of mothers who had experienced prolonged periods of maternal deprivation in childhood as a result of being raised in impersonal institutions. As adults these women were observed with and interviewed about their own children and compared with a group of mothers whose childhood had not been similarly disrupted. Table 35 shows the results for one of the various measures taken, namely the summary rating of parenting quality arrived at for the mothers of both groups. Two conclusions become evident. First, four times as many of the deprived mothers were rated as "poor" in their parental style compared with the normally reared group of mothers; as shown by measures of more specific aspects, they tended to be considerably less sensitive, were rather more negative and also more ineffective in controlling their children. In this sense the findings suggest that these

Table 35   Ratings of parenting quality in deprived and nondeprived mothers

	Deprived mothers	*Nondeprived mothers*
Good	31	48
Intermediate	29	41
Poor	40	11

Source: Adapted from Dowdney et al. (1985)

women's history had put them at risk as parents. However, the second conclusion is that this is by no means an inevitable consequence. Thus, before one assumes that deprivation breeds deprivation, it is noteworthy that nearly one-third of these mothers had been assessed as "good," that in many respects the two groups did not differ and that gross defects of parenting were found in only a few of the deprived mothers. The mere fact of early deprivation is thus not sufficient on its own to cause parenting difficulties as an adult; other factors are also involved. It is noteworthy that just the same conclusions arise in the case of child abuse: it has been estimated that only about a third of abused children become abusing adults (Kaufman & Zigler, 1987) – an incidence that is vastly greater than that among nonabused individuals but that also shows there is nothing inevitable about the developmental outcome of such a childhood history.

The same applies to other groups that have been identified as "at risk" for parenting deficiencies but where again not all individuals are necessarily affected. One such group are teenage mothers: as has repeatedly been shown, parenting deficiencies occur more frequently in this group than among older mothers. For example, in an observational study of feeding and play with their 6-month-old babies adolescent mothers were found to be less expressive, less positive, less patient, and less vocal than older mothers observed under the same conditions (Culp, Culp, Osofsky, & Osofsky, 1991). These are typical findings; it is therefore not surprising that children of teenage mothers are generally considered to be at a disadvantage both cognitively and socially. What is less certain, however, is whether these are consequences that are directly attributable to the nature of the relationship with the mother, or whether other factors play a part. Teenage mothers, after all, are not only young but also mostly single, often poor and ill-educated, frequently without sufficient support from others and, as a result of their early parenthood, more likely to be at a disadvantage as far as social, educational, employment, and financial chances are concerned (Furstenberg, Brooks-Gunn, & Chase-Lonsdale, 1989). It is therefore possible that the effects on the child of the mother's age are at least in part due to these aspects and not solely to those associated with emotional immaturity and lack of experience. To take one of the aspects mentioned, poverty: the capacity for supportive, consistent, and involved parenting can easily be diminished as a result of the many life stresses associated with economic hardship (McLoyd, 1990); under such conditions parents are more likely to be irritable and depressed and consequently become less available, less patient and less loving in their interactions with their children.

Parents suffering from psychiatric and related disorders are a group that is particularly prone to parenting difficulties. Both mental retardation (Dowdney & Skuse, 1993) and alcoholism (von Knorring, 1991) in parents tend to be associated with aberrant child rearing practices and increased rates of behavior disorders in the children. However, most research has concentrated on maternal depression and its implications for children – largely because of the high prevalence of the condition. As has been repeatedly demonstrated, the interactions of such mothers with their children are characterized by reduced sensitivity and responsiveness, lack of reciprocity, flat emotional tone and a general absence of spontaneity and interest (Puckering, 1989). Depressed parents may be physically present but tend to be psychologically absent, and accordingly their children have been shown to suffer an increase in risk for the development of psychopathology by a factor of at least 2 or 3 (Dodge, 1990). Yet again, just as with teenage mothers, we find that explaining the link between parental characteristics and child development is by no means a straightforward matter, for the mechanisms behind the association may take many different forms: genetic transmission, disruptive parenting (which itself encompasses a great variety of different aspects), imitation, marital discord, parental absence through prolonged hospitalization, and social isolation. According to findings by N. B. Miller et al. (1993), of particular importance is the way in which parental depression affects the marital relationship, for it was that which these investigators found to be more closely associated with the development of preschool children's behavior problems than other factors. However, it is also noteworthy, that when the study was repeated with a sample of early adolescents the association between family variables and child outcome was not as marked – presumably because by then children were more autonomous and more involved in social groups other than the family.

Child characteristics play a part in affecting the adequacy of parenting in so far as some children are just more difficult to bring up than others. There is a natural inclination to look for causes of parental inadequacy within the parent; however, as we have seen repeatedly, what transpires between parent and child is determined as much by the latter as by the former, and particularly where the child is atypical in some respect the rearing task is a much more onerous one and thus more likely to go off course.

We have already discussed the problems encountered in relating to a child that, by virtue of blindness or having Down's syndrome, does not display the usual emotional expressions (pp. 58–9). Under these circumstances "reading" the child is much more difficult; when the child cannot send clear signals it is much more likely that the parent will respond inappropriately and that an asynchronous pattern of interaction is set up. In addition, being a parent of a retarded or handicapped child produces psychological consequences such as low self-esteem, depression, and aggressive feelings which are likely to have adverse effects on the relationship with the child; the sheer knowledge of having brought an atypical child into the world thus affects the parent's state of well-being and will in turn bring about distortions in the way the child is cared for.

One group that is especially at risk for child abuse are prematurely born infants (Belsky & Vondra, 1989). Again the reason appears to be that such children are more difficult to bring up, at least in the early months of life. As we saw in chapter 3, premature children do not make easy social partners: their behavior tends to be disorganized and therefore more difficult to respond to, their cry is often high-pitched and obnoxious, they take a long time before becoming capable of social skills such as eye contact and smiling, and in addition their appearance may be unattractive in comparison with baby norms. As they also tend to be fretful and difficult to soothe, and as it is often not easy to establish an acceptable sleep rhythm, parents can sometimes become discouraged, develop feelings of inadequacy and frustration and, under certain conditions, express these feelings in the form of abuse. Even when parental reactions take a less extreme form it is often difficult to respond to a premature infant in an appropriate manner (Eckerman, Oehler, Medvin, & Hannan, 1994). In most cases the problem is a temporary one, confined to the period of infancy after which the behavior of prematurely born children gradually becomes more organized and predictable. During that period, however, the effect of the child on the parent is such that caretaking may well become distorted in certain respects.

Social context factors are the third group of influences to take into account in attempts to explain parental deviance. In a stress-free environment a family may well function quite satisfactorily on the basis of its own resources; at times of difficulty, however, the availability of sources of help from outside the family becomes important and affects not just the parents as individuals but also the quality of the relationships within the family, including that with the child. It is surely no coincidence that social isolation is so frequently reported as a characteristic of abusive families (Garbarino & Crouter, 1978). Thus the extent to which families are embedded in social networks, comprising relatives, friends, and neighbors as well as formal agencies and organizations, has a bearing on what transpires between parent and child. All are potential sources of support, whether that involves information (e.g. about child care), practical action like the provision of adequate housing, or simply a shoulder to cry on. They function as buffers against stress and so enable the parents to devote themselves more easily to the child's care.

There are many demonstrations of an association between emotional support and the quality of parenting (Cochran et al., 1990). Those parents who receive more support behave towards their children with greater warmth and more consistency, are able to provide more effective discipline and yet be less punitive, respond to their children with greater sensitivity, have more positive attitudes about child rearing, show greater affection and are more likely to have securely attached children. Unfortunately it is the parents who are already at risk – teenage mothers, unmarried or divorced women, psychiatrically ill parents, and so forth – who tend to have smaller networks and thus fewer outside resources to draw on. Take single mothers: as Cochran et al. have shown, such women tend to have fewer individuals to turn to for help than mothers in two-parent families, the difference being most marked with respect to relatives, i.e. the people one can expect to be most likely to offer support (table 36). As Cochran and his colleagues also found, the size of the network reported by the single mothers was closely related to their perception of the child: the smaller the network the more negative was the mothers' attitude when asked "Is your child easy or difficult to raise?" Those with least support apparently were most uncomfortable in their parenting role – a finding that held for both blue collar and white collar families and not only for the United States sample referred to in the table but also a Swedish sample similarly investigated.

Table 36   Size of social network of one-parent and two-parent families

	Single mothers		Mothers in two-parent families	
	Blue collar	White collar	Blue collar	White collar
Relatives	5.5	6.6	8.8	11.1
Neighbors	2.7	3.5	3.0	4.5
Others	4.1	8.2	3.5	7.4
Total	12.3	18.3	15.3	23.0

Source: Adapted from Cochran et al. (1990)

There can be little doubt that the explanation of parental pathology can take many forms, depending on the individual case. Moreover, in most instances it is a *combination* of influences that is responsible for producing aberrant behavior, even though the relative importance of each influence may vary. An episode of physical abuse, for example, may be triggered by the child's incessant crying; the fretfulness can stem from the difficult temperament with which the child is endowed; such behavior is experienced as stressful and impinges on parents too young and immature to cope satisfactorily; the parents' ability is in any case impaired by the many other stresses which they face; and in view of their social isolation they need to cope with these problems on their own despite inadequate personal resources. Such a family is thus exposed to a multiplicity of risks, making the provision of constructive help no easy task.

Socialization Processes

Socialization refers to those processes whereby the standards of any given society are transmitted from one generation to the next. Acquisition of such standards is one of the principal tasks of childhood, and how children come to conform to them and eventually adopt them as their own is thus the basic issue in the study of socialization. Not that this process starts with general moral principles of the "thou shalt not . . ." kind, for these are much too abstract for young children to grasp. Instead, it begins with such highly specific and concrete instances of behavior as using a spoon instead of one's fingers for eating, not snatching toys from another child, and being kind to the new baby. How adults go about imposing these requirements, and how children come to conform to them, are questions to which developmental researchers have for long sought satisfactory answers.

Theoretical Assumptions

Socialization is an adult-initiated process, but the extent to which the child also plays a part has been the subject of much controversy in the past. Historically a number of models of the socialization process have influenced our thinking, each based on a particular concept of the basic nature of children; each therefore also making certain assumptions about the role the parent plays in the rearing of children; and each leading to different kinds of research (see summary in table 37).

(1) *Laissez-faire model* The French thinker Jean-Jacques Rousseau, writing in the 18th century, based his assumptions about the bringing up of children on the belief that each child arrives in the world preformed, with all basic aspects of personality already laid down and having merely to unfold in the course of subsequent development. It follows that the child's caretakers have but a limited part to play; as Rousseau asserted, "everything is well when it leaves the Creator's hands, everything degenerates in the hands of man." The task of parents is thus one of *laissez-faire* (leave alone) – of confining themselves, that is, to providing a maximally permissive environment in which children's potential can unfold. Educationalists such as Pestalozzi, Froebel, and A. S. Neill subsequently adopted this principle by setting up schools in which, by means of a largely unstructured environment, children can give free expression to their spontaneous interests and activities and where socialization is thus primarily a self-initiated process. It follows that research efforts influenced by this model would concern themselves little with adults' behavior: their role is too minimal; instead, attention would be largely on the child and the manner in which preformed abilities come to manifest themselves in overt behavior.

(2) *Clay molding model* At the opposite extreme we have a view of the child as wholly unformed at birth, like a lump of clay that adults can mold into any shape they decide upon. In time the shape will set, and the form it takes will then be wholly

Table 37 Models of socialization of children

Model	Concept of child	Parental practices	Ensuing research
Laissez-faire	Preformed	Leave alone	Plotting norms of development
Clay molding	Passive	Shaping and training	Effects of rewards and punishment
Conflict	Antisocial	Discipline	Parent–child conflicts
Mutuality	Participant	Sensitivity and responsiveness	Reciprocity in social interaction

explicable in terms of whatever caretakers did during the child's impressionable years. To understand how socialization comes about one must therefore concentrate wholly on the behavior of the caretakers: it is their rewards and punishments, their ways of habit training and their example that account for the final product. The child's individuality is thus neglected and all suggestions of innate potential denied. Children are seen as passive, infinitely malleable, and totally at the mercy of the molding process, while developmental change is explained solely in terms of environmental input to the child. ,

(3) *The conflict model*   According to this view children are not passive; from the beginning they have wishes and desires of their own which impel them to behave in certain ways. Unfortunately these ways are antithetical to society; they bring children into conflict with their caretakers, whose task is then to compel them to give up their natural preferences and adopt all sorts of unnatural modes of behavior regarded as desirable by adults. While this view has a historical basis in the notion that children are originally evil and that it is the task of their caretakers to curb their sinful tendencies, it has its modern counterpart too, especially in the writings of Freud. He in particular propagated the view that human nature is essentially antisocial, that children are initially creatures whose instinctual drives are of a selfish, destructive nature and thus incompatible with living in society. Freud's conception of socialization is thus of a conflict model: parents are characterized predominantly in terms of prohibitions, commands, threats, and exhortations; children are painted as aggressive, selfish, fearful, and in due course guilt-ridden. Research inspired by this model would accordingly focus mainly on parent–child conflicts, seeing these as engendered by the child's antisocial nature on the one hand and the parents' role in curbing primitive impulses on the other.

(4) *The mutuality model*   The influence of the above three models has been undermined by more recent findings, of which two in particular are relevant, both of which we have repeatedly encountered in this book. First, it is apparent that children are far from passive; from the earliest age they take an active part in their own upbringing. A view of the child as *participant* is thus a more appropriate one. Second, mutual adaptation, not conflict, is the basic theme that runs through the course of parent–child interaction. Far from starting off as an antisocial being that must be coerced into sociability the infant begins life pre-adapted for social interaction. A model of socialization based on parent–child mutuality is thus indicated, and it is this on which the more recent work is based that we shall discuss below.

Cognitive Socialization

Traditionally cognition used to be treated as a set of functions that develop within human beings as a result of maturation and individual learning experiences. Cognitive functions were treated as beneath-the-skin events; the focus was entirely on the individual, and while it was admitted that certain "outside" events such as gross neglect could interfere with the development of cognitive processes little credence was given to the notion that the child's social transactions may be an essential part of cognitive growth and that they can provide the foundations for its emergence.

Much of the credit for changing this view is due to Vygotsky (1978), whose work first appeared in Russian in the 1930s but was not discovered and translated in Western countries till several decades later. Cognitive skills, according to Vygotsky, have a social origin: they must first be performed jointly with a competent adult before they come under the child's control. Thus all higher psychological functions, including thinking, learning, and problem solving, appear first on an *intermental* plane, i.e. in the course of interacting with another person, before they become internalized and the child is able to perform them on an *intramental* plane. Social interactions therefore form the primary context in which the child is initiated to the more mature ways of thinking current in each society, and cognitive functioning can only grow under the guidance of adults willing to support, direct, and organize the child's activities in such a way that the child can participate in increasingly complex ways until eventually able to function independently. Not that children are merely passive receivers of adult guidance: they seek, select, and structure the assistance of those around them in learning how to solve problems, and to be effective the adult must therefore be aware of and follow the child's own motivations to learn. Cooperative activity is thus the hallmark of individual mental growth.

One way in which children contribute to such cooperative activity is by signaling their readiness to learn. Interaction with adults in problem solving situations can only be of benefit if the child has achieved some specified level of competence. Accordingly Vygotsky proposed the *zone of proximal development* (ZPD) to define the range within which adult guidance is likely to be most effective. The boundaries of the ZPD are determined by the gap between what children can do on their own and what they can achieve when acting as the junior partner of a more knowledgeable person. It is thus a region of sensitivity to guidance where the child is uncertain and looking for help and is therefore most susceptible to adult instruction. Only interactions that occur within the ZPD are said to bring about cognitive change. The ability of adults to pitch their tutorial efforts within this zone is thus a crucial factor in helping the child to progress to independence, and the competent tutor is someone who is capable of determining this zone for any given child and a given task, providing the necessary help and guidance and then gradually withdrawing support as the child becomes capable of performing independently. Mutual cooperation is thus the key to mental growth: on the one hand children actively seek help and communicate their requirements to those around them, and on the other hand adults sensitively respond by first offering support but then progressively withdrawing it as the child achieves the necessary competence to cope alone.

The research instigated by this account (e.g. Rogoff, 1990; Rogoff, Mistry, Gonen, & Mosier, 1993) has focused on interactions, not on individuals, treating adult and child as a problem solving dyad. Work carried out by D. Wood (1988; D. Wood & Middleton, 1975) provides a good example of this approach. Mothers of 4-to-5-year-olds were asked to teach their children to put together a construction toy – a task too difficult for these children to do alone but one which they were able to accomplish with "good" tuition. What is good tuition? On the basis of detailed observations of how mothers went about their task, Wood suggests that mothers who relied exclusively on demonstration, or mothers who merely attempted to talk children through the task, had little success; when subsequently asked to put the toy together on their own these children achieved little. The mothers of children who learned most were those who taught their children "contingently," that is at each step the mother monitored what the child was able to do, adapted both the nature and level of her help accordingly and in this way made any help she offered contingent upon the child's understanding of previous levels of instructions. When the child failed she offered more support; when the child succeeded she offered less support, and the extent to which such a "contingent-shift" rule was applied turned out to be predictive of the child's subsequent skill on this task.

In our previous discussion of the onset of language skills (pp. 120ff.) we noted that these develop optimally in the context of *joint involvement episodes* (JIEs), i.e. one-to-one encounters in which adult and child pay joint attention to and jointly act upon some specific topic. We can now extend this notion to functions other than language; following on from Vygotsky it appears that such encounters, in which children can make their first attempts at some new skill on the basis of the adult's support and feedback, provide the requisite context for the growth of higher cognitive functions generally. Whether Vygotsky was right in proposing that the *long-term* development of cognition is crucially dependent on the child's experience of these encounters remains uncertain. What is clear is that in JIEs children's behavior is often richer and more complex than at other times. JIEs, that is, can elicit a child's optimal and developmentally most advanced performance.

The evidence for this proposition (reviewed in Schaffer, 1992) relates to various cognitive functions such as attention, problem solving, and symbolic play. Take attention – a function that has traditionally been treated as though it were purely an individual property, untouched by interpersonal experience. Yet it has been apparent for some time that children's attentional capacity varies according to social context. Dunn and Wooding (1977), for example, observed 2-year-old children at home and found the length of their attention bouts to be significantly greater when playing with the mother than when playing on their own. However, such correlational data leave open the question of whether the mother was in fact responsible for bringing about this effect; experimentally varying the adult's involvement in the child's play is one way to ascertain this. A study by Parrinello and Ruff (1988) did so by assigning adults to either low, medium, or high levels of involvement in the play of 10-month-old infants, the levels varying according to the manner and frequency with which toys were offered, the amount of the adult's talk and her physical proximity. As table 38 shows, the infants' attention span did vary with the amount of adult involvement,

Table 38 Mean length of infants' attention episodes (in seconds)

	Low	Medium	High
	Adult involvement level		
Low attenders	2.71	4.05	3.50
High attenders	4.70	5.12	4.67

Source: Adapted from Parrinello & Ruff (1988)

though the effect was greatest at medium rather than at high levels (perhaps the latter were too overpowering). But the effect also varied from one infant to another: infants who had earlier been classified as low spontaneous attenders while playing on their own were found to benefit significantly more from adult involvement than infants classified as high spontaneous attenders.

We can conclude that children's performance can be raised to more optimal levels by an adult's involvement but that the extent of this effect varies according to characteristics of the child. This is borne out by other studies too, such as those that have examined children's play behavior. In the early years play goes through some marked developmental changes that reflect the child's cognitive competence. Thus in infancy play is generally of a *sensorimotor* nature, in that the child explores toys merely for the pleasure of sensation. Subsequently play becomes *functional*, i.e. the child assigns objects the function they are designed for (blocks are for building, cars for pushing, etc.). Eventually play becomes *symbolic*, in that the child can use toys to represent other objects and engage in pretend play. Various scales have been developed to chart children's progression in play maturity (e.g. Belsky & Most, 1981; Nicolich, 1977); these differ in the number of levels describing that progression, but historically all were used to examine play as an essentially solitary activity and yielding a "pure" indication of the child's cognitive growth.

Play, however, frequently occurs in social interaction contexts, and there are signs that a partner, under certain conditions at least, can elicit higher maturity levels from a child than shown in solitary play. Slade (1987), for instance, during observations of toddlers at home found that both the level of play and the length of play episodes increased when the mother participated in the child's activities in contrast to periods when the child played alone. The effect depended, however, on the nature of the mother's participation, being greater when she actively entered into the child's play activities and encouraged by means of explicit suggestions. Merely providing a verbal commentary was not as effective. Again, however, we find that child characteristics also play a part in determining the effectiveness of the adult's help, and of these the child's age is a particularly important influence. This is well illustrated in a study by O'Connell and Bretherton (1984). Children at two ages, 20 and 28 months, were observed playing on their own and in a joint session with the mother. When their play activities were categorized into three main groupings corresponding to sensorimotor, functional, and symbolic play it was found that the diversity of activities within these categories increased significantly when the mother joined in. The maternal effect differed, however, according to the child's age: at 20 months sensorimotor and functional play actions were affected by the mother's presence; at 28 months only symbolic play was thereby fostered. As the mothers provided guidance to an equal extent with respect to all categories of play one must conclude that the children quite systematically selected from the constant flow of suggestions those that fitted in with their own capabilities. At the earlier age sensorimotor and functional play predominated; children then used the mother's assistance for these two kinds of activities. At 28 months, on the other hand, they had become capable of the rather more advanced symbolic type of play and accordingly took advantage of those suggestions which helped them to perform at that level. It was thus the *child* who determined the effectiveness of the mother's instructions, many of which may not have been particularly suitable at that developmental stage but which the child simply ignored.

There can be no question that much of cognitive growth is initially propelled by spontaneous changes within the child that are an inherent part of development. Thus children set the agenda; as Vygotsky stressed, there is little point in instruction until the child reaches the ZPD. The adult's role is not to create new cognitive processes; it is rather to facilitate, direct, and extend those that have already appeared. During the early years this is brought about most effectively in contexts of joint involvement, i.e. in one-to-one exchanges where adults can provide the support that children require for more advanced performance and where they can negotiate with the child what activities to carry out and what meanings to attach to these activities. Responsibility for tackling the problem can then gradually be transferred from adult to child as the latter internalizes the adult's strategies and instructions. The term *scaffolding* has been used to designate such adult activities, meaning thereby the "process that enables a child or novice to solve a problem, carry out a task or achieve a goal which would be beyond his unassisted efforts" (D. Wood, Bruner, & Ross, 1976). It is a useful umbrella term to describe a wide range of adult actions. In some respects it is misleading in that it implies a rigid structure or one that does not involve the child; however, Wood and his colleagues use the term to denote the continuous revision of action in response to the child's ongoing activity that an adult undertakes, thus denoting a highly flexible process. It is this which is said to be the crucial element in helping the child towards independent behavior.

There is much in this account which remains uncertain: how the internalization occurs whereby children manage to adopt adults' behavior as their own; whether all cognitive functions need social priming to the same degree; what the most effective adult forms of involvement are and how these should vary according to age and other child characteristics. What is clear is that this approach bears out the mutuality model of socialization we described above, and that it is applicable to cognition as much as to other aspects of behavior. The idea that *social* skills require an interpersonal context for their acquisition and development can no doubt be readily accepted; on the other hand, the proposal that *cognitive* abilities are similarly tied to a social context does not have the same intuitive appeal and has in the past been rejected in favor of searches for purely intrapersonal processes responsible for the course of development. There is, however, increasing evidence that social interactive experiences do affect cognitive growth, that their influence in the early years is most effectively transmitted in the context of what we have referred to as joint involvement episodes, and that they entail the mutual cooperation of a participant child and a sensitive adult.

The case of early number development

One cognitive function that illustrates the need to consider social aspects in attempts to understand its development is numeracy. The idea that a child's *literacy* has social roots has been grasped by educators for quite some time; the interest shown in the role of joint picture book reading (e.g. DeLoache & DeMendoza, 1987) is one example. Involvement in such an activity with a parent enables the young child to learn that pictures and text are meaningful, to become acquainted with some of the conventions of literacy (e.g. holding books upright and turning pages in sequence) and to acquire the necessary motivation to look at books by finding out that they are fun. It is thus no surprise that the extent of children's experience of such a joint activity can predict their later reading ability, as well as foster their language development (Whitehurst et al., 1994).

The growth of numeracy skills, on the other hand, has for the most part been treated as a purely intrapersonal development. Such research has thrown valuable light on the way in which children begin to construe the world in quantitative terms and on the principles which underlie their number concepts at different ages (Hughes, 1986). However, it neglects the fact that from the beginning children are exposed to adult conversations that are full of references to number, made quite spontaneously and with no particular intent to teach (Durkin, Shire, Crowther, & Rutter, 1986). In addition, a great

many social activities go on at home which involve children in number-related ideas (Saxe, Guberman, & Gearhart, 1987): songs and rhymes (e.g. "One, two, buckle my shoe"), informal games (e.g. counting toes or fingers), competitions (such as number of times children can skip up and down), household activities (e.g. getting the child to help with measuring out ingredients in cooking), or such other domestic routines as laying a table or choosing a particular TV channel. Thus children's developing cognitive competencies to deal with number are given every opportunity in the course of daily life to become interwoven with the way in which society makes use of numeracy.

This process has been examined at a more detailed level in observations of mothers playing number games with children. Saxe and colleagues (1987) asked mothers of preschool children to teach them various counting and number reproduction tasks, thereby treating mother and child as a problem solving dyad and as a result finding many similarities to other joint involvement interactions such as those on attention and symbolic play described above. Mothers generally adjusted the level and kind of guidance given to the child's ongoing number activity: they would, for instance, recognize the type of difficulty experienced by the child at any given moment and respond with instructions tailored to that difficulty. Following an error by the child they shifted to more specific instructions;

following a successful move they adjusted the complexity level of their guidance upwards. Mothers of less able children simplified the task more by breaking it down into smaller and easier components; mothers also simplified their instructions when confronted by more difficult tasks. At the same time children adjusted their behavior in the light of the mother's input, making use of her efforts to cope with a number task that they could not solve on their own. Thus mothers created teaching contexts in which, on the basis of a continuous process of mutual adjustment, they were able to convey to their children some of the specific skills required to tackle number problems and do so in a context of playful, motivating interaction.

This is a very different orientation to one which suggests that children try to figure out on their own the nature of number. It is apparent that any account of the origins of numeracy must include reference to the part this concept plays in the child's social exchanges; we need to look not just at the child but also at the child's caretakers and their joint interaction if we are to understand how number understanding becomes a meaningful aspect of the cognitive repertoire.

Emotional Socialization

As we saw in chapter 2, emotional development proceeds from a biological basis. The primary emotions appear to be universal and the manner of their expression innate. Yet, just as with cognitive functions, the child's encounters with other people can shape and redirect emotional behavior, ensuring that it comes to conform with the customs and expectations of caretakers. There is considerable variation among social groups as to what is acceptable: different cultures have evolved different rules for emotional display; within any one society there are differences among families in the emotional climate that they have established; and in each case adults act, both consciously and unconsciously, to steer the child into ways of expressing, managing, and even talking about emotions that conform to the customs of their particular group. Not that this can be done arbitrarily: characteristics such as the child's age and temperament put constraints on adults' efforts. How emotional socialization takes place will therefore depend on the child's characteristics as well as the goals and values of the adult; here too a process of mutual negotiation is required to bring about the kind of behavior that makes people acceptable and predictable.

Cross-cultural studies provide the most vivid evidence concerning the socialization of emotion. This is seen especially in the *display rules* that every society has evolved, i.e. the conventions that govern the overt expression of emotion, and the actions taken to enforce them. Consider the following examples:

(1) While keeping emotional impulses in check is emphasized in all societies, the manner of doing so shows considerable variation. Hendry (quoted by P. L. Harris, 1989), a social anthropologist working in Japan, went along to her son's kindergarten in order to observe local practices and found that staff laid considerable emphasis on

the checking of emotional displays. Crying, for example, was actively discouraged and persistent criers teased or ostracized. In disputes over toys older children were expected to give in to younger ones and, in a quarrel, encouraged to apologize. The children's attention was drawn to how the victim of aggression felt and in this way urged to inhibit their emotional outbursts. Staying on good terms and playing harmoniously was the goal which these children were constantly urged to attain; whatever their inner feelings, overt displays of such negative emotions as anger and jealousy were regarded as unacceptable and to be suppressed. The result, as Ekman (1972) found, is that in public Japanese adults are much less likely to display emotions than Westerners, even though in private, when they believe themselves unobserved, they express them just as readily.

(2)   The people of Ifaluk, an island in the Western Pacific, illustrate another aspect of emotional socialization, namely the direction of emotional behavior through the use of language (Lutz, 1987). Different societies construe emotions in different ways, and one of the tasks of parents is therefore to convey to children sets of terms, together with the meaning ascribed to them, which their society uses to highlight particular feelings. To the Ifaluk the term *metagu* is central in this respect: it is the fear or anxiety which prevents undue excitement and inhibits aggression. Excitement in children is regarded as leading to misbehavior; adults must therefore react to it with anger which will arouse *metagu* in the child. In so far as Ifalukians value cooperation, sharing, and obedience they stress the development of feelings associated with *metagu* in the child and use the term to direct the child's attention to the importance of inhibiting disruptive and aggressive behavior.

(3)   Our third example is one we described in chapter 3, namely the approach of the Gusii of Kenya to emotional socialization (LeVine et al., 1994). These people, as we saw, regard the expression of any strong feeling as disruptive to social life: elaborate social rules have therefore been developed to avoid all overt expression of emotions, particularly by means of gaze aversion and the use of bland countenance. This is already evident in mothers' treatment of their infants: Gusii mothers do stimulate their infants, but their repertoire consists mostly of repetitive vocalizations, taps, headnods, and fixed facial expressions, all administered in order to achieve a flat, even, and affectless interaction.

Such cross-cultural evidence shows that socialization affects emotional development in various ways. For one thing, it sets limits to the extent to which emotionality in general should be expressed: in societies such as the Gusii the limits are considerably lower than found in Western countries and children from an early age are encouraged to inhibit all but the mildest expression of feeling. Second, some emotions are given greater prominence in certain cultures than is found elsewhere: the Ilongot, a tribe of former headhunters in the Philippines, see anger and passion as positive virtues and encourage them accordingly by means of their child rearing practices (Rosaldo, 1980). Third, the norms for displaying emotions in particular situations are also largely culture-specific: as we saw above, in Japan group interactions are not regarded as occasions for fostering individual assertiveness as in the West but for encouraging cooperation and giving way. And finally, children's emotions are managed through the use of verbal labels. As we noted for the Ifaluk, particular societies cut up the emotional spectrum in ways that fit in with their sets of values; by labeling certain kinds of emotions children's awareness of these are sharpened and their behavior accordingly channeled in culturally appropriate ways.

While parents in any given society share culturally defined values there is still plenty of room for variation in the kind of emotional climate that distinguishes each family. The daily interactions which children experience within the family, whether as participants or as observers, are often of a highly emotional nature. Such experiences are thought to bring about important consequences for children's affective development.

This is most apparent at the extremes of the emotional continuum, namely when, on the one hand, a family member suffers from depression and the prevailing emotional tone is thereby flattened and, on the other hand, when interactions within the family are marked by sustained conflict and anger (P. L. Harris, 1994). As to depression, we have already seen that such a condition can markedly alter parents' style of interaction with their children, producing a general lack of affect and damping down all the feelings of fun and excitement which a child would normally experience during the exchange. In so far as depressed parents tend to be critical, unsupportive, and intrusive their children are more likely to encounter negative than positive emotions, particularly when the depressed parent is the main caretaker. The impact on the child is likely to be greatest during the first two years or so, for it is then that the capacities to regulate emotion and arousal emerge – a development that takes place primarily in the context of social interaction and that, initially at least, requires the support of the child's more mature partners. But what if that support is not forthcoming because of the parent's psychological unavailability? As the evidence (reviewed by Cummings & Davies, 1994) shows, even in infancy parental depression brings about a reduction in positive affect. There are fewer smiles, more gaze aversion, and less interest in surroundings: in short, the infant acts "depressed." What must be of particular concern is that such a behavioral style is not just shown when interacting with the depressed parent but is generalized to other people. This is illustrated in figure 18, based on a study by Field and colleagues (1988) in which the reactions of 3- to 6-month-old infants were observed while in face-to-face interactions with the mother and also with a female stranger. Not only did infants with depressed mothers show considerably less positive behavior with the mother but, compared to infants with nondepressed mothers, they were also less positive to the stranger. As the latter in turn then tend to respond less positively a vicious circle is set up which may well perpetuate the child's symptomatology. Muted emotion, social withdrawal, anxiety, and passivity have all been reported as occurring more frequently among children of depressed parents than in other children, and though the

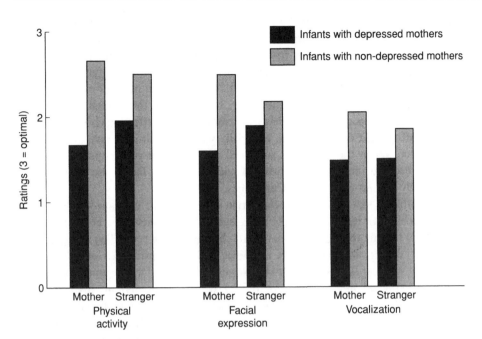

Figure 18 Behavior ratings of infants with depressed and nondepressed mothers, interacting with the mother or with a stranger (adapted from Field et al., 1988)

association between parental and child psychopathology may be brought about in various ways, there can be little doubt that children's emerging capacities to control and modulate their own emotions can be seriously affected by the parent's emotional disturbance.

As to conflict, the consequences for children's emotional development when exposed to continuous confrontation and aggression in others may also be marked (Cummings, 1994). Under such circumstances the effects are mostly of the "externalizing" kind, i.e. children too become aggressive, with anger as the predominant emotion in their interpersonal relationships. However, other types of reaction also occur, including passivity and withdrawal. It is not yet clear why there are such individual differences; it may be that the impact of the same event on children of different temperament produces varying results. What is clear is that adults' anger, particularly if frequent and sustained, has the effect of interfering in the development of children's own emotional control, and heightened aggression especially may result if children are given no encouragement to check their impulsive tendencies. This applies whether children are witnesses of conflict between their parents or whether they themselves are the victims of violence, though the effect is greatest when they experience both. Experimental studies, in which adults simulate angry conflict in front of children, confirm the effect: subsequently children are more likely to hit playmates, fight for toys, and indulge in verbal aggression. As Cummings, Ianotti, and Zahn-Waxler (1985) found, the consequences are greatest for children already aggressively inclined. When pairs of children observed adults interacting first in a friendly and then in an angry manner, those children who had previously been categorized as highly aggressive showed a much greater increase in aggression to their peers than did other children (see table 39). This was even more pronounced when the procedure was repeated a month later. It seems that the arousal generated by witnessing other people's conflict has a general disruptive effect on children's capacity to regulate their own emotions, especially when they already have difficulties in this respect. When the stress is a sustained one, far from getting used to conflict, children become increasingly sensitized and thus more likely also to behave in emotionally inappropriate ways (Cummings, 1994).

It is unlikely that emotional socialization can simply be explained by reinforcement, teaching, or imitation. These processes may play some part: after all, parents do attempt to train their children to control their impulses, rewarding and punishing them accordingly, and they do set examples with their own behavior (Thompson, 1994). But such explanations tend to be one-sided: they neglect the mutual regulation and negotiation of mood that occur during all social interactions, involving both partners and thus constituting an *emotional dialog*. Studies of such dialogs (e.g. by Denham, 1993), in which measures are taken of a mother's and child's emotional displays as they continuously change in the course of an interaction episode, have shown the extent to which both partners respond to each other's expressions with appropriate, matching expressions of their own. Happiness in the child, for example, is followed by happiness in the mother; fear, on the other hand, by tenderness. From the child's point of view this means that the mother's emotions are predictable; from the mother's point of view it means that she can engage in *affect coaching*, i.e. manipulate her child's emotional state by the manner of her response.

While coaching reflects the adult's personal and cultural values which the child is expected to adopt, the bidirectional nature of emotional dialogs must be emphasized. Adults respond to children as well as children to adults; whatever efforts an adult makes to steer a child in certain directions are constrained by the child's predisposition. What is effective with a placid child may not work with an excitable child; what

Table 39   Time spent in aggressive acts following episodes of adults' positive and angry interactions

	Nonaggressive children	*Moderately aggressive children*	*Highly aggressive children*
Adults' positive interaction	0.90	7.95	13.00
Adults' angry interaction	7.70	10.57	50.19

Source: Adapted from Cummings et al. (1985)

is appropriate for a 6-year-old may not be so for a 15-year-old; and how a parent goes about the task of affect direction at any given moment will depend on what the child is doing at that time. Thus, like other aspects of development, emotional socialization is based on the mutuality of parent and child and not on a one-sided imposition of one upon the other.

Emotional dialogs are nonverbal exchanges of facial, gestural, and other affective signals and take place from infancy on. However, once a child becomes able to talk *dialogs about emotion* form a new means whereby adults can influence the course of affective development. From about 18 months on references to feeling states (e.g. "frightened," "hurt," "sad") appear in children's talk – first in relation to their own feelings, later on in relation to the feelings of others too (Bretherton et al., 1986). By age 2 most children not only spontaneously refer to feelings but will also enter into lively discussion about them with parents: about their causes, about their effects on the child and about ways to change them (Dunn, Bretherton, & Munn, 1987). Such conversations give parents the opportunity to share with children their interpretations of particular emotional experiences, to discuss their significance and to articulate their causes. Take the following example (from Dunn et al. 1987) concerning a 24-month-old child whose older sibling has just been showing him a book with pictures of monsters:

Child:	Mummy, Mummy.
Mother:	What's wrong?
Child:	Frighten.
Mother:	The book?
Child:	Yes.
Mother:	It's not frightening you!
Child:	Yes!
Mother:	It did, did it?
Child:	Yes.

This excerpt shows that, as a result of the child being able to verbalize his feelings, the mother can share the experience, sympathize with his fear and pinpoint the cause. She is thus in a position to influence the child's appraisal of the situation by explaining, reassuring, or (if she had so chosen) reinforcing his fear and in this way channeling future emotional expression.

Mothers differ considerably in the extent to which they talk about feelings to their children, and these differences are related to differences in the extent to which young children themselves communicate verbally about feeling states. According to Dunn et al. (1987), an intriguing sex difference becomes evident in this respect, in that mothers give greater encouragement to their daughters to talk about emotion than they do to their sons. This is found as early as 18 months, and already by 24 months the sex difference is found in the children's own talk: girls are more ready to refer to emotions than boys. A further study by Dunn, Brown, and Beardsall (1991) suggests that differences in family discourse about feelings may have considerable implications for children's later social behavior. Measures of the frequency of such talk, taken when the children were 3 years old, were found to be closely related to a measure of social sensitivity taken at age 6. Thus children who grew up in families in which such feeling-state talk was frequent were as 6-year-olds better at making judgments about other people's emotions than were children who had been less involved in such talk. It may well be that verbal discussion about others' feelings alerts children to their significance, enables them to reflect upon the role of emotions and thus sensitizes them to the range of behavior whereby people express them. Language is therefore a crucial medium with which emotional socialization is accomplished.

Summary

Families as Systems

- Families are ideal contexts for the socialization of children. However, research on nontraditional families had shown that conformity to one specific family norm is by no means essential to children's well-being.
- Systems theory, when applied to the family, stresses the importance of studying the components, i.e. individual members and their relationships, in the context of the whole family unit. It follows that what happens in one part of the system has repercussions in other parts – as seen, for example, in the mutual influence of the parents' marital relationship and the child's well-being.
- Families are dynamic units that change in response to outside events and that reorganize themselves when confronted with internal changes. The latter is illustrated by the transition to parenthood on the birth of a baby, requiring renegotiation of existing relationships.

The Nature of Parenting

- Parents can be characterized in terms of universal, culture-specific and individual attributes. While parenting has a genetic base, it is also a flexible system greatly influenced by social pressures.
- Efforts to categorize parental styles have drawn attention to two major dimensions, i.e. permissiveness/restrictiveness and warmth/hostility.
- According to Baumrind, parenting can best be described in terms of a taxonomy of authoritarian, permissive, authoritative, and rejecting-neglecting styles. Authoritative parenting tends to be associated with the most and rejecting-neglecting parenting with the least degree of competence in children.
- The parental styles of mothers and fathers differ in various respects. There is, however, no evidence that females are biologically prepared to a greater degree for the task of child care than males.

- How parents behave depends in part on their beliefs about the nature of child development. Such belief systems are influenced both by the parents' cultural background and their personality, but their relationship with parental behavior and with child development is not a close one because of the operation of many additional influences.
- Deviant and inadequate parenting takes many forms. To understand its causation three kinds of factors need to be taken into account: parental characteristics, child characteristics, and the social context of the relationship. Parents' aberrant behavior is usually brought about by a multiplicity of risks.

Socialization Processes

- Socialization refers to the transmission from one generation to another of a society's standards of beliefs and behavior. It has been conceptualized in different ways, of which the principal are the laissez-faire model, the clay molding model, the conflict model, and the mutuality model. The last of these is currently considered as the most satisfactory in the light of empirical findings.
- The development of cognitive functions is one area in which socialization processes operate. Vygotsky's theory, which stresses a progression from "intermental" to "intramental" functioning, is one attempt to explain how this occurs; research based on his views has shown how adults provide helpful input to children attempting to master tasks, e.g. through "scaffolding" activities performed during one-to-one interaction.
- Emotional development is the other major area illustrating socialization influences. As cross-cultural studies show, different societies have different rules for the display of emotions, and these need to be learned early in childhood.
- Even within any one society children's daily social interactions can provide them with markedly differing emotional experiences, with important consequences for their affective development. This is illustrated, for example, by families where a parent suffers from depression and the emotional tone is therefore flattened; it is also seen in cases of sustained family conflict, where the unchecked display of adult aggression can interfere in the development of children's own emotional control.
- The way in which adult and child exchange affective signals in the course of social interaction (their "emotional dialog") helps to explain the course of emotional socialization. Another means is the talk about emotions which occurs with increasing frequency between parents and their preschool children.

Chapter 6

From Other-control to Self-control

In the course of development children must learn to assume responsibility for their own behavior. How they do so is a problem of profound theoretical interest, for the emergence of the capacity for self-regulation is one of the hallmarks of childhood and represents an achievement of great complexity. It is also a problem with considerable practical implications, for failure to develop such a capacity can result in impulsive, egocentric, and antisocial beings who in later life continue to express their every whim and demand the instant gratification that one would normally expect only in very young children.

Initially children must rely on others to perform regulating functions for them. Thus young infants cannot easily calm themselves when upset; the mother must soothe and comfort. Children around the age of 3 are notorious for their inability to tolerate frustration, and their consequent temper tantrums; others must distract, bribe, discipline, or use whatever techniques are appropriate to control children's emotions for them. And inner standards of behavior, which act as guiding principles even in the absence of external sanctions, take the whole of childhood to fully develop; until they do, children's caretakers must ensure that the demands of society are made explicit and that children conform accordingly. Thus adults play a crucial part in helping children to achieve control over their own behavior; it is only through initial dependence on others that a child can develop autonomy.

How adults carry out this task, and how their actions interweave with the child's growing capability, is a problem to which much attention has been given. A useful developmental scheme for the very beginnings of self-regulation has been provided by Kopp (1982) and is illustrated in table 40. Children, according to this proposal, go through a series of phases in the early years in each of which they face certain specific developmental challenges that they must meet as a step towards acquiring control over their own behavior. Thus in the first phase, extending over the initial 2 or 3 months, the problem of regulation involves safeguarding the infant from stimulation that is too strong and which will therefore have too great an arousing effect. Caregivers have a vital role in protecting and soothing, though already the infant has devices such as comfort sucking available that will also help in reducing arousal. During the next phase, between about 3 and 9 months, the infant needs to learn how to adjust behavior to external circumstances such as objects reached for and grasped; the type of control required is a primitive one referred to by Kopp as *modulation*, in that it is not conscious or intentional. Deliberate control does not appear till the third phase, i.e. from the end of the first year on; it is then that the child becomes able to comply with commands. At this age compliance is tied to the here-and-now directives of the caregiver; these have no effect in the adult's absence for the child cannot as yet internalize commands; however, in so far as children may choose either to comply or not to comply a definite advance of self-regulating abilities is indicated. This is taken considerably further during the next phase, for from about 2 years on children do become able to behave according to adult directives even when on their own. The first signs of the all-important capacity for *internalization* have thus appeared. These are initially somewhat fragile; during Kopp's last phase, from about 3 years on, they become more firmly established, and particularly so if adults treat the child in a consistent and sensitive manner and thus allow the child to learn what is socially acceptable and what is not.

Thus on the one hand there are certain cognitive prerequisites which appear as part of the child's maturational timetable and which set the agenda for each phase. With the appearance of intentionality, for example, compliance becomes possible, for then children can begin to make deliberate choices whether to follow the adult's directive or not. Similarly the onset of representational thinking and recall memory make internalization possible; by their means children free themselves from the here-and-now and act on the basis of past experiences. And on the other hand caregivers must help the child in meeting each challenge; they need to provide whatever form

Table 40   Phases of children's self-regulation

Phases	Approximate ages (months)	Features
Neurophysiological modulation	0–2/3	Modulation of arousal
Sensorimotor modulation	3–9+	Change ongoing behavior in response to environment
Control	12–18+	Intentional behavior, conscious awareness of action
Self-control	24+	Representational thinking and recall memory; behave according to social expectations in absence of adult
Self-regulation	36+	Strategy production, conscious introspection, flexibility of control to meet changing situational demands

Source: Adapted from Kopp (1982)

of support is required at that phase of development to complement the child's fragile control capacities and thus make it possible to move on to the next step.

Parental Control Techniques and Child Compliance

The end result of socialization in childhood is an individual who has internalized the norms of society and uses them as a guide to conduct. However, the development of a moral conscience is a long-drawn-out process; initially children conform to social requirements because parents exert control over them and expect them to comply with their demands. As we saw from Kopp's scheme, compliance becomes possible at the end of the first year when children begin to make intentional choices, but however far in time such a step may be from a fully developed moral sense it is almost certainly essential to the eventual formation of an internalized conscience (Kochanska, 1991). How parents get children to do things is a topic of interest in its own right; it is also one that may lead to greater understanding of children as their own moral controllers.

Compliance and Noncompliance

At its simplest, compliance is doing what you are told to do. Parents have certain goals and standards which they know the child will not meet unless directed to do so: faces must be washed, television switched off at a particular time and siblings have to stop fighting. By virtue of their greater power parents enforce these rules and expect their children to obey. Thus compliance is required for smooth parent–child inter-action; no wonder that noncompliance is one of the most frequent reasons for psychiatric referral of young children (Forehand & McMahon, 1981). According to G. R. Patterson and colleagues (1989), early noncompliance can be the beginning of a chain of events which include coercive family interactions, poor peer relationships, delinquency, and various conduct problems in later life. Compliance is thus a highly valued and desirable trait.

Yet the incidence of noncompliance to parental directives, even in perfectly normal and well-functioning children, is considerable. Rates ranging from 20 to 40 percent have been reported for young children in different studies (Forehand, 1977), and according to G. R. Patterson and Forgatch (1987) a rate as high as 50 percent can be regarded as acceptable for 10- to 11-year-old boys. Moreover, in many instances parents do not appear to be greatly concerned by noncompliance: between one-quarter and one-third of the time mothers merely ignore it; alternately they just repeat their request (Lytton, 1979; C. D. Nelson & Stockdale, 1985). More forceful efforts, resulting in confrontation and conflict, are much less frequent. It seems that a certain level of noncompliance is tolerable to parents.

There are in fact a number of reasons why young children's failure to comply should not be merely seen in a negative light. Spitz (1957) once identified the acquisition of the ability to say "no" in the second year of life as "beyond doubt the most spectacular intellectual and semantic achievement during early childhood." From an immediate point of view a parent no doubt regards compliant behavior as desirable; from a longer term point of view, however, the child's ability to assert itself and go against the wishes of the parent is a desirable expression of growing autonomy. Noncompliance can thus serve positive functions in social development by providing an opportunity for children (1) to assert their independence within the context of the parent–child relationship, and (2) to develop social skills and strategies to express their autonomy in a socially acceptable way (Kuczynski, Kochanska, Radke-Yarrow, & Girnius-Brown, 1987). Thus during the first three years noncompliance may simply be manifested as negativism; however, in due course children must learn more indirect and tactful ways of expressing their opposition to other people's wishes. As Kuczynski and Kochanska (1990) found when tracing the course of children's non-compliance during the first five years, a considerable array of strategies of increasing sophistication is gradually assembled, reflecting children's growing skill in asserting themselves in the face of opposition and in persuading adults to comply with the child's wishes (see table 41). Whereas at first children's only possible response is to say "no," in time they become capable of bargaining and negotiating; noncompliance, that is, may well reflect social competence when expressed in these more advanced ways and can therefore be regarded as a positive achievement. It is worth adding that the same authors also found evidence that a high rate of compliance is sometimes associated with maladjustment; the notion that compliance is "good" and that non-compliance is "bad" is clearly a simplistic one.

Table 41 Children's noncompliance strategies

Strategy	Description
Passive noncompliance	Child ignores mother's directive
Simple refusal	Overt refusal to comply; expressed verbally (e.g. "No, I won't") or nonverbally (e.g. shakes head)
Direct defiance	Verbal or nonverbal opposition, accompanied by anger (e.g. throws pillow after told not to)
Excuses	Explanations for not complying (e.g. "I am too little" or "It doesn't need washing")
Bargains	Attempts to change or limit terms of directive (e.g. "Later" or "I will if I get a cookie")
Negotiation	Bargaining and excuses

Source: Adapted from Kuczynski & Kochanska (1990)

Both compliance and noncompliance increase with age in the first few years. Yet the most marked changes are not so much in the overall rate but in the way in which these response systems are organized. In a study by B. E. Vaughn, Kopp, and Krakow (1984) children between 18 and 30 months were observed in a number of situations in which they were expected to follow their mothers' directives. Among the youngest children compliance was found only sporadically; thereafter it was more clearly demonstrated and showed a marked increase. Most notably, however, at 30 months compliance was characterized by much greater coherence: children now showed consistency in their behavior across tasks; individual differences in keeping with other developmental achievements were clearly evident; and the children could thus be regarded as more predictable than at earlier ages. Similarly with noncompliance: this too increased in overall rate; the older children were thus both more compliant and more noncompliant than the younger. Again, however, it was organizational changes that were most prominent: with increasingly sophisticated cognitive and language skills children's noncompliance through simple avoidance decreased over age; noncompliance by means of arguing, on the other hand, increased as the children used their new abilities to vigorously filibuster in the face of their mothers' directives. As Kuczynski and Kochanska (1990) found for children up to the age of 5, what appears to change is not the motive to assert autonomy but the skill with which it is expressed.

The Role of Caregivers

How do parents get children to do things? In the past a "clash of wills" paradigm dominated our thinking: parents, by virtue of their superior power, were thought to assert themselves more or less forcefully in order to steer their children willy nilly in directions unilaterally determined by the adult. More recent research has shown that reality is rather more complex. Clashes of will do occur, of course, but parental control techniques take a far more varied, more subtle, and often less dictatorial form than previously suggested.

Control techniques refer to all those behaviors employed by one person to change the ongoing course of another's activity. Their function is to channel that activity in certain directions, inhibiting some tendencies but enhancing others. They are usually directed towards immediate, not long-term consequences, i.e. to obtain a child's compliance with the parent's wish at the time rather than to bring about the internalization of the values underlying the request made. Yet it is probable that long-term consequences are brought about by humdrum, everyday controls: there is certainly a considerable amount of evidence available to suggest that the particular form of parental controls influences not only immediate compliance but also subsequent internalization and self-control (Stafford & Bayer, 1993).

In general, parental controls have been found most effective in obtaining the child's compliance if the following conditions are met (Rocissano, Slade, & Lynch, 1987):

1   parents are willing to allow the child a degree of control in the interaction;
2   parents use the child's interests and ongoing actions as a guide to their requests and directives;
3   the interaction takes place against the background of a warm and supportive relationship.

Thus the more coercive the control techniques are on which a parent relies and the less an attempt is made to maintain a degree of reciprocity with the child, the greater is the likelihood that compliance will not be obtained and that internalization of values will not be facilitated (Putallaz & Heflin, 1990). Admittedly we cannot be certain that techniques effective in promoting immediate compliance are necessarily the same as those required for longer term effects; however, Kuczynski (1984) found that even in immediate situations 4–year-old children whose mothers used high-power techniques were less compliant than children with less assertive mothers. Moreover, the more often high-power techniques are used by parents the less frequently will children comply over time. Suggestions, according to Lytton and Zwirner (1975), are more effective than direct commands; negative controls (threats, criticism, physical intervention, and anger) were found by Crockenberg and Litman (1990) to be associated with defiance; and persuasive strategies (e.g. explanation and bargaining), when employed by parents with older children, are reported by Kuczynski et al. (1987) as more likely to bring about compliance than direct and forceful methods. As Crockenberg and Litman put it, techniques are effective if they not only give the child clear information as to what is wanted but also invite power sharing, for in this way implicit recognition is given that the child is a person separate from the parent with his or her own needs and wishes. Thus "Would you pick up the toys, please?" is indeed a question and not just an indirect command, as it gives the child a choice to adopt the mother's goal or not and so reinforces the sense of autonomy while at the same time eliciting compliance. Direct confrontation may produce neither result.

One of the most effective ways of gaining a child's compliance is to work within the child's own frame of reference. As Schaffer and Crook (1979, 1980) found, when mothers want the child to carry out some action on a particular object they tend carefully to time their interventions to ensure that the child's attention is already focused on that object. Controls, that is, do not descend in bolt-out-of-the-blue fashion; instead, mothers monitor the child's focus of interest and act when the time is right. If the child's attention is elsewhere the mother will either employ an attention attracting device (pointing, tapping, verbally labeling, etc.) in order to orient the child appropriately, or else she will wait until the child spontaneously attends to the object. Only then will she request action. Under such circumstances compliance is far more likely than when a mother takes no notice of the child's present activity and tries to impose her own interests. Topic sharing is thus a necessary condition for obtaining compliance; to bring this about requires sensitivity on the part of the parent to the child's state. Again, recognition of the child as a separate person is thereby implicated.

Sensitivity is also shown in the way in which parents adjust their controls to the child's developmental status. With very young children nonverbal forms of conveying requests are prominent; as children get older there is increasing reliance on verbal means (Schaffer, Hepburn, & Collis, 1983). This reflects parents' adaptation to their children's increasing capacity to understand language; physical supports are thus phased out as verbal communications become effective by themselves (Kuczynski et al., 1987). At first sight the observation, made by Hepburn and Schaffer (1983; see also Schaffer, 1984) that mothers already issue verbal directives to infants just 5 months old, i.e. long before they become capable of compliance, seems to contradict the notion of parental sensitivity. However, closer inspection reveals that few of these controls are genuine but are either a comment on something the child is already doing (e.g. "Pick it up," said after the child started picking up a toy), or a comment on something the mother herself is doing (e.g. "Sit up," said while putting the child in a sitting position), or a "joke control," i.e. one asking for an action quite inappropriate to the 5-month-old infant's competence level and known by the mother to be so (e.g. "Get into your bath"). It is perhaps surprising that adults indulge in such apparently unrealistic requests; however, this appears to reflect a general tendency on the part of parents to involve their young children in interactive formats long before the child can properly participate in them. There are advantages for both partners in such seeming lack of realism: for the child it provides plenty of experience of that format, providing the chance to learn about the demand characteristics of other people's requests before becoming capable of responding independently; and for the parent it makes it easier to judge when the child has reached that point and when responsibility for compliance can be handed over. Thus even such pseudo-controls have a purpose.

The content of parental requests, i.e. what it is they want children to do, is perhaps the most obvious area where one would expect developmental change to take place. Yet, despite the light this aspect can throw on the nature of the goals and values parents set out to transmit, surprisingly little attention has been paid to this topic. An exception is a longitudinal study by Gralinski and Kopp (1993) of a group of children followed up during the preschool period, whose mothers were asked to report on the rules for everyday standards of behavior that they attempted to enforce at different ages. As the findings show, there is a progression along the lines of LeVine's (1974) proposal that socialization is initially concerned with anything to do with the child's safety and survival and that only later do parents move on to transmitting family and cultural standards. Thus in the second year, when a child had just become mobile, mothers' control talk was full of prohibitions about touching things that are dangerous, climbing on to furniture, or running out into the street. With age these decreased, and instead mothers' concern was expressed more in rules relating to interpersonal matters ("Share toys," "Be nice to your sister," "Don't hurt the cat"). Eventually mothers shifted to rather more elaborate rules associated with social norms ("Wait until I finish talking," "Say please") and with self-care ("Wash your face," "Don't take off your shoes"). All types of rules convey to the child what is acceptable or not; the sheer amount of pressure enforcing these may not change drastically over age, but what does change is the content of the mothers' rules and this, as Gralinski and Kopp note, was found by them impressively to dovetail with the children's developmental advances. Such changes in the nature of rules and control issues are found throughout childhood. Thus in adolescence (G. W. Peterson, Rollins, & Thomas, 1985) compliance during the early teenage years tends to be sought mostly in such routine matters as household duties and dressing habits; in later adolescence parents' concerns switch more to topics such as dating or alcohol use. But at whatever age and with respect to whatever issue of control, compliance is most easily obtained when it takes place in the context of a well functioning, reciprocal relationship.

The case of communicating controls to deaf children

When a child suffers from a communication disorder such as deafness the customary strategies of control may no longer be effective. Under normal circumstances the switch from nonverbal to verbal means of control during the first few years generally happens almost automatically as parents adjust to the child's rapidly increasing capacity for language comprehension. But what if the child's deafness blocks the usual communication channel? How are parents to convey their requests under such circumstances and what effect will different modes of communication have on the parent–child relationship generally?

In cases of communication problems the overall quality of the parent–child relationship tends, in some respects, to be distinctive. Thus Schlesinger and Meadow (1972) observed the interaction patterns of mothers and their deaf children, aged 3 to 7, and concluded that the mothers tended to be rather more "inflexible, controlling, didactic, intrusive, and disapproving" when compared with the mothers of hearing children. The presence of such an apparently negative style was confirmed by Brinich (1980) in a rather more detailed examination: again the mothers of deaf children were found to show an emphasis on didactic controls, resorting to instructions and commands rather than to more subtle means such as suggestions. Not surprisingly, these mothers had to resort to much more attention-attracting behavior than mothers with hearing children; thus, in order to ensure that the child was watching her face the mother first had to orient the child towards her. More surprisingly, these mothers talked just as much as mothers of hearing children; though their speech was stylistically distinctive its amount was by no means diminished.

These findings were taken still further in a study by Henggeler, Watson, and Cooper (1984), again involving both deaf and hearing children between 3 and 7 years of age. The deaf children's mothers were found to use considerably more nonverbal means of control – they pointed, pantomimed, physically guided, and facially signaled more in order to have their children comply. Yet at the same time they also used more verbal means of control than found among the hearing children's mothers; however, this occurred only during free play and not during a teaching session. This is unexpected: mothers are normally more relaxed in the former than in the latter situation, yet the deaf children's mothers appeared to be *less* concerned about obtaining compliance during the teaching session – possibly because they were trying to shield the child from experiencing failure.

As Brinich points out, a more directive style has also been found in mothers of mentally handicapped children, and it may well be that in any situation where reciprocal communication breaks down the adult adapts by taking over control of the interaction. This means, however, that she becomes more coercive in her way of relating to the child – a style that, as we have seen, is not conducive to eliciting compliance. A vicious circle may well be set up then, in which the mother, desperate to get the child to comply, becomes increasingly coercive and is thus led to adopt the very style that is unlikely to achieve this end. Thus parents of deaf children are confronted by a dilemma in communicating with them that reaches further than the child's hearing problems and encompasses the relationship as a whole. A much greater use of directiveness and controls, as well as a less harmonious relationship in general, have been consistently demonstrated when hearing parents are paired with deaf children (Koester, 1994). Just why this is so, however, remains a matter of contention, and explanations put forward have ranged from the parents' negative emotional reaction to their child's deafness to heightened efforts to maintain the child's attention and overcome any delays in language development.

Learning Social Rules

Children do not just *act* in accordance with adults' wishes; they also try to *make sense* of the requirements they are supposed to meet. Efforts to make sense appear surprisingly early: they become evident as soon as the second year, and from then on children increasingly form hypotheses as to what is demanded from them and why, as they figure out just what it is that these messages signify about the social world in which they live.

It is in the context of the family that children first learn about the rules that regulate interpersonal behavior. Each family has its routines and conventions; the family may be a microcosm of society, but it is through a few intimate interpersonal relationships that children's initial acquaintance with the dos and don'ts of that society takes place. A child aged 3, asked if hitting other children is good or bad, will know the socially correct answer; at that age children may not yet be able to explain or justify their response but they do know that certain standards of behavior are expected of them and that sanctions will be imposed if they do not conform. The groundwork for the development of morality is thus laid.

The Emergence of Standards

Some time during the second year children become aware that they, other people, and also physical objects are meant to meet particular normative standards. As Kagan (1981) first noted in the course of some casual observations, children during the latter half of the second year often show a considerable preoccupation with flawed, broken, or dirty objects: a crack in the plastic base of a toy telephone, a small tear in some clothing or a piece of dirt on a chair. In order to test these findings more systematically Kagan observed children around $1\frac{1}{2}$ years of age in a laboratory playroom with a set of toys, some of which were purposely flawed: an animal with a head missing, a broken pencil, a boat with holes in the bottom, and a doll with streaks on the face. Before $1\frac{1}{2}$ years no child showed any sign of concern about these flaws; subsequently children not only paid undue attention to the affected toys but also made explicit comments such as "Yuk," "Fix it," and "Broke." The children were, it seems, not only aware of but sometimes upset by the failure of the toys to meet particular standards of perfection. The same attitude was also found to emerge around that age with respect to personal standards. When children were shown various actions performed by an adult that were just beyond their own competence to carry out (making a doll ride a horse, wash a doll's face, etc.) those older than 18 months frequently showed distress at their inability to repeat the action and so meet the standard set by the adult.

Thus some time during the second year children begin to show awareness of standard, of the violation of standards, and of their own failure to meet adults' expectations. Not that all violations are a source of comment and upset; prior experience of parental disapproval, especially when expressed with considerable emotional force, will direct the child's attention to that event and make failure to meet the required standard a personally meaningful experience. Yet children do not just mechanically reflect the adult's expectations; even at that age there are already signs that a child can generate its own standards. Kagan quotes the example of a 2-year-old girl who became upset because she had a small doll and a large toy bed and could not find a small toy bed that she regarded as more appropriate for the doll. The girl, that is, was evaluating her action in terms of what is "right"; inability to meet the requirement was judged by her as failure and caused distress. However, whether standards are imposed by others or by oneself, behavior comes increasingly to be dominated by success or failure to meet whatever requirements have been set. Thus from age 2 there is a sharp increase in children's interest in what is permitted and what is prohibited; certain actions or events can now be classified as improper; and evaluative language such as "good" and "bad" appears more and more frequently in the comments that children spontaneously make about their experiences.

The growth of language skills during the second year means that children can start to verbalize their concerns about standards and discuss them with adults. Dunn (1988), observing children in their homes, confirmed Kagan's finding that during the second year increasing interest is shown in objects that are broken, dirty, or out of place; she also noted that such objects then often form the start of a conversation with the mother (figure 19). For that matter mothers, apparently aware of their children's growing interest, were also found to draw the child's attention to such things and did so with increasing frequency in the course of the second year. Thus anything flawed or torn frequently became a topic for discussion, giving the adult the opportunity to explain to the child the reasons for that condition and what, if anything, could be done to rectify it. Take the following example quoted by Dunn involving an 18-month-old child who has brought a toy frog to the mother and is pointing to a tear in it:

Mother: I think he's sprung a leak, hasn't he, John?
Child: (*points again to tear*)
Mother: Oh yes, I see. (*tries to mend frog*)
Child: No.
Mother: Well, I'm trying to mend it.
Child: Look. (*points again to frog*)
Mother: Yes, it's mended.
Child: No. (*shakes head*)
Mother: It jolly well is mended.
Child: (*shakes head, points to further hole*) Look.

As we have noted before, parent–child conversations make a most useful vehicle for children to express their concerns, share them with an adult and be guided to socially appropriate ways of dealing with the situation. Thus in the course of discussion children are able not only to display their newly found ideas of perfection but also to

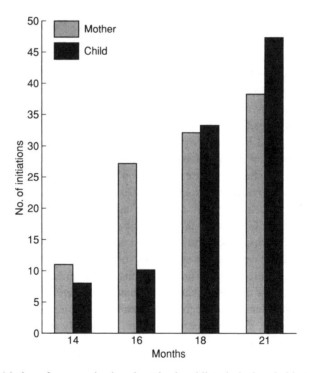

Figure 19   Initiation of communication about broken/dirty/misplaced objects, by child and mother (from Dunn, 1988)

test them out against the standards of other people and learn what to do about any violations and shortcomings. The acquisition of the idea of standards is, in the first place, a cognitive achievement: it involves the child being able to make a mental comparison of "how it is" with "how it ought to be," and it is this ability which first appears some time in the middle of the second year. Once the ability is in place children may generate their own standards; for the most part, however, adults supply them, and it is no coincidence that from the middle of the second year on parents markedly increase the expectations conveyed to their children with regard to standards of personal conduct.

Family Routines as Learning Opportunities

As part of their everyday living children are surrounded by messages about what is allowed and expected and what is not. Parents already begin to send such messages in infancy, though usually in a half-joking manner ("I wish you wouldn't do that, you disgusting baby"). These messages show a sharp increase in the second and third years when children become mobile and more competent, but they continue right through into adolescence when once again rules of social behavior account for much of parental discourse. The topics of the messages will, of course, vary from age to age. As Dunn (1988) has shown, in the preschool years they include such things as whether it is acceptable to put toys down the toilet, pull the cat around by its tail, destroy a brother's castle of blocks, or jump up and down on the sofa wearing muddy boots. With an adolescent the discussion is more likely to concern the use of alcohol or drugs, contact with the opposite sex, and the keeping of hours. Issues become salient as the child passes from one developmental stage to another and wants to try out different patterns of behavior. In all cases, however, the purpose is to convey to the child some social rule which will regulate that child's conduct; as a result the child will acquire knowledge concerning such principles as possession, sharing and turn-taking, age and sex roles, personal hygiene, and politeness.

Rules are learned in the first place in the context of family routines. The conventions surrounding meals, outings, television viewing, and bedtimes provide plenty of opportunity for finding out what is regarded as acceptable behavior, for rules are initially not abstract principles (e.g. "you must be clean") but are tied to particular, recurrent family customs (e.g. "you must wash your hands before dinner"). But such learning is neither bloodless nor mindless: for one thing, it often occurs in situations that are emotionally highly charged and where conflict around a rule is a particularly marked feature; and for another children do not merely obey or imitate automatically but from the second year on discuss, question, and reflect upon the rules which they are expected to follow. These two aspects deserve more detailed consideration.

Family life, by its very nature, is an emotional affair; when a child's learning is embedded in family relationships it will inevitably occur in the midst of much joy and excitement but also amongst strife and dispute. An important function of such emotion is to heighten children's awareness of their experience: whether the emotion is positive or negative the child is more likely to recall what occurred in an affectively charged situation than an emotionally neutral one. Thus Zahn-Waxler, Radke-Yarrow, and King (1979) found that what mattered about mothers' explanations about the importance of not hurting others was not so much the content of their explanation but rather the emotional intensity with which they expressed themselves: it was that which predicted the children's subsequent prosocial behavior. Particular experiences, that is, are tagged with affective labels, and these labels are thought by some to play a decisive role in the way in which behavior is affected by past learning (Maccoby & Martin, 1983).

The importance of an emotional component in bringing about learning is probably one reason why disputes with others are of such significance in shaping children's social understanding. Because of all the attention paid to the adverse effects of persistent marital conflict on children's well-being it is easy to overlook the positive contribution which family arguments can make when they take place against a background of sound relationships, and yet the experience of arguing about some particular issue does have beneficial effects – especially when the child is directly involved and when the dispute is resolved. As A. R. Eisenberg (1992) found when observing 4-year-olds and their mothers, disputes are a frequent feature of the interaction of such couples, yet mostly they are not disruptive of the relationship nor are they normally accompanied by any intense anger – indeed they often end with one or the other party (more often the mother) dropping the issue for the sake of peace. Disputes help children to assert their independence: they can pursue conflict without risking the mother's anger. At the same time they often force mothers to state rules in a very explicit form, such as in this example quoted by Eisenberg:

> *Child:*   (*offers biscuit dough*) Taste it.
> *Mother:* No, I don't want to right now, sweetie. (*Three further exchanges, with child demanding and whining*)
> *Child:*   (*whines*) Please.
> *Mother:* (*angry*) Ethan! You need to learn that when somebody tells you no, that's what they mean.

For that matter, children are also forced to learn that they are expected to advance rules for their own behavior, as illustrated by the following exchange:

> *Mother:* You're gonna go to school next year.
> *Child:*   No.
> *Mother:* How come?
> *Child:*   I don't wanna go.
> *Mother:* Why?
> *Child:*   Because I don't wanted to.
> *Mother:* There has to be a reason.

The mother, by conveying to the child that simply not wanting to go to school is not sufficient and that more precise reasons need to be forthcoming, is indoctrinating the child in the social convention that school attendance is obligatory and that only the most persuasive of reasons can break this rule.

There are other lessons that can also be learned from participating in family disputes, in particular how to conduct such disputes. Thus children need to learn the rules for negotiation: they need, for example, to find out that opposition cannot usually be stated by merely saying "no" but that they must develop the art of reasoned argument. In addition they have to develop skills for assuming (or for avoiding) responsibility for the transgression of rules; they must know how to produce justifications for their actions; and they must learn how to summon help from an adult in a dispute with another child that they are in danger of losing. Such skills appear surprisingly early: getting the mother's help in a conflict with a sibling is already evident at age 2 (Dunn, 1988), and by age 3 children can produce quite sophisticated justifications for their behavior in disputes – justifications which refer not only to their own needs and requirements but also to the consequences of their actions and even quite explicitly to the existence of social rules (Dunn & Munn, 1987).

The fact that children quite early on become aware of and show great fascination with social rules illustrates the second point we must stress: rule acquisition is not a mindless activity but involves the child in actively interpreting the meaning adults are attempting to convey. The very fact that children ask "why" when told what to do means that they are no longer content to accept directives at their surface but are searching for the underlying regularities which tie each directive to some kind of social meaning. Take the following conversation of a 4-year-old with her mother (again taken from A. R. Eisenberg, 1992):

Child: Can we go to that park?
Mother: Well, you didn't wear your shoes. You wore your ballet slippers.
Child: Well, that's okay.
Mother: No, because your ballet slippers aren't made to play outdoors in. They'll get torn up.
Child: But can I wear my shoes?
Mother: Well, we won't do that this weekend because it's beginning to get dark and in some places even parks are kind of dangerous after it gets dark.
Child: Why?
Mother: Well, because sometimes bad people come out at night and do things . . . .

What is significant about this conversation is not just that the child has the opportunity to learn a great deal about the way the world works but also that it is the child that is actively inquiring, arguing, and pushing the mother to elaborate on reasons for particular courses of action. By age 4 at any rate the child appears to have learned that conduct is regulated by social rules and in consequence is now busily searching for and constructing sets of such rules.

Yet even before then children already show concern about rule-regulated behavior. Dunn (1988) plotted the number of references made by children between 18 and 36 months to reasons and justifications for their actions during disputes, and found these to increase steadily over this period (figure 20). At the same time mothers also increased their explicit references to social rules, presumably in parallel to their expectations as to the children's ability to understand. Conversations about what is permitted and what forbidden thus form an early feature of mothers' and children's interactions; by their means children can explore the nature of rules, test their limits and investigate the likely sanctions for transgression without actually having to engage in the relevant behavior. And for their part mothers can clearly articulate what the rules are which they expect their children to observe – all in a playful, conversational context quite unthreatening to the child. It also appears that the greater the number of references to social rules which a mother habitually employs the more likely it will be that her child will show relatively mature behavior in interpersonal situations (Dunn & Munn, 1986).

Thus children come to realize that there are shared conceptions as to what is good and what is naughty, and they often act these out in pretend play. At first their

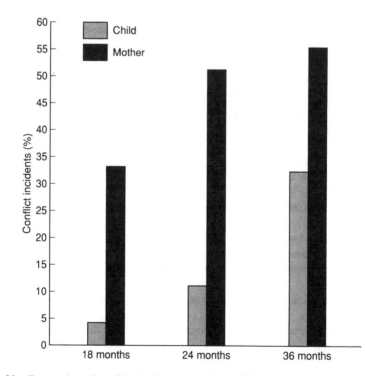

Figure 20   Proportion of conflict incidents in which child and mother reason/justify their actions (from Dunn, 1988)

understanding is only partial and intuitive rather than complete and explicit; from the third year, however, they become increasingly able to verbalize rules and to insist on their application (at least when in the child's own interest!). Phrases such as "my turn" and "that's not yours" show that the child has acquired an understanding, at a practical level at any rate, that social behavior is ordered in certain ways, that these ways need to be observed by all members of the group and that failure to observe will bring about certain predictable but usually unpleasant consequences. They may question the rules, joke about them, or quite deliberately break them, but the basic idea of a rule is now firmly embedded in their mind.

Children's opportunity to acquire such social learning is intimately dependent on the kind of environment in which they spend their everyday life. The fact that the family can provide a particularly suitable learning context is well illustrated in a study by B. Tizard and Hughes (1984), in which a group of 4-year-old London children were observed both at home with their mothers and at nursery school with members of staff. In certain respects at least the home turned out to be a far more effective environment for the acquisition of knowledge about the way the world works than the nursery school. Simply by being around the mother, by participating in everyday activities such as shopping and housework and visiting, but most of all by talking and arguing and endlessly asking questions, the children were constantly being provided with information relevant to growing up in our culture. Take one typical exchange:

Mother: What do you want a drink of?
Child: Rosehip. [*i.e. rosehip syrup*]
Mother: Oh, you've just had a drink [of that].
Child: Rosehip. (*firmly*)
Mother: Right, one more drink of rosehip, and then we've got to keep the rest for Tessa, all right? (*Tessa is the baby sister*)
Child: Why?
Mother: Because Tessa can't drink orange squash, and things like you can.
Child: Why can't she?
Mother: Because it's all too sweet for her. Not good for babies, that sort of thing. It's not good for anybody really, but we still drink it. When we go to [*the supermarket*] we'll get you a drink of your own.
Child: Why? . . .
Mother: Because the rosehip costs a lot of money.
Child: Is Tessa going to drink it all?
Mother: Tessa only drinks a little weeny bit, so it lasts quite a long time, but if you drink it you drink about a whole bottle a day.

A conversation such as this shows the mother to be a highly dedicated teacher, who, by explaining an ordinary, everyday activity can convey to the child information about babies' feeding habits, the cost of drinks, the need to go to the supermarket if more drink is needed, and so forth. It also shows the child to be a highly curious learner, and "why" questions, at this age at least, thus form a constant feature of parent–child conversations.

The nursery schools in which Tizard and Hughes observed these same children were in many respects a different world, and despite their stated educational aims did not stimulate the same curiosity. Thus the children asked far fewer "why" questions; their answers to questions put to them by adults tended to be brief; and conversations generally appeared emotionally flat in comparison with those at home. Nursery schools, of course, have different aims and foster these through play and group interaction, yet when it comes to conveying information about the social world the home turns out to be an extraordinarily effective learning context. Five factors are singled out by Tizard and Hughes to account for this:

1   The home is the center of a very extensive range of activities, concerned with both domestic tasks and events in the outside world. The range of experiences to be discussed is thus far wider than found in nursery school.
2   At home adult and child share a common past; a present event can thus be linked to previous experience and so made more meaningful. In nurseries conversations tend to be almost entirely about the here-and-now.
3   In the majority of families there are few children and there is therefore little competition for the mother's attention. Thus far more one-to-one interactions take place there than in nurseries, where the adult has to divide her time among a much larger group.
4   At home learning is often embedded in contexts of great meaning to the child, in that activities involve things of intense interest to the individual which it would be difficult to duplicate in the group activities of the nursery school.
5   Finally, at home the teacher–learner relationship is a highly emotional one – unlike the rather impersonal relationships found in nurseries. This may at times hinder learning, but for the most part it allows the child to keep near the mother and ensures a much freer expression of questions and concerns.

For preschool children the learning potential of the home is thus very considerable. By no means all families are able to provide this potential: where the mother is depressed, or where the family is cut off from the rest of the community, or where there are many siblings closely spaced such learning cannot easily take place. Under more ideal conditions, however, the home has the advantage not only of providing lots of interesting and meaningful information but also of stirring the child's curiosity through showing willingness to satisfy that curiosity.

Siblings' Contribution

With increasing age children's conceptions of rules become more differentiated as they learn that what is acceptable may vary from one situation to another and from one individual to another. Family life offers a particularly good chance of finding out that rules may be applied differently in different relationships, especially as interactions with siblings are in certain respects conducted along very different lines from those prevailing with parents.

The extent to which siblings influence each other must not be underestimated. They spend a lot of their time together; they share many of their experiences; they observe each other participating in other relationships; and their relationship with each other is often an intensely emotional one. Even the fact that they are mismatched for age provides the ideal context for learning. In a series of follow-up observations over a three-year period Abramovitch and her colleagues (Abramovitch, Corter, & Lando, 1979, 1986; Pepler, Abramovitch, & Corter, 1981) found a great deal of interaction among the sibling pairs they observed and were struck by how rich and varied that interaction generally was. Rivalry certainly existed, yet positive forms of interaction tended to predominate in most pairs. Thus prosocial acts (helping, sharing, cooperating) were found in both older and younger siblings; there was much imitation, mostly on the part of the younger member; and each pair had worked out a reciprocal relationship in which the older child was usually the initiator and the younger one the follower and submitter. Changes in frequency and complexity of behavior occurred in all individual children as they grew older; the balance within each pair, however, generally remained the same.

Observations such as these show that siblings are important individuals in each other's lives. What is more, their relationship is unique and differs in many respects from that found between parent and child. This is well illustrated by analyses of children's conversations (J. R. Brown & Dunn, 1992). When the mother is the partner the talk is mainly about caretaking activities; when a sibling is partner talk is often about playful and humorous situations where children share jokes or tease each other in a way rarely found in mother–child conversations. In the preschool period references to feelings during talk with the mother tend to show a marked decrease; in talk with the sibling, on the other hand, they increase. What is more, while mothers talk mainly about the child's feelings siblings almost always talk about their own. Each conversational partner, that is, fulfills a different function: in one case supporting the child's attempts to understand and come to terms with his or her own feelings; in the other drawing the child's attention to another individual's inner life. Similarly with fantasy play (Dunn, 1993): whereas mothers only infrequently join children in such play and then usually as didactic spectators, siblings often act as full partners in a shared pretend world that can become increasingly rich and fantastic and provide endless amusement to both participants.

It is apparent that the interaction of siblings has a special significance for cognitive and social development that is different from that of the parent–child interaction. Children get to know about social rules concerning such matters as possession, fairness, sharing, and turn-taking during play with siblings; making up their own rules as they go along gives the enterprise extra jest. Take the following example (from Dunn, 1988):

Three-year-old playing bouncing ball with older sibling:
Sibling: Can I have a go? Can I do that? May I?
Child: When I have had two goes.
Sibling: Yes, it's your turn so . . . so you have two goes. And I am four so I have four
       goes. Yes! I have four goes. (*A few minutes later Child tries to get ball back*)
Sibling: No! I have four goes. Four.
       (*Child gets ball back, sibling again requests turn*)
Sibling: Can I have a go?
Child: No. When I have had eight goes. 'Cos I'm. . . .

The very fact that siblings tend to be close in age gives an extra edge to their rule construction: issues of fairness and justice are so much more important in a relationship tinged with rivalry than one, such as that between parent and child, where one partner is so obviously more powerful than the other. The sheer fun derived from joint play, as well as the need to work out shared goals, provide the motivation to cooperate according to some mutually agreed rule system, and where such a system is not already in existence children will happily construct it to suit their particular purpose. And for that matter it is joint fun too that lies behind siblings' conversations about "naughty" words or their trying out of "rude" actions: transgression in the company of another, equally delighted child provides a safe way of finding out what forbidden fruit tastes like.

Just what siblings learn from each other depends on the age and sex composition of each dyad, and perhaps even more on the fit of the two individual children's temperament (Munn & Dunn, 1989). The range of differences among sibling relationships is substantial: the frequency of conflict incidents between siblings in a sample studied by Dunn (1993) ranged from 0 to 56 episodes per hour; in the same group a measure of the connectedness of their verbal communications ranged from 18 percent of conversational turns to 100 percent. There are therefore limits to the generalizations one can make about sibling relationships; indeed the individuality of each relationship may well have profound long-term implications for personality development. In any case, peer relationships are far from static: as the children grow older and their competencies and outside interests change the nature of their relationship also changes. During middle childhood, according to findings by Buhrmester and Furman (1990), siblings become more egalitarian in status, and while there is little change in the degree of affection that pairs have for each other between 8 and 17 years a decline in companionship is commonly found during this period. Such a decline probably reflects the increasing involvement with peers outside the home and suggests a lessening of mutual influence.

What does distinguish sibling relationships in general is that they are characterized by a mixture of *complementary* and *reciprocal* features (Dunn, 1993). Complementary features are most evident in the parent–child relationship, where the older individual plays a role that is different from but interrelated with that of the younger one. Reciprocal features are found in peer interaction: both individuals play similar, matching parts. Among siblings there is a difference in knowledge and power, yet that difference is not so great that the two children cannot sometimes play and talk together on the same level. It is this combination of features that makes sibling relationships potentially so influential: on the one hand the older child can act as teacher, guide, and model to the younger; on the other hand, however, both children share interest and competence to a sufficient degree to tackle jointly the task of social understanding.

The case of handicapped siblings

Whereas siblings normally have little difficulty in evolving a finely balanced relationship on the basis of relative age and competence, that balance is considerably more difficult to achieve when one of the children is mentally and/or physically handicapped. While much depends on the nature and severity of the handicap as well as on the children's ages, the relationship is frequently a much more difficult one to establish and likely to show a rather different mixture of complementary and reciprocal features than found in comparable but nonhandicapped pairs.

Two studies illustrate this pattern: one by Abramovitch, Stanhope, Pepler, and Corter, (1987) on Down's syndrome children and the other by Dallas, Stevenson, and McGurk (1993) on children with cerebral palsy. In both the behavior of the handicapped child towards the sibling was found to be comparable in certain respects to that of the second-born child in a normal family, regardless of whether the handicapped sibling was in fact the older or the younger of the pair. The normal child, that is, always had to take the role of the first-born – initiating interactions, setting an example, and being generally directive and facilitative towards the other child. Normal children were often considerably more positive and nurturant than those

in other sibling pairs: in both studies more prosocial behavior was found in such children than among nonhandicapped pairs – possibly because of parental example, or because the handicapped child was less of a rival, or because the passivity characterizing many handicapped children evoked such behavior. That passivity was seen in all aspects of social responsiveness in both Down's syndrome and cerebral palsied children: there was less prosocial behavior, less aggression and a generally reduced responsiveness, seen for example in the difficulty these children had in sustaining social interaction and their consequent tendency to withdraw.

All this made the task of the nonhandicapped sibling very much more difficult, and especially so when the child was the younger of the pair. Under such circumstances a reversal of roles was called for, but in all pairs the nonhandicapped child tended to adopt a far more directive manner in order to compensate for the handicapped sibling's disability. Thus the mode of interaction was a clearly hierarchical one in virtually all cases; whatever their relative ages the relationship in these sibling pairs was based on complementary rather than reciprocal features and as a result often lacked the diversity and excitement found in other dyads.

Convention and Morality

The rules which regulate social behavior take various forms, but one fundamental distinction which, according to Turiel (1983), is already made by quite young children is that between rules pertaining respectively to social convention and to morality. Take the following two statements:

"If he wants to be a member of our group he must wear a yellow jacket."

"He should not hit younger children."

The former expresses an arbitrary norm. It is dependent on the particular group which has adopted it and can easily be changed by its members. Thus conventional rules are a matter of choice; they are specific to certain settings such as families, schools, or peer groups and they serve to maintain a particular social system in predictable ways. Rules relating to morality, on the other hand, are universal; they are valid whether there is a social consensus or not, for they refer to ethical standards common to humanity and are thus obligatory. Transgression of a social convention may offend other members of the group; transgression of a moral prescription, however, is a violation of principles that guarantee the rights and welfare of others.

According to Turiel, children learn to make the distinction between these two categories from a quite early age because of the different types of social interaction that they involve. Conventions are dogmatically taught, being handed down by authority. Initially they may be regarded as universal; it does not take long, however, before children realize that the done thing in one's own family is not necessarily the done thing in any other family. Moral principles, on the other hand, are acquired because children perceive that certain actions have consequences for other people that are intrinsically harmful: witnessing a younger child being hit is sufficient to show that such an act, in whatever social context, is undesirable. Thus children begin to construct two quite different domains of knowledge about the social world and its functioning.

A considerable number of studies have produced empirical support for Turiel's proposition. For instance, Nucci and Nucci (1982) observed children aged 6 to 13 years at school in situations where moral or social convention rules were transgressed by other children, and found that the way in which they reacted to the two kinds of transgression differed. For one thing, they were much more likely to respond to moral transgression than to the violation of, say, a school rule. For another, the type of response differed: retaliation in the case of moral violation was common but seen as inappropriate to transgression of conventions. Also their statements about the two differed: when a moral rule was violated they commented on the injury or loss experienced by the victim, pointed out the unjust nature of the act or requested the transgressor to consider how it would feel to be the victim. When a conventional rule was violated they were more likely to ask transgressors to refrain, remind them of the rule or to ridicule them. When interviewed the children's comments confirmed that they saw the two kinds of events as quite different: moral transgressions were judged wrong whether the school had a rule or not; transgression of conventions, however, were known to be rule dependent.

In general, both the behavior and the thinking of children with respect to the two classes of transgression differ sharply. Asked, for example, how wrong it would be to commit certain acts – stealing, hitting, eating with fingers, addressing a teacher by first name, and so on – children in the Nucci and Nucci study quite consistently viewed moral transgressions as more serious, giving as their reason the harm inflicted on others. Violations of conventions were usually seen as just impolite or disruptive. When asked if it would be all right to steal in a country that had no rules about stealing, school-aged children almost invariably condemned such an act. Asked if it would be acceptable to play a game by different rules if all participants agreed to the change, virtually all children responded that the rules could then be changed. Thus moral rules are regarded as more binding and their transgression as more serious than is the case with social rules. The distinction becomes evident from about the age of 3 (Smetana & Braeges, 1990); at that age it is usually made on the basis of how general the rules are, that is, whether they are universal or context specific. Thus preschoolers know that stealing is wrong in all situations, and they also quickly learn that moral behavior is not dependent on any particular set of rules and any particular authority figure.

Not all would agree that the distinction between the two kinds of transgression is as absolute as Turiel and his associates have suggested (e.g. Rest, 1983). What this work does show is that children clearly do not learn about social rules in a mindless way but that, quite on the contrary, they try from an early age to understand them and attempt to see their underlying sense, and that in consequence they make distinctions between them based on the way in which they are experienced in the course of social interaction.

Prosocial and Antisocial Behavior

For a long time an essentially negative view of children prevailed in psychological theory. This was largely due, first to Freudian, and later to Piagetian writing: the child emerged from these accounts as a selfish, self-centered, aggressive, and uncooperative being, with little interest in other people in their own right and little understanding of anyone else's needs and requirements. Early accounts of young children tended accordingly to dwell on the negative side: when Lois Murphy (1937) published her observations of peer interaction among preschool children she maintained that aggressive and selfish behavior outnumbered positive actions such as sharing and helping by a ratio of eight to one. That young children often are aggressive and selfish in an unbridled manner not usually found among older individuals, and that positive social actions tend to be less frequent and more fleeting than later on, cannot be doubted. However, to maintain that children are by nature incapable of cooperating with or caring about others until the age of 6 (as Piaget asserted) flies against empirical evidence.

Such evidence has accumulated in plenty over the last few decades, and the term "prosocial" has been coined in order to group together all aspects of helping, caring, sharing, cooperation, and sympathy (Hay, 1994). Signs of these are evident from at least the second year on; the fact that they emerge so early in life represents a very remarkable achievement. Thus it is no longer a matter of asking whether children are basically prosocial or antisocial but rather of determining the conditions under which one or the other kind of behavior can be found – whatever the child's age.

Empathy and Altruism

To act in a manner that benefits another person with no obvious self-gain, i.e. to behave altruistically, involves the vicarious sharing of emotion with that person in order to understand his or her need. The term *empathy* is used to designate such sharing; it has been defined by M. L. Hoffman (1987) as an affective response more appropriate to someone else's situation than one's own. Thus a child who feels sad when another is sad or happy when another is happy is showing empathy; being on the same emotional wavelength means that the child can take whatever action is appropriate in rendering help and understanding. Empathy and altruism are thus closely associated, even though it is possible for one to occur without the other.

A developmental analysis of empathy has been offered by M. L. Hoffman (e.g. 1987) and is outlined in table 42. It involves four broad steps, each of which reflects the cognitive capacities the child has attained at that time. Thus initially, when infants cannot even differentiate other from self, they are incapable of "true" empathy with another person; an infant may begin to cry when hearing another child cry but this is through contagion or some other primitive mechanism and is merely an involuntary, global reaction. Subsequently, as the sense of self and of other becomes increasingly differentiated, children's empathic feelings become more and more sophisticated: they can mirror more closely the precise emotions of the other person; they can distinguish among a wider and more subtle range of feelings; they can, thanks to developing language abilities, represent to themselves more easily the other's specific requirements; and from late childhood or adolescence on, when they conceive of others as continuing individuals with separate histories and identities, they can experience the appropriate feelings of empathy by being able to imagine another's state even when no immediate cues of distress are available.

Much support for Hoffman's developmental scheme is available from empirical studies, though most of these have examined the early stages of empathy. The second year in particular has been singled out as the time when the first recognizable signs of empathy are found and also when children begin to act with clearly altruistic purposes in mind. Observations by Rheingold (1982; Rheingold, Hay, & West, 1976) provide a vivid illustration of the fact that anyone prepared to look for prosocial behavior can find plenty of examples even at that early stage. Thus Rheingold noted that children as young as 18 months were willing to share their toys with others and did so by spontaneously giving or showing them to mothers, fathers, and even to

Table 42 Stages in the development of empathy

Stage		Age at start	Characteristics
1	Global empathy	In first year	Others are not yet perceived as distinct from the self, therefore another's distress is confounded with own unpleasant feelings. Infants thus act as though what happened to another infant is happening to themselves
2	"Egocentric" empathy	In second year	The child is now aware that another person and not the self is in distress, but the other's internal states are still assumed to be the same as the child's own
3	Empathy for another's feelings	About 2 or 3	The child becomes aware that others have distinct feelings and responds to these in non-egocentric ways
4	Empathy for another's life condition	Late childhood	Children perceive others' feelings not just as momentary reactions but as expressions of their general life experience. The emphatically aroused affect is thus combined with a mental representation of the other's general condition, and the child responds differently to transitory and chronic states of distress

Source: Adapted from M. L. Hoffman (1987)

unfamiliar people. The fact that they did so without prompting, direction, or praise seems to indicate, Rheingold believed, that this is a "natural" behavior and contradicts the notion of egocentrism as the prime motive at that age. Similarly spontaneous helping can be observed in such young children: when Rheingold asked adults to carry out a variety of common household tasks (setting a table, making up a bed, dusting and sweeping, and so forth) she found many of the children to join in promptly and enthusiastically and, as their verbalizations showed, with the clear motive of helping rather than merely playing. Thus they would use the word "help"; or they would comment "fold clothes"; or they might assert "I can do it," and in this way indicate that they were aware of themselves as actors who were working with others to a common end. As Rheingold suggested, young children enjoy being with other people, take an interest in their activities, like imitating these and joining in, and are also obviously pleased when they get recognition and praise for such activities.

It is, however, when confronted by another person's distress that a child's prosocial tendencies become most evident. A series of reports by Zahn-Waxler, Radke-Yarrow and their colleagues (e.g. Radke-Yarrow, Zahn-Waxler, & Chapman,

1983; Zahn-Waxler, Radke-Yarrow, & King, 1979; Zahn-Waxler, Radke-Yarrow, Wagner, & Chapman, 1992) have documented the onset and developmental course of children's concern for others, both when the child is personally responsible for the other's distress and when acting as a mere bystander. The children's mothers were trained to act as observers, and over the course of the second year they accordingly recorded their child's reactions to any naturally occurring situation in which another person expressed distress. As their reports show clearly, even at the beginning of the second year another person's emotional upset is already a significant event, eliciting not only intense interest and occasionally reactive crying but also the beginnings of attempts to provide comfort. These took a predominantly physical form (e.g. hugging or patting), but already by the middle of the second year they had not only increased in frequency (as seen in table 43) but were also now expressed in such different ways as verbal comfort (e.g. "You be okay"), advice ("Be careful"), help (giving bottle to a crying baby), sharing (of food with a sibling) and distraction. At the same time the mothers also noted signs of empathic concern such as seen in facial expressions (e.g. looking sad) or in vocalizations (e.g. "I'm sorry") which also increased in frequency over age but were, not surprisingly, rather less evident when the child had personally caused the other's distress. Concern for others, both as an emotional response to upset (empathy) and as a behavioral attempt to alleviate (altruism) can therefore be found from the beginning of the second year; children, we can conclude, feel responsible for others at a very early age, and it may well be that these early forms of caring and remorse are precursors of the more mature manifestations of compassion and conscience that are seen in older children.

While prosocial behavior subsequent to the second year initially shows a definite increase in frequency, no such straightforward trend is found during the middle or later years of childhood (Radke-Yarrow et al., 1983). Hay (1994) has argued that there is an actual decline in prosocial activity between the ages of 3 and 6; others (see N. Eisenberg, 1989) find a more complex picture, in that the incidence of such behavior varies according to situation, measure, and gender. What certainly changes

Table 43 Children's responses to others' distress during the second year of life

	Distress caused by child (age in months)			Other distress situations (age in months)		
	13–15	*18–20*	*23–25*	*13–15*	*18–20*	*23–25*
Altruistic behavior	0.07	0.10	0.52	0.09	0.21	0.49
Empathic concern	0.03	0.03	0.14	0.09	0.10	0.25

Scores represent mean proportion of distress episodes to which child responded.
Source: Adapted from Zahn-Waxler et al. (1992).

is the nature and organization of prosocial behavior – a change that has much to do with the increasingly sophisticated cognitive capacities of children. One of these refers to developmental advances in role-taking skills, i.e. the ability to assume the perspective and part of another person. Such advances are particularly marked in mid-childhood and, as M. L. Hoffman (1984) has pointed out, enable children increasingly to differentiate between their own and others' emotional states. As a result they become capable of experiencing compassion or "sympathetic distress" – a feeling characterized by the individual's cognitive understanding of the other person's condition and thus different from the more primitive empathic distress experienced by the younger child. Cognitive awareness also aids children to respond to other people's emotions in diverse ways, beyond undifferentiated personal distress; insight into their condition means that children, as they grow older, are more likely to appreciate that particular emotions are linked to particular situations and to provide types of help and comfort tailored to such situational demands. Not that cognitive interpretations always lead to more effective interventions: Caplan and Hay (1989) found that 3- to 5-year-old children in nursery school paid attention to and were often upset by another child's distress and yet rarely offered help. When subsequently interviewed about these episodes they explained that this was because an adult was present and that it was therefore not up to them to offer help. Here we have a clear illustration of the fact that empathy does not invariably give rise to altruistic behavior but depends on such other aspects as the individual's interpretation of the situation as a whole. With increasing age the relationship between empathy and altruism becomes a more predictable one (N. Eisenberg & Miller, 1987); for that matter, individual differences in prosocial behavior generally become more stable (Hay, 1994). It is as though over age the whole behavior system becomes more firmly organized and integrated into the individual's personality. At the same time children also become more capable of explaining and justifying their prosocial actions. When N. Eisenberg (1982) questioned 4- to 5-year-old children about their motives for helping or sharing, using a series of hypothetical situations presented in story-form, she obtained a large number of hedonistic reasons – the children, that is, referred to the benefit that they themselves would gain from their actions. Interviewed again 18 months later the children produced far fewer hedonistic reasons and instead explained their behavior more in terms of altruistic factors (and thereafter also increasingly with reference to abstract goals). Yet even at 4 years of age children referred to altruistic motives too; they did mention the needs of others and so demonstrated that their mental representations as well as their actions were at least to some extent other-oriented.

Individual Differences in Prosocial Behavior

There are marked differences between children in the extent to which they empathize with others and in their manifestation of altruistic behavior. Initially these differences are relatively unstable; in the first two or three years little consistency is found across time and situation, and the degree to which one aspect of prosocial behavior is related to another (say helping with sharing) is also limited (Hay, 1994). It is also during this period of relative instability that empathy and altruism are especially susceptible to environmental influence (Robinson, Zahn-Waxler, & Emde, 1994).

Parents often spend much effort in attempting to ensure that their children become generous, helpful, and caring individuals, for in our society at least these are socially approved behaviors that bring credit to child and parent alike. It seems obvious therefore that we should turn to an examination of socializing patterns in order to explain individual differences in prosocial tendencies. Before we do, however, let us note that there are indications that genetic determinants also play a part. These come primarily from studies of adults (e.g. Rushton et al., 1986), where comparisons of identical and nonidentical twins point to greater similarities among the former than the latter on measures of empathy and altruism. A similar comparison by Zahn-Waxler, Robinson, and Emde (1992), carried out on twins in their second year, came up with somewhat mixed results. Maternal reports on the children at two ages, 14 and 20 months, showed strong evidence of heritability in such indications of prosocial behavior as efforts to help or comfort and expressions of concern; however, when the children were directly observed for their reactions to simulated distress scenes at the same two ages, the evidence was rather more equivocal. It may well be that a similar investigation, held at an age of greater stability of prosocial behavior, would have yielded more definite support for genetic determinants.

Whatever the role of innate factors, the socialization practices of parents undoubtedly account for much of the variation in children's prosocial tendencies. Cross-cultural comparisons make this point particularly clearly, as illustrated in a classical study by Beatrice and John Whiting (1975). The Whitings systematically observed children aged 3 to 10 in six small communities located in Kenya, India, the Philippines, Okinawa, Mexico, and the United States, and in each obtained measures of the children's altruistic as well as their egoistic behavior. The rate of altruism varied significantly among the cultures, with the American children scoring lowest on all three of the aspects of altruism singled out and those from the Kenyan, Philippine, and Mexican communities scoring highest. As the Whitings demonstrate, these group differences can be linked to the particular socialization practices that prevail in each cultural setting. Three aspects are noteworthy:

1   the number of tasks which are assigned to children;
2   the mother's work responsibilities outside the home;
3   the size of the family.

In those communities that assign many tasks to children (especially those involving care of younger siblings), that expect mothers to spend much time working in the fields, and where the size of the family makes it especially important for older siblings to help, altruism was highest. In such societies children are accustomed from an early age to consider the common good, actively to engage in a range of prosocial functions, and to learn that such behavior is "for real," that is, that it makes a genuine contribution to the welfare of the family. Under such circumstances children develop an altruistic orientation to social life and to behave quite early on in a spontaneously helpful manner. As the Whitings concluded, altruism is highest in those societies that need altruism most; when the conditions of life are such that mutual helpfulness is essential for survival parents will ensure that children learn to behave accordingly at as early a stage as possible.

In Western society, with its much more individualistic orientation, altruism does not play the same essential role and the pressures on children to develop such a trait are therefore not as great. Nevertheless, they do exist and take a variety of forms. As Grusec (1991) found when she asked mothers of 4- and 7-year-olds to report on their own reactions to their children's prosocial behavior, this frequently took the form of social approval, whether verbal (e.g. "That was a nice thing to do") or gestural (e.g. a nod or a pat). What is noteworthy, however, is that the type of response expected by some psychological theories hardly ever occurred: the mothers rarely used any form of material reinforcement; also they rarely engaged in deliberate empathy training, i.e. by directing children's attention to the effects of their behavior on the other person. A conventional learning account is thus not applicable to the development of altruism – a conclusion strengthened by the finding that the mothers often did not react at all to the child's prosocial behavior or at best just acknowledged it briefly.

Yet it has also become clear, as a result of studies such as those by Zahn-Waxler, Radke-Yarrow, and King (1979) and Robinson, Zahn-Waxler, and Emde (1994), that some types of parental behavior are more closely associated with the development of children's prosocial tendencies than other types. These are:

1 *The provision of clear rules and principles*   As Zahn-Waxler and her colleagues found, mothers who explain the rules of behavior explicitly ("You don't bite people!") and who are also quite clear about the consequences of the child's actions ("If you hit Susan it will hurt her") are most likely to foster prosocial behavior. Children are thus given guidelines that they can transfer to other situations, whereas unexplained prohibitions ("No, don't do that!") cannot be so used.

2 *Emotional conviction on the part of the parent*   According to Zahn-Waxler et al., explanations ought *not* to be delivered in a calm and cool manner. On the contrary, whenever the basic cognitive message is embellished by the parent with intensity of feeling the child is more likely to appreciate the importance of that message. Thus mothers who expressed themselves forcefully, even at times harshly, were found in that study to have the children with the highest rates of altruism.

3 *Attributing prosocial qualities to the child*   Children who are frequently told that they are "helpful" or "generous" or "kind" will internalize these attributions as qualities of their own perceived personality and accordingly live up to their reputation. Children thus come to appreciate that motivation in social situations comes from internal sources; where children perceive their good behavior to be instigated only by external agents they are unlikely to be "good" when that external agent is absent.

4 *Modeling by parent*   Demonstrating altruistic behavior to children is probably one of the more important functions of a parent. While imitation is no longer thought to play the vital role which social learning theory once ascribed to it, the principle that actions speak louder than words is a powerful one in explaining adults' impact on children. In any case, the mother who frequently models altruistic behavior to other people is also likely to be the mother who behaves in an empathic way to her own child.

5 *Empathic caregiving to child*   This brings us to what may well be the most essential attribute, i.e. the existence of a warm and responsive relationship between parent and child. Those parents who behave in a loving, accepting manner towards their children are most likely to have children with high rates of prosocial behavior. This no doubt accounts for the demonstrated relationship between the formation of secure attachments in infancy and the subsequent capacity for empathy with others (Waters, Wippman, & Sroufe, 1979). The overall family climate in which the child is brought up thus provides the background for the development of feeling about other people; where such a background is combined with the more specific techniques listed above the chances are greatest that prosocial behavior will develop freely.

Let us emphasize, however, that there is no one specific formula for producing altruistic children. A major reason for this is that the outcome does not just depend on whatever input socializing agents provide; it depends also on the child. In part this is due to preexisting characteristics such as those provided by the child's genetic make-up (though not the child's gender: note that there is little convincing evidence for the common belief in the existence of sex differences in empathy and altruism – see N. Eisenberg & Strayer, 1987). Largely, however, it is due to the child's own role while actively participating in prosocial behavior: the very fact that the child is engaged in prosocial activity provides the opportunity of learning by doing. Children monitor their own behavior; they can thus perceive themselves as helpful and able to benefit others, and through self-evaluation conclude that such behavior is worth repeating and incorporating as a permanent part of the self. Other people's praise for such actions and their example will, no doubt, help to propel the child along such a course; it would be a mistake, however, to regard these external forces as the only developmental influences. Children's own cognitions and feelings about the activities in which they are engaged must also be taken into account.

The case of empathy development in physically abused children

Parental maltreatment of children is known to give rise to various problems in the children's subsequent socioemotional development. In particular one can expect deficits in their prosocial skills to become apparent – children who receive harsh treatment from their caregivers are unlikely to feel concern about the distress of others. The example set to them by their parents is certainly not one to help them in this respect: when Frodi and Lamb (1980) showed videotapes of crying infants to mothers who had abused their children they found these women to express not only less sympathy than other mothers but also feelings of annoyance. Abusive parents, it seems, are unlikely to create a home climate in which empathy with others is fostered.

Physically abused children show various disturbances in their social behavior. George and Main (1979), for example, found 1- to 3-year-old abused toddlers in day care centers to show more aggression than was observed in nonabused children, displaying this not only to peers but also to staff whom the abused children harassed with assaults or threats of assault. They also turned away from all friendly overtures by the adults, this not being a type of contact with which they could cope. Thus the abused children came to resemble their parents, first in having problems controlling their aggressive feelings and second in acquiring a reputation as difficult and therefore becoming socially isolated.

Several studies have concerned themselves specifically with abused children's reactions to others' distress. Main and George (1985), for instance, in their comparison of abused and nonabused toddlers, found that children in the latter group responded to distress with signs of concern, empathy, and sadness in about one-third of such incidents. The abused children occasionally engaged in mechanical comforting movements, i.e. they might pat the distressed child but without any indication of emotional concern. In no instance was any genuine sympathy displayed, and instead these children frequently responded with physical aggression, threats, or anger. Such behavior is, of course, regarded as socially quite inappropriate and must give rise to worry about the children's future development. However, a report by Klimes-Dougan and Kistner (1990), also based on observations of abused and nonabused children in day care, holds out some hope. Again *inappropriate* behavior was found more frequently among the abused group in response to another child's distress, including withdrawal from or aggression towards such a child. Yet when the frequency of *appropriate* responses was plotted (i.e. any attempt to alleviate distress by offering some form of comfort or help), no difference was found between the two groups: the abused children too showed the socially acceptable kind of behavior. It may well be relevant that these children were somewhat older than those studied by Main and George, i.e. preschoolers of 3 to 5 rather than toddlers, and that they had spent a period of 1 to 2 years in the day care center and thus had had quite a lot of experience of contact with nonabusive caregivers and nonabused peers, providing them with more appropriate ways of responding to distress.

Aggression: Nature and Development

What is aggression? It is often talked of as something undesirable, an antisocial tendency which is unfortunately part of human nature but which children must quickly be taught to control and redirect. Yet the very fact that it is part of human nature means that it has been of adaptive value in the history of our species; without the capacity for aggression we would not have survived. Nevertheless, there can be no doubt that high levels of individual aggression can constitute a danger to the social order; all aggression may not be antisocial and much depends on both target and level, but in every society some degree of control is required.

Let us note, however, that societies vary in the extent to which they value or condemn aggressiveness and that their child rearing practices accordingly reflect these values. The Great Whale River Eskimos stress peace and harmony in their social relationships, do not condone any kind of violence among their members and therefore actively discourage all forms of aggressive behavior in their children (Honigmann, 1954). The Mundugumor of eastern New Guinea, on the other hand, used to be cannibals who had little compunction about killing other people; parents in that society encouraged their children from the beginning to be independent, combative and emotionally unresponsive to others (M. Mead, 1935). In our own society toughness is valued more in some subcultures than in others; generally, however, it is agreed that some checking of aggressiveness is essential and that one of the principal tasks of parents, teachers, and other caregivers must be to ensure that children learn from an early age on to control their hostile impulses.

We can best define aggression as any behavior that is designed to harm others. This seems a relatively innocuous definition; in fact there has been much controversy about the term and just what actions should be covered by it (Archer & Browne, 1989). Must the *intention* to do harm be an essential feature, or, given the difficulty of knowing others' intentions, ought an act be judged purely on the basis of the results it produces? Should the context be taken into account? For instance, a man killing another in a drunken brawl is no doubt acting aggressively, but what about a man killing another on the battlefield? And how is one to distinguish between aggressiveness and assertiveness – do they shade into each other or are they distinct phenomena? Here, at least with respect to one aspect seen in young children, we do have an answer, for in a now classic study Blurton Jones (1972) demonstrated that there are distinct differences between children's aggression and an assertive play style referred to as "rough-and-tumble." As detailed records of facial and bodily movements show, aggression is composed of *frown, fixate, hit, push, and take-tug-grab*; whereas rough-and-tumble is characterized by *laugh-playface, run, jump, hit-at and wrestle*. The two patterns are thus morphologically dissimilar; they also tend to occur in different contexts, i.e. aggression is found in disputes over toys while rough-and-tumble is not. Moreover, children who frequently engage in one kind of activity do not necessarily do so in the other. Such a distinction can be important. Take, for example, statements about sex differences in aggression: when the two patterns are not differentiated boys, who tend to engage in rougher forms of play than girls, are judged to be considerably more aggressive; when the distinction is made that difference, though still evident, is much reduced.

Aggression can take many forms: it may be verbal or physical, carried out in groups or individually, be accompanied by strong emotions or coldly executed, and be carefully targeted or indiscriminate. A distinction that has been found particularly useful in research on aggression is that between the following two categories:

1 *hostile aggression*, i.e. those acts for which the major goal is to inflict harm or injury on the victim;
2 *instrumental aggression*, i.e. actions that are aggressive in form and may harm another person but that are motivated by nonaggressive reasons.

The distinction, it should be noted, depends on the individual's intent, not on the act itself: in hostile aggression hurting is an end in itself; in instrumental aggression it is a means to a quite different end such as obtaining an object that the aggressor wants. The difference, as Hartup (1974) has pointed out, is not a conceptually clean one and yet is useful, primarily because in tracing the development of aggression over age the two types show a different course.

We can summarize developmental changes in aggression under four headings: amount, type, elicitors and cognitions.

Amount   The overall trend is for aggression in the interchanges of children to decrease over age (Parke & Slabey, 1983). This is certainly evident in the preschool years; for example Holmberg (1980) found 50 percent of all actions directed by 1-year-old children to other children could be classified as coercive, whereas at $3\frac{1}{2}$ years the incidence was down to 17 percent. Later on in childhood, however, there are indications that aggressiveness is once again on the increase: according to Cairns (1986) both observed and self-reported aggressive acts increase between the ages of 9 and 14, though this was found only for males and not for females. The sex difference, however, may be due to the way in which aggressiveness is manifested: whereas in the boys investigated it was directly expressed as confrontation, in the girls it took more subtle forms such as social ostracism and alienation.

Type   Not surprisingly, as children get older there is a tendency for aggression to become increasingly expressed in verbal rather than physical form. The 2-year-old has little choice but to express anger through direct bodily action; by the age of 10 shaming, humiliating, sarcasm, and teasing have all been added to the repertoire of responses for hurting others. What also changes, however, is the balance between hostile and instrumental aggression. Hartup (1974), observing groups of 4–6- and 6–7-year-olds over a period of time, found that the decline in the frequency of aggressive incidents was almost entirely due to decreases in instrumental aggression; hostile aggression changed little except in form (for example, when insulted older children return the insult rather than retaliate by hitting the other child). Aggression, it seems, is used in different ways as children become older: initially it is often a chance byproduct, as when a 2-year-old attempts to grab a toy from another child; subsequently, however, it evolves into a deliberate, interpersonal action targeted at specific individuals.

Elicitors   In so far as aggression is employed in the service of the individual's goals and in so far as these goals change with age, so the situations to which the individual reacts aggressively also change. Thus the very young child's conflicts are mainly with other children and concern the possession of toys; increasingly they come also to involve parents and center around routines – meals, bathing, bedtime, and so forth. In later childhood group membership begins to play a part: children no longer fight just for individual goals but also for those which affect the gang or other peer group which now-influences the child's style of life.

Cognitions   Increasingly children's behavior is influenced by their interpretation of events, and in particular by their attribution of motives to others. This applies especially to their growing insight into the reasons underlying the actions of those in opposition to the child. The older child has sufficient role taking skill to be able to put himself in the place of another and will thus be more able to anticipate the likely action taken by an opponent. As a result aggressive behavior can be more sophisticated and subtle – at least in those situations where strong emotion does not sweep the individual away on a tide of direct violence. Increasing cognitive involvement brings with it greater control over behavior; the chances of inhibiting primitive impulses increase, though the ability to deliberately plan aggressive action and thus to make it more effective also increases.

From a very early age individual differences are already apparent in the level of children's aggressiveness. Hay and Ross (1982) observed pairs of 21-month-old children on four consecutive days and found, first, considerable variation from child to child in the frequency with which conflicts were initiated and second, that these differences remained stable over time: the number of initiations of conflicts during the first three days predicted the number of initiations on the fourth day, whether the child was paired with the same or a different partner. But what about long-term stability? Is aggressiveness a persistent trait? Will the aggressive preschool child become an aggressive adolescent and adult? By and large the answer seems to be *yes*. After reviewing 16 studies that had all examined this issue Olweus (1979) concluded that there is considerable evidence for a substantial degree of stability over a period of years and that the extent of this is comparable to the stability found for intelligence test scores. Consistency from one situation to another was also frequently reported in the studies Olweus reviewed. The most impressive evidence, however, comes from a 22-year follow-up of over 600 children, conducted by Eron (1987; see also Huesmann,

Eron, Lefkowitz, & Walder, 1984). The children were seen first at age 8, when those who had been rated as aggressive by peers also viewed themselves as aggressive, were more likely to rate others as aggressive and in general looked upon the world as an aggressive place. Seen again at age 18, these aggressive children had by and large become aggressive youths: high levels of early aggressiveness, for instance, predicted later antisocial behavior, as seen in the finding that those who had been rated as aggressive in childhood were three times more likely to have a police record at age 18 than other individuals. When seen once more at age 30 those who had been highly aggressive at 8 were still highly aggressive on measures of personality characteristics; they were also more likely to have engaged in criminal activities, to have been prosecuted for traffic violations, to have behaved violently towards their spouse, and customarily to engage in severe punishment of their children. Early aggressiveness, it seems, has a good chance of turning into severe antisocial behavior in adulthood – a finding confirmed by Farrington (1991), who undertook a similar long-term follow-up of an English sample and also found that, at least in the case of males, aggressiveness in mid-childhood was a significant predictor of antisocial activities in adults.

This does not mean, of course, that aggressiveness is rigidly fixed from an early age and is resistant to all change. Although a persistent trait, it can be influenced by experience, and the possibility of treatment and control can therefore be considered. As Eron (1987) points out, it may well be that in early childhood certain attitudes and standards are learned with respect to social relationships and that it is these which persist and account for the stability over age in aggressiveness; therefore, if one wants to change the level of aggressiveness it is these attitudes which one must focus on. Pertinent here is Eron's finding that measures of early prosocial behavior are negatively related to later antisocial aggressiveness: thus one could consider aggression and prosocial behavior as opposite problem solving strategies which the child acquires early in life. If one is learned well it is unlikely that the other will be learned.

Such a cognitive approach to the analysis of aggression has been taken considerably further in work by Kenneth Dodge (1986). In attempting to understand children's information processing and response selection in situations that might provoke aggressive behavior, Dodge began with the assumption that it is not the situation itself but the individual's interpretation of that situation which needs to be addressed. Different individuals may perceive the same stimulus as either hostile or benign: highly aggressive boys, for instance, are likely to attribute hostile intent to another child who, say, knocks down some toys; nonaggressive boys, on the other hand, will see the same incident as accidental. The former are therefore more likely to retaliate aggressively, provoking further hostility and dislike from other children and thus confirming the aggressive child in his belief that others have hostile intentions; this in turn will make him all the more ready to behave aggressively on future occasions. A vicious circle is thus set up, beginning with the attributions made by the aggressive child.

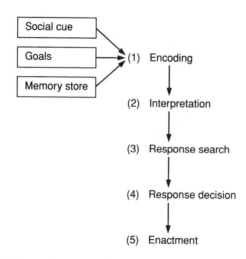

Figure 21   Dodge's information processing model (adapted from Dodge, 1986)

Figure 21 illustrates the information processing model that Dodge has proposed to account for the series of steps involved in this procedure. How a child responds depends on the processing and interpretation of information at each of these steps. Thus, in the first place, the child must *encode* the information provided, that is, attend to and assimilate what is happening (e.g. his toys have been knocked down by another child). This process is influenced not only by what he sees and hears (the social cues) but also by his memory store of similar events and by such general goals as wanting to make friends or wanting to demonstrate his toughness. The second step involves *interpretation*, i.e. the child must make sense of what he has seen and decide, for example, whether the peer acted deliberately or accidentally. It is here in particular that attributional bias plays a part and that aggressively inclined children will be more likely to perceive hostile intent in others' actions. Next, a *response search* takes place: the child must generate possible reactions to what he has seen in the light of his interpretation of the event. Differences occur among children in the number of possibilities they can conjure up; the more socially skilled child will have available a greater range, while the highly aggressive child may have only a single response to call on which he employs in a stereotyped and apparently unthinking manner. A *response decision* process follows: if the child can generate a number of possible responses he must now determine which is the most appropriate; the more he is able to consider the possible consequences of each the more informed will be the choice made. Finally the child *enacts* the chosen response, and here too there will be individual differences in the skill with which this is carried out.

One might think that all this makes what is often an apparently spontaneous and impulsive act into something that is highly complex, intellectual, and deliberate. However, Dodge is anxious to stress that the sequence of processes involved in fact occurs very rapidly and often at an unconscious level. It is possible, however, experimentally to isolate the different steps and investigate how individuals such as highly aggressive boys operate at each one. In this way Dodge and his colleagues have demonstrated that the same aggressive act performed by different individuals may be the result of quite different processes: for example, a deficit in social skills in one case and an attributional bias resulting in misinterpretation of information in another. These differences, moreover, may arise at any one of the sequence of steps outlined. Clinical intervention, aimed at reducing the level of aggressiveness in children, must therefore be based on a detailed diagnosis of what the child's skills and biases are at each of the steps before any efforts to retrain or reorient the child can take place.

The case of bullying

Children's aggression takes many forms, but one of the most common is bullying. As reviews by Olweus (1993) and P. K. Smith (1991) have shown, large-scale investigations in various countries suggest an incidence of up to one in five children for being bullied and up to one in ten for bullying others. It is thus a very widespread phenomenon; it can also be an extremely distressing one for the victims, resulting in extreme cases in suicide.

According to Olweus (1993), bullying takes two forms which he calls direct and indirect. The former refers to physical attacks on children; the latter to behavior such as social ostracism or spreading nasty rumors. Boys indulge more in direct, girls in indirect bullying; and whereas the incidence tends to decrease somewhat with age this applies less to indirect forms. While it can involve just one aggressor and one victim, more often several children participate in the bullying act though some may merely play relatively passive roles. Not surprisingly, it occurs mainly at school.

The typical bully is usually a highly aggressive individual, as seen in behavior towards adults as well as children. Bullies try to domineer over others; they have little capacity for empathy; and their bullying is often part of a general antisocial, rule-breaking behavior pattern. When Olweus followed up such children into adult life he found that the incidence of criminality and alcohol abuse was considerably greater than among other individuals. The typical victim, on the other hand, suffers primarily from a lack of assertiveness (Schwartz, Dodge, & Coie, 1993). Such children rarely initiate conversations or attempt to persuade others to change their behavior in any way; they spend a lot of time in passive play; they tend to be anxious, insecure, and quiet, with low self-esteem. In so far as these characteristics are to be found before they become involved in being bullied it seems that they are a cause rather than an effect of such treatment. Certain children, that is, are more likely to elicit bullying by virtue of inherent personality features such as unassertiveness, at least when paired with the highly aggressive type of child who is looking for victims. Yet, as Perry, Kusel, and Perry (1988) found, aggression and victimization do not necessarily run in parallel: there is a subgroup of so-called "provocative victims" who are also aggressive as well as hyperactive and lacking in concentration, and whom others find so irritable that these children too fall quite easily victim to bullying.

Various intervention programs have been implemented to cope with this problem (see P. K. Smith & Thompson, 1991). The most extensive is one initiated by Olweus (1993), which relies on a variety of measures designed to heighten awareness of bullying and to involve parents and teachers in directly dealing with it. These measures are at the level of the school (e.g. better supervision of playtime), at the level of the class (e.g. role playing) and at the level of the individual (e.g. talks with both bullies and victims). An evaluation of this program indicates a considerable success rate, i.e. a reduction of bullying incidents of 50 percent or more and also a reduction of such other antisocial behavior as vandalism and truancy.

Biological and Social Determinants of Aggressive Behavior

What are the origins of aggression? A number of theories have been put forward to provide answers; they differ in a variety of ways but in particular in the weight they give to innate determinants as opposed to experience.

(1)   *Freud's instinct theory*   According to Sigmund Freud (1930) aggression is derived from an inborn tendency to destroy – a *death instinct*, as he referred to it. This tendency is usually directed outward towards other people or property; occasionally it may also be directed inward and result in self-mutilation or even suicide. Like all instincts aggression, according to Freud, works according to a hydraulic model: energy builds up over time until it reaches a level where it must be discharged. This can be done in socially acceptable ways, e.g. through sport activities, or in ways disapproved by society such as violence. It follows that one way of controlling aggression is through *catharsis*, that is, by providing individuals with the opportunity to discharge the excessive energy through harmless means. In fact it has been shown that such treatment does not work; moreover, the hydraulic model is a largely discredited idea and few people now consider Freud's account of aggression to be of use.

(2)   *Lorenz's ethological theory*   Lorenz (1966) also saw aggression in instinctual terms, though he tied the term closely to overt behavior units that, because of their adaptive value, have become part of the genetic inheritance of the species. As such the tendency is part of the "big four" – hunger, sexuality, flight, and aggression – and, like the others, has evolutionary value by ensuring that the strongest and fittest will survive. Humans are equipped with a basic fighting urge directed against other members of the species – an urge that is often expressed in ritualized form and that may be triggered by certain quite specific releasing stimuli. Lorenz's account is thus based on observational material and has the advantage of a cross-species perspective. However, he too put his faith in a hydraulic model; and like Freud the picture he presents is an essentially pessimistic one: aggression, being a basic instinct, is an inevitable part of our nature; it must be discharged, and to do so in a way that is not primitive and destructive is a far from easy undertaking.

(3)   *The frustration–aggression hypothesis*   Originally put forward by a group of learning theorists (Dollard et al., 1939), this view sees aggression as the inevitable result of frustration. People have particular goals; when goal-directed behavior is blocked they respond with anger and hostility. The connection between frustration and aggression is a learned one: when children discover that aggression alleviates frustration in that it may remove the block and bring about the desired goal they are likely to repeat the aggressive actions under similar circumstances (Sears, 1958). Such a notion has a certain common sense appeal and for a time enjoyed considerable popularity. Its disadvantage is, however, that it overstates the case: frustration does not always lead to aggression, and for that matter aggression is not always caused by frustration.

(4)   *Bandura's social-learning theory*   Bandura (1973) placed greater emphasis on experiential influences on aggressive behavior than any of the other theorists we have mentioned. According to him aggression is like other types of social behavior in that it is acquired either through direct learning or through observation. The former occurs when a child's aggressive acts are reinforced – whether by getting its way or by simply attracting attention. If such acts are found to work then the child is likely to repeat them. However, Bandura gave most prominence to observational learning: when children see others behave aggressively, especially other people whom they admire, and when they note that their behavior produces results, they are likely to imitate them and also behave aggressively under similar circumstances. There is a wealth of evidence (much of it produced by Bandura and his colleagues) that children can acquire aggressive actions by observing others, and much of the concern about the possible effects of violence seen on television derives from this demonstration. Yet this does not explain why different children react differently to the same scenes of violence: it has been suggested, for instance, that girls tend to show a decrease in aggressiveness after viewing television violence whereas boys show an increase (Schuck et al., 1971). An interaction of environmental and organismic factors appears to be at work in determining the child's response, and most of the existing theories have failed to do justice to the full complexity of this interaction and thus fail to provide a satisfactory explanation.

There is no doubt that organismic factors play a substantial part in accounting for individual differences in aggressiveness. The study by Rushton and colleagues (1986), to which we referred above (p. 274) as demonstrating a genetic influence on prosocial characteristics, found that aggressiveness too is thus affected. Measures of aggression, obtained from adult identical and nonidentical twin pairs, indicated that a considerable part of the variance among individuals was directly due to heredity. However, if the subjects' parents are themselves genetically predisposed to aggressive behavior they are also more likely to reinforce, model, or otherwise provide environments that enhance aggressiveness in their children; environmental influences are thus confounded with genetic influences. In addition, as we saw in our discussion of behavior genetics in chapter 2, we need to bear in mind the possibility that children may themselves actively create their own environments in keeping with their individual characteristics: aggressive children are thus likely to consort with other aggressive children, especially in later childhood and adolescence, and thereby maintain and reinforce the tendencies with which they were born. The fact that early measures of temperament can predict subsequent aggressiveness is no doubt also a reflection of genetic factors that can affect behavior in various ways at different ages: irritability, high activity level, irregularity, and distractibility in infancy have all been designated as precursors of later aggressiveness (J. E. Bates, 1987; Bates et al., 1991).

The tendency for aggressiveness to be greater in males than in females has often been used as an argument for the influence of biological factors. However, the following points need to be borne in mind.

- The difference applies to physical more than to verbal aggression.
- Opinion is far from unanimous: while many studies have reported a sex difference others have failed to find it (Hyde, 1984).
- The evidence that males are more aggressive because of hormonal influences, with particular reference to testosterone, is far from conclusive (Huston, 1983).
- Even if one could show that greater male aggressiveness is a reliable phenomenon one cannot conclude that it is the result of biological factors. The possibility that it is due to adults' different treatment of boys and girls must also be considered.

The last point needs emphasis, for it leads us to consider the role that socialization may play in shaping aggressiveness in the course of children's development. Aggression, it appears, is tolerated more easily when shown by boys than by girls. In a study by Condry and Ross (1985) adults were asked to observe two children playing roughly in the snow and then to rate the amount of aggression they saw. As the children were dressed in bulky snowsuits it was impossible to tell their gender; however, half of the observers were told that they were boys and half that they were girls. As the findings for both male and female observers show, less aggression was recorded for so-called boys than for so-called girls; the *same behavior*, shown by the *same children*, was perceived as nonaggressive in "boys" but as aggressive in "girls." The point where we begin to label rough play as aggressive appears to differ for the two sexes; our tolerance for what is permissible is clearly greater in the case of boys, and the pressure on girls to behave nonaggressively is therefore likely to be more intense.

The influence that parents exert in general on the developmental course of their children's aggression has received much attention (Parke & Slabey, 1983). The following parental characteristics have been found to be associated with high levels of aggressiveness in children:

- *Rejection by parents*   According to Olweus (1980), aggression in adolescent boys is closely related to their mothers' attitude to them: where the mother is indifferent or outright rejecting the son is more likely to show a higher degree of aggression than when the mother is warm and accepting. Rejecting parents, we can assume, will not take much interest in the child's efforts to develop self-control; in the absence of reward for such efforts the child has little motivation to curb hostile impulses and as a result will remain at a developmentally retarded emotional level.

- *Parental permissiveness*   When parents are overly permissive they will fail to set clear limits to the child's aggressiveness; consequently the child feels free to directly express impulses with the apparent approval of the parents. Thus the mother's permissiveness of aggression was found by Olweus (1980) to be another factor that predicted level of aggressive behavior in adolescent boys: the more lax the mother in her attitude the greater the level of her son's aggression was likely to be.

- *Parental modeling of aggression*   As we saw in the account of Bandura's social learning theory of aggression, children are likely to imitate other people's actions, and particularly those of their parents. Highly aggressive children have repeatedly been found to have highly aggressive parents: for example, Huesman and colleagues (1984) found that the stability of aggression over two generations, when measured at comparable ages for parent and child, was very high; Eron, Huesman, and Zell (1991) even found evidence for such consistency over three generations. There are several possible explanations for such a relationship, including genetic effects; however, the repeated demonstration that children can acquire behavior patterns through observational learning suggests that this may well be at least one of the ways in which parents influence their children's aggressiveness.

- *Parental punishment*   When physical punishment is frequent, erratic, and inconsistent, high levels of aggression may result (Eron, Walder, & Lefkowitz, 1971; Eron & Huesman, 1984). Again the influence of models may be pertinent here; however, it has also been shown that the effects vary with the child's level of aggressiveness: when nonaggressive children are punished they are likely to suppress their hostile behavior, but highly aggressive children when punished will persist or even increase their aggressive tendencies (Eron et al., 1971).

- *Parental reward of aggression*   Under some circumstances parents take definite pride in their children's aggression. As Bandura and Walters (1959) showed, parents of highly aggressive adolescent boys punished their sons for any form of hostility directed at the parent; however, they actively encouraged and condoned aggression towards other boys. In this way parents conveyed to their children that certain kinds of aggression are acceptable and so helped to perpetuate such behavior.

Thus a number of parental characteristics show a strong relationship to the likelihood that children will develop aggressive tendencies. But let us bear in mind that correlations are of limited value in understanding how such a development comes about: they do not demonstrate that parents *cause* such behavior in their children. For one thing, the cause–effect sequence may go in the opposite direction: children who by nature are aggressively inclined may elicit certain kinds of reactions in their parents such as a highly punitive or a rejecting attitude. And for another, both parental and child behavior may have a common basis such as a similar genetic predisposition. Other approaches than the correlational one, such as one that examines in detail the specific to-and-fro of family interactions, are therefore needed to provide insight into the dynamics underlying the development of aggression.

The work of Gerald Patterson and his associates (e.g. G. R. Patterson, 1982; Patterson, De Baryshe, & Ramsey, 1989) provides an excellent example of this kind of alternative. Children known to be highly aggressive were observed at home interacting with other family members and compared with relatively nonaggressive children. These observations, according to Patterson, show clearly that an escalating pattern of coercion characterizes interactions in the families of the aggressive children, as illustrated by the following steps:

1   the child acts in an aggressive manner (e.g. a boy defies the mother's request to tidy up his room);
2   the mother responds with some form of hostile behavior (e.g. she shouts at her son);
3   the child reacts by stepping up his own hostility (e.g. he yells back);
4   the mother too increases her own aggressiveness (e.g. by physically punishing the boy);

and so on.

Each aggressive act can be seen as an attempt to switch off the noxious behavior of the other person, but by means which generally have just the opposite effect. If the child lives in an atmosphere where little positive stimulation (encouragement, praise, affection, and so forth) is available, he is likely to resort to the kind of behavior that does attract attention, i.e. disruptive activity, and once he embarks on that course others in such a family are likely to respond in a way that will increase the child's own level of aggressiveness. Mutual provocation is thus typical of the families from which highly aggressive children come; the behavior of the individuals involved has, according to Patterson, a *coercive* quality in that it elicits further aggression; and the children's aggressive behavior is perpetuated because it is often the only way in which they can obtain attention or compliance from others or that enables them to escape from an otherwise unstimulating and boring environment, even at the cost of punishment. Children who for one reason or another are already highly aggressive will therefore escalate their aggression rather than decrease it in the face of punishment, because in this way they at least gain recognition. And once children's behavioral style is established it has repercussions in other areas of life: they are likely to be rejected by many of their peers and will therefore join deviant groups; this in turn will make a delinquent career more likely; and in so far as this will provide them with recognition and at least short-term satisfaction they are unlikely to invest effort in academic achievement and so will become school failures.

There are many reasons why certain parents and certain children get into the patterns of repeated negative reinforcement with each other that Patterson observed. Some have to do with the parents' own history: when they themselves were raised with poor disciplinary techniques they may well repeat the pattern with their own children. Others have to do with prevailing levels of stress: where this is high even normally raised parents may resort to child rearing techniques that are far from optimal and provoke family aggression. The child's temperament also plays a part, for children with an inherent tendency towards aggressiveness are more likely to elicit harshness in their parents than are other children. And when all these factors come together one is especially likely to find the kind of setting that will give rise to the more severe cases of children's conduct problems. All this, Patterson suggests, results from the establishment of *coercive cycles*, where any small increase in the intensity of either the parent's or the child's aggressiveness is matched by the other person; family members thus become locked into a pattern of mutual negative reinforcement.

An analysis such as this has two advantages. First, it provides insight into family dynamics and draws attention to the factors responsible for the development of childhood aggression. And second, it points to a course of treatment – one which Patterson and his colleagues have pioneered and for which they claim some measure of success. Such a course, they suggest, must begin with an extensive period of home observation in order to determine the nature of each family's coercive cycles. Subsequent measures depend on this initial diagnosis, but they are likely to include the retraining of parents with a view to equipping them with different interaction skills: for instance, to use "time out" methods to stop the child's coercive actions and to give rewards for "good" behavior rather than punishment for "bad" behavior. They are also likely to include attempts to teach children self-control and to help them acquire insight into the causes and effects of their aggressive actions. Let us emphasize, however, that whatever course of treatment is chosen all involve a *family systems* orientation: the social interaction model advanced by Patterson puts the onus on the way in which the family functions as a whole and on the total set of exchanges within it rather than on the individual pathologies of either parents or children.

The case of violence on television and in video games

No one would suggest that what goes on in the family is the only source of aggressiveness in children. In particular, violence portrayed on television has been singled out as a possible contributor, especially as children tend to spend such a large proportion of their time viewing TV programs. Alarmist statements about the damaging effects on children abound, but are these justified?

Despite several decades of research the answer

remains uncertain. There is no doubt that *short-term* effects can be demonstrated: show one group of children a series of violent TV programs and another group (comparable in their initial level of aggressiveness) some neutral programs; measure the amount of aggression displayed subsequently in a play situation, and almost invariably the former group will behave in a more aggressive manner towards others than the latter (Wood, Wong, & Chackere, 1991). But the evidence for *long-term* effects is more ambiguous. This is largely because of the difficulty of demonstrating a *causal* relationship: does a lot of exposure to violent TV bring about children's aggressiveness or do children already predisposed to aggression choose to watch a great many such programs? Eron (1987), in the 22-year longitudinal study we have already referred to, measured the amount of TV violence that children at the age of 8 customarily viewed and found it to be strongly related to the aggression and criminality found in the same individuals at age 18. But he also found that the 8-year-olds who viewed most violence were already more aggressive than other children, suggesting a circular process: on the one hand, aggressive children prefer violent television, and on the other hand violence on television causes them to be more aggressive. It appears that TV violence does need to be taken seriously but it also seems that it is far from playing the crucial role which some people have attributed to it (Singer, 1989).

Violent video games (the so-called video nasties) are of more recent origin than television

and so far less research into their influence is available. Yet there are reasons for rather greater concern, for whereas television viewing is an essentially passive activity playing games demands active participation, and it is the children themselves who are often placed in the role of killer and maimer. Again short-term effects have been demonstrated. For example, Silvern and Williamson (1987) measured children's aggressive behavior in a free play situation and then asked them either to play a violent video game ("Space Invaders") or to watch a violent cartoon on television. Subsequently further measures of aggression were taken. These showed that, in comparison with the baseline measures, playing the video game had resulted in a significant rise in aggressiveness; however, this turned out to be no greater than that brought about by viewing the violent cartoon.

From a review of the relevant literature Griffiths (1991) concluded that a majority of the studies – especially on young children as opposed to those in their teenage years – show that children *do* become more aggressive after playing violent video games. But there are still problems to be sorted out with regard to the definition of "violence" – for instance, is "Tom and Jerry" to be regarded as harmful, seeing that it is one of the most violent cartoons ever made? And above all, we need to learn about long-term effects: there are those who argue that children may actually become immune after a lot of exposure to violence, but at present such statements are at best speculative.

Moral Development

The end product of socialization is an individual who can distinguish right from wrong and is prepared to act accordingly. Such an individual can be said to have acquired a sense of morality, that is, he or she will behave in ways that uphold the social order and will do so through inner conviction and not because of a fear of punishment. As we have seen, parents and other caregivers devote much effort to controlling children and getting them to comply with adult standards, but whereas compliance is dependent on external sanctions morality is based on the individual's own firmly held beliefs as to how people should behave in society. There may well be a link between early compliance and later moral development: empirical evidence provided by Kochanska (1991) shows that the extent of toddlers' compliance to their mothers' socialization demands predicts the development of conscience six years later. The acquisition of a conscience is a sign that the child has now learned that activities such as cheating, lying, and stealing are wrong; an inner voice rather than the parent's authority is henceforth the child's guide to behavior; the principles whereby human beings regulate their affairs have become internalized.

How moral internalization occurs is a central problem in the study of social development. It is a complex process and our knowledge is still limited. But one thing is clear: it is not a matter of blind acceptance of adult standards, of passively learning what others didactically teach. As with all other aspects of socialization, the child's active nature in selecting, interpreting, and making sense of the information provided must be emphasized. Morality is constructed by the child out of social experience, shaped by the cognitive understanding of which the child is capable at particular points of development. Part of that experience is what other people do and say; morality is, after all, handed down from one generation to another and children's sense of right and wrong is dependent on a learning process initiated by adults. Nevertheless, a crucial role is also played by the way in which children interpret the moral principles conveyed to them, and how their understanding changes in the course of development before they become capable of truly mature moral thinking has thus been of particular interest to psychologists.

Piagetian Theory

Much of the credit for the emphasis on the child's active nature in constructing moral principles goes to Piaget, whose book *The moral judgment of the child* (1932) provided not only a wealth of empirical material regarding the way in which children think about moral issues but also a theory about how their thinking is transformed in the course of development. Piaget studied a number of aspects. One concerned the nature of social rules and their validity, and for this purpose he joined children in playing games such as marbles in order to find out what children's conceptions were about these rules. Thus he would ask questions such as "Where do these rules come from?" "Must everyone obey a rule?" "Can these rules be changed?", and repeat them for children of different ages in order to trace the transformations in children's understanding with greater cognitive maturity. Another aspect concerned what children mean by such transgressions as lying, stealing, and damaging property; and yet another referred to children's concepts of authority and the origins of justice.

Piaget was particularly interested in the role that *intent* plays in children's thinking about moral transgression. He would therefore tell them pairs of stories, each of which was about a child bringing about some undesirable outcome but in one of which this resulted from the child's intentional naughtiness while the other was purely accidental. The following is an example:

(A)   A little boy who is called John is in his room. He is called to dinner. He goes into the dining room. But behind the door there was a chair, and on the chair there was a tray with fifteen cups on it. John couldn't have known that there was all this behind the door. He goes in, the door knocks against the tray, bang go the fifteen cups and they all get broken!

(B)   Once there was a little boy whose name was Henry. One day when his mother was out he tried to get some jam out of the cupboard. He climbed up on to a chair and stretched out his arm. But the jam was too high up and he couldn't reach it and have any. But while he was trying to get it he knocked over a cup. The cup fell down and broke.

The child was then asked to say whether John or Henry was the naughtier one and to explain the reasons for the choice made.

Piaget concluded from all the various findings presented in his book that in the first four years or so children are still in a *premoral period*. At that time there is little conception of what a rule is and what purpose it serves. When playing marbles, for instance, children do so initially in an uncoordinated way and subsequently make up their own rules. Ideas about right and wrong are still arbitrary; the choice of wrong-doer when presented with pairs of stories such as the above tends to be random. After the age of 4 or 5, however, children's ideas become much more systematic. They then enter the stage of *moral realism* – so called because judgments tend to be based on the real or objective damage done. John would thus be regarded as the naughtier of the two children because he broke 15 cups whereas Henry only broke one cup. The intention behind the action is thus neglected. The child also sees rules as absolutes: they are made by authority (parents, God, the police, etc.) and are sacred and unalterable. Right and wrong are thus defined for evermore by whatever rules exist. Around the age of 9 or 10 this absolute view gives way to a more relative one, as children become capable of *moral subjectivism*. Children then come to appreciate that rules are arbitrary agreements which can be challenged and changed by consent. They will now find Henry the naughtier of the two children: an individual's subjec-tive motives and intentions are the criterion whereby wrongdoing is judged rather than the amount of damage resulting from the action. They also no longer believe, as they did at the earlier stage, that punishment must invariably follow any misdeed but see it as only a possible consequence which one can escape by not being detected. Thus the three-stage progression (summarized in table 44) brings the child from a point where there is little appreciation of the principles behind such features of social life as fairness, justice, and authority to a fully developed, mature conception of these ideas which the child can articulate and use as guides for social interaction.

Table 44 Piagetian stages of moral understanding

Stage	Age range (years)	Characteristics
Premoral	Up to 4	No understanding of rules or of the bases of right and wrong
Moral realism	4 to 9 or 10	Actions judged by material outcome. Rules emanate from authority; can't be changed. Wrong is whatever adults forbid
Moral subjectivism	From 9 or 10	Actions judged according to intentions. Rules made by people; can be changed by mutual agreement. Wrong is transgression of moral principles

Children's progression along this stage sequence is, according to Piaget, determined by two factors: their cognitive abilities and their social experience. The former refers primarily to the egocentrism which characterizes young children's thinking and which prevents a child taking into account another person's intentions. Only when children become capable of appreciating that various, quite diverse perspectives can prevail will they be able to understand that different sets of people can draw up different sets of rules and that there is therefore nothing absolute about these. Piaget believed (controversially) that this change does not come about till mid-childhood and it is therefore not till after then that a different moral orientation can be adopted. Subsequent research has cast doubt on this assertion (Rest, 1983), in particular as it has been shown that children can take into account other people's intentions at a much earlier age. In part, the problem also arises from Piaget's methodology, for in his pairs of stories he confounds intention and amount of damage done. When this is disentangled by, for instance, telling children pairs of stories where amount of damage is held constant and only intention is varied, much younger children show that they can base their judgment on the actor's inner motives (e.g. Imamoglu, 1975).

As to social experience, the topic of moral judgment provides one of the very few instances where Piaget is willing to acknowledge the role of interpersonal influences on children's development. What is more, Piaget was very specific as to the nature of this influence, for he insisted that it is interaction with peers rather than with adults that enables children to progress from moral realism to moral subjectivism. When playing with others of the same age children will frequently get involved in conflicts as to how games should be played and what social rules should be applied to their play. As everyone has equal status there is considerable pressure on children to compromise, thereby acknowledging that others can also have a valid point of view even though that may be different from the child's own. *Interpersonal conflict* thus gives rise to *cognitive conflict*, which Piaget saw as the vehicle for all developmental progress. Children, that is, need to resolve in their own minds the discrepancies between their own and others' ideas and do so by accepting that rules are merely social contracts dependent on mutual consent and not on some all-powerful authority. They move thus from an absolute to a relative, more flexible conception of morality.

Piaget himself provided little evidence that interaction with peers plays the crucial role in moral development that he assigned to it. However, there are indications that peer interaction can, to some extent at least, be more effective than interaction with an adult. Kruger (1992) paired 8-year-old children with either an age mate or with the mother, and asked each dyad to discuss two specific moral dilemmas with a view to reaching consensus. The children's moral reasoning ability was assessed both before and after the discussion. As the post-tests show, those who had been paired with a peer made significantly more progress on moral reasoning and showed greater superiority in this respect than those who had been paired with an adult. The reason for this difference became apparent when Kruger examined what went on during the discussion: in sessions with an adult children tended to be passive and rarely produced spontaneous contributions; in sessions with an age mate, on the other hand, they actively argued, generated many spontaneous statements, and tried hard to resolve the problem set for them. In general, the greater the number of spontaneous arguments the children were able to generate the greater was the sophistication of their subsequent moral reasoning, and while this applied to the sessions with an adult too those with an age mate were provided with a setting more suited to active participation and thus to greater progress.

Piaget's theory of moral development has been extremely influential, particularly because of its emphasis on the child's constructive role and its demonstration that children's conceptions of morality may differ markedly from those of adults. However, the theory has also encountered criticisms, many of which concern the methodology Piaget employed to generate the data on which the theory is based. For example, the stories presented in his moral dilemmas tend to be too long and complex for young children and to involve hypothetical situations far removed from their own experience. When these obstacles are removed it is generally found that children show advanced reasoning at much earlier ages than Piaget had proposed. There has also been criticism of the monolithic nature of Piaget's stages: according to other investigators children do not necessarily belong to either one stage or another but may give situation-specific responses, focusing (for example) sometimes on intention and sometimes on amount of damage when presented with pairs of transgression stories. And finally, Piaget's developmental scheme has been found wanting in sophistication: it is based on only three stages, focuses primarily on just one transition (that from realism to subjectivism), and suggests that moral development reaches maturity in mid-childhood, with no further progress to the made thereafter. Subsequent work has tried to remedy these deficiencies.

Kohlberg's Theory

By far the best known scheme following on from Piaget's work is that by Lawrence Kohlberg (e.g. 1969, 1976). It represents a more fine-grained approach which analyzes individuals' responses in much greater detail and scores them according to a much more complex system that has taken over 20 years to develop. Instead of 3 stages there are 6, and these extend moral development right into adulthood. Like Piaget, however, Kohlberg stresses the child's constructive role in thinking about moral issues, and like Piaget he also sees moral development as closely bound up with the child's cognitive development.

Table 45 summarizes the sequence of six stages which Kohlberg uses as a framework for moral development. These are grouped under three levels, referring respectively to preconventional, conventional, and postconventional morality.

1   *Preconventional morality*   At this level morality is a matter of what other people tell the child to do. Doing right involves obedience to those in authority; rules are whatever it is they demand. The first stage conforms closely to Piaget's moral realism, in that the seriousness of transgression is judged by the amount of

Table 45   Kohlberg's stages of moral development

Level 1:   Preconventional morality
Stage 1:   Punishment-and-obedience orientation
What is right is whatever others permit; what is wrong is what others punish. There is no conception of rules. The seriousness of a violation depends on the magnitude of the consequence.
Stage 2:   Individualism and instrumental orientation
Rules are followed only when it is in the child's immediate interest. Right is what gains rewards or when there is an equal exchange ("you scratch my back and I'll scratch yours").

Level 2:   Conventional morality
Stage 3:   Mutual interpersonal expectations, relationships, and conformity
"Being good" means living up to other people's expectations, having good intentions, and showing concern about others. Trust, loyalty, respect, and gratitude are valued.
Stage 4:   Social system and conscience
"Right" is a matter of fulfilling the actual duties to which you have agreed. Social rules and conventions are upheld except where they conflict with other social duties. Contributing to society is "good."

Level 3:   Postconventional morality
Stage 5:   Social contract or utility and individual rights
People hold a variety of values and opinions, and while rules are relative to the group these should be upheld because they are part of the social contract. Rules that are imposed are unjust and can be challenged. Some values, such as life and liberty, are non-relative and must be upheld regardless of majority opinion.
Stage 6:   Universal ethical principles
Self-chosen ethical principles determine what is right. In a conflict between law and such principles, it is right to follow one's conscience. The principles are abstract moral guidelines organized into a coherent value system.

damage done; in the second stage, however, the child is just beginning also to consider people's intention.

2   *Conventional morality*   Individuals at this level judge the morality of acts in terms of their conformity to the rules or norms prevailing in the group to which they belong. Rules are obeyed at stage 3 primarily in order to obtain approval from others; at stage 4 they are obeyed in order to comply with the law and formal customs. Judgments are now based on people's intentions; Piaget's moral subjectivism is thus incorporated into the scheme at this point.

3   *Postconventional morality*   While individuals at this level broadly accept the rules of society they give precedence to more basic ethical principles, which they are willing to uphold even when they clash with the law of the land (the conscientious objector in wartime, willing to go to jail rather than be conscripted to fight, is an example). This is particularly marked at stage 6 where, unlike the previous stage, there is strict adherence to universal principles of ethics and justice and where the individual experiences no conflict in adhering to these rather than to the country's legal requirements.

Kohlberg assessed children's (and adults') moral development by presenting them with stories containing moral dilemmas. The best known example is the "Heinz" story.

In Europe, a woman was near death from a special kind of cancer. There was one drug that doctors thought might save her. It was a form of radium that a druggist in the same town had recently discovered. The drug was expensive to make, but the druggist was charging $2,000, or 10 times the cost of the drug, for a small (possibly life-saving) dose. Heinz, the sick woman's husband, borrowed all the money he could, about $1,000, or half of what he needed. He told the druggist that his wife was dying and asked him to sell the drug cheaper or to let him pay later. The druggist replied "No, I discovered the drug, and I'm going to make money from it." Heinz then became desperate and broke into the store to steal the drug for his wife.

Should Heinz have done that?

Kohlberg devised an elaborate scoring system to allocate his subjects to particular stages, but in doing so he took little notice of the answer to his question at the end of the story but instead concentrated on the reasons given. These he explored in a detailed interview following each story, and it was on the basis of the nature of the justifications so provided that he postulated the developmental scheme outlined above. Table 46 provides some examples of the sort of answers given to the "Heinz" story that typically occur at the three levels of moral development (note that some answers argue *for* stealing the drug and others *against* but that this is irrelevant in the scoring system).

While Kohlberg did not set out to provide precise age norms for the stages postulated, research has shown that *preconventional* reasoning is the dominant mode

Table 46 Examples of answers to Kohlberg's moral dilemma

Preconventional level

"He should steal the drug because if he lets his wife die he will get into trouble" (stage 1)

"You may not get much of a jail sentence if you steal the drug, but your wife will probably die before you get out so it won't do you much good" (stage 2)

Conventional level

"No one will think you're bad if you steal the drug, but your family will think you're inhuman if you don't" (stage 3)

"It's natural for Heinz to want to save his wife, but it's still always wrong to steal" (stage 4)

Postconventional level

"You can't have everyone stealing when they get desperate. The ends may be good, but the ends don't justify the means" (stage 5)

"If you don't steal the drug and let your wife die you'd always condemn yourself for it afterwards. You wouldn't have lived up to your own standards of conscience" (stage 6)

---

throughout early and mid-childhood and is still to be found in many adolescents (as well as among adult criminal offenders). All such individuals see moral rules as embodied in external authority, to be obeyed because of the unpleasant consequences of not doing so. *Conventional* morality emerges in mid-adolescence and remains the norm for the majority of adults; it indicates that the individual has internalized rules, regards them as his or her "own" and follows them out of conviction. *Postconventional* morality, which gives precedence to self-chosen ethical principles over social convention, is rare, even amongst intelligent adults; indeed there is some question as to whether stage 6 thinking is to be found in more than a handful of saintlike persons. These developmental trends are illustrated in figure 22, which is taken from a longitudinal study by Kohlberg and his colleagues (Colby, Kohlberg, Gibbs, & Lieberman, 1983) of a group of boys followed up over a 26-year period from the age of 10 to 36.

The same longitudinal study also illustrates a number of other features of Kohlberg's developmental scheme, all of which have attracted interest from other researchers too:

Sequential ordering   According to Kohlberg an individual passes through the various stages in fixed order. Moral reasoning at lower levels lays the foundation for reasoning at higher levels; stages cannot be skipped and progression is therefore orderly. This has largely been borne out by empirical data: Colby et al., for instance, found all their subjects proceeded through the developmental stages in the hypothesized sequence; no one skipped a stage, and in only 6 percent of instances was a regression observed in the stage at which individuals reasoned at different ages. Studies by others (e.g. Walker, 1989) have resulted in similar findings.

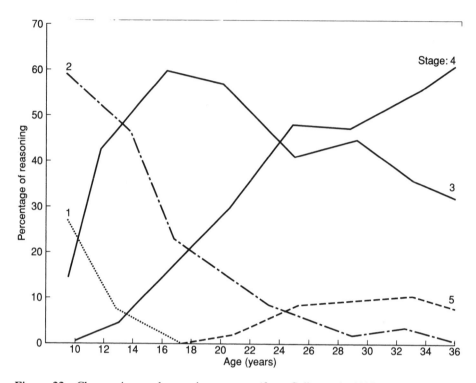

Figure 22   Changes in moral reasoning over age (from Colby et al., 1983, p. 46)

Relationship to cognitive development   The level at which children are able to reason about moral issues is, according to both Kohlberg and Piaget, determined by the cognitive stage which they have attained. Thus preconventional thinking is rooted in the young child's egocentrism; conventional thinking requires the ability to assume the perspective of others; and postconventional thinking calls for the highest level of cognitive development, i.e. the use of formal operations. By and large empirical investigations confirm this relationship, with particular reference to perspective taking (Rest 1983): a certain minimum of cognitive ability is required before a child can cope with reasoning about moral problems at a given level. But let us stress that that minimum does not guarantee comparable moral ability: it may be a *necessary* but is not a *sufficient* condition; exposure to relevant social experiences are also required.

Consistency   If moral reasoning is based on particular cognitive structures then the way in which individuals approach different moral problems should reveal similar types of thinking. This assumption too has been largely borne out. Colby et al. (1983), for example, found that the majority of their subjects obtained scores for the different moral dilemmas administered which placed them either at the same or at most at two adjoining stages. And Walker (1989) found similar consistency when comparing answers to Kohlberg's dilemmas on the one hand and to real-life dilemmas generated by the subjects themselves from their own experience on the other hand.

Universality   The relationship to cognitive development should also mean that the sequence of Kohlberg's stages must be identical in all cultures. If cognitive development is universal (as Piaget maintained and as is generally accepted) then moral development should be also. From a review of 45 studies carried out in 27 countries Snarey (1985) concluded that the invariant sequence of moral stages first found among North Americans also takes place in other societies and that stage skipping and stage regression are rarely reported anywhere. All in all, it appears that people in quite diverse cultural environments "have come to maintain structurally similar principles of human dignity, equality, and the value of life," and that the way in which we approach morality is indeed a reflection of the human condition. However, what does differ from one culture to another is the height of moral reasoning attained. As Snarey noted in his review, postconventional reasoning is even rarer in many societies than it is in North America; young people reared in the Israeli kibbutz system, on the other hand, were found to display this type of thinking to a significantly greater extent – possibly because of the communal emphasis and the greater investment in preserving social solidarity prevalent in that type of environment.

Kohlberg's theory of moral understanding is one of the most influential contributions to child development made in recent decades. While based on Piagetian views it greatly extends these and, after stimulating a very large body of research, its principal proposals remain unchallenged. Its benefits, moreover, include not only some fascinating insights into children's and adults' understanding of social issues but also the implementation of various practical measures such as moral education programs designed for "morally retarded" individuals (Schaefli, Rest, & Thoma, 1985).

Yet the theory has not escaped criticism. Kohlberg's methodology, like Piaget's, has been condemned by some writers, in particular because the stories presented to children are complex and refer to unfamiliar and therefore meaningless aspects of life. Under such circumstances children's abilities can easily be underestimated. The theory has also been criticized for focusing solely on *reasoning* about moral issues, that is, dealing exclusively with cognitive aspects and having little to say either about the strong emotions that often accompany moral decisions or about the behavior resulting from all that cerebral activity. In addition it has been pointed out that Kohlberg confines himself to only some aspects of morality, i.e. justice and fairness, and that his dilemmas therefore deal solely with wrongdoing. Children's reasoning about *prosocial* issues is not dealt with – an omission which N. Eisenberg (1986) has set out to rectify. And finally Gilligan (1982) has accused Kohlberg of being male-biased, in that his theory is primarily based on studies of boys whose moral orientation is not necessarily representative of that of females. Girls, according to Gilligan, mainly adopt a *care orientation*, i.e. they have been brought up to value nurturance, empathy, and a concern for others, and their approach to moral issues is thus dominated largely by a sense of "goodness." Boys, on the other hand, tend to be pushed towards independence, assertiveness, and achievement; for them moral dilemmas represent conflicts between different parties which social rules must resolve, and as a result they tend to adopt a *justice orientation*. It follows that the Kohlberg scoring scheme underestimates girls' moral reasoning ability – hence Gilligan's accusation of male bias. However, reviews of the literature on moral reasoning have failed to substantiate these arguments: Walker (1984) examined 77 studies that provided data about both males and females and found no consistent sex differences in the level of reasoning employed. In this respect, as in most others, Kohlberg's theory remains intact.

Moral Conduct and its Link with Moral Understanding

To think about morality is one thing; to act morally is another. But are the two linked? Does a mature level of moral understanding guarantee a high level of moral conduct?

Kohlberg's own view is clear. As he put it: "One can reason in terms of principles and not live up to those principles" (Kohlberg, 1975). In other words, one cannot expect a one-to-one correspondence: an individual may know what is right and yet behave dishonourably. Nevertheless, it is difficult to believe that the two realms, knowledge and behavior, are totally separate and that attainment in the one does not affect the nature of the other. Indeed Kohlberg himself agreed that the two are more likely to show consistency as the individual reaches higher levels of cognitive maturity – an argument bolstered by his finding that among students capable of postconventional moral reasoning only 15 percent cheated when they were given the opportunity, whereas 70 percent of students reasoning at the preconventional level did so. Yet even here we have evidence of only a trend: the exceptions in both groups are as noteworthy as the majorities, and to predict from knowledge to action is clearly an uncertain undertaking.

One problem is that moral conduct is in itself not necessarily a wholly consistent characteristic. To some extent at least people vary from one situation to another: an individual who would not under any circumstances deceive family and friends may have no compunction about misleading the income tax authorities. An old study by Hartshorne and May (1928–30) illustrates such inconsistency. As part of their "Character Education Inquiry" they investigated the extent to which 10,000 children aged 8–16 could be tempted to lie, cheat, or steal in a variety of situations. For example, on scholastic tests children had the opportunity surreptitiously to consult an answer key or fill in additional items after the official end of the test. Similarly on athletic tests in the sports field children could cheat by, for example, putting in a self-reported result higher than that actually achieved. In all cases, however, arrangements had been made to obtain the child's real achievement and, by comparing that with the reported score, obtain a measure of cheating. Other situations presented the children with the opportunity to tell lies or to steal some small amounts of money, both again easily detected by the investigators. Thus an "honesty score" could be derived from each situation, but when Hartshorne and May compared the various scores obtained by the children they found little consistency. A child who cheated under one set of circumstances did not necessarily cheat, lie, or steal under other sets. Honesty, Hartshorne and May concluded, is not a consistent character trait but is situation-specific. While this has been questioned by other researchers who have found some degree of consistency and who therefore do believe in the existence of a stable disposition underlying moral behavior, the results of the Hartshorne and May study draw attention to the fact that an individual's honesty is influenced by many situational and motivational factors and that consistency of moral conduct cannot therefore be taken for granted.

Demonstrating consistency between moral understanding and moral conduct is an even more hazardous business. It is noteworthy that children who cheated in Hartshorne and May's study were just as likely to assert that cheating is wrong as children who did not cheat. In a review of studies using mainly the Kohlberg dilemmas to test for moral understanding and a considerable variety of measures to assess moral behavior, Blasi (1980) found a somewhat mixed picture. The clearest results came from research on the moral reasoning of juvenile delinquents, which most studies reported to be well below that of nondelinquents (see the case of juvenile delinquents' moral development, below). Research involving other aspects of children's moral conduct (such as cheating, resistance to temptation, and returning a lost object) generally showed some relationship to moral reasoning but the correlations found were mostly low. The same applies to studies of altruistic behavior: children reasoning at more advanced levels are more likely to help, share, and cooperate with others than children of lower maturity; again, however, the association is a tenuous one and by no means consistent from one situation to another.

We must conclude that moral conduct may well be influenced by the level of moral understanding reached by the individual but that it is far from being the only or necessarily the main determinant. Other factors also play a part: for example peer pressure to engage in particular activities, the cost to oneself of certain courses of action as calculated by the individual, and the influence of other personality characteristics such as ego-strength or the ability to resist temptation. These and other influences all need to be taken into account if one is to explain why an individual adopts some particular moral stance under a given set of circumstances.

The case of juvenile delinquents' moral development

If there is a link between understanding and conduct then it should be especially apparent in those who break the law. Quite a number of studies have therefore been conducted with juvenile delinquents in order to investigate whether they function at a lower level of moral understanding, as given by the Kohlberg scale, than law abiding young people of a similar age.

One of the first studies was by Kohlberg (1969) himself. Adolescent boys with a history of antisocial behavior were asked to respond to moral dilemmas such as the "Heinz" story and their answers compared with those of nondelinquents. The delinquents were found consistently to use preconventional types of reasoning; their notions of right and wrong tended to be associated with external authority rather than stemming from internal conviction as was mostly the case with the nondelinquents. Kohlberg attributed this to the inconsistent and frustrating child rearing experiences which the parents of the former group had adopted, though this was based on speculation rather than direct evidence.

Subsequent studies, as reviewed by Blasi (1980) and by J. R. Nelson and colleagues (1990), have largely confirmed the finding that delinquents do tend to function at more immature levels of moral understanding than controls matched for age, social class, and general intelligence. Yet the relationship is by and large only a moderate one, for there is considerable variability between subjects and, for that matter, also within subjects in their reasoning about different moral dilemmas. As Jurkovic (1980) concluded, the supposed moral immaturity of juvenile delinquents has not been unequivocally demonstrated; offenders are morally a heterogeneous group and their variability appears to be related to all sorts of personality, situational, and motivational influences. A failure in moral understanding alone cannot therefore explain delinquent behavior; a distinction is necessary between an individual's underlying moral capabilities and the application of these. One problem is that delinquency is a very broad category, and it may therefore be of help to investigate specific subgroups such as violent as contrasted with nonviolent offenders. We also do not know whether the moral reasoning of delinquents is fixated at an early level or whether it is merely progressing at a slower rate than that of nondelinquents – a problem which only longitudinal studies can illuminate (J. R. Nelson et al., 1990).

Various attempts have been made to advance delinquents' understanding through programs of moral education, including one by Kohlberg and his associates. The success of these has been, at best, moderate. This is not surprising, given the fact that understanding and conduct are not closely associated. To focus only on cognitive aspects of morality is to neglect all the social and personality factors that also play a part in determining delinquent behavior, and it is only from an understanding of the interplay of all these aspects and by taking all into account when mounting ameliorative action that one can hope for any measure of success.

Developing a Conscience

One of the hallmarks of maturity is that the individual progresses from unquestioning obedience to external authority to a state of moral autonomy. Rules and values become internalized, social norms are accepted as one's own, and conscience, that "still small voice," now comes to determine choices between alternative courses of behavior. How that comes about, and especially how *internalization* is accomplished and what *conscience* consists of, have for long been a matter of speculation and inquiry.

One answer was provided by Freud. Children love parents but also fear and hate them, for they are sources not only of comfort and security but also of control and frustration. But feelings of hostility towards love objects are not permissible, and to resolve the ensuing conflict children take over their parents' prohibitions and internalize them as though they were their own. Conscience is thus based on "identification with the aggressor" – though as this results in a highly emotionally charged structure of a largely unconscious nature Freud preferred the term *superego* to the more rational "conscience." In this way children retain their parents' affection and at the same time develop a mechanism whereby they will punish themselves whenever transgression gives rise to guilt. The hostility previously felt towards the parents is now directed inward, and fear of guilt rather than fear of punishment is the motive that impels children to act in accord with social standards.

As M. L. Hoffman (1988) has pointed out, Freud's account receives little support from research. For instance, the hypothesis that moral internalization depends on identification with a punitive parent is not borne out: as we shall see below, disciplinary techniques that are based on force are *less* effective in fostering moral development than techniques based on love and reasoning. But for the most part Freud's theory is a difficult one to test: it was derived originally from observations of adult patients and is not couched in terms that easily lend themselves to empirical investigation. In more recent times much effort has therefore been devoted to investigating aspects of moral internalization that do lend themselves to objective study. Take the following aspects of behavior, each one of which can be regarded as an overt index of internalization:

- the child is able to resist temptation, even when no adult is present;
- the child shows signs of shame and embarrassment after transgression;
- the child offers to make reparation for wrongdoing;
- the child confesses and accepts responsibility for a misdeed;
- the child spontaneously adopts a morally "right" course, even at some personal cost.

Let us consider the first-mentioned in this list, for the *resistance-to-temptation* paradigm was at one time a popular method of investigating the operation of some aspects of children's conscience (e.g. Parke, 1974). It generally involves bringing children to a laboratory observation room, one at a time, showing them some attractive toys and informing them that they must not touch these but can play with some other, unattractive toys. After a period of play in the presence of the experimenter, during which the child may be "punished" for transgression (e.g. by setting off a noxious buzzer or by a verbal rebuke) the child is left alone but observed through a one-way window in order to ascertain whether the rule is violated or not. In this way one can investigate the effects of different disciplinary techniques such as type of instruction and nature and timing of punishment and compare how children of different ages behave under such circumstances.

There must be some doubt whether such artificial laboratory conditions recreate the real-life situations in which children's conscience struggles normally occur. Nevertheless, the procedure has been useful in drawing attention to several points. First, age changes occur in the ability to resist temptation in that younger children show no hesitation in touching the forbidden toys the moment the experimenter has left and no guilt when caught doing so; with age there is increasing hesitation and greater signs of guilt. This is hardly surprising; what has also become apparent is the speed with which this development occurs in the preschool period. Second, at quite an early age there are already wide-ranging individual differences among children in the ability to resist temptation; those who resist longer also tend to show remorse, apologize, and freely confess after transgression to a greater extent than other children (Sears, Rau, & Alpert, 1965). And third, it has been shown that providing even quite young children with a *rationale* for not touching the toys is more effective than *punishment*; most effective, however, is a combination of *both* methods. The kind of rationale that ought to be employed depends on the child's age: 3-year-olds are most influenced by telling them the toy can easily break and should therefore not be touched; telling them the toy belongs to another child is of little use. Five-year-olds, on the other hand, are more influenced by the latter explanation; notions of property rights are now meaningful and do affect what the child regards as right or wrong (Parke, 1974). We can conclude that the most effective explanation is that which most closely matches the child's ways of thinking about moral rules at that particular stage of development.

At what age do children develop a conscience? Kochanska and colleagues (1994) obtained reports from mothers of preschool children about two kinds of behavioral manifestations: *affective discomfort*, i.e. feelings of guilt, anxiety concerning deviation, and remorse associated with actual or potential wrongdoing, and *behavioral control*, i.e. the ability to refrain from wrongdoing and to exercise restraint, and supplemented these reports with observation of the children in a temptation situation. Their findings suggest that around age 3 a significant shift takes place, in that a marked increase then occurs in these various indices. Yet some signs of conscience can be found even earlier: reparation and confession, for instance, were seen in some children around the 18- to 24-month age range – the age, that is, when the awareness of standards first emerges.

Internalizing moral norms and developing a guilt-producing conscience is clearly a highly complex process about which we still have much to learn. What has been found so far suggests the following developmental sequence:

1 The initial and most basic prerequisite is the formation of the self. This will, at the very least, enable children to attribute acts of wrongdoing to themselves and will make it possible for them to think of themselves in terms of "*I* am good/*I* am naughty."

2 A further, very early development concerns the awareness of standards. In the second year, as we have seen, children become aware that certain standards, including those of personal conduct, need to be met; failure to meet them can be upsetting.

3 Once parents see that children are aware of standards and are able to comply with directives they will increasingly exert socialization pressures. Children then begin to react to parental disapproval with generalized distress.

4 The generalized distress gives way in due course to more differentiated feelings as children become capable of experiencing shame, embarrassment, and other such "personal" emotions.

5 As the resistance-to-temptation experiments have shown, children at first require an adult's presence to refrain from carrying out a forbidden act. However, the ability to resist temptation becomes increasingly firm from the early preschool years on. This is evident above all when the child is under no immediate supervision; in addition, the length of time children can resist increases as does their resolve when confronted with greater temptation (e.g. even more attractive toys or even less chance of being caught).

6 Eventually the child no longer needs explicit adult forbiddance but refrains from certain activities spontaneously, i.e. on the basis of self-generated prohibitions. If for any reasons these are transgressed the child will show manifestations of guilt, admit that punishment is justified and be willing to provide reparation.

The proper functioning of society, as well as the mental health of its individual members, require that this developmental progression takes place smoothly and completely. Unfortunately this is not always the case. *Psychopaths* are individuals who have never learned to experience guilt; they appear to be without conscience and are thus more likely to get involved in antisocial activities. Despite much effort little is known as yet about the circumstances which give rise to this syndrome. However, let us also stress that there are individuals who suffer from the opposite condition, i.e. too strict a conscience. Such people are likely to suffer from crippling anxiety, to be plagued by (apparently groundless) guilt feelings and to have erected all sorts of neurotic defense mechanisms to cope with these emotions. It was such patients that set Freud speculating about the origins of the superego, and they remain among the most frequent referrals to psychotherapists.

Socialization Influences on Moral Development

It is generally assumed that the kinds of child rearing techniques and attitudes which parents display are likely to have marked effects on the rate and nature of moral internalization. The most consistent attempt to investigate and conceptualize this influence is found in the work of Martin Hoffman (e.g. 1977, 1988).

According to Hoffman the techniques parents use can be grouped under the following three headings:

1 *Love-oriented discipline*   In order to get children to conform parents using this kind of technique will withhold affection and approval whenever the child misbehaves. They will, for example, ignore the child, turn their back, refuse to speak or listen, isolate the child, explicitly state a dislike for the child, or threaten to leave the child. Love withdrawal has an intensely punitive quality, for ultimately it means abandonment or separation and that, for a highly dependent child, can be extremely frightening and could thus be a powerful motive to obey.

2 *Power-assertive discipline*   This refers to techniques which rely on the parents' superior power over the child. Included here are physical punishment, withholding of privileges, and any verbal means whereby parents impose their will on the child (e.g. "Do it because I tell you to!"). Instead of fear, these are likely to give rise to anger and resentment.

3 *Inductive discipline*   Included here are all those techniques that involve giving children explanations for requiring them to behave in a particular way. It is thus a non-punitive strategy, which relies on providing children with a cognitive rationale in order to convince them to conform. Examples include appeals to the child's pride (e.g. "Be like a big boy!"), concern for others (e.g. "You would hurt her!"), and pointing out the physical requirements of the situation. The appeal is thus to the child's understanding rather than to emotions of fear or anger.

Most parents make use of all three types of discipline, and even in any one disciplinary episode they may show a mixture of the three. Nevertheless there are consistent differences in the extent to which individual parents prefer to rely on one particular technique rather than on the other two, and according to Hoffman these differences in the dominant type of discipline are associated with the kind of moral development that one finds in their children. Thus in a typical study (e.g. M. L. Hoffman & Salzstein, 1967) parents are interviewed and asked to discuss how they would respond in various specific situations common to family life, e.g. the child breaks or damages something of value, or the parent learns that the child is doing badly in school. The parents' responses are then analyzed to determine the extent to which each of the three disciplinary techniques is relied on in such situations. Parental preference can thereupon be related to various indices of the child's moral development, including measures of guilt obtained from the way children complete a story about a child's transgression, ratings by classmates of the child's consideration for others, and teachers' reports on the child's tendency to confess after wrongdoing and accept responsibility.

The following generalizations emerge from such correlational results:

1 Frequent use of *inductive* techniques by parents is associated with moral maturity in children. This applies particularly to what Hoffman called "other-oriented" inductions, i.e. those in which the implications of the child's behavior for other people are pointed out. In comparison with the other two kinds of discipline induction is most effective in bringing about the internalization of moral standards.

2 When parents' predominant technique involves the use of *power* the child is likely to develop a moral orientation that is based on fear of detection and punishment. Instead of relying on internal standards the child's behavior is largely governed by external sanction; moral development is thus inhibited by much punishment.

3 The use of *love withdrawal* as the principal kind of discipline shows no consistent relationship to moral orientation – a finding that contradicts the Freudian hypothesis that the internalization of morality is determined by the possible loss of parental love.

What makes induction so effective? Several possible reasons have been put forward by Hoffman. First, control through explanation helps children to generalize the rule, so that they can apply it to future occasions as well. Second, by pointing out the consequences parents enable children to anticipate feelings of guilt should they act in the prohibited manner. Children are made to appreciate that the responsibility lies with them; it is therefore up to them to act in the required manner. And third, it may be that inductive techniques make it easier for children to dissociate the message from its original source, the parent, than is the case with the other two techniques; the content is thus remembered without associating it with the originating circumstances, and internalization is thereby fostered.

As Hoffman himself has pointed out, there are methodological shortcomings to the studies on which his conclusions are based. In so far as these studies rely on interview material, parents may give distorted accounts of their behavior in order to present themselves favorably (the "social desirability effect"). When the parents are also asked to supply information about the child's reactions, findings that emerge about associations with disciplinary methods may well be contaminated by their stemming from a single source. In addition, we need to consider the possibility that the emphasis on induction may be specific to older children and be less effective in children too young to be influenced by explanation. And finally, we must note that moral development is treated as a unitary phenomenon and that different aspects of morality are considered to respond similarly to particular socializing influences – an assumption which may well be unjustified and which requires further examination.

However, of most concern is the correlational nature of this work, which makes it difficult to infer cause–effect sequences. One cannot, that is, be sure that the way in which children develop a moral sense is directly due to their parents' treatment; it may be that the adoption of one kind of discipline rather than another is dictated by the nature of the child. As Kochanska (1991) has suggested, the temperamental qualities with which children are born may well play an important role in the child's own moral socialization. For example, children who by nature are anxious are likely to be more responsive to their parents' socialization efforts; reprimands for transgression will arouse considerable internal tension and discomfort, and guilt can therefore easily develop as a consequence of even quite mild disciplinary measures. On the other hand children who are temperamentally unperturbable are more likely to need more forceful methods of child rearing; having a relatively low anxiety level, they are more difficult to socialize and low-key parental strategies are therefore not sufficient. Findings by Kochanska give some support to these proposals and indicate that generalizations about the effects of various disciplinary techniques cannot be made without taking into account the individuality of children. In short, what works for one may not work for another. Indeed, as a result of this kind of consideration Grusec and Goodnow (1994) have suggested that what matters is not so much parents' use of any one particular type of disciplinary technique as the *flexibility* they show in adapting their message to the characteristics of the child as well as to the kind of misdeed perpetrated. The active nature of the child is thereby emphasized: children are more likely to internalize the message if they perceive it clearly and judge it as appropriate to the misdeed, and parents ought therefore to ensure that whatever action they take matches both the child and the child's wrongdoing.

Summary

- The progression from other-control to self-control is one of the most important themes of childhood. It is dependent both on the development of certain cognitive prerequisites and on the support provided by adult caregivers.

Parental Control Techniques and Child Compliance

- The capacity for compliance with others' demands emerges at the end of the first year. It is a highly valued trait, required for smooth parent–child interaction; nevertheless, the capacity for noncompliance can also serve positive functions. With age the rate of both compliance and noncompliance increases; the organization of both also becomes more coherent.
- Control techniques refer to the actions caretakers employ to obtain children's compliance. They are most effective if applied with sensitivity in the context of a reciprocal interaction with the child; used in this way they are also more likely to facilitate the internalization of values than more coercive techniques.

Learning Social Rules

- During the second year children become aware of the importance of meeting particular normative standards for behavior and appearance. This awareness, and children's interest in violating standards, are reflected in their conversations, which parents can use to extend children's ability to understand the social rules set up to guide their behavior.

- The conventions surrounding family routines provide a particularly useful means of learning rules as to what is acceptable and what is not. The emotions with which such routines are often imbued help in this respect; even family arguments are of use in conveying to young children how to conduct and to resolve disagreements.
- Children are far from passive in rule learning; they actively attempt to make sense of their social world and how it functions by questioning and challenging and by testing the limits through deliberate noncompliance.
- Interaction with siblings is a further arena for the acquisition of rule governed behavior. Such interactions fulfill different functions from those with parents, as shown by analyses of conversations: issues of justice and fairness, for instance, are much more to the fore, so that children learn more about cooperation, sharing and turn-taking than they do from their parents. Parent–child relationships are primarily marked by complementary features; sibling relationships, on the other hand, contain mostly reciprocal features.
- Rules pertain either to social convention or to morality. The former involve arbitrary group norms, whereas the latter are universal in nature. Children from quite a young age are capable of making this fundamental distinction in the nature of social behavior.

Prosocial and Antisocial Behavior

- Signs of empathy, altruism, and other forms of prosocial behavior are evident from the second year on. With further cognitive development these become more sophisticated, as summarized in Hoffman's four-stage scheme.
- Individual differences in prosocial behavior are to some extent genetically determined; parental socializing practices, however, play a major part, as seen in cross-cultural comparisons and in the analysis of the facilitating effects of different kinds of parental behavior. Children themselves, however, are also actively involved in shaping their own prosocial activities.

Aggression: Nature and Development

- Aggression takes many forms, but a useful distinction can be made between hostile aggression, characterized by the intention to hurt the victim, and instrumental aggression, which is motivated by other reasons.
- Developmental changes in aggression are to be found in various respects. Thus with age overt manifestations tend to decrease and take a verbal rather than a physical form; the decrease, however, is primarily in instrumental aggression. Individual differences in aggressiveness, found at an early age, tend to remain stable, making possible the long-term prediction of antisocial behavior.

- An information processing model by Dodge shows that any individual aggressive act can be spelled out in terms of a sequence of interpretive and decision making stages, and that at any one point in this sequence individual differences may arise.

Biological and Social Determinants of Aggressive Behavior

- Among attempts to account for the origins of aggression are Freud's instinct theory, Lorenz's ethological theory, the frustration–aggression hypothesis and Bandura's social-learning theory. Accounts differ in the weight they give to biological and social factors respectively.
- The role of biological influences is indicated by evidence that aggressiveness is genetically based. However, the generalization that there are sex differences in aggressiveness is less soundly established.
- Social influences are illustrated by the various aspects of parental rearing practices associated with individual differences in children's aggressiveness. But a correlational approach cannot provide proof of causation; a social interaction analysis such as Gerald Patterson's is required to yield insight into the dynamics underlying the development of aggression.

Moral Development

- Children construct morality out of their social experience in accord with their cognitive understanding. Piaget in particular stressed this constructive role, and to describe the development of children's understanding proposed a three-stage sequence consisting of a premoral period, a stage of moral realism, and a stage of moral subjectivism.
- A more sophisticated scheme has been put forward by Kohlberg, involving a more differentiated sequence extending right into adulthood and based on three levels referring respectively to preconventional, conventional, and postconventional morality.
- A conscience is developed as a result of internalizing adults' rules and values. Various indices of conscience development, such as the ability to resist temptation, have been worked out; they indicate a marked increase around the age of 3. Of the three kinds of disciplinary techniques parents use, i.e. love-oriented, power-assertive, and inductive, the latter is associated with the most advanced conscience development.

Chapter 7

Extrafamilial Influences

Psychologists' attempts to explain the nature of socialization were at one time almost wholly confined to the family, indeed initially to the mother's relationship with her child. It was only gradually that other sources of influence came to be considered: first, from within the family, the father and the child's siblings; subsequently sources outside the family such as peers, the school, and the media. The belief that the mother is the principal, even the sole force involved in the socialization process ("matricentric thinking," as Lamb, 1978, called it) gave way to the realization that from the beginning children are embedded in a network of social relationships involving a diversity of individuals, each of whom has to be recognized as exerting some sort of influence on the course of the child's development. The family may be the first context in which the child learns about the social world, but it is not the only one and beyond the early years there may well be circumstances when other contexts come to play a part that is just as vital in accounting for children's behavior.

This change in our thinking is due to a number of factors. One is the failure of parental practices to account for variations in children's personality development (Maccoby & Martin, 1983). On their own at least, parents' child rearing techniques have been found to have only limited explanatory power, and the move away from Freudian theory was to a considerable extent due to the resulting disillusionment with any attempt that limits the search for the forces underlying development to parents and to the early years. But another factor is the reality of social life; today, mothers are no longer confined to the home; many go out to work and thus share the child's care with other people (relatives, friends, day care staff) from an early age. And if children attend some form of day care they encounter an influence that becomes increasingly important once they progress through preschool settings to school, namely that of other children. Even the school itself, as a social system with its own sets of rules and demands and customs, requires children to adapt their behavior in ways not required in the family. Add to that the influence that television and other modern media may exert, and one must acknowledge that children's development is indeed shaped by multiple forces.

Extrafamilial influences have so far received somewhat uneven attention in research, with by far the most given to peer relationships. Also so far most effort has been devoted to describing each type of influence in its own right, with far fewer attempts made to integrate them into a wider picture of *joint* efficacy. Yet socializing agents do not function in isolation: mother and father, for instance, do not impinge on the child separately, with additive effects, but have a combined and integrated influence, and in just the same way there are links between children's relationships with parents and their relationships with peers that may well take all sorts of varied and complex forms. We have still much to learn about such links, but the essential point remains: it is the relationships between different sets of children's experiences that one must attend to and not just each separate set on its own.

Peer Relationships

Nature and Function

A useful distinction has been made between two types of relationships, each of which contributes something uniquely to a child's development and both of which should therefore be experienced (Hartup, 1989).

- *Vertical relationships* are those which are formed with an individual with greater knowledge and power than possessed by the child and therefore mostly involve someone older such as a parent or a teacher. The interactions on which they are based tend to be mainly of a complementary nature: the adult controls, the child submits; the child seeks help, the adult offers it. The roles played are thus interlinked but the behavior patterns whereby they are expressed differ. The main function of vertical relationships is to provide the child with security and protection, as illustrated by the child's attachment to the parent. They also enable children to gain knowledge and acquire skills, as seen in the teacher–child relationship.
- *Horizontal relationships* are formed with individuals having the same social power as the child's; they are egalitarian in nature and the interactions on which they are based are reciprocal rather than complementary. This is seen, for example, in the games which children play together: one hides, the other seeks; one throws a ball, the other catches it. The roles can then be reversed, for the partners have similar abilities. Yet the function of horizontal relationships is to give children the opportunity to learn those skills that can be acquired only among equals, such as those involving cooperation and competition, and experience in interacting with other children thus fulfills certain unique functions which cannot be fulfilled by vertical relationships.

The distinction is, of course, not an absolute one: the relationship with an older sibling, for example, contains both complementary and reciprocal elements. Nevertheless, peer relationships make certain unique contributions to children's development and do so just because the partner is of equal status – as seen in Piaget's proposal that children grow out of egocentric modes of thinking through being confronted with others' perspectives in the course of peer interaction. Family relationships are not egalitarian, and just for that reason cannot teach children as effectively as can peer groups skills such as turn-taking, sharing, leadership qualities, or how to cope with hostility and bullying.

Thus children help to socialize each other. The peer group is, in fact, in many respects a miniature society in its own right, seen most clearly in the gangs that some adolescents form and that exert great power over their individual members. These are subcultures, each characterized by its own set of rules and social organization, and while some of them may adopt sets of values deviant from those of society as a whole they do at least fulfill the function of enabling their members to acquire skills of conformity, loyalty, and cooperation. In so far as such groups may have a definite structure they also enable their members to learn about the nature of social organization and the way in which leaders and followers relate in orderly fashion.

There is, however, another reason why the distinction between vertical and horizontal relationships, useful though it may be, should not be regarded as an absolute one. Occasionally the peer group can take over certain functions that normally belong to the adult–child system, such as the provision of attachment-derived comfort and security. The most famous example is one provided by Anna Freud and Sophie Dann (1951) and concerns a group of six 3-year-old children who, at the end of the Second World War, were found living by themselves in a concentration camp. While they were still infants their parents had been killed in Nazi gas chambers, and although they received intermittent care from other inmates, most of whom were also subsequently killed, the children more or less brought themselves up. In the two years or so before liberation they stuck together tightly as a group and developed fierce ties of loyalty to one another.

When found after the war and transferred to a refuge in England they were in many respects extremely disturbed. They were wild, restless, destructive, and above all hostile to all adults with whom they came into contact. With each other, however, they behaved quite differently. As Freud and Dann put it, these children

> had no other wish than to be together and became upset when they were separated. . . . No child would remain upstairs while the others were downstairs. . . . If anything of the kind happened, the single child would constantly ask for the other children, while the group would fret for the missing child. . . . There was no occasion to urge the children to "take turns"; they did it spontaneously. They were extremely considerate of each other's feelings. . . . At mealtimes handing food to the neighbour was of greater importance than eating oneself.

In short, the children had developed intense feelings of attachment to each other of the kind that normally are developed towards parents. Their emotional security was totally dependent on the physical availability of the other children, and it was within the context of these peer relationships that they also learned sensitivity to the needs of others. The fact that the children eventually became capable of establishing positive relationships with adults and in due course were capable of leading normal lives was, one must assume, due to the fact that the peer group took over functions that adults failed to supply. However, under the usual circumstances of child rearing in the Western world the emotional needs of children in the first years are catered for in vertical relationships; horizontal relationships assume a later and different kind of importance.

In the course of development children's contact with peers gradually increases while that with adults decreases. When S. Ellis, Rogoff, and Cromer (1981) observed children aged 1 to 12 years at home and outdoors in order to establish the identity of their companions they found that at a remarkably early age children began to interact more frequently with other children than with adults (see figure 23). However, the sheer fact of being with someone is only part of the story; the feelings of closeness the child experiences with the companion is another. Levitt, Guacci-Franco, and Levitt (1993) interviewed children aged 7 to 14 in order to establish the people they considered to be close to them and generally to play an important part in their lives, and found that at all ages members of the immediate family were regarded as being closest. From about 10 years onwards the extended family was also increasingly mentioned, but at adolescence a marked increase occurred in the extent to which peers were referred to as sources of emotional support. What is notable, however, is that even at the youngest ages friends were often included among the individuals the child felt close to – a finding that applied equally to both sexes and to all the ethnic groups included in the study. The importance of peer relationships to these children is thus apparent.

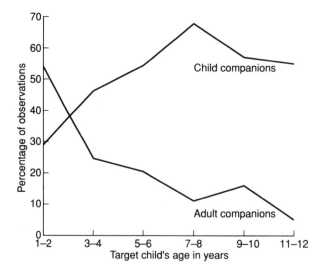

Figure 23   Child and adult companions at different ages (from Ellis et al., 1981)

The case of culture and its effects on peer relationships

Both the nature and the extent of peer relationships are influenced by the type of society in which the child is brought up. As Whiting (1986) showed when comparing 20 communities from many parts of the world, the amount of time that children spend in the company of different individuals (mothers, fathers, relatives, age mates, older children, and so forth) varies greatly, depending on such factors as the basic economy and settlement pattern characterizing each society and the household and family composition prevalent in that community. Take the Kung Bushmen of the Kalahari Desert in Botswana (Konner, 1975). Children there are brought up in small family groups living a nomadic existence; their opportunities for play with children of the same age are therefore limited, and nearly all social interactions other than those with adults are thus with siblings and cousins. This is typical of hunter-gatherer societies generally, yet the same pattern can be found in some Western communities too: as Whiting points out, children living on isolated farms in northern Norway will spend all their time with parents and siblings, and even when they go to school the number of children there is usually so small that education takes place in mixed-age groups. Thus in many societies it is in the non-peer, multi-age group of juveniles that children spend most of their time, and it is often that group that assumes considerable responsibility for the supervision and socialization of its younger members.

In industrial societies peer groups have only relatively recently become important, namely with the introduction of compulsory schooling. The system of grading means that children of the same age spend much of the day together, and it is often in the classroom setting that they form friendships which ensure that their out-of-school activities are dominated by the peer group too. Moreover, the increasing demand for day care and nursery facilities for preschool children and the upward extension of the school leaving age mean that the present generation of children spend an even larger proportion of the early life span in the company of peers. In some cultural settings the emphasis on the peer group is taken even further: as cross-national comparisons of nursery school regimes have shown (Tobin, Wu, & Davidson, 1989), group belongingness and group cooperation are emphasized to a far greater extent in the upbringing of quite young children in China and Japan than in the United States, where individualism is valued more. An even more extreme example is the kibbutz system of rearing children, in so far as these live from the beginning, not with their parents, but separately with a cohort of age mates. By spending almost the entire day in the company of the same small group of peers children are encouraged to develop values such as cooperation and selfless dedication to collective goals rather than pursue their own individual aims through interpersonal competition – an intention that, according to some reports (e.g. Hertz-Lazarowitz, Fuchs, Sharabany, & Eisenberg, 1989; Shapira & Madsen, 1974) appears to have succeeded in producing personalities with the desired characteristics.

Thus the precise role which the peer group plays in a child's development is to a considerable extent dependent on the culture in which that child is brought up. Parents are almost universally involved in child rearing, but the part played by peers is subject to far greater variation from one society to another. Our following account of peer relationships is primarily geared to Western practices; it should be borne in mind, however, that these are culture-specific and that both the extent of peer interaction and the purpose to which it is put are an expression of our particular institutions and values.

Developmental Trends

How children relate to their peers is determined by many factors: temperamental characteristics such as, in particular, the child's sociability; the child's past experience of encounters with age mates; the familiarity of the partner and the existence of any friendship bonds between the two; the circumstances under which the interaction occurs (task related or not; the availability of toys; the presence of adults, etc.); and the function which the child's particular culture has assigned to peer interaction. But above all peer relationships are influenced by the developmental stage which the child has attained and the kinds of social skills that can therefore be employed when interacting with another individual of similar status. It follows that peer relationships go through certain orderly developmental sequences and that they can be expected to show various specific sets of characteristics at different age periods. We can summarize these as follows.

(1)   *Infancy*   As early as 3 months infants show interest in other babies, looking at them for longer periods than at an adult and making more abrupt, excited movements (Fogel, 1979). But it is doubtful whether the other child is seen as anything more than an interesting object that elicits various exploratory responses, and it is not till the second half of the first year that interactive behavior emerges. Initially such interactions take a very simple form: child A, for instance, holds out a toy to child B; child B touches or takes the toy but without looking at child A, and the sequence ends there. Even these very primitive interactions occur only rarely in the first year: according to Vandell, Wilson, and Buchanan (1980) they can be found on average about once every four minutes at 6 months and about once every three minutes at 9 and 12 months. Unreciprocated approaches, however, are common: in the study by Vandell and colleagues they occurred on about 47 percent of occasions. Thus the main difficulty at this age appears to consist in linking behavior to that of the partner: overtures are not reciprocated and social contacts are still largely one-way affairs.

(2)   *The toddler period*   From the second year onwards peer interactions become both more frequent and more complex (Howes, 1987). Reciprocal play is seen more often; sequences of linked behavior become longer; and children now can exchange roles as well as turns. Games thus become possible in which, for example, one partner runs and the other chases or one hides and the other seeks, with children taking turns at the roles they play. Increasingly children also become capable of incorporating toys into their social activities, attending to both object and partner at the same time. By the end of the second year pairs of children spend more time in social than in solitary play; they also spend more time with the peer even when the mother is present (Eckerman, Whatley, & Kutz, 1975). But social behavior is also becoming more differentiated and adjusted to the nature of the child's companion: Ross and Lollis (1989) found children as young as 20 months, paired with previously unfamiliar

peers, to show distinctive patterns of social interaction which varied consistently according to partner. These variations emerged gradually in the course of a number of play sessions, though interestingly they became evident in positive social interactions but not in conflict sequences, where behavior remained stereotyped irrespective of the identity of the other child.

(3) *The preschool years* Increasingly the capacity for symbolic play and the development of verbal skills transform the nature of peer interaction. Children can now communicate meaning; they can share knowledge about their activities; they are able to engage in a wide range of pretend play; and they can negotiate with one another the rules determining the structure of their games. They also become able to engage in group play with several simultaneous partners rather than participate only in dyadic play with one partner. Thus social behavior in general increases markedly during this period – an increase illustrated in figure 24 (based on findings by P. K. Smith, 1978) in which a distinction is made between solitary play, parallel play (i.e. activities carried out by children next to each other with similar toys but without direct interaction), and group play (i.e. all forms of social participation). While parallel play remained fairly constant over the nine-month period during which these 3-year-olds were observed, solitary play decreased as the children became more confident and skilled in participating in each other's play activities.

(4) *Childhood* With school entry children's opportunities to interact with others of the same age increase considerably, and the developmental trends we have already noted in the nature of their peer relationships become much more marked (Hartup, 1983). Increases occur in the ability to communicate information and meaning and in cooperative and sharing skills. At the same time children become much more proficient in "reading" others' emotional states, motives, and intentions; interactions can thus be more precisely tailored to the characteristics of the partner; and children can more easily participate in joint tasks which require them to coordinate their efforts in order to reach a common goal or even a goal that only the partner wants to achieve. Egocentrism, in Piaget's sense, is certainly left well behind. But children are also now much more choosy in their partners: not only are groups almost exclusively same-sex in composition but friendships between pairs of children become very much more meaningful and sustained. Social groups are thus no longer ad hoc affairs, formed through chance encounters; children of like minds seek each other out and then further sustain each other's interests. This applies even to the motivation to learn and achieve at school, as found in a study by Kindermann (1993) of 9- and 10-year-old children. For one thing, at the start of the school year these children tended to affiliate with others who shared their particular level of academic motivation; for another, at the end of the year the groups had reorganized in such a way that each had preserved its motivational level, despite considerable turnover of individual members. By mid-childhood the peer group has thus clearly attained an important role in the lives of individual children.

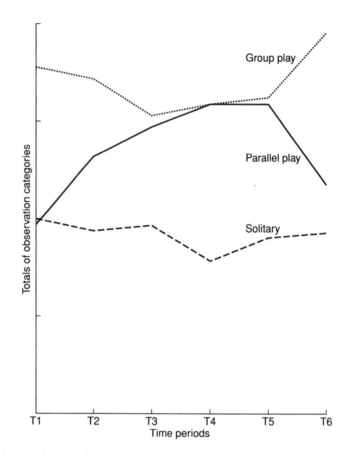

Figure 24   Developmental changes for three types of play (Adapted from Smith, 1978, group 1 measures only)

(5) *Adolescence*   Relationships with peers become even more critical during the adolescent years. As a transitional phase to adult society the kinds of relationships established at this time may well serve as prototypes for subsequent relationships, and though such an assertion is difficult to prove it does underline the vital role which peers now play. One arena in which this is seen is in heterosexual relationships, for mixed-sex groups now reappear and are soon followed by the formation of mixed-sex couples. How to relate to the opposite sex is thus part of the learning process. Another part refers to the use of the peer group as a reference group. Adolescence is often a time of considerable uncertainty, both about the self and about society in general, and peers can provide both support and guidance in defining one's role and one's values. It is therefore not surprising to find that conformity to the peer culture rises sharply in early adolescence, waning only in the approach to adulthood when the individual has a more firmly established sense of identity (Berndt, 1979). The extent

to which that conformity brings young people into conflict with their parents can easily be overstated: divergence is often confined to relatively minor matters such as dress or taste in music, and in general peer pressure is more likely to be against antisocial activity than towards it (B. B. Brown, Clasen, & Eicher, 1986). All this means that the function of the peer group undergoes some marked changes in adolescence, as seen in the answers which 10- to 16-year-olds gave to S. F. O'Brien and Bierman (1988) to questions about their perception of peers and how they were influenced by them. The 10-year-olds defined peer groups in terms of shared activities and behavior (e.g. "They hang around together"; "They act tough"); by age 16, however, shared attitudes have become the main criterion. At all ages peers were valued for providing companionship and support; the older adolescents, however, also mentioned their role in supporting feelings of self-worth (e.g. "You feel needed, secure in who you are"; "If they don't accept you, you might feel something is wrong with you").

In summary, peer interactions in the course of childhood tend to become more *frequent*, more *sustained*, more *complex*, more *intimate*, and more *cohesive*. These are general trends; however, there are considerable variations among children in the kind of relationships they form, and to these we turn next.

Popular, Rejected, and Neglected Children

By far the most attention has been given to differences between children in popularity with peers. Whether a child is popular or unpopular has considerable implications for that individual's well-being at the time; what has also become clear is that the nature of acceptance or rejection by the peer group can have more far reaching implications with respect to future adjustment and mental health.

To ascertain a child's popularity psychologists have used a variety of *sociometric techniques* (Hymel, 1983). Thus children may be given a list of class mates' names or photos and asked "Who would you most like to play with?" or they may be asked questions about each individual class mate such as "How much would you like to be with (play with, work with, etc.) this child?" and thus produce ratings for the child on a scale of like–dislike. On the basis of such peer nominations the degree of any given child's popularity can then be ascertained.

Initially popularity was regarded as a unidimensional continuum, at one end of which children are generally accepted by their group while at the other end they are rejected. Further work has shown that more subtle distinctions are required (Dodge, 1983; A. F. Newcomb, Bukowski, & Pattee, 1993); in particular that unpopular children fall into two very different categories, namely *rejected* and *neglected* children. The former are actively disliked; the latter may not be popular but they are not disliked. In most studies three groups have therefore been compared, namely popular (or accepted), rejected, and neglected children, though "average" children and sometimes also "controversial" children (i.e. those who are liked by some and disliked by others) have also been added.

As seen in table 47, the three main groups are characterized by distinct behavioral profiles. Popular children are liked because they have outgoing, friendly personalities, are skilled at interacting both in dyadic and in group settings and can take the lead in activities without undue aggression. Rejected children are inept in peer interaction: many of them indulge in inappropriate and disruptive behavior and are often antisocial and aggressive towards others, and though they may frequently attempt to join group activities they tend to be rebuffed because of their aversive characteristics. Neglected children are also inept in peer interaction: they tend to avoid dyadic encounters and spend more time with larger groups; however, because of their shyness they mostly play on their own, rarely asserting themselves or showing aggression towards others.

Do children become unpopular because they have certain personality characteristics and are therefore not accepted by their peers, or are those characteristics caused

Table 47 Behavioral profiles of popular, rejected, and neglected children

Popular children
- Positive, happy dispositions
- Physically attractive
- Lot of dyadic interaction
- High levels of cooperative play
- Willing to share
- Able to sustain an interaction
- Seen as good leaders
- Little aggression

Rejected children
- Much disruptive behavior
- Argumentative and antisocial
- Extremely active
- Talkative
- Frequent attempts at social approaches
- Little cooperative play, unwilling to share
- Much solitary activity
- Inappropriate behavior

Neglected children
- Shy
- Rarely aggressive; withdraw in face of others' aggression
- Little antisocial behavior
- Not assertive
- Lot of solitary activity
- Avoid dyadic interaction, more time with larger groups

by their exclusion from children's groups? The latter explanation, though not perhaps as obvious as the former, is certainly a plausible one: the rejected child cannot develop social interaction skills and will therefore behave ineptly, unable to share and cooperate and indulging instead in eye-catching behavior such as talkativeness and hyperactivity in order to obtain entry to peer groups. Similarly neglected children may become shy and solitary just because they are neglected. In order to sort out the cause–effect sequence Dodge (1983; Dodge, Coie, Pettit, & Price, 1990) set up groups from previously unacquainted children (mostly in the 6- to 8-year range), assessed their personality characteristics at the beginning and then observed how, in a series of meetings, their social status gradually began to emerge. The findings show clearly that children bring characteristics with them which then cause others to respond in particular ways. This is especially evident in the case of children who become rejected: they tend to engage in the sort of behavior which is unlikely to bring positive reactions from peers, such as aggressiveness, uncooperativeness, and social ineptness, seen especially in their initial approaches to others. Contrast that with children who turn out to be popular: from the beginning they display skillful behavior in group entry and in the management of social interactions; this makes them generally acceptable and quickly establishes their popular status. Yet this does not mean that we must exclude the other explanation: the social experiences which children have in peer groups may well reinforce the dispositions which brought about these experiences in the first place, strengthening them and thus making it in turn even more likely that they will encounter further such experiences.

If such a circular feedback system is in operation we can expect continuity in children's social status: once rejected (or neglected or popular) always rejected (or neglected or popular). Some support for this expectation is found in a five-year follow-up study by Coie and Dodge (1983) of groups of third-graders and fifth-graders. Yearly sociometric data for these children showed considerable stability, even though they changed school during this time and puberty intervened. The year-to-year stability was greatest in the case of rejected children: they were least likely to change their status. As the length of the test–retest interval increased stability coefficients decreased somewhat; again, however, this was less evident in the case of rejected children.

It is therefore rejected children who must give rise to greatest concern. There are indications that neglected children, when transferred to a different peer group, may become accepted by their new companions; rejected children, on the other hand, are likely to retain their social status (A. F. Newcomb, Bukowski, & Pattee, 1993). Moreover rejected children, in certain respects at least, tend to think of themselves in negative terms (Malik & Furman, 1993), i.e. as less competent socially, as more anxious and as having fewer positive expectations from interpersonal relationships. Yet many rejected children are also unrealistic in their self-concepts: according to C. J. Patterson, Kupersmidt, and Griesler (1990) such children tend to have inflated views of the extent to which they are accepted by their peers – a distortion which no doubt serves to protect them against painful reality.

What is of most concern, however, is the growing body of evidence which shows that rejected children are liable to develop serious adjustment problems later in life, with particular reference to externalizing difficulties, i.e. those involving aggression, conduct disorders, and antisocial behavior. Poor quality of peer relationships in childhood, it appears, is predicative of subsequent psychological maladjustment; in particular, children who are rejected by their age mates constitute an at-risk group. Among the long-term consequences that have been found are poor academic achievement, dropout from school, juvenile delinquency, violence, adult criminality, and certain forms of psychopathology (Kupersmidt, Coie, & Dodge, 1990; Parker & Asher, 1987). A study by Kupersmidt and Coie (1990) illustrates the link between peer rejection and subsequent problems. These investigators followed up 11-year-old children for seven years in order to compare popular, average, neglected, and rejected children on various outcome measures in late adolescence. The findings (as illustrated in figure 25) show clearly that rejected children turned out to be most at risk: they were twice as likely to have become truants as other children; they were also more likely to have dropped out of school or been suspended or to have been kept back a class; by late adolescence they were three times more likely to have come into contact with the police than average children (something which popular children had avoided altogether); and in general the likelihood that the rejected children had developed some sort of nonspecific problem, whether at school or outside, was far greater than that of any other group. Neglected children, on the other

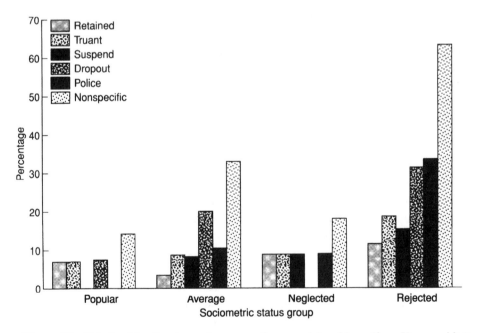

Figure 25   Relationship of sociometric status to future social problems (from Kupersmidt & Coie, 1990)

hand, showed little indication that they were at risk for the development of social maladjustment.

To find a link between early peer status and subsequent adjustment is useful but not enough: one also needs to explain how it is brought about. There are various possibilities: perhaps both poor peer relationships and later maladjustment are the result of a more general psychological disturbance; or it may be that peer rejection gives rise to deviant socialization experiences which in turn lead to a deviant lifestyle; or possibly the lack of social support makes rejected children more vulnerable to stress and thus more likely to become maladjusted. As yet we do not know enough to arrive at any definite conclusions, but in the meantime let us note one other possibility for which there is at least some support and which highlights the crucial role of aggressive tendencies in rejected children. In fact, not all rejected children are characterized by aggression, and when one compares those who are aggressive with those who are not it turns out that the former are considerably more at risk for later social maladjustment than the latter. Thus, when Kupersmidt and Coie (1990), in the study we have just described, compared the predictive powers of measures of aggression with measures of rejection they found the former to be a more accurate index of the extent to which children in their mixed racial sample developed behavior problems than the latter. As we saw in chapter 6, aggressiveness is a relatively persistent trait throughout childhood and is associated with externalizing problems such as truancy, delinquency, and violence – i.e. the problems which characterize rejected children. Add to that the fact that children, rejected by their ordinary peer group, frequently become involved in antisocial groups where they find ready acceptance of their aggressive behavior (Dishion, Patterson, Stoolmiller, & Skinner, 1991), and one can see that aggressiveness in rejected children may well play a vital part in linking peer status with later outcome.

But what about the subgroup of rejected children who are not aggressive? What accounts for their social status? Work by Rubin and his colleagues (e.g. K. H. Rubin, LeMare, & Lollis, 1990; K. H. Rubin & Coplan, 1992) draws attention to the role of *social withdrawal*: a pattern, that is, characterizing children who are behaviorally inhibited to a marked extent, are extremely unassertive in their social interactions and who thus become isolated and rejected by their peers for their unwillingness to join in with others. As a result they too are at risk for the development of psychological problems. Take a study by Hymel, Rubin, Rowden, and LeMare (1990), in which 7-year-old children were assessed on a large number of measures, including sociometric peer ratings, and followed up over a three-year period. Those classified as rejected because of aggressiveness were found to develop *externalizing* problems (involving interpersonal hostility, lack of impulse control and distractibility) – a finding which replicates that of other studies we have mentioned. Rejected children characterized by social withdrawal also developed difficulties but these were of an *internalizing* nature, i.e. fearfulness, anxiety, and withdrawal. These findings therefore suggest that withdrawn children are also an at-risk group, though for a different kind of behavioral pathology.

Peer relationships take many varied forms and it is therefore not surprising that the original classification according to degree of popularity was soon found inadequate and that finer distinctions were required. Thus unpopular children were divided into those who are rejected and those who are neglected; then a further subdivision was proposed for rejected children, i.e. rejected-aggressive and rejected-withdrawn children. No doubt yet other distinctions will need to be made as a result of further research, but what has become very apparent is that the kind of relationships which are formed with peers can offer an insight into the coping mechanisms which children employ in adjusting to their social world, and that the nature of these mechanisms can tell one quite a lot about the likely development of later adjustment problems.

The case of treatment for peer relationship difficulties

In view of the importance of peer relations, both at the time and prognostically, it would be useful to intervene in those cases where children fail to establish proper relationships with the aim of bringing about some improvement in their interpersonal abilities. Various kinds of approaches have been explored to this end (Malik & Furman, 1993), of which those involving the training of specific social skills are the most prominent.

Such programs generally start off by diagnosing the child's particular difficulties and then by breaking down the required skills into specific components. Thus in situations such as joining other children in their ongoing activity or cooperating with others in carrying out a particular task certain strategies are required to bring about acceptance, and while most children adopt these automatically some require help in doing so in an appropriate manner. Different programs adopt different methods in offering such help. In some programs children watch films in order to learn certain skills from models which they then, after discussion with a trainer, practice in similar situations. In others children role-play social situations while the adult comments on their techniques and, by making them aware of problems as they arise, helps to modify their behavior as required. Alternately a reinforcement approach is adopted, based on praise of

"right" and disapproval of "wrong" actions. And in still others a cognitive model underlies the treatment offered, in that it is assumed that the child's difficulties with peers result from misinterpreting social situations and that treatment must therefore consist of counteracting such processing deficiencies through discussion and coaching.

Reports about the effectiveness of programs provide somewhat mixed results (Furman & Gavin, 1989). To some extent this is a matter of how effectiveness is measured: whether, for example, in terms of specific behavior changes or more generally in growing peer acceptance. Also how soon the measures are taken will influence the results obtained. A further consideration is the nature of the peer problem tackled: highly aggressive children, for instance, are least responsive to treatment (Coie & Koepple, 1990). But as to the basic question regarding the kind of program that produces the best results, the indications are that those based on a combination of modeling, reinforcement, practice, and cognitive approaches are most effective (Ladd & Mize, 1983). A great deal still needs to be learned about how to produce change in established social patterns; in the meantime there is at least enough promise in existing work to regard this as an enterprise well worth the effort.

Friendship and Loneliness

Being popular and having friends are not the same thing. On the one hand, it is quite possible for a generally popular child not to have any special friends, and on the other hand a considerable proportion of unpopular children do have one or two friends. In a study of nearly 900 children aged 8 to 10 years from a Midwestern community in the United States whose peer status had been assessed, 45.3 percent of low-accepted, 82.3 percent of average-accepted and 93.8 percent of high-accepted children reported that they had at least one best friend (Parker & Asher, 1993). Thus a relationship between popularity and having friends does exist but is far from perfect. Almost half of the least popular children in this large sample did have friends, while a few of the most popular ones were friendless. It means that friendship is a topic that deserves investigation in its own right.

This is especially so because having friends is important to the great majority of children, and without them they may experience intense loneliness. According to self-report measures containing items such as "It's easy for me to make new friends at school" and "I have nobody to talk to in class" something like 10 percent of children in the 8- to 11-year age range in one American sample reported feeling lonely (Asher, Parkhurst, Hymel, & Williams, 1990). The subjective experience of *feeling* rejected may not always follow actually *being* rejected, but whatever its origin it can give rise to considerable suffering, and in adolescence in particular is associated with depression and a sense of being in limbo, and when the child is deprived of any feeling of social belongingness a loss of self-esteem tends to follow. "You feel like you're an outsider," "It seems like no one wants you," "It's like you're the only one on the moon" – these statements reveal the intense emotions aroused when children feel excluded.

It is perhaps no wonder that children miss having friends, for psychologically this relationship fulfills a number of important functions, of which the provision of companionship and sheer fun is the most obvious immediate benefit to children. When Foot, Chapman and Smith (1977) asked pairs of children to watch some humorous cartoons together they found that friends got much more enjoyment out of the experience than nonfriends: the former laughed and smiled more, there was more talking and looking at each other, and in general friends showed greater social responsiveness and more "response matching," i.e. a sharing of mood and behavior. However, there are also other, more distal functions. Hartup (1992) lists the following:

1   friendships are contexts in which children can acquire or elaborate basic social skills like social communication and cooperation;
2   they provide children with self-knowledge as well as knowledge about other people and about the world;
3   they give children emotional support in the face of stress; and
4   they are forerunners of subsequent relationships (romantic, marital, and parental) in that they provide experience of handling intimacy and mutual regulation.

None of these functions is wholly unique to friendship; the friendless child can still develop in ways acceptable to society. But friendships provide an arena where feelings of self-worth are promoted to an extent that, especially from preadolescence on, is not found in other relationships and where intimate disclosure is possible that young people often find difficult with family members.

But what do children themselves think friendship is all about? When children are asked questions such as "What is a friend?" or "Why do you have friends?" their answers show progressive changes as they become older (e.g. Bigelow & La Gaipa, 1980; Furman & Bierman, 1983). In preschool and early school years friends are seen as playmates with whom children can share certain activities ("Tommy is my friend because we play together") or simply in terms of propinquity ("He lives next door"). Subsequently, in mid-childhood, shared values and tastes are emphasized ("We both like pop music"), as well as reciprocated liking of each other's company. Finally, from about 12 years on, friendships are thought about in terms of opportunities for exchanging secrets, sharing feelings, and expecting help with psychological problems ("You need someone you can tell anything to, all kinds of things that you don't want to spread around"). These changes reflect the cognitive changes in self- and other-understanding that we talked about in chapter 4. Initially children judge people in concrete terms – the activities they engage in, their appearance, their location, and so forth. Subsequently they become able to infer others' emotional states and think about them in terms of permanent psychological dispositions. Eventually relationships as such can be thought about and friendship comes to be defined as a special tie that makes self-disclosure possible among intimately connected individuals (Youniss, 1980).

The nature of friendship shows other developmental changes. First, when do friendships begin to play a part in children's lives? The answer depends largely on how one defines friendship. Observations in day care settings have shown that some children in their second year already show preferences in their choice of playmate that remain constant over a whole year (Howes, 1987). However, such choices, dependent on familiarity and compatibility, are usually limited to particular settings and activities; it is not till the fourth year that they become more clear-cut and differentiated (Hartup, 1992). Friendships also become more common then: according to Hinde, Titmus, Easton, and Tamplin (1985) about half of the 4-year-olds they observed had at least one "strong associate," that is, children with whom they spent at least 30 percent of their time when both were together in nursery school. About a third of these children had more than one such a relationship. After school entry this number increases sharply: in one study (Reisman & Shorr, 1978) children in second grade named about four friends each; in seventh grade this number had gone up to about seven each. In adolescence there is again a slight decline in the number of friends (Hartup, 1992), though this is compensated for by the increased depth of the relationships formed. Friendships also become more stable in later childhood: when Berndt and Hoyle (1985) asked children in the first and in the fourth grades at the beginning of the school year to name their best friends and then repeated their question at the end of the year, they found 54 percent of the younger and 76 percent of the older children named the same individuals. In many cases, of course, friendships last much longer, though to a considerable extent that depends on opportunity to meet, whether through being in the same class or living in the same neighborhood.

The most marked developmental change, however, concerns the use to which friendship is put, and this is most evident with respect to self-disclosure and the sharing of private feelings and thoughts. It is this which characterizes the difference between children's and adolescents' friendships, for the latter show an intimacy which does not occur in earlier years (Youniss, 1980). This is partly a reflection of the change from involvement with parents to involvement with peers: conversations with friends, for instance, reveal a readiness for self-disclosure that is not found in conversations with parents (Youniss & Smollar, 1985). This occurs especially among girls: pairs of girls who are best friends are more prepared to share secrets and reveal things about themselves than is found in male pairs or, for that matter, in the mixed sex pairs that become increasingly prevalent during adolescence (Dolgin & Kim, 1994). It has been suggested that the reason for this sex difference is that girls are more oriented towards interpersonal relationships while boys are primarily interested in action and achievement. This is speculative; what is clear is that among adolescents generally friendships come to assume a deeper and more profound meaning than existed before, and that by the same token a lack of friends gives rise to more intense feelings of loneliness than can be found at any time in earlier years.

A large number of studies show that being without friends is associated with a variety of more or less undesirable developmental outcomes. These are summarized in table 48. Let us, however, note three provisos when examining these associations. First, friendlessness may be a purely temporary state; while that may give rise to feelings of loneliness it is unlikely to be related to any more lasting emotional problem. Second, while friendless children in general are a group at risk by no means all are affected; some children do not seem to need friends for healthy psychological development. And third, it is at present difficult to sort out cause from effect in the association between friendlessness and developmental conditions: it may be that lack

Table 48 Conditions associated with friendlessness

Children without friends are more likely
- to have emotional problems
- to lag behind other children in perspective taking abilities
- to be less altruistic
- to have deficiencies in such social skills as group entry, cooperative play, and conflict management
- to be generally less sociable
- to show poorer school adjustment
- to make fewer educational gains

of friendship experience brings about deficiencies in social skills, emotional problems, and so forth; it is, however, also possible that children having such problems are less attractive to peers and therefore less likely to make friends.

Peer Cooperation

It is easy to concentrate on the negative aspects of peer interaction – the conflicts, fighting, and rivalry that undoubtedly do occur whenever children come together, and neglect the positive aspects that may be less dramatic but that really form the core of children's relationships with one another. This is indeed what happened in the history of peer research, which in its early phases gave the impression that peer interaction was just a constant battleground. It is only comparatively recently that the balance has been corrected and that we have come to learn about children cooperating together, children helping each other, children learning from each other, and children being cared for and socialized by other children.

A notable example is found in *peer collaborative learning* – a phenomenon that has attracted considerable research interest of late (e.g. C. Howe, 1993) and that has wide-ranging theoretical and educational implications. In the past there was a general assumption that the knowledge and skills which children acquire in the course of development are handed down from adults, be they parents or teachers; that other children are simply irrelevant in this respect; and that educational practice must therefore reflect this one-way, downward process of transmission. It has become increasingly apparent, however, that such an assumption is misleading, for as a growing body of research is showing, the possibility that children can contribute substantially to each other's intellectual development cannot be ignored. As Foot, Morgan, and Shute (1990) point out, it is a myth that children are only *recipients* of help and instruction; they too are capable of playing a very real part as instructors and helpers if only given the opportunity and responsibility.

It is useful to distinguish between three types of peer collaborative learning (Damon & Phelps, 1989):

1   *Peer tutoring*   This refers to those situations in which one child helps another by providing instruction and guidance. Strictly speaking this is not collaborative learning, for the children stand in a teacher–learner relationship vis-à-vis each other; in practice, however, the teaching child also frequently benefits from the experience. Furthermore, in so far as the teaching child is often older than the learner child the two, strictly speaking, are not peers. What matters, however, is that there is a certain degree of asymmetry in the knowledge possessed by the pair and it is around this that their interaction revolves.

2   *Cooperative learning*   In this arrangement children are organized by a teacher into groups or teams, each of which is assigned a problem or task which the team must tackle jointly. They may do so by breaking the task down into parts for

which particular individuals assume responsibility; all members, however, have a common goal and are presumably motivated to achieve this by a team spirit that they have acquired. Thus the children inspire and support each other; success depends on their joint effort.

3   *Peer collaboration*   Instead of one child learning from another, more experienced one (as in peer tutoring), both children are equally ignorant at the start of the task. There is no teacher who passes down knowledge to a learner; the relationship between the two participants is a wholly symmetrical one and based on mutual interest and trust rather than on authority. The learning process is thus a matter of joint discovery: by active discussion and exchange of ideas, and by sharing their own partial and incomplete perspectives, the children eventually reach a solution when neither would have been able to do so alone. Having to interact with someone who has a different view of the problem challenges children to examine their own ideas, and as a result a new approach may emerge which is more appropriate as solution than the children's individual conceptions. Two heads, it seems, are better than one.

The distinction between these three types is not wholly a mutually exclusive one; nevertheless, it is a useful one in drawing attention to different features of the joint learning process. By far the most interest in recent years has been aroused by the third type, i.e. peer collaboration, for the notion that children working *jointly* can make intellectual advances which are beyond them when working alone and, moreover, that they can do so without any input from a more knowledgeable person is an intriguing one which is now supported by a considerable body of research. Much of this work originated in studies carried out by Willem Doise and his colleagues (e.g. Doise & Mugny, 1984; Doise, 1990). The research design adopted in these studies generally involved a pre-test in which the child's basal performance level was established, followed by random assignment to either a dyadic or an individual problem-solving condition. This was succeeded by a post-test when the child's performance on that problem was again assessed in an individual session. Most of Doise's tasks involved the traditional conservation problems which Piaget investigated in individual children; other investigators, however, have also employed such diverse tasks as spatial coordination, legal thinking, moral reasoning, and mathematics, as well as computer-based learning assignments (Crook, 1992). The findings from the majority of these studies show that dyadic performance is superior to solo performance: when naive children tackle a problem together they advance more in their understanding than when they work on their own. This is found not only on immediate post-tests but subsequently, indicating that a real intellectual advance has occurred. A 6-year-old child, for instance, who on a pre-test shows no awareness of the conservation of quantity, can gain insight into this concept and correctly solves other quantity conservation problems after working together with another 6-year-old who initially was just as ignorant.

Let us note, however, that the superiority of joint over solo performance does not occur invariably. It depends on a number of conditions which are outlined in table 49. Some of these concern the child's standing vis-à-vis the task; others refer to aspects of the interpersonal relationship of the two partners. Peer interaction, we must conclude, is of benefit to learning, but not under all conditions.

How can we explain the effectiveness of peer collaboration? It cannot be due to either instruction or imitation, as both children are equally incompetent to begin with. According to Doise, the mechanism responsible for change is *sociocognitive conflict*, which occurs when a child comes up against another (though not necessarily correct) viewpoint in the course of joint problem solving that differs from the child's own. Mental restructuring is then required, in so far as the child must coordinate the partner's ideas with his or her own, and from this an approach to the problem may emerge that is not only different from but more advanced than the child's previous approach when working alone. However, this cannot happen merely through the passive presentation of alternative viewpoints; children must be actively engaged in opposing their particular opinion and reasoning with those of their partner. Such confrontation is disturbing, and the children therefore attempt to reduce the disturbance by coordinating their respective viewpoints – a coordination which brings about a reorganization of each child's individual ideas. Social interaction thus becomes a source of cognitive progress by virtue of the sociocognitive conflict it engenders (Doise, 1990).

Not all agree that it is the element of conflict that is the crucial mechanism which accounts for the effects produced by peer interaction. On the contrary, Damon and Phelps (1989) argue that *cooperation* is the key facilitator, pointing to studies that

Table 49   Variables influencing the effectiveness of peer collaboration

Variable	*Nature of influence*
	Peer collaboration is likely to be hindered if:
Age	Children are too young (i.e. up to early preschool years) to engage in constructive dialogue
Task difficulty	The task is too difficult in relation to the children's cognitive level
Between–children discrepancy	The children differ greatly in their respective base levels of understanding the problem
Dominance–passivity	One child is too domineering and/or the other child is too passive for cooperative behavior to emerge
Conflict intensity	The relationship is too conflictual for a joint solution to be possible
Interpersonal acquaintance	The children are too unfamiliar and wary in their relationship to explore each other's thinking and share their own ideas

Sources: Foot et al. (1990); C. Howe (1993)

show an inverse relationship between amount of peer disagreement and subsequent cognitive progress. Thus children who disagreed with one another the most were least likely to make progress, whereas children who accepted one another's view were the most likely to advance. In fact the two positions are not as far apart as they seem (Kruger, 1993): as analyses of children's dialog in such situations show, conflict is not just a matter of head-on confrontation but an extended discourse that explores the reasoning behind the different viewpoints presented. Thus the pairs of 8-year-olds whom Kruger studied while discussing the resolution of moral dilemmas spent time both agreeing and disagreeing. On the one hand they produced ideas for the partner to respond to, offered information about ideas, and helped each other in accepting or rejecting particular solutions. On the other they also criticized each other's ideas, pointing out the shortcomings of the peer's suggestions and pushing forward their own, allegedly better proposals. It seems that what matters is that the child encounters multiple perspectives on the same problem which must then somehow be reconciled. Precisely how much conflict or cooperation is involved in this process is of less consequence than the need to integrate the various perspectives into one final product. *Cooperative co-construction* is thus the key, and this occurs whenever two (or more) individuals explore each others' thoughts in order then to create a new, joint outcome.

The case of science education through peer interaction

If peer interaction can promote the growth of understanding with respect to problems such as conservation and sociomoral issues, what about its contribution to "real" educational topics of the kind taught in school? In a series of studies Howe and her colleagues (C. Howe, Tolmie, & Rodgers, 1990, 1992; Tolmie, Howe, Mackenzie, & Greer, 1993) investigated not just whether but by what means peer interaction enables children to learn about scientific concepts such as those involved in understanding why objects float or sink and what accounts for the speed of objects down an incline.

Children in the 8- to 12-year range were first given a pre-test in order to assess their initial conceptions of such phenomena. They were then assigned to groups of four, some of which contained children with similar and others with different kinds of conceptions. Each group was given a set of problems (e.g. having to predict whether a metal key and a plastic ring would float or sink in different types of liquid) and asked to discuss these in order to come to an agreed answer. No adult was present during these group sessions, but the children were videotaped in order to record both their behavior and their comments ("I think it'll float because it's got air inside"; "It'll not go very far because the slope isn't very steep"; etc.). Post-tests were subsequently administered, immediately following the group sessions and several weeks later, in order to see whether the children's understanding had improved in comparison with their pre-test performance.

The results show that such improvement did indeed take place. However, the advance was found on the later post-test rather than that immediately following the group session, presumably because of the need for consolidation of the insights gained. Time is thus required before the benefits appear. In addition, improvement was evident in those groups which were composed of children with initially differing rather than similar conceptions, supporting the Piagetian assertion that children can construct concepts at a higher level through joint discussion but only when they approach the problem from initially differing points of view. Even quite young children do not approach problems such as those posed in these studies with a completely blank mind; they already have certain preconceptions which may be quite inadequate but which enable them to compare their ideas with other children's inadequate ideas and, through the ensuing discussion, jointly produce a superior solution which each child then assimilates into his or her understanding of the problem.

These results suggest that science education too can benefit from the use of peer interaction. This may be hard to accept because of the convention that children only progress as a result of explicit instruction from more knowledgeable teachers. It appears, however, that the mutual help provided by children, equally ignorant though they may be at first, must not be neglected; group discussion among peers can also have a place in the curriculum.

Interface of Peer and Family Relationships

Families and peers provide the two main arenas wherein children's socialization takes place. In the past each has been investigated in its own right; however, what occurs in one inevitably has implications for the other. This applies especially to the influence of parent–child relationships on peer relationships, and though no doubt the reverse influence pattern can also be found it is to the former that most attention has recently been given (see Parke & Ladd, 1992; K. H. Rubin, 1994).

The links between the two systems take various forms, of which three are most notable (Parke et al., 1989):

1   parental socialization strategies, in so far as these bring about certain characteristics in children which are then displayed in social interactions, including those with peers;
2   parents' explicit education of their children in peer interaction: parents, that is, instruct their children in the most appropriate ways of playing with others and support and maintain the relationships formed;
3   parents function as managers of their children's social lives: they provide opportunities for contact with other children and thus actively determine both the extent of that contact and with whom it takes place.

It is important to bear in mind that the parents' influence can be both positive and negative. Take the last mentioned parental function, that of manager. On the one hand, parents can take such positive steps as enrolling the child in a preschool group, inviting other children to the home, or sending the child to summer camp – all ways designed to provide opportunities for contact with peers. On the other hand, they may disrupt the child's friendships by moving away from the neighborhood or placing the child in another school; alternately, a possessive parent may simply discourage the child from having contacts with others outside the home. What is apparent is that the processes linking a child's two kinds of relationships, those with parents and those with peers, can take a considerable variety of forms, some of which may be more important at certain developmental stages than at others.

There is a further distinction which we can usefully make in trying to understand the nature of the linkage. This is between *direct* and *indirect* influences of the one system on the other (Ladd, 1992). *Direct* influences are mainly those which relate to parents as educators and managers of their children's peer related activities (the second and third types listed above); here the parent is trying quite explicitly to guide the child towards certain kinds of interaction with others, thus facilitating (or hindering) the child's attempts to enter the peer culture. Such a role is particularly evident in the early preschool years when most children begin to make more extensive contacts outside the home. It is seen, for example, in the finding that preschoolers whose parents actively initiate peer contacts tend to have more friends and more consistent partners than children whose parents do not involve themselves in such arrangements; the former children are also more likely to be accepted by their classmates when they enter kindergarten (Ladd & Golter, 1988). The parents' influence is also seen at a more subtle level in, for instance, the way in which they intervene in their children's play with others: as Ladd and Golter found in their sample, the more intrusive and controlling the mothers were the more likely it was that their children failed to develop the necessary skills for social play. Those children, on the other hand, whose mothers were less directive, content to watch from a distance and intervene only occasionally, tended to show a greater degree of social competence.

Indirect influences take many forms, but in general they are based on the assumption that the quality of parenting experienced in the family will affect the nature of the child's peer relationships. One example we referred to in chapter 3 when discussing the consequences of forming secure or insecure attachments to the mother: according to some studies (e.g. Elicker, Englund, & Sroufe, 1992) the quality of the mother–infant relationship is a reliable predictor of the child's later peer relationships, and as that quality may be determined by the mother's sensitivity to her baby in the early months an association appears to exist between certain maternal characteristics and the child's later ability to form peer relationships – an indirect relationship indeed, but one believed to be mediated by the internal working models which, as we saw, are established through attachments and tend to be generalized to other relationships formed by the child. Such a link has not been confirmed by all studies (Lamb & Nash, 1989), but if it does exist it is presumably based on the confidence which the child derives from a secure initial attachment and which will then carry over to other social spheres.

Various other aspects of parental child rearing techniques have also been associated with the development of peer competence (see Ladd, 1992; and Putallaz &

Heflin, 1990, for summaries). Some of these involve global parental styles such as authoritativeness; others refer to the type of discipline used by parents (e.g. induction versus power assertion); and still others, usually derived from direct observation, describe the specific practices parents employ in interacting with their children – the amount of their directiveness, the extent to which they elicit positive affect, their ability to sustain play activities, and so on. The main characteristics which emerge from this work as capable of fostering children's competence with peers are:

- *parental warmth*, endorsed by many studies as a major contributor to the way in which children interact with other children;
- *parental control*, which ideally should be moderate in degree, as both excessive and inadequate control have been found to lead to aggressiveness in children and thence to rejection in the peer group;
- *parental involvement*, i.e. parents should be interested in and responsive to the activities of their children, who will then develop the inner security which can help in becoming socially accepted;
- a *democratic attitude*, because when this prevails in the family children are more likely to develop the necessary interactive skills required for egalitarian relationships such as those found in peer groups.

One other type of indirect influence linking family and peer systems is the parent's personality. To take one example: Kolvin and colleagues (1977) found that a significant relationship existed between mothers' sociability and the extent to which their children were rejected or neglected by peers. Thus mothers low on sociability (as measured by their contacts with neighbors) were more likely to have unpopular children than more sociable mothers – a difference presumably brought about by the different child rearing techniques used by sociable as opposed to unsociable women.

The chain of influences suggested by this account is illustrated in figure 26 by the solid arrows. The child rearing methods adopted by parents are those which they find congenial in relation to their own personality characteristics. These techniques help to shape the child's personality, and this in turn will determine how the child behaves with peers and the status attained in the peer group. Yet, as one so often finds, such a one-way causal sequence is probably oversimplified. We know, for example, that child rearing methods are affected not only by the parent's but also the child's personality characteristics. We have also discussed the likelihood that a child's acceptance or rejection by peers will react back on that child, possibly producing lasting changes in behavior patterns. And finally we must take into account the possibility that a child's behavior in the peer group may not be influenced by child rearing experiences but by the genetic factors which are shared with the parent. That family and peer systems are linked cannot be doubted; the nature of that linkage, however, and the way it is produced clearly require highly complex explanations.

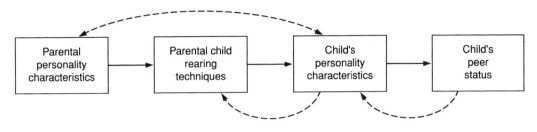

Figure 26   Links between family and peer system

The Child in Society

Family and peer group are in many respects the most immediate contexts in which children's development occurs, but there are many other sets of social influences that also play a decisive role in that development. Some of these, such as the school to which a child goes, impinge on children directly, in that the child comes into immediate contact with and so experiences them at first hand. Others have an indirect influence; these are social conditions which are mediated primarily by the child's interpersonal relationships and thus become meaningful through other people's reactions to them. A country's economic conditions, for example, are an abstraction far removed from a child's experience, yet poverty and unemployment can profoundly transform children's lives because of their impact on the parents and thus on the kind of upbringing which they provide for their children. In the same way race and ethnicity are abstractions which are translated into direct influences on a child by the way in which other people respond to them.

A noteworthy attempt to provide a theoretical framework in which to place all such social influences has been made by Bronfenbrenner (1979). His *ecological systems theory* emphasizes the fact that children's development can only be understood if closely related to the particular environmental settings which they experience, whether directly or indirectly. There is a multiplicity of such settings, but according to Bronfenbrenner these may best be viewed as a set of nested systems, each inside the next, rather like a set of Russian dolls. As shown in figure 27, there are four layers that one can usefully distinguish:

1   *Microsystems* are the immediate settings of a child's life which have a direct impact on experience. Families, peer groups, day care centers, and schools are the most common examples.
2   *Mesosystems* refer to the links between microsystems. As we saw in the case of the family and the peer group, what happens in one may well affect what happens in the other, and the relationships between them must therefore also be taken into account. Similarly family and school: the linkages between the two settings are many and experience in one may well profoundly affect the child's experience in the other.

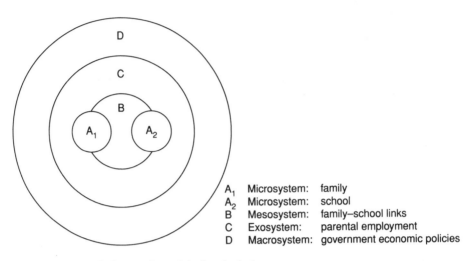

A₁   Microsystem: family
A₂   Microsystem: school
B   Mesosystem: family–school links
C   Exosystem: parental employment
D   Macrosystem: government economic policies

Figure 27   Bronfenbrenner's model of ecological systems

3   *Exosystems* are those settings in which the child does not directly participate but which do affect the way the microsystem functions. Examples are the parents' employment and work experience: what happens there will influence the child via the parents' reaction to them.

4   *Macrosystems* are the final level. These are furthest removed from the child's direct experience and yet may ultimately have some very profound effects. Social values, ideologies, and political institutions (such as reflected, for instance, in government economic decisions) are amongst these; explicit or implicit policies regarding such matters as race and class are further examples. Macrosystems contain all the other levels and their influence permeates through all.

One of the main points emphasized by this way of viewing the child's environment is the close interdependence between levels. Most research in the past has confined itself to examining the impact of immediate settings, yet (to take an example) the warmth and interest a parent shows towards a child may well be closely related to the parent's job satisfaction, which in turn is dependent on government policies concerning such matters as conditions of employment and the provision of child care facilities. To do justice to the complexity of interdependent influences in any one investigation is extraordinarily difficult; it is therefore no wonder that most of what we know about social influences on children is somewhat piecemeal, and that it is only of late that efforts have been made to link up the various levels.

The Social System of the School

Of the various social institutions that we shall consider the school is a particularly significant one. Not only do children spend a large amount of time there – *Fifteen thousand hours*, as the title of one report (Rutter, Maughan, Mortimore, & Ouston, 1979) reminds us – but the school is also the child's first introduction to a quite different kind of system to that of the family. It is very much larger, it is more formally organized, and the purpose that it serves and the roles that people play within it are different from those the child has been used to at home. The primary function of the school may be to help children advance academically, but the learning opportunities it provides encompass much more than is represented by the content of lessons. In order to run efficiently schools must have sets of rules which are found, for example, in timetables that have to be followed, codes of discipline that need to be obeyed and regulations about conduct and appearance which children are expected to know. Schools therefore need to convey not only academic knowledge but also the social norms which enable the institution to run effectively.

What is "effectiveness" when applied to schools and what determines it? A great deal of research effort has been devoted to providing an answer (see review by Sylva, 1994), and table 50 lists the principal characteristics where a measure of agreement has now been reached as to how effective schools can be differentiated from ineffective. What is noteworthy, however, is that these specific characteristics usually occur together: effective schools are high and ineffective schools are low on the majority of them. Thus schools provide a particular "ethos" which distinguishes each as a whole, and it is this which accounts for the effects produced on its children.

A study by Rutter and colleagues (1979) provides some clear support for this notion. It is based on 12 secondary schools in London, attended mostly by working class children among whom quite a few came from disadvantaged backgrounds. Information about the children's background and achievements was gathered from records and tests, and data were also obtained from attendance records and teachers' ratings of classroom behavior. Four main "outcome" measures were constructed: academic achievement, misbehavior, attendance rate, and delinquency. Considerable differences among the 12 schools were found in these measures; as, moreover, these were correlated to a high degree a general impression of effectiveness was created. So

Table 50   Characteristics differentiating effective from ineffective schools

- Strong educational leadership
- High expectations of student achievement
- Emphasis on basic skills
- An orderly climate
- Regular evaluation of students' progress
- Homework assigned regularly
- Firm but not severe discipline
- Widespread opportunities for children to take responsibility
- High proportion of teacher time interacting with class as a whole
- Clear feedback to students on their performance
- Ample use of praise of good performance

Source: Based on Rutter (1983); and Sylva (1994)

what is responsible for these differences among schools? Neither the children's family background nor their personal characteristics on entry to the school could account for them; there was also no relationship with such physical features of the school as age of buildings, space, size of school or size of class. Instead, "school processes" provided the answer, i.e. those aspects of a school which relate to its social organization, pattern of personal relationships and style of group management. These referred to such specific matters as the degree of academic emphasis, the availability of teachers for consultation, the system of rewards and punishment, the extent to which children were given responsibility and the amount of time teachers spent on educational topics as opposed to extraneous matters, and were measured by means of interviews with teachers, questionnaires and observations of classroom activities. There were altogether 39 of such measures, and in combination they were found to be more closely related to the outcome variables than were any of them individually. In short, they added up to a particular *ethos* which distinguished individual schools; the effectiveness of schools depended on that ethos, and how children behaved at school was thus largely a function of the psychological environment which they experienced in the school they attended.

There are many specific aspects of school organization that have been investigated in their own right, and none more so than the "traditional" versus "open" dichotomy. Traditional classrooms are those where children sit at rows of desks facing the teacher, where teaching is by means of formal instruction addressed to the whole class, and where a fixed curriculum determines what is taught. In open classrooms a different physical arrangement prevails: there are various areas for each educational activity and children move around the room, working individually or in small groups. There is also a different curricular arrangement, in that teachers are more flexible in what is taught and rely less on formal instruction and more on student initiative. The two approaches represent different educational philosophies, but evaluation of their relative effectiveness is made difficult by the fact that different kinds of parents (and children) opt for one or the other. Furthermore, their effectiveness depends on the children's age, in so far as the open system is more suited for younger children; it also depends on the task, in so far as illustrating difficult concepts or the need to transmit a lot of factual information tends to be easier in traditional classrooms (Rutter, 1983). Personality differences also play a role, for some children do better in one kind of regime than the other. Sweeping generalizations about the relative advantages of the two systems are thus unjustified, and it is therefore no wonder that research has come up with frequently conflicting results. A review by P.L. Peterson (1979) of a large number of studies concerned with this problem concluded that measures of achievement gave children from traditional schools a slight advantage, whereas children in open schools were superior in creative thinking and independence. The differences in all these aspects, however, were slight and unimpressive and give little support to the more fervent advocates of either approach.

The effects of school organization become most apparent during transitions from one type of system to another, as seen when children are transferred from preschool to elementary school, and then again on entry to secondary school. At each step the child is confronted with a new system with different rules, requirements, and norms; in each case the new school is generally larger, more work oriented and more formal; and on each occasion the child is expected to make the adaptation to the new system speedily and with little explicit guidance. The following details illustrate what was involved for one typical American group of children going from elementary to junior high school (Simmons, Burgeson, & Careton-Ford, 1987):

> The mean school size increases from 466 to 1,307, and the mean number of children in one's grade from 59 to 403. Instead of one main teacher and a small, stable set of children in one's class, the school becomes bureaucratized and departmentalized, with teachers, classrooms, and often classmates constantly changing over the course of the day. . . . Feelings of anonymity among students increase sharply – feelings of knowing nobody and being known by no one. . . .

As Simmons et al. point out, this transition unfortunately occurs when many children have to make other transitions too, the most important of which is heralded by the onset of puberty, with its implications for physical appearance and for social relationships with the opposite sex. Some children may also happen to be confronted by other changes at that time, e.g. moving to a new neighborhood, parental divorce, or joining a stepparent family. According to Simmons and colleagues' findings, the more transitions have to be negotiated within the same time period the greater is the likelihood of negative consequences, especially with respect to self-esteem and especially so in girls. Other investigators have found somatic rather than psychological consequences (Hirsch & Rapkin, 1987); also not all agree with an earlier assertion by Simmons, Blyth, Van Cleave, and Bush (1979) that the school transition is a more potent threat to children's adjustment than puberty. Many children, of course, manage these transitions very successfully; nevertheless, moving from one kind of school environment to another is a potentially stressful event and, as far as the move to secondary school is concerned, its timing to coincide with puberty changes is an unfortunate one.

Schools do not, of course, just influence children's academic achievement. Rutter, Maughan, Mortimore, and Ouston (1979), as we saw, included among their outcome variables also misbehavior, delinquency, and attendance rate, and it would be easy to add to that list quite a number of measures relating to emotional adjustment and to social relationships with both peers and teachers. The influence of schools on a child's self-image, however, is of particular significance. This is already evident at the preschool level: the reason why preschool education is effective has less to do with the specific things that children learn and much more with the self-esteem that they can develop in successfully accomplishing tasks (Sylva, 1994). No wonder that the fostering of positive self-images in children has frequently been advocated as a school's major aim, for children who have succeeded in this respect are more likely to persist in the face of failure, be less likely to truant, remain in school longer, and do more work on their own outside school. Unfortunately there are indications that schools frequently fall short in the help they give children in this respect. According to one survey study (Dunkin & Biddle, 1974) teachers use praise no more than 6 percent of the time, and even some kindergarten teachers use reprimand significantly more than praise (Berkeley, 1978). There are, of course, great differences between teachers and between schools in this respect; it does seem, however, that the balance between positive and negative feedback provided to children, with its implications for the kind of academic self-image the children come to construct, may form a crucial component of school effectiveness. Yet such a self-image is not merely an outcome of schooling; children making the home-to-school transition already have certain attitudes and varying degrees of confidence which will affect their response to school. As Entwisle, Alexander, Pallas, and Cardigan (1987) found when they studied this transition, children's academic self-image may emerge during this time but it does so in different ways in the two sexes according to tendencies already present when they first arrive in school. Girls, that is, were already strongly influenced by the stereotypic sex-role notions about mathematical abilities: although they did as well in mathematics as boys they did not consider their achievements in this area to be relevant to the academic self-image they were forming. Girls also depended strongly on the evaluations of their parents, whereas boys appeared to be more independent, in that their self-image showed little relationship to parental expectations and was closer to the evaluations they themselves formed of their performance. The kinds of marks they were getting in mathematics played a particularly prominent role in this respect. Thus the relationship between schooling and self-image is a reciprocal one: schools do influence children's developing image of themselves as more or less effective students; on the other hand how children respond to school experiences is affected by preexisting ideas about the self which are already there on school entry.

In so far as these ideas will largely reflect home influences, we have here one instance of the way in which family and school are interlinked. While both family and school are *microsystems*, in Bronfenbrenner's terminology, the relationship between the two brings us to a consideration of *mesosystems*. These emphasize the principle that children's development cannot be understood by reference to isolated social settings but that their interconnectedness must also be taken into account. Most of the research on family–school links has addressed the following three questions:

1   How does the family create an active learning environment, both before school entry and subsequently?
2   How do parents instill motivation in their children to succeed in academic matters?
3   How do parents get involved in their children's school experiences?

There is now ample evidence to indicate that, with regard to each of these three aspects, parents' interests and involvement in their children's school performance can have powerful effects (Hess & Holloway, 1984; Scott-Jones, 1984). The means whereby this is accomplished include a great many parental techniques: verbal stimulation, especially at the preschool level; encouragement of literacy and of numeracy; active involvement in homework; arranging trips to libraries; formal and informal contacts with teachers; help in choice of courses; prompt action to deal with problems in school, and so on. These are mostly management strategies; above all, however, it is the parents' expectations and beliefs concerning their children's educational achievement that are linked to school progress. There are even suggestions from several studies that such expectations and beliefs are better predictors of how well children do in school than what actually goes on in the school itself (e.g. Entwisle & Hayduk, 1982; H. W. Stevenson & Newman, 1986). However that may be, the link between family and school is a firm one.

Admittedly, in most studies that link is based on a correlation, and a simple cause-and-effect relationship (parental effort and belief as cause; child success as effect) cannot therefore be inferred automatically. Other explanations are also conceivable. For one thing, children doing well at school may encourage parents to pay more attention to their academic work; the cause-and-effect relationship, that is, goes in the opposite direction. And for another, the association of parents' behavior and children's achievement may be due to a common basis such as shared intelligence, as a result of which parents and children are equally inclined to participate in educational activities. However, intervention studies whereby parental actions are experimentally modified, show that what parents do can have an effect on children's school performance. Take a study by J. Tizard, Schofield, and Hewison (1982): parents of 7- and 8-year-olds were trained to have their children read aloud to them at regular intervals, while another group of children of comparable reading achievement received no such treatment. After a year the children's abilities were once more assessed; those who had received the extra attention were found to have made significantly more progress in reading than the children from the comparison group. This does not rule out either of the other two explanations we have mentioned, but does indicate that at least one component of the family–school link refers to the effects parents exert, for better or worse, on children's educational achievement.

The case of Asian versus American schooling

The way in which school influences, in conjunction with those from the home, combine to produce particular educational outcomes is well illustrated by some cross-cultural work on the learning of mathematics. In a series of reports H. W. Stevenson and his colleagues (and Lee, 1990; et al., 1990; Stigler, Lee, & Stevenson, 1987) have described the achievements of children in China, Japan, and the United States in this subject area and examined some of the factors that account for the different rates of progress found in the three countries.

When large numbers of first and fifth graders in each country were administered educational achievement tests it became apparent that the Asian children far outperformed their American counterparts in mathematics, though not in reading. This was already evident in the first grade; by the fifth grade the differences were even greater. Among 20 fifth-grade classrooms in each country, the average score on mathematics tests obtained by children in the highest scoring American classroom was below that of all Japanese classrooms and of all but one Chinese classrooms. The difference is thus a substantial one; in so far as there are reasons to believe the results are nationally representative they must give rise to concern among American educators.

What accounts for these findings? Observations in classrooms supply part of the answer. In the Asian countries teachers appeared to be better prepared for the teaching of mathematics, placed greater value on such teaching, organized their lessons more efficiently and were able to endow their classrooms with greater liveliness and variety. In addition, a substantially greater amount of time was devoted to mathematics teaching in the two Asian countries; thus the mean number of hours spent on this subject per week in the fifth grade was 3.4 in the United States, 11.4 in China, and 7.6 in Japan. The total amount of time spent by children in school did not differ; it was rather that greater prominence was given to mathematics in the Asian countries than in the United States. There were also differences in how classrooms were organized: the Japanese and Chinese children spent the majority of their time working together as a class whereas American children spent more time working on their own or in small groups. The children's attention to work-related activities tended to be greater and more continuous in the Asian than in the American classrooms, reflecting the different management styles of the teachers. Most important, however, were the actual expectations which the teachers had regarding their children's achievements: these were consistently higher in both China and Japan and were backed up by the teachers' demands on the children.

In this respect the teachers were expressing a general attitude regarding the importance of mathematics which appears to prevail in each of the three societies. This attitude also emerged from interviews with the children's mothers. Those in China and Japan, like the teachers, had higher expectations of their children than American mothers; they were more critical and less easily satisfied with their children's performance, despite the fact that the Asian children outscored American children. Mothers in China and Japan dedicated themselves to their child's schoolwork, as seen by the space, funds, and time allocated to the child and also in their involvement in homework and in their readiness to relieve the child of help with family chores. American mothers had broader goals: they wanted their children to be more generally involved in a wide range of activities and were less concerned purely with academic performance. These mothers also believed that a child's success at school is primarily determined by innate abilities; the Asian mothers, on the other hand, regarded effort as the most important factor. Not surprisingly, given the combined effects of home and school, the children's attitudes reflected these cultural differences. The American children did not especially like school; nevertheless, they tended to be satisfied with their progress and thought they were meeting the expectations of both parents and teachers. They also defined success more in terms of reading than mathematics. Asian children were less easily satisfied: like their elders they too believed in the importance of effort, took note of adults' high standards, and accepted the need to work hard to meet these. There were no signs that they were under stress as a result of such attitudes or that there was any other psychological price to pay for adopting this orientation. In due course the Asian children developed strong internal motivation towards learning and achievement, again reflected particularly in their progress in mathematics.

Parental Unemployment and Child Poverty

In Western countries children rarely have any direct contact with their parents' work experience; the setting in which fathers and often mothers too spend a large part of their lives tends to be an unfamiliar one which does not immediately impinge on the child's awareness. Yet what occurs there can have profound implications for the family as a whole and for children's psychological development in particular. Using Bronfenbrenner's terminology, parental employment constitutes an *exosystem*: its effects on children, that is, are indirect, being transmitted through the parents' reactions and through the spending power available to the family. This does not, however, lessen their impact.

A vivid illustration of this chain of consequences is found in a series of reports by Elder and his colleagues on the implications of fathers' loss of employment as a result of sudden shifts in a country's economy (e.g. R. D. Conger et al., 1992, 1993; Elder, Conger, Foster, & Ardelt, 1992). In the 1980s an agricultural crisis severely hit a large part of Midwestern America, resulting in farm foreclosures, major wage declines, reduced work opportunities, and large-scale unemployment. Such conditions have long been known to produce family breakdown, physical and mental health problems, and antisocial behavior; the precise steps whereby they filter down to affect children's well-being are spelled out in the reports by Elder and his group as a result of observing over 200 families, each containing at least one adolescent child, as they went through such a crisis. A conceptual model, illustrated in figure 28, provides an overview of these steps. The sequence begins with drastic changes in the parents' employment conditions involving, in particular, a sharp reduction in income. This puts the family as a whole under considerable economic pressure, thereby changing its lifestyle and disrupting accustomed habits. When parents find that bills can no longer be paid and that material necessities cannot be purchased they become depressed and demoralized, and as a result relationships within the family begin to deteriorate. On the one hand marital conflict increases, and on the other hand there are adverse effects on parenting. Parents, that is, become more distant, less supportive, harsher and more irritable in the treatment of their adolescent children, who in turn deteriorate in their psychological adjustment.

By investigating all the various steps in this sequence Elder's group was able to demonstrate that the crucial effect on children was the parents' altered behavior towards them. Financial pressures per se obviously did have an impact too, in changing the lifestyle of these young people and reducing their own purchasing powers. However, the primary influences were the disrupted parenting practices which they now encountered and which were found to equal degree in mothers and in fathers. The effects on the children that emerged from this study were varied; they included a greater incidence of emotional and conduct problems, a deterioration in social behavior, and a diminished sense of self-esteem. Increases in loneliness, depression, and antisocial tendencies can also occur under such circumstances.

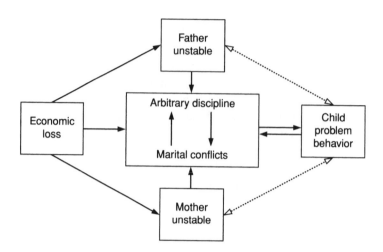

Figure 28 Model of links between economic conditions and child adjustment (from Elder & Caspi, 1988)

One other consequence for children and adolescents of particular significance is Elder's finding that behavior at school was adversely affected; both the relationship with teachers and academic performance, as reflected in grade points, worsened. Once again we see that experiences in one life setting have implications for what happens in other settings: changing conditions in the parent's workplace may affect children's behavior not only in the family but also at school. We have already seen that the transition from one kind of school to another can present difficulties; a study by Flanagan and Eccles (1993) shows that this presents particular problems to children affected by parental employment crises. Eleven-year-old children, who were followed up over a two-year period as they passed from elementary to junior high school, were divided into four groups: a *stable* group whose families experienced no adverse employment conditions during this time; a *deprived* group, who reported continuous unemployment right through this period; a *declining* group, which experienced a layoff or demotion at some point within the two years of the study; and a *recovery* group where reemployment following layoff occurred during this time. Measures of the children's social adjustment were taken both before and after the transition to the new school. As figure 29 shows, how children fared in the course of the transition was markedly affected by their parents' employment problems. There was a general trend for adjustment scores to drop following entry to the new school; on the other hand, those of the recovery children actually rose somewhat to approach the level of the stable group. Most notable, however, is the sharp drop found in the declining group: children confronted at home with their parents' loss of work and income experienced most difficulty in making the change from one school to another. Again we see that having to make two transitions simultaneously tends to be particularly stressful; such children are affected even more adversely than those from the deprived group whose experience of family hardship is of a more long-term nature.

This does not mean, of course, that chronic economic hardship is of little consequence – on the contrary, the evidence that poverty produces cumulative ill-effects of a far-ranging nature is highly convincing. As has become apparent, even in so-called affluent countries such as the United States the scale of poverty among children is distressingly high. In 1991, 21.8 percent of American children lived in families with incomes below the official poverty level (Huston, McLoyd, & Coll, 1994) – an increase of one-third compared with the rate two decades earlier. Poor children tend to be disproportionally represented in certain sectors of the community, in particular among ethnic minorities and single-parent households, and are often subjected to a multiplicity of disadvantages including poor schooling, inadequate health care and nutrition, slum housing, and life among violent and unsupportive adults. It is therefore not surprising to find that such children are a group at psychological risk: the chances that any child from a poverty background will develop behavior problems, antisocial tendencies, and educational retardation are vastly greater than for a child from a more affluent background. Such effects are evident from very early on; however, they become especially visible in adolescence when educational failure, a high dropout rate, unemployment, crime and delinquency, and unwanted pregnancy characterize a very much higher proportion of young people from poor than from affluent backgrounds (Huston, 1991).

Poverty can exert its effects in various ways. For example, if there is not enough

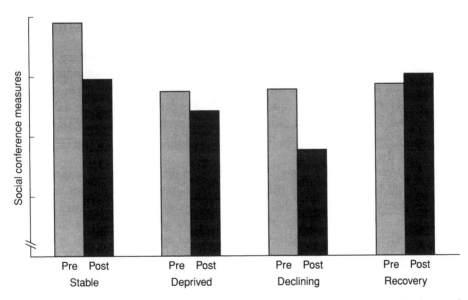

Figure 29   Relation of parental work status to children's social competence at school pre and post the transition to junior high school (adapted from Flanagan & Eccles, 1993)

money then there will not be enough toys or books or other cognitively stimulating materials, and the child's school achievements will thus be adversely affected by such home inadequacies. For that matter, poor children are more likely to go to unsatisfactory schools: even at the preschool level the probability that children from low-income families are exposed to insensitive and harsh teaching practices is greater than it is for children from more advantaged families (Phillips et al., 1994). Again, however, as in the case of sudden income loss, it is through the effects on the parents' mental state and consequently their socializing practices that poverty primarily influences children's psychological development. As McLoyd (1990) has put it: "Poverty and economic loss diminish the capacity for supportive, consistent, and involved parenting and render parents more vulnerable to the effects of negative life events." The distress experienced by parents living on inadequate income reduces the quality of care, psychological as well as physical, which they are able to provide for their children: caught up in their own feelings of helplessness and depression their task of fostering a strong, supportive relationship with the child is a very much harder one.

Studies of parenting in poor families have drawn attention to three aspects that are particularly prominent under such conditions (Huston, 1991; McLoyd, 1990; Sampson & Laub, 1994):

1 *Harsh discipline*   A climate of hostility among family members has commonly been reported for households beset by financial difficulties. This manifests itself in marital conflicts; it is also seen in the often erratic and threatening disciplinary techniques used by parents. There is greater reliance on physical punishment and coercion to gain the child's compliance, and in general an authoritarian style tends to characterize the parent–child relationship.

2 *Inadequate supervision*   Poor homes are often chaotic and disorganized, for parents caught up in their own problems have little energy to bring order to their lives. This is reflected in the supervision of children, which tends to be inconsistent and careless and which thus exposes them to danger both within and outside the home. Undesirable peer group influences in particular are more likely to play a part in such children's lives; the attractions of the street are often greater than those of the home.

3 *Weak parent–child attachments*   Poverty reduces the likelihood of forming sound emotional bonds, for when parents are preoccupied with problems involving food, housing, and health they may be less sensitive and responsive to their children – qualities that, as we have seen, are said to foster the growth of attachments. Reduced attentiveness and a lack of warmth are known to be associated with children's aggression; this in turn makes them less lovable and thus further diminishes the possibility of close bonds being formed.

While poverty is undoubtedly a risk factor to children's psychological health, we must bear in mind that a considerable proportion of children reared under such conditions escape damage and develop into well-functioning individuals. A combination of circumstances accounts for this. For one thing, the stresses of poverty do not invariably lead to inadequate parenting: some parents can cope even under great adversity, especially so if they receive backing from other people such as friends and relatives, and are therefore able to provide a normally supportive environment for their children. And for another, factors within the children themselves also play a part, as they do in the face of any type of stress, in that by virtue of their inborn characteristics some children show greater resilience to adversity than others and are able to surmount difficulties that more vulnerable individuals are not able to meet (Rutter, 1987). What appears to be crucial is the effect on a child's self-image. For many children poverty reduces self-esteem: they perceive that they and their families are no longer in control of their own fate; they realize that consequently they are inferior in relation to other's lifestyles and opportunities, and as a result feelings of depression, worthlessness, and low self-esteem tend to develop (Lempers, Clark-Lempers, & Simons, 1989). These are particularly evident in adolescence, when social comparison comes to play a prominent part in an individual's self-image. A good many adolescents who cannot afford the material things that their peers spend money on may well feel inferior and rejected, especially in a consumer society that places great value on the possession of such things (McLoyd, Jayaratue, Caballo, & Borquez, 1994). And yet there are other young people, from similar circumstances, who do find a way out and do gain self-respect. Sometimes this is brought about by resorting to antisocial behavior: activities such as burglary probably have less to do with wanting to acquire other people's belongings than with attempts to gain a sense of achievement. But that may also be gained by following more acceptable pathways, as happens when, for instance, the young person has some intellectual, athletic, or artistic talent that can lead to fulfillment and emotional satisfaction, or when opportunities arise to participate in community schemes designed to help the old, the sick, or the handicapped. Thus poverty does not have invariant consequences; it represents a considerable handicap for many but is one which some can manage to surmount by finding ways of preserving self-respect.

Ethnic Minorities

In virtually every society there are majority and minority groups, and whether an individual belongs to the former or the latter may have considerable psychological consequences. In a very few cases, such as in South Africa during the apartheid period, a minority group may have power and privilege; more often than not quality-of-life indicators show minorities to be at a decided disadvantage in most spheres of life. Occasionally, as in Nazi Germany, this may take extreme forms of brutality and persecution; more often than not it creates conditions under which children's development compares unfavorably with that found among the majority, constituting a handicap of more or less serious severity. Thus, as in the case of poverty, events at a macro-level filter down to the individual child: how society is stratified will affect the behavior of all its members, whether they belong to the majority or to a minority. Differences in race and ethnicity are the main criteria for stratification; it is primarily these which we shall consider.

One implication as far as children are concerned is that the conditions of family life may differ according to their social group membership. Take African-Americans – the minority group that has attracted more research than any other. These children's early experience tends to be shaped in a disproportionally large number of cases by the following features:

(1)   *Poverty*   Whereas 21.8 percent of all children living in the United States in 1991 were classified as poor, the comparable figure for African-American children was 45.9 percent (and 40.4 percent for those of Hispanic origin). The poverty experienced by such children is more likely to be long-term; it is less likely to be alleviated by institutional support for families than is found among poor European-Americans (Huston, McLoyd, & Coll, 1994). As we have seen, poverty has wideranging implications for children's development and tends to diminish their long-term chances in life.

(2)   *Single-parenthood*   More than half of all African-American children live in families headed by a lone parent (usually the mother); this is about three times as many as found among European-American children (Tolson & Wilson, 1990). Single-parenthood is associated with a variety of stresses; once again poverty is foremost. Children raised in mother-only families are less likely to do well at school, are more likely to be implicated in antisocial activities and have poorer occupational opportunities on leaving school than offspring of intact families (McLanahan, Astone, & Marks, 1991).

(3)   *Extended family structure*   While many African-American families do not contain a father, they often do include other kin. About 10 percent of African-American children under age 18 live with their grandparents – three times as many compared with white children; 53 percent of the African-American elderly population share a residence with a relative as compared to 40 percent of the white elderly population (Harrison et al., 1990). Unlike father absence the extended family represents a source of strength: thus a three-generational structure signifies stability over time; the ready availability of grandparents provides support to harassed mothers; and children are given the opportunity for a wider range of social interactions and choice of attachment figures. Black grandmothers in particular tend to be much more closely involved in the upbringing of children than their white equivalents, especially so in single-parent households (Pearson, Hunter, Engswinger, & Kellam, 1990), and the children benefit accordingly by doing better in school and having fewer behavior problems than black children with lone mothers.

(4)   *Authoritarian parenting style*   A higher proportion of African-American parents adopt an authoritarian style in bringing up their children (Dornbusch et al., 1987). This may well be a reaction to the life stresses experienced by these parents, but whatever the origin, such a style involves the creation of a particular family climate that is distinguished by high demands and low responsiveness and that is also associated with poorer school grades than are other parental styles. The authoritative parenting style, on the other hand, which is generally associated with positive child outcomes, tends to be somewhat less common among African-American than among European-American families (Steinberg et al., 1994)

There are other features which distinguish African-American families, but the above are among the most common. They indicate that ethnicity affects the family microsystem in particular ways, exposing children growing up therein to certain kinds of distinctive experiences. Of course not all African-American families are so characterized, many having a lifestyle similar to that of the white majority. Moreover, other ethnic minorities, even those also living in the United States, have their own cultural, social, and economic characteristics and so provide quite different contexts for their children's development. However, there is one aspect of experience that the members of virtually all minority groups share, and that is the high probability of encounters with prejudice.

Prejudice directed against other groups, especially those whose members are visibly different in appearance, is unfortunately highly prevalent and can be found even among young children. It can appear as early as 3 or 4 years of age and, at least according to some research, becomes more marked until about 7 years when it declines again to some extent (Aboud, 1988). For example, G. M. Vaughn (1964), working in New Zealand, showed children pairs of photographs of a white child and a Maori child, asking "Which child would you choose for a playmate?" The percentage of white children who chose the Maori photo was 25 at age 4 years, 0 at 6 and 8 years, 30 at 10 years and 40 at 12 years. Powlishta, Serbin, Doyle, and White (1994), in a study of English Canadian children between 5 and 13 years, found clear signs of prejudice against French Canadian children throughout the age range, even though the main difference separating the two groups is only that of language; the extent of prejudice, however, did decline somewhat with age. It is highly likely that estimates of the incidence of prejudice in childhood are affected, first, by the particular groups (ethnic or otherwise) investigated and second by the measures employed to this end (e.g. observations of social interaction, choice of photo or doll, assigning evaluative adjectives to group members, and so on). What is certain is that prejudice is a manifestation of a general trend to categorize people and to regard negatively all those social categories to which the individual does not belong – even when groups are experimentally established on purely arbitrary criteria (e.g. under- versus overestimators of dots). According to Tajfel (1978) we do this for the sake of self-enhancement; by mentally establishing ethnic as well as other social categories we can, in the first place, assign an identity to ourselves and secondly make comparisons between our own and other groups which result in a highly positive evaluation of the former and a negative attitude to the latter. The need for self-enhancement is thus at the root of prejudice. In some individuals this need is, for one reason or another, greater than in others and the extent of prejudice will vary accordingly.

Prejudice is encountered in many forms. Among children name calling is the most frequent (Troyna & Hatcher, 1992), though racial harassment can also assume more violent expressions such as bullying and physical attacks. But it is often the more subtle and unintentional forms of discrimination, such as those which a child may encounter from adults at school, that can have the most far-reaching effects. This is already seen at a preschool level, as found in an observational study, conducted in Scotland, by Ogilvy and colleagues (1992) of white nursery teachers' interactions with Asian (mainly Pakistani) and white children. Two different styles became evident: with Asian children the adults assumed a highly controlling manner, issuing a lot of directives and giving the children few options; with white children they were less didactic, more relaxed, and less negative. The teachers also tended to be more responsive to the white children, so providing them with more contingent reciprocal interaction than the Asian children experienced. It may well be that such different styles are adopted quite unconsciously; what is certain is that the one shown to the Asian children is much less likely to foster active learning than the one shown to the white children.

A study in England by Sonuga-Barke and colleagues (1993), again involving white and Asian children, illustrates the same unconscious biases at work. Teachers of 6- to 7-year-old boys rated each child for activity level, using standardized questionnaires and interviews for this purpose. Groups of hyperactive and nonhyperactive (control) subjects were thus identified, whereupon objective measures of activity such as actometers strapped to the boys' arm or leg and neurological tests were obtained from each child. When the teachers' subjective assessments were compared with the objective measures, a bias emerged in the way the two ethnic groups had been judged: teachers consistently overestimated the Asian boys' levels of activity and inattention relative to those of the white boys. Arm and leg activity, for instance, as measured by the actometers, showed Asian boys to be well below the activity level of their white counterparts; indeed the Asian boys judged to be hyperactive had activity levels that were little different from those of white control boys (figure 30). It seems that the degree of deviance ascribed by teachers to a particular behavior pattern varies as a function of the child's ethnic background.

Given such experiences, it is no wonder that children from minority groups become highly self-conscious about their status. Belonging to a particular social group, and being able to define oneself in terms of that group, may have many advantages for a child, but when that group is subject to adverse discrimination and is looked down upon by the rest of society there may be unfortunate consequences for the way in which children define and evaluate themselves.

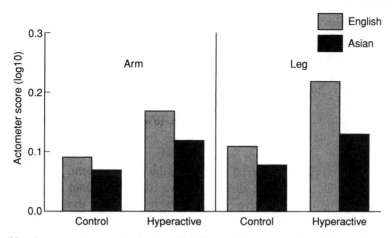

Figure 30 Actometer scores obtained by English and Asian boys (from Sonuga-Barke et al., 1993)

How do children construct an ethnic identity? According to Phinney (1990), several components are involved in this process:

1 *Self-identification*: what ethnic label does the child use for him/herself and how "correct" is that label?
2 *Evaluative attitude*: does the child feel positively or negatively about being a member of a particular group?
3 *Sense of belonging*: does the child have strong bonds with its group?
4 *Ethnic involvement*: does the child participate in the social life and cultural practices of the group?

We know most about the first two of these aspects, and most of that knowledge has been derived from research on African-American children's self-concept.

Such research has grown through several phases. Up to the early 1960s it was taken for granted that black children in the United States compare themselves negatively to white children and grow up feeling "inferior." A series of studies initiated by Clark and Clark (1940) showed, first, that awareness of one's own and others' ethnicity is already developing during the preschool years (and rather earlier in minority children than in other children). Thus, given a white and a black doll and asked to "point to the doll which is most like you," more than a third of 3-year-olds were already able to respond correctly. In addition, it was found that black children, when given the choice between the colours black and white, consistently preferred white; when shown pictures of black and white people they evaluated the whites more positively than the blacks; and when asked to point to "the doll that is the nice doll" the majority of the black children picked out the white one. These results, repeatedly confirmed in studies carried out up to the 1960s (see Spencer, 1983), seemed to show that the attitudes held by the majority to one's ethnic group were consistently reflected in the child's developing attitude to itself: the concept of *self-hatred* was even used to describe how such children reacted to the social pressures they experienced.

Subsequently, however, doubts arose as to the meaning and generality of these findings. Criticisms were expressed regarding both the methods used and the interpretations attached to the findings (e.g. Banks, 1976; Bennett, Dewberry, & Yeeles, 1991), but even more to the point later studies (e.g. Stephan & Rosenfield, 1979) obtained different results. When based on children born in the United States from the mid-1960s onwards a reversal of findings became apparent: blacks expressed preference for the color black; their evaluative comments about black individuals were positive; and self-evaluative comments were similar to those made by white children. It may be that differences in methodology help to account for this change; more likely a new sociopolitical climate bringing about reduced racial discrimination is the crucial factor. The dominant majority (i.e. whites) need not be the group from which a child derives its norms; thus children who are taught by their parents about black history and the civil rights movement develop pride in their racial identity and acceptance of their own ethnic group (Spencer, 1983). How children make sense of their membership of a minority group is therefore not just a reflection of the majority view in their society; more immediate experiences in the family constitute a more powerful source of influence. It is thus perfectly possible for minority children to be aware of their underprivileged status in society and yet not internalize these values as part of their self-concept. As Spencer pointed out, a distinction is necessary between *group identity*, assessed by so-called preference measures which indicate the child's evaluation of his or her group, and *personal identity* as assessed by self-esteem measures. The former has often been found to show "white bias" on the part of black children; however, there is no evidence from the latter that black children's image of themselves as persons is any less positive than can be found for the rest of the population (Cross, 1985).

It is primarily in adolescence that the issue of ethnic identity assumes importance for individuals and may become a focus of acute self-consciousness. It is also then that ethnicity, as a result of cognitive developments, becomes elaborated into a quite complex psychological system – a process further described in table 51. However, even in the early years children's ethnic conception, both of themselves and of others, changes and is transformed in keeping with cognitive status. Thus, whereas the preschool child classifies people according to aspects of external appearance such as skin color, the school child begins to take more subtle characteristics into account, including customs, religion, and food. Ethnic identity is at first a very simple concept: the preschooler will say: "I am Mexican because my mother says so," accepting without question the label provided and knowing little about its connotations. But already at an early school level a child is more likely to say: "I am Mexican because my parents come from Mexico," with at least some limited awareness of the geographical and historical foundation to such a statement. Yet even then children's hold

Table 51 Stages in ethnic identity formation during adolescence

Stage	Age	Characteristics
1 Unexamined ethnic identity	Preadolescence	Lack of exploration of ethnic concepts. Values of majority passively accepted.
2 Ethnic identity search	Early adolescence	Seeking to understand what ethnicity means for oneself. Questioning old attitudes. May include heightened political consciousness and outrage.
3 Ethnic identity achievement	Late adolescence	Clear, confident sense of one's own ethnicity. Uncertainties resolved and commitments made. Ethnicity internalized.

Source: Based on Phinney (1993)

on ethnicity is superficial; for instance, not till the age of 9 or 10 will children realize that black persons remain black even though they put on white makeup or a blond wig (Aboud, 1988). Thus ethnicity develops in the trail of cognitive development, though the content of ideas about it are largely shaped by the child's experiences in family and society.

Among the various implications of minority group membership particular attention has been paid to the effects on educational achievement. Concern that some ethnic groups perform worse at school than others has been expressed in various countries. In the United States, for example, a large number of studies have shown that African-American students "generally earn lower grades, drop out more often, and attain less education than do whites" (Mickelson, 1990); similarly in Britain the Swann Report (1985), a government initiated investigation into ethnic minority children's educational attainment, found that children of Afro-Caribbean origin for the most part performed well below the level reached by white children. That same report also found, however, that children of Asian origin are generally as competent as white students are – a finding mirrored by American studies of children from Japanese-American families who often outperform their white classmates (Matute-Bianchi, 1986). What applies to one minority group clearly need not apply to another.

Further research has shown that there are other constraints to sweeping generalizations about ethnic minority children's educational achievements. For example, there are indications that educational underachievement varies not only according to race but also according to gender, with African-American boys showing the lowest grade averages as well as the highest incidence of school behavior problems (Simmons, Black, & Zhou, 1991). There are further indications that educational difficulties apply to some aspects of school performance but not to others: Entwisle and Alexander (1990), for example, found African-American children at the point of school entry not to do as well as white children on tests of mathematical reasoning but just as well on tests of mathematical computation. And H. W. Stevenson, Chen, and Uttal (1990), in a comparison of African-American, Hispanic-American and white children over the first five grades of school, found that one must also take into account certain changes over time: children from the two minority groups scored initially below the level of the white children in mathematics but were no longer significantly different after five years of schooling. This did not, however, apply to their reading performance where ethnic differences remained evident throughout this period.

It is apparent that ethnic differences in educational achievement are rather more elusive than was thought at one time. Yet a justified concern about the danger of underachievement on the part of minority children remains, and a variety of explanations have been put forward to account for this phenomenon. These include the following:

1   inherited differences in intelligence between ethnic groups;
2   specific cognitive and linguistic deficits;
3   low achievement need, possibly due to lack of parental interest or to the anti-academic orientation of the peer group;
4   differences in cultural values of the ethnic group, with particular reference to the value placed on educational success;
5   discriminatory practices in educational institutions;
6   low self-esteem;
7   poverty and deprivation.

There is as yet little consensus about the role which these various factors play, and while some are clearly more contentious than others the lack of empirical data makes any conclusion premature. Ethnic differences in school achievement have been labeled "a phenomenon in search of an explanation" (Sue & Okazaki, 1990), though one could also argue that at present the phenomenon has rather too many explanations.

The case of children of mixed race

The main challenge of ethnicity lies in the formation of an identity appropriate to one's group. This can present difficulties when that group forms a minority in society; when the child is of mixed race and, so to speak, has a foot in each camp the strains can well be greater. Mixed race individuals have often been looked down upon and greeted with distaste; labels such as "mulatto," "half-caste," and "half-breed" give expression to such feelings. While there are indications that the number of such individuals is increasing in many countries, their total remains small and their place in society often ill-defined.

A study by B. Tizard and Phoenix (1993) throws some light on the way in which mixed race individuals come to shape their self-identity. A group of 15- to 16-year-old adolescents, each with one white and one black (usually Caribbean) parent, were interviewed and compared with both a group of white and a group of black youngsters. All the young people had been born in Britain and were living in London, though the black parents were for the most part immigrants. Lengthy interviews were also held with parents.

The main interest of the research workers lay in how these young people of mixed race thought about and identified themselves. Did they think they were white, or black, or some distinct category in between? Did they feel allegiance to one ethnic group rather than another? Was identity formation a particularly difficult affair for them, creating confusion and stress? Inevitably, there was some diversity within the group, as seen in the labels which they assigned to themselves. Somewhat less than half thought of themselves as "black"; most of the rest as "mixed" or "brown," with a few as "more white than black." Yet these were not hard-and-fast identities: many of the mixed race youngsters appeared to switch backwards and forwards between identifications, often according to the demands of a particular situation. For the most part, however, they resisted pressure to be either black or white because they felt themselves to be *both*; they also did not want to alienate a parent by choosing one or the other, and thus settled for something in between which they then endowed with positive qualities.

Nevertheless, the proportion who wished they were another color was twice as large as in the group with two black parents. While some of the young people regarded their status as interesting or exotic, others referred to the hostility that they sometimes met from both black and white people and which confused and upset them. Thus the amount of strain involved in identity formation was clearly greater in the mixed race group than even in the minority black group – a strain which some tried to resolve by adopting multiple ethnic identities while others still seemed uncertain just where they belonged in the scheme of things.

Children's Construction of Society

Social systems such as families and peer groups are immediately accessible to children's experience, and working out how they function is thus not too difficult a task. But the society in which a child lives is also composed of a great many more remote and abstract systems: political institutions, for example, such as those involved in national government and local community; economic institutions such as stores and banks; and geographical entities such as the country and city to which a child belongs. These too need to be understood as part of social development; in so far as they are not directly experienced, mastery of such concepts may take longer and involve more complex processes.

Consider a child's comprehension of geographical terms. As Jahoda (1963, 1964) found when studying Scottish children between 6 and 11 years of age, their ideas of the relationship between the city (Glasgow), country (Scotland), and nation (Britain) in which they lived were initially quite confused. Some of the youngest children could not even conceive of their city as an entity that was all around them; asked where Glasgow was they produced answers such as "It is down in X street." Even when they became aware of it as a proper unit there were still difficulties in relating it to Scotland, which they tended to think of as "outside" Glasgow. And even when that relationship had been mastered there were still problems about fitting Britain into the total scheme: Britain, according to some children, was seen as somehow "beside" Scotland, or described as "sort of Scotland – another name for it." Thus at first the children's responses reveal an almost complete ignorance about the wider geographical and social world surrounding them; only gradually do they acquire the conceptual tools enabling them to organize their environment meaningfully; and not till the age of 10 or 11 do they fully comprehend the hierarchical relationship between the concepts of city, country, and nation. In so far as such concepts form part of a child's developing self-identity, these more remote aspects appear to enter that identity in a meaningful way at a relatively late age.

Comprehension of economic institutions, such as commerce and banking and the role that money plays, is an even more complex and long-drawn-out process. From an early age children go shopping with their parents, yet their ideas of what goes on in shops – why, for instance, money is handed over and why often money is handed back – are at first primitive and limited in scope. For example, a 6-year-old, interviewed about shopping transactions, seemed to view these as a game-like ritual (Jahoda, 1984):

Interviewer: What do you do when you buy something?
Child: Give the shoplady the money.
Interviewer: What does she do with it?
Child: Gives the money back.
Interviewer: Is it the same money?
Child: Yes.
Interviewer: Where does the milk in the shop come from?
Child: Cows – the man brings it.
Interviewer: Does the lady have to pay for the milk?
Child: The lady pays the man and the man pays the lady because he gives her milk.

It takes some time before children realize that money and goods are exchanged in such a way that the shopkeeper is left with fewer goods but with more money at the end of the transaction. However, it is not till the age of 7 or 8 that children realize, first, that the people doing the selling have a job for which they get paid, and second, that the shops also have to pay for the goods they receive. But even then children have still not grasped the idea of profit; mostly they assume that the price to the shop is the same as that charged to the customer. Only from about age 10 onwards will children begin to understand that there are three distinct sub-systems, referring respectively to supplier–shop, shop–customer, and shop–sales staff relationships, and it is only then that children learn how these are coordinated to form one system. Not till then can they gain real insight into the way in which this particular aspect of society functions.

Developments such as these are not merely a matter of the child obtaining information as to how these systems work. As Jahoda (1984) noted from his observations, the children were not just repeating things they had learned at school or been told at home. Rather, they were faced with questions from the interviewer that were quite new to them, and they actively tried to fit together whatever information happened to be at their disposal in order to produce some sort of sensible answer. They adopted, that is, a *constructive* approach – one that was constrained not only by lack of information but also by the child's cognitive limitations in getting to grips with abstractions and complex interrelationships. No wonder, given such limitations, 6-year-olds interpret shopping transactions in terms of their own experience, seeing them as gamelike exchanges and egocentrically viewing shops as simply places one goes to in order to get things. Nevertheless, when confronted with problems about the way in which various parts of society work, children are frequently seen actively trying to make sense of what is happening in order to reconcile discrepancies and explain peculiarities, and then quite suddenly in the course of the interview spontaneously to gain insight and develop understanding. Ideas about society, that is, do not merely progress from ignorance to knowledge on the basis of accumulated information; instead, such ideas are actively constructed in somewhat the same way that Piaget described with respect to the child's developing understanding of the physical world. Take the following exchange (Jahoda, 1984):

Interviewer:	Does the shoplady have to pay for the bread (she sells)?
Child:	No.
Interviewer:	So the bread is just given to the shops?
Child:	(*pauses, then laughs*) No – they'll pay for it.

This child, it seems, is old enough to have appreciated the difficulty of maintaining his original view when confronted with the implications; in the light of that conflict he abandoned his previous position and so spontaneously graduated to a higher level of understanding.

A developmental scheme outlining the nature of children's understanding of society has been proposed by Furth (1980), on the basis of investigating a considerable range of societal concepts, including shopping transactions, the roles played by such individuals as doctors and teachers, and the functions of government and community. The following stages make up Furth's scheme:

1 *(5–6 years): No understanding* Children have no systematic framework for interpreting the societal events they observe. All items of information about the social world are treated in isolation or are merely interpreted in the light of purely personal considerations. Thus money is thought to be freely available, and money transactions are regarded as an empty ritual without precise meaning.

2 *(7–8 years): Understanding some basic functions* Children begin to understand those aspects of society of which they have direct experience. They know that

money serves as a means of exchange for goods; they have learned why some of their money is sometimes returned as change; but they do not know what the shopkeeper does with the money. Anything not within their immediate experience is inexplicable: thus a child, asked to explain the functions of a mayor, replied that "he is the one that gives you permission to climb Mount Everest."

3   *(9–11 years): Understanding part-systems*   Logical coherence is now attempted in children's explanations of how social systems work. Children can infer relationships (such as that between shopkeeper and supplier) without the benefit of direct observation. However, they can apply this attitude only to limited systems; complex interrelationships are still beyond their comprehension. One boy, for example, understood that a headteacher has financial responsibilities for his school; asked then how he obtains the money the boy explained that the headteacher probably works in another school and gets paid from there.

4   *(Beyond 11 years): Logical understanding*   From now on children understand the basic mechanisms involved in societal functions. By applying formal logical thinking they can work out how various social systems work, and only lack of knowledge still limits the range of their understanding. Thus they know why we have a government and how it fulfills its role, even though they cannot yet explain the various details of the process. Also their thinking about the general needs of society and its traditions and symbols remains somewhat concrete and therefore unsystematic. Thus stage 4 is by no means the end point; further development is required to reach adequate and mature understanding of social institutions, though in fact many adults fail to get much further than this stage.

Of the various stages the third one is probably of most psychological interest, for it is then that children start to make inferences beyond their direct experience and to construct theories about how societal events can function. Their theories may be partial and inadequate; they show, however, that children are not content with passively taking in information but that they approach their social world creatively and productively.

Summary

Peer Relationships

- Children form two kinds of relationships: vertical and horizontal. The former are with individuals of greater knowledge and power than the child's; the latter are with those having the same power, such as peers. The distinction, though not absolute, draws attention to different kinds of contributions made by the child's partners to development.

- Various orderly developmental sequences are to be found in children's contacts with peers right through from infancy to adolescence. Thus their interactions become more frequent, more sustained, more complex, more intimate, and more cohesive.

- To describe individual differences in the nature of the relationships children make with peers, a category system has been employed which classifies children as popular (or accepted), neglected, or rejected. Each of these types is associated with certain personality characteristics.

- Early peer status can predict later psychological adjustment. This is particularly evident in the case of rejected children, who are most at risk for subsequent social maladjustment. Rejected children characterized by aggression are likely to develop externalizing problems; those characterized by withdrawal may develop internalizing problems.

- Friendships, especially from the preadolescent years on, fulfill a number of important functions the nature of which changes with age, ranging from shared activities in the preschool years to shared tastes in mid-childhood and shared feelings and disclosure in adolescence. Being without friends can be associated with some undesirable developmental outcomes.

- The positive value of peer relationships is seen clearly in peer collaborative learning, of which three types can be distinguished: peer tutoring, cooperative learning, and peer collaboration. Most interest has focused on the last, which shows that children working jointly can make intellectual advances well beyond them when working alone.

- Mutual influences exist between children's family relationships and their peer relationships. This is especially evident with regard to the way in which parental actions affect the nature and amount of contact with peers. The links between the two systems take both a direct form, where parents try deliberately to shape the child's peer interactions, and an indirect form, in that the quality of parenting affects the nature of the child's peer relationships.

The Child in Society

- Bronfenbrenner's ecological systems theory serves to draw attention to the multiplicity of social influences that impinge on children's development and orders them into various levels: microsystems, mesosystems, exosystems, and macrosystems. The interdependence of these levels is emphasized by the model.

- The school is a specially prominent social system affecting children's behavior. Each individual school provides a particular ethos, and it is this rather than any specific characteristics which brings about these effects. This is also seen on transition from one school system to another – a change which calls for considerable readjustment, especially when it occurs in conjunction with other stressful events such as puberty.

- Links between the two systems of home and school take many forms; their nature can have considerable implications for children's academic motivation and progress and for the development of their self-image.

- Children may have only indirect contact with their parents' work experience, yet the world of employment is another social system with potentially profound implications for children. This is well illustrated by Elder's studies of father's loss of work; by taking a family systems approach these show that there are consequences for the family as a unit, for relationships within that unit, and for the various individuals in it including children. The latter are affected primarily by the parents' altered behavior towards them, the effects being evident even outside the family, for example at school.

- Economic conditions that produce child poverty can have cumulative ill-effects on development of a far-ranging nature. Again many of these are mediated by family processes, in that the nature of parenting is often profoundly altered in poverty-stricken families. While affected children are thus at risk many do escape, the crucial factor being the way in which children preserve their self-image.

- One further social system providing a context for development is found in ethnicity. How society is stratified and what group a child belongs to can produce multiple influences, seen most clearly in children belonging to ethnic minorities. Here too much depends on the conditions of family life, but also on the way children build up a self-identity in the face of prejudice from majority groups.

- How children are affected by their society is also a matter of how they construe that society. Such understanding, especially of the more remote economic and political parts, develops only slowly in the course of childhood. A developmental scheme outlining this process has been put forward by Furth, emphasizing the constructive role children play in their theorizing about the nature of society.

Chapter 8

Social Experience and its Aftermath

So far we have examined children's social development primarily from a contemporaneous perspective, rather than asked about its significance for the individual's future status. In this chapter we turn to the latter issue and investigate how early development is connected with outcome in maturity. What role do childhood events play in determining adult personality? Do early experiences leave irreversible effects that manifest themselves in later years? Is there a continuity from childhood to adulthood and, if so, how does such continuity manifest itself and by what means is it brought about? In short, what is the significance of childhood?

These are extraordinarily complex questions, and it will come as no surprise that as yet we have no definitive answers to them. Yet they are also extremely important questions, for as we saw right at the beginning of this book one of the motives for studying childhood is to determine what the process of development leads to. Children, that is, are not only studied for their own sake but also because eventually they become adults. To be able to predict from early status to final outcome could have many advantages, not least because it would enable us to intervene with preventative action in cases of high risk. No wonder that a great deal of effort has been devoted to tracing the course of development from the beginning to the end of childhood, and to attempts to establish how mature personality characteristics are connected to preceding events. Many of the earlier explanations were, in retrospect, rather simplistic in the developmental models on which they were based; more recent attempts have begun to demonstrate that the connection between *early* and *late* is often a highly complex one and that efforts to predict from one to the other need to take into account a considerably greater number of factors than was thought necessary at one time.

Reversible or Irreversible?

Infantile Trauma and Critical Periods

The notion that the early years are the most impressionable ones seems at first sight almost a matter of common sense. Surely, the younger the child the greater must be the susceptibility to experience, and the idea that traumatic events occurring at that time leave irreversible effects on the developing personality was thus readily accepted even in the form in which Freud advanced it.

Freud became convinced of the importance of infancy experiences through his attempts to trace the origins of neurotic disorders. As he put it:

> It seems that neuroses are only acquired during early childhood (up to the age of six), even though their symptoms may not make their appearance until much later. . . . Analytic experience has convinced us of the complete truth of the common assertion that the child is psychologically father of the man and that the events of its first years are of paramount importance for its whole subsequent life.   (S. Freud, 1949)

On the basis of "memories" obtained from adult patients in the course of therapy it is possible, Freud believed, to reconstruct the nature of early experience and to determine those events to which infants are maximally responsive. These are primarily of a somatic nature: the struggle of the baby to obtain the maternal breast, the frustrations of scheduling and of weaning, the anger experienced during toilet training. As we saw in chapter 1, whether any such experience is stressful or not depends on the libidinal phase the child is passing through at the time: thus in the oral phase the child's main concern is with activities like sucking, swallowing, and biting, and should excessive frustration be encountered during such activities the child will remain fixated at that stage and as an adult manifest a particular personality constellation (the "oral character") distinguished by such features as extreme dependence, passivity, and "mouth habits" like drinking, smoking, and overeating. A straightforward continuity thus exists between early experience and later outcome: traumatic events in infancy leave irreversible effects that manifest themselves in adulthood, and though Freud himself worked backwards from his adult patients to their childhood it should, in theory at least, be possible to predict forwards from infant traumata to pathology in later life.

However, as reviews such as that by Caldwell (1964) have shown, empirical investigations have failed to substantiate such an association. Rigid scheduling of feeds, early and sudden weaning, interference with comfort sucking habits – these and other alleged traumata in infancy bear little relationship to the nature of personality in maturity. There are various possible reasons for this failure. For one thing, Freud relied for his evidence on adults' memories, and the reliability of information so obtained is, at best, controversial (Brewin, Andrews, & Gotlieb, 1993). For another, the very fact that these adults were all psychologically disturbed introduced various complications and made generalization difficult. But most of all we must question the belief that the specific events selected by Freud were indeed so traumatic that they left irreversible effects on the developing personality, irrespective of all other considerations such as, for example, the interpersonal context in which these events occurred. Contrast this with Erik Erikson's (1963) view of the effects of early experiences. In his opinion the main thing that a child acquires as a result of being fed or otherwise cared for in a particular manner is a sense of trust or mistrust in the caregiver, which is then carried forward to subsequent developmental stages and has implications for the way in which these are negotiated. The emphasis is thus on general interpersonal qualities rather than on specific experiences, and instead of treating the early event in isolation it is embedded in the wider context of subsequent development – a point that is, as we shall see, particularly important if one is to understand the significance of early experience.

Freud's formulation can be regarded as a version of the *critical period hypothesis,* though put forward long before this was formalized by Lorenz (1935) as part of ethological theory. Based originally on his observations of the "imprinting" phenomenon, which referred to the tendency of certain species of birds to form an attachment to the parent only within a sharply delimited period soon after hatching, Lorenz believed that critical periods represent developmental phases of maximum susceptibility to certain kinds of influence. Learning at this time occurs easily and quickly: in imprinting, for example, the animal will form a strong bond to the parent after only a brief exposure to it. That learning, moreover, is of a permanent, irreversible nature: if the animal is exposed to a biologically "incorrect" object such as a human being or a member of some other species it will not be possible subsequently to shift the attachment to the parent; alternately, if the animal is kept in isolation and forms no attachment during this time it will remain a social isolate all its life. Critical periods are sharply delimited, at least in the case of the birds which Lorenz studied; what happens then affects the animal throughout its subsequent life course.

This view, like Freud's, is an extreme expression of the notion that early experience is irreversible. In fact subsequent work by ethologists has shown that, even when applied to lower species such as birds, it is not tenable in such an all-or-none form. The limits of critical periods have not been found to be as immutable as Lorenz believed, nor is the learning that then occurs as permanent as he thought it was. As a result, the term *sensitive periods* has come to be preferred, for as Hinde (1963) put it, it seems that we are merely concerned with changing *probabilities* of certain forms of learning, so that periods of maximum probability may be surrounded by periods of reduced probability.

Nevertheless, there has been much discussion as to whether critical (or sensitive) periods are to be found in human development. For example, the onset of attachments has been linked to states of developmental readiness, with the further implication that the child remains in this state for only a limited period of time and that delay beyond it makes attachment formation impossible. This was stated in its most explicit form by John Bowlby (1951), who proposed that any child deprived of the opportunity to form attachments will develop an "affectionless character," that is, be permanently unable to establish meaningful relationships with others. But, inspired by Lorenz's findings, Bowlby further proposed that the opportunity to form attachments *must* occur in a sharply delimited period early on in development. Citing as evidence a series of studies of children who had spent their first few years in impersonal institutions before being fostered, he declared that:

> Even good mothering is almost useless if delayed until after the age of $2\frac{1}{2}$ years.

It follows that the formation of the first attachment can be delayed somewhat beyond the usual age in the first year, but that nevertheless there is a definite limit beyond which no amount of the "right" kind of experience is effective if the child has been deprived before then: the child is bound to develop the affectionless character. There is thus a critical period in those first $2\frac{1}{2}$ years: whatever happens or fails to happen then will affect the individual for ever after.

Evidence obtained more recently does not bear out this view. This is well illustrated by B. Tizard (1977; Hodges & Tizard, 1989) in a follow-up study of children who had been admitted to an institution in the early weeks of life and had remained there for their first few years. During this time they were cared for by such a large number of different people that they had virtually no opportunities to establish an attachment to anyone; emotionally they were kept, so to speak, on ice. Subsequently, however, the children were adopted, the adoption occurring very much later than is normally advised, in some cases taking place as late as 7 years and in all instances well beyond the end of Bowlby's critical period. On follow-up, first at age 8 and then again at 16, various assessments were carried out, but especially of the children's capacity to form social relationships with others. In some respects the children compared unfavorably with a normally reared comparison group: for example, they tended to be overfriendly and even affectionate with strangers and at school were less popular with other children and had fewer friends. Yet in the majority of cases relationships within the adoptive family were good: the children soon began to show real affection to their new parents and this developed quickly into close attachment bonds. None resembled the stereotype of the ex-institutional child described by Bowlby; there was thus no indication that a delay as long as several years had produced the "affectionless character."

The oldest child in Tizard's study was 7 years when adopted, and we have no evidence as to what happens in cases where the delay is even greater. All we can conclude is that the critical-period notion, that there is a sharply delimited range (ending, say, in the third year) beyond which children are no longer able to develop emotional attachments to anyone, is not supported by these findings. The die is by no means cast just because children have missed the usual age for attachment formation; a better guideline to follow would be "it is never too late."

The case of Genie

The acquisition of language has also been discussed in the light of the critical-period hypothesis. Language, according to some writers, is crucially dependent on the "right" sort of experience (i.e. speech input from others) at the "right" sort of time – though apart from the fact that this must occur in early childhood there is little agreement as to what its limits are. The difficulty with this notion lies in confirming it, and the rare instances of children who miss out on language experience during the early years do not provide unequivocal evidence because the children miss out on so much else as well.

The best known example is provided by Genie, a girl brought up in virtual isolation in her home in Los Angeles from the second year onwards and not discovered till the age of 13. Her father, a mentally sick man with a hatred for children, confined Genie in a small room and refused to let anyone speak to her. Thus for a period of about 12 years she heard no speech at all – neither from other people nor from radio or television. When discovered she was extremely disturbed emotionally, quite inept socially, physically retarded and also malnourished. Yet efforts to teach her to speak (documented in detail by Curtiss, 1982) did have some success:

she learned single words, began to string them together to form sentences and used speech meaningfully to communicate with others. Yet what she learned remained extremely limited. She was unable to grasp many of the most basic concepts of grammar (e.g. putting "-ed" at the end of verbs to express the past tense); word order gave her trouble; she did not learn how to ask questions; and even her intonation remained abnormal. After six years of living with a foster family her speech was still deviant to a very marked degree.

Whether observations such as these shed any light on the question of a critical period for language acquisition must be doubted, despite the claims and counterclaims that have been made: a single-case study, where there are so many other complicating factors and where the evidence of language acquisition is so equivocal, is hardly likely to resolve such a complex issue. According to Lenneberg (1967) the critical period for language acquisition lasts until puberty – a span of criticality so long that the concept loses all sense. Like the research on attachment formation, data about language acquisition give little reason to confirm the usefulness of the critical-period hypothesis in understanding the nature of human development.

Acute Stress

Early experiences, we can conclude, do not necessarily produce irreversible effects just because they are early. But what of those highly stressful events that children may encounter at any time in the course of development – traumatic experiences that, because of the intensity of their impact, cause much upset at the time and may well be remembered for years to come? Do they bring about changes in a child's personality that may be of a long-term nature?

Let us consider what is surely one of the worst experiences a child may encounter, namely the suicide of a parent. Two psychiatrists, Shepherd and Barraclough (1976), investigated a group of such children, following them up over a period of several years after the event and comparing their progress with that of a control group from a similar social background. There was no doubt that all children were much affected at the time of the suicide and that this was experienced by them as a major trauma. When seen several years later the group as a whole was characterized by a considerably greater incidence of psychological problems than the comparison group; more significant, however, was the fact that among the children there was great variation in their long-term reactions to this experience. Some were markedly disturbed and gave cause for concern, yet others were functioning normally and showed no sign of maladjustment despite the fact that the circumstances of the suicide had been just as traumatic. The reason for this difference, according to Shepherd and Barraclough, could be found in the general pattern of the children's lives in which that specific event was embedded: where the dead parent had been alcoholic or violent or markedly abnormal and where such behavior caused marital and other family problems children were much more likely to show emotional scars years later than in those cases where the parent's troubles had remained reasonably self-contained. The traumatic experience itself, that is, had to be seen in the context of the quality of life experienced by the child over the years.

Investigations of the impact of other kinds of stressful events lead to similar conclusions. Take the effects on children of natural disasters such as earthquakes, volcanic eruptions, hurricanes, floods, and fires – all extremely frightening at the time and responsible for much short-term upset, yet not necessarily the cause of long-term damage (Saylor, 1993). A study of the effects on children of a brushfire in Australia that had devastated a vast area, destroying many homes and farms and killing huge numbers of livestock, can serve as an example (McFarlane, 1988). When assessed at various points in the two–year period following the disaster, it was found that for the group as a whole the trauma was a significant though not overwhelming cause of psychological disorder in the children. About a fifth of the 240 children investigated were regarded as disturbed two years later; the remainder appeared to be functioning normally. Again we find that the traumatic event per se need not bring about long-term damage, and again there are indications that the event must be seen in the context of more lasting experiences. In this instance these experiences referred primarily to the way in which the children's parents reacted to the disaster: the greater their disturbance (as a result of loss of home, livelihood, income, etc.) the greater the likelihood the child was disturbed too. It seems that the extreme stress that is experienced at one specific point of time will produce long-term effects if, but only if, it leads to further problems that maintain the impact of the initial trauma. Parents whose whole lifestyle has been destroyed may well create a different emotional atmosphere for the child to grow up in subsequently; when they suffer from severe post-traumatic stress their ability to provide psychological support for the child will consequently be impaired. If the child is later found to manifest some degree of disturbance it is more likely that the factor responsible is the continuing adversity, such as family atmosphere and parental mood, rather than the impact of the single trauma, however horrific at the time. And, seeing that any one traumatic episode may be embedded in many different kinds of family contexts, the outcome can be quite diverse, with long-term effects primarily dependent on what preceded and what followed that specific episode (A. M. Clarke & Clarke, 1976).

One relatively common experience in early childhood that causes great distress at the time is separation from the parents, such as when a child is admitted to hospital or taken into public care. Children within the age range of approximately 6 months and 5 years are particularly vulnerable; any break in the bond whereby the parent is no longer readily available constitutes a considerable trauma for such children and especially so if it involves the child being looked after by unfamiliar people in an unfamiliar environment (Schaffer, 1990). Yet it has also become evident that a temporary separation on its own is unlikely to damage the child's development in the long term; once the bond is restored there may be a period of regressive behavior and insecurity, but provided this is met with by competent, sensitive parenting the child will soon resume normal behavior. On the other hand, *repeated* separations do have an effect which tends to be cumulative, as Quinton and Rutter (1976) noted when relating children's psychological adjustment scores to their hospitalization experiences. Single hospital admissions were not found to be associated with any form of psychological disturbance in later years whereas repeated admissions did show such an association, and especially as their number and length increased. This is in keeping with the common finding that the more risk factors a child encounters the greater is the likelihood of long-term psychopathology (Masten & Coatsworth, 1995): after any one stress children are no more likely to have behavior problems than children who have not encountered any stresses; the combination of two or more stresses, on the other hand, progressively increases the probability that the child will develop psychopathology.

There is one further finding by Quinton and Rutter that is relevant to us, namely that the likelihood of an adverse outcome of separation experiences is greatest in the case of those children who come from a disadvantaged home. Children who for one reason or another are already insecure or troubled are the ones most likely to be damaged by such experiences: thus, when their family background is characterized by conflict and their relationships are already insecure, even single and temporary separations produce a disproportionately severe effect. Yet again we must conclude that it is not the specific trauma but the family situation which existed before and to which the child will return that is the crucial influence in determining subsequent pathology.

Chronic Adversity

In the light of findings such as those described above the search for the antecedents of adult difficulties has switched from acute and early trauma, impinging on the child at one specific point of time, to chronic experiences which adversely affect the child over periods of years. Early experience does have a special significance: as A. M.

Clarke and Clarke (1976) put it, it is *foundational* in character in that it tends to set the tone for subsequent experience. Thus one unfortunate event may well lead to further unfortunate events, representing the first link in a chain the end result of which is pathology. It is, however, the chain as a whole that is more likely to be responsible for this outcome rather than any one link; what is more, it has also become apparent that there is nothing inevitable about this outcome: chains can be broken and pathology averted.

A striking example of both the damaging effects of chronic adversity and the possibility of reversing these effects is provided by the impact on children of extreme deprivation of parental care. Wayne Dennis (1973), in a classical study of children reared for the first six years of their lives in a Middle Eastern orphanage (referred to as the Creche), described graphically the consequences of the drastic lack of individual care to which these children were subjected. From the early weeks of life these children were rarely talked to, played with, or even picked up; feeding often involved a bottle propped up on a pillow; opportunities to leave their crib, let alone their room, were few; and in general the level of environmental stimulation provided in the Creche was vastly below that which we usually regard as desirable. As a result Dennis observed progressive deterioration in the children's developmental status – from a mean Developmental Quotient of 100 at the beginning of the first year (indicating average functioning) to a mere 53 at the end of the first year (i.e. 12-month-old infants were performing at the level of 6-month-old infants). This severe retardation continued throughout the stay in the Creche: for example, more than half the children were still not able to sit up at 21 months of age and less than 15 percent were able to walk by the age of 3. Children of apparently good potential had thus become retarded to an extreme degree as a result of their treatment throughout infancy and early childhood.

When the children reached the age of 6 they were transferred to another institution more suitable for older children – the girls to one and the boys to another. Some children had also by then been placed in adoptive families. Further assessment showed that the girls continued to function at the same grossly retarded level: at the age of 16 they had a mean IQ of approximately 50 and were obviously mentally handicapped to a quite severe degree. The boys, on the other hand, fared much better: they obtained a mean IQ of about 80, indicating that they were now performing within the normal range. Though somewhat below average, they appeared to have made a marked recovery. This applied even more so to the adopted children – indeed those adopted before the age of 2 obtained an average IQ of 95 in their teens. Why the difference between the institutionalized girls and the other two groups? The answer appears to lie in the kind of environment in which the children lived after the age of 6. The girls' institution was every bit as barren as the first in which they had been reared; their deprivation simply continued. The boys' institution, for one reason or another, was very much more stimulating: it was better staffed, had far more educational and recreational facilities and provided the children with much more individual attention. This applied, of course, even more so to the adopted children who lived normal family lives. Thus extreme deprivation of parental care produced severe retardation, and where it continued throughout childhood that retardation also continued. However, even after 6 years the effects proved to be largely reversible: the damage brought about even by such long-term adversity was not permanent (see figure 31).

Dennis examined only intellectual effects and we know nothing about other aspects of these children's personalities. Yet there are indications from other studies that similar conclusions apply there too. This is strikingly shown in reports by Koluchova (1976a, 1976b) on a pair of twin boys in Czechoslovakia who, from infancy on, were brought up by their father and stepmother in a state of gross deprivation and isolation. To quote from Koluchova's report:

> The boys grew up in almost total isolation, separated from the outside world; they were never allowed out of the house or into the main living rooms. . . . They lived in a small, unheated closet, and were often locked up for long periods in the cellar. They slept on the floor on a polythene sheet and were cruelly chastised. They used to sit at a small table in an otherwise empty room, with a few building bricks which were their only toys.

This regime continued until the boys were discovered at the age of 7 years and rescued from their plight. Their psychological state at that time was parlous: they were barely able to walk, could communicate with each other only by gestures, were extremely frightened of any new experience, and had few social skills which they could use in relating to either the children or the adults that they now encountered in the outside world. After a period in a children's home the boys were placed with two middle-aged sisters who became their foster parents and devoted their lives to their care. Gradually the children acquired enough intellectual and language skills to

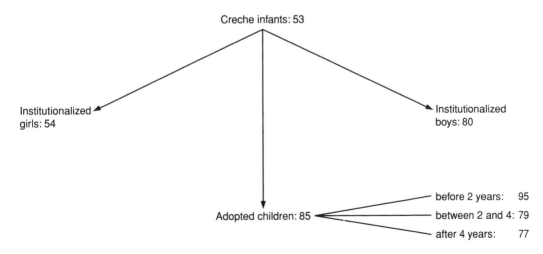

Figure 31   IQs of children deprived of parental care (based on Dennis, 1973)

enable them to attend school; gradually they showed that they were of normal intelligence and could benefit from education; and gradually they also acquired the social skills to enable them to live with others in a normal fashion. The improvement continued: at age 23 they had graduated from a technical high school and were working as electricians; they had caught up scholastically by then and cognitively and emotionally appeared to be normal (A. D. B. Clarke & Clarke, 1984). Again, a prolonged experience that produced a horrendous degree of pathology was found to be reversible in its consequences. What we do not know, of course, is how much longer the children's deprivation would have had to go on for before it eventually left irreversible effects.

Such experiences are fortunately rare, but there are other forms of chronic adversity that, while less severe, are very much more common. Being raised in an atmosphere of family conflict is perhaps the most notable example – one that has been highlighted by the great increase in divorce which brings to an end about 1 in every 3 marriages and which involves a very large number of children (about 40 percent of children being born now in the United States will, according to some calculations, experience the divorce of their parents some time before the age of 16). More often than not divorce is associated with periods of parental conflict that may well have gone on for years before the parents separate and that sometimes continue afterwards too, and as has been amply demonstrated the total experience can cause considerable distress to children caught up in it.

The effects of parental divorce on children have been summarized by a number of writers (e.g. Amato, 1993; Emery, 1982; Hetherington, 1993; Wallerstein, Corbin, & Lewis, 1988). The main findings are:

- Nearly all children, whatever their age, are adversely affected by this experience, at least in the short term.
- The nature, severity, and duration of effects vary greatly from one child to another.
- There is some evidence that the immediate effects are greater among boys than among girls.
- There are also indications that these effects are most marked in mid-childhood rather than in the preschool period or in adolescence.
- The effects manifest themselves outside the home as well as inside, and involve relationships with siblings and peers as well as with parents.
- Many children gradually adjust after two or three years following the divorce, though this is influenced by a large constellation of factors including the continuity of contact with the noncustodial parent, the financial status of the single-parent family and therefore its lifestyle, and whether the custodial parent remarries and a congenial stepfamily is formed.
- As to long-term effects, there is still disagreement on such matters as the children's own marital relationships in adulthood and the likelihood of their divorce.

Just what about the total divorce experience brings about adverse effects in children? A great many factors are involved, all of which play some part, but there is now ample evidence that the critical factor is exposure to parental conflict before, during, and also often after the parents' separation and formal divorce (Amato & Keith, 1991; Emery, 1982). This conclusion is supported by the following findings:

- Children from intact families where there is conflict show more behavior problems than children from intact families without conflict.
- Children from broken (i.e. one-parent) families that are conflict-free are better adjusted than children from intact but conflict-ridden families.
- Children who have lost a parent through divorce are more likely to show adverse effects than children who have lost a parent through death.
- Children whose divorcing parents have managed to avoid overt conflict are less at risk for the development of behavior problems than those whose parents did engage in conflict.
- The more conflict there is in a family the greater is the likelihood of undesirable consequences for the child.
- Behavior problems often appear long before the parents' divorce.

The last point is perhaps the most convincing. When Block, Block, and Gjerde (1986, 1988) followed up a large group of children from the age of 3 they found, first, that children whose parents had recently divorced were more likely to be psychologically disturbed than children whose parents remained together, and second, that the origins of such disturbance could be traced back to a period long before the parents actually separated. The so-called effects of parental divorce, that is, occurred well before the divorce, and the responsible factor is therefore not so much the break in the relationship brought about by the dissolution of the marriage as the atmosphere of discord and tension that existed while the parents were still living together. As Block and colleagues found, parents who eventually divorce tend to disagree more among themselves about child rearing methods than other parents; they are also less supportive with and less interested in their children – a result, presumably, of their marital problems which spill over into the relationship with the child.

Why does conflict between parents have such destructive effects on children? Answers have been sought both through observational and interview studies and by means of laboratory investigations in which children's reactions to simulated conflict are recorded (Cummings, 1994). One thing the latter show clearly is that children, exposed to repeated incidents of conflict, do not get used to it: on the contrary, they become *sensitized* in showing increasingly greater reactivity. Thus their emotional arousal will be elicited more quickly, more intensely, and for a longer period on subsequent occasions than initially; the fact that they know what to expect makes things worse, not better. When children are exposed to such scenes day in, day out over a period of months or years, their own capacity to regulate their emotions is likely to become impaired: instead of gradually gaining control over emotional displays such as aggression they will continue to express them overtly, encouraged by the behavior which their parents model for them.

The emotional arousal experienced by children witnessing their parents' fighting and arguing, as well as the example set thereby, are *direct* effects. There are also *indirect* effects: marital conflicts can bring about distortions in family relationships, and it is these distortions that may then produce further behavior problems. From a child's point of view it is the changes in the quality of parenting produced by marital difficulties that are of most consequence (J. M. Jenkins & Smith, 1991). When parents are under stress as a result of marital problems the relationship with the child also suffers. The effects include inconsistent discipline, increased intrusiveness and control, less affection in some cases and (to compensate for its lack in the marital relationship) overwhelming affection in others, and lack of adequate supervision due to the parent's preoccupation (Belsky, Youngblade, Rovine, & Volling, 1991; Holden & Ritchie, 1991). Marital conflict, reduced quality of parenting, and children's behavior problems thus go hand in hand.

Table 52 Conditions ameliorating children's adverse reactions to parental divorce

1 Reduction of parental conflict
   Even after divorce the parents must in many cases continue to make joint decisions about the child. The establishment of smooth working relationships is thus essential for the child's well-being

2 Regular contact with the noncustodial parent
   Continuation of the relationship with the parent no longer regularly living with the child is nearly always essential, even after the custodial parent's remarriage

3 The well-being of the custodial parent
   Much depends on his or (more often) her success in adjusting to single parenthood, especially as this will affect the ability to provide a stable, supportive environment for the child

4 Maintenance of the family's lifestyle
   The majority of single-parent families are financially worse off. The more this can be avoided the more undesirable consequences for the child can also be avoided

5 Avoidance of disruption of child's life over and above parental separation
   Moving to a new neighborhood, a new house, and a new school, with the consequent loss of friends and other local support, often follow parental divorce. Again it helps to avoid such additional stresses

6 In case of remarriage, the establishment of a positive relationship with the stepparent
   Remarriage has been found to bring about both positive and negative consequences for children. Much depends on the quality of relationships established in the new family

Source: Based on Emery (1982); Hetherington (1993); Hetherington et al. (1989); Wallerstein et al. (1988)

There is no doubt that the experience of chronic parental disharmony can have deleterious effects on children. However, two qualifications need to be added. First, not all children are equally affected: as J. M. Jenkins and Smith (1991) found, some children even in homes characterized by a great deal of conflict are able to cope and escape pathology. Coping mechanisms can take many forms; J. M. Jenkins, Smith, and Graham (1989), for instance, found that seeking contact with a sibling, confiding in friends, offering comfort to parents and interpreting parental quarrels as beneficial were among the strategies which 9- to 12-year-old children employed. The second qualification refers to the fact that even when children have been exposed to marital discord for a lengthy period adverse effects need not be permanent. As we noted above in summarizing the findings of research on divorce, children usually recover two to three years after the parents' separation and learn to adjust to their new way of life. But this outcome is not inevitable; it depends on the "right" conditions being present, and much effort therefore needs to be spent on finding what these ameliorating conditions are (see table 52 for some examples).

There are other examples of chronic adversity which are known to produce psychopathology in children, though parental conflict is probably the most common and certainly the most thoroughly investigated. Alcoholism in parents is one: it too impinges on children both directly, i.e. through the scenes created by the parent, and indirectly by means of distorted parent–child relationships. Yet, as M. O. West and Prinz (1987) point out in their summary of research on this topic, by no means all children from alcoholic homes are inevitably doomed to psychological disorder. Parental alcoholism does not occur in a vacuum: its effects may be mitigated or exacerbated by other factors prevailing in the family (of which marital conflict is one) which *in toto* determine the outcome. In itself a parent's alcoholism is a risk factor, but risks can be averted and do not necessarily lead to unfortunate end results. The identification of risk factors is essential, but equally essential is to understand the processes that lead some children to develop psychopathology when exposed to risk and others to avoid such an outcome.

The case of parental conflict and juvenile offending

To illustrate the effects of exposure to parental conflict on one particular outcome, i.e. children's delinquent behavior in early adolescence, let us turn to a study by Fergusson, Horwood, and Lynskey (1992), based on a birth cohort of New Zealand children who had been followed up throughout childhood. Information was obtained from over 700 of this group about the (mostly minor) offenses committed by them during the age period 11 to 13; at the same time data were also collected regarding both parental conflict and such family changes as separation, reconciliation, and remarriage.

A close relationship emerged from the findings between parental conflict and children's rate of offending: the more children had been exposed to prolonged arguments between their parents or witnessed incidents of physical assault the more likely it was that they had engaged in some delinquent behavior in early adolescence. However, exposure to family change showed no such relationship: children, that is, who had experienced parental separation in the absence of overt discord showed low rates of offending. The crucial role of conflict is thus once again indicated.

This does not mean, of course, that all children exposed to conflict will inevitably become offenders. Even within this group there was considerable variability in this respect, and Fergusson and his colleagues found some evidence that this was because parental conflict affected those children most who were, for one reason or another, already predisposed to developing delinquent behavior. Thus the greatest impact appeared to be on children who had shown an early history of conduct problems – i.e. externalizing behavior such as aggressiveness, disobedience, and truancy. For instance, boys with an exposure to parental conflict plus high levels of early conduct problems were found to have a 90 percent chance of offending; on the other hand, girls with no exposure to conflict and low levels of early problem behavior had a close to zero probability of committing offenses before the age of 13.

Thus parental conflict puts children at risk, at least with respect to one kind of undesirable outcome, i.e. juvenile delinquency. But it is also clear that there is no simple one-to-one relationship between these two variables; the outcome is not an invariable one but depends on other aspects too.

Multiple Outcomes

The belief that particular childhood experiences will invariably lead to particular outcomes in adulthood is clearly an oversimplified notion. Predicting from early life to later end points has turned out to be a futile exercise; even long-term adversity need not produce irreversible effects. The methodological approach whereby one compares a group of children who have had a particular unfortunate experience with a group without such an experience may be of use in spotting risk factors; it is of no use, however, in understanding why some children escape that risk and others do not. For instance, it has been established that approximately one in three of physically abused children will develop into an abusing adult (Kaufman & Zigler, 1987); in so far as this is an incidence rate vastly above that for the population as a whole children who have undergone such an experience must be considered a risk group for this kind of outcome. Yet one cannot neglect the fact that two out of the three will *not* become abusing adults; it is necessary therefore to consider what distinguishes these two from the first child. Methodologically, a focus is thus required on individual differences within the affected group in order to understand the specific processes whereby the same experience can lead to a diversity of outcomes. We have already seen that long-term effects are very much dependent on life experiences subsequent to early adversity; tracing the chain reactions and examining each link in the chain should thus provide an insight into how individual children eventually develop their mature personality characteristics. In addition we also need to take into account the factors that make for greater vulnerability to stress in some children than in others, whose resilience when confronted by similar misfortune leads to a more favorable outcome.

Vulnerability and Resilience

As every study of children's behavior under stress shows, in the face of apparently identical circumstances there is great variability in reaction. Some individuals are completely bowled over; others emerge relatively unscathed. What accounts for such differences?

At one time the attention of both research workers and professionals charged with the care of children focused entirely on *victims* – those who have succumbed to deprivation, maltreatment, abuse, and stress. This is hardly surprising, for these children are obviously in urgent need of help. It is only more recently that attention has also been given to *survivors* – the children who also encountered trauma yet came through relatively unharmed. The trauma itself is thus not a sufficient cause of subsequent pathology; other factors also play a part, including both *risk factors*, that is, those that increase the probability of some undesirable outcome as a result of exposure to stress, and *protective factors*, which have the opposite result in buffering children against such outcomes. A lot of effort is now being devoted to the search for such factors, for understanding why children differ in their standing along the vulnerability–resilience continuum will make it easier to predict the outcome of stress experiences and should also help in our efforts to prevent undesirable outcomes.

One of the most influential studies in this endeavor is that conducted by Emmy Werner (1989, 1993; E. E. Werner & Smith, 1982). It involves the follow-up of all 698 babies born in one year on the Hawaiian island of Kauai, on whom information was subsequently collected when they were 2, 10, 18, and 32 years old. A substantial number of these children were reared under conditions of considerable adversity: about half grew up in poverty, and many encountered such additional serious risk factors as pre- and perinatal complications, parental mental illness or alcoholism, and disruption of the family unit. It is therefore not surprising to find that a large proportion developed behavior problems of some kind. What is also notable is the further finding that other children, equally exposed to such adversities, appeared to remain unscathed throughout childhood, adolescence, and early adulthood. Thus about two-thirds of the high-risk children did develop serious psychological or educational problems at some point in childhood, acquired a criminal record or became pregnant in adolescence, and had mental health difficulties in their thirties. The remaining one-third, however, developed very differently: they coped with life at home, succeeded in school, managed to lead a useful social life, and grew into competent, confident and caring young adults. Why the difference?

One factor (to which we have already drawn attention in this connection in chapter 2) is the children's *sex*. In their first decade boys tended to be less resilient than girls in the face of a wide variety of physiological and psychosocial stresses. At birth more boys than girls encountered perinatal difficulties, and of those children with the most serious complications a greater proportion of boys died. In subsequent years boys were more likely to develop behavior problems, encounter difficulties at school, require medical help for serious illness, come to the attention of mental health services, and acquire a delinquency record. In the second decade this pattern changed: by age 18 more boys than girls had improved, and any new problems appeared more frequently among girls than boys. Nevertheless, overall in the course of childhood females appeared to cope rather more successfully with the various stresses they encountered than males.

Another factor, one which played a particularly significant part throughout childhood, was the children's *temperament*. "Easy" infants were likely to become resilient children; "difficult" infants frequently turned out to be highly vulnerable to life's stresses. Even in the first year the resilient children had elicited positive attention from others; they were described as affectionate, cuddly and good natured, with fewer eating and sleeping problems, and throughout early childhood they were more likely to elicit approval and support from adults and be involved in positive interactions with peers. Many of the vulnerable children, on the other hand, continued to be regarded as difficult; their effect on others was often negative and they were thus less likely to experience the supportive relationships which might have stood them in good stead when faced with adversity. No wonder that, as adults, they were found to have developed a less positive self-concept and to be less responsible, assertive, and achievement-oriented than the resilient children.

Werner noted quite a number of other factors which also distinguished vulnerable and resilient children. For instance, resilient children were more likely to have grown up in families with four or fewer children, with a space of two years or more between themselves and their next sibling; fewer had experienced prolonged separations early in life; more had the opportunity to form close bonds with family members; and more sought and found emotional support outside the family, such as from relatives, teachers, and friends. The presence of an intact family unit throughout childhood was especially significant as a protective factor; it helped to explain, for example, why youths who had become involved in minor delinquent activities did not go on to a more serious criminal career as adults. Other studies have added to the list of factors that influence children's reactions to stress; table 53 lists the most important.

As a result of studies such as Werner's we can point to a number of conclusions about the nature of vulnerability and resilience (Masten, 1994; Rutter, 1987):

- Some of the factors responsible for children's differing responsiveness to adversity reside within the child; others operate from outside. The former include inborn characteristics such as sex, temperament and intelligence, and also acquired personality features such as the self-esteem that a child develops. The

377 Social Experience and its Aftermath 377

Table 53 Examples of factors influencing children's susceptibility to stress

Factors operating from "within" child

Sex

girls are less vulnerable than boys in early childhood, but more so in adolescence

Temperament

children with "easy" temperament withstand stress better than those with "difficult" temperament

Intelligence

children capable of good academic achievement preserve their self-esteem better despite adversity in other spheres of life

Birth condition

children exposed to birth complications, prematurity, etc., require extra support to develop personal resources for coping with stress

Factors operating from "outside" child

Family harmony

children from conflict-free families are less likely to be harmed by stress than children from conflictual families

Close attachments

supportive relationships protect children; even one good relationship with a parent can buffer the child against the adverse effects of an unsatisfactory relationship with the other parent

Parental caregiving styles

styles such as the authoritative one which foster children's self-esteem provide the confidence to face up to adversity

Availability of substitute caregivers

the beneficial influence of alternate figures such as grandparents is an insurance against the loss of support from parents

Separation

children leading a stable, predictable existence develop more means to deal with life problems

Number and spacing of children in family

when children do not have to compete to an inordinate degree for parental attention they are more likely to develop personal resources for coping with stress

Parental psychopathology

children whose parents are psychologically unavailable because of mental illness or addiction may be less secure and more vulnerable

Poverty

the large number of stresses associated with poverty makes children more susceptible to any problematic experience

latter refer to environmental influences, including family relationships, lifestyle, and separation experiences.

• Child factors and environmental factors do not operate in isolation but interact in various ways. For instance, an easy temperament makes it more likely that the parents will form a warm, supportive relationship with the child; such a relationship in turn will then become a protective factor.

- Vulnerability is not a unitary entity; assessing an individual's reactions to one type of adversity does not necessarily enable one to predict that person's reactions to another type. Stability from one situation to another cannot therefore be taken for granted.
- Variability over time may also occur. Vulnerable children can develop resilience; resilient children may become vulnerable. On the other hand, where the child's experience reinforces the lessons of the past continuity is more likely. Thus success breeds success: a child who has coped well with adversity will be more confident in tackling new stresses, and by the same token unfortunate past experiences may well make it more difficult for a child to cope with future adversity.
- The effects of past history on current behavior are channeled through an individual's self-esteem. Successful outcomes provide self-confidence and raise children's belief that they are able to cope; unsuccessful outcomes have the opposite effect.
- Understanding the sources of vulnerability and resilience helps us in planning intervention strategies aimed at preventing or at least minimizing ill-effects on children exposed to stress. Masten (1994) lists four basic strategies for this purpose: (1) reducing children's vulnerability, e.g. through eliminating poverty or preventing birth complications, (2) reducing exposure to stress, e.g. by providing mediation services to divorcing parents and so lessening their conflict, (3) increasing the availability of resources to children at risk, e.g. by alerting teachers to the needs of vulnerable children, and (4) mobilizing protective processes, e.g. by fostering positive relationships with parents.

The case of parental support as a protective factor in adolescence

Let us examine in more detail what is perhaps the most important protective factor, namely the support that parents provide at times of difficulty. As has been repeatedly established, parenting that is warm and supportive gives rise to all sorts of beneficial effects, and while social support from virtually any source (peers, teachers, relatives, etc.) can be of help, that received from parents tends to be the most effective buffer in the face of stress (Belle, 1989). Even just one good relationship with a parent can bring this about, and may indeed protect the child against the ill-effects of a poor relationship with the other parent (Rutter, 1979).

The start of adolescence is often the time when support is particularly badly needed. As we previously saw, multiple stresses then impinge on the child as a result of puberty and school changes, with implications for the individual's self-concept, body image, peer relationships and emotional adjustment. These tend to affect girls more severely than boys, as seen in the incidence of depressive symptoms: whereas during childhood this is somewhat greater among males, from the age of 12 or 13 on such symptoms become more prevalent among females (Ge et al., 1994). The reason for this change is not clear, though there are indications that in adolescence girls tend to be more exposed to stressful events and more upset by them when they occur. In any case, while boys remain at the same level, girls' vulnerability continues to increase (Petersen, Sarigiani, & Kennedy, 1991).

Despite the fact that in adolescence peer relationships assume a much greater importance than hitherto, when faced with severe stresses young people still regard parents as the main source of support. As established by several studies (e.g. Ge et al., 1994; Petersen et al., 1991), closeness with parents moderates the negative effects of adverse life events; the relationship with a sympathetic parent appears to provide the "arena of comfort" that adolescents require (Simmons, Burgeson, & Careton-Ford, 1987). There is some uncertainty whether the effect is found for both sexes or only for girls, and whether it applies only to the relationship with the mother or equally to that with the father; what is certain is that parents can act as a buffer against general life events and that the kind of relationship established with them can make all the difference in adolescents' ability to cope even with such specific stresses as, for example, the problems caused by diabetes (Hauser, Vieyra, Jacobson, & Wertlieb, 1985).

In so far as adolescence is often a troublesome time there is an urgent need to find effective ways of reducing stress and the resulting symptomatology. The precise means whereby parents can exercise their protective function must therefore be identified. According to Sandler, Miller, Short, and Wolchnik (1989), they do so primarily through three processes: enhancing their children's self-esteem, so that their sense of worthiness is not impaired by any apparent failure to cope; giving direct assistance in tackling the source of stress in a constructive manner; and reinforcing their feeling of security through providing them with a warm and accepting relationship. In so far as the parent–child relationship tends to change with the onset of puberty it appears to be those parents who are capable of maintaining closeness in the face of this change that are most likely to succeed in their protective function.

Developmental Pathways

Rather than attempt directly to link early experience with later personality functioning in a one-to-one fashion, the particular developmental pathways that lead by multiple steps from one to the other need to be investigated. And rather than expect all children to follow the same pathways allowance must be made for a diversity of experiences guiding children to different outcomes. Longitudinal studies that trace the whole sequence and so fill in the time gap are thus necessary; these are time-consuming and the results from only a few are as yet available.

Among the best known of such studies are two that were launched in California around 1930, namely the Oakland Growth Study based on children born around 1920–1 and the Berkeley Guidance Study based on children born in 1928–9. By chance, both samples were exposed to a prolonged period of severe adversity, brought about by the Great Depression which hit very many families in that area in the early 1930s and caused large-scale unemployment and considerable financial hardship. The impact on the families, as plotted in a series of follow-up investigations, has been described in detail in a number of reports by Glen Elder and his colleagues (e.g. Elder, 1974; Elder & Caspi, 1988); here we shall focus primarily on the implications for the children's development of this natural experiment.

These implications varied according to both the children's age and their sex. The Oakland group were already entering adolescence at the time of the crisis, and as a result of the sudden income loss they became involved in the various shifts of economic and domestic roles that took place in these families. Fathers who were no longer breadwinners became peripheral figures, and responsibilities increasingly evolved to the mother but also to the adolescent children. Mothers, particularly when they were able to pick up a job, assumed more power and authority, but as conditions worsened the adolescents also became more valuable. They were required to help meet the increased work and economic needs of these deprived households, and particularly among the sons a large number did manage to obtain paid jobs, albeit of a part-time and unskilled nature, while girls became primarily involved in household duties. As a result these young people, in contrast to those who did not take on extra responsibilities, reached the status of adulthood much more rapidly: having had to leave the world of childhood behind sooner they became more independent, more effective, and more oriented to adult values than others of their age. However, the effect differed for boys and girls. Boys, as a result of obtaining jobs outside the family, freed themselves at a relatively early age from the traditional constraints of parental control; in addition, they frequently responded to the stresses of family life by becoming involved in peer activities and thus spending a large part of their time outside the home. When seen in later years as adults they had retained their faith in industriousness and were less inclined to flounder from one job to another. The girls, on the other hand, became homebound as a result of their increased domestic duties; moreover, lack of money meant they had less to spend on clothes, cosmetics, and other items valued in adolescence, and in consequence they tended sharply to reduce their outside social activities such as dating. When seen in subsequent years they had become women with a strong orientation to home and family; they valued home making and parental responsibilities, and they had also married earlier and had children sooner than their peers from nondeprived backgrounds. Thus despite the considerable difficulties encountered in their adolescence both boys and girls gained in personal growth, though in different ways. Having found that they were needed and that they had a real contribution to make even at that relatively early age they responded by growing up more quickly.

The children from the Berkeley study were considerably younger when the Great Depression hit their families. As preschoolers they were much more dependent on their parents and consequently more vulnerable to family instability. The effects on them were thus more negative than those on the Oakland adolescents: not only did they develop various behavior problems at the time but even in adolescence they were found to be less confident and to hold lower aspirations and therefore to perform more poorly scholastically. However, this was much more marked in boys than in girls: the latter, as found in many other studies, appeared to be less vulnerable during early childhood to the effects of stress; they were also less affected than the boys by the changed relationship with the father, whose frustrations and tensions were likely to make him very much more punitive and rejecting than he had been before the crisis.

There is thus a causal sequence from economic hardship to the children's adjustment, this being affected in both direct and indirect ways by the parents' reactions to the crisis. Unemployment and financial problems bring about mood changes in the parents to which children will respond in various negative ways. As a result of these changes parents' treatment of their children will also change; in addition the relationship between mother and father may deteriorate under the stress of their situation. Both these influences will raise the risk of behavior problems developing in the children, and a more problematic child will in turn make the parents more tense and thus more punitive and arbitrary in their treatment of that child.

A later study by Elder, to which we referred in chapter 7 (see p. 343), described the reactions of a different sample of families to another economic crisis, namely the breakdown in agriculture which Midwestern America experienced in the 1980s. There are a number of differences in findings between the two sets of studies; nevertheless, the crucial role that altered parental behavior plays in affecting the outcome for children receives strong confirmation there (Elder, Conger, Foster, & Ardelt, 1992). In particular, there too the increased hostility and punitiveness of fathers under stress from economic hardship was found to increase the likelihood of aggressive behavior and depressed feelings developing in the children. Thus the adverse effects of financial problems encountered by the family do not necessarily impinge directly on children; reduced spending money may have some consequences, but it is the disorganizing effects on family relationships above all that provide the vital link between adversity and outcome for these children. The effects on the father's (and to a lesser extent the mother's) mood, together with any marital tensions that developed, mediated the way in which the economic stresses impinged on the child through the changes produced in parenting practices. There was, of course, nothing inevitable about this sequence: where parents managed to remain calm, resolved their marital conflicts and continued to care for the child in a consistent way children were protected from the psychological costs of the crisis; where, on the other hand, the economic stress adversely affected the parents' mood and thereby their child rearing practices, and where fathers in particular assumed a hostile and rejecting attitude, the children were put at risk. Thus by investigating the period intervening between adversity and outcome and by disentangling the various elements characterizing the families it is possible to locate the crucial links and so account for the fact that different children can end up differently after the same experience.

The quality of family relationships and the nature of parenting have emerged as the vital mediating processes from other investigations too. An example is the series of studies by George Brown and his colleagues (e.g. G. Brown, 1988; G. Brown,

Harris, & Bifulco, 1986; T. Harris, Brown, & Bifulco, 1986) on the childhood antecedents of depression in adult women. It has long been thought that one such antecedent of depression may be the loss of a parent during childhood, yet research that has merely attempted to link the one with the other has come up with contradictory and inconclusive results. The virtue of Brown's studies is that the influence of other, intervening experiences has also been taken into account. The findings show, first of all, that women who had lost a mother either through death or through prolonged separation before the age of 17 were at risk for the development of clinical depression; this did not apply to loss of father. Second, the women at greatest risk were those who had experienced "aberrant" separations, that is, those brought about not by death or even divorce but by the mother's neglect or rejection. The circumstances in which the loss occurred, with particular reference to the quality of the parenting that the child had received, appeared to matter more than the loss per se. And third, the most influential factor leading to subsequent depression was the lack of satisfactory parental care *following* the loss which many of the children experienced. Thus when one compares women who had lost a mother but who did receive adequate subsequent care with women who had not lost a parent the rate of depression was no greater among the former than the latter (see table 54); similarly, the reason that loss of father put these women at less of a risk was that the children were very much more likely to remain at home and continue to receive adequate care than after the loss of the mother. We can conclude that losing a mother in childhood predisposes the individual to depression in later years, but only if it leads to later lack of proper parental care. The specific event, that is, assumes importance if it brings about an unsatisfactory situation of a *chronic* nature for the child.

Let us note one further finding by the Brown group. Loss of mother, particularly when brought about for "aberrant" reasons, was found to increase the chances of the child being put on a conveyor belt of ever-greater adversity. As shown in figure 32, the mother's loss increased the chances 3.6-fold of subsequent poor care arrangements. This was associated with a 2.5 times increase in the likelihood of a premarital pregnancy, which in turn made it more probable that the girl would not advance socially and that she would marry an undependable man. Lack of parental care also increased the chances that the girl would develop feelings of helplessness, and

Table 54 Rate of depression among women according to childhood experience of loss

Type of loss	Adequate care (%)	Inadequate care (%)
Death of mother	10	34
Separation from mother	4	36
Death of father	0	0
Separation from father	12	50
No loss of either parent	3	13
No loss of mother	4	21

Source: Based on T. Harris et al. (1986)

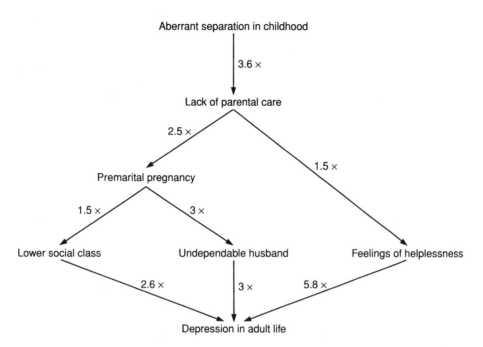

Figure 32 Pathways from "aberrant" separations in childhood to adult depression (from Rutter, 1989, based on data from G. W. Brown et al., 1986)

together these various strands greatly raised the likelihood that the final outcome in adult life would be clinical depression. The pathway from childhood experience to adult outcome may thus involve a whole sequence of steps, each of which is made more likely by what preceded it.

However, let us also stress that there is nothing inevitable about such a downward progress. Chains of adversity can be broken at any point, for each link in the chain is open to other influences that could sever the chain (Rutter, 1989). Much depends on the way in which life-transitions are managed, for these may either reinforce the previous adverse experiences or else offer an escape route. We have already seen this in the case of the institutionalized children described by Dennis (1973): when routinely transferred at the age of 6 from one orphanage to another the girls continued to live under conditions of extreme deprivation; the boys, on the other hand, fortuitously went to a much more stimulating institution and so were able to escape their fate of intellectual deterioration. A study by Quinton and Rutter (1988) illustrates well the importance of such life-transitions and how they are negotiated. Its aim was to see whether parental breakdown in one generation leads to parental breakdown in the next generation, that is, do children deprived of adequate parenting in turn become depriving parents? Accordingly, women who had spent a large part of their childhood in institutions because of the breakdown of their family were assessed with respect to the adequacy of their own parenting skills. The findings show that there was indeed a difference between these mothers and a comparison group of normally brought up women, in that the former tended to be less sensitive, less supportive, and not as warm in their relationships with their children. The pathway whereby this end result was brought about is illustrated in figure 33; it shows the various intervening steps that lead from the breakdown in parenting experienced by the mother as a child to her own parenting problems, and illustrates how each set of deviant circumstances can make it more likely that the next set is brought about.

Yet again we need to draw attention to the exception: by no means all the women who came from a deprived background showed deficiencies as parents. As a group they were more at risk; within the group, however, there was marked variability in outcome, and this could be accounted for by examining the various links making up the chain of circumstances leading from childhood experience to adult behavior. To take one example (figure 34): some of the girls had much more positive school experiences than others, due to a combination of good intelligence and good schooling. Such girls were three times more likely in late adolescence and early adulthood to be capable of proper planning in their choice of careers and of marriage partner. This meant they were twelve times more likely to marry for positive reasons, which in turn increased the chances fivefold that their marital relationship would be a supportive one. As a result their chances increased threefold that they would show generally good social functioning, including being able to act as caring parents.

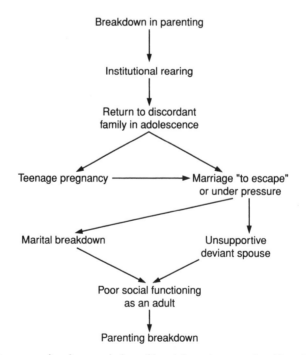

Figure 33   Intergenerational transmission of breakdown in parenting (from Rutter, 1989)

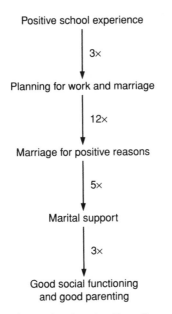

Positive school experience

3×

Planning for work and marriage

12×

Marriage for positive reasons

5×

Marital support

3×

Good social functioning
and good parenting

Figure 34   One route for escaping early adversity (from Rutter, 1989)

These findings help to clarify why similar adverse experiences early in life can give rise to multiple outcomes. An adverse experience may launch an individual on a particular developmental pathway that could lead to later problems; however, as we have seen repeatedly, the end result also depends on intervening experiences and amongst these the negotiation of *transition points* turns out to be of particular importance. At each transition point the individual is confronted with alternatives from which one course needs to be selected: to stay on at school or to leave; to obtain an unskilled job or to undertake further study or training; to keep an unplanned baby or to have it adopted; to marry a particular partner or not; and so forth. Selection among alternatives may not be a matter of free choice; only too often the individual is swept along by the force of circumstances. However, these are circumstances prevailing at that time, not just those encountered in early life, and in so far as there are many transition points to be negotiated and many influences determining which course is selected at each of them, a much more varied and much more dynamic picture emerges of developmental pathways than that which rigidly associates early adversity with one particular end result.

Continuity and Discontinuity

Should we think of psychological development as a continuous process, one that forms an uninterrupted sequence where later characteristics arise out of earlier ones, or should we regard it as a series of steps and transformations, each of which involves a replacement of previous structures with little obvious connection between the old and the new? The question has given rise to heated argument, for it is concerned not only with the kind of overall view we take of the nature of development but also with the practical issue of predictability. If later psychological manifestations arise directly out of earlier ones prediction should be easy; if development means periodic reorganization children's early characteristics may bear little relationship to their adult personality. While few would adopt either of these extreme views the extent to which we should stress continuity or discontinuity remains a matter of contention.

In certain senses, of course, there is bound to be both continuity and discontinuity. On the one hand, nobody doubts that in certain fundamental respects a child remains the "same"' throughout development; on the other hand development, by definition, is about change. There are many kinds of change: some are merely quantitative, such as the increase in vocabulary that takes place over age; others involve the adoption of a qualitatively quite different approach to the environment, such as the changeover from sensorimotor to symbolic thinking; and still others refer to the emergence of completely new structures, such as the onset of focused attachments in infancy. These changes are inevitable; the problem therefore is how a child can at one and the same time remain basically the same while changing drastically. When continuity is assessed simply in terms of the identical manifestation of behavior at different ages, one finds that relationships between early and later personality measures tend to be positive but rarely strong, especially so when measures obtained in infancy are used (Emde & Harmon, 1984). A major reason for such poor predictability is that the same tendency may be overtly expressed in quite different ways at different ages: aggression, for example, is generally manifested in direct physical form in early childhood but in verbal form in the later years. Similarly, developmental quotients obtained in infancy bear virtually no relationship to intelligence quotients in later childhood; on the other hand quite different aspects of infants' information processing efficiency do predict later intellectual status (McCall & Carriger, 1993). What we therefore need to search for is not so much identity as coherence, for the same psychological structure can manifest itself in quite different ways at different ages and yet demonstrate a predictable sequence (Sroufe & Jacobovitz, 1989). The relationship between a secure attachment in infancy and subsequent competence in peer interaction is one such example; that between hyperactivity, inattentiveness, and impulsiveness in early childhood and high aggressiveness in later childhood is another. Alternately, one may search for the sources of continuity in broad personality styles, each one of which may manifest itself in different ways at different ages, but nevertheless retain throughout the same characteristic approach to environmental challenge (see table 55 for an example). Continuity is thus said to reside at "inner" levels, whatever transformations there may be at overt levels – in just the way that the tadpole remains the same animal even when it has changed into a frog. It is therefore the extent to which meaningful and consistent links exist over the developmental course that provide the answer to the question of continuity, and in so far as such links can

Table 55   Continuity of three interactional styles from childhood to adulthood

Style	Manifestation in childhood	Manifestation in adulthood
Ill-temperedness	Explosive temper tantrums in reaction to frustration and authority	Irritable; moody; occupationally downward mobile; truculent with superiors
Shyness	Emotionally inhibited; uncomfortable in social settings; slow in contacts	Unassertive; reluctant to act; unwilling to commit self; slow in entering stable career, marriage, and parenthood
Dependence	Tendency to seek attention, company, approval; demanding; intense attachments	Warm; insightful; socially poised; satisfactory marriage; "on time" with career, marriage, and parenthood

Source: Based on Caspi et al. (1990)

be brought about in various ways it can be a long and arduous task to demonstrate their existence.

Predicting Psychopathology

Questions of continuity are at their most urgent when they refer to deviant development. Behavior problems can be found from a very early age on; when they occur they give rise not only to concern in their own right but also to worry as to their significance with respect to the future. Does children's early status predict their later condition? Is there a link between childhood disturbance and adult psychopathology? Or are early problems mostly of a transient nature and of little predictive value? Answers to such questions could have considerable practical implications, for if, say, such problems do bear a relationship to later deviance the search for effective means of intervention in childhood needs to be redoubled. It also then becomes important to identify the kinds of problems that are most likely to persist and the types of conditions that maintain them in order to target interventionist action more effectively.

However, the area of psychopathology illustrates only too well the sort of complexities that surround the continuity issue. For example, problems do not necessarily persist in the same form; when new problems develop are they the old ones in new form or is there no relationship between them? Furthermore, what applies to one kind of psychological disturbance may not apply to another: different symptoms may have different predictive significance and generalizations about psychopathology as a whole would therefore not be justified. And in addition variables such as children's sex, their developmental status, and the age span over which prediction is to take place must also be taken into account. The greatest degree of continuity tends to be found in the area of antisocial behavior (B. Martin & Hoffman, 1990): chronic adolescent delinquents tend to have been children who started antisocial behavior early on and engaged in the greatest variety of such activities, and though the patterns largely change from fighting and disobedience to theft and addiction the antisocial trend often persists. Such persistence may show impressive duration, as the two longitudinal studies by Eron (1987) and by Farrington (1991), carried out in the United States and in England respectively, demonstrate with such consistency: highly aggressive 8-year-old boys are very likely to become violent men 25 years later. By and large *externalizing* conditions (conduct disorders, delinquency, aggression, and other forms of acting out against the environment) do show a greater tendency to persist than *internalizing* conditions (i.e. behavior characterized by inhibition, withdrawal, and problems within the self). This is seen in a study by Fischer, Rolf, Hasazi, and Cummings (1984), in which a sample of over 500 children was first assessed during the preschool period and then again 7 years later. For both sexes externalizing symptoms found at the earlier age showed a significant continuity with externalizing symptoms at the later age. No such stability over age was found for internalizing behavior. Let us emphasize, however, that even with respect to the externalizing syndrome the relationship between earlier and later status was far from perfect. As the authors of this study put it, "what impresses one about these results is the flexibility and plasticity of development that they seem to imply, such that discontinuity rather than significant continuity in behavioral expression . . . seems to be the norm."

It seems therefore that our main focus should be less on the *extent* of continuity in psychopathology and more on the *conditions* under which continuity and discontinuity are to be found. Various studies throw some light on this question. For example, Richman, Stevenson, and Graham (1982) found approximately 7 percent of a sample of London 3-year-old children to be moderately or severely disturbed and a further 15 percent to be mildly disturbed. Five years later it was found that 61 percent of these disturbed children still had significant psychological difficulties. In general, boys' problems were more likely to persist than girls', and children with moderate or severe problems had a greater persistence rate than those with mild problems. Continuity was provided more by some symptoms than by others: thus restlessness and high activity in particular were signs of poor outcome, leading to antisocial behavior at the older age. This is in keeping with other findings concerning the externalizing syndrome; however, Richman and her colleagues also found such internalizing symptoms as early fearfulness to show a marked association with later neurotic difficulties. In addition, they noted that the mothers of the problem children themselves had higher rates of psychological disturbance throughout the five years of the follow-up, and the parents also had more marital difficulties and more physical ill health.

Just what part a child's family situation plays in the maintenance of psychopathology cannot, of course, be ascertained from such correlational data. However, a strong possibility is that that part is a direct one: i.e., that adverse home conditions of long-term duration continue to feed the child's problems and provide little opportunity for escape. It may be, on the other hand, that parental and child difficulties stem from the same genetic origins; it may also be that there is a self-perpetuating tendency in the child's problems, especially because of the feedback effect of a difficult child on an emotionally vulnerable parent. That environmental effects do need to be taken into account is suggested by findings obtained by Egeland, Kalkoske, Gottesman, and Erickson (1990). In their follow-up of preschool children to early school age these investigators found considerable continuity in adaptation: children identified as competent at the earlier age mostly continued to function in a competent fashion, whereas preschool children with behavior problems tended still to have problems several years later. Yet there were exceptions: some of the competent preschoolers later developed psychological difficulties, and some of those with early problems subsequently showed good adjustment. By investigating the family circumstances of these exceptions Egeland and his colleagues were able to show that discontinuity could be accounted for by either changes in the mother (such as in any depressive symptoms shown by her), or changes in the family's life circumstances (such as income problems), or changes in the overall quality of the home environment. When any of these markedly improved the child's psychological condition benefited; when they deteriorated the child's mental health was also adversely affected. Continuity, it seems, is to some degree dependent on environmental stability, perhaps especially so in the early years; this environmental stability is closely linked to the family situation, and this in turn is by and large a matter of parents' behavior towards their children and any changes that occur therein.

Finding continuity is, of course, easier for broadly defined categories of psychopathology than for highly specific symptoms. Some findings concerning the latter are illustrated in table 56; from it we see that there is a great deal of fluctuation in the common behavior problems that are to be found in the preschool period. Variability both from one age period to another and from one symptom to another is considerable; clearly for many children behavior problems are short-lived, though for some the difficulties can persist over rather longer periods of time. Contrast this with the

Table 56   Some continuities of early behavior problems from one age to another

	Percentage of children continuing			
	From 1 to 1½ years	*From 1½ to 2 years*	*From 2 to 3 years*	*From 3 to 4½ years*
Night waking	41	54	25	14
Poor appetite	–	23	65	–
Food faddiness	–	25	31	–
Temper tantrums	–	–	45	34

Source: After S. Jenkins, Owen, Bax, & Hart (1984)

internalizing and externalizing categories, each of which encompasses a very wide range of syndromes and symptoms. As children get older they may well exchange one behavioral manifestation for another, developmentally more appropriate one; continuity at the symptom level will then be broken but is not at the category level.

It may be, however, that the most successful attempts to predict psychopathology will not be confined to searching for earlier signs of psychopathology but will instead draw on more general aspects of personality functioning in early life. Take peer status: as we have seen, the nature of a child's relationships with other children has considerable predictive power with respect to subsequent socioemotional adjustment. As a number of studies have shown, rejected children are especially at risk for the development of serious adjustment problems later in life, with particular reference to externalizing difficulties (e.g. Kupersmidt & Coie, 1990). Or take attachment security: while results here are somewhat more mixed, a number of studies have found indications that insecurely attached infants are more likely to develop behavior problems at later ages than those securely attached (see Belsky & Nezworski, 1988). For both peer status and attachment security the reason for the link with later adjustment still needs to be clarified; it is no coincidence, however, that both refer to interpersonal relationships, for the quality of these even in early life is already highly distinctive and may well provide one of the principal clues as to what is to come.

Mechanisms of Development

The model of development that has generally been found most acceptable, and that seems most able to make sense of the available evidence concerning the influence of early experience, is the *transactional* one, as described by Sameroff and Chandler (1975) in a seminal review of early risk factors. Such a view takes the place of *linear* models, which assume that particular characteristics of a child or of a child's environment in early life enable one to make long-term predictions and, in their own right, make it possible to specify the outcome in maturity. This, as we have seen, is not possible: children with identical characteristics or experience can end up very different, just as the same outcome may be achieved via a multiplicity of routes. Take one of the risk factors that Sameroff and Chandler discuss: prematurity. The likelihood that such children will develop various cognitive and social deficiencies is greater than it is for full-term infants; yet by no means all such children develop abnormally. Prematurity per se does not enable us to predict how a child will function in the years to come, nor is the degree of prematurity related to children's later psychological status. It is only by also taking into account the environment in which premature children are reared that prediction becomes possible: where parents provide the kind of experiences that offset potential ill effects the outlook is favorable; where, on the other hand, such experiences are adverse the ill effects will be given full rein. The same applies to other kinds of prenatal and perinatal complications, at least those that have not resulted in obvious brain damage: such children are only at risk if reared in certain kinds of depriving family environments. The environment, together with the child's early condition, must therefore be taken into account if one is to understand the course of development. Concentrating only on the child's condition at birth, as do linear models, provides poor predictive power.

The variable that Sameroff and Chandler found to provide the best summary explanation of environmental effects is social class. In socially advantaged families children who have suffered early complications show few residual effects in the long term; children with identical pathology reared in disadvantaged families, on the other hand, do show adverse effects. However, to understand the processes involved in bringing about these diverse consequences one must go beyond summary variables like social class and examine the attitudes and behavior of parents towards their at-risk infant in reducing or maintaining the child's deficits. The transactional model stresses that both child and parent bring particular characteristics to every interactive episode; that both child and parent are psychologically changed as a consequence of interacting; and that these effects are cumulative and their long-term outcome thus a function of a multiplicity of interactive influences (figure 35 illustrates this continuous process of interaction and change). Development is therefore not statically determined by some specific event irrespective of the effects it produces on the particular environment: it is a dynamic process of mutual modification of child and social environment.

To do proper justice to the transactional view we should, ideally, be able to spell out details of the following three aspects:

1 the characteristics that children bring to the business of development as part of their inherent endowment;
2 the identity and nature of the environmental forces that help to shape the developmental course;
3 the way in which these two sets of influences interact and determine the eventual product.

As yet, our knowledge is still limited with respect to all three aspects, though the advent of behavior genetics in particular has given a considerable boost to the search for relevant answers. This is perhaps most obvious in the case of the first set of

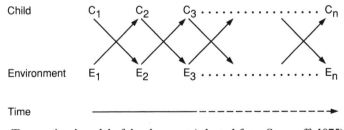

Figure 35 Transactional model of development (adapted from Sameroff, 1975)

influences, those contributed by the child's nature. As we have seen at various points in this book, genetic factors play a considerable role, first of all, in shaping children's *individuality*; characteristics such as sex and various temperamental qualities are obvious examples. In addition, however, it is apparent that children arrive in the world with powerful inborn programs that determine to a large extent the *species-typical* course of their development, i.e. those aspects of psychological growth that are common to all children. Early development in particular is marked by the appearance of such genotypic milestones as the onset of attachments, the ability to point at interesting objects with the index finger, the emergence of words, and so forth.

Following a proposal by the biologist C. H. Waddington (1957), the principle of *canalization* may be used to describe the extent to which an individual's development is shaped by these inherent programs. Development, according to Waddington, can be likened to a marble rolling down a hillside, its course determined by the depth of the gullies or canals characterizing that hillside. Where these are deep the marble is bound to remain in the gully: development here is highly canalized as a result of powerful genetic determinants, and the chances of environmental forces steering the marble in other directions is limited. At other places, however, gullies are more shallow and experience can therefore more easily affect the developmental course. The extent to which canalization affects behavior varies with age: it is especially obvious in infancy, when the individual is most buffered against the influence of idiosyncratic experience; it is also then that strong *self-righting* tendencies ensure that the individual will quickly recover from adverse experience and return to the preordained developmental pathway. However, canalization also varies from one facet of development to another. Thus it is most evident with respect to physical aspects, as seen in the individual's self-righting following malnutrition, whereby the child is enabled quite speedily to return to its normal body weight once proper nourishment has been restored. Some psychological aspects are also deeply canalized, in particular those referring to sensory, perceptual, and motor functions; others, however, are more easily steered off course, and among these many social functions are especially prone to the effects of experience (Cairns, 1991).

As to the second set of influences we listed, i.e. those stemming from the environment, much of recent research in developmental psychology has been devoted to attempts increasingly to refine our understanding of environmental concepts. Originally these were crude and global: culture, social class, income group, family type, and other such "address" labels, as Bronfenbrenner and Crouter (1983) referred to them, were used to designate the types of experience that impinge on children. These have now given way to more specific and precise notions, which not only do justice to the actual, concrete experiences that affect children but which can also lead us to an understanding of the processes involved in child–environment interaction. The search for such variables has brought us above all to interpersonal relationships, for it is primarily in their context that children acquire and perfect so many of the skills required for social living. How others communicate with the child; how they help out with the task of emotional control; what disciplinary techniques they customarily resort to – it is the study of such experiences that has made it possible to learn not just about the products but also the processes of socialization. It is also perhaps ironic that some of the most interesting proposals regarding environmental influences have come from advances in behavior genetics – a science generally associated with the study of organismic influences. Yet take the suggestion that the salient environmental forces that affect individual development are of a nonshared and not a shared kind, i.e. that in order to understand individual differences we must explain why children within the same family are so different from one another, and that it is therefore influences that work within rather than between families that require our attention (Dunn & Plomin, 1990). We have here a very good indication of the fact that the analysis of the environment does not have to be a separate enterprise from the analysis of the individual.

This brings us to the third consideration, namely the interaction of organismic and environmental influences, and here our need for further knowledge is greatest. Earlier efforts to understand the factors responsible for psychological differences among individuals concentrated on the relative contributions made by heredity on the one hand and environment on the other. Two conclusions emerged from this work: first, that a genetic component can be found in nearly all behavioral characteristics, and second that this rarely amounts to more than 50 percent of the variance and often considerably less (Plomin & McClearn, 1993). However, as long ago as 1958 Anastasi called for a move beyond questions concerned with *how much* variance is accounted for by genetic and environmental factors respectively and for a consideration instead of *how* these two sets of influences co-act during development. That the two are intimately connected and that they should not be thought of as a dichotomy is no longer doubted; the nature of the connection, however, remains to be spelled out. As Plomin (1994b) put it, it is the hyphen in the nature–nurture formula that now requires our attention above all.

Not that there is any shortage of proposals! One of the most provocative is one we mentioned in chapter 2, that is, Scarr's (1992) suggestion that as long as children receive "good-enough" parenting their development is determined primarily by inherited characteristics. The environment, that is, needs to be supportive; as long as it fulfills this basic function children will develop according to their potential. Nature has not left the developmental course at the mercy of chance experience; the experiences that are necessary are those that are likely to occur in any average expectable environment, and only those of an extreme nature, such as gross deprivation, will cause interference. This is a far cry from the traditional view of parents as all-powerful shapers of their children's development – a view which tends to pay little more than lipservice to any kind of inherent determinants, preferring to focus on "outer" (and therefore visible) environmental forces and assigning to them the ultimate responsibility for the child's personality growth. Scarr's views have aroused some fierce opposition from those who do believe that the details of parental practices affect development, even within the normal range of child rearing behavior (e.g. Baumrind, 1993; Wachs, 1993), and who argue that there is considerable evidence to show that what parents do or fail to do can have crucial effects on their children. Let us, however, return to the distinction between *species-typical* development and the development of *individuality*, for it is to the former that Scarr's argument primarily applies rather than the latter. There is little evidence that the unfolding of universal programs, containing such milestones as the appearance of attachment, pointing, and language, are affected by the details of parental behavior; these are maturationally driven changes that will be found in any normally supportive social environment. There is considerably more evidence that individual differences in the manner in which these developments manifest themselves and the use to which they are put (as seen, for example, in the quality of children's attachments or the communicative purposes of their gestural and verbal expressions) can be influenced by the nuances of the child's rearing environment.

What is now generally accepted is that any attempt to understand the child–environment interaction must note that the direction of influence is not merely from environment to child but also from child to environment. Children, that is, by virtue both of their inherent make-up and their accumulated experience, tend to construct their own environments by selecting and even creating those settings that are compatible with their individual characteristics. As Scarr (1992) put it, children actively engage in "niche-picking"; they ensure thereby that they can function in surroundings that provide them with opportunities to give full and comfortable rein to their talents and personality features. We can see this clearly in children's choice of friends: where there is the opportunity to choose, children are likely to associate with those of their peers whose characteristics are in keeping with their own. However, it is also seen in other spheres, such as choice of school subjects, of sports activities and of hobby clubs. In each case children actively construct their own experiences by determining the nature of the environment that provides them with the best opportunities for self-fulfillment. Thus the environment is not merely something foreign imposed on the child from outside; it is an integral part of the child's make-up which, through the child's efforts, becomes increasingly more integrated in the course of development.

We see here a more general trend to which we have repeatedly referred in this book. Children's social development is a highly active process as far as children themselves are concerned: far from being pushed and pulled by whatever environmental forces they happen to encounter they are busy from the beginning in selecting and rejecting, evaluating and interpreting, and constructing and changing both the social and the nonsocial aspects of their surroundings. Environmental determinism is clearly not an acceptable view. For that matter, genetic determinism is not acceptable either: children are not blindly propelled by their inheritance; as we have seen, genetic determinants can offer only partial explanations for individual differences and so leave much to be accounted for. Models of development must therefore be based on a multi-dimensional system of influences, and these need to include the child's self-generated efforts. There are contributions, that is, from within the self as well as from the genes and from the environment. Thus a basic developmental task that all children need to undertake is the construction of a self-concept; it is a task to which children turn from a very early age; and once such a concept is in existence, even in rudimentary form, it exerts a marked influence on the child's choice of action courses. Questions such as "Will I like it?", "What will it do for me?", and "What will others think if I do this?" increasingly influence the choice made. Children thereby gain control of their own fate, increasingly so as they become more skilled in evaluation and deliberation, and efforts to understand the course of children's development must thus include the subjective meaning which children attach to their experience.

Summary

Reversible or Irreversible?

- The notion that certain kinds of early experiences produce irreversible effects was advanced by Freud but has not been substantiated by subsequent research. Similarly Lorenz's critical-period hypothesis has had to be modified; in particular Bowlby's application of it to human attachment formation has not been borne out by research on late-adopted children.
- Highly stressful experiences encountered by children may produce marked psychopathology at the time. Single episodes, however, rarely produce long-term consequences on their own; their consequences must be seen in the context of more continuous experiences such as an altered family climate.
- Even chronic adversity does not invariably result in permanent damage. As seen in studies of children exposed to long-term deprivation, ill-effects can be reversed through drastic changes in rearing conditions. This is borne out by studies of the effects of family conflict, which is considered the crucial element in producing adverse effects on children experiencing parental divorce: here too such effects need not be permanent but can be reversed under certain conditions.

Multiple Outcomes

- The reason that not all children succumb to adverse experiences is that factors other than the experience itself play a part. These take the form both of risk factors and protective factors, many of which have now been identified through research.
- One set of factors accounting for children's variable response to stress refers to their resilience/vulnerability – a characteristic at least partially of an inherent origin, as reflected in temperamental and sex differences. Other factors influencing this characteristic stem from the child's experience, such as the quality of family relationships.

- Attempts to use early experience in order to predict long-term outcome have proved unsuccessful. Instead, the developmental pathways that individuals take from one to the other need to be traced by means of longitudinal studies, thus investigating all links in the chain rather than just the first and the last. In this way it becomes possible to account for the fact that different children end up differently after experiencing the same adverse conditions.
- Such studies show that chains of adversity can be broken at various points, and that in particular the final outcome depends on the way in which certain life-transitions are negotiated. The study of developmental pathways thus points to a much more varied and dynamic process than any attempt to see early experience as an all-formative influence on personality development.

Continuity and Discontinuity

- Development involves both continuity and discontinuity, though the emphasis to be given to each remains a matter of contention. To some extent this is a matter of the level of analysis employed: at an overt, behavioral level continuity in various individual difference parameters has been shown to be poor; at a process or style level, on the other hand, continuity is easier to demonstrate.
- Being able to predict later psychopathology from childhood characteristics would have many advantages, but straightforward links have so far not been found. Most continuity exists with respect to the development of antisocial behavior; externalizing symptoms on the whole tend to persist more than internalizing symptoms. Continuity is most likely under conditions of environmental stability.
- Efforts to explain developmental progression benefit from being based on a transactional model, whereby the mutual and progressive interaction of child characteristics and environmental characteristics is taken into account. A multidimensional system of influences is therefore required, and this needs to include the child's self-generated efforts.

References

Aber, J. L., & Cicchetti, D. (1984). The socio-emotional development of maltreated children. In H. Fitzgerald, B. Lester, & M. W. Yogman (Eds.), *Theory and research in behavioral pediatrics* (Vol. 2). New York: Plenum.

Aboud, F (1988). *Children and prejudice*. Oxford, UK: Blackwell.

Abramovitch, R., Corter, C., & Lando, B. (1979). Sibling interaction in the home. *Child Development, 50*, 997–1003.

Abramovitch, R., Corter, C., Pepler, D. J., & Stanhope, L. (1986). Sibling and peer interaction: A final follow-up and a comparison. *Child Development, 57*, 217–229.

Abramovitch, R., Stanhope, L., Pepler, D., & Corter, C. (1987). The influence of Down's syndrome on sibling interaction. *Journal of Child Psychology and Psychiatry, 28*, 865–879.

Achenbach, T. M. (1978). *Research in developmental psychology: Concepts, strategies, methods*. New York: Free Press.

Acredolo, L., & Goodwyn, S. (1988). Symbolic gesturing in normal infants. *Child Development, 59*, 450–466.

Ahrens, R. (1954). Beitrag zur Entwicklung des Physiognomie unter Mimikerkenntnis. *Zeitschrift experimentelle und angewande Psychologie, 2*, 412–454.

Ainsworth, M. D. S., Blehar, M. C., Waters, E., & Wahl, S. (1978). *Patterns of attachment*. Hillsdale, NJ: Erlbaum.

Altmann, J. (1974). Observational study of behavior: Sampling methods. *Behavior, 49*, 227–267.

Amato, P. R. (1993). Children's adjustment to divorce: Theories, hypotheses and empirical support. *Journal of Marriage and the Family, 55*, 23–38.

Amato, P. R., & Keith, B. (1991). Parental divorce and the well-being of children: A meta-analysis. *Psychological Bulletin, 110*, 26–46.

Amsterdam, B. (1972). Mirror self-image reactions before age two. *Developmental Psychobiology, 5*, 297–305.

Anastasi, A. (1958). Heredity, environment and the question "How?" *Psychological Review, 65*, 197–208.

Archer, J. (1992). *Ethology and human development*. Brighton, UK: Harvester Wheatsheaf.

Archer, J., & Browne, K. (Eds.). (1989). *Human aggression: Naturalistic approaches*. London: Routledge.

Archer, J., & Lloyd, B. (1985). *Sex and gender*. Cambridge, UK: Cambridge University Press.

Aries, P. (1973). *Centuries of childhood*. Harmondsworth, UK: Penguin.

Asher, S. R., Parkhurst, J. T., Hymel, S., & Williams, G. A. (1990). Peer rejection and loneliness in childhood. In S. R. Asher & J. D. Coie (Eds.), *Peer rejection in childhood*. Cambridge, UK: Cambridge University Press.

Aslin, R. N. (1987). Visual and auditory development in infancy. In J. D. Osofsky (Ed.), *Handbook of infant development*, 2nd ed. New York: Wiley.

Astington, J., Harris, P., & Olson, D. (1988). *Developing theories of mind*. New York: Cambridge University Press.

Bailey, J. M., Bobrow, D., Wolfe, M., & Mikach, S. (1995). Sexual orientation of adult sons of gay fathers. *Developmental Psychology, 31*, 124–129.

Bakeman, R., & Gottman, J. M. (1987). Applying observational methods: A systematic view. In J. D. Osofsky (Ed.), *Handbook of infant development*, 2nd ed. New York: Wiley.

Baldwin, A. L. (1980). *Theories of child development*, 2nd ed. New York: Wiley.

Baldwin, J. M. (1987). *Social and ethical interpretations in mental development.* New York: Macmillan.

Bandura, A. (1973). *Aggression: A social learning analysis.* Englewood Cliffs, NJ: Prentice-Hall.

Bandura, A. (1977). *Social learning theory.* Englewood Cliffs, NJ: Prentice-Hall.

Bandura, A. (1982). Self-efficacy mechanism in human agency. *American Psychologist, 37,* 122–147.

Bandura, A. (1986). *Social foundations of thought and action: A social-cognitive theory.* Englewood Cliffs, NJ: Prentice-Hall.

Bandura, A., Ross, D., & Ross, S. A. (1961). Transmission of aggression through imitation of aggressive models. *Journal of Abnormal and Social Psychology, 63,* 575–582.

Bandura, A., & Walters, R. H. (1959). *Adolescent aggression.* New York: Ronald Press.

Bandura, A., & Walters, R. H. (1963). *Social learning and personality development.* New York: Holt, Rinehart, & Winston.

Banks, W. C. (1976). White preferences in blacks: A paradigm in search of a phenomenon. *Psychological Bulletin, 83,* 1179–1186.

Barenboim, C. (1981). The development of person perception in childhood and adolescence: From behavioral comparisons to psychological constructs to psychological comparisons. *Child Development, 52,* 129–144.

Barnard, K. E., Bell, H. L., & Hammond, M. A. (1984). Developmental changes in maternal interactions with term and preterm infants. *Infant Behavior and Development, 7,* 101–113.

Barnett, M. A. (1987). Empathy and related responses in children. In N. Eisenberg & J. Strayer (Eds.), *Empathy and its development.* Cambridge, UK: Cambridge University Press.

Baron-Cohen, S. (1991). The theory of mind deficit in autism: How specific is it? *British Journal of Developmental Psychology, 9,* 301–314.

Baron-Cohen, S., Leslie, A. M., & Frith, U. (1985). Does the autistic child have a "theory of mind"? *Cognition, 21,* 37–46.

Baron-Cohen, S., Leslie, A. M., & Frith, U. (1986). Mechanical, behavioural and intentional understanding of picture stories in autistic children. *British Journal of Developmental Psychology, 4,* 113–125.

Barrett, K. C., & Campos, J. J. (1987). Perspective on emotional development II: A functionality approach to emotion. In J. D. Osofsky (Ed.), *Handbook of infant development,* 2nd ed. New York: Wiley.

Bates, E., O'Connell, B., & Shore, C. (1987). Language and communication in infancy. In J. D. Osofsky (Ed.), *Handbook of infant development,* 2nd ed. New York: Wiley.

Bates, J. E. (1980). The concept of difficult temperament. *Merrill-Palmer Quarterly, 26,* 299–319.

Bates, J. E. (1983). Issues in the assessment of difficult temperament: A reply to Thomas, Chess, and Korn. *Merrill-Palmer Quarterly, 29,* 89–97.

Bates, J. E. (1986). The measurement of temperament. In R. Plomin & J. Dunn (Eds.), *The study of temperament: Changes, continuities, and challenges.* Hillsdale, NJ: Erlbaum.

Bates, J. E. (1987). Temperament in infancy. In J. D. Osofsky (Ed.), *Handbook of infant development,* 2nd ed. New York: Wiley.

Bates, J. E., Bayles, K., Bennett, D. S., Ridge, B., & Brown, M. M. (1991). Origins of externalizing behavior problems at eight years of age. In D. Pepler & K. Rubin (Eds.), *The development and treatment of childhood aggression.* Hillsdale, NJ: Erlbaum.

Baumrind, D. (1967). Child care practices anteceding three patterns of preschool behavior. *Genetic Psychology Monographs, 75,* 43–88.

Baumrind, D. (1971). Current patterns of parental authority. *Developmental Psychology Monographs, 4,* 1–101.

Baumrind, D. (1973). The development of instrumental competence through socialization. In A. D. Pick (Ed.), *Minnesota symposia on child psychology* (Vol. 7). Minneapolis: University of Minnesota Press.

Baumrind, D. (1991). The influence of parenting style on adolescent competence and substance use. *Journal of Early Adolescence, 11,* 56–95.

Baumrind, D. (1993). The average expectable environment is not good enough: A response to Scarr. *Child Development, 64,* 1299–1317.

Becker, W. C. (1964). Consequences of different kinds of parental discipline. In M. L. Hoffman & L. W. Hoffman (Eds.), *Review of child development research* (Vol. 1). New York: Russell Sage Foundation.

Bell, R. Q. (1968). A reinterpretation of the direction of effects in studies of socialization. *Psychological Review, 75,* 81–95.

Bell, S. M. (1970). The development of the concept of the object as related to infant–mother attachment. *Child Development, 41,* 291–311.

Belle, D. (Ed.). (1989). *Children's social networks and social supports.* New York: Wiley.

Belsky, J. (1981). Early human experience: A family perspective. *Developmental Psychology, 17*, 3–23.

Belsky, J. (1984). Marriage, parenting, and child development. In J. Belsky, R. M. Lerner, & G. M. Spanier (Eds.), *The child in the family*. Reading, MA: Addison Wesley.

Belsky, J., & Isabella, R. A. (1988). Maternal, infant, and social-contextual determinants of attachment security. In J. Belsky & T. Nezworski (Eds.), *Clinical implications of attachment*. Hillsdale, NJ: Erlbaum.

Belsky, J., & Most, R. K. (1981). From exploration to play: A cross-sectional study of infant free play behavior. *Developmental Psychology, 17*, 630–639.

Belsky, J., & Nezworski, T. (Eds.). (1988). *Clinical implications of attachment*. Hillsdale, NJ: Erlbaum.

Belsky, J., & Rovine, M. (1987). Temperament and attachment security in a strange situation: An empirical rapprochement. *Child Development, 58*, 787–795.

Belsky, J., & Rovine, M. J. (1988). Nonmaternal care in the first year of life and the security of infant–parent attachment. *Child Development, 59*, 157–167.

Belsky, J., & Vondra, J. (1989). Lessons from child abuse: The development of parenting,. In D. Cicchetti & V. Carlson (Eds.), *Child maltreatment*. Cambridge, UK: Cambridge University Press.

Belsky J., Youngblade, L., Rovine, M., & Volling, B. (1991). Patterns of marital change and parent–child interaction. *Journal of Marriage and the Family, 53*, 487–498.

Bem, S. L. (1974). The measurement of psychological androgyny. *Journal of Consulting and Clinical Psychology, 42*, 155–162.

Bem, S. L. (1981). Gender schema theory: A cognitive account of sex typing. *Psychological Review, 88*, 354–364.

Benbow, C. P., & Stanley, J. C. (1983). Sex differences in mathematical reasoning ability: More fads. *Science, 222*, 1029–1031.

Bennett, M., Dewberry, C., & Yeeles, C. (1991). A reassessment of the role of ethnicity in children's social perception. *Journal of Child Psychology and Psychiatry, 32*, 969–982.

Berkeley, M. V. (1978). *Inside kindergarten*. Unpublished doctoral dissertation, Johns Hopkins University (quoted in Entwisle, Alexander, Pallas, & Cardigan (1987), see below).

Berman, P. W. (1980). Are women more responsive than men to the young? A review of developmental and situational variables. *Psychological Bulletin, 88*, 668–695.

Berman, P. W., & Goodman, V. (1984). Age and sex differences in children's responses to babies: Effects of adults' caretaking requests and instructions. *Child Development, 55*, 1071–1077.

Berndt, T. J. (1979). Developmental changes in conformity to peers and parents. *Developmental Psychology, 15*, 608–616.

Berndt, T. J., & Hoyle, S. G. (1985). Stability and change in childhood and adolescent friendships. *Developmental Psychology, 21*, 1007–1015.

Best, D. L., Williams, J. E., Cloud, M. J., Robertson, L. S., Edwards, J. R., Giles, H., & Fowles, J. (1977). Development of sex-trait stereotypes among young children in the United States, England, and Ireland. *Child Development, 48*, 1375–1384.

Bettes, B. A. (1988). Maternal depression and motherese: Temporal and intonational features. *Child Development, 59*, 1089–1096.

Bigelow, B. J., & La Gaipa, J. J. (1980). The development of friendship values and choice. In H. C. Foot, A. J. Chapman, & J. R. Smith (Eds.), *Friendship and social relations in children*. Chichester, UK: Wiley.

Bishop, D. V. M. (1993). Autism, executive functions, and theory of mind: A neuro-psychological perspective. *Journal of Child Psychology and Psychiatry, 34*, 279–294.

Blakemore, J. E. D., La Rue, A. A., & Olejnik, A. B. (1979). Sex-appropriate toy preferences and the ability to conceptualize toys as sex-role related. *Developmental Psychology, 15*, 339–340.

Blasi, A. (1980). Bridging more cognition and moral action: A critical review of the literature. *Psychological Bulletin, 88*, 1–45.

Block, J., Block, J. H., & Gjerde, P. F. (1988). Parental functioning and the home environment in families of divorce. *Journal of the American Academy of Child and Adolescent Psychiatry, 27*, 207–213.

Block, J. H., Block, J., & Gjerde, P. F. (1986). The personality of children prior to divorce: A prospective study. *Child Development, 57*, 827–840.

Block, J. H., Block, J., & Morrison, A. (1981). Parental agreement–disagreement on child rearing orientation and gender-related personality correlates in children. *Child Development, 52*, 965–974.

Blurton Jones, N. (Ed.). (1972). *Ethological studies of child behaviour*. London: Cambridge University Press.

Boles, D. B. (1980). X-linkage of spatial ability: A critical review. *Child Development, 51,* 625–635.

Bonvillian, J. D., Orlansky, M. D., & Novack, L. L. (1983). Developmental milestones: Sign language acquisition and motor development. *Child Development, 54,* 1435–1445.

Bornstein, M. H. (1985). How infant and mother jointly contribute to developing cognitive competence in the child. *Proceedings of the National Academy of Sciences, 82,* 7470–7473.

Bornstein, M. H. (1989). Cross-cultural developmental comparisons: The case of Japanese-American infant and mother activities and interactions. *Developmental Review, 9,* 171–204.

Bornstein, M. H. (Ed.). (1991). *Cultural approaches to parenting.* Hillsdale, NJ: Erlbaum.

Bornstein, M. H., & Ruddy, M. (1984). Infant attention and maternal stimulation: Prediction of cognitive and linguistic development in singleton and twins. In H. Bonma & D. G. Bonwhuis (Eds.), *Attention and performance.* London, UK: Erlbaum.

Bouchard, T. J., & McGue, M. G. (1981). Familial studies of intelligence: A review. *Science, 212,* 1055–1059.

Bowlby, J. (1951). *Maternal care and mental health.* Geneva, Switzerland: World Health Organization.

Bowlby, J. (1969). *Attachment and loss. Vol. 1: Attachment.* London, UK: Hogarth Press.

Bowlby, J. (1973). *Attachment and loss. Vol. 2: Separation: Anxiety and anger.* London, UK: Hogarth Press.

Bowlby, J. (1980). *Attachment and loss. Vol. 3: Loss, sadness and depression.* London, UK: Hogarth Press.

Brackbill, Y. (1958). Extinction of the smiling response in infants as a function of reinforcement schedule. *Child Development, 29,* 115–124.

Bretherton, I. (1984). Social referencing and the interfacing of minds: A commentary on the views of Feinman and Campos. *Merrill-Palmer Quarterly, 30,* 419–427.

Bretherton, I. (1985). Attachment theory: Retrospect and prospect. In I. Bretherton & E. Waters (Eds.), Growing points of attachment theory and research. *Monographs of the Society for Research in Child Development, 50* (Serial No. 209).

Bretherton, I., & Beeghly, M. (1982). Talking about internal states: The acquisition of an explicit theory of mind. *Developmental Psychology, 18,* 906–921.

Bretherton, I., Fritz, J., Zahn-Waxler, C., & Ridgeway, D. (1986). Learning to talk about emotions: A functionalist perspective. *Child Development, 55,* 529–548.

Bretherton, I., McNew, S., & Beeghly-Smith, M. (1981). Early person knowledge as expressed in gestural and verbal communication: When do infants acquire a "theory of mind"? In M. E. Lamb & L. R. Sherrod (Eds.), *Infant social cognition.* Hillsdale, NJ: Erlbaum.

Brewin, C. R., Andrews, B., & Gotlieb, I. H. (1993). Psychopathology and early experience: A reappraisal of retrospective reports. *Psychological Bulletin, 113,* 82–98.

Bridges, K. M. B. (1932). Emotional development in early infancy. *Child Development, 3,* 324–341.

Brinich, P. M. (1980). Childhood deafness and maternal control. *Journal of Communication Disorders, 12,* 75–81.

Brody, G. H., Pillegrini, A. D., & Sigel, I. E. (1986). Marital quality and mother–child and father–child interactions with school-aged children. *Developmental Psychology, 22,* 291–296.

Brody, G. H., Stoneman, Z., McCoy, J. K., & Forehand, R. (1992). Contemporaneous and longitudinal associations of sibling conflict with family relationships assessments and family discussions about sibling problems. *Child Development, 63,* 391–400.

Bronfenbrenner, U. (1977). Toward an experimental ecology of human development. *American Psychologist, 82,* 513–531.

Bronfenbrenner, U. (1979). *The ecology of human development.* Cambridge, MA: Harvard University Press.

Bronfenbrenner, U., & Crouter, A. (1983). The evolution of environmental models in developmental research. In W. Kessen (Ed.), *Handbook of Child Psychology* (Vol. 1), 4th ed. New York: Wiley.

Brooks, J., & Lewis, M. (1976). Responses to strangers: Midget, adult and child. *Child Development, 47,* 323–332.

Broughton, J. (1978). Development of concepts of self, reality and knowledge. *New Directions for Child Development, 1,* 75–100.

Brown, B. B., Clasen, D. R., & Eicher, S. A. (1986). Perceptions of peer pressure, peer conformity dispositions, and self-reported behavior among adolescents. *Developmental Psychology, 22,* 521–530.

Brown, G. (1988). Causal paths, chains and strands. In M. Rutter (Ed.), *Studies of psychosocial risk: The power of longitudinal data.* Cambridge, UK: Cambridge University Press.

Brown, G. W., Harris, T. O., & Bifulco, A. (1986). The long term effects of early loss of parent. In M. Rutter, C. E. Izard, & P. B. Read (Eds.), *Depression in young people*. New York: Guilford.

Brown, J. R., & Dunn, J. (1991). "You can cry mum": The social and developmental implications of talk about internal states. *British Journal of Developmental Psychology, 9*, 237–256.

Brown, J. R., & Dunn, J. (1992). Talk with your mother or your sibling? Developmental change in early family conversations about feelings. *Child Development, 63*, 336–349.

Bruner, J. S. (1977). Early social interaction and language acquisition. In H. R. Schaffer (Ed.), *Studies in mother–infant interaction*. London: Academic Press.

Bruner, J. S. (1983). *Child's talk: Learning to use language*. Oxford, UK: Oxford University Press.

Buhrmester, D., & Furman, W. (1990). Perception of sibling relationships during middle childhood and adolescence. *Child Development, 61*, 1387–1398.

Bullock, M., & Lutkenhaus, P. (1990). Who am I? Self-understanding in toddlers. *Merrill-Palmer Quarterly, 36*, 217–238.

Burke, J. D., Borus, J. F., Burns, B. J., Millstrom, K. H., & Beasley, M. C. (1982). Changes in children's behavior after a natural disaster. *American Journal of Psychiatry, 139*, 1010–1014.

Buss, A. H., & Plomin, R. (1984). *Temperament: Early developing personality traits*. Hillsdale, NJ: Erlbaum.

Cairns, R. B. (1986). An evolutionary and developmental perspective on aggressive patterns. In C. Zahn-Waxler, E. M. Cummings, & R. Ianotti (Eds.), *Altruism and aggression*. Cambridge, UK: Cambridge University Press.

Cairns, R. B. (1991). Multiple metaphors for a singular idea. *Developmental Psychology, 27*, 23–26.

Caldwell, B. M. (1964). The effects of infant care. In M. L. Hoffman & L. W. Hoffmann (Eds.), *Review of child development research*. New York: Russell Sage Foundation.

Campos, J. D., Barrett, K. L., Lamb, M. E., Goldsmith, H. H., & Stenberg, C. (1983). Socioemotional development. In M. M. Haith (Ed.), *Handbook of Child Psychology, Vol 2: Infancy and Developmental Psychology*. New York: Wiley.

Caplan, M. Z., & Hay, D. F. (1989). Preschoolers' responses to peer distress and beliefs about bystander intervention. *Journal of Child Psychology and Psychiatry, 30*, 231–242.

Carey, W. B. (1986). Clinical interactions of temperament: Transitions from infancy to childhood. In R.

Plomin & J. Dunn (Eds.), *The study of temperament: Changes, continuities, and challenges*. Hillsdale, NJ: Erlbaum.

Case, R. (1991). Stages in the development of the young child's first sense of self. *Developmental Review, 11*, 210–230.

Casler, L. (1961). Maternal deprivation: A critical review of the literature. *Monographs of the Society for Research in Child Development, 26*, (2, Whole No. 80).

Caspi, A., Elder, G. H., & Herbener, E. S. (1990). Childhood personality and the prediction of life-course pattern. In L. N. Robins & M. Rutter (Eds.), *Straight and devious pathways from childhood to adulthood*. Cambridge, UK: Cambridge University Press.

Cicchetti, D., & Beeghly, M. (1987). Symbolic development in maltreated youngsters: An organizational perspective. In D. Cicchetti & M. Beeghly (Eds.), *Symbolic development in atypical children*. San Francisco: Jossey-Bass.

Cicchetti, D., & Sroufe, L. A. (1976). The relationship between affection and cognitive development in Down's syndrome infants. *Child Development, 47*, 920–929.

Clark, K. B., & Clark, M. P. (1940). Skin color as a factor in racial identification and preference in Negro preschool children. *Journal of Social Psychology, 11*, 156–169.

Clarke, A. D. B., & Clarke, A. M. (1984). Constancy and change in the growth of human characteristics. *Journal of Child Psychology and Psychiatry, 25*, 191–210.

Clarke, A. M. & Clarke, A. D. B. (1976). *Early experience: Myth and evidence*. London: Open Books.

Clarke-Stewart, K. A. (1978). And daddy makes three: The father's impact on mother and young child. *Child Development, 49*, 466–478.

Clarke-Stewart, K. A. (1989). Infant daycare: Maligned or malignant? *American Psychologist, 44*, 266–273.

Cobb, N. J., Stevens-Long, J., & Goldstein, S. (1982). The influence of televised models on toy preferences in children. *Sex Roles, 8*, 1075–1080.

Cochran, M., Larner, M., Riley, D., Gunnarson, L., & Henderson, C. R. (Eds.). (1990). *Extending families: The social networks of parents and their children*. Cambridge, UK: Cambridge University Press.

Cohen, D. (1979). *J. B. Watson: The founder of behaviourism*. London: Routledge & Kegan Paul.

Cohen, L. J, & Campos, J. J. (1974). Father, mother,

and stranger as elicitors of attachment behavior in infancy. *Developmental Psychology, 10*, 146–154.

Cohn, J., & Tronick, E. (1983). Communicative rules and the sequential structure of infant behavior during normal and depressed interaction. In E. Tronick (Ed.), *The development of human communication and the joint regulation of behavior.* Baltimore: University Park Press.

Cohn, J. F., Campbell, S. B., Matias, R., & Hopkins, J. (1990). Face-to-face interactions of postpartum depressed and nondepressed mother–infant pairs at 2 months. *Developmental Psychology, 26*, 15–23.

Coie, J. D., & Dodge, K. A. (1983). Continuities and changes in children's social status. A 5-year longitudinal study. *Merrill-Palmer Quarterly, 29*, 261–282.

Coie, J. D., & Koepple, G. K. (1990). Adapting intervention to the problems of aggressive and disruptive rejected children. In S. R. Asher & J. D. Coie (Eds.), *Peer rejection in childhood.* Cambridge, UK: Cambridge University Press.

Colby, A., Kohlberg, L., Gibbs, J., & Lieberman, M. (1983). A longitudinal study of moral judgment. *Monographs of the Society for Research in Child Development, 48* (1–2, Serial No. 200).

Collis, G. M. (1977) Visual co-orientation and maternal speech. In H. R. Schaffer (Ed.), *Studies in mother–infant interaction.* London: Academic Press.

Collis, G. M., & Schaffer, H. R. (1975). Synchronization of visual attention in mother–infant pairs. *Journal of Child Psychology and Psychiatry, 16*, 315–320.

Condry, J., & Condry, S. (1976). Sex differences: A study of the eye of the beholder. *Child Development, 47*, 812–819.

Condry, J. C., & Ross, D. F. (1985). Sex and aggression: The influence of gender label on the perception of aggression in children. *Child Development, 53*, 1008–1016.

Conger, J. J. (1991). *Adolescence and youth: Psychological development in a changing world*, 4th ed. New York: Harper & Row.

Conger, R. D., Conger, K. J., Elder, G. H., Lorenz, F. O., Simons, R. L., & Whitbeck, L. B. (1992). A family process model of economic hardship and adjustment of early adolescent boys. *Child Development, 63*, 526–541.

Conger, R. D., Conger, K. J., Elder, G. H., Lorenz, F. O., Simons, R. L., & Whitbeck, L. B. (1993). Family economic stress and adjustment of early adolescent girls. *Developmental Psychology, 29*, 206–219.

Cooley, C. H. (1902). *Human nature and social order.* New York: Charles Scribner.

Coon, H., Fulker, D. W., Defries, J. C., & Plomin, R. (1990). Home environment and cognitive ability of 7-year-old children in the Colorado adoption project: Genetic and environmental etiologies. *Developmental Psychology, 26*, 459–468.

Cooper, R. P., & Aslin, R. N. (1990). Preference for infant-directed speech in the first month after birth. *Child Development, 61*, 1584–1595.

Coopersmith, S. (1967). *The antecedent of self-esteem.* San Francisco: Freeman.

Cowan, C. P., & Cowan, P. A. (1992). *When partners become parents.* New York: Basic Books.

Cowan, P. A., & Hetherington, E. M. (Eds.). (1991). *Family transitions.* Hillsdale, NJ: Erlbaum.

Cox, M. (1986). *The child's point of view.* Brighton, UK: Harvester.

Crain, W. (1992). *Theories of development: Concepts and applications*, 3rd ed. New York: Prentice-Hall.

Crockenberg, S. B. (1981). Infant irritability, mother responsiveness, and social support influences on the security of infant–mother attachment. *Child Development, 52*, 857–865.

Crockenberg, S., & Litman, C. (1990). Autonomy as competence in 2-year-olds: Maternal correlation of child defiance, compliance and self-assertion. *Developmental Psychology, 26*, 961–971.

Crook, C. (1992). Cultural artefacts in social development: The case of computers. In H. MuGurk (Ed.), *Childhood social development: Contemporary perspectives.* Hove, UK: Erlbaum.

Cross, W. E. (1985). Black identity: Rediscovering the distinction between personal identity and reference groups orientation. In M. B. Spencer, G. K. Brookes, & W. R. Allen (Eds.), *Beginnings: The social and affective development of black children.* Hillsdale, NJ: Erlbaum.

Crowell, J. A., & Treboux, D. (1995). A review of adult attachment measures: Implications for theory and research. *Social Development, 4*, 294–327.

Culp, R. E., Culp, A. M., Osofsky, J. D., & Osofsky, H. J. (1991). Adolescents' and older mothers' interaction patterns with their six-month-old infants. *Journal of Adolescence, 14*, 195–200.

Cummings, E. M. (1994). Marital conflict and children's functioning. *Social Development, 3*, 16–36.

Cummings, E. M., & Davies, P. T. (1994). Maternal depression and child development. *Journal of Child Psychology and Psychiatry, 35*, 73–112.

Cummings, E. M., Ianotti, R. J., & Zahn-Waxler, C.

(1985). The influence of conflict between adults on the emotions and aggression of young children. *Developmental Psychology, 21*, 495–507.

Curtiss, S. (1982). *Genie: A psycholinguistic study of a modern-day "wild child."* New York: Academic Press.

Dallas, E., Stevenson, J., & McGurk, H. (1993). Cerebral-palsied children's interactions with siblings – I. Influence of severity of disability, age and birth order. *Journal of Child Psychology and Psychiatry, 34*, 621–648.

Damon, W., & Hart, D. (1982). The development of self-understanding from infancy through adolescence. *Child Development. 53*, 841–864.

Damon, W., & Hart, D. (1988). *Self-understanding in childhood and adolescence.* New York: Cambridge University Press.

Damon, W., & Phelps, E. (1989). Strategic uses of peer learning in children's education. In T. J. Berndt & G. W. Ladd (Eds.), *Peer relationships in child development.* New York: Wiley.

Daniels, D., Dunn, J., Furstenberg, F. F., & Plomin, R. (1985). Environmental differences within the family and adjustment differences within pairs of adolescent siblings. *Child Development, 56*, 764–774.

Darwin, C. (1859). *On the origin of species.* London: John Murray.

Darwin, C. (1872). *The expression of emotions in man and animals.* London: John Murray.

Dasen, P. R., & Heron, A. (1981). Cross-cultural tests of Piaget's theory. In H. C. Trandis & A. Heron (Eds.), *Handbook of cross-cultural psychology* (Vol. 4). Boston: Allyn & Bacon.

Dawkins, R. (1976). *The selfish gene.* London: Oxford University Press.

DeCasper, A. J., & Fifer, W. P. (1980). Of human bonding: Newborns prefer their mothers' voices. *Science, 208*, 1174–1176.

DeCasper, A. J., Lecanuet, J.-P., Bunuel, M.-C., Granier Deferre, C., & Maugeais, R. (1994). Foetal reactions to recurrent maternal speech. *Infant Behavior and Development, 17*, 159–164.

DeCasper, A. J., & Spence, M. J. (1986). Prenatal maternal speech influences newborns' perception of speech sounds. *Infant Behavior and Development, 9*, 133–150.

DeLoache, J. S., & DeMendoza, O. A. P. (1987). Joint picture book interactions of mothers and 1-year-old children. *British Journal of Developmental Psychology, 5*, 111–124.

de Mause, L. (Ed.). (1974). *The history of childhood.* New York: Psychohistory Press.

Denham, S. A. (1993). Maternal emotional responsiveness and toddlers' social-emotional competence. *Journal of Child Psychology and Psychiatry, 34*, 715–728.

Dennis, W. (1973). *Children of the Creche.* New York: Appleton-Century-Crofts.

Dennis, W., & Dennis, M. G. (1941). Infant development under conditions of restricted practice and minimum social stimulation. *Genetic Psychology Monographs, 23*, 147–155.

deVries, M. W. (1984). Temperament and infant mortality among the Masai of East Africa. *American Journal of Psychiatry, 141*, 1189–1194.

Dishion, T. J., Patterson, G. R. Stoolmiller, M. & Skinner. M. L. (1991). Family, school, and behavioral antecedents to early adolescent involvement with antisocial peers. *Developmental Psychology, 27*, 172–180.

Dixon, S., Tronick, E., Keefer, C., & Brazelton, T. B. (1981). Mother–infant interaction among the Gusii of Kenya. In T. M. Field, A. M. Sostek, P. Vietze, & P. H. Leiderman (Eds.), *Culture and early interaction.* Hillsdale, NJ: Erlbaum.

Dodge, K. A. (1983). Behavioral antecedents of peer social status. *Child Development, 54*, 1386–1389.

Dodge, K. A. (1985). Facets of social interaction and the assessment of social competence in children. In B. H. Schneider, K. H. Rubin, & J. E. Ledingham (Eds.), *Children's peer relations: Issues in assessment and intervention.* New York: Springer.

Dodge, K. A. (1986). Social information-processing variables in the development of aggression and altruism in children. In C. Zahn-Waxler, E. M. Cummings, & R. Ianotti (Eds.), *Altruism and aggression.* Cambridge, UK: Cambridge University Press.

Dodge, K. A. (1990). Developmental psychopathology in children of depressed mothers. *Developmental Psychology, 26*, 3–6.

Dodge, K. A., Coie, J. D., Pettit, G. S., & Price, J. M. (1990). Peer status and aggression in boys' groups: Developmental and contextual analysis. *Child Development, 61*, 1289–1309.

Dodge, K. A., Pettit G. S., McClaskey, C. L., & Brown, M. M. (1986). Social competence in children. *Monographs of the Society for Research in Children, 51* (2, Serial No. 213).

Doise, W. (1990). The development of individual competences through social interactions. In H. C.

Foot, M. J. Morgan, & R. H. Shute (Eds.), *Children helping children*. Chichester, UK: Wiley.

Doise, W., & Mugny, G. (1984). *The social development of the intellect*. Oxford, UK: Pergamon Press.

Dolgin, K. G., & Kim, S. (1994). Adolescents' disclosure to best and good friends: The effects of gender and topic intimacy. *Social Development, 3*, 146–157.

Dollard, J., Doob, L. W., Miller, N. E., Mowrer, D. H., & Sears, R. R. (1939). *Frustration and aggression*. New Haven, CT: Yale University Press.

Donaldson, M. (1978). *Children's minds*. London: Fontana.

Dornbusch, S. M., Ritter, P. L., Liederman, P. H., Roberts, D. F., & Fraleigh, M. J. (1987). The relation of parenting style to adolescent school performance. *Child Development, 58*, 1244–1257.

Dowdney, L., & Skuse, D. (1993). Parenting provided by adults with mental retardation. *Journal of Child Psychology and Psychiatry, 34*, 25–48.

Dowdney, L., Skuse, D., Rutter, M., Quinton, D., & Marzek, D. (1985). The nature and quality of parenting provided by women raised in institutions. *Journal of Child Psychology and Psychiatry, 26*, 599–626.

Dunham, P. J., Dunham, F., & Curwin, A. (1993). Joint-attentional states and lexical acquisition at 18 months. *Developmental Psychology, 29*, 827–831.

Dunkin, M. J., & Biddle, B. J. (1974). *The study of teaching*. New York: Holt, Rinehart, & Winston.

Dunn, J. (1988). *The beginning of social understanding*. Oxford, UK: Blackwell.

Dunn, J. (1993). *Young children's close relationships*. Newbury Park, CA: Sage.

Dunn, J., Bretherton, I., & Munn, P. (1987). Conversations about feeling states between mothers and their young children. *Developmental Psychology, 23*, 132–139.

Dunn, J., Brown, J., & Beardsall, L. (1991). Family talk about feeling states and children's later understanding of others' emotions. *Developmental Psychology, 27*, 448–455.

Dunn, J., & Kendrick, C. (1982a). *Siblings: Love, envy and understanding*. Cambridge, MA: Harvard University Press.

Dunn, J., & Kendrick, C. (1982b). Temperamental differences, family relationships, and young children's response to change within the family. In R. Porter & G. M. Collins (Eds.), *Temperamental differences in infants and young children*. London: Pitman.

Dunn, J., & Munn, P. (1986). Sibling quarrels and maternal intervention: Individual differences in understanding and aggression. *Journal of Child Psychology and Psychiatry, 27*, 583–595.

Dunn, J., & Munn, P. (1987). Development of justification in disputes with mother and sibling. *Developmental Psychology, 23*, 791–798.

Dunn, J., & Plomin, R. (1990) *Separate lives: Why siblings are so different*. New York: Basic Books.

Dunn, J., Plomin, R., & Daniels, D. (1986). Consistency and change in mothers' behavior towards young siblings. *Child Development, 57*, 348–356.

Dunn, J., & Wooding, C. (1977). Play in the home and its implications for learning. In B. Tizard & D. Harvey (Eds.), *Biology of play*. London: Heinemann.

Durkin, K., Shire, B., Crowther, R. D., & Rutter, D. (1986). The social and linguistic context of early number word use. *British Journal of Developmental Psychology, 4*, 269–288.

Dweck, C. S. (1986). Motivational processes affecting learning. *American Psychologist, 41*, 1040–1048.

Eagly, A. H. (1987). *Sex differences in social behavior: A social-role interpretation*. Hillsdale, NJ: Erlbaum.

Easterbrooks, M. A. (1989). Quality of attachment to mother and to father: Effects of perinatal risk status. *Child Development, 60*, 825–830.

Easterbrooks, M. A., & Emde, R. N. (1988). Marital and parent–child relationships: The role of affect in the family system. In R. A. Hinde & J. Stevenson-Hinds (Eds.), *Relationships within families*. Oxford, UK: Clarendon Press.

Eaton, W. O., & Enns, L. R. (1986). Sex differences in human motor activity level. *Psychological Bulletin, 100*, 19–28.

Eaves, L. J., Eysenck, H. J., & Martin, N. G. (1989). *Genes, culture, and personality: An empirical approach*. San Diego, CA: Academic Press.

Eckerman, C. O., & Oehler, J. M. (1992). Very-low birthweight newborns and parents as early social partners. In S. L. Friedman & M. D. Sigman (Eds.), *The psychological development of low birthweight children*. Norwood, NJ: Ablex.

Eckerman, C. O., Oehler, J. M., Medvin, M. B., & Hannan, T. E. (1994). Premature newborns as social partners before term age. *Infant Behavior and Development, 17*, 55–70.

Eckerman, C. O., Whatley, J. L., & Kutz, S. L. (1975). The growth of social play with peers during the second year of life. *Developmental Psychology, 11*, 42–49.

Eder, R. (1990). Uncovering young children's psychological selves: Individual and developmental differences. *Child Development, 61*, 849–863.

Edwards, C. P., & Whiting, B. (1977). *Sex differences in children's social interaction.* Unpublished report to the Ford Foundation.

Egeland, B., Kalkoske, M., Gottesman, N., & Erickson, M. F. (1990). Preschool behavior problems: Stability and factors accounting for change. *Journal of Child Psychology and Psychiatry, 31*, 891–910.

Ehrhardt, A. A., & Baker, S. W. (1974). Fetal androgens, human central nervous system differentiation, and behavioral sex differences. In R. C. Friedman, R. M. Rickard & R. L. van de Wiele (Eds.), *Sex differences in behavior.* New York: John Wiley.

Eiduson, B. T., Kornfein, M., Zimmerman, I. L., & Weisner, T. S. (1982). Comparative socialization practices in traditional and alternative families. In M. Lamb (Ed.), *Non traditional families: Parenting and child development.* Hillsdale, NJ: Erlbaum.

Eisenberg, A. R. (1992). Conflicts between mothers and their young children. *Merrill-Palmer Quarterly, 38*, 21–43.

Eisenberg, N. (1982). The development of reasoning regarding prosocial behavior. In N. Eisenberg (Ed.), *The development of prosocial behavior.* New York: Academic Press.

Eisenberg, N. (1986). *Altruistic emotion, cognition, and behavior.* Hillsdale, NJ: Erlbaum.

Eisenberg, N. (Ed.). (1989). *Empathy and related emotional responses.* San Francisco: Jossey-Bass.

Eisenberg, N., & Miller, P. A. (1987). The relation of empathy to prosocial and related behavior. *Psychological Bulletin, 101*, 91–119.

Eisenberg, N., Murray, E., & Hite, T. (1982). Children's reasoning regarding sex-typed toy choices. *Child Development, 53*, 81–86.

Eisenberg, N., & Strayer, J. (1987). *Empathy and its development.* Cambridge, UK: Cambridge University Press.

Eisenberg, N., Wolchnik, S. A., Hernandez, R., & Pasternack, J. F. (1985). Parental socialization of young children's play: A short-term longitudinal study. *Child Development, 56*, 1506–1513.

Ekman, P. (1972). Universal and cultural differences in facial expressions of emotion. In J. Cole (Ed.), *Nebraska symposia on motivation.* Lincoln: University of Nebraska Press.

Ekman, P., & Friesen, W. (1978). *Facial action coding system.* Palo Alto, CA: Consulting Psychologists Press.

Ekman, P., & Oster, H. (1979). Facial expressions of emotions. *Annual Review of Psychology, 30*, 527–554.

Elder, G. H. (1974). *Children of the great depression.* Chicago: University of Chicago Press.

Elder, G. H., & Caspi, A. (1988). Economic stress in lives: Developmental perspectives. *Journal of Social Issues, 44*, 25–45.

Elder, G. H., Conger, R. D., Foster, E. M., & Ardelt, M. (1992). Families under economic pressure. *Journal of Family Issues, 13*, 5–37.

Elicker, J., Englund, M., & Sroufe, L. A. (1992). Predicting peer competence and peer relationships in childhood from early parent–child relationships. In R. D. Parke & G. W. Ladd (Eds.), *Family–peer relationships: Modes of linkage.* Hillsdale, NJ: Erlbaum.

Ellis, R., & Wells, G. (1980). Enabling factors in adult–child discourse. *First Language, 1*, 46–62.

Ellis, S., Rogoff, B., & Cromer, C. C. (1981). Age segregation in children's social interaction. *Developmental Psychology, 17*, 399–407.

Ember, C. R. (1973). Feminine task assignment and the social behavior of boys. *Ethos, 1*, 424–439.

Emde, R. N., & Harmon, R. J. (Eds.). (1984). *Continuities and discontinuities in development.* New York: Plenum Press.

Emery, R. E. (1982). Interparental conflict and the children of discord and divorce. *Psychological Bulletin, 92*, 310–330.

Entwisle, D. R., & Alexander, K. L. (1990). Beginning school math competence: Minority and majority comparisons. *Child Development, 61*, 454–471.

Entwisle, D. R., Alexander, K. L., Pallas, A. M., & Cardigan, D. (1987). The emergent academic self-image of first graders: Its response to social structure. *Child Development, 58*, 1190–1206.

Entwisle, D. R., & Baker, D. P. (1983). Gender and young children's expectations for performance in arithmetic. *Developmental Psychology, 19*, 200–209.

Entwisle, D. R., & Hayduk L. A. (1982). *Early schooling: Cognitive and affective outcomes.* Baltimore: Johns Hopkins University Press.

Erikson, E. H. (1963). *Childhood and society*, 2nd ed. New York: Norton.

Eron, L. D. (1987). The development of aggressive behavior from the perspective of a developing behaviorism. *American Psychologist, 42*, 435–442.

Eron, L. D., & Huesmann, L. R. (1984). The relation of prosocial behavior to the development of aggression and psychopathology. *Aggressive Behavior, 10*, 201–212.

Eron, L. D., Huesmann, L. R., & Zell, A. (1991). The role of parental variables in the learning of aggression. In D. J. Pepler & K. H. Rubin (Eds.), *The development and treatment of childhood aggression.* Hillsdale, NJ: Erlbaum.

Eron, L. D., Walder, L. O., & Lefkowitz, M. M. (1971). *Learning of aggression in children.* Boston: Little, Brown.

Fagot, B. I. (1978). The influence of sex of child on parental reactions to toddler children. *Child Development, 49*, 459–465.

Fagot, B. I. (1985). Beyond the reinforcement principle: Another step towards understanding sex role development. *Developmental Psychology, 21*, 1097–1104.

Fagot, B. I., & Hagan, R. (1991). Observations of parent reactions to sex-stereotyped behaviors: Age and sex effects. *Child Development, 62*, 617–628.

Fagot, B. I., & Leinbach, M. D. (1989). The young child's gender schema: Environmental input, internal organization. *Child Development, 60*, 663–672.

Fantz, R. L. (1961). The origin of form perception. *Scientific American, 204*, 66–72.

Fantz, R. L., & Nevis, S. (1967). Pattern preferences and perceptual-cognitive development in early infancy. *Merrill-Palmer Quarterly, 13*, 77–108.

Farrington, D. P. (1991). Childhood aggression and adult violence: Early precursors and later-life outcomes. In D. J. Pepler & K. H. Rubin (Eds.), *The development and treatment of childhood aggression.* Hillsdale. NJ: Erlbaum.

Feinman, S. (1982). Social referencing in infancy. *Merrill-Palmer Quarterly, 28*, 445–470.

Feldman, S. S., & Aschenbrenner, B. (1983). Impact of parenthood on various aspects of masculinity and femininity: A short-term longitudinal study. *Developmental Psychology, 19*, 278–289.

Feldman, S., & Brown, N. (1993). Family influences on adolescent male sexuality: The mediational role of self-restraint. *Social Development, 2*, 15–35.

Ferguson, C. A. (1978). Talking to children: A search for universals. In J. H. Greenberg (Ed.), *Universals of human language.* Stanford, CA: Stanford University Press.

Fergusson, D. M., Horwood, L. J., & Lynskey, M. T. (1992). Family change, parental discord and early offending. *Journal of Child Psychology and Psychiatry, 33*, 1059–1076.

Fernald, A., & Morikawa, H. (1993). Common themes and cultural variations in Japanese and American mothers' speech to infants. *Child Development, 64*, 637–656.

Feshbach, N. D. (1987). Parental empathy and child adjustment/maladjustment. In N. Eisenberg & J. Strayer (Eds.), *Empathy and its development.* Cambridge, UK: Cambridge University Press.

Field, T. (1978). Interaction behaviors of primary versus secondary caretaker fathers. *Developmental Psychology, 14*, 183–184.

Field, T. (1987). Affective and interactive disturbances in infants. In J. D. Osofsky (Ed.), *Handbook of infant development*, 2nd ed. New York: Wiley.

Field, T., Healy, B., Goldstein, S., Perry, S., Bendell, D., Schanberg, S., Zimmerman, E. A., & Kuhn, C. (1988). Infants of depressed mothers show "depressed" behavior even with nondepressed adults. *Child Development, 59*, 1569–1579.

Fischer, M., Rolf, J. E., Hasazi, J. E., & Cummings, L. (1984). Follow-up of a preschool epidemiological sample. *Child Development, 55*, 137–150.

Flanagan, C. A., & Eccles, J. G. (1993). Changes in parents' work status and adolescents' adjustment at school. *Child Development, 64*, 246–257.

Floyd, F. J., & Zmich, D. E. (1991). Marriage and the parenting partnership: Perceptions and interactions of parents with mentally retarded and typically developing children. *Child Development, 62*, 1434–1448.

Fogel, A. (1977). Temporal organization in mother–infant face-to-face interaction. In H. R. Schaffer (Ed.), *Studies in mother–infant interaction.* London: Academic Press.

Fogel, A. (1979). Peer vs mother directed behavior in 1- to 3-month-old infants. *Infant Behavior and Development, 2*, 215–226.

Fogel, A. (1991). *Infancy*, 2nd ed. St Paul, MN: West Publishing.

Fogel, A., & Hannan, T. E. (1985). Manual actions of nine to fifteen-week old human infants during face-to-face interaction with their mothers. *Child Development, 56*, 1271–1279.

Fogel, A., Nwokak, E., Dede, J. Y., Messinger, D., Dickson, K. L., Matusov, E., & Holt, S. A. (1992). Social process theory of emotion: A dynamic system approach. *Social Development, 1*, 122–142.

Fonagy, P., Steele, H., & Steele, M. (1991). Maternal representations of attachment during pregnancy predict the organization of infant–mother attachment at one year of age. *Child Development, 62,* 891–905.

Foot, H. C., Chapman, A. J., & Smith, J. R. (1977). Friendship and social responsiveness in boys and girls. *Journal of Personality and Social Psychology, 35,* 401–411.

Foot, H. C., Morgan, M. J., & Shute, R. H. (1990). Children's helping relationships: An overview. In H. C. Foot, M. J. Morgan, & R. H. Shute (Eds.), *Children helping children.* Chichester, UK: Wiley.

Forehand, R. (1977). Child noncompliance to parental requests: Behavioral analysis and treatment. In M. Hersen, R. M. Eisler, & P. M. Miller (Eds.), *Progress in behavior modification* (Vol. 5). New York: Academic Press.

Forehand, R. L., & McMahon, R. J. (1981). *Helping the noncompliant child.* New York: Guilford Press.

Fox, N. A., & Fein, G. G. (Eds.) (1990). *Infant day care: The current debate.* Norwood, NJ: Ablex.

Fox, N. A., Kimmerly, N. L., & Schafer, W. D. (1991). Attachment to mother/attachment to father: A meta-analysis. *Child Development, 62,* 210–225.

Fraiberg, S. H. (1977). *Insights from the blind.* New York: Basic Books.

Freedman, D. (1974). *Human infancy: An evolutionary perspective.* Hillsdale, NJ: Erlbaum.

Freud, A., & Dann, S. (1951). An experiment in group upbringing. *Psychoanalytic Study of the Child, 6,* 127–168.

Freud, S. (1930). *Civilisation and its discontent.* London: Hogarth Press.

Freud, S. (1949). *An outline of psycho-analysis.* London: Hogarth Press.

Frisch, H. L. (1977). Sex-stereotypes in adult–infant play. *Child Development, 48,* 1671–1675.

Frith, U. (1989). *Autism: Explaining the enigma.* Oxford, UK: Blackwell.

Frodi, A. M., & Lamb, M. E. (1980). Child abusers' responses to infant smiles and cries. *Child Development, 51,* 239–241.

Frodi, A. M., Lamb, M. E., Leavite, L. A., & Donovan, W. L. (1978). Fathers' and mothers' responses to infant smiles and cries. *Infant Behavior and Development, 1,* 187–198.

Frodi, A., & Thompson, R. (1985). Infants' affective responses in the Strange Situation: Effects of pre-maturity and of quality of attachment. *Child Development, 56,* 1280–1290.

Furman, W., & Bierman, K. L. (1983). Developmental changes in young children's conceptions of friendship. *Child Development, 54,* 549–556.

Furman, W., & Gavin, L. A. (1989). Peers' influence on adjustment and development: A view from the intervention literature. In T. J. Berndt & G. W. Ladd (Eds.), *Peer relationships in child development.* New York: Wiley.

Furstenberg, F. F., Brooks-Gunn, J., & Chase-Lonsdale, L. (1989). Teenaged pregnancy and childrearing. *American Psychologist, 44,* 313–320.

Furth, H. (1980). *The world of grown-ups: Children's conceptions of society.* New York: Elsevier.

Galambos, N. L., Almeida, D. M., & Peterson, A. C. (1990). Masculinity, femininity and sex role attitudes in early adolescence: Exploring gender intensification. *Child Development, 61,* 1915–1933.

Garbarino, J. A., & Crouter, A. (1978). Defining the community context for parent–child relations: The correlates of child maltreatment. *Child Development, 49,* 604–616.

Ge, X., Lorenz, F. O., Conger, R. D., Elder, G. H., & Simons, R. L. (1994). Trajectories of stressful life events and depressive symptoms during adolescence. *Developmental Psychology, 30,* 467–483.

George, C., & Main, M. (1979). Social interactions of young abused children: Approach, avoidance and aggression. *Child Development, 50,* 306–318.

Gesell, A. (1933). Maturation and the patterning of behavior. In C. Murchison (Ed.), *A handbook of child psychology,* 2nd ed. Worcester, MA: Clark University Press.

Gilligan, C. (1982). *In a different voice: Psychological theory and women's development.* Cambridge, MA: Harvard University Press.

Goldberg, W. A., & Easterbrooks, M. A. (1984). The role of marital quality in toddler development. *Developmental Psychology, 20,* 504–514.

Goldfield, B. A., & Reznick, J. S. (1990). Early lexical acquisition: Rate, content, and the vocabulary spurt. *Journal of Child Language, 17,* 171–183.

Goldin-Meadow, S., & Morford, M. (1985). Gesture in early child language: Studies of deaf and hearing children. *Merrill-Palmer Quarterly, 31,* 145–176.

Goldsmith, H. H., & Campos, J. J. (1982). Toward a theory of infant temperament. In R. M. Emde & H. J. Harmon (Eds.), *The development of attachment and affiliation systems*: New York: Plenum Press.

Goldsmith, H. H., & Campos, J. J. (1986). Fundamental issues in the study of early temperament: The Denver twin temperament study. In M. E. Lamb, A. J. Brown, & B. Rogoff (Eds.), *Advances in developmental psychology* (Vol. 4). Hillsdale, NJ: Erlbaum.

Golombok, S., & Fivush, R. (1994). *Gender development*. Cambridge, UK: Cambridge University Press.

Goodnow, J., & Collins, W. A. (1990). *Development according to parents: The nature, sources and consequences of parents' ideas*. Hove, UK: Erlbaum.

Goossens, P. A., & van IJzendoorn, M. H. (1990). Quality of infants' attachments to professional caregivers: Relation to infant–parent attachment and day-care characteristics. *Child Development, 61*, 832–837.

Gottesman, I. I. (1993). Origins of schizophrenia: Past as prologue. In R. Plomin & G. E. McClearn (Eds.), *Nature, nurture and psychology*. Washington, DC: American Psychological Association.

Gottfried, A. E., & Gottfried, A. W. (Eds.). (1988). *Maternal employment and children's development*. New York: Plenum.

Gralinski, J. H., & Kopp, C. B. (1993). Everyday rules for behavior: Mothers' requests to young children. *Developmental Psychology, 29*, 573–584.

Greenberg, M. T., Cicchetti, D., & Cummings, E. M. (Eds.). (1990) *Attachment in the preschool years*. Chicago: University of Chicago Press.

Griffiths, M. D. (1991). Amusement machine playing in childhood and adolescence: A comparative analysis of video games and fruit machines. *Journal of Adolescence, 14*, 53–73.

Grossmann, K., Grossmann, K. E., Spangler, G., & Unzner, L. (1985). Maternal sensitivity and newborns' orientation responses as related to quality of attachment in Northern Germany. In I. Bretherton & E. Waters (Eds.), Growing points of attachment theory and research. *Monographs of the Society for Research in Child Development, 50* (1–2, Serial No. 209).

Grusec, J. (1991). Socializing concern for others in the home. *Developmental Psychology, 27*, 338–342.

Grusec J. E., & Goodnow, J. J. (1994). Impact of parental discipline methods on the children's internalization of values: A reconceptualization of current points of view. *Developmental Psychology, 30*, 4–19.

Guardo, C. J., & Bohan, J. B. (1971). Development of a sense of self-identity in children. *Child Development, 42*, 1909–1921.

Gustafson, G. E., Green, J. A., & West, M. J. (1979). The infant's changing role in mother–infant games: The growth of social skills. *Infant Behavior and Development, 2*, 301–308.

Hall, J. A., & Halberstadt, A. G. (1980). Masculinity and femininity in children: Development of the Children's Personal Attributes Questionnaire. *Developmental Psychology, 16*, 270–280.

Hamilton, W. D. (1964). The genetical theory of social behaviour. *Journal of Theoretical Biology, 7*, 1–52.

Happe, F. (1994). *Autism: An introduction to psychological theory*. London: UCL Press.

Hareven, T. K. (1984). Themes in the historical development of the family. In R. D. Parke (Ed.), *Review of child development research, Vol. 7: The family*. Chicago: University of Chicago Press.

Harkness, S., & Super, C. M. (1992). Parental ethnotheories in action. In I. E. Sigel, A. V. McGillicuddy-De Lisi, & J. J. Goodnow (Eds.), *Parental belief systems: The psychological consequences for children*, 2nd ed. Hillsdale, NJ: Erlbaum.

Harlow, H. F. (1958). The nature of love. *American Psychologist, 13*, 673–685.

Harlow, H. F., & Zimmerman, R. R. (1959). Affectional responses in the infant monkey. *Science, 130*, 421–432.

Harris, M., Jones, D., Brooks, G., & Grant, J. (1986). Relations between the non-verbal context of maternal speech and rate of language development. *British Journal of Developmental Psychology, 4*, 261–268.

Harris, P. L. (1989). *Children and emotion*. Oxford, UK: Basil Blackwell.

Harris, P. L. (1994). The child's understanding of emotion: Developmental change and the family environment. *Journal of Child Psychology and Psychiatry, 35*, 3–28.

Harris, T., Brown, G., & Bifulco, A. (1986). Loss of parent in childhood and adult psychiatric disorder: The role of lack of adequate parental care. *Psychological Medicine, 16*, 641–659.

Harrison, A. O., Wilson, M. N., Pine, C. J., Chan, S. Q., & Buriel, R. (1990). Family ecologies of ethnic minority children. *Child Development, 61*, 347–362.

Hart, D., Fegley, S., Chan, Y. H., Mulvey, D., & Fischer, L. (1993). Judgments about personal identity in childhood and adolescence. *Social Development, 2*, 66–81.

Hart, S. N., & Brassard, M. R. (1987). A major threat to children's mental health: Psychological maltreatment. *American Psychologist, 42*, 160–165.

Harter, S. (1982). The perceived competence scale for children. *Child Development, 53*, 87–97.

Harter, S. (1987). The determinants and mediational role of global self-worth in children. In N. Eisenberg (Ed.), *Contemporary topics in developmental psychology*. New York: Wiley.

Harter, S., & Barnes, R. (1981). Children's understanding of parental emotions. Unpublished manuscript, quoted by Harter, S. (1983), Developmental perspectives on the self-system. In E. M. Hetherington (Ed.), *Handbook of child psychology* (Vol. 4). New York: Wiley (1983).

Hartshorne, H., & May, M. S. (1928–30). *Studies in the nature of character* (Vols. I–III). New York: Macmillan.

Hartup, W. W. (1974). Aggression in childhood: Developmental perspective. *American Psychologist, 29*, 336–341.

Hartup, W. W. (1983). Peer relations. In P. H. Mussen (Ed.), *Handbook of child psychology* (Vol. 4). New York: Wiley.

Hartup, W. W. (1989). Social relationships and their developmental significance. *American Psychologist, 44*, 120–126.

Hartup, W. W. (1992). Friendships and their developmental significance. In H. McGurk (Ed.), *Childhood social development: Contemporary perspectives*. Hove, UK: Erlbaum.

Hauser, S. T., Vieyra, M. A. B., Jacobson, A. M., & Wertlieb, D. (1985). Vulnerability and resilience in adolescence: Views from the family. *Journal of Early Adolescence, 5*, 81–100.

Hay, D. F. (1994). Prosocial development. *Journal of Child Psychology and Psychiatry, 35*, 29–72.

Hay, D. F., & Ross, H. S. (1982). The social nature of early conflict. *Child Development, 53*, 105–113.

Hebb, D. O. (1946). On the nature of fear. *Psychological Review, 53*, 250–275.

Henderson, N. D. (1982). Human behavior genetics. *Annual Review of Psychology, 33*, 403–440.

Henggeler, S. W., Watson, S. M., & Cooper, P. F. (1984). Verbal and nonverbal maternal controls in hearing mother–deaf child interaction. *Journal of Applied Developmental Psychology, 5*, 319–329.

Hepburn, A., & Schaffer, H. R. (1983). Les contrôles maternels dans la prime enfance. *Enfance, 1–2*, 117–127.

Hertz-Lazarowitz, R., Fuchs, I., Sharabany, R., & Eisenberg, N. (1989). Students' interactive and noninteractive behaviors in the classroom: A comparison between two types of classroom in the city and the kibbutz in Israel. *Contemporary Educational Psychology, 14*, 22–32.

Hess, R. D., & Holloway, S. D. (1984). Family and school as educational institutions. In R. D. Parke (Ed.), *Review of child development research* (Vol. 7). Chicago: University of Chicago Press.

Hetherington, E. M. (1988). Parents, children and siblings: Six years after divorce. In R. A. Hinde & J. Stevenson-Hinde (Eds.), *Relationships within families*. Oxford, UK: Clarendon.

Hetherington, E. M. (1993). An overview of the Virginia Longitudinal Study of divorce and remarriage with a focus on early adolescence. *Journal of Family Psychology, 7*, 39–56.

Hetherington, E. M., Stanley-Hagan, M., & Anderson, E. R. (1989). Marital transitions: A child's perspective. *American Psychologist, 44*, 303–312.

Higgins, E. T., & Parsons, J. E. (1983). Stages as subcultures: Social-cognitive development and the social life of the child. In E. T. Higgins, W. W. Hartup, & D. N. Ruble (Eds.), *Social cognition and social development*. New York: Cambridge University Press.

Hinde, R. A. (1963). The nature of imprinting. In B. B. Foss (Ed.), *Determinants of infant behavior* (Vol. 2). London: Methuen.

Hinde, R. A. (1974). *The biological bases of human social behavior*. New York: McGraw-Hill.

Hinde, R. A. (1979). *Towards understanding relationships*. London: Academic Press.

Hinde, R. A. (1982). *Ethology*. London: Fontana.

Hinde, R. A. (1983). Ethology and child development. In P. H. Mussen (Ed.), *Handbook of child psychology* (Vol. 2). New York: Wiley.

Hinde, R. A. (1987). *Individuals, relationships and culture*. Cambridge, UK: Cambridge University Press.

Hinde, R. A. (1992). Human social development: An ethological/relationship perspective. In H. McGurk (Ed.), *Childhood social development: Contemporary perspectives*. Hillsdale, NJ: Erlbaum.

Hinde, R. A., & Herrmann, J. (1977). Frequencies, durations, derived measures and their correlations in studying dyadic and triadic relationships. In H. R. Schaffer (Ed.), *Studies in mother–infant interaction*. London: Academic Press.

Hinde, R. A., Titmus, G., Easton, D., & Tamplin, A. (1985). Incidence of "friendship" and behavior with strong associates versus non-associates in preschoolers. *Child Development, 56*, 234–245.

Hirsch, B. J., & Rapkin, B. D. (1987). The transition to junior high school: A longitudinal study of self-esteem, psychological symptomatology, school life, and social support. *Child Development, 58,* 1235–1243.

Hirshberg, L. M., & Svejda, M. (1990). When infants look to their parents: 1. Infants' social referencing of mothers compared to fathers. *Child Development, 61,* 1175–1186.

Hodges, J., & Tizard, B. (1989). IQ and behavioral adjustment of ex-institutional adolescents. *Journal of Child Psychology and Psychiatry, 30,* 53–76.

Hoffman, L. W. (1988). Cross-cultural differences in child rearing goals. In R. A. LeVine, P. M. Miller, & M. M. West (Eds.), *Parental behavior in diverse societies.* San Francisco: Jossey-Bass.

Hoffman, L. W. (1989). Effects of maternal employment in the two-parent family. *American Psychologist, 44,* 283–292.

Hoffman, M. L. (1977). Moral internalization: Current theory and research. In L. Berkowitz (Ed.), *Advances in experimental social psychology* (Vol. 10). New York: Academic Press.

Hoffmann, M. L. (1984). Interaction of affect and cognition in empathy. In C. E. Izard, J. Kagan, & R. Zajonc (Eds.), *Emotions, cognitions and behavior.* Cambridge, UK: Cambridge University Press.

Hoffman, M. L. (1987). The contribution of empathy to justice and moral judgment. In N. Eisenberg & J. Strayer (Eds.), *Empathy and its development.* Cambridge, UK: Cambridge University Press.

Hoffman, M. L. (1989). Moral development. In M. H. Bornstein & M. E. Lamb (Eds.), *Developmental psychology: An advanced textbook,* 2nd ed. Hillsdale, NJ: Erlbaum.

Hoffman, M. L., & Salzstein, H. D. (1967). Parent discipline and the child's moral development. *Journal of Personality and Social Psychology, 5,* 45–47.

Holden, G. (1988). Adults' thinking about a child-rearing problem: Effects of experience, parental status and gender. *Child Development, 59,* 1623–1632.

Holden, G. W., & Ritchie, K. L. (1991). Linking extreme marital discord, child rearing and child behavior problems: Evidence from battered women. *Child Development, 62,* 311–327.

Holden, G. W., & Zambarano, R. J. (1992). Passing the rod: Similarities between parents and their young children in orientations toward physical punishment. In I. E. Sigel, A. W. McGillicuddy-De Lisi, & J. J. Goodnow (Eds.), *Parental belief systems: The psychological consequences for children,* 2nd ed. Hillsdale, NJ: Erlbaum.

Holmberg, M. C. (1980). The development of social interchange patterns from 12–42 months. *Child Development, 51,* 448–456.

Honigmann, J. J. (1954). *Culture and personality.* New York: Harper.

Horn, J. M. (1983). The Texas adoption project: Adopted children and their intellectual resemblance to biological and adoptive parents. *Child Development, 54,* 268–275.

Horn, J. M., Lochlin, J. C., & Willerman, L. (1979). Intellectual resemblance among adoptive and biological relatives: The Texas adoption project. *Behavior Genetics, 9,* 177–208.

Howe, C. (1981). *Acquiring language in a conversational context.* London: Academic Press.

Howe, C. (Ed.). (1993). Peer interaction and knowledge acquisition. *Social Development, 2,* No. 3.

Howe, C., Rodgers, C., & Tolmie, A. (1990). Physics in the primary school: Peer interaction and the understanding of floating and sinking. *European Journal of Psychology of Education, 5,* 459–475.

Howe, C., Tolmie, A., & Rodgers, C. (1992). The acquisition of conceptual knowledge in science by primary school children: Group interaction and the understanding of motion down an incline. *British Journal of Developmental Psychology, 10,* 113–130.

Howe, M. J. A. (Ed.). (1990). *Encouraging the development of exceptional skills.* Leicester, UK: British Psychological Society.

Howe, M. J. A. (1990). *Sense and nonsense about hothouse children.* Leicester, UK: British Psychological Society.

Howes, C. (1987). Social competence with peers in young children: Developmental sequences. *Developmental Review, 7,* 252–272.

Howlin, P., & Yule, W. (1990). Taxonomy of major disorders in childhood. In M. Lewis & S. M. Miller (Eds.), *Handbook of developmental psychopathology.* New York: Plenum.

Hubbard, J. A., & Coie, J. D. (1994). Emotional correlates of social competence in children's peer relationships. *Merrill-Palmer Quarterly, 40,* 1–20.

Huesman, L. R., Eron, L. D., Lefkowitz, M. M., & Walder, L. O. (1984). Stability of aggression over time and generations. *Developmental Psychology, 20,* 1120–1134.

Hughes, M. (1986). *Children and number.* Oxford, UK: Basil Blackwell.

Huston, A. C. (1983). Sex typing. In P. H. Mussen (Ed.), *Handbook of child psychology* (Vol. 4). New York: John Wiley.

Huston, A. C. (1985). The development of sex-typing. *Developmental Review, 5*, 1–17.

Huston, A. C. (Ed.). (1991). *Children in poverty: Child development and public policy*. New York: Cambridge University Press.

Huston, A. C., McLoyd, V. C., & Coll, C. G. (1994). Children and poverty: Issues in contemporary research. *Child Development, 65*, 275–282.

Hyde, J. S. (1984). How large are gender differences in aggression? A developmental meta-analysis. *Developmental Psychology, 20*, 722–736.

Hymel, S. (1983). Preschool children's peer relationships: Issues in sociometric assessment. *Merrill-Palmer Quarterly, 29*, 237–260.

Hymel, S., Rubin, K. H., Rowden, R., & LeMare, L. (1990). Children's peer relationships: Longitudinal predictions of internalizing and externalizing problems from middle to late childhood. *Child Development, 61*, 2004–2021.

Imamoglu, E. M. (1975). Children's awareness and usage of intention cues. *Child Development, 46*, 39–45.

Imperato-McGinley, J. (1979). Androgens and the evolution of male-gender identity among male pseudo-hermaphrodites with 5-reductase deficiency. *New England Journal of Medicine, 300*, 1233–1270.

Imperato-McGinley, J., Guerro, L., Gautier, T., & Peterson, R. E. (1974). Steroid 5-reductase deficiency in man. *Science, 186*, 1213–1216.

Isabella, R. A. (1993). Origins of attachment: Maternal interactive behavior across the first year. *Child Development, 64*, 605–621.

Isabella, R. A., Belsky, J., & von Eye, A. (1989). Origins of infant–mother attachment: An examination of interactional synchrony during the infant's first year. *Developmental Psychology, 25*, 12–21.

Izard, C. E. (1971). *The face of emotion*. New York: Appleton-Century-Crofts.

Izard, C. E. (1977). *Human emotions*. New York: Plenum.

Izard, C. E. (1979). *The maximally discriminative facial movement coding system (Max)*. Newark, DE: University of Delaware.

Izard, C. E., & Malatesta, C. Z. (1987). Perspectives on emotional development I: Differential emotions theory of early emotional development. In J. D. Osofsky (Ed.), *Handbook of infant development*, 2nd ed. New York: Wiley.

Jackson, E., Campos, J. J., & Fischer, K. W. (1978). The question of decalage between object permanence and person permanence. *Developmental Psychology, 14*, 1–10.

Jacobsen, T., Edelstein, W., & Hofman, V. (1994). A longitudinal study of the relation between representatives of attachment in childhood and cognitive functioning in childhood and adolescence. *Developmental Psychology, 30*, 112–124.

Jahoda, G. (1963). The development of children's ideas about country and nationality. *British Journal of Educational Psychology, 33*, 143–153.

Jahoda, G. (1964). Children's concepts of nationality: A critical study of Piaget's stages. *Child Development, 35*, 1081–1092.

Jahoda, G. (1984). The development of thinking about socioeconomic systems. In H. Tajfel (Ed.), *The social dimension*. Cambridge, UK: Cambridge University Press.

James, W. (1892). *Psychology: The briefer course*. New York: Harper.

Jenkins, J. M., & Smith, M. A. (1991). Marital disharmony and children's behavior problems: Aspects of a poor marriage that affect children adversely. *Journal of Child Psychology and Psychiatry, 32*, 793–810.

Jenkins, J. M., Smith, M. A., & Graham, P. J. (1989). Coping with parental quarrels. *Journal of the American Academy of Child and Adolescent Psychiatry, 28*, 182–189.

Jenkins, S., Owen, C., Bax, M., & Hart, H. (1984). Continuities in common behavior problems in preschool children. *Journal of Child Psychology and Psychiatry, 25*, 75–89.

Johnson, M. H., & Morton, J. (1991). *Biology and cognitive development: The case of face recognition*. Oxford, UK: Blackwell.

Jones, E. (1953-7). *The life and work of Sigmund Freud* (Vols. 1–3). New York: Basic Books.

Jurkovic, G. J. (1980). The juvenile delinquent as a moral philosopher: A structural developmental perspective. *Psychological Bulletin, 88*, 709–727.

Kagan, J. (1978). *Infancy*. Cambridge, MA: Harvard University Press.

Kagan, J. (1981). *The second year: The emergence of self-awareness*. Cambridge, MA: Harvard University Press.

Kagan, J. (1982). *Review of research in infancy*. New York: Grant Foundation Publication.

Kagan, J., Reznick, J. S., & Snidman, N. (1986). Temperamental inhibition in early childhood. In R. Plomin & J. Dunn (Eds.), *The study of temperament: Changes, continuities, and challenges*. Hillsdale, NJ: Erlbaum.

Kagan, J., Reznick, J. S., & Snidman, N. (1987). The physiology and psychology of behavioral inhibition in children. *Child Development, 58*, 1459–1473.

Kaila, E. (1932). The reactions of the infant to the human face. *Annals Universitie Abo., 17*, 1–114.

Kanner, L. (1943). Autistic disturbance of affective contact. *Nervous Child, 2*, 217–250.

Katz, P. A., & Ksansuak, K. R. (1994). Developmental aspects of gender role flexibility and traditionality in middle childhood and adolescence. *Developmental Psychology, 30*, 272–282.

Kaufman, J., & Cicchetti, D. (1989). Effects of maltreatment on school-age children's socio-emotional development: Assessments in a daycamp setting. *Developmental Psychology, 25*, 516–524.

Kaufman, J., & Zigler, E. (1987). Do abused children become abusive parents? *American Journal of Orthopsychiatry, 57*, 186–192.

Kaye, K. (1977). Toward the origin of dialogue. In H. R. Schaffer (Ed.), *Studies in mother–infant interaction*. London: Academic Press.

Kaye, K., & Fogel, A. (1980). The temporal structure of face-to-face communication between mothers and infants. *Developmental Psychology, 16*, 454–464.

Keller, A., Ford, L. H., & Meacham, J. A. (1978). Dimensions of self-concept in preschool children. *Developmental Psychology, 14*, 483–489.

Kerr, M., Lambert, W. M., Stattin, H., & Klackenberg-Larsson, I. (1994). Stability of inhibition in a Swedish longitudinal sample. *Child Development, 65*, 138–146.

Kessen, W. (1965). *The child*. New York: Wiley.

Kinard, E. M. (1980). Emotional development in physically abused children. *American Journal of Orthopsychiatry, 50*, 686–696.

Kindermann, T. A. (1993). Natural peer groups as contexts for individual development: The case of children's motivation in school. *Developmental Psychology, 29*, 970–977.

Kinsbourne, M., & Hiscock, M. (1983). The normal and deviant development of functional lateralization of the brain. In P. H. Mussen (Ed.), *Handbook of child psychology* (Vol. 2). New York: John Wiley.

Klimes-Dougan, B., & Kistner, J. (1990) Physically abused preschoolers' responses to peers' distress. *Developmental Psychology, 26*, 599–602.

Klinnert, M. D. (1984). The regulation of infant behavior by maternal facial expression. *Infant Behavior and Development, 7*, 447–465.

Kochanska, G. (1991). Socialization and temperament in the development of guilt and conscience. *Child Development, 62*, 1379–1392.

Kochanska, G., DeVet, K., Goldman, M., Murray, K., & Putnam, S. P. (1994). Maternal reports of conscience development and temperament in young children. *Child Development, 65*, 852–868.

Koester, L. S. (1994). Early interactions and the socioemotional development of deaf infants. *Early Development and Parenting, 3*, 51–60.

Kohlberg, L. (1966). A cognitive developmental analysis of children's sex-role concepts and attitudes. In E. E. Maccoby (Ed.), *The development of sex differences*. Stanford, CA: Stanford University Press.

Kohlberg, L. (1969). Stage and sequence: The cognitive-developmental approach to socialization. In D. A. Goslin (Ed.), *Handbook of socialization theory and research*. Chicago: Rand-McNally.

Kohlberg, L. (1975). The cognitive-developmental approach to moral education. *Phi Delta Kappa*, June, 670–677.

Kohlberg, L. (1976). Moral stages and moralization: The cognitive-developmental approach. In T. Lickona (Ed.), *Moral development and behavior*. New York: Holt, Rinehart, & Winston.

Koluchova, J. (1976a). Severe deprivation in twins: A case study. In A. M. Clarke & A. D. B. Clarke (Eds.), *Early experience: Myth and reality*. London: Open Books.

Koluchova, J. (1976b). A report on the further development of twins after severe and prolonged deprivation. In A. M. Clarke & A. D. B. Clarke (Eds.), *Early experience: Myth and reality*. London: Open Books.

Kolvin, I., Garside, R., Nicol, R., Leitch, I., & Macmillan, A. (1977). Screening school children for high risk of emotional and educational disorder. *British Journal of Psychiatry, 131*, 192–206.

Konner, M. (1975). Relations among infants and juveniles in comparative perspective. In M. Lewis & L. A. Rosenblum (Eds.), *Friendship and peer relations*. New York: Wiley.

Konner, M. (1982). Biological aspects of the mother–infant bond. In R. Emde & R. H. Harmon (Eds.), *The development of attachment and affiliative systems*. New York: Plenum Press.

Kopp, C. B. (1982). Antecedents of self-regulation: A developmental perspective. *Developmental Psychology, 18*, 199–214.

Korn, S. J., Chess, S., & Fernandez, P. (1978). The impact of children's physical handicaps on marital quality and family interaction. In R. Lerner & S. Spanier (Eds.), *Child influences on marital and family interaction*. New York: Academic Press.

Korner, A. F., & Grobstein, R. (1966). Visual alertness as related to soothing in neonates: Implications for maternal stimulation and early deprivation. *Child Development, 37*, 867–876.

Korner, A. F., & Thoman, E. B. (1970). Visual alertness in neonates as evoked by maternal care. *Journal of Experimental Child Psychology, 10*, 67–78.

Kotelchuck, M., Zelazo, P. R., Kagan, J., & Spelke, E. (1975). Infant reactions to parental separations when left with familiar and unfamiliar adults. *Journal of Genetic Psychology, 126*, 255–262.

Kruger, A. C. (1992). The effect of peer and adult–child transactive discussions on moral reasoning. *Merrill–Palmer Quarterly, 38*, 191–211.

Kruger, A. C. (1993). Peer collaboration: Conflict, cooperation or both? *Social Development, 2*, 165–182.

Kuczaj, S. A. (1986). Discussion: On social interaction as a type of explanation of language development. *British Journal of Developmental Psychology, 4*, 289–300.

Kuczynski, L. (1984). Socialization goals and mother–child interaction: Strategies for long-term and short-term compliance. *Developmental Psychology, 20*, 1061–1073.

Kuczynski, L., & Kochanska, G. (1990). Development of children's noncompliance strategies from toddlerhood to age 5. *Developmental Psychology, 26*, 398–408.

Kuczynski, L., Kochanska, G., Radke-Yarrow, M., & Girnius-Brown, O. (1987). A developmental interpretation of young children's non-compliance. *Developmental Psychology, 23*, 799–806.

Kuebli, J., & Fivush, R. (1992). Gender differences in parent–child conversations about past emotions. *Sex Roles, 27*, 683–698.

Kuhn, D., Nash, S. C., & Brucker, L. (1978). Sex role concepts of two- and three-year olds. *Child Development, 49*, 445–451.

Kupersmidt, J. B., & Coie, J. D. (1990). Preadolescent peer status, aggression and school adjustment as predictors of externalizing problems in adolescence. *Child Development, 61*, 1350–1362.

Kupersmidt, J. B., Coie, J. D., & Dodge, K. A. (1990). The role of poor peer relationships in the development of disorder. In S. Asher & J. Coie (Eds.), *Peer rejection in childhood*. New York: Cambridge University Press.

Ladd, G. W. (1992). Themes and theories: Perspectives on processes in family–peer relationships. In R. D. Parke & G. W. Ladd (Eds.), *Family–peer relationships: Modes of linkage*. Hillsdale, NJ: Erlbaum.

Ladd, G. W., & Golter, B. S. (1988). Parents' management of preschoolers' peer relations: Is it related to children's social competence? *Developmental Psychology, 24*, 109–117.

Ladd, G. W., & Mize, J. (1983). A cognitive social learning model of social skill training. *Psychological Review, 90*, 127–157.

LaFreniere, P., Strayer, F. F., & Gaulthier, R. (1984). The emergence of same-sex affiliative preferences among preschool peers: A developmental/etiological perspective. *Child Development, 55*, 1958–1965.

Lamb, M. E. (1977) Father–infant and mother–infant interaction in the first year of life. *Child Development, 48*, 167–181.

Lamb, M. E. (1978). Qualitative aspects of mother- and father–infant attachments. *Infant Behavior and Development, 1*, 265–275.

Lamb, M. E. (1981). *The role of the father in child development*. New York: Wiley.

Lamb, M. E., & Nash, A. (1989). Infant–mother attachment, sociability and peer competence. In T. J. Berndt & G. W. Ladd (Eds.), *Peer relationships in child development*. New York: Wiley.

Lamb, M. E., Thompson, R. A., Gardner, W., & Charnov, E. L. (1985). *Infant–mother attachment: The origins and developmental significance of individual differences in Strange Situation behavior*. Hillsdale, NJ: Erlbaum.

Langlois, J. H., & Downs, A. C. (1980). Mothers, fathers, and peers as socialization agents of sex-typed play behaviors in young children. *Child Development, 51*, 1237–1247.

Leinhardt, G., Seewald, A. M., & Engel, M. (1979). Learning what's taught: Sex differences in instructions. *Journal of Educational Psychology, 71*, 432–439.

Lempers, J. D., Clark-Lempers, D., & Simons, R. L. (1989). Economic hardship, parenting, and distress in adolescence. *Child Development, 60*, 25–39.

Lenneberg, E. H. (1967). *Biological foundations of language*. New York: Wiley.

Leonard, S. P., & Archer, J. (1989). A naturalistic investigation of gender constancy in three- to four-year-old children. *British Journal of Developmental Psychology, 7*, 341–346.

Leslie, A. M. (1987). Pretence and representation: The origins of "theory of mind." *Psychological Review, 94*, 412–426.

Lester, B. M., Hoffman, J., & Brazelton, T. B. (1985). The rhythmic structure of mother–infant interaction in term and preterm infants. *Child Development, 56*, 15–27.

LeVine, R. A. (1974). Parental goals: A cross-cultural view. In H. J. Leichter (Ed.), *The family as educator*. New York: Teachers College Press.

LeVine, R. A. (1988). Human parental care: Universal goals, cultural strategies, individual behavior. In R. A. LeVine, P. M. Miller, & M. M. West (Eds.), *Parental behavior in diverse societies*. San Francisco: Jossey-Bass.

LeVine, R., Dixon, S., LeVine, S., Richman, A., Leiderman, P. H., Keefer, C. H., & Brazelton, T. B. (1994). *Child care and culture: Lessons from Africa*. Cambridge, UK: Cambridge University Press.

Levitt, M. J., Guacci-Franco, N., & Levitt, J. L. (1993). Convoys of social support in childhood and early adolescence: Structure and function. *Developmental Psychology, 29*, 811–818.

Levy-Shiff, R. (1994). Individual and contextual correlates of marital change across the transition of parenthood. *Developmental Psychology, 30*, 591–601.

Lewis, C. (1986). The role of the father in the human family. In W. Sluckin & M. Herbert (Eds.), *Parental behaviour*. Oxford, UK: Blackwell.

Lewis, M. (1990). Social knowledge and social development. *Merrill-Palmer Quarterly, 36*, 93–116.

Lewis, M. (1992). *Shame: The exposed self.* New York: Free Press.

Lewis, M., Alessandri, S. M., & Sullivan, M. W. (1992). Differences in shame and pride as a function of children's gender and task difficulty. *Child Development, 63*, 630–638.

Lewis, M., & Brooks-Gunn, J. (1979). *Social cognition and the acquisition of self.* New York: Plenum.

Lewis, M., Feiring, C., McGuffog, C., & Jaskir, J. (1984). Predicting psychopathy in six-year-olds from early social relations. *Child Development, 55*, 123–136.

Lewis, M., Sullivan, H. W., Stanger, C., & Weiss, M. (1989). Self-development and self-conscious emotions. *Child Development, 60*, 146–156.

Liben, L. S., & Signorella, M. L. (1993). Gender-schematic processing in children: The role of initial interpretations of stimuli. *Developmental Psychology, 29*, 141–149.

Lips, H. M. (1988). *Sex and gender*. Mountainview, CA: Mayfield.

Lipsitt, L. P. (1963). Learning in the first year of life. In L. P. Lipsitt & C. C. Spiker (Eds.), *Advances in child development and behavior*, Vol. 1. New York: Academic Press.

Livesley, W. J., & Bromley, D. B. (1973). *Person perception in childhood and adolescence*. London: Wiley.

Livson, N., & Peskin, H. (1980). Perspective on adolescence from longitudinal research. In J. Adelson (Ed.), *Handbook of adolescent psychology*. New York: Wiley.

Locke, J. (1693). *Some thoughts concerning education*, 4th ed. London: A. & J. Churchill.

Loeber, R. (1982). The stability of antisocial and delinquent child behavior: A review. *Child Development, 53*, 1431–1446.

Loehlin, J. C. (1982). Are personality traits differentially heritable? *Behavior Genetics, 12*, 417–428.

Loehlin, J. C., Horn, J. M., & Willerman, L. (1981). Personality resemblance in adoptive families. *Behavior Genetics, 11*, 309–330.

Loehlin, J. C., Horn, J. M., & Willerman, L. (1989). Modeling IQ change: Evidence from the Texas adoption project. *Child Development, 60*, 993–1004.

Loftus, E. F. (1993). The reality of repressed memories. *American Psychologist, 48*, 518–537.

Lorenz, K. (1935). Der Kumpan in der Umwelt des Vogels. *Journal für Ornithologie, 83*, 137–213, 289–413.

Lorenz, K. (1965). *Evolution and modification of behavior*. Chicago: University of Chicago Press.

Lorenz, K. (1966). *On aggression*. London: Methuen.

Lutz, C. (1987). Goals, events and understanding in Ifaluk emotion theory. In D. Holland & N. Quinn (Eds.), *Cultural models in language and thought*. Cambridge, UK: Cambridge University Press.

Lytton, H. (1979). Disciplinary encounters between young boys and their mothers and fathers: Is there a contingency system? *Developmental Psychology, 15*, 256–268.

Lytton, H. (1980). *Parent–child interaction: The socialization process observed in twin and singleton families*. New York: Plenum.

Lytton, H., Conway, D., & Sauve, R. (1977). The impact of twinship on parent–child interaction. *Journal of Personality and Social Psychology, 35*, 97–107.

Lytton, H., & Zwirner, W. (1975). Compliance and its

controlling stimuli observed in a natural setting. *Developmental Psychology, 11*, 769–779.

Maccoby, E. E. (1980). *Social development*. New York: Harcourt Brace Jovanovich.

Maccoby, E. E. (1990). Gender and relationships: A developmental account. *American Psychologist, 45*, 513–520.

Maccoby, E. E., & Jacklin, C. N. (1974). *The Psychology of sex differences*. Stanford, CA: Stanford University Press.

Maccoby, E. E., & Jacklin, C. N. (1980). Sex differences in aggression: A rejoinder and reprise. *Child Development, 51*, 964–980.

Maccoby, E. E., & Jacklin, C. N. (1987). Gender segregation in childhood. In H. W. Reese (Ed.), *Advances in child development and behavior* (Vol. 4). Orlando, FL: Academic Press.

Maccoby, E. E., & Martin, J. A. (1983). Socialization in the context of the family: Parent–child interaction. In E. M. Hetherington (Ed.), *Handbook of child psychology. Vol. IV: Socialization, personality, and social interaction*. New York: Wiley.

Macfarlane, A. (1975). Olfaction in the development of social preferences in the human neonate. In R. Porter & M. O'Connor (Eds.), *Parent–infant interaction*. Amsterdam: Elsevier.

Mahler, M., Pine, F., & Bergman, A. (1975). *The psychological birth of the human infant*. New York: Basic Books.

Main, M., & Cassidy, J. (1988). Categories of response to reunion with the parent at age 6: Predictable from infant attachment classifications and stable over a 1-month period. *Developmental Psychology, 24*, 415–426.

Main, M., & George, C. (1985). Response of abused and disadvantaged toddlers to distress in playmates: A study in the day care settings. *Developmental Psychology, 21*, 407–412.

Main, M., Kaplan, N., & Cassidy, J. (1985). Security in infancy, childhood, and adulthood: A move to the level of representation. In I. Bretherton & E. Waters (Eds.), Growing points of attachment theory and research. *Monographs of the Society for Research in Child Development, 50* (1–2, Serial No. 209).

Main, M., & Solomon, J. (1985). Discovery of an insecure disorganized/disoriented attachment pattern. In M. Yogman & T. B. Brazelton (Eds.), *Affective development in infancy*. Norwood, NJ: Ablex.

Malatesta, C. Z., Culver, C., Tesman, J. R., &

Shepard, B. (1989). The development of emotion expression during the first two years of life. *Monographs of the Society for Research in Child Development, 54* (1–2, Serial No. 219).

Malik, N. M., & Furman, W. (1993). Problems in children's peer relations: What can the clinician do? *Journal of Child Psychology and Psychiatry, 34*, 1303–1326.

Marcus, D. E., & Overton, W. F. (1978). The development of cognitive gender constancy and sex role preferences. *Child Development, 49*, 434–444.

Marquis, D. P. (1941). Learning in the neonate: The modification of behavior under three feeding schedules. *Journal of Experimental Psychology, 29*, 263–282.

Martin, B., & Hoffman, J. A. (1990). Conduct disorders. In M. Lewis & S. M. Miller (Eds.), *Handbook of developmental psychopathology*. New York: Plenum.

Martin, C. A., & Johnson, J. E. (1992). Children's self-perceptions and mothers' beliefs about development and competencies. In I. E. Sigel, A. V. McGillicuddy-De Lisi, & J. J. Goodnow (Eds.), *Parental belief systems: The psychological consequences for children*, 2nd ed. Hillsdale, NJ: Erlbaum.

Martin, C. L. (1989). Children's use of gender-related information in making social judgments. *Developmental Psychology, 25*, 80–88.

Martin, C. L. (1993). New directions for investigating children's gender knowledge. *Developmental Review, 13*, 184–204.

Martin, C. L., & Halverson, C. F. (1981). A schematic processing model of sex typing and stereotyping in children. *Child Development, 52*, 1119–1134.

Martin, C. L., & Halverson, C. F. (1983). The effects of sex-typing schemas on young children's memory. *Child Development, 54*, 563–574.

Martin, C. L., & Little, J. K. (1990). The relations of general understanding to children's sex-typed preferences and gender stereotypes. *Child Development, 61*, 1427–1439.

Martin, C. L., Wood, C. H., & Little, J. K. (1990). The development of gender stereotype components. *Child Development, 61*, 1891–1904.

Masataka, N. (1993). Motherese is a signed language. *Infant Behavior and Development, 15*, 453–460.

Masten, A. S. (1994). Resilience in individual development: Successful adaptation despite risk and adversity. In M. C. Wang & E. W. Gordon (Eds.), *Educational resilience in inner-city America*. Hillsdale, NJ: Erlbaum.

Masten, A. S., & Coatsworth, J. D. (1995). Competence, resilience, and psychopathology. In D. Cicchetti & D. Cohen (Eds.), *Manual of developmental psychopathology*. New York: Cambridge University Press.

Matute-Bianchi, M. E. (1986). Ethnic identities and patterns of school success and failure among Mexican-descent and Japanese-American students in a California High School. *American Journal of Education, 91*, 233–255.

Maurer, D. (1985). Infants' perception of facedness. In T. M. Field & N. A. Fox (Eds.), *Social perception in infants*. Norwood, NJ: Ablex.

McCall, R. B. (1977). Challenges to a science of developmental psychology. *Child Development, 48*, 333–344.

McCall, R. B., & Carriger, M. S. (1993). A meta-analysis of infant habituation and recognition performance as predictors of later IQ. *Child Development, 64*, 57–79.

McCarthy, J. D., & Hodge, D. R. (1982). Analysis of age effects in longitudinal studies of adolescent self-esteem. *Developmental Psychology, 18*, 372–374.

McCartney, M., Scarr, S., Phillips, D., Grajek, S., & Schwartz, J. C. (1982). Environmental differences among day care centers and their effects on children's development. In E. F. Zigler & E. W. Gordon (Eds.), *Day care: Scientific and social policy issues*. Boston: Auburn House.

McDevitt, S. (1986). Continuity and discontinuity of temperament in infancy and early childhood: A psychometric perspective. In R. Plomin & J. Dunn (Eds.), *The study of temperament: Changes, continuities, and challenges*. Hillsdale, NJ: Erlbaum.

McFarlane, A. C. (1988). Recent life events and psychiatric disorder in children: The interaction with preceding extreme adversity. *Journal of Child Psychology and Psychiatry, 29*, 677–690.

McFarlane, A. C., Poliansky, S. K., & Irwin, C. (1987). A longitudinal study of the psychological morbidity in children due to a natural disaster. *Psychological Medicine, 17*, 727–738.

McGuire, S., Neiderhiser, J. M., Reiss, D., Hetherington, E. M., & Plomin, R. (1994). Genetic and environmental influences on perceptions of self-worth and competence in adolescence: A study of twins, full siblings and step-siblings. *Child Development, 65*, 785–799.

McLanahan, S. S., Astone, N. M., & Marks, N. F. (1991). The role of mother-only families in reproducing poverty. In A. C. Huston (Ed.), *Children in poverty: Child development and public policy*. Cambridge, UK: Cambridge University Press.

McLoyd, V. C. (1990). The impact of economic hardship on black families and children: Psychological distress, parenting, and socioeconomic development. *Child Development, 61*, 311–346.

McLoyd, V. C., Jayaratue, T. E., Caballo, R., & Borquez, J. (1994). Unemployment and work interruption among African American single mothers: Effects on parenting and adolescent socioemotional functioning. *Child Development, 65*, 562–589.

McNally, S., Eisenberg, N., & Harris, J. D. (1991). Consistency and change in maternal child-rearing practices and values: A longitudinal study. *Child Development, 62*, 190–198.

Mead, G. H. (1934). *Mind, self and society*. Chicago: University of Chicago Press.

Mead, M. (1935). *Sex and temperament in three primitive societies*. New York: Morrow.

Mead, M. (1962). A cultural anthropologist's approach to maternal deprivation. In *Deprivation of maternal care: A reassessment of its effects*. Geneva, Switzerland: World Health Organization.

Mednick, S. A., Moffitt, T. E., & Stack, S. (1987). *The causes of crime: New biological approaches*. New York: Cambridge University Press.

Messer, D. J. (1978). The integration of mother's referential speech with joint play. *Child Development, 49*, 781–787.

Mickelson, R. (1990). The attitude-achievement paradox among black adolescents. *Sociology of Education, 63*, 44–61.

Miller, N. B., Cowan, P. A., Cowan, C. P., Hetherington, E. M., & Clingempeel, W. G. (1993). Externalizing in preschoolers and early adolescents: A cross-study replication of a family model. *Developmental Psychology, 29*, 3–18.

Miller, P. H., & Aloise, P. A. (1989). Young children's understanding of the psychological causes of behavior: A review. *Child Development, 60*, 257–285.

Miller, S. A. (1988). Parents' beliefs about children's cognitive development. *Child Development, 59*, 259–285.

Minde, K., Perrotta, M., & Marton, P. (1985). Maternal caretaking and play with full-term and premature infants. *Journal of Child Psychology and Psychiatry, 26*, 231–244.

Minuchin, P. (1988). Relationships within the family: A systems perspective on development. In R. A.

Hinde & J. Stevenson-Hinde (Eds.), *Relationships within families*. Oxford, UK: Clarendon Press.

Money, J. (1987). Sin, sickness, or status? Homosexual gender identity and psychoneuroendocrinology. *American Psychologist, 42*, 384–399.

Money, J., & Ehrhardt, A. A. (1972). *Man and woman, boy and girl*. Baltimore: Johns Hopkins University Press.

Montemayor, R., Eisen, M. (1977). The development of self-conceptions from childhood to adolescence. *Developmental Psychology, 13*, 314–319.

Morelli, G. A., & Tronick, E. Z. (1992). Efe fathers: One among many? A comparison of forager children's involvement with fathers and other males. *Social Development 1*, 36–54.

Morgan, G. A., & Ricciuti, H. N. (1969). Infants' responses to strangers during the first year. In B. M. Foss (Ed.), *Determinants of infant behaviour* (Vol. 4). London: Methuen.

Munn, P., & Dunn, J. (1989). Temperament and the developing relationship between siblings. *International Journal of Behavioral Development, 12*, 433–451.

Munroe, R. H., Shimmin, H. L., & Munroe, R. L. (1984). Gender understanding and sex role preference in four cultures. *Developmental Psychology, 20*, 673–682.

Murphy, C. M., & Messer, D. J. (1977). Mothers, infants and pointing, a study of a gesture. In H. R. Schaffer (Ed.), *Studies in mother–infant interaction*. London: Academic Press.

Murphy, L. (1937). *Social behavior and child personality*. New York: Columbia University Press.

Neill, A. S. (1962). *Summerhill*. London: Gollancz.

Nelson, C. A. (1962). The recognition of facial expressions in the first two years of life: Mechanisms of development. *Child Development, 58*, 889–909.

Nelson, C. A., & Ludemann, P. M. (1989). Past, current, and future trends in infant face perception research. *Canadian Journal of Psychology, 43*, 183–198.

Nelson, C. D., & Stockdale, D. F. (1985). Maternal control behavior and compliance of preschool children. *Parenting Studies, 1*, 11–18.

Nelson, J. R., Smith D. J., & Dodd, J. (1990). The moral reasoning of juvenile delinquents: A meta-analysis. *Journal of Abnormal Child Psychology, 18*, 231–239.

Nelson, K. (1973). Structure and strategy in learning to talk. *Monographs of the Society for Research in Child Development, 38* (Serial No. 149).

Newcomb, A. F., Bukowski, W. W., & Pattee, L. (1993). Children's peer relations: A meta-analytic review of popular, rejected, neglected, controversial and average sociometric status. *Psychological Bulletin, 113*, 99–128.

Newcombe, N. S., & Baenninger, M. (1989). Biological change and cognitive ability in adolescence. In G. R. Adams, R. Montemayor, & T. P. Gullotta (Eds.), *Biology of adolescent behavior and development*. Newbury Park, CA: Sage.

Newson, J., & Newson, E. (1974). Cultural aspects of childrearing in the English-speaking world. In M. P. M. Richards (Ed.), *The integration of a child into a social world*. Cambridge, UK: Cambridge University Press.

Nicolich, L. M. (1977). Beyond sensori-motor intelligence: Assessment of symbolic maturity through analysis of pretend play. *Merrill-Palmer Quarterly, 23*, 89–99.

Ninio, A. (1988). The effects of cultural background, sex and parenthood on beliefs about the timetable of cognitive development in infancy. *Merrill-Palmer Quarterly, 34*, 369–388.

Nucci, L. P., & Nucci, M. S. (1982). Children's social interactions in the context of moral and conventional transgressions. *Child Development, 53*, 403–412.

O'Brien, M., & Huston, A. C. (1985). Development of sex-typed play behavior in toddlers. *Developmental Psychology, 21*, 866–871.

O'Brien, S. F., & Bierman, K. L. (1988). Conception and perceived influence of peer groups: Interviews with preadolescents and adolescents. *Child Development, 59*, 1360–1365.

O'Connell, B., & Bretherton, I. (1984). Toddlers' play alone and with mother: The role of maternal guidance. In I. Bretherton (Ed.), *Symbolic play: The development of social understanding*. London: Academic Press.

Ogilvy, C. M., Boath, E. H., Cheyne, W. M., Jahoda, G., & Schaffer, H. R. (1992). Staff–child interaction styles in multi-ethnic nursery schools. *British Journal of Developmental Psychology, 10*, 85–97.

Olsen-Fulero, L. (1982). Style and stability in mother conversational behaviour: A study of individual differences. *Journal of Child Language, 9*, 543–564.

Olweus, D. (1979). Stability and aggressive reaction patterns in males: A review. *Psychological Bulletin, 86*, 852–875.

Olweus, D. (1980). Familial and temperamental determinants of aggressive behavior in adolescent boys:

A causal analysis. *Developmental Psychology, 16,* 644–666.

Olweus, D. (1993). *Bullying at school: What we know and what we can do.* Oxford, UK: Blackwell.

O'Malley, P. M., & Bachman, J. G. (1983). Self-esteem: Change and stability between ages 13 and 23. *Developmental Psychology, 19,* 257–268.

Orlansky, H. (1949). Infant care and personality. *Psychological Bulletin, 46,* 1–48.

Paikoff, R. L., & Brooks-Gunn, J. (1991). Do parent-child relationships change during puberty? *Psychological Bulletin, 110,* 47–66.

Papousek, H. (1961). Conditioned head rotation references in infants in the first months of life. *Acta Paediatrica, 50,* 565–576.

Parke, R. D. (1974). Rules, roles and resistance to deviation: Recent advances in punishment, discipline and self-control. In A. D. Pick (Ed.), *Minnesota symposia on child psychology* (Vol. 8). Minneapolis: University of Minnesota Press.

Parke, R. D. (1978). Parent–infant interaction: Progress, paradigms and problems. In G. P. Sackett (Ed.), *Observing behavior* (Vol. 1). Baltimore: University Park Press.

Parke, R. D. (1981). *Fathering.* London: Collins; Cambridge, MA: Harvard University Press.

Parke, R. D., & Ladd, G. W. (Eds.). (1992). *Family–peer relationships: Modes of linkage.* Hillsdale, NJ: Erlbaum.

Parke, R. D., MacDonald, K., Burkes, V., Carson, J., Bhavnagis, N., Barth, J., & Beitel, A. (1989). Family and peer systems: In search of the linkages. In K. Kreppner & R. M. Lerner (Eds.), *Family systems and life-span development.* Hillsdale, NJ: Erlbaum.

Parke, R. D., & Slabey, R. G. (1983). The development of aggression. In P. H. Mussen (Ed.), *Handbook of child psychology* (Vol. 4). New York: Wiley.

Parker, J. G., & Asher, S. R. (1987). Peer relations and later personal adjustment: Are low-accepted children at risk? *Psychological Bulletin, 102,* 357–389.

Parker, J. G., & Asher, S. R. (1993). Friendship and friendship quality in middle childhood: Links with peer group acceptance. *Developmental Psychology, 29,* 611–621.

Parmalee, A. H., Wenner, W. H., & Schulz, H. R. (1964). Infant sleep patterns from birth to 16 weeks of age. *Journal of Pediatrics, 65,* 576–582.

Parrinello, R. M., & Ruff, H. A. (1988). The influence of adult intervention on infants' level of attention. *Child Development, 59,* 1125–1135.

Pasley, K., & Ihinger-Tallman, M. (Eds.). (1984).

Remarriage and step-parenting. *Special Issue of Family Relations. 33,* No. 3.

Patterson, C. J. (1992). Children of lesbian and gay parents. *Child Development, 63,* 1025–1042.

Patterson, C. J., Kupersmidt, J. B., & Griesler, P. C. (1990). Children's perceptions of self and of relationships with others as a function of sociometric status. *Child Development, 61,* 1335–1349.

Patterson, G. R. (1982). *Coercive family processes.* Eugene, OR: Castilia Press.

Patterson, G. R., De Baryshe, D., & Ramsey, E. (1989). A developmental perspective on antisocial behavior. *American Psychologist, 44,* 329–335.

Patterson, G. R., & Forgatch, M. (1987). *Parents and adolescents: Living together.* Eugene, OR: Castilia Press.

Pearson, J. L., Hunter, A. G., Engswinger, M. E., & Kellam, S. G. (1990). Black grandmothers in multigenerational households. *Child Development, 61,* 434–442.

Pedlow, R., Sanson, A., Prior, M., & Oberklaid, F. (1993). Stability of maternally reported temperament from infancy to 8 years. *Developmental Psychology, 29,* 998–1007.

Pepler, D. J., Abramovitch, R., & Corter, C. (1981). Sibling interaction in the home: A longitudinal study. *Child Development, 52,* 1344–1347.

Perner, J. (1988). Higher-order beliefs and intentions in children's understanding of social interaction. In J. W. Astington, P. L. Harris, & D. R. Olson (Eds.), *Developing theories of mind.* Cambridge, UK: Cambridge University Press.

Perner, J., Ruffman, T., & Leekam S. R. (1994). Theory of mind is contagious: You catch it from your sibs. *Child Development, 65,* 1228–1238.

Perry, D. G., & Bussey, K. (1979). The social learning theory of sex differences: Imitation is alive and well. *Journal of Personality and Social Psychology, 37,* 1699–1712.

Perry, D. G., Kusel, S. J., & Perry, L. C. (1988). Victims of peer aggression. *Developmental Psychology, 24,* 807–814.

Perry, D. G., White, A. J., & Perry, L. C. (1984). Does early sex typing result from children's attempts to match their behavior to sex role stereotypes? *Child Development, 55,* 2114–2121.

Petersen, A. C., Sarigiani, P. A., & Kennedy, R. E. (1991). Adolescent depression: Why more girls? *Journal of Youth and Adolescence, 20,* 247–271.

Peterson, G. W., Rollins, B. C., & Thomas, D. L. (1985). Parental influence and adolescent conformity: Compliance and internalization. *Youth and Society, 16*, 397–420.

Peterson, P. L. (1979). Direct instruction reconsidered. In P. L. Peterson & H. J. Walberg (Eds.), *Research in teaching.* Berkeley, CA: McCutchan.

Phillips, D. A., Voran, M., Kisker, E., Howes, C., & Whitebrook, M. (1994). Child care for children in poverty: Opportunity or inequity? *Child Development, 65*, 472–492.

Phinney, J. S. (1990). Ethnic identity in adolescents and adults: Review of research. *Psychological Bulletin, 108*, 499–514.

Phinney, J. S. (1993). A three-stage model of ethnic identity development in adolescence. In M. E. Bernal & G. P. Knight (Eds.), *Ethnic identity: Formation and transmission among Hispanics and other minorities.* Albany, NY: State University of New York Press.

Piaget, J. (1929). *The child's conception of the world.* New York: Harcourt Brace Jovanovich.

Piaget, J. (1932). *The moral judgment of the child.* London: Routledge & Kegan Paul.

Piaget, J. (1950). *The psychology of intelligence.* London: Routledge & Kegan Paul.

Piaget, J. (1951). *Play, dreams and imitation in childhood.* London: Routledge & Kegan Paul.

Piaget, J. (1952). *The origin of intelligence in the child.* London: Routledge & Kegan Paul.

Piaget, J. (1954). *The child's construction of reality.* London: Routledge & Kegan Paul.

Piaget, J., & Inhelder, B. (1956). *The child's conception of space.* London: Routledge & Kegan Paul.

Pickens, J., & Field, T. (1993). Facial expressivity in infants of depressed mothers. *Developmental Psychology, 29*, 986–988.

Pipp, S., Easterbrooks, M. A., & Brown, S. R. (1993). Attachment status and complexity of infants' self- and other-knowledge when tested with mother and father. *Social Development, 2*, 1–14.

Pipp, S., Fischer, K. W., & Jennings, S. (1987). The acquisition of self- and mother-knowledge in infancy. *Developmental Psychology, 23*, 86–96.

Plomin, R. (1986). *Development, genetics, and psychology.* Hillsdale, NJ: Erlbaum.

Plomin, R. (1987). Developmental behavioral genetics and infancy. In J. Osofsky (Ed.), *Handbook of infant development*, 2nd ed. New York: Wiley.

Plomin, R. (1990). *Nature and nurture: An introduction to human behavioral genetics.* Pacific Grove, CA: Brooks/Cole.

Plomin, R. (1994a). Nature, nurture, and social development.

ment. Social Development, 3, 37–53.

Plomin, R. (1994b). The Emanual Miller Memorial Lecture 1993: Genetic research and identification of environmental influence. *Journal of Child Psychology and Psychiatry, 35*, 817–834.

Plomin, R. (1995). Genetics and children's experiences in the family. *Journal of Child Psychology and Psychiatry, 36*, 33–68.

Plomin, R., & Bergeman, C. S. (1991). The nature of nurture: Genetic influence on "environmental" measures. *Behavioral and Brain Science, 14*, 373–427.

Plomin, R., Corley, R., DeFries, J. C, & Fulker, D. W. (1990). Individual differences in television viewing in early childhood: Nature as well as nurture. *Psychological Science, 6*, 371–377.

Plomin, R., & Daniels, D. (1987). Why are children in the same family so different from each other? *Behavioral and Brain Sciences, 10*, 1–16.

Plomin, R., & DeFries, J. C. (1985). *Origins of individual differences in infancy.* New York: Academic Press.

Plomin, R., DeFries, J. C., & McClearn, G. E. (1990). *Behavioral genetics: A primer*, 2nd ed. New York: W. H. Freeman.

Plomin, R., Loehlin, J. C., & DeFries, J. C. (1985). Genetic and environmental components of "environmental" influences. *Developmental Psychology, 21*, 391–402.

Plomin, R., & McClearn, G. E. (Eds.). (1993). *Nature, nurture and psychology.* Washington, DC: American Psychological Association.

Plomin, R., & Rowe, D. C. (1979). Genetic and environmental etiology of social behavior in infancy. *Developmental Psychology, 15*, 62–72.

Pomerleau, A., Malcuit G., & Sabetier, C. (1991). Child rearing practices and parental beliefs in three cultural groups of Montreal: Quebecois, Vietnamese, Haitian. In M. H. Bornstein (Ed.), *Cultural approaches to parenting.* Hillsdale, NJ: Erlbaum.

Power, T. G., & Parke, R. D. (1982). Play as a context for early learning: Lab and home analyses. In L. M. Laosa & I. E. Sigel (Eds.), *Families as a learning environment for children.* New York: Plenum.

Powlishta, K. K., Serbin, L. A., Doyle A.-B., & White, D. R. (1994). Gender, ethnic and body type biases: The generality of prejudice in childhood. *Developmental Psychology, 30*, 526–536.

Pratt, M. W., Hunsberger, B., Pancer, S. M., Roth, D., & Santolupo, S. (1993). Thinking about parenting: Reasoning about developmental issues across the lifespan. *Developmental Psychology, 29,* 585–595.

Prechtl, H. F. R. (1958). The directed head turning response and allied movements of the human body. *Behaviour, 13,* 212–242.

Prior, M. (1992). Childhood temperament. *Journal of Child Psychology and Psychiatry, 33,* 249–280.

Puckering, C. (1989). Maternal depression. *Journal of Child Psychology and Psychiatry, 30,* 807–878.

Putallaz, M., & Heflin, A. H. (1990). Parent–child interaction. In S. R. Asher & J. D. Coie (Eds.), *Peer rejection in childhood.* Cambridge, UK: Cambridge University Press.

Pye, C. (1986). Quiche Mayan speech to children. *Journal of Child Language, 13,* 85–100.

Quinton, D., & Rutter, M. (1976). Early hospital admissions and later disturbances of behaviour. *Developmental Medicine and Child Neurology, 18,* 447–459.

Quinton, D., & Rutter, M. (1988). *Parental breakdown: The making and breaking of intergenerational links.* Aldershot, UK: Gower.

Radin, N. (1982). Primary caregiving and role-sharing fathers. In M. Lamb (Ed.), *Non-traditional families: Parenting and child development.* Hillsdale, NJ: Erlbaum.

Radke-Yarrow, M., Zahn-Waxler, C., & Chapman, M. (1983). Children's prosocial dispositions and behavior. In P. H. Mussen (Ed.). *Handbook of child psychology* (Vol. 4). New York: Wiley.

Reisman, J. M., & Shorr, S. I. (1978). Friendship claims and expectations among children and adults. *Child Development, 49,* 913–916.

Rest, J. R. (1983). Morality. In P. H. Mussen (Ed.). *Handbook of child psychology. Vol. 3: Cognitive development.* New York: Wiley.

Rheingold, H. L. (1982). Little children's participation in the work of adults, a nascent prosocial behavior. *Child Development, 53,* 114–125.

Rheingold, H. L., & Cook, K. (1975). The content of boys' and girls' rooms as an index of parent behavior. *Child Development, 46,* 459–463.

Rheingold, H. L., & Eckerman, C. O. (1970). The infant separates himself from his mother. *Science, 168,* 78–83.

Rheingold, H. L., & Eckerman, C. O. (1973). Fear of the stranger: A critical examination. In H. W. Reese (Ed.), *Advances in child development and behavior* (Vol. 8). New York: Academic Press.

Rheingold, H. L., Gewirtz, J. L., & Ross, H. W. (1959). Social conditioning of vocalizations in the infant. *Journal of Comparative and Physiological Psychology, 52,* 68–73.

Rheingold, H. L., Hay, D. F., & West, M. J. (1976). Sharing in the second year of life. *Child Development, 47,* 1148–1158.

Ribble, M. A. (1944). Infantile experiences in relation to personality development. In J. McV. Hunt (Ed.), *Personality and the behavior disorders.* New York: Ronald Press.

Richardson, J. G., & Simpson, C. H. (1982). Children, gender and social structure: An analysis of the contents of letters to Santa Claus. *Child Development, 53,* 429–436.

Richman, N., Stevenson, J., & Graham, P. (1982). *Preschool to school.* London: Academic Press.

Ricks, M. H. (1985). The social transmission of parental behavior: Attachment across generation. In I. Bretherton & E. Waters (Eds.), Growing points of attachment theory and practice. *Monographs of the Society for Research in Child Development* (1–2, Serial No. 209).

Riese, M. L. (1990). Neonatal temperament in monozygotic and dizygotic twin pairs. *Child Development, 61,* 1230–1237.

Robinson, J. L., Zahn-Waxler, C., & Emde, R. (1994). Patterns of development in early empathic behavior: Environmental and child contributional influences. *Social Development, 3,* 125–145.

Rocissano, L., Slade, A., & Lynch, V. (1987). Dyadic synchrony and toddler compliance. *Developmental Psychology, 23,* 698–704.

Rogoff, B. (1990). *Apprenticeship in thinking: Cognitive development in social context.* New York: Oxford University Press.

Rogoff, B., Mistry, J., Gonen, A., & Mosier, C. (1993). Guided participation in cultural activity by toddlers and caregivers. *Monographs of the Society for Research in Child Development, 58* (8, Serial No. 236).

Rosaldo, M. Z. (1980). *Knowledge and passion.* Cambridge, UK: Cambridge University Press.

Ross, H. S. & Lollis, S. P. (1987). Communication within infant social games. *Developmental Psychology, 23,* 241–248.

Ross, H. S., & Lollis, S. P. (1989). A social relations analysis of toddler peer relationships. *Child Development,* 1082–1091.

Rotenberg, K. J. (1982). Development of character constancy of self and other. *Child Development, 53,* 505–515.

Rothbart, M. K., Ziaie, H., & O'Boyle, C. G. (1992).

Self-regulation and emotion in infancy. In N. Eisenberg & R. A. Fabes (Eds.), *Emotion and its regulation in early development*. San Francisco: Jossey-Bass.

Rowe, D. C., & Plomin, R. (1981). The importance of nonshared environmental influences in behavioral development. *Developmental Psychology, 17,* 517–531.

Rubin, J. S., Provenza, F. J., & Luria, Z. (1974). The eye of the beholder: Parents' views on sex of newborns. *American Journal of Orthopsychiatry, 5,* 353–363.

Rubin, K. H. (Ed.). (1994). From family to peer group: Relations between relationships systems. *Social Development, 3,* No. 3.

Rubin, K. H., & Coplan, R. (1992). Peer relationships in childhood. In M. Bornstein & M. Lamb (Eds.), *Developmental psychology: An advanced textbook*. Hillsdale, NJ: Erlbaum.

Rubin, K. H., LeMare, L. J., & Lollis, S. (1990). Social withdrawal in childhood: Developmental pathways to peer rejection. In S. R. Asher & J. D. Coie (Eds.), *Peer rejection in childhood*. Cambridge, UK: Cambridge University Press.

Ruble, D. N. (1987). The acquisition of self-knowledge: A self-socialization perspective. In N. Eisenberg (Ed.), *Contemporary topics in developmental psychology*. New York: Wiley.

Rushton, J. P., Fulker, D. W., Neale, M. L., Nias, D. K., & Eysenck, H. J. (1986). Altruism and aggression: The heritability of individual differences. *Journal of Personality and Social Psychology, 50,* 1192–1198.

Rutter, M. (1979). Protective factors in children's response to stress and disadvantage. In M. W. Kent & J. E. Rolf (Eds.), *Primary prevention of psychopathology* (Vol. 3). Hanover, PA: University Press of New England.

Rutter, M. (1983). School effects on pupil progress: Research findings and policy implications. *Child Development, 54,* 1–29.

Rutter, M. (1987). Psychosocial resilience and protective mechanisms. *American Journal of Orthopsychiatry, 57,* 316–331.

Rutter, M. (1989). Pathways from childhood to adult life. *Journal of Child Psychology and Psychiatry, 30,* 23–51.

Rutter, M. (1992). Nature, nurture and psychopathology. In B. Tizard & V. Varma (Eds.), *Vulnerability and resilience in human development*. London: Jessica Kingsley.

Rutter, M., Maughan, B., Mortimore, P., & Ouston, J. (1979). *Fifteen thousand hours: Secondary schools and their effects on children*. London: Open Books.

Rutter, M., & Robins, L. N. (Eds.) (1990). *Straight and devious pathways from childhood to adulthood*. Cambridge, UK: Cambridge University Press.

Sagi, A., Lamb, M. E., Lewkowicz, K. S., Shoham, R., Doir, R., & Estes, D. (1985). Security of infant–mother, –father, and –metapelet attachments among kibbutz-reared Israeli children. In I. Bretherton & E. Water (Eds.), Growing points of attachment theory and research. *Monographs of the Society for Research in Child Development, 50* (1–2, Serial No. 209).

Sameroff, A. J. (1975). Early influences on development: Fact or fancy? *Merrill-Palmer Quarterly, 21,* 267–294.

Sameroff, A. J. (1983). Developmental systems: Contexts and evolution. In W. Kessen (Ed.), *Handbook of child psychology: Vol. 1. History, theory, and methods*. New York: Wiley.

Sameroff, A. J., & Chandler, M. J. (1975). Reproductive risk and the continuum of caretaking casualty. In F. D. Horowitz (Ed.), *Review of child development research* (Vol. 4). Chicago: University of Chicago Press.

Sameroff, A. J., & Feil, L. (1985). Parental conceptions of development. In I. Sigel (Ed.), *Parental belief systems*. Hillsdale, NJ: Erlbaum.

Sameroff, A. J., & Fiese, B. H. (1992). Family representations of development. In I. E. Sigel, A. V. McGillicuddy-De Lisi, & J. J. Goodnow (Eds.), *Parental belief systems: The psychological consequences for children*, 2nd ed. Hillsdale, NJ: Erlbaum.

Sameroff, A. J., Seifer, R., Barocas, B., Zax, M., & Greenspan, S. (1987). IQ scores of 4-year-old children: Social environmental risk factors. *Pediatrics, 79,* 343–350.

Sampson, R. J., & Lamb, J. H. (1994). Urban poverty and the family context of delinquency: A new look at structure and process in a classic structure. *Child Development, 65,* 523–540.

Sander, L. W., Stechler, G., Burns, P., & Julia, H. (1970). Early mother–infant interaction and 24-hour patterns of activity and sleep. *Journal of the American Academy of Child Psychiatry, 9,* 103–123.

Sander, L. W., Stechler, G., Burns, P., & Lee, A. (1979). Change in infant and caregiver variables over the first two months of life. In E. B. Thomas (Ed.), *Origins of the infant's social responsiveness*. Hillsdale, NJ: Erlbaum.

Sandler, I. N., Miller, P., Short, J., & Wolchnik, S. A. (1989). Social support as a protective factor for children in stress. In D. Belle (Ed.), *Children's social networks and social supports*. New York: Wiley.

Saxe G. B., Guberman, S. R., & Gearhart, M. (1987). Social processes in early number development. *Monographs of the Society for Research in Child Development, 52* (2, Serial No. 216).

Saylor, C. F. (Ed.). (1993). *Children and disasters*. New York: Plenum.

Scarr, S. (1992). Developmental theories for the 1990s: Development and individual differences. *Child Development, 63*, 1–19.

Scarr, S., & Kidd, K. H. (1983). Developmental behavior genetics. In P. H. Mussen (Ed.), *Handbook of child psychology (Vol. 2). Infancy and developmental psychobiology*. New York: Wiley.

Scarr, S., & McCartney, K. (1983). How people make their own environments: A theory of genotype – environmental effects. *Child Development, 54*, 424–435.

Scarr, S., & Weinberg, R. A. (1980). Calling all camps! The war is over. *American Sociological Review, 45*, 859–865.

Scarr, S., & Weinberg, R. A. (1983). The Minnesota adoption studies: Genetic differences and malleability. *Child Development, 54*, 260–267.

Schaefer, E. S. (1959). A circumplex model for maternal behavior. *Journal of Abnormal and Social Psychology, 59*, 226–235.

Schaefli, A., Rest, J. R., & Thoma, S. J. (1985). Does moral education improve moral judgment? A meta-analysis of intervention studies using the Defining Issues Test. *Review of Educational Research, 55*, 319–352.

Schaffer, H. R. (1958). Objective observations of personality development in early infancy. *British Journal of Medical Psychology, 31*, 174–183.

Schaffer, H. R. (1966). The onset of fear of strangers and the incongruity hypothesis. *Journal of Child Psychology and Psychiatry, 7*, 95–106.

Schaffer, H. R. (1974). Cognitive components of the infant's response to strangers. In M. Lewis & L. A. Rosenblum (Eds.), *The origins of fear*. New York: Wiley.

Schaffer, H. R. (Ed.). (1977). *Studies in mother–infant interaction*. London: Academic Press.

Schaffer, H. R. (1984). *The child's entry into a social world*. London: Academic Press.

Schaffer, H. R. (1987). The social context of psychobiological development. In H. Rauh & H. C. Steinhausen (Eds.), *Psychobiology and early development*. Amsterdam: North Holland/Elsevier.

Schaffer, H. R. (1989). Language development in context. In S. von Tetzchner, L. S. Siegel, & L. Smith (Eds.), *The social and cognitive aspects of normal and atypical language development*. New York: Springer-Verlag.

Schaffer, H. R. (1990). *Making decisions about children: Psychological questions and answers*. Oxford, UK: Blackwell.

Schaffer, H. R. (1992). Joint involvement episodes as contexts for cognitive development. In H. McGurk (Ed.), *Childhood social development: Contemporary perspectives*. Hove, UK: Erlbaum.

Schaffer, H. R., & Crook, C. K. (1979). Maternal control techniques in a directed play situation. *Child Development, 50*, 989–996.

Schaffer, H. R., & Crook, C. K. (1980). Child compliance and maternal control techniques. *Developmental Psychology, 16*, 54–61.

Schaffer, H. R., & Emerson, P. E. (1964a). The development of social attachments in infancy. *Monographs of the Society for Research in Child Development, 29* (3, Whole No. 94).

Schaffer, H. R., & Emerson, P. E. (1964b). Patterns of response to physical contact in early human development. *Journal of Child Psychology and Psychiatry, 5*, 1–13.

Schaffer, H. R., Greenwood, A., & Parry, M. H. (1972). The onset of wariness. *Child Development, 43*, 165–175.

Schaffer, H. R., Hepburn, A., & Collis, G. M. (1983). Verbal and nonverbal aspects of mothers' directives. *Journal of Child Language, 10*, 337–355.

Schieffelin, B. B., & Ochs, E. (1983). A cultural perspective on the transition from prelinguistic to linguistic communication. In R. M. Golinkoff (Ed.), *The transition from prelinguistic to linguistic communication*. Hillsdale, NJ: Erlbaum.

Schlesinger, H. S., & Meadow, K. P. (1972). *Sound and sign: Childhood deafness and mental health*. Berkeley, CA: University of California Press.

Schneider, B. H. (1993). *Children's social competence in context*. Oxford, UK: Pergamon.

Schneider-Rosen, K., & Cicchetti, D. (1984). The relationship between affect and cognition in maltreated infants: Quality of attachment and the development of self-recognition. *Child Development, 55*, 648–658.

Schneider-Rosen, K., & Cicchetti, D. (1991). Early self-knowledge and emotional development: Visual self-recognition and affective reactions to mirror self-image in maltreated and non-maltreated toddlers. *Developmental Psychology, 27*, 471–478.

Schneider-Rosen, K., & Rothbaum, F. (1993). Quality of parental caregiving and security of attachment. *Developmental Psychology, 29*, 358–367.

Schratz, M. (1978). A developmental investigation of sex differences in spatial (visual analytic) and mathematical skills in three ethnic groups. *Developmental Psychology, 14*, 263–267.

Schuck, S. Z., Schuck, A., Hallam, E., Mancini, F., & Wells, R. (1971). Sex differences in aggressive behavior subsequent to listening to a radio broadcast of violence. *Psychological Reports, 28*, 931–936.

Schwartz, D., Dodge, K. A., & Coie, J. D. (1993). The emergence of chronic peer victimization in boys' play groups. *Child Development, 64*, 1755–1772.

Schwartz, G. M., Izard, C. E., & Ansal, C. E. (1985). The 5-month old's ability to discriminate facial expressions of emotions. *Infant Behaviour and Development, 8*, 65–77.

Scott-Jones, D. (1984). Family influence on cognitive development and school achievement. In E. Gordon (Ed.), *Review of research in education*. Washington, DC: American Educational Research Association Press.

Sears, R. R. (1958). Personality development in the family. In J. M. Seidman (Ed.), *The child*. New York: Holt, Rinehart, & Winston.

Sears, R. R., Maccoby, E. E., & Levin, H. (1957). *Patterns of child rearing*. Evanston, IL: Row, Peterson.

Sears, R. R., Rau, L., & Alpert, R. (1965). *Identification and child rearing*. Stanford, CA: Stanford University Press.

Selman, R. L. (1980). *The growth of interpersonal understanding*. New York: Academic Press.

Serbin, L. A., Powlishta, K. K., & Gueko, J. (1993). The development of sex typing in middle childhood. *Monographs of the Society for Research in Child Development, 58* (2, serial No. 232).

Serbin, L. A., & Sprafkin, C. (1986). The salience of gender and the process of sex typing in three- to seven-year-old children. *Child Development, 57*, 1188–1199.

Shantz, C. U. (1983). Social cognition. In J. H. Flavell & E. M. Markman (Eds.), *Handbook of child psychology* (Vol. 3). New York: Wiley.

Shapira, A., & Madsen, M. C. (1974). Between- and within-group cooperation and competition among kibbutz and non-kibbutz children. *Developmental Psychology, 10*, 140–145.

Shepherd, D. M., & Barraclough, B. M. (1976). The aftermath of parental suicide for children. *British Journal of Psychiatry, 129*, 267–276.

Siegal, M. (1987). Are sons and daughters treated more differently by fathers than by mothers? *Developmental Review, 7*, 183–209.

Sigel, I. E. (1992). The belief–behavior connection: A resolvable dilemma? In I. E. Sigel, A. V. McGillicuddy-De Lisi, & J. J. Goodnow (Eds.), *Parental belief systems: The psychological consequences for children*. Hillsdale, NJ: Erlbaum.

Silvern, S. B., & Williamson, P. A. (1987). The effects of video game play on young children's aggression, fantasy and prosocial behavior. *Journal of Applied Developmental Psychology, 8*, 453–462.

Simmons, R. G., Black, A., & Zhou, Y. (1991). African-American versus White children and the transition to junior high school. *American Journal of Education, 99*, 481–520.

Simmons, R. G., Blyth, D. A., Van Cleave, E. G., & Bush, D. M. (1979). Entry into early adolescence: The impact of school structure, puberty, and early dating on self-esteem. *American Sociological Review, 44*, 948–967.

Simmons, R. G., Burgeson, R., & Careton-Ford, S. (1987). The impact of cumulative change in early adolescence. *Child Development, 58*, 1220–1234.

Singer, D. G. (1989). Caution: Television may be hazardous to a child's mental health. *Developmental Behavioral Pediatrics, 10*, 259–261.

Skinner, B. F. (1953). *Science and human behavior*. New York: Macmillan.

Slabey, R. G., & Frey, K. G. (1975). Development of gender constancy and selective attention to same-sex models. *Child Development, 46*, 849–856.

Slade, A. (1987). A longitudinal study of maternal involvement and symbolic play during the toddler period. *Child Development, 58*, 367–375.

Sluckin, W. (1972). *Imprinting and early learning*, 2nd ed. London: Methuen.

Smetana, J. G., & Braeges, J. L. (1990). The development of toddlers' moral and conventional judgments. *Merrill-Palmer Quarterly, 36*, 329–346.

Smith, C., & Lloyd, B. (1978). Maternal behavior and perceived sex of infant: Revisited. *Child Development, 49*, 1263–1265.

Smith, P. K. (1978). A longitudinal study of social participation in preschool children: Solitary and parallel play re-examined. *Developmental Psychology, 14*, 517–523.

Smith, P. K. (1991). The silent nightmare: Bullying and victimization in school year groups. *The Psychologist, 4*, 243–248.

Smith, P. K., & Thompson, D. A. (Eds.). (1991). *Practical approaches to bullying*. London: David Fulton.

Snarey, J. R. (1985). Cross-cultural universality of social-moral development: A critical review of Kohlbergian research. *Psychological Bulletin, 97*, 202–232.

Snow, M. E., Jacklin, C. N., & Maccoby, E. E. (1983). Sex-of-child differences in father–child interaction at one year of age. *Child Development, 54*, 227–252.

Sokolov, J. L. (1993). A local contingency analysis of the fine-tuning hypothesis. *Developmental Psychology, 29*, 1008–1023.

Sollie, D., & Miller, B. (1980). The transition to parenthood at a critical time for building family strengths. In N. Stinnet & P. Knaub (Eds.), *Family strengths: Positive models of family life*. Lincoln: University of Nebraska Press.

Sonuga-Barke, E. J. S., Minocha, K., Taylor, E. A., & Sandberg, S. (1993). Inter-ethnic bias in teachers' ratings of childhood hyperactivity. *British Journal of Developmental Psychology, 11*, 187–200.

Sorce, J. F., & Emde, R. N. (1982). The meaning of infant emotional expressions: Regularities in caregiving responses in normal and Down's syndrome infants. *Journal of Child Psychology and Psychiatry, 23*, 145–158.

Spencer, M. B. (1983). Children's cultural values and parental child-rearing strategies. *Developmental Review, 3*, 351–370.

Spitz, R. A. (1957). *No and yes: On the genesis of human communication*. Madison, CT: International Universities Press.

Spitz, R. A., & Wolf, K. M. (1946). The smiling response: A contribution to the ontogenesis of social relationships. *Genetic Psychology Monographs, 34*, 57–125.

Spock, B. (1948). *Baby and child care*. New York: Duell, Sloan & Pearce.

Sroufe, L. A., & Jacobovitz, D. (1989). Diverging pathways, developmental transformations, multiple etiologies and the problem of continuity in development. *Human Development, 32*, 196–203.

Stack, D. L., & LePage, D. E. (1996). Infants' sensitivity to manipulation of maternal touch during face-to-face interactions. *Social Development, 5*, 41–55.

Stafford, L., & Bayer, C. L. (1993). *Interaction between parents and children*. Newbury Park, CA: Sage.

Stebbing, G. (1982). *Darwin to DNA: Molecules to humanity*. San Francisco: Freeman.

Steinberg, L., Lamborn, S. D., Darling, N., Mounts, N. S., & Dornbusch, S. M. (1994). Over-time changes in adjustment and competence among adolescents from authoritative, authoritarian, indulgent and neglectful families. *Child Development, 65*, 754–770.

Stephan, W. G., & Rosenfield, D. (1979). Black self-rejection: Another look. *Journal of Educational Psychology, 71*, 708–716.

Stern, D. N. (1985). *The interpersonal world of the infant*. New York: Basic Books.

Stevenson, H. W. (1965). Social reinforcement of children's behavior. In L. P. Lipsitt & C. C. Spiker (Eds.), *Advances in child development and behavior* (Vol. II). New York: Academic Press.

Stevenson, H. W., Chen, C., & Uttal, D. H. (1990). Beliefs and achievement: A study of black, white, and Hispanic children. *Child Development, 61*, 508–523.

Stevenson, H. W., & Lee, S. (1990). Contexts of achievement. *Monographs of the Society for Research in Child Development, 55* (1–2, Serial No. 221).

Stevenson, H. W., Lee, S., Chen, C., Lummis, J., Stigler, J., Fan, L., & Ge, F. (1990). Mathematics achievement of children in China and the United States. *Child Development, 61*, 1053–1066.

Stevenson, H. W., Lee, S., & Stigler, J. (1986). Mathematics achievement of Chinese, Japanese and American children. *Science, 231*, 693–699.

Stevenson, H. W., & Newman, R. S. (1986). Longterm prediction of achievement attitudes in mathematics and reading. *Child Development, 57*, 646–659.

Stevenson, M. R., & Black, K. N. (1988). Paternal absence and sex-role development: A meta-analysis. *Child Development, 59*, 793–814.

Stigler, J. W., Lee, S., & Stevenson, H. W. (1987). Mathematics classrooms in Japan, Taiwan, and the United States. *Child Development, 58*, 1272–1285.

Stipek, D., Recchia, S., & McClintic, S. (1992). Self-evaluation in young children. *Monographs of the Society for Research in Child Development, 57* (1, Serial No. 226).

Sue, S., & Okazaki, S. (1990). Asian-American educational achievement: A phenomenon in search of an explanation. *American Psychologist, 45*, 913–920.

Sullivan, H. S. (1947). *Conceptions of modern psychiatry*. Washington, DC: White Foundation.

Swann Report (1985). *Education for all*. London: HMSO, Cmnd 9453.

Sylva, K. (1994). School influences on children's development. *Journal of Child Psychology and Psychiatry*, *35*, 135–170.

Tajfel, H. (1978). Social categorization, social identity and social comparison. In H. Tajfel (Ed.), *Differentiation between social groups*. London: Academic Press.

Tamis-LeMonda, C. S., & Bornstein, M. H. (1989). Habituation and maternal encouragement of attention in infancy as predictors of toddler language, play, and representational competence. *Child Development*, *60*, 738–751.

Tauber, M. A. (1979). Sex differences in parent–child interaction styles during a free-play session. *Child Development*, *50*, 981–988.

Taylor, M. C., & Hall, J. A. (1982). Psychological androgyny: A review and reformulation of theories, methods and conclusions. *Psychological Bulletin*, *92*, 347–366.

Tellegen, A., Lybben, D. T., Bouchard, T. J., Jr., Wilcox, K. J., Seal, N. L., & Rich, S. (1988). Personality similarity in twins reared apart and together. *Journal of Personality and Social Psychology*, *54*, 1031–1039.

Thomas, A., & Chess, S. (1977). *Temperament and development*. New York: Bremner/Mazel.

Thomas, A., & Chess, S. (1982). Temperament and follow-up to adulthood. In R. Porter & G. M. Collins (Eds.), *Temperamental differences in infants and young children*. London: Pitman/Ciba.

Thomas, A., & Chess, S. (1986). The New York Longitudinal Study: From infancy to early adult life. In R. Plomin & J. Dunn (Eds.), *The study of temperament: Changes, continuities and challenges*. Hillsdale, NJ: Erlbaum.

Thomas, A., Chess, S., & Birch, H. G. (1968). *Temperament and behavior disorders in children*. New York: New York University Press.

Thomas, A., Chess, S., & Korn, S. J. (1982). The reality of difficult temperament. *Merrill-Palmer Quarterly*, *28*, 1–20.

Thompson, R. A. (1994). Emotion regulation: A theme in search of definition. In N. A. Fox (Ed.), The development of emotion regulation: Biological and behavioral consideration. *Monographs of the Society for Research in Child Development*, *59* (2–3, Serial No. 240).

Thompson, R. A., Lamb, M. E., & Estes, D. (1982). Stability of infant–mother attachment and its relationship to changing life circumstances in an unselected middle-class sample. *Child Development*, *53*, 144–148.

Tinbergen, N. (1951). *The study of instinct*. Oxford, UK: Oxford University Press.

Tizard, B. (1977). *Adoption: A second chance*. London: Open Books.

Tizard, B., & Hughes, M. (1984). *Young children learning: Talking and thinking at home and at school*. London: Fontana.

Tizard, B., & Phoenix, A. (1993). *Black, white or mixed race?* London: Routledge.

Tizard, J., Schofield, W. N., & Hewison, J. (1982). Collaboration between teachers and parents assisting children's reading. *British Journal of Educational Psychology*, *52*, 1–15.

Tobin, J. J., Wu, Y. H., & Davidson, D. H. (1989). *Preschool in three cultures: Japan, China, and the United States*. New Haven, CT: Yale University Press.

Tolmie, A., Howe, C., Mackenzie, M., & Greer, K. (1993). Task design as an influence on dialogue and learning: Primary school group work with object flotation. *Social Development*, *2*, 183–201.

Tolson, T. F. J., & Wilson, M. N. (1990). The impact of two- and three-generational black family structure on perceived family climate. *Child Development*, *61*, 416–428.

Tomasello, M., & Farrar, M. J. (1986). Joint attention and early language. *Child Development*, *57*, 1454–1463.

Tomasello, M., Manule, S., & Kruger, A. C. (1986). Linguistic environment of one- to two-year-old twins. *Developmental Psychology*, *22*, 169–176.

Tomasello, M., & Todd, J. (1983). Joint attention and lexical acquisition style. *First Language*, *4*, 197–212.

Trevarthen, C. (1977). Descriptive analyses of infant communicative behaviour. In H. R. Schaffer (Ed.), *Studies in mother–infant interaction*. London: Academic Press.

Trevarthen, C., & Hubley, P. (1978). Secondary intersubjectivity. In A. Lock (Ed.), *Action, gesture and symbol*. London: Academic Press.

Tronick, E. Z. (1989). Emotions and emotional communication in infants. *American Psychologist*, *44*, 112–119.

Tronick, E. Z., Morelli, G. A., & Winn, S. (1987). Multiple caretaking of Efe (Pygmy) infants. *American Anthropologist*, *89*, 96–106.

Troyna, B., & Hatcher, R. (1992). *Racism in children's lives*. London: Routledge.

Turiel, E. (1983). *The development of social knowledge: Morality and convention*. Cambridge, UK: Cambridge University Press.

Vandell, D. L., Wilson, K. S., & Buchanan, N. R. (1980). Peer interaction in the first year of life: An examination of its structure, content and sensitivity to toys. *Child Development, 51*, 481–488.

van IJzendoorn, M. H., Juffer, E., & Duyvesteyn, M. G. C. (1995). Breaking the intergenerational cycle of insecure attachment: A review of the effects of attachment-based interventions on maternal sensitivity and infant security. *Journal of Child Psychology and Psychiatry, 36*, 225–248.

van IJzendoorn, M. H., & Kroonenberg, P. (1988). Cross-cultural patterns of attachment: A meta-analysis of the Strange Situation. *Child Development, 59*, 147–156.

Vaughn, B. E., Block, J. H., & Block, J. (1988). Parental agreement on child rearing during early childhood and the psychological characteristics of adolescents. *Child Development, 59*, 1020–1033.

Vaughn, B. E., Egeland, B., Sroufe, A. L., & Waters, E. (1979). Individual differences in infant–mother attachment at twelve and eighteen months: Stability and change in families under stress. *Child Development, 50*, 971–975.

Vaughn, B. E., Goldberg, S., Atkinson, L., Marcovitch, S., MacGregor, D., & Seifer, R. (1994). Quality of toddler–mother attachment in children with Down's syndrome: Limits to interpretation of Strange Situation behavior. *Child Development, 65*, 95–108.

Vaughn, B. E., Kopp, C. B., & Krakow, J. B. (1984). The emergence and consolidation of self-control from eighteen to thirty months of age: Normative trends and individual differences. *Child Development, 55*, 990–1004.

Vaughn, B. E., Lefever, G. B., Seifer, R., & Barglow, P. (1989). Attachment behavior, attachment security and temperament during infancy. *Child Development, 60*, 728–737.

Vaughn, G. M. (1964). The development of ethnic attitudes in New Zealand school children. *Genetic Psychology Monographs, 70*, 135–175.

Vibbert, M., & Bornstein, M. H. (1989). Specific associations between domains of mother–child interaction and toddler referential language and pretense play. *Infant Behavior and Development, 12*, 163–184.

von Knorring, A. L. (1991). Children of alcoholics. *Journal of Child Psychology and Psychiatry, 32*, 411–421.

Vygotsky, L. S. (1978). *Mind in society: The development of higher psychological processes*. Cambridge, MA: Harvard University Press.

Wachs, T. D. (1993). The nature–nurture gap: What we have here is a failure to collaborate. In R. Plomin & G. E. McClearn (Eds.), *Nature, nurture, and psychology*. Washington, DC: American Psychological Association.

Waddington, C. H. (1957). *The strategy of the genes*. London: Allen & Son.

Walker, L. J. (1984). Sex differences in the development of moral reasoning: A critical review. *Child Development, 55*, 677–691.

Walker, L. J. (1989). A longitudinal study of moral reasoning. *Child Development, 60*, 157–160.

Wallerstein, J. S., Corbin, S. B., & Lewis, J. M. (1988). Children of divorce: A 10-year study. In E. M. Hetherington & J. D. Arasteh (Eds.), *Impact of divorce, single parentship and step-parentship on children*. Hillsdale, NJ: Erlbaum.

Walters, G. C., & Grusec, J. E. (1977). *Punishment*. San Francisco: Freeman.

Waters, E. (1978). The reliability and stability of individual differences in infant–mother attachment. *Child Development, 49*, 483–494.

Waters, E., & Sroufe, L. A. (1983). Social competence as a developmental construct. *Developmental Review, 3*, 79–97.

Waters, E., Wippman, J., & Sroufe, L. A. (1979). Attachment, positive affect, and competence in the peer group: Two studies in construct validation. *Child Development, 50*, 821–829.

Watson, J. B. (1913). Psychology as a behaviorist views it. *Psychological Review, 20*, 158–177.

Watson, J. B. (1919). *Psychology from the standpoint of a behaviorist*. Philadelphia: Lippincott.

Watson, J. B. (1925). *Behaviorism*. New York: People's Institute Publishing Company.

Watson, J. B. (1928). *Psychological care of infant and child*. New York: Norton.

Weinraub, M., Clemens, L. P., Sockloff, A., Ethridge, T., Graceley, E., & Myers, B. (1984). The development of sex role stereotypes in the third year: Relationships to gender labeling, gender identity, sex-typed toy preference and family characteristics. *Child Development, 55*, 1493–1506.

Weisner, T. S. & Gallimore, R. (1977). My brother's keeper: Child and sibling caretaking. *Current Anthropology, 18*, 169–190.

Weisner, T. S., & Wilson-Mitchell, J. E. (1990). Nonconventional family life-styles and sex typing in six-year-olds. *Child Development, 61,* 1915–1933.

Wellman, H. M. (1990). *The child's theory of mind.* New York: Bradford Books/MIT Press.

Wellman, H. M., & Banerjee, M. (1991). Mind and emotion: Children's understanding of the emotional consequence of beliefs and desires. *British Journal of Developmental Psychology, 9,* 191–214.

Wellman, H. M., & Gelman, S. A. (1987). Children's understanding of the nonobvious. In R. J. Sternberg (Ed.), *Advances in the psychology of human intelligence* (Vol. 4). Hillsdale, NJ: Erlbaum.

Wells, G. (1985). *Language development in the preschool years.* Cambridge, UK: Cambridge University Press.

Wenar, J., & Coulter, J. B. (1962). A reliability study of developmental histories. *Child Development, 33,* 453–462.

Werner, E. E. (1989). High-risk children in young adulthood: A longitudinal study from birth to 32 years. *American Journal of Orthopsychiatry, 59,* 72–81.

Werner, E. E. (1993). Risk, resilience and recovery: Perspectives from the Kauai longitudinal study. *Development and Psychopathology, 5,* 503–575.

Werner, E. E., & Smith, R. S. (1982). *Vulnerable but invincible: A longitudinal study of resilient children and youth.* New York: McGraw Hill.

Werner, H., & Kaplan, B. (1963). *Symbol formulation: An organismic developmental approach to language and the expression of thoughts.* New York: Wiley.

West, M. M., & Konner, M. J. (1976). The role of the father: An anthropological perspective. In M. Lamb (Ed.), *The role of the father in child development.* New York: Wiley.

West, M. O., & Prinz, R. J. (1987). Parental alcoholism and childhood psychopathology. *Psychological Bulletin, 102,* 204–218.

White, L., & Brinkerhoff, D. (1981). The sexual division of labor: Evidence from childhood. *Social Forces, 60,* 170–181.

Whitehurst, G. J., Arnold, D. S., Epstein, J. N., Angell, A. L., Smith, M., & Fischel, J. E. (1994). A picture book intervention in day care and home for children from low-income families. *Developmental Psychology, 30,* 679–689.

Whiting, B. B. (1986). The effects of experience on peer relationships. In E. Mueller & C. Cooper (Eds.), *Process and outcome in peer relationships.* New York: Academic Press.

Whiting, B. B., & Edwards, C. P. (1988). *Children of different worlds: The formation of social behavior.* Cambridge, MA: Harvard University Press.

Whiting, B. B., & Whiting, J. W. M. (1975). *Children of six cultures: A psycho-cultural analysis.* Cambridge, MA: Harvard University Press.

Wilson, E. O. (1975). *Sociobiology.* Cambridge, MA: Harvard University Press.

Wilson, R. S. (1983). The Louisville twin study: Developmental synchronics in behavior. *Child Development, 54,* 298–316.

Wilson, R. S., & Matheney, A. P. (1986). Behavior-genetics research in infant temperament: The Louisville twin study. In R. Plomin & J. Dunn (Eds.), *The study of temperament: Changes, continuities and challenges.* Hillsdale, NJ: Erlbaum.

Wimmer, H., & Perner, J. (1983). Beliefs about beliefs: Representation and constraining function of wrong beliefs in young children's understanding of deception. *Cognition, 13,* 103–128.

Wolff, P. H. (1966). The causes, controls and organization of behavior in the neonate. *Psychological Issues, 5,* (Monograph No. 17).

Wolkind, S., & de Salis, W. (1982). Infant temperament, maternal mental state and child behavior problems. In R. Porter & G. Collins (Eds.), *Temperamental differences in infants and young children.* CIBA Foundation Symposium 89. London: Plenum.

Wood, D. (1988). *How children think and learn.* Oxford, UK: Basil Blackwell.

Wood, D., Bruner, J. S., & Ross, G. (1976). The role of tutoring in problem solving. *Journal of Child Psychology and Psychiatry, 17,* 89–100.

Wood, D., & Middleton, D. (1975). A study of assisted problem solving. *British Journal of Psychology, 66,* 181–191.

Wood, W., Wong, F. Y., & Chackere, N. (1991). Effects of media violence on viewers' aggression in unconstrained social interaction. *Psychological Bulletin, 109,* 371–383.

Wynne-Edwards, V. C. (1962). *Animal dispersion in relation to social behaviour.* Edinburgh, UK: Oliver & Boyd.

Yogman, M. W., Dixon, S., Tronic, E., Adamson, L., Als, H., & Brazelton, T. B. (1976). *Development of infant social interaction with fathers.* Paper presented at the meeting of the Eastern Psychological Association, New York.

Youniss, J. (1980). *Parents and peers in social development.* Chicago: University of Chicago Press.

Youniss, J., & Smollar, J. (1985). *Adolescents' relations with mothers, fathers, and friends.* Chicago: University of Chicago Press.

Zahn-Waxler, C., & Radke-Yarrow, M. (1982). The development of altruism: Alternative research strategies. In N. Eisenberg (Ed.), *The development of prosocial behavior.* New York: Academic Press.

Zahn-Waxler, C., Radke-Yarrow, M., & King, R. A. (1979). Child-rearing and children's prosocial initiations toward victims of distress. *Child Development, 50,* 319–330.

Zahn-Waxler, C., Radke-Yarrow, M., Wagner, E., & Chapman, M. (1992). Development of concern for others. *Developmental Psychology, 28,* 126–136.

Zahn-Waxler, C., Robinson, J. L., & Emde, R. (1992). The development of empathy in twins. *Developmental Psychology, 28,* 1038–1047.

Zaslow, M. J., & Hayes, C. D. (1986). Sex differences in children's response to psychosocial stress: Toward a cross-context analysis. In M. Lamb, A. Brown, & B. Rogoff (Eds.), *Advances in developmental psychology* (Vol. 4). Hillsdale, NJ: Erlbaum.

Zaslow, M. J., & Rogoff, B. (1981). The cross-cultural study of early interaction: Implications from research in culture and cognition. In T. Field, A. Sostek, P. Vietze, & H. Leiderman (Eds.), *Culture and early interaction.* Hillsdale, NJ: Erlbaum.

Author Index

Subject Index